T0033748

SOUTH LANARKSHIRE
Leisure & Culture

www.library.southlanarkshire.gov.uk

**South Lanarkshire Libraries**

This book is to be returned on or before the last date stamped below or may be renewed by telephone or online.

**Delivering services for South Lanarkshire**

18 MAY 2017    100719

26 JUL 2017

SOUTH LANARKSHIRE LIBRARIES
BOOK SALE

- 1 AUG 2019

341.22

CAMBUSLANG LIBRARY
27 MAIN STREET
CAMBUSLANG
GLASGOW
G72 7EX
TEL: 0141 584 2530

JT12344/Dec13

# THE GUARDIANS

L122/1 5

(C⁺. F. H. Jullien)

M. Sakenobé · M. Kastl · M. Weaver · M. Merlin · M. Rappard · M. Catastini · Comte de Penha Garcia · M. Palacios · Lord Lugard · Mlle Dannevig · Marquis Théodoli Président · M. Van Rees Vice-Président · M. Orts

LA COMMISSION PERMANENTE DES MANDATS
(Genève, novembre 1929)

— 71 —

RHODES HOUSE LIBRARY
LUGARD PAPERS

**Frontispiece.** Permanent Mandates Commission, 1929. Seated, left to right: Sir Frederick Lugard, Valentine Dannevig, Marquis Alberto Theodoli, D. F. W. Van Rees, and Pierre Orts. Standing, left to right: Nobumichi Sakenobe, Ludwig Kastl, William Weaver, Martial Merlin, William Rappard, Count de Penha Garcia, Vito Catastini, and Leopoldo Palacios.

# THE GUARDIANS

## THE LEAGUE OF NATIONS AND
## THE CRISIS OF EMPIRE

SUSAN PEDERSEN

OXFORD
UNIVERSITY PRESS

# OXFORD
## UNIVERSITY PRESS

Great Clarendon Street, Oxford, OX2 6DP,
United Kingdom

Oxford University Press is a department of the University of Oxford.
It furthers the University's objective of excellence in research, scholarship,
and education by publishing worldwide. Oxford is a registered trade mark of
Oxford University Press in the UK and in certain other countries

© Susan Pedersen 2015

The moral rights of the author have been asserted

First Edition published in 2015

Impression: 1

All rights reserved. No part of this publication may be reproduced, stored in
a retrieval system, or transmitted, in any form or by any means, without the
prior permission in writing of Oxford University Press, or as expressly permitted
by law, by licence or under terms agreed with the appropriate reprographics
rights organization. Enquiries concerning reproduction outside the scope of the
above should be sent to the Rights Department, Oxford University Press, at the
address above

You must not circulate this work in any other form
and you must impose this same condition on any acquirer

British Library Cataloguing in Publication Data

Data available

Library of Congress Control Number: 2014954172

ISBN 978–0–19–957048–5

Printed in Great Britain by Clays Ltd, St Ives plc

Links to third party websites are provided by Oxford in good faith and
for information only. Oxford disclaims any responsibility for the materials
contained in any third party website referenced in this work.

C460287253

It isn't to harm the slave, that we say he must be ruled...but because it is better for everyone to be ruled by divine reason, preferably within himself and his own, otherwise imposed from without... This is clearly the aim of the law, which is the ally of everyone. But it's also our aim in ruling our children, we don't allow them to be free until we establish a constitution in them, just as in a city, and—by fostering their best part with our own—equip them with a guardian and ruler similar to our own to take our place. Then, and only then, we set them free.

Plato, *Republic*, Book IX
(trans. G. M. A. Grube)

# Contents

## PART IV. BETWEEN EMPIRE AND
## INTERNATIONALISM, 1933–39

# List of Illustrations

# List of Tables and Maps

# Principal Players

For administrators of the Mandated Territories, see Appendix II.

## IN THE COLONIAL AND FOREIGN MINISTRIES

Leo Amery (1873–1955), passionate British imperialist, Conservative and League critic; Colonial under-secretary, 1919–21; Colonial Secretary, 1924–29

Robert de Caix (1869–1970), architect of French Middle East strategy; Secretary of the *Comité de l'Asie française*; in High Commission (Beirut) until 1923; at the Quai d'Orsay, 1923–39

Fritz Grobba (1886–1973), German orientalist and diplomat; in Foreign Ministry, 1926–32; German Ambassador to Iraq, 1932–39

Halewyck de Heusch (1876–1950), Director-General of Political and Administrative Affairs, Belgian Ministry for the Colonies

William Ormsby-Gore (1885–1964), British politician; at the Arab Bureau, 1916–17; liaison to the Zionist Commission, 1918; British member of the PMC, 1921–22; colonial under-secretary, 1922, 1924–29; Colonial Secretary, 1936–38

## IN THE LEAGUE SECRETARIAT

Vito Catastini (1879–?), Italian colonial official; member of Mandates Section from 1921, Chef de Section, 1925–29, Director, 1929–37

Sir Eric Drummond (1876–1951), Foreign Office civil servant; Private Secretary to A. J. Balfour at the Peace Conference; First Secretary-General of the League of Nations, 1919–33; subsequently British Ambassador to Italy

Huntington Gilchrist (1891–1975), American member of Secretariat, 1919–28; in Mandates Section, 1924–28; later involved in United Nations

Edouard de Haller (1897–1957), Swiss member of Mandates Section, 1928–40; Director, 1938–40

William Rappard (1883–1958), Swiss-American political scientist, internationalist, and professor; Director of the Mandates Section, 1920–24; Member of the Mandates Commission, 1925–39

## ON THE MANDATES COMMISSION

Valentine Dannevig, Norwegian school director; Scandinavian member of PMC, 1928–39

Alfredo Freire d'Andrade (1859–1929), soldier and Governor-General of Mozambique, Portuguese member of PMC, 1921–28

Ludwig Kastl (1878–1969), colonial administrator, German South West Africa, 1910–20; in reparations section, Foreign Ministry; Director of Consortium of German Industries; German member of PMC, 1927–29

Frederick Lugard (1858–1945), colonial administrator and Governor-General of Nigeria; author of *The Dual Mandate in British Tropical Africa*; British member of PMC, 1923–36

Martial Henri Merlin (1860–1935), Governor-General, French West Africa; French member of PMC, 1926–34

Pierre Orts (1872–1958), diplomat, professor, and advisor to the Belgian colonial ministry; Belgian member of PMC, 1921–39; PMC Vice-President, 1934–37 and President, 1937–39

Leopoldo Palacios (1876–1952), social reformer and professor; Spanish member of PMC, 1924–39

Alberto Theodoli (1873–1955), aristocrat, diplomat, politician, and banker; Italian member and President of PMC, 1921–37

D. F. W. Van Rees (1863–1934), colonial official and legal member of the Dutch Council of the Indies; Dutch member and Vice-Chairman of PMC, 1921–34

## INTERNATIONALISTS AND NATIONALISTS, PETITIONERS, AND POTENTATES

Abdullah bin Husayn (1882–1951), Emir of Transjordan, 1921–46; King of Jordan, 1946–51

Sultan al-Atrash (1891–1982), leader of the Druze Revolt in Syria, 1925–26

Shakib Arslan (1869–1946), Druze aristocrat, pan-Islamist and intellectual; Secretary and Geneva representative of the Cairo-based Syro-Palestinian Congress

Dantès Bellegarde (1877–1966), Delegate to the League of Nations for the Republic of Haiti, 1921–22, 1930

Raymond Leslie Buell (1896–1946), American scholar of Africa, peripatetic researcher, Director of the Foreign Policy Association, and author of *The Native Problem in Africa* (1928)

Ralph Bunche (1904–1971), Harvard-trained political scientist at Howard University; involved in US planning for postwar order 1941–46; later director of the UN Trusteeship Council

W. E. B. Du Bois (1868–1963), African-American intellectual, political leader, and pan-Africanist

Faysal bin Husayn (1883–1933), leader of the Arab Revolt; King of Syria, 1920, expelled by French; King of Iraq, 1921–33

Hajj Amin al-Husayni (1897–1974), Mufti of Jerusalem, 1921–37

J. H. Harris (1874–1940), humanitarian; Organizing Secretary, Anti-Slavery Society, 1910–40

Michael Leahy (1901–1977), Australian explorer and prospector in New Guinea

Abraham Morris (?–1922), Bondelswarts leader, fought in Nama war against Germans, 1903–6; Scout for South African forces, 1915; killed resisting South African administration

Yuhi V Musinga (?–1944), King of Rwanda, 1896–1931, deposed by the Belgians

Olaf Frederick Nelson (1883–1944), copra trader and leader of the Samoan Mau movement

Heinrich Schnee (1871–1949), Governor of German East Africa, 1912–18; later leader of German colonial movement; joined Nazi Party, 1932

A. J. Toynbee (1889–1975), world historian and British internationalist; Director of Studies, Royal Institute of International Affairs, 1925–55; favoured conciliation of Germany, 1930s

Chaim Weizmann (1874–1952), President, World Zionist Organization, 1920–31, 1935–46; later President of Israel

Quincy Wright (1890–1970), American political scientist and Professor of International Law, University of Chicago; author of *Mandates under the League of Nations* (1930)

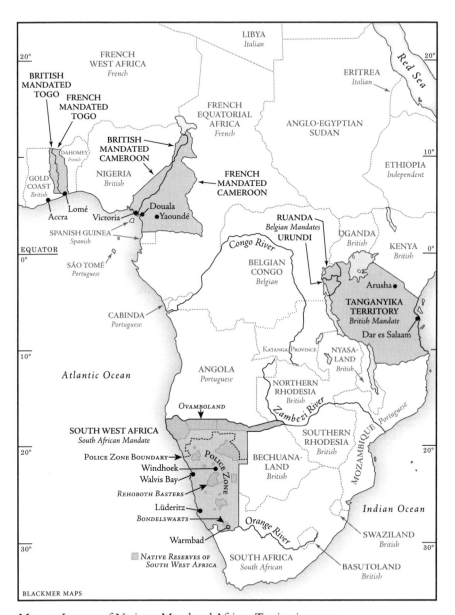

**Map 1.** League of Nations: Mandated African Territories, 1922

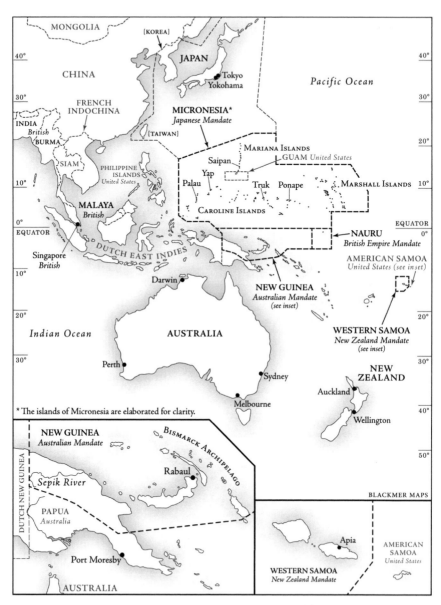

**Map 2.** League of Nations: Mandated Pacific Territories, 1932

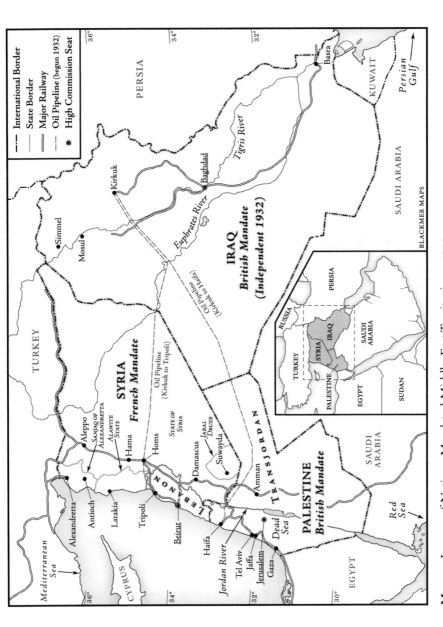

**Legend**
- – · – International Border
- —— State Border
- —— Major Railway
- – – – Oil Pipeline (begun 1932)
- ⊙ High Commission Seat

**Map 3.** League of Nations: Mandated Middle–East Territories, c. 1932

BLACKMER MAPS

**Table 1.** Population and Size of Mandated Territories

## Mandated Territories: Size and Population
### (as counted and classified by the mandatory powers)

| | Territory | Size (km²) | 1921 Population | | 1938 Population | |
|---|---|---|---|---|---|---|
| **"A" MANDATES** | Palestine Mandate | | | | | |
| | *Palestine only* | 27,009 | 589,177 | Moslems | 997,000 | Arabs |
| | | | 83,790 | Jews | 411,000 | Jews |
| | | | 71,464 | Christians | 27,000 | Others |
| | | | 7,617 | Others (1922) | | |
| | *Transjordan only* | 90,000 | 200,000 | (1924 estimate) | 300,214 | |
| | Syria and Lebanon | 202,500 | | | | |
| | *Syria only* | | 1,509,000 | Settled | 2,715,107 | |
| | | | 250,000 | Bedouins | | |
| | *Lebanon only* | | 570,000 | | 850,000 | |
| | Iraq | 438,000 | 2,850,000 | (1927)[1] | *Independent* | |
| **"B" MANDATES** | Cameroon (British)[2] | 88,266 | 600,000 | (estimate) | 857,227 | |
| | Cameroon (French) | 429,750 | 1,877,113 | Natives | 2,606,281 | Natives |
| | | | 1,570 | Non-natives | 3,227 | Non-natives |
| | | | | (1926 estimate) | | |
| | Togo (British)[2] | 33,772 | 187,939 | | 370,327 | |
| | Togo (French)[2] | 52,000 | 698,130 | (estimate) | 780,170 | |
| | Tanganyika | 932,364 | 4,107,000 | Natives | 5,214,000 | Africans |
| | | | 19,700 | Non-natives | 9,345 | Europeans |
| | | | | | 33,784 | Asians |
| | Ruanda/Urundi | 53,200 | 3,000,000 | (estimate) | 3,752,742 | |
| **"C" MANDATES** | South West Africa | 822,909 | 208,605 | Non-whites | 261,138 | Non-whites |
| | | | 19,432 | Whites | 30,941 | Whites |
| | Western Samoa | 2,934 | 32,601 | Natives | 54,160 | Natives |
| | | | 3,821 | Europeans | 3,599 | Europeans |
| | New Guinea | 240,864 | 214,136 | Natives counted | 581,342 | Natives counted |
| | | | 2,927 | Non-natives | 6,283 | Non-natives |
| | Nauru | 30 | 1,084 | Nauruans | 1,661 | Natives |
| | | | 266 | Pacific Islanders | 1,533 | Chinese |
| | | | 497 | Chinese | 206 | Others |
| | | | 119 | Europeans | | |
| | Japanese Mandated Islands | 2,149 | 48,494 | Natives | 50,868 | Natives |
| | | | 3,200 | Japanese (1921) | 70,141 | Japanese |
| | | | | | 119 | Others |

[1] Estimated at 1,500,000 Shias; 1,150,000 Sunnis; 88,000 Jews; 79,000 Christians; and 27,000 Yezidis. 12 *PMCM,* 21.

[2] Figures include Africans only; non-Africans numbered fewer than 1,000.

Source: Peter Anker, *The Mandates System: Origin—Principles—Application* (Geneva, 1945).

# Introduction

## Guardians Assemble

On 4 October 1921, William Rappard welcomed the Permanent Mandates Commission of the League of Nations to Geneva for its first session. Rappard, a thirty-eight-year-old Swiss professor, had been named Director of the Mandates Section in the League Secretariat a year earlier. He was, that is, the international official appointed to help the new Commission get on with its job, to review the imperial powers' administration of those African, Pacific, and Middle Eastern territories seized from Germany and the Ottoman Empire during the First World War. Large, ruddy, curly-haired, and inveterately cheerful, Rappard looked like a Swiss farmer—but he was efficient, capable, and effortlessly trilingual, held degrees in economics and law, and had an expansive network of liberal internationalist friends. He was passionately committed to the League of Nations, established through the signing of the Versailles Treaty more than two years earlier.

That those occupied territories would be governed under League oversight had been one of the Peace Conference's most bitterly contested decisions. Every allied power wanted compensation for war losses and suffering; most thought annexation of their conquests no more than their due. Only reluctantly did they bend to American pressure and the wave of internationalist and anti-imperialist sentiment sweeping the globe, and even so they kept their obligations, and the League's powers, limited and vague. Article 22 of the Covenant loftily decreed that 'advanced nations' would administer 'peoples not yet able to stand by themselves under the strenuous conditions of the modern world' according to the principle that 'the well-being and development of such peoples form a sacred trust of civilization', but included few practical details. The mandatory powers were to report annually on their administration, and a permanent commission was established to review them. The Covenant had nothing to say, however, about how long mandatory control was to last, how it might be ended, or indeed what the League was to do if the governing power failed to uphold the principles of the 'sacred trust'.

The mandates system was thus, as Rappard admitted to the Commission in his opening remarks, at best a compromise between partisans of imperial annexation and those who wanted all colonies placed under international control. It was a compromise, moreover, that had very nearly come apart. Once the American Senate rejected the Versailles Treaty and Warren Hastings had succeeded Woodrow Wilson as President, imperial statesmen had seen little need to hold to concessions made under very different conditions. Promises to consult Middle Eastern populations on the choice of mandatory power had long been abandoned. Territories had been assigned to their occupiers (or, in the case of France's rule over Syria, to the power willing to force its claims). By 1921, Rappard admitted, that disposition was 'an accomplished fact' and could not be undone.[1] Worse, those ostensible 'mandatories' had proven reluctant to negotiate the terms of their rule and quite uninterested in establishing the oversight apparatus at all. Only fierce criticism of their prevarication and foot-dragging at the first and second annual League assemblies in 1920 and 1921—criticism engineered in part by Rappard himself—had forced the League Council finally to convene the new Commission.

Yet, whether the eight men and one woman whom Rappard welcomed to Geneva in October 1921 could bring the imperial powers to heel was very much an open question. Appointed by the Council but usually on the recommendations of governments, most were retired diplomats or former colonial officials. All but one hailed from states with colonial empires and four from powers ruling territories the Commission was to oversee. All but the Japanese member were white Europeans; only the Scandinavian member was female. And while all were appointed as 'independent experts', ostensibly for their 'personal qualities' and not as representatives of their states, most had close ties to, or were even under direct instructions from, their governments. The Italian member was a former colonial under-secretary greatly offended by Italy's lack of a mandate. The Belgian member had successfully negotiated his country's claim to retain Rwanda and Burundi. The Portuguese member was an unblushing advocate of forced labour for African men. Small wonder the African American intellectual W. E. B. Du Bois had buttonholed Rappard a few weeks earlier to urge that a 'man of African descent' be added to the Commission. No such appointment had been, or would ever be, made.[2]

This should not surprise. By 1921 it was growing clear that, whatever purposes the mandates system had been devised to serve, extending the right of national self-determination was not one of them. Populations placed under mandate responded by resisting its imposition almost as strenuously as had the imperial powers. Arab nationalists thought they had been promised independence and not 'tutelage'; Samoans insisted they were quite as civilized as their New Zealand 'tutors' and well able to 'stand alone'. Just a few months before the Commission assembled, an influential delegation of now-exiled Arab notables had called on Rappard to protest that allied pledges of self-determination had been violated. Having overthrown Faysal bin Husayn's fragile Arab state, France was imposing colonial rule on Syria; Britain was supporting a policy of Jewish immigration in Palestine against the desires of the Arab majority.[3] Through contacts with anti-slavery campaigners, Rappard had also heard appeals against French mandatory rule from Duala elites in Cameroon and Ewe traders in Togo. He knew, too, how very little had come of any of those protests. Indeed, under direct orders from his boss, the League's first Secretary General Sir Eric Drummond, he had helped to suppress some of them.

William Emmanuel Rappard, League official and lawyer, was no anti-imperialist. Few Western liberals, in 1921, were. He did not think the occupied areas ready for self-government; the language of civilizational stages, of 'backward' peoples and Western guidance, fell easily from his lips. But Rappard was, nonetheless, an internationalist. He believed international collaboration could assuage national antagonisms; he thought 'native peoples' should be governed in their own interests and not those of the imperial powers. A year in post had cost him some illusions, but it had not dented his beliefs. And, importantly, that year had taught him much. By nature an open-hearted and outspoken man, he had acquired caution, diplomacy, and a measure of guile. He had learned to argue from texts rather than principles, and to wring from the Covenant every possible ounce of authority. He had learned the skills of confidential consultation and careful leaking. He had found allies—in the Secretariat, in the humanitarian and international organizations eager to lend the League a hand, in the American universities and foundations, and above all in the new British member of the Commission, a young idealist named William Ormsby-Gore. And Rappard had one crucial asset, the Mandates Commission—a body that, however cautious its members, was authorized by the Covenant to advise the Council on 'all matters' (and Rappard would always stress that crucial word, 'all') relating to the fulfilment of the mandates. The Mandates Commission, Rappard was certain, could be the tool through which the imperial order would be transformed. 'It was impossible to overestimate the importance' of their work, Rappard told the startled members. The Commission 'marked the beginning of an epoch in Colonial history'.[4]

This book argues that Rappard was right. This quixotic and near-forgotten effort to subject imperial rule to international control had profound effects, although they were not quite those that its architects and advocates expected. Mandatory oversight was supposed to make imperial rule more humane and therefore more legitimate; it was to 'uplift' backwards populations and—so its more idealistic supporters hoped—even to prepare them for self-rule. It did not do these things: mandated territories were not better governed than colonies across the board and in some cases were governed more oppressively; claims by populations under League oversight for political rights were more often met with repression than conciliation. Historians who have located the system's significance in its impact on local administration have remained too indebted to the binary frameworks of imperial history, and have left its crucial dynamics and effects unexplored.[5]

To grasp why the League mattered, we must begin elsewhere: in Geneva, with the Mandates Commission, the Secretariat officials who supported it, and the emerging and far-flung network seeking to reach and sway it. For, what was new and transformative about the mandates system was not the rhetoric of the civilizing mission, which all imperial powers employed, nor even ruling practices on the ground, which mirrored those in colonies. What was new, rather, was the apparatus and level of international diplomacy, publicity, and 'talk' that the system brought into being. Put bluntly, League oversight could not force the mandatory powers to govern mandated territories differently; instead, it obliged them to *say* they were governing them differently. Imperial statesmen and officials had to face wearying, detailed, and often acrimonious interrogations in Geneva, often with experts briefed by humanitarian lobbies or rival foreign ministries posing questions, and a host of journalists, petitioners, and even nationalist leaders waiting outside the door.

The mandates system, in other words, was a vehicle for what we might call 'internationalization'—the process by which certain political issues and functions are displaced from the national or imperial, and into the international, realm. Not administration but rather the work of legitimation moved to Geneva, as imperial powers strove to defend—and others to challenge— their authority. This level of conflict was unexpected, for the mandatory apparatus had first been conceived, as the Secretariat official Philip Noel-Baker put it, as 'an organ of constructive co-operation on colonial matters'[6]—as a vehicle, in other words, for collaboration among the imperial powers themselves. But how internationalization works depends on who is in the international room, and the crowd holding entry tickets to Geneva, while certainly largely European and almost entirely white, was nevertheless too large, too polyglot, and—over time—too riven with antagonisms, to be marshalled behind a single banner. Buffeted by claims to national self-determination from outside Europe and demands for revision of the Versailles settlement within it, its deliberations and decisions amplified by critics, scholars, and the press, the mandates system of the League of Nations became the site and stake of a great international argument over imperialism's claims.

In the history of the mandates system we thus recover the role of the League of Nations as an agent of geopolitical transformation. For decades following its demise in the late 1930s, the League was not remembered in this way. It was the institution that was supposed to end war, and that tragically failed to do so. But in the last decade—no doubt because we too now live in an increasingly networked but also uncertain and multipolar world— historians have been looking back at the League with new eyes. In doing so, we have come to appreciate how complex and consequential this first great experiment in international government really was. The League cannot be treated as if it were a state, possessed of a clear decision-making structure and coercive power. Instead, it is better understood as a force field, one made up of shifting alliances, networks, and institutions, which a host of actors entered and sought to exploit.[7] Three institutions in particular structured that field.

First was the Assembly: the committee of the whole, the ostensible parliament of the world. Of course, with much of Africa and Asia under European rule, the League Assembly was much smaller and very much whiter than the United Nations is today. Its global reach was limited, for the United States never formally joined (although most Latin American states did), Germany was admitted only in 1926, Turkey in 1932, and the Soviet Union in 1934—by which point the states most determined to overturn the Versailles order were exiting.[8] And yet, precisely because it was born at a

moment of territorial disarray, the League was always imagined as something more than a meeting ground for sovereign states: it was to rise above
national hatreds and defend nothing less than 'civilization' itself. In November
1920 and every September thereafter, delegates from the fifty-odd member
states, with a train of journalists, lobbyists, and well-wishers, swept into
Geneva, turning this placid bourgeois town into the world capital of rhetoric, diplomacy, and style. Potentates and socialites dispensed patronage
at competitively lavish receptions; politicians from small states sought to
cut a figure and play to audiences at home; and a few famous League
personalities—Czechoslovakia's Eduard Beneš, Belgium's Paul Hymans,
China's Wellington Koo—exercised influence beyond the 'throw-weight' of
their states. This world was beautifully and poignantly memorialized by the
Hungarian cartoonists Alois Derso and Emery Kelen, and by the great
German-Jewish photographer Erich Salomon (later killed at Auschwitz), its
triumphs and tragedies—the admission of Germany, Emperor Haile Selassie's
eloquent denunciation of the Italian subjection of Ethiopia—captured by
the border-dissolving new medium of film.[9] Even the British imperialist
Leo Amery, who loathed the League and—as we shall see—did his best to
weaken it, remembered his Assembly session fondly, recalling the Spanish
delegate exclaiming, when a champagne cork went off with a loud pop at
one festive lunch, 'Voilà l'artillerie de la Société des Nations!'[10] That was
true: the League's power lay, not in arms, but in the simple fact that it
brought the statesmen of the world, well-oiled by drink, into a public arena
where they had to perform civility and espouse internationalism, whatever
their private or even political inclinations.[11]

Behind closed doors and in more rarefied circles, League politics could
have a harder edge. A second institution, the League Council, dominated
politically if not numerically by the great powers, met regularly (around
four times a year) and decided which issues would be addressed—and, more
particularly, not addressed. The scramble to secure Council seats among
those states that weren't great powers, but sometimes thought they were,
was brutal. Only the Scandinavians amicably traded off; other states doubted
their interests were safe in the hands of anyone but themselves. Spain and
Brazil both threatened to leave the League if they weren't given permanent
seats when Germany got one on entry in 1926 (and Brazil did so); hypersensitive Poland used various ruses to hang on to a seat for the whole of the
League's life. Sir Eric Drummond, who thought the Council unquestionably
the nerve centre of the whole project, wearied himself with these negotiations,

the Council growing larger and losing effectiveness as it grew.[12] The great powers responded by withdrawing for private discussions on the side—the 'Locarno tea-parties' much deplored by those excluded but that Drummond shrewdly realized were essential if the powers were to tolerate the League system at all.

But if the Assembly tried to set the agenda and the Council to rein it in, actual responsibility for carrying out policy rested with a third institution, the Secretariat. Drummond had begun building the Secretariat in London, drawing especially on the able men (and, if nearly always in lesser posts, the able women) who had staffed the wartime agencies of allied cooperation. In October 1920 that incipient bureaucracy, complete with baggage and children, boarded a special hired train at Victoria Station and headed for Geneva. The move reinforced its members' sense of election. A League school and a League radio station were founded; affairs and marriages bloomed; and a distinctive ethos—egalitarian, cosmopolitan, sexually emancipated—ruled. Of course, 'spying' would become a major problem too, with ostensibly impartial officials reporting back to their foreign ministries, but by the early 1920s Drummond had created something entirely new: a truly international bureaucracy, structured by function and not by nationality, loyal to an international charter, and capable of efficiently managing a complex programme. This is the structure of the United Nations to this day.[13]

These three institutions were crucial, but when commentators began referring to a 'Geneva spirit'—'l'esprit de Genève'—they meant something more. For the impact of the League was sustained and magnified by the host of international commissions, organizations, lobbies, and experts who were incorporated into aspects of its work or simply volunteered their services. Limited in size and resources (the Secretariat counted only about seven hundred individuals at its height), the League drew on the expertise of, and sometimes simply devolved authority onto, a host of swiftly internationalizing civic and voluntary organizations. Clever officials like Ludwig Rajchman at the Health Section or Rachel Crowdy at the Social Section exploited their close ties to American foundations or international philanthropies to supplement modest budgets and staff. As such projects proliferated and voluntary organizations moved offices to Geneva, nations-who-would-be-states, experts seeking jobs, scholars seeking subjects, and lobbies seeking recognition all clamoured to make their voices heard.[14] The Secretary General presided over that cacophony but did not control it. No one did: that was the whole point.

The peacemakers of 1919, watching the rise of that noisy, polyvalent world, felt a sense of ambivalence and sometimes trepidation. They had thought of the League as a tool for great-power collaboration, but with the Americans and the Soviets outside, the Germans excluded at French insistence, and too many voluble third-rank politicians, pacifists, and 'cranks' massed on the Geneva stage, they doubted it could ever play that role. The League was 'more likely to become a centre of intrigue than a real benefit to the peace of the world', British Prime Minister David Lloyd George complained in December 1920;[15] his Cabinet Secretary Sir Maurice Hankey—the man first offered Drummond's job, but who had rejected it as less important than the work of coordinating British imperial policy— deplored 'the dangerous tendency of the League Secretariat to arrogate to itself too much power'.[16] The two floated schemes to replace the League with a new organization centred on the great powers and sought to bypass the League through the 'diplomacy by conference' of those years—the Washington Conference, the Genoa Conference, and so forth.

Yet the League could not be sidelined. Partly this was because it had the only competent international staff around, so much so that Drummond, in 1922, was belatedly asked to dispatch his teams of translators and typists and précis-writers to Genoa to manage the conference that had tried to exclude them.[17] Partly the League was sustained by the hopes of the millions who joined the national League of Nations societies founded to support it, who signed petitions or protested when their governments violated its norms, who studied the Covenant text or went to lectures about its work, who reverently toured its headquarters in Geneva.[18] But the League also survived because it addressed—indeed, was forced by its member states and constrained by the Covenant to address—issues that no government would or could take on alone.

William Rappard, who knew the institution so well, captured the scope of its activities in a 1925 book aptly titled *International Relations as Viewed from Geneva*. In terms of its mission, Rappard explained, there were really three separate Leagues of Nations.[19] The first he called the 'League to Outlaw War'. This was the League whose provisions absorbed governments and international lawyers as they sought to give teeth to the Covenant; that brought statesmen and officials together to discuss disarmament; and that intervened with more or less success in territorial conflicts—between Sweden and Finland, Greece and Bulgaria, Columbia and Peru, and a host of others—before succumbing to the triple blows of the Manchuria Crisis, the Second Disarmament Conference, and the Italo-Ethiopian War. It is this League on which such hopes were pinned, that was disparaged after 1945, and that people today still have in mind when they say that the League 'failed'.[20]

Alongside this beset world of security conferences and international crises, however, there were two other Leagues of Nations. There was a 'technical' League working to combat the proliferating hazards and traffics of an increasingly interconnected world. This League set standards for air traffic, radio transmission, and child welfare; organized the Austrian bailout and standardized economic data; combated sexual and drug trafficking; dealt with Russian refugees and negotiated the Greek-Turkish population exchange; pioneered development missions to China and Liberia; set up research stations to track epidemic diseases; and ran institutes and conferences to promote economic and intellectual cooperation. This League never 'declined' and only expanded, steadily promoting the authority and elevating the role of those new international actors, the 'expert' and what we would today call the NGO. The political scientist David Mitrany, who had close ties to League officials, had these operations in mind when, during the Second World War, he crafted his 'functionalist' theory of how cooperation on mundane activities might create networks that would promote peace.[21] It is this League that laid the foundation for the institutions of global governance we have today, and that is now the focus of so much historical interest.[22]

And, finally, there was a third League, what one might call the 'world-orderers' League, which worked to adjudicate relations of sovereignty. Rappard, conscious of how many territorial decisions had been made in 1919—and how difficult those were proving to enforce—called this third, inelegantly, 'the League to execute the Peace Treaties'. That League ran plebiscites in or attempted to adjudicate certain disputed areas (Memel, Silesia, Vilna, Mosul, Alexandretta) and administered others (Danzig, the Saarland). It also ran two enormously consequential regimes set up to stabilize and legitimate the decisions reached in Paris and Lausanne. One of these was the minorities regime, a system through which the League Council, guided by Secretariat officials, sought to hold a dozen new or reconstituted East European or Balkan states to promises of minority rights they had made as the price of sovereignty;[23] the second was the mandates system. This League, like the others, changed over time, especially in response to Germany's 1926 entry and then exit only seven years later. It became, in the eyes of some, the

League to *overcome* the peace treaties, with not only Germany but also other states and internationalists trying to use those regimes to challenge and change that settlement. By the mid-1930s the minorities regime had crumbled under that revisionist onslaught, but the mandates system continued, re-emerging in 1945 as the United Nations Trusteeship System.

This book is the first comprehensive history of the mandates system— that is, of the League's effort to manage the imperial order—written in over fifty years.[24] It treats the system as a whole, attending to all seven mandatory powers and all of the fourteen mandated territories scattered through Africa, the Pacific, and the Middle East. It also examines how strategies and struggles over the mandated territories emerged and were played out in three different realms—those of imperial and great-power interests and diplomacy, of the League's officials and norms, and of the balance of forces within the territory itself. These arenas were not, of course, distinct. They were fluid, cross-cutting, and bumped up against one another all the time. Indeed, it is precisely by studying those interactions that our story emerges.

It is a story that will take us to many parts of the world—the windswept scrublands north of South Africa's Orange River, famine-blighted hilltops in Rwanda, Baghdad's public garden at the moment of independence, Syria's Jabal Druze under siege. We will accompany the Samoan trader Olaf Nelson as he gathered signatures against New Zealand's rule, the African American scholar Ralphe Bunche as he headed to Togo to pursue his dissertation research, and the prospector Mick Leahy as he marched into the New Guinea highlands, leaving death and wonder in his wake. But always, those travels will bring us back to Geneva. For Geneva was where quarrels over the mandated territories ended up: it was where Nelson sent his petitions, where Bunche began his research, where Leahy found himself denounced as a murderer. League bodies adjudicated those arguments through internationally mandated public procedures and flexible private diplomacy, through rigorous textual analysis and personal lobbying and pressure. Officials worked hard at times to keep matters quiet, but without much success, for not only was the League founded on the principle of public openness, its institutions were too large and too riven by national and ideological rivalries and loyalties to keep secrets well. National officials shared information with Secretariat officials (and vice versa); disaffected inhabitants sent exposés to humanitarian organizations and political allies. And much made its way into the columns of a vigilant press.

All mandatory powers and all mandated territories were affected by this process of internationalization. They were not, however, all equally affected, nor did League bodies or indeed the Western newspaper-reading public pay all equal mind. This is not, then—it cannot be—a history of political developments in each mandated territory. Such accounts must inevitably be local; they cannot privilege events that reverberated internationally over others critical to developments within the territory itself. A history of international change must do that, however. It must examine those moments when argument and conflict spilled beyond the individual state or empire, landed in the League force field, and went on to affect what we might call the global order as a whole. This book therefore tracks those events and controversies—revolts and famines, certainly, but also debates over 'trusteeship', 'civilization', 'independence', and 'sovereignty'—that reverberated through Geneva and forced an international response. Territories that were lightning rods for controversy (pre-eminently South West Africa and Palestine, though also at particular points Syria, New Guinea, French-mandated Cameroon, Western Samoa, Tanganyika, Rwanda, and Iraq) thus receive sustained attention; those that drew little international scrutiny (the Japanese Islands, British-mandated Cameroon, British- and French-mandated Togo, and Nauru) are only fitfully visible. The eyes of Geneva turned to follow catastrophes and crises; its ears bent to hear particularly strident or eloquent voices. Our eyes and ears will follow them.

Before we begin that tour, however, we must understand how the mandates system emerged and worked. Part One provides that account, looking in three chapters at the roles played by imperial contestation, bureaucratic innovation, and pressure from below in shaping the character of the mandates system. Intended by its Anglo-American founders to serve as a vehicle for inter-imperial collaboration, one that would be in the hands of government officials and that would generalize Anglo-American norms, it was rescued and reshaped—once those founders lost interest—by a group of (largely British) internationalists, humanitarians, and League officials one level down. The system that emerged was much less statist and much more genuinely international than anticipated. It was more dependent on the Secretariat, and that Secretariat was more independent than expected as well. Finally, the system was more open to pressure from various groups claiming to speak either for inhabitants or for 'public opinion'—such pressure flowing to Geneva through a surprisingly open petition process.

The book then traces how League oversight affected the imperial order from the First World War until the Second. As we shall see, geopolitical conditions and tensions, especially what one might call a first 'Cold War' between the powers that made and those that challenged the Versailles settlement, set the bounds within which the League system worked. Indeed, in the period from 1922 until the late 1920s, treated in Part Two, the mandates system served largely to mitigate Anglo-French antagonisms, to promulgate a paternalistic definition of 'trusteeship', and to push claims to 'self-determination' off the table. Chapters on the League's handling of risings and civil disobedience movements in South West Africa, Syria, and Western Samoa lay out this retreat in detail.

Yet the mandates system did not remain in this Anglo-French cul-de-sac, for German entry into the League in 1926 unleashed a new dynamic. One might say that the Germans seized the role the Americans had abdicated, for as the major European power without an empire—and, moreover, as the former sovereign of many of the mandated territories—Germany was determined that if she could not regain her colonies, she could at least fight to realize those 1919 promises of international control, open economic access, and a roadmap towards independence. The chapters in Part Three track the fierce debates within and outside the League over sovereignty, free labour, and possible moves to independence, a story that culminates in Britain's prescient decision to move Iraq from mandate status to a clientelist form of statehood.

That move could perhaps have been a harbinger of future developments, but the economic crisis, German withdrawal in 1933, and the subsequent erosion of the League's authority placed this attempt to develop international norms about empire under considerable strain. As the chapters in Part Four show, after 1935 that project fell into crisis on every level. Italy's attack on Ethiopia that year undermined Western claims to civilizational superiority even within the West, while allied willingness to contemplate colonial concessions to Germany—that is, to contemplate returning one or more territories inhabited by non-whites to a Nazi state—further eroded the legitimacy of the mandates system. When the Commission grew sharply critical of British policy in Palestine, even Britain—hitherto the League's main protector—lost faith in the project of imperial 'internationalization'. By 1939 the mandates system had very few defenders.

It had had, however, profound effects. If international oversight—as opposed to alien rule more generally—left only light traces on some territories, in others those dynamics of scrutiny and publicity had a real impact. Britain's inability in Palestine to back away from a Zionist pledge that most of its High Commissioners came to think misguided, Belgium's decision to entrench ethnic divisions as a tool of labour control in Rwanda and Burundi, and South Africa's inability to annex lightly populated South West Africa: all these attest to the way a Geneva-based culture of international lobbying and debate created new risks for imperial states and at times changed what they wanted. Those local effects were variable and do not conform to any single pattern. Yet, in the system as a whole we find a logic and a teleology.

The mandates system made imperial governance more burdensome and brought normative statehood nearer. This was not what its architects and officials had intended. To the contrary, they sought at every turn to uphold imperial authority and strengthen the prestige and legitimacy of alien, non-consensual rule. The problem was that the internationalization inherent in League oversight worked against those purposes. By offering a platform for wordy humanitarians, belligerent German revisionists, and nationalists determined to expose the brutalities of imperial rule, the mandates system not only undermined imperial authority but also—possibly more importantly—led at least some within the European empires to question whether direct rule was so desirable anyway. That most local inhabitants had no affection for the mandates system seems apparent. Over time, however, many within the imperial powers lost their sympathy for it as well. After all, since the Mandates Commission readily upheld other forms of imperial incursion, failing to prevent massive alienation of native land and insisting that the mandated territories be opened to international concessions and trade, was formal administrative control really necessary? Small wonder that Britain—the most 'global' of the imperial powers—chose to craft in Iraq a form of independence that seemed far less troublesome.

After 1945 the movement towards normative statehood would accelerate. In 1920 there were some fifty independent states; today there are two hundred. Colonies and protectorates, condominiums and trust territories, those trailing appendages of empire, have vanished from the globe. Yet if statehood is now ubiquitous, its makeup is varied indeed. Some states set their own rules, but others lack not only that 'monopoly over the legitimate use of force' which the great German sociologist Max Weber considered the foundation of statehood but also the capacity to provide their citizens with basic services and rights. Their leaders retort that they are as subjected by global corporations and international lending bodies as they once were by imperial states. We live in a world of formally independent states of very varying capacity, and if we look back to the mandates system, we can see this order emerging.

# PART I

# Making the Mandates System

# ONE

## Of Covenants and Carve-Ups

I am very doubtful myself about the success of the League of Nations, but I have no doubt whatever that, if it is to be an effective instrument at all, it can only be so *by virtue of the influence of the British Empire and America* . . . We must try to extend the *pax Britannica* into a *pax mundi*.

Lord Milner, 14 August 1919[1]

[Henry] Simon frankly said that he saw no real difference between a colony and such mandated area. This is the French view. As Peretti said to me later in Paris: 'You will see what these mandates will develop into in ten years.'

Diary of George Louis Beer, entry for 10 August 1919[2]

When elephants fight, the grass suffers.

East African proverb[3]

On the USS *George Washington* in the icy mid-Atlantic in December 1918, George Louis Beer felt the weight of the world on his shoulders. Beer, a forty-six-year-old former businessman and lecturer in British history at Columbia University, was part of the 100-man delegation accompanying Woodrow Wilson on his mission to bring Europe a just and lasting peace. Beer had been the colonial policy expert on 'The Inquiry', that wartime cabal of American academics assembled to plan the settlement; his particular responsibility was to secure the 'free, open-minded, and absolutely impartial adjustment of all colonial claims' promised in the fifth of Wilson's Fourteen Points. Annexation of the conquered German and Ottoman territories had been ruled out of the question, and through 1918 proposals had emerged to place 'backwards' or 'derelict' peoples under international control. But it was still far from clear what that international system might look like.

A methodical and serious-minded man, and with little to do on board ship but eat large meals and take the odd constitutional on deck, Beer hoped to use the voyage to hammer out a plan. But he found the atmosphere on board—he recorded in his diary—'highly undemocratic and unsociable': Wilson kept to his stateroom; it was almost impossible for anyone to get to him. And when Beer finally managed to sit him down for a serious talk, he found his chief's ideas vague at best. The German colonies were to be the 'common property' of that dream project, a League of Nations, with actual administration entrusted to some small non-imperial state. Wilson thought the Scandinavians might do a good job.[4]

Beer's own ideas weren't well developed, but he was fairly certain this wouldn't work. He agreed with Wilson on the fundamentals. Like Wilson, he thought the occupied territories could not be returned, for 'nothing could be more ignoble than...to turn over millions of helpless natives to the tender mercies of Germany'.[5] Like Wilson too, he never considered the prospect of Africans governing themselves. 'The negro race,' Beer had opined in one memorandum for The Inquiry, 'has hitherto shown no capacity for progressive development except under the tutelage of other peoples'.[6] He too thought the work of 'tutelage' had to be internationalized, distinguished from imperial rule, and carried out under open public scrutiny and according to humane and progressive norms.

But Beer hardly thought the small nations of Europe well equipped to carry forward such a plan. What could the Norwegians possibly know about governing colonies? It wasn't just their lack of experience that troubled him. Beer took nineteenth-century ideas about the relative value of different European peoples and civilizations very seriously indeed. At the Peace Conference he would be horrified to see 'Germans, Magyars, and Italians...being sacrificed to people whose cultural value was infinitely less'; he thought it 'far preferable to have Poles under Germans and Jugo-Slavs under Italians than the contrary'.[7] And when it came to governing colonies, Beer was persuaded that one nation provided the model for the world to follow. 'Native rights were most carefully and effectively protected' in the British colonies, and Britain was also the power most committed to those free trading economic policies that the United States thought crucial to future peace.[8] Why not use the League to generalize the British Empire's excellent practices?

Unsurprisingly, British politicians, internationalists, and humanitarians saw it mostly that way as well. By the time Wilson sailed, the British were, metaphorically speaking, in the mid-Atlantic, ready to greet him. The continental settlement reached at Versailles, heavily shaped by French interests and anxieties, would seek above all to contain Germany; the colonial settlement, however, was an Anglo-American product. It looked the way it did because the British were so desperate for an American alliance, but also because American preferences and ideals could be reconciled most easily with British imperial practices. But if the affinity between American and British interests structured the mandates system from the start, it also left the system more vulnerable when the Americans pulled out. By late 1919 the French were openly seeking to subvert an international regime that they perceived—rightly—to be structured against them. The mandates regime that was born at the Peace Conference was nearly dead by 1920, making our first story one of an infanticide barely averted. That system would survive, but it would change, sustained not by American idealism or imperial collusion but rather, much more precariously, by the authority of the League itself.

## The great wartime scramble

No one thought the territories that changed hands in the early years of the First World War would become the harbingers of a new order. They were just booty. For two centuries European empires had adjusted their holdings and borders through global war, sugar islands and princely states changing hands with a shifting balance of power. Why should this war be any different?

While the German armies fought their way through Belgium and dug in in Flanders and northern France, allied and Dominion armies moved to occupy Germany's colonial possessions. Germany's undefended Samoan islands were surrendered to a landing party of New Zealand troops on 29 August 1914. The phosphate island of Nauru was turned over to the HMAS *Melbourne* on 9 September, and some three weeks later, after a short fight, the capital of Germany's holdings in New Guinea and the Bismarck Archipelago fell to an Australian naval force. The Australians then pressed forward towards the equator, only to discover that the Japanese had already sent warships to capture the Caroline, Mariana, and Marshall Islands. By mid-October, all Germany's Pacific possessions were in allied hands.[9]

Ousting Germany from Africa took longer. British and French troops swiftly occupied Togoland and the Cameroonian port of Duala, but the well-equipped German forces in the interior resisted. Not until early 1916 would they pass into Spanish territory. The South West African campaign ran into trouble too, for some troops mutinied rather than take up arms against fellow whites; only in spring 1915 was a new invasion mounted and Windhoek taken. The campaign for German East Africa proved most troublesome of all. For four years the clever German General Paul von Lettow-Vorbeck and his capable African askaris tied up British and South African forces in a guerrilla campaign waged throughout East Africa. That campaign, and the opportunistic seizure of Rwanda and Burundi by a rapacious Belgian force, left famine and devastation in its wake.[10]

None of those conquerors thought they would leave anytime soon. South Africa extended its rail line north and began handing out land to white settlers; Australia doubled the number of New Guinean indentured labourers on seized copra plantations. By 1916, when the British government first appointed an interdepartmental committee to think through policy towards the captured territories, annexationist sentiment was strong. Although the representative from the General Staff warned that the balance of power required a 'strong Teutonic state' in Central Europe, and that Germany would become resentful and hard to manage if not accorded a colonial sphere, his objections were swiftly quashed. Whether to amplify imperial holdings (as with German East Africa), to provide booty and buffers for the Dominions (as with the Pacific territories and South West Africa), or simply as bribes for importunate allies (the plan for Togo and Cameroon), the German colonies should all be retained—a decision confirmed by a War Cabinet Committee on 'Territorial Desiderata' in the spring of 1917.[11]

'What we have we hold': a time-honoured imperial policy that won French and Belgian support as well. Since the French Cabinet and public were transfixed by the carnage on the Western Front, the articulation of colonial aims was left to officials and lobbyists, whose ambitions now grew unchecked. That the German colonies would not be restored went without saying, but when Emmanuel de Peretti and Albert Duchêne, respectively heads of the African departments at the French Foreign and Colonial Ministries, invited Belgian colonial officials Octave Louwers and Pierre Orts to Paris in September 1917 for a private conversation, those assembled swiftly found points of agreement. One was that it was imperative to sweep away the Berlin and Brussels Acts that had established free trade and common norms in the Congo basin, so that European powers might hold their African territories in full sovereignty. Another was that Britain, with its irritating penchant for international agreements and free trade, was likely to be the main impediment. Remember Duchêne and Orts: we shall meet them again wearing new and ill-fitting 'League of Nations' hats.[12]

But the German colonies were not the only prize. The allies were also dismembering and squabbling over the Ottoman Empire. The secret Treaty of London of April 1915 brought Italy into the war with a promise of parts of Southern Anatolia as well as 'equitable compensation' in Africa while leaving the Middle Eastern provinces to Britain and France.[13] All powers, however, found it hard to make good on these plans. Britain's Indian Army had attacked Mesopotamia early in the war, only to find itself mired in a draining campaign that would last four years and cost over 90,000 (mostly Indian) casualties.[14] New surrogates were needed, and in 1915 one was found in Sharif Husayn, ruler of the Hejaz, restive under Ottoman overlordship and willing to lend Britain aid in exchange for recognition of his own sovereign claims. Notes between Husayn and the High Commissioner in Egypt, Sir Henry McMahon, cemented the alliance (and unleashed a century of recriminations), an 'Arab Bureau' of intelligence officers in Cairo

**Figure 1.1** Faysal bin Husayn, King of Syria (1920) and of Iraq (1921–33).

coordinated strategy and paid the subsidies, and Husayn's able and magnetic third son Faysal (Figure 1.1) occupied himself with the dangerous work of cultivating Syrian nationalists in famine-ridden and Ottoman-controlled Damascus. The Arab Revolt began in June 1916 with attacks on Ottoman garrisons and supply lines in and around Mecca, Medina, and Ta'if.[15] Remember Faysal: his gamble on British support would win him a crown and a country, but not the one he or his followers had wanted.

In France, Robert de Caix, the aristocratic, Catholic secretary of the powerful and well-connected *Comité de l'Asie française*, noted that Anglo-Arab alliance with trepidation. France had powerful interests in the Levant. By 1914, France had guaranteed the autonomy of the Christian community of Mount Lebanon for half a century, French companies handled much of the silk trade, French had become a lingua franca for the educated class, and there were 40,000 children enrolled in French schools.[16] Now, de Caix's imperial lobby hoped to bring the whole of Syria—and, if possible, Palestine too—under France's wing. But France had no troops to spare for Middle Eastern adventures and had to use diplomacy to stake its claims. While McMahon parlayed with Husayn, the French diplomat and colonialist François Georges-Picot negotiated with the British Middle East expert Sir Mark Sykes. The controversial agreement that bore their name, finalized in May 1916 but not made public until a year later, stipulated that France would establish 'such direct or indirect administration or control as they desire' in Lebanon and a swathe of territory running from Celicia to Armenia, that Britain would have similar freedom in Mesopotamia, and that much of coastal Palestine would be placed under international control. True, the agreement conceded that the two powers would uphold 'an independent Arab State or a Confederation of Arab States' in the interior, but divided that region into two 'zones' within which France in the north and Britain in the south would have exclusive rights.[17]

In 1916 most British and virtually all French officials thought these promises of Arab statehood would never come due. It was a moment of sweeping but ambiguous pledges. The following November saw the most famous of them, issued in the peculiar form of a letter from British Foreign Secretary Arthur Balfour to the English Zionist, Baron Rothschild. 'His Majesty's Government,' so it read, 'view with favour the establishment in Palestine of a national home for the Jewish people, and will use their best endeavours to facilitate the achievement of this object, it being clearly understood that nothing shall be done which may prejudice the civil and religious rights of existing non-Jewish communities in Palestine, or the rights and political

status enjoyed by Jews in any other country'—sixty-eight words that have
yielded a century of controversy.[18] In the spring of 1918, just months after
British imperial forces under General Edmund Allenby entered Jerusalem, a
Zionist Commission arrived in Palestine to begin planning the new 'homeland'. It was led by Chaim Weizmann, the brilliant Zionist politician and
research chemist—Russian Jew by birth, British by affiliation—who had
emerged as the movement's most adept leader. Remember Weizmann: he
too would gamble on British support and win a state, and it would be the
one he wanted.

So it was that by the autumn of 1918, when German and Ottoman resistance collapsed and Germany asked for an armistice, all the German colonies
and the Ottoman Arab provinces were under allied occupation. They were
a disparate collection of lands: save for the accident of having changed hands
in a war fought for European interests, they had nothing in common. Tiny
Nauru was a few kilometres wide, South West Africa larger than France.
Rwanda and Burundi were densely populated, but the enormous expanse
that became Tanganyika contained only some four million people, mandate
Palestine fewer than a million, arid South West Africa a few hundred thousand. They were unlike in climate, resources, economic development, social
structure, and indeed their prior experience of colonial rule, for whereas
the Middle East territories had at least had Ottoman institutions and Arab
culture in common, Germany had not governed its overseas territories
according to a single plan. South West Africa's indigenous population had
been brutally subjugated to make way for white settlement, but the sophisticated and rank-conscious Samoans had been treated cautiously, and most
New Guineans probably never knew they were under German rule. And
yet, in the interwar years, these disparate and far-flung territories would
have one experience in common. They would be governed under the oversight of the League of Nations.

## The Emergence of the Mandates Plan

To explain how that wartime scramble gave way, within a year, to a plan
to entrust 'civilized' peoples with the benevolent 'tutelage' of the rest, we
have to look beyond imperial statesmen and their machinations. There is a
reason for this. Faced with the Bolshevik challenge and an American public
unwilling to fight a war for imperial aims, a vain and bookish American
President promised a peace of a new kind, a peace without annexations or

indemnities, overseen by a new global body, the League of Nations. That 'Wilsonian moment', as we know, elicited a response that Wilson never imagined, with mobilized publics from Korea to Poland to Samoa—not to mention the populations already taking matters into their own hands in the Middle East—deciding that the President's stirring words applied to them.[19]

To fight the tiger or to ride it? It is enormously consequential that the British government decided, not for the last time, that they had no alternative but to be on the Americans' side. Indeed, not only were British officials and intellectuals already fully engaged in a transatlantic dialogue about the creation of a League of Nations, but when it came to the particular question of how to reform imperial practice, the British were out ahead.[20] This was the case partly because British politicians were constrained by the same liberal political culture that both hampered and empowered Wilson. Unlike France and Belgium, Britain too had entered the First World War without being directly attacked, justifying that engagement as a defence of the rights of small states and the principles of international law. Parliamentary oversight and pressures for greater democratic control of foreign policy were strong and openly annexationist sentiments widely deplored. True, the African conquests were welcomed even by liberals, but only as a means of saving natives from the depredations of the Hun. As early as 1916 the Anti-Slavery Society, the most vocal and well placed of humanitarian lobbies, thus raised the question of how 'the child races of the world' were to be protected at the war's end; and if the Society found it 'absurd' to imagine that 'Mandingos, Hereros, Polynesians, Fiots, Fans, and Kikuyus' might sit beside 'Russian, French and German diplomats' to decide their fate,[21] one year later it had changed its mind. In 1917 and early 1918 the Society, the Labour Party, and an influential slice of liberal opinion all came to agree that Africans should be consulted directly about their wishes and a system of 'international control' established to safeguard their rights.[22]

Most thought these principles entirely compatible with British imperial rule. Ideas of imperial tutelage or 'trusteeship' had a long genealogy, with the history of British anti-slavery cited as evidence of the empire's role in generalizing humanitarian norms.[23] Secure in its assumptions of moral leadership, British politicians were comfortable stating that, as Lloyd George promised in June of 1917, 'the wishes, the desires, and the interests' of the people of the former German colonies 'must be the dominant factor in settling their future government'.[24] Six months later, on 5 January 1918, in a speech given three days *before* Wilson's 'Fourteen Points' address, the Prime

Minister confirmed not only that the peoples of the Middle East deserved to have their 'separate national conditions' recognized, but also that native 'chiefs and councils' of the former German colonies were 'competent to consult and speak for their tribes and members'.[25] Such consultation was, after all, expected to show only a strong preference for British rule. The main problem the British would face, one Foreign Office official remarked smugly, was that 'we cannot hope to take into the British sphere all the peoples in the world who would doubtless like to enter it'.[26]

Which leads us to another reason why Britain found Wilsonian ideas easy to accommodate: because they dovetailed so nicely with British imperial practice. British statesmen had always hunted diligently for 'native rulers' with whom they could ally and trade; a preference for 'indirect rule' marked the imperium at many turns. Various princes and potentates should indeed run their own affairs, guided by British residents or consuls and with the Royal Navy keeping the global peace: this was much the best (and cheapest) approach. But what imperial statesmen tended to mean by that was—as Colonial Secretary Lord Milner (here speaking of Arabia) patiently explained to Lloyd George in 1919—that the native state 'should be kept out of the sphere of European political intrigue and within the British sphere of influence: in other words, that her independent native rulers should have no foreign treaties except with us.'[27] Indeed, the Arab Bureau had been set up to extend British hegemony along such lines.

But in the process something unexpected happened. Some of those British officials began to take Wilsonian language to heart. Consider William Ormsby-Gore, a young Conservative army officer from an aristocratic family seconded to the Arab Bureau in 1916. Ormsby-Gore had found Egyptian politics discouraging—'we rule here by fear & not by love or gratitude or loyalty'[28]—but his work building the alliance with Husayn convinced him that a new approach was possible. The Sykes-Picot agreement profoundly shocked him. 'We make professions of defending and helping small & oppressed nations,' he protested to one of his superiors. If then 'we parcel out between our allies & ourselves vast tracts of countries which do not want us . . . we shall have to admit that the Ramsay Macdonalds, Trevelyans & Shaws at home, and our doubting Indian critics in India, knew us better than we knew ourselves'.[29] Britain should win friends by embracing self-determination, and should do so, he thought (warmheartedly if not entirely logically), for both Arabs and Jews. Recalled to London in 1917, Ormsby-Gore became part of the circle that crafted the Balfour Declaration

and in spring 1918 was sent to Palestine with Chaim Weizmann and the
Zionist Commission (Figure 1.2) to try to 'get the Arab & Jewish leaders to
come to some agreement regarding their respective rights and powers in
future'.[30] Remember Ormsby-Gore: we will soon meet him again, looking
to Geneva to carry forward those projects.

Of course, the British embrace of self-determination was often more
cynical than that. The Sykes-Picot agreement had been struck when the
Ottomans were still in control, but by the end of 1918 virtually the whole
of the Middle East was in British hands. Success bred greater ambitions, as
a host of policymakers began to think that the French might be pushed
aside and the British Empire hold sway over a corridor of colonies and
'native states' running from India to the Cape. When Allenby held back
his troops that December and let Faysal enter Damascus on a white horse
before him, as when British officials read out the Anglo-French Declaration
promising to establish 'National Governments and administrations deriving
their authority from the initiative and free choice of the indigenous popu-

**Figure 1.2** Chaim Weizmann, in white suit, and the Zionist Commission to
Palestine, Spring 1918. First two officers on the left: Edwin Samuel (son of Herbert
Samuel) and William Ormsby-Gore.

lations', they were making a bid for their own hegemony as well. As Lord Curzon, then Lord President of Council, pithily put it in one Cabinet committee meeting, the British were going to 'play self-determination for all it is worth' to secure their imperial gains.[31]

Out of this potent brew of liberal internationalism, imperial humanitarianism, and sheer territorial acquisitiveness the British proposals for the mandates system emerged.[32] There was still no consensus. South African Prime Minister Jan Christiaan Smuts made one influential case for the British Empire as a model for the League in his December 1918 pamphlet, *The League of Nations: A Practical Suggestion*. But Smuts' florid production was in fact an effort at containment, for he restricted international control to the Middle East alone, since the German colonies were all 'inhabited by barbarians, who not only cannot possibly govern themselves, but to whom it would be impracticable to apply any ideal of political self-determination'.[33] The Anti-Slavery Society thought otherwise, and even some within the Colonial Office were prepared to accept that the League should have the right to visit territories, terminate mandates, and adjudicate disputes between states. Indeed, if the League thought such stipulations should extend to all colonies, one official noted that 'Britain at any rate would have no objections to raise.'[34]

But the French would. Through December of 1918 French officials watched the emerging Anglo-American alliance with mounting rage. To their mind, France had won its right to territorial compensation at Verdun, and Britain's attempt to change the rules of the game amounted to treason. France needed West Africa to provide soldiers in any future war, and at the Quai d'Orsay (the Foreign Ministry) Robert de Caix thought Faysal's new Syrian state little more than a British surrogate.[35] But when French diplomats tried to get their British counterparts to come to a bilateral agreement before the Americans arrived, they found their erstwhile allies evasive and difficult. The British, having cast in their lot with Wilson, would use that alliance to force acceptance of a mandates system no one else wanted.

## The waxing and waning of Wilsonianism

In January 1919 the various national delegations settled into the grand Parisian hotels and got to work. George Louis Beer thought they operated very differently. The British were well prepared, and Beer found the atmosphere at the Hotel Majestic refreshingly 'democratic', with 'all the big political personages from all corners of the Empire' eating together in the dining room.[36] The French were poorly prepared but it hardly mattered, for Prime Minister Georges Clemenceau paid no attention to his ministers and ignored their advice.[37] Beer's own American delegation was most paradoxical. Wilson had arrived with dozens of experts and reams of reports and plans, but once in place he ignored them. A story was going round, Beer recorded in frustration in March, that when the American experts had good ideas they took them to the French, who passed them to the British, who finally brought them to Wilson.[38]

That the British would mediate between the moralizing Americans and the rest became clear as soon as the colonial settlement came up. The United States, France, Britain, Italy, and Japan readily agreed on 24 January that the German colonies would not be given back, but Wilson's proposal to administer them under League mandate won support only from Lloyd George, and even he suggested that the Pacific and South African territories be exempted. The Dominions and the Japanese ministers vociferously agreed, and the French Colonial Minister Henry Simon stated on 27 January that while France was willing to apply the 'open door' and to protect the native population, she claimed a 'right to sovereignty' in order to carry out 'her work of civilization'. The Peace Conference had been in session for ten days, and already anti-annexationism was in tatters. 'The world would say that the Great Powers first portioned out the helpless parts of the earth, and then formed a League of Nations,' Wilson interjected angrily. No one would have confidence in a League constructed on that basis.[39]

Lloyd George scrambled for compromise. He thought the mandates system worth saving, not only in order to keep Wilson on board, but—as he told the British Empire Delegation—for sound imperial reasons as well. Lord Robert Cecil, the maverick Conservative and internationalist who became Wilson's main British partner in the project to frame the League of Nations, agreed: the proposed standards prevailed in the British Empire anyway but would force reform on 'the badly-governed colonies of France and Portugal'. On 27 January, Smuts had insisted on the need to limit the mandates system to the Middle East territories where people could 'speak for themselves', but Lloyd George now thought the system could—if there were different levels of mandate—be extended.[40] Australia's fiery Welsh Prime Minister Billy Hughes still carped and caviled, but by leaning on Wilson and the Dominion premiers alike, Lloyd George won agreement.

On 30 January 1919 the Supreme Council agreed that the Ottoman Middle East and the former German colonies, being inhabited by 'peoples not yet able to stand by themselves under the strenuous conditions of the modern world', would be administered by 'advanced nations' on the principle 'that the well-being and development of such peoples form a sacred trust of civilization'. Three levels of mandate were defined. 'A' mandates would be drafted for the communities formerly under Ottoman rule, who had 'reached a stage of development where their existence as independent nations can be provisionally recognized', and who were therefore to be rendered 'advice and assistance' by a mandatory selected in consideration of their own wishes. 'B' mandates would be applied to Germany's ex-colonies in East, West, and Central Africa, which would be governed under various humanitarian principles and would grant equal economic access to all League states. Finally, a set of territories that 'owing to the sparseness of their populations, or their small size, or their remoteness from the centres of civilisation, or their geographical contiguity to the mandatory state'—the Peacemakers had the Pacific territories and South West Africa in mind—could be administered as under 'C' mandates as 'integral portions' of the mandatory power's own territory. The French were still unhappy with the planned proscription on militarization, but when Lloyd George breezily assured Clemenceau that provided they did not 'train big nigger armies for the purposes of aggression' they could recruit at will, France too accepted the mandates system in principle.[41]

The decisions reached on 30 January would hold. There would be a mandates system, with three levels of 'mandate' and with the obligations of the administering power and the rights of the subject populations varying by level. The language and structure agreed that day would become Article 22 of the League Covenant. But much was still unclear—including which nations would act as 'mandatories', which national communities in the Middle East would come into the system (the situation of the Armenians, Kurds, and indeed of Anatolia itself being still in limbo), and the precise conditions under which mandatories would rule. In theory, the Supreme Council of the allied powers was to decide those questions, and certainly it heard much testimony about them. The 'Big Four'—and then, when Italy walked out, the 'Big Three'—listened to Belgium's appeal to retain Rwanda and Burundi, to the Italians' exigent demands, and to Chaim Weizmann's case for Zionist rights in Palestine. They heard Emir Faysal's appeal for international recognition of his fragile government in Damascus, American academics' warning of the utter opposition by Syrians to French rule, the Maronite patriarch's case for a 'greater Lebanon' under French protection, and the flowery perorations of a francophile Syrian delegation organized by the Quai d'Orsay. On 20 March they agreed to send an international Commission (which France and Britain then boycotted) to discern the views of the Middle Eastern populations. They let J. H. Harris, the energetic Secretary of the British Anti-Slavery Society—doing his best, one civil servant complained, to have the Society 'recognized as one of the Great Powers'—argue for stringent international oversight, a proscription on land transfers, and the establishment of some sort of 'Court of Appeal' before which native representatives could be heard.[42] They did not grant an audience to the first Pan-African Congress, convened in Paris by W. E. B. Du Bois to assert the rights of peoples of African descent to be consulted about the continent's fate, although Du Bois did meet with Beer and a few other advisors to Wilson.[43] Appeals for consultation or autonomy were coming in from populations across Africa, the Middle East, and the Pacific, but the Council did not acknowledge them.[44]

Until 7 May, however, no further decisions were made. Instead, the principals turned to their seconds to sort out matters behind the scenes. Wilson left negotiations over mandates to Beer and his confidential advisor, 'Colonel' Edward House, Clemenceau to his Colonial Minister, Henry Simon, and Lloyd George to his Colonial Secretary, Viscount Alfred Milner, who was called over to Paris to craft a system with which all parties could agree. Milner had mixed feelings about that. One of the great imperial proconsuls of the Edwardian period, he had been an expansionist High Commissioner in South Africa and the patron of a talented group of young imperial officials before serving as part of the tight cabal guiding war policy under Lloyd George. He had emerged from the First World War certain that Britain's imperial power and not much else shielded the world from anarchy, and while he was willing to gamble on a 'League of Nations', Milner, like Smuts, thought of it mostly as a mechanism for universalizing British norms and practices. A pragmatist and a patriot, he had read the reports of Lloyd George's coercion of the Dominions' premiers 'not without anxiety', believing that whatever was done elsewhere, South West Africa and the Pacific colonies 'should be handed over *simpliciter* to the British flag'.[45]

The first job of the British Empire's delegation, Milner thus decided, was to 'try to clear our own minds as to what we wanted' before worrying about the complexities of negotiations with the other powers. In a crucial memo-randum dated 8 March, he recast the system as a British imperialist might. He left the 'A' territories aside, for as the war in the Middle East was con-tinuing, nothing much could be done there but to wait and see. When it came to Africa, however, Milner began by pushing League sovereignty—central to Wilson's conception—off the table. Sovereignty was a technical question of interest to lawyers alone, he argued rather disingenuously: the crucial point was that 'actual authority' would be exercised entirely by the mandatory power, which was 'in the position of a man receiving a property subject to certain servitudes'. This was a formula that implicitly still vested sovereignty in the imperial power, and indeed, in the case of the 'C' man-dates, Milner thought those servitudes so slight that the territory could be incorporated into the administering state. Nor could he see any particular impediment to bringing a 'B' mandate (he was thinking here of East Africa) into administrative union with a neighbouring colony. In sharp contrast to the plans circulated by the Anti-Slavery Society, Milner made no attempt to define the League's powers, clearly feeling that the less said about that the better.[46] From some early meetings with Henry Simon and Albert Duchêne, Milner knew how little the French liked the idea of League oversight, but in his system at least, there was little 'oversight' to which they could object.[47]

On 7 May the Supreme Council finally allocated the African mandates. Unsurprisingly, occupiers were everywhere confirmed as mandatories, although the whole of German East Africa (including Rwanda and Burundi, now occupied by Belgium) went to Britain, and Britain and France were asked to make a joint recommendation about Togo and Cameroon.[48] Milner then tried to settle all the remaining questions. He and Simon met repeat-edly with the Italians and together resisted their extensive North African claims.[49] He met with the Belgian delegation, and—to the disgust of Beer, his own Under-Secretary Leo Amery, Lord Curzon (soon to take over as Foreign Secretary), and the Anti-Slavery Society, all of whom had the lowest possible opinion of Belgian colonial rule—was persuaded by the impec-cably prepared Pierre Orts to let Belgium retain Rwanda and Burundi.[50] And he met bilaterally with Simon about Togo and Cameroon, initially amicably agreeing that the 'small strips' of Togo should simply be incorp-orated into the neighbouring French and British colonies, 'without any ques-tion of a mandate',[51] only to be told by Lloyd George that the Supreme Council had by no means agreed that West Africa could be excused from the regime.[52] Had Milner and Simon been left to their own devices, they might have made short work of the mandates system altogether.

**Figure 1.3** East African *Schutztruppen* on parade in Berlin, 2 March 1919, led by Paul von Lettow-Vorbeck. Heinrich Schnee, last Governor of German East Africa, is third, in the dark uniform.

But as Lloyd George realized, the allies needed the mandates system, for it was the only defence against a charge of simple annexation. On 7 May, the very day the territories were allocated, the German delegation received the draft peace terms, which provoked mass meetings, protests, and a week of 'national mourning'.[53] The 'war guilt' clause and the territorial losses in the East probably hit hardest, but the requirement that Germany renounce the overseas colonies was also a blow. Two months earlier, Germany's 'undefeated' General Paul von Lettow-Vorbeck had led the just-repatriated East African *Schutztruppe* in their colonial uniforms through cheering crowds in Berlin (Figure 1.3). Germany's colonies, the German delegation insisted, were now more necessary than ever, providing vital raw materials, markets, and space for settlement to the shrunken new Republic. Moreover, 'as one of the great civilized races, the German people have the right and duty to co-operate... in the education of undeveloped races, the common task of civilized humanity', and would willingly govern 'in trust'.[54] The allies retorted that Germany had forfeited that civilizational standing entirely. It had unleashed a war that was 'the greatest crime against humanity and the freedom of peoples that any nation, calling itself civilized, has ever consciously committed'. The record of German colonial rule made it impossible 'to entrust to her the responsibility for the training and education of their inhabitants'.[55] Few phrases would rankle more.

And with that, on 28 June 1919, Germany's new Social Democratic government was constrained to sign the treaty, at a ceremony that also brought the League of Nations into effect. But while the Covenant was included in that text, the mandates were not, for Milner hadn't secured agreement. Although a Commission under his chairmanship was kept in session in London through July and early August, it still made little progress.[56] One problem was the dogged Japanese objection to the omission of the 'open door' clause from the 'C' mandate texts—a decision taken to enable Australia to maintain its exclusion of non-whites[57]—but a second and more intractable one was that the French now hoped to dispense with the system altogether. As the Foreign Office's legal advisor explained, the French intended to make liability for military service universal across French West Africa and did not want to be bound by any agreement that might make that difficult,[58] nor would they discuss 'A' mandates at all.[59] After a final meeting of the Commission on 5 August, which the French boycotted, Milner gave up.[60] The French were determined to 'just be squatters,' he reported privately to Foreign Secretary A. J. Balfour, and 'like other squatters they will, by mere lapse of time, become owners'.[61]

Milner didn't much care. He was an imperialist far more than a League man and was also one of the few who didn't think the British should try, as he put it, to 'diddle the French out of Syria'.[62] But for those British statesmen committed to the League, not to mention those committed to Faysal, French prevarication was profoundly worrying. Robert Cecil, Balfour, and the newly appointed Secretary General of the League, Sir Eric Drummond, all urged Milner to keep the Commission in session to draft the Middle East mandates—with a clause, Cecil helpfully suggested, specifying that each territory was now 'an independent state under the guarantee of the League of Nations', language entirely unacceptable to both Britain and France.[63] Eight months earlier, with France's position in the Middle East negligible and Wilson ascendant, Britain had rebuffed French overtures; now, with the American star waning, it was the French turn to put Britain off. Milner was about to go to Egypt to devise a new constitutional settlement, and Cecil now suggested that he set the standard by placing Egypt under mandate—a request that generated one of Milner's most astute letters.

'I have... always been favourable to the "mandate" principle,' Milner told Cecil—not least because he regarded it as 'nothing more than the clothing in a definite form and investing with international authority of the kind of system which we have in practice been trying to work out in Egypt'. Indeed, if other Ottoman areas had been put under mandate, Britain might well consider whether to 'complete the edifice' by putting Egypt on the same footing. But no such mandates had yet been created, and:

> We really cannot go on playing at this game of mandates all by ourselves. Before I would agree to putting any portion of the world, which we at present control, under a mandate, I should want to feel much surer than I do that the mandatory system is going to work. At present, it is not too much to say that nothing has been done to make it a reality except what we have done (I might almost say what *I* have done), and that we have not succeeded in imposing its restrictions upon anybody but ourselves.

The French, Milner noted, had 'firmly declined to accept one fundamental provision of the mandate which happened not to suit them', and had since made clear that they were disinclined to accept a mandate in West Africa at all.

And who was going to make them do so? No one but Britain and the United States really wished to make the League of Nations a reality, and the United States 'seems to me less and less inclined to put any weight into the effort to make it an effective force'. Britain could not therefore afford to quarrel with France, nor should it accept all the nuisance of giving people 'who object to being governed at all... the right to haul you over the coals before an international tribunal' unless by doing so they established the authority of the League 'all round'. Milner had every intention of trying to give Egypt a constitution 'on what I might call mandatory lines' but would not open Egypt up to international interference unless there was some chance of the regime being accepted by other powers.[64] And with that, he left for Egypt.

What Milner failed to acknowledge, of course, was that the 'fundamental provision' to which the French objected—the ban on military recruiting—was one that undermined French security while leaving British power intact. West Africa was the French Empire's main reservoir of military manpower, as India (and not Africa) was Britain's—and one can imagine Britain's response had France proposed demilitarizing the Indian subcontinent in the interests of world peace. With the election of the right-wing Bloc National government in November 1919, with Wilson and the troublesome Monsieur Beer back in the United States, and with Senegalese and Moroccan troops arriving in the Levant, France had little reason to compromise.

That winter the prospects of the mandates system reached a nadir. The Versailles Treaty was running into trouble in Congress; although few knew this, Wilson had suffered a debilitating stroke and would never regain his strength. Mercifully, the League's supporters could not foresee how vindictively the United States would turn on its offspring: in 1922 and 1923 the Republican administration of Warren Harding would leave its letters unanswered while compelling each mandatory power to negotiate a separate treaty guaranteeing the United States equal rights in each territory—a wearying process that further delayed ratification of the mandate texts.[65] But March 1920 was bad enough, for the US Senate rejected the Treaty for the final time and George Louis Beer—the man slated to head the Mandates Section in Geneva—suddenly died. The mandates system as an Anglo-American project was over.

## Creating facts on the ground

American retreat made one thing crystal clear: Britain and France would have to reconcile. With no prospect of an American presence in Armenia or Anatolia, the British swiftly concluded that their bread would after all be buttered on the same side as the French. The Sykes-Picot agreement once again providing the framework, British officials accepted that they could not interfere in the French 'zone'. In return, they made clear that Palestine was none of France's business. Between late 1919 and early 1921, in a series of often acrimonious private meetings and by creating 'facts on the ground', the two imperial powers came to terms (Figure 1.4).

The public face of that agreement was the San Remo conference of April 1920. There, the Supreme Council finally allocated the Middle East mandates. Mesopotamia and Palestine went to Britain, and Syria (including Lebanon) to France; the two powers also initialled a secret agreement granting France a quarter of Iraqi oil. Yet, what was achieved at San Remo was not the common programme imagined by Wilson and Smuts but something more like an agreement to disagree. Thus, while the French and the Italians made clear their dislike of the Zionist cast of the Palestine mandate and objected especially to language pledging to safeguard only the non-Jewish population's 'civic and religious' and not their 'political' rights, they accepted Curzon's strained claim that 'in the British language all ordinary rights were included in "civil rights"'.[66] Weizmann, present at San Remo, was euphoric: the agreement was 'as significant as the Balfour Declaration'.[67] In return, the British confirmed their disengagement from Syria.

**Figure 1.4** Allies at odds: First conference of Hythe, May 1920. Left to right: Philip Sassoon, General Weygand, Marshal Foch, Field Marshal Sir Henry Wilson, ?, David Lloyd George, Philip Kerr, Alexandre Millerand, François Marsal, Austen Chamberlain, G. Camelqueck, and Maurice Hankey.

The two powers then moved to create the Middle Eastern states and borders they desired. In the French zone the disposition was largely the brainchild of Robert de Caix, now appointed Secretary General to the new High Commissioner to Syria, the devoutly Catholic veteran of the Moroccan campaigns General Henri Gouraud. Together, from their base in Beirut, Gouraud and De Caix would remake the map of Syria. Their first act was to ensure a separate existence for Lebanon. A separate Lebanon, Faysal had told the American commissioners sent to discern local views in July 1919, was 'an unnatural idea' inspired by the occupying French: 'Syria' was a national unit, of which Lebanon was an integral part. Not all inhabitants of what became 'Lebanon' agreed, with the Maronite community of Mount Lebanon particularly anxious about Faysal's agenda. Adept lobbying by

**Figure 1.5** Architects of mandate Syria: General Gouraud and François Georges-Picot, front and centre, on the steps of the Eglise latine, Beirut, 23 November 1919; Robert de Caix in a dark suit directly behind and to the right of Picot.

Patriarch Hawayik won a promise from Clemenceau in November 1919 of an independent Lebanon, and at Gouraud's insistence largely Moslem areas claimed by 'our Lebanese clients...the main foundation for our influence in Syria' (including the Biqa valley, Beirut, and Tripoli) were placed within it (Figure 1.5).[68] On 1 September 1920, Gouraud announced the establishment of 'Greater Lebanon' under French mandate.[69]

By then, the Faysali state had also been swept away. The Commission led by the Americans Henry King and Charles Crane which had travelled through Syria and Palestine in the summer of 1919 had concluded that the Syrian population was implacably opposed to French rule, but its report was never made public and—except in mobilizing local opinion—had no effect.[70] Through 1919, Allenby had kept some 45,000 British troops in Syria, compared to a mere 8,000 for France,[71] but towards the end of the year those forces began pulling out, leaving Faysal to make the best deal with the French that he could. Summoned to Paris in October, he was read out terms. France would recognize the 'independence' of the Arab state, but

in exchange French advisors would organize its administration, army, and police; France would defend its borders and handle its foreign relations; and
economic concessions would be granted preferentially to France—a requirement in violation of Article 22 itself.[72] Most reluctantly, Faysal accepted this
ultimatum—'he had been handed over tied by feet and hands to the French,'
he told one British officer[73]—but Syrian nationalists did not. On 8 March
1920, the day the US Senate rejected the Versailles Treaty, a Syrian General
Congress meeting in Damascus proclaimed Syria an independent state 'within
its natural boundaries'—that is, including Lebanon and Palestine—and named
Faysal its king.[74] When the San Remo decision to confer the mandate on
France was announced the next month, Faysal refused to accept it.[75]

Gouraud and De Caix would not let that defiance stand. The Quai d'Orsay
had already secured an absolute commitment of British non-intervention,
whatever action the French took,[76] and that May, De Caix negotiated an
armistice with Turkey—a move, Faysal wrote Lord Curzon, that signalled
Gouraud's intention 'to find some excuse for starting military operations
against my Government in Damascus' (Figure 1.6).[77] He was right: in a long

**Figure 1.6** King Faysal, on a white horse, inspecting troops in front of the Hotel
Baron, Aleppo, June 1920.

memorandum outlining his plans for Syria, De Caix had already decided on the expulsion of the Faysali government. 'Not only was a Sharifian monarchy something artificial and absolutely alien to the traditional aspirations and divisions in the country', but it had also been dreamed up by 'English Arabophiles' as a weapon to use against France. The English aim, De Caix wrote bitterly, had been to arouse Arab nationalism in Syria while keeping Mesopotamia untainted, 'and thus to use it to expel France from Syria'. No compromise was possible: instead, France must oust Faysal and divide up the territory. Lebanon and the Kurdish and Turkish areas would be given separate administrations, while Syria itself would be carved up into eight or nine loosely federated statelets. It was entirely a plan to divide and rule.[78]

With French troop strength now up to 80,000, the denouement came only days later. London having instructed Allenby not to respond to Faysal's appeals,[79] on 24 July 1920 the Sharifian forces battled French Senegalese and Moroccan troops for some eight hours on the plains of Maysalun outside Damascus (Figure 1.7). Artillery and aircraft were heavily used, Gouraud reported to Paris, and Faysal's war minister was found dead on the field.[80]

**Figure 1.7** General Gouraud, on a white horse, inspecting French Senegalese troops before the battle of Maysalun, July 1920.

In Britain, the news was received with consternation. In the House of Commons a few days earlier, Ormsby-Gore and Cecil had denounced French behaviour as absolutely in conflict with the principles of the Covenant, but were told shortly that Britain had no grounds for complaint. France was merely seeking to enforce order and ensure respect for the mandate—precisely the same policy that Britain was pursuing in Mesopotamia.[81] Lord Curzon, who had just replaced Balfour as Foreign Secretary, had a quiet word with Philippe Berthelot, Secretary General at the Quai d'Orsay, saying that Britain had obligations to Faysal and would not view his 'disappearance... without some concern'—but beyond this warning, Britain would not intervene.[82] Faysal and his supporters fled and within days were in Palestine.

The Mesopotamian parallel was an apt one, for in the summer of 1920 the British zone was also in flames. The Anglo-French declaration of November 1918 promising local self-government had been read out in Baghdad as in Damascus and Jerusalem, but the acting Civil Commissioner there, army officer Sir Arnold Wilson, was persuaded that the local Arabs had no desire for self-government and had imposed an 'Indian' style of direct administration instead. That summer, the Shi'a tribes of the Euphrates allied with urban (mostly Sunni) nationalists to unleash a major rising aimed at forcing out the infidel occupiers. By November the British had re-established control, but only through heavy use of air power and at the cost of some £40 million.[83]

Yet even as costs mounted and battles raged, those distinctive British ideas about 'independence' reasserted themselves. 'The time has gone by when an Oriental people will be content to be nursed into self-government by a European power,' one Foreign Office advisor had written in May 1920; given those awakened national feelings, 'direct administration' in the Middle East was out of the question.[84] Its cost was too high anyway: militarily and financially overstretched, already struggling to find money and men for campaigns in Ireland, India, Egypt, and Eastern Europe, British ministers in London—and still more a restive British House of Commons—viewed Britain's Mesopotamian commitments as a costly extravagance. As the French poured troops into Syria, British ministers and officials in Iraq searched for another model.[85]

A genuine feeling of compunction towards Faysal also shaped British thinking. 'Faysal alone of all Arabian potentates has any idea of [the] practical difficulties of running a civilized government,' Sir Arnold Wilson wrote only a week after that monarch's expulsion from Damascus. Might Faysal be offered Mesopotamia instead?[86] Curzon agreed, and in early August he and Lloyd George informed the new French premier Alexandre Millerand and Philippe Berthelot of this plan. Millerand was, predictably, horrified. The British should understand 'how impossible it would be for the French Government to let Feisul, who had behaved in a traitorous manner to the French, occupy Mesopotamia'. The British, however, were not willing to back down. They were pouring blood and treasure into the sands in Iraq, Lloyd George told Millerand bluntly, and could no longer afford it. Moreover, while they had not protested when the French had ousted Faysal from Damascus, considering this none of their business, they had made a promise to establish an Arab state and intended to keep it.[87] Gouraud's fierce protests from Syria had no effect.[88] In Iraq, British political officers began organizing declarations by notables in their region in favour of Faysal's candidacy (no easy business in the Kurdish north, one sourly recalled).[89] On 23 August 1921, wearing a military uniform rather than his customary Arab dress, Faysal was crowned king of Iraq.

Palestine, too, was restive in the spring of 1920, its public life already marked by a pattern of rival mobilization by Zionists and the urban Arab population. In early April celebrations of the Muslim festival of Nebi Musa degenerated into a terrible pogrom, with Jewish self-defence units mobilizing in response.[90] The news that the Balfour Declaration was to be incorporated into the Palestine mandate aroused 'great excitement' among Palestine's still almost 90 per cent Arab population, and Allenby warned from Egypt that Muslims would regard the 'appointment of a Jew as first Governor, even if he is a British Jew, as handing country over at once to a permanent Zionist Administration'.[91] Sir Herbert Samuel, a former Liberal Home Secretary and English Zionist (he had been present at San Remo to ensure the inclusion of the Balfour Declaration in the mandate), arrived to take over as High Commissioner anyway, and Britain's long and futile attempt to win Arab consent to Jewish immigration began (Figure 1.8). But Samuel's other effort at conciliation was more lasting: the formation of Transjordan.

In 1920 the disposition of the swathe of land east of the Jordan River was still far from certain. The region was sparsely inhabited and about half the population, estimated around 230,000, were nomadic Bedouins. According to the Sykes-Picot agreement, the region lay in the British zone, but insofar as it had come under state control at all, Faysal, who had won the allegiance

**Figure 1.8** Herbert Samuel's arrival in Jaffa as the first High Commissioner, 30 June 1920.

of local shaykhs by providing mediation, subsidies, and services, had governed its northern regions from Syria.[92] The collapse of that regime led to the re-establishment of tribal authority and some efforts by the French to exert influence as well. Samuel was eager to establish British authority, and with grudging consent from London he travelled to Salt in August 1920 to win the consent of notables to post British political officers in the territory.[93] But there were Hashemite interests to consider too. That November, Husayn's second son Abdullah arrived in Ma'an with an armed force of 300 to defend the family claim. Driven by his presence, anxieties about French influence, and the imperative need to keep costs down, a second 'Sherifian solution' took shape.[94]

★ ★ ★

In March 1921 virtually everyone who was anyone in British Middle Eastern policy met in Cairo. The new Colonial Secretary, Winston Churchill, attended along with a host of Britain's top military brass, and Percy Cox and Herbert Samuel, High Commissioners respectively for Iraq and Palestine, brought their most important officials. There, the 'Sharifian solution' was ratified. Britain would support an Arab government in Iraq; the Royal Air Force would be entrusted with defence, 'pacifying' the Kurdish and tribal populations from the air; an Anglo-Iraq Treaty would be negotiated regulating the relations of the two states; and Faysal would be offered the throne. The group was less sure about Abdullah, but they agreed to give him a trial in Transjordan, supported by a British subsidy and British officers.[95]

Watching this process from Beirut was, of course, Robert de Caix, and at the end of March he travelled to Jerusalem for a word with Churchill, who was meeting there with Samuel and Abdullah following the Cairo Conference (Figure 1.9). He was supposed to smooth Anglo-French relations, but how could he do that when the policies of the two states were so diametrically opposed? In allying with the Arabs, De Caix warned, 'England was playing with a force that it would not be able to master', one that would inevitably affect France as well. Churchill retorted that France's expulsion of Faysal had caused Britain difficulties of its own, and that Britain was as free to organize administrations in its zone as the French had shown themselves to be in theirs.[96]

**Figure 1.9** Architects of mandate Palestine in Jerusalem, 28 March 1921: Emir Abdullah, Herbert Samuel, and Winston Churchill.

And there we must leave the two imperial powers in 1921, glowering at one another across the Sykes-Picot line. They had come, finally, to terms, accepting the relative spheres set by occupation in Africa and by secret treaty in the Middle East. But the idea that they were colluding could not be more far-fetched, for they were hardly even on speaking terms, and the system they were supposed to be running—the mandates system—was scarcely to be seen. Its Anglo-American foundation had crumbled, and French antipathy to the whole project ran unchecked. But its supporters—at this stage a polyglot assortment of (mostly British) internationalists, humanitarians, and lawyers, with the odd League official thrown in—still had one trick up their sleeves. 'Conversation *à deux* gives opportunities for unreasonableness on the part of one of the negotiators which would not present themselves if there were outside participants,' Robert Cecil advised shrewdly: it was time to bring more voices into the room.[97] And where were those to be found? If the mandates system were to become a reality, Britain would have to look to Geneva.

# TWO

## Rules of the Game

Monsieur Avenol [French Deputy Secretary General] said that . . . the Secretariat . . . had no administrative or executive power of its own, nor had its members the duty, or the right, of initiating policy . . . All power of initiative thus rested in the Members [States] of the League.

Professor Rappard, while admitting the officially impersonal character of the Secretariat, set against this the position in actual fact, namely, the very real influence of members of the Secretariat upon opinion in League matters, and in particular the recognised system whereby the Council's decisions were prepared by its servants—its intelligent and responsible servants—in the Secretariat.

League of Nations Directors' Meeting Minutes, no. 74, 28 February 1923[1]

By the summer of 1920 the mandates system was a naked and shivering shadow of its Wilsonian self. Occupiers had been named 'mandatories', but not a single mandate text had been agreed nor any oversight apparatus set up. Promises to consult local wishes—much less to build national governments—had been broken and those who contested the new dispensation exiled or crushed. But if that crackdown cemented allied control, it disillusioned and angered internationalists across the globe. 'The system of Mandates did not appear to have been received with very much sympathy by public opinion,' the Italian representative pointed out at the eighth meeting of the League Council held in San Sebastian, Spain, in early August 1920, four months after the San Remo decisions. 'The Mandates were regarded as convenient fictions of a temporary character.'[2] It was far from clear that the system would amount to anything at all.

And indeed, it could well have ended then and there. That it did not owed less to those ostensible architects of the mandates system, Wilson, Smuts, Lloyd George, and Milner—none closely involved in mandate matters by

1920 anyway—than to the quiet persistence of a much less flamboyant and largely forgotten group of men: the early officials of the League Secretariat. Bureaucrats are unglamorous historical actors. But to turn programmes into practices, especially when the visionaries have either left the stage or turned petulant, demands a particular sort of character and capacity. In 1920 three men who cast their lot with the League—its first Secretary General, Sir Eric Drummond, his confidential assistant, Philip Baker, and the first Director of the Mandates Section, William Rappard—rescued the near-expiring mandates regime. They had the support of key (mostly British) statesmen as well, but they considered the work their job and brought to the task all those skills—networking, planning, report-writing, alliance-building, compromising—on which successful administration depends. Bureaucracy, more than idealism, tamed the demons of power. In 1920 the allied powers did very largely as they liked; by 1922 they were grudgingly learning new rules. To understand how this transformation happened, we move back to London in 1919, where a punctilious Scot began building a new model army.

## Drummond, Baker, and the Secretariat

Nothing the League produced was more quietly revolutionary than the international Secretariat. There was no real precedent. When statesmen gathered to transact business before 1914, they did so in private, with at most a secretary or two to keep minutes and draft communiqués. Follow-up was left (or not) to individual states. The League, however, was to meet regularly and would need a staff. The Covenant thus stipulated that a permanent Secretariat be established and in an annex named the first Secretary General to head it: Sir Eric Drummond.

A career Foreign Office official who had acted as Arthur Balfour's unobtrusive right-hand man at the peace conference, Drummond was chosen when no leading statesman seemed appropriate or available and Sir Maurice Hankey decided to remain Cabinet Secretary. Drummond was forty-three in 1919. A gangly, droopy-eyed Scottish aristocrat (in 1937 he became the seventh Earl of Perth), he was, the catty Spanish head of the disarmament section remarked, the only man he'd ever met who looked entirely natural in plus fours. Yet Drummond's languorous mien was deceptive, for he proved to be highly organized, meticulous, good at selecting staff (especially in the early days), and able to mediate disputes and deliver bad news without

**Figure 2.1** Sir Eric Drummond as Secretary General.

offence. True, in contrast to a strong-minded figure like Dag Hammarskjöld, Drummond was self-effacing to a fault, much more the secretary than the general (as the joke went). But, landed the task of creating an institution from scratch, and with no precedent for his role, his innate caution (which was not servility) proved an asset. He had the rare distinction of leaving his office with a higher reputation than when he assumed it (Figure 2.1).[3]

In the summer of 1919, once the Versailles Treaty was signed, Drummond settled into a suite of rooms near Whitehall and began mapping out the structure of the Secretariat and hiring staff. Sir Maurice Hankey, before turning the post of Secretary General down, had sketched out a structure intended to facilitate great-power collaboration, with separate bureaus for French, British, American, Italian, and Japanese under-secretaries, each bringing their own national staff.[4] But Drummond, remarkably, broke with this statist vision. Rather than structure the Secretariat by nation, Drummond organized it by function, with separate sections—the Legal Section, the Economic and Financial Section, the Mandates Section, and so forth—established to support each of the organization's key areas of work. Still more boldly, he decided to create a genuinely international officialdom, a body of men and women not lent from national bureaucracies but rather hired *de novo* and owing loyalty to the League alone. Not that the Secretariat was 'neutral' exactly. A group of tried wartime collaborators provided its spine, with Drummond entrusting the Political Section to the historian Paul Mantoux, who had served as Clemenceau's interpreter at the Peace

Conference; the Economic Section to the Oxford economist Sir Arthur Salter; the Information Section to the French journalist Pierre Comert; the Legal Section to the Dutch jurist Joost van Hamel; and the particularly tricky task of running the minorities regime to the able Norwegian diplomat Erik Colban. But there were unusual or visionary appointments too, notably of Dame Rachel Crowdy, who had made a name organizing Britain's voluntary nursing service in France during the First World War, as head of the Social Section; and at Crowdy's urging, of the brilliant Polish epidemiologist Ludwig Rajchman at the Health Section.[5] The knowledge that they were to serve the League and not their state attracted a young and overwhelmingly progressive staff, and if Drummond shunted most of the female applicants off into the clerical services, he thereby secured the Secretariat an enviable reputation for accuracy and professionalism.

The Mandates Section was to go to George Louis Beer, but Beer had returned to New York once the Milner Commission ceased to meet, and as US participation grew uncertain, his interest in the post declined. When Beer refused an urgent request in October 1919 to return to London to restart the faltering negotiations over mandates, Drummond turned for help to a bright young official (and later Nobel Peace Prize Laureate) seconded from the Foreign Office, Philip Baker (later Noel-Baker).[6] Baker was to handle matters until Beer's return. But since Beer never returned, until the Secretariat's move to Geneva in the summer of 1920 and William Rappard's appointment as Director that October—that is, for more than a year—whatever the League did on mandates was very largely Baker's work.[7]

Baker was far to the left of Drummond politically, but he had the kind of formation, connections, and intimate understanding of British officialdom's rules of the game that made for easy collaboration between the two. Baker had been a brilliant undergraduate at Cambridge and an Olympic runner, and had been decorated for valour while serving with a Friends ambulance brigade in the First World War. After 1918 he turned into what we might call one of the Zeligs of international politics, the unidentified but vaguely familiar face just behind the minister in official photographs. He had been Robert Cecil's confidential assistant and secretary to the Commission drafting the Covenant at the Peace Conference and then secretary to Milner's Mandates Commission, roles that had left Baker with a better knowledge of the positions of each of the mandatory powers than anyone else. Drummond knew his young collaborator would try to push those powers in a more progressive direction, but he could also trust Baker to respect the enabling fiction of British government: that politicians take decisions, and officials simply provide technical assistance. None of the key documents about mandates issued by the Council or the Secretary General carry Baker's name. In the League archives, his initials are on every draft.

Baker began by helping those British politicians and officials—A. J. Balfour in August 1919, Drummond in September, Sir Cecil Hurst and Lord Curzon later that winter—who were trying to bring the French back to the drafting table.[8] But those bilateral efforts went nowhere, convincing Baker that the League Council had to take up the mandate question itself. Joost van Hamel, the Dutch head of the Secretariat's Legal Section, assured Drummond that the Council had the authority to do so, for when it had proven impossible to include the mandates in the Treaty of Versailles, a short line of text had been added to Article 22 stating that the degree of control exercised by the mandatory would be 'explicitly defined in each case by the Council'.[9] In the spring of 1920, now wearing a 'League' hat, Baker persuaded Drummond to sign an uncharacteristically sharp ultimatum that went to the Council,[10] and at its session at San Sebastian in August the Council approved what became known (after the name of the Belgian minister who presented it) as the Hymans Report, which set the framework for the League's oversight regime. True, the American rejection of the Treaty in March dictated many concessions. The responsibility for allocating territories, defining borders, and indeed drafting the mandates themselves were all ceded to the allied powers, and it was agreed that the great-power dominated Council, and not the more progressive Assembly, was responsible for oversight. Yet, for all that, the Hymans Report stipulated both that the League was rightly concerned not only with matters specifically mentioned in the mandate texts but rather with 'the whole material and moral situation of the peoples under the Mandate', and that the Mandates Commission must include a majority of members from non-mandatory powers. The Council then asked the allied powers for the mandate texts, so that the work of supervision could begin.[11]

Thus by the autumn of 1920, very largely at the Secretariat's insistence, the Council had agreed to bring the system into effect. Drummond and Baker had been able to force the issue because, while ostensibly international officials, they had easy and confidential relations with a host of British officials and statesmen. Indeed, at this stage, the Secretariat was as much an outpost of the British Foreign Office as anything else, and the decision to shift responsibility from the Supreme Allied Council to the League Council a sharply pragmatic response to American withdrawal. Having lost the American alliance, the British would look to the League Council to stabilize the colonial settlement. Drummond knew, however, that English dominance bred resentment and had to be curtailed if the League was to thrive. He transferred Baker out of the section six months later, but before Baker left he played one final, dangerous game, stoking the desire of the League Assembly to make the 'sacred trust' real.

## Cecil, Nansen, and the Assembly

In August 1920, Drummond made an advance trip to Geneva, where he negotiated the purchase of the 200-room lakefront hotel that would house the League for the next sixteen years. Relocation to neutral Switzerland—and not, as had been proposed, to 'liberated' Brussels—signalled the determination of the new institution to rise above the hatreds of war and reinforced the Secretariat's sense of distinction. A few short weeks later, on 15 November—later than anticipated, the Council having waited in vain for the United States to join—the First League Assembly met. Forty-two member states sent delegations, and a host of officials, lobbyists, journalists, delegates from would-be member states and simple well-wishers showed up as well. Delegates were swiftly enmeshed in a web of meetings, as six separate committees got to work on issues ranging from the admission of new states, to the tasks of the technical sections, to the organization of the Secretariat, to such 'hot button' questions as Armenian refugees or the use of economic blockades. There was plenty of socializing too, with national delegations hosting competitively lavish receptions.[12]

The League Assembly could not become (as the United Nations General Assembly would) a platform for anti-colonial nationalists and a force behind decolonization. It was too European-dominated and too white. With the anomalous exception of India, imperial possessions had no voice. Yet the Assembly was a place where small states could speak up: its ethos was democratic and its Wilsonian sympathies were acute. Arriving in Geneva that November, many delegates also had reason to worry that the great powers were about to sweep Wilson's key accomplishment, the mandates system, under the rug. They knew about Sharif Husayn's unavailing appeals to Britain and the League, and Baker had made sure that their dossiers contained copies of the Hymans Report and the San Sebastian decisions through which the Council claimed responsibility for mandates.[13] In those dossiers was also found a sharp protest issued by the German government.[14] Many delegates sympathized with the German claim that the Council was usurping powers laid on the League as a whole (and thus on the Assembly); privately, indeed, British officials did too. A fight was brewing for control of the mandates system.

At the Assembly mandates fell under the Sixth Committee, which dealt with security and armaments. Paul Hymans was on that committee, but so too were the unpredictable Robert Cecil, the famed Norwegian humanitarian and explorer Fridtjof Nansen (who was named chair of its mandates subcommittee), numerous members from smaller states, and the ubiquitous Baker as 'Recording Secretary'. The Committee immediately asked to review the mandate texts, but the Council prevaricated, only agreeing at the last minute to pass them along on condition that the committee not mention them in open session.[15] Nansen and Cecil, however, refused to be cowed, and on the Assembly's last day they proposed a resolution calling on the mandatory powers to bring the system into effect immediately.

That brought A. J. Balfour to his feet, and the conflict between Council and Assembly (and between imperial and international interests) into open view. 'The responsibility for dealing with the Mandates,' Balfour told the Assembly shortly, 'lay with the Council alone.' As the British representative on that body, he would consider himself 'absolutely free to consider these problems on their merits, unrestricted by anything which the Assembly might do'. The meeting was then treated to a very English public spat, with Cecil (Balfour's cousin) retorting that Balfour's own Committee had already agreed that the Assembly was free to discuss any League matter. The resolution passed, but the delegates implicitly accepted that the Council would not be coerced and would 'reserve to itself full liberty' in dealing with it.[16]

The Council had thus confirmed its control—and yet the Assembly's public criticism had its effect. Now on the defensive, the Council approved a constitution for the Permanent Mandates Commission (PMC), telegraphed the mandatory powers to submit their mandate drafts, and on 17 December brought the 'C' mandates into effect. Over the next few months, it extracted the draft 'B' mandates and appointed the members of the Mandates Commission—including, as the Assembly had requested, a woman. Real oversight then shifted to the Commission, but the Assembly never lost interest in the system it had done much to midwife. Each year its Sixth

Committee would review the report of the Mandates Commission and until 1934 its conclusions were discussed in plenary session. The Assembly could throw its weight behind the Commission whenever it came under attack; individual delegates could denounce repressive acts in mandated territories or dilate on the evils of imperialism in front of a packed hall. The blunt language with which the South African delegates described their new charges—'peoples sunk in barbarism for untold centuries',[17] for example—didn't play well in the cosmopolitan world of the Assembly. The mandatory powers often found themselves on the defensive.

The Assembly was able to play this important early role for several reasons. The public nature of its procedures mattered; so too did the fact that Cecil, out of office at this stage and trying to build a kind of 'centre party', was willing to play an independent, gadfly role.[18] But Cecil could also count on Baker to keep him informed: indeed, it is not too much to say that League officials shaped—even engineered—the Assembly's response. Baker's loyalty to Cecil and support for the Assembly against the Council had a cost, however, for Drummond concluded that Baker could not be trusted to run the Disarmament Section (a job Baker thought he had been promised); Baker, who had always thought it wrong for a British national (or a national of any mandatory power) to be in charge of the mandates section, then decided to leave the Secretariat altogether.[19] With Baker gone, much would depend on the character of the Mandates Section's new Director.

## Rappard and the Mandates Section

On 9 October 1920, just before that First Assembly and the Secretariat's move to Geneva, Drummond had asked William Emmanuel Rappard, a Swiss academic and internationalist, to accept the role of Director.[20] This was a bold choice and one Drummond probably came to regret. The problem wasn't just that Rappard—a big, warm, quick-witted bear of a man—was anything but a bureaucrat at heart. It was also that Rappard, like Baker, was a true Wilsonian and had very different ideas from Drummond about how the League should work. Drummond thought the League could smooth collaboration among the great powers, whereas for Rappard it was a way to hold those powers accountable to a democratizing world. The two would clash many times during the four years Rappard spent in the Secretariat, and Rappard almost always lost. He was, after all, directly responsible to

Drummond, whose authority was absolute. Yet, straining at Drummond's leash, Rappard managed to imbue the Mandates Section and the Mandates Commission with a measure of his own independence and idealism.

Rappard was born in New York in 1883 into a Swiss merchant family, returning to Switzerland at the age of seventeen. Trilingual in French, German, and English, he studied economics and law in Geneva and completed a doctorate there in 1908. He was an inveterate traveller, though, spending time and making friends at universities across Europe as well as at Harvard, where he was Assistant Professor of Economics from 1911 until 1913. He then took a Professorship in Geneva but kept a finger in many other pies, undertaking long missions to Washington, London, and Paris on behalf of the Swiss government during the war. A warm exponent of Wilsonian ideas, he negotiated both Swiss entry into the League and the agreement to make Geneva its seat.[21] Rappard had qualms about working under Drummond, with whom he had had an unhappy misunderstanding about another possible post, but his friends (including Jean Monnet, then French Deputy Secretary General) and his own desire to see a Swiss among the top officials persuaded him to accept.[22]

Tensions between Rappard and Drummond were visible almost from Rappard's first day in the Secretariat. Like Baker, Rappard thought the Council had to be pushed to come to agreement with the Americans and approve the mandates—and in this, even if grudgingly, Drummond supported him.[23] But Rappard also wanted to make sure that those texts conformed to Article 22 'in letter and in spirit', as the Covenant's supporters were wont to say. That there was cause for worry became apparent as the 'B' mandate texts trickled into the Secretariat in the winter of 1920. In a concession to the Dominions, the 'C' mandates had included a clause allowing the mandatory power to administer the territory 'as an integral part of his territory', and the introduction of a similar clause into the Togo and Cameroon mandates had been the price of French agreement to hold those territories under mandate at all. Now, the Belgians introduced a similar clause into the mandate for Rwanda and Burundi, breezily passing that change off as a minor administrative matter.[24] Baker and Rappard were not fooled. All 'B' drafts save Britain's East Africa mandate, Baker wrote, would now 'require very considerable modification by the Council of the League if they are really to conform to the letter and spirit of Article 22'. The clauses on slavery, forced labour, liquor traffic, and land should all be tightened, but that clause allowing administrative union had to be done away with altogether or the distinction between 'B' mandates and 'C' mandates would almost disappear.[25]

But with all mandatory powers save the Dominions on the Council, would the Council really tighten up those texts? Rappard thought that unlikely, and, like Baker before him, began to cast about for allies behind the scenes. From the fracas at the first assembly and his own reading of the British press, Rappard knew how angry and betrayed many well-placed internationalists and humanitarians in Britain felt about the long delay in bringing the mandates system into effect. In early 1921 he began privately collaborating with two of the most vocal—the indefatigable Organising Secretary of the Anti-Slavery Society, J. H. Harris, and the former Arab Bureau member and now Conservative MP, William Ormsby-Gore. Both men, recall, had been at the Peace Conference (Harris to press the anti-slavery cause, Ormsby-Gore as part of Milner's entourage); both had become passionate supporters of the mandates ideal; and both were now doing all they could—in private, in Parliament, through the League of Nations Union, and in the press—to give it flesh.[26] By January 1921, Rappard was asking Harris's advice about how best to address the issues of the liquor traffic, arms, and slavery in the 'B' mandate texts; remarkably, and in sharp contrast to the racist assumptions underpinning much humanitarian thought, Harris told him that he disapproved of disarming the native population 'because a totally disarmed population tends to make the Administration domineering', and that he also thought it hardly ' "playing the game" to say that the native should not have spirits but the white man may'.[27] Ormsby-Gore also wrote to Rappard, repudiating claims of African incapacity and downplaying the significance of the distinction between 'A' and 'B' territories altogether. 'You will probably think my ideas...revolutionary' but the mandatory power should be 'merely the temporary guardian or trustee exercising such trusteeship on behalf of the League, with a view to the development of each mandatory area'—in Africa as well as the Middle East—'into an independent state.'[28] Rappard professed himself 'most happy' to hear this, but noted that 'there is no doubt whatever that your conception is very far from being shared by the Governments of the Mandatory Powers themselves'.[29] Harris and Ormsby-Gore responded by stepping up their public pressure on the British government to publish the mandate texts.

Rappard's collusion with English internationalists irritated Drummond. He told Rappard *not* to send the draft 'A' and 'B' mandates for review to the newly appointed members of the Permanent Mandates Commission, and when Rappard let slip that Ormsby-Gore thought the Commission had every right to see those texts, Drummond said he was sorry Rappard had discussed the matter outside the Secretariat at all.[30] But with the Council so secretive and Drummond so cautious, to whom could Rappard turn but Britain's outspoken internationalists? 'Never more than at the present moment,' he wrote to Ormsby-Gore in March, 'have I felt that the future of the mandatory system and of the League of Nations as a whole rests primarily on the shoulders of their friends in Great Britain.'[31] Drummond still refused to let the Commission see those drafts—'certain members' of the League being 'very tenacious of the Council's sole right' to define those texts.[32] At the Second Assembly in the summer of 1921, however, Rappard, Cecil, and Nansen together exploited delegates' anger at the fact that the mandates *still* had not been approved to extract a pledge from the mandatory powers to send reports to the newly appointed Permanent Mandates Commission immediately.[33]

These efforts could only do so much to compensate for genuine great-power agreement. Sympathetic as Britain's Colonial Office and even the Foreign Office were to mandate principles (which they had largely shaped), and irritated as the British government truly was with American obstruction and French foot-dragging, the British would not and could not impose the system on their own. Not until 18 July 1922, after the allies had reached agreement with the United States and almost four years after the Armistice, did the Council finally approve the 'B' mandates—and these texts included those proto-annexationist clauses that Baker and Rappard had found so objectionable.[34] Yet Rappard's networking did have an effect, enabling key British supporters to shape League policy on mandates even after Baker was gone. A circular pattern was established in which Secretariat officials shared confidential information with national political figures, who then put pressure on their governments to take action at Geneva. With Rappard in charge and the League heavily dependent on British goodwill, this pattern worked to Britain's advantage. But as the Secretariat grew 'leakier' and geopolitical tensions more intense, the web of connections would become harder to manage.

While fighting the Covenant's corner from 1920 to 1924, Rappard also set up the Mandates Section and hired its first staff. Compared to the economic, political, and information sections, the Mandates Section was small, but it grew as its responsibilities expanded. Most non-clerical work at the

**Figure 2.2** William Rappard, seated far right, with Vito Catastini and the staff of the Mandates Section.

League was entrusted to what was called the First Division staff, a category that included both the high officials and the 'Members of Section' who were the workhorses of the League. (Baker, for all his contacts and initiative, had been a Member of Section.) For two years the Mandates Section contained only two First Division members, Rappard and the Italian Vito Catastini (who replaced Baker in mid-1921), supplemented by two to three secretaries (Figure 2.2). In 1923 a third Member was added, and when Rappard resigned in 1924 the American Huntington Gilchrist was transferred from the Minorities Section to keep the strength at six—three First Division staff and three secretaries. In the period following German entry into the League of Nations, two additional First Division staff members (neither German) were added; by June 1932 the Mandates Section had, with secretaries, a staff of ten. It shrunk slightly in size in the late 1930s but did not go into precipitous decline until the crisis of 1939–40.

As a politically sensitive section, Mandates was to be staffed by nationals of the non-mandatory powers. With the exception of Baker and the clerical staff (who were mostly British, French, and Swiss), this precept was strictly followed. This did not keep the section free from national intrigue, for although Italy was not a mandatory power, it certainly wished to become one, and Catastini, formerly an official at the Italian Colonial Office and part of the Italian delegation at the Peace Conference, reported straight to Rome.[35] Yet Rappard enforced an ethos of impartiality (which, in his case, meant sharing information with British internationalists but not usually British officials), and several members who spent long periods in the section—the Dane F. T. B. Friis from 1923 to 1930, the American Huntington Gilchrist from 1924 to 1928, the Swiss Edouard De Haller from 1928 to 1940, and the Norwegian Peter Anker through much of the 1930s—sustained its reputation for competence and dedication. If anything, Rappard worked staff to exhaustion. When a Commission member complained in 1922 that some typists sent from the central pool had been insubordinate, their supervisor exploded. His typists had worked until midnight for two weeks without complaint. Perhaps next year the Commission might 'be induced to regard the Secretariat more or less as mandated territory, and to look a little more closely into the welfare of the natives'?[36]

Complaints like these were few. Unlike some other sections (especially the Social Section, where Rachel Crowdy was given a tiny, barely competent staff), Mandates ran smoothly. In the mid-1920s the section took on administrative responsibilities for the League's anti-slavery work, but its main job was always to support the Mandates Commission. The section set the schedule for the sessions, arranged for travel and accommodation of members, collected annual reports from the mandatory powers (and wrote nagging letters when they were late), kept and checked the Commission's voluminous minutes, received and kept track of all petitions, made sure the Commission's reports were sent in a timely manner to the Council, and compiled a vast array of other material (laws, treaties, speeches, scholarly articles, protests), sending a selection each month to the members of the PMC.[37]

Rappard took that task of gathering information very seriously, consulting Harris and his academic friends to identify regional newspapers able to reveal local opinion. Regular perusal of the *Gold Coast Leader*, *The Pacific Islands Monthly*, the *Windhoek Advertiser*, and other out-of-the-way publications gave members of the Commission and League officials alike a sharp and often critical optic on the mandatory power's administration and sometimes on their own deliberations. Galvanized by the 1925 Syrian rising, and aware that the news in the European press was 'extremely scarce and often unreliable', in the late 1920s Rappard, Catastini, and Gilchrist went to considerable trouble to find someone able to translate articles from Arabic newspapers published in Beirut, Damascus, Jerusalem, Jaffa, Cairo, and Baghdad.[38] The Mandates Section kept track of the proliferating scholarly literature on mandates too, working with the League library to amass an impressive collection and to issue regular, and increasingly lengthy, bibliographies.[39] Many doctoral students and academics, among them such important African American intellectuals as Ralph Bunche and Alain Locke, spent time perusing that collection.

Under Rappard's energetic direction, section officials often crossed the boundary between bureaucratic support and policy planning, and between impartial analysis and advocacy. Officials not only wrote the reports of those (relatively few) Commission members too busy or lazy to do the work themselves and briefed the Council members and Assembly delegates who were named 'rapporteur' on mandates, but also consciously worked to enhance the system's authority and reputation. Rappard published and lectured on international relations in three languages and willingly read works on the mandates system by Quincy Wright, A. J. Toynbee, and other prominent scholars before publication. Gilchrist, whom Drummond used to keep in contact with Raymond Fosdick and other prominent American supporters of the League (and whose salary as a mere 'Member of Section' almost equalled that of Catastini, his ostensible chief), briefed American statesmen and philanthropists during visits to the United States. Section officials also punctiliously answered the many letters that politicians, academics, activists, and philanthropists wrote to the League about mandates and received visitors who showed up in person. Cosmopolitan and welcoming, the Mandates Section became known as a place where Zionists, Arab nationalists, Pan-Africanists, and German revisionists—not to mention Rappard's huge network of academic and political friends—could find a cordial reception.

If the Mandates Section was his special responsibility, Rappard also set the practices of the Commission itself. Demonstrating a confidence in his role that many wished Drummond would show, Rappard opened each session with a short report summarizing developments and outlining tasks. He had the good sense to present himself only as its tool—'Does a man owe gratitude to his pen?'[40]—but he led the Commission as much as he served it. It was thanks to Rappard, the Chairman Marquis Theodoli quipped at the first session, that they 'had enjoyed such a terrible visit in the beautiful town of Geneva, where his tireless activity had not given them a single day's respite, but had supplied them every day with a newly prepared task'.[41] Rappard's dedication galvanized even the indolent or cynical; long after he left the Secretariat, he still held the Commission together. He corresponded with many members for decades.

In 1924 Rappard was offered the post of Vice-Rector at the University of Geneva and resigned from the Secretariat.[42] He was an academic at heart and may have wearied of his battles with Drummond. The Commission members were devastated, first begging Rappard to hold both positions simultaneously, an option Drummond had already ruled out,[43] and then dispatching a weighty delegation to request that Rappard be appointed an 'extraordinary' member.[44] Given the strength of feeling, the Council agreed, and in June 1925 Rappard attended his first session as a member. Resident in Geneva, already knowledgeable about every aspect of the Commission's work, and possessed of confidential contacts throughout the Secretariat, Rappard immediately became its leading presence. He served on the Commission for the rest of its life.

Drummond professed 'keen satisfaction' with Rappard's new role,[45] but he never appointed anyone of his caliber again. Catastini took over Rappard's duties at the rank of 'Chef de Section' and at about half Rappard's salary until finally promoted to Director in 1929. Catastini held this position until 1935, when he was let go under staff rules limiting top positions to six years (exceptions being made only for powerful figures like Rajchman at Health, Salter at Economics, or Colban at Minorities); the correct but uninspiring Swiss official, Edouard de Haller, succeeded him. By the 1930s the Mandates Section was mostly going through the motions, but that didn't particularly matter, both because Rappard had set those motions and because initiative had long shifted to the Mandates Commission, the linchpin of the whole system.

## The Permanent Mandates Commission

The existence of the Mandates Commission was prescribed in the League Covenant. It was 'to receive and examine the annual reports of the Mandatories and to advise the Council on all matters relating to the observance of the mandates', and the British and American officials at the Peace Conference

immediately began planning its size, structure, and powers. George Louis
Beer, for example, envisioned a body of some three dozen government representatives, experts, and League officials, divided into separate committees for
the African and Ottoman territories.[46] When the United States turned against
the League those plans were scaled far down, but Baker, drawing up modified
proposals in the run-up to the First Assembly, urged Drummond at least to
make sure that its members were not 'obscure under-secretaries' appointed by
governments but 'men of experience, weight and reputation', whose scope of
activity would be left open.[47] The constitution approved by the Council in
November 1920 bent over backwards to safeguard the prerogatives of the
mandatory powers anyway. They were entitled to have a representative present when the Commission discussed a territory; any 'observations' it made
must be sent to that representative for comment before being transmitted to
the Council; and the Council was required to publish those comments alongside the Commission's 'observations' and reports.[48]

And yet some shred of Baker's idealism remained even in this denatured
text. All nine members of the PMC were to be named by the Council, and
if that was a disappointment to the Assembly, it was surely better than a
Commission made up of government representatives. They were, further, to
be appointed 'for their personal merits and competence' and were not to
hold any government office; only four were to be nationals of the mandatory
powers (a stipulation that effectively excluded the three Dominions holding
mandates from representation); and an official of the International Labour
Organization could attend all sessions.[49] Finally, the Commission was left free
to 'regulate its own procedure subject to the approval of the Council'. Those
powers, modest as they seem, greatly disquieted the French Colonial Minister,
Albert Sarraut, when he learned his government had agreed to them. A body
composed mostly of members from non-mandatory states would surely tend
towards 'theoretical' or even 'rash' judgements. Demands and protests would
gather around it. There would be endless trouble.[50]

How realistic were Sarraut's fears? On the simplest level, they seem
absurd, for when the Council appointed the first members in February
1921, most were colonial officials if anything more hard-bitten than Sarraut
himself. Much more radical appointees had been suggested. Labour's Arthur
Henderson nominated the Anti-Slavery Society's J. H. Harris and the Fabian
colonial expert Leonard Woolf. The Swiss-based Bureau International pour
la Défence des Indigènes proposed their long-serving President René
Claparède.[51] The Second Pan-African conference held in Paris in September

1921 asked that a coloured member be added—a request supported publicly at the 1921 Assembly by the Haitian delegate Dantès Bellegarde and privately by Baker, who thought the Council should consider 'this [W. E. B.] Dubois [sic], about whom everybody is talking'.[52] But none of these proposals succeeded, for the Council usually let the various Foreign Offices do the choosing. Unsurprisingly, none was inclined to name an armchair philosopher, much less an anti-colonial radical, and only Sweden was willing to 'waste' its slot on the token woman.

The Mandates Commission thus was very much an imperialists' club. Of nine members, five were recently retired colonial governors, ministers, or high officials. The French member, Jean-Baptiste Paul Beau, at sixty-four the oldest, had held various diplomatic posts in the Far East, culminating in a long spell as Governor General in Indochina. The Portuguese member, Alfredo Augusto Freire d'Andrade, age sixty-one in 1921, had had a long career in Portuguese Africa, culminating as Governor General of Mozambique. Daniel François Willem van Rees, the Dutch member, age fifty-eight, had followed his father into service in the Dutch East Indies, and was, on his retirement in 1914, Vice President of the Dutch Council of the Indies. The Italian member, the Marquis Alberto Theodoli, forty-seven in 1921, was an engineer and banker who had served as Italy's representative on the Commission on Ottoman Public Debt, briefly as Under-Secretary of State for the Colonies in Francesco Nitti's Liberal administration, and been part of the Italian delegation at the Peace Conference. Perhaps the ultimate insider was, however, the Belgian member, none other than Pierre Orts, aged forty-seven. A lawyer and diplomat from a family of lawyers and diplomats, Orts served as a legal advisor to the king of Siam and then as a confidential councillor in the Belgian colonial ministry—in which role, as we know, he managed to persuade Milner to overturn the Supreme Council's initial decision and cede Rwanda and Burundi to Belgium.[53] All five of these members remained on the Commission for at least five years and most for much longer.[54]

The Spanish, Japanese, Swedish, and British members ran a bit less true to type. Spain, given a member after the American Cameron Forbes declined to join, treated the post as a sinecure and appointed two diplomats in quick succession, each of whom served for only one session and the second of whom named his successor.[55] Yet, unorthodox as this was, it produced in Leopoldo Palacios, a liberal professor and social reformer aged forty-eight on his appointment in 1924, the Commission's only long-serving defender of the principle of national self-determination. The first Japanese member, Kunio Yanagita, forty-six in 1921, a sometime parliamentary official who had travelled in Micronesia and published works on folklore and ethnology, was also unusually progressive and open-minded. But he served for only three sessions and was succeeded by two diligent but orthodox Foreign Ministry officials.[56] Sweden put forward the candidacy of Anna Bugge-Wicksell, age fifty-nine in 1921, a veteran women's suffrage and peace campaigner, who made it her 'particular business to care for and speak for' the 'helpless' women and children of the mandated territories. She was succeeded by the like-minded Valentine Dannevig, in her fifties when she joined the PMC, the director of a Norwegian girls' school and one of the founders of the Norwegian branch of the Women's International League for Peace and Freedom.[57]

But the most surprising choice was the British member, none other than Baker and Rappard's co-conspirator, William Ormsby-Gore. Not only was Ormsby-Gore at age thirty-six by some distance the youngest member, but, with his wartime experience in Cairo and Palestine, he was also the most knowledgeable about the Middle East. Officials at the Foreign and Colonial Offices had wanted to give the prominent former Governor General of Nigeria, Sir Frederick Lugard, the job, but Winston Churchill, taking over as Colonial Secretary in February 1921, wished to placate backbench Conservatives disenchanted with Lloyd George.[58] Ormsby-Gore's appointment heartened the Anti-Slavery Society and delighted Rappard.[59] As we shall see, confidential collaboration between these two did much to set the Commission's early course. But Ormsby-Gore was too ambitious and talented to remain outside the British government for long. He resigned in late 1922 to become Under-Secretary of State for the Colonies in Andrew Bonar Law's Conservative administration, making space finally for Lugard, aged sixty-five. When France appointed Martial Henri Merlin, Governor General of French West Africa from 1918 to 1923, to succeed Beau in 1926 (when Merlin was sixty-six), the Mandates Commission began to resemble a spa for retired African governors.

And yet, the Mandates Commission proved a more independent body than anyone could have predicted. Not that it welcomed theorists and radicals. The very few members who had such inclinations, notably the Spaniard Palacios, never had much influence. To the contrary, it was precisely because the members of the Commission were well integrated into their country's imperial and foreign-policy establishments that they proved hard to control. Men who had governed colonies were disinclined to take dictation from politicians, and when Germany gained a seat in 1927 (appointing in succession two serious-minded economic experts, Ludwig Kastl and Julius Ruppel), members became even more self-consciously independent. But the Commission's unruliness was compounded too by three formal attributes: that its members served without term; that it derived its authority from written texts; and that its deliberations were published and publicized.

First, the lack of term limits made for an extraordinarily stable membership. Only twenty-eight people, including the two successive ILO representatives, Harold Grimshaw and William Weaver (both dedicated reformers with ties to the anti-slavery world), served on the Commission for the whole of its twenty years of active existence. The Italian Theodoli served for sixteen years, the Swiss Rappard and the Spaniard Palacios for fifteen, the Dutchman Van Rees for fourteen, Lugard for thirteen, the Norwegian Valentine Dannevig for eleven, and Orts for the whole of the Commission's life. The Commission's membership, moreover, fluctuated most in the first and last years of its existence. For the nine years from 1926 until 1935 it exhibited a Politburo-like fixity, with only fifteen people circulating through its eleven seats. Indeed, between 1930 and 1935 not a single new member joined and only one—the German member—left. Members clung to their positions, resigning only when incapacitated or when their governments ordered them out (Table 2). Older members died in harness.

That long service meant that members developed camaraderie and expertise. At the second session, responsibility for different topics—liquor traffic, labour, education, public health, the 'open door'—was shared among members, and if some rather neglected their homework, others avidly threw themselves into it. Perhaps bored or lonely at the close of prominent careers, some devoted extraordinary amounts of time to the Commission—a dedication that turned the Dutch member Van Rees, for example, into the pre-eminent legal authority on mandates and a short-tempered scourge of the representatives he interrogated. Members took on the task of explaining the system to their compatriots, contributing articles, lectures, and—in the case of Van Rees and Palacios—massive legal studies to a burgeoning scholarly literature.[60] Yet, as members came to know one another well, cross-national alliances developed too. Rappard, Lugard, and Orts sat together and often acted as a bloc; in the 'German period' the Swiss, German, Spanish, and Scandinavian members sometimes joined together to put the members

**Table 2.** Members of the Permanent Mandates Commission, by Nationality.

## Members of the Permanent Mandates Commission, by Nationality

Source: Minutes of the Permanent Mandates Commission, 1921–1939.

| International Labor Organization (ILO) | Germany | Switzerland | Scandinavia | Spain | Portugal | Japan | France | Belgium | United Kingdom | Netherlands | Italy | Month/Year | Meeting Number |
|---|---|---|---|---|---|---|---|---|---|---|---|---|---|
| Grimshaw | | | Bugge-Wicksell | | | | Beau | Orts | | Van Rees | Theodoli | 10/1921 | 1 |
| | | | | Pina | Freire d'Andrade | Yanagita | | | | | | 8/22 | 2 |
| | | | | Palacios | | Yamanaka | | | Ormsby-Gore | | | 7/23 | 3 |
| | | | | | | | | | Lugard | | | 6/24 | 4 |
| | | | | | | | | | | | | 10/24 | 5 |
| | | Rappard | | | | | | | | | | 6/25 | 6 |
| | | | | | | | | | | | | 10/25 | 7 |
| | | | | | | | Merlin | | | | | 2/26 | 8 |
| | | | | | | | Roume | | | | | 6/26 | 9 |
| | | | | | | | | | | | | 11/26 | 10 |
| | | | | | | | | | | | | 6/27 | 11 |
| | Kastl | | | | | | | | | | | 10/27 | 12 |
| | | | Dannevig | | | Sakenobe | | | | | | 6/28 | 13 |
| | | | | | de Penha Garcia | | | | | | | 10/28 | 14 |
| | | | | | | | | | | | | 7/29 | 15 |
| Weaver | Ruppel | | | | | | | | | | | 11/29 | 16 |
| | | | | | | | | | | | | 6/30 | 17 |
| | | | | | | | | | | | | 6/30 | 18 |
| | | | | | | | | | | | | 11/30 | 19 |
| | | | | | | | | | | | | 6/31 | 20 |
| | | | | | | | | | | | | 10/31 | 21 |
| | | | | | | | | | | | | 11/32 | 22 |
| | | | | | | | | | | | | 6/33 | 23 |
| | | | | | | | | | | | | 10/33 | 24 |
| | | | | | | | | | | | | 6/34 | 25 |
| | | | | | | | | | | | | 10/34 | 26 |
| | | | | | | | Manceron | | | Van Asbeck | | 6/35 | 27 |
| | | | | | | | | | | | | 10/35 | 28 |
| | | | | | | | | | Hailey | | | 5/36 | 29 |
| | | | | | | | Giraud | | | | | 10/36 | 30 |
| | | | | | | | | | | | | 5/37 | 31 |
| | | | | | | | | | Hankey | | | 6/37 | 32 |
| | | | | | | | | | | | | 11/37 | 33 |
| | | | | | | | | | | Hailey | | 6/38 | 34 |
| | | | | | | | | | | | | 10/38 | 35 |
| | | | | | | | | | | | | 6/39 | 36 |
| | | | | | | | | | | | | 12/39 | 37 |

from mandatory states on the defensive. Familiarity could produce dislike too—the indolent and uncooperative French member, Martial Merlin, made few friends—but over time, a kind of *esprit de corps* developed.

The heart of that spirit was a commitment to the Commission's second key characteristic, which members tended to call independence or impartiality but that would be better thought of as legalism or textualism. Most members agreed with the Swede Anna Bugge-Wicksell that the Commission 'like Caesar's wife, must not even be suspected';[61] they were proud that they sat, as Theodoli put it, 'as free men'.[62] It is important to realize, however, that that 'independence' was a public stance. It did not prevent members from instinctively defending imperial styles to which they had devoted their lives or from consulting privately with their governments before the sessions. Virtually all members from great or mandatory powers did so; what varied was the flagrancy of that collaboration. Here, the French members were very much on one side, for all saw their role *tout court* as to defend French interests as the Quai d'Orsay saw them—a job they performed doggedly but so transparently that they forfeited authority within the Commission itself. By contrast, Orts, Theodoli, and to a degree even Lugard and the German members, *performed* impartiality, scrupulously citing League texts or Council decisions—and not national interest or even common sense— when making their case. Textualism became the language politics was forced to speak. Not only Commission members but also mandatory powers and legal scholars, humanitarians, and petitioners, spoke of 'spirit' and 'letter', cited chapter and verse.

That textualism was necessary, finally, because the Commission worked amid a swirl of publicity. Except for one staged plenary meeting per session devoted to some general question (public health, for example), the Commission met in private, for even the most critical—Theodoli, the German members—realized the accredited representatives would hardly speak publicly about 'delicate' questions.[63] Yet members also recognized that they needed to cultivate public interest and threaten public exposure in order to be effective. From the outset, it was taken as read that the Commission's report to the Council, observations on the territories, reports on petitions, and minutes (which, even when 'corrected', were full of revealing information) should all be published. Those publications went to all League governments, but copies were also sent, usually for free, to deposit libraries in some forty-six countries, to public and university libraries (especially in the United States), to international and humanitarian organizations, to several hundred newspapers and periodicals across the globe, and to a select group of colonial officials, humanitarians, journalists, and scholars.[64]

As mandatory powers grew conscious of the intense interest of an international public in their affairs, they scrambled to rein in the Commission's powers. Suggestions that it might visit particular territories were swiftly turned down (although Rappard, Orts, Theodoli, the German Julius Ruppel, and a few other individual members did make trips on their own);[65] as we shall see in Chapter 7, all mandatory powers also banded together in the mid-1920s to deny the Commission the right to grant oral audiences to petitioners or experts. Yet, armoured by that rhetoric of impartial service, the Commission successfully defended its foundational right to consider outside information and to publish its views. Of course, the Commission had 'no other duty than to submit to the Council such observations as may be suggested to us by the reports of the mandatory Powers,' Theodoli said piously in response to one such attack, but 'it would certainly be most regrettable that our observations, which are the fruit of laborious enquiries carried out in a spirit of goodwill and the highest impartiality, should not be made known to public opinion and, in particular, to its great organ, the Assembly of the League of Nations'.[66] With the mandatory powers so sensitive, the Commission was usually unable to *solicit* outside information, but its right to *receive* the flood of material sent to it could not be denied. Sometimes the Commission would ignore that material anyway, but its existence as a focus for claim-making and complaint had profound and sometimes unexpected effects.

How did the Commission do its work? Members received the annual reports of the mandatory powers at their homes. They were to use those to draw up questions about their specific area of responsibility and were to write an initial report on any petitions for which they had been named 'rapporteur'. Once in Geneva, the Commission reviewed the government report and any relevant petitions about each territory with a representative of the mandatory power. The Commission met alone in the last day or two to draft their own report and their 'observations' on each territory, which were then sent to the mandatory powers for comment before being delivered to the Council. The Commission's work was then finished, although Theodoli or Van Rees was invited to attend the Council session at which its report was discussed, often as much as six months later. There, a representative of one of the non-mandatory powers on the Council summarized the report, thanked the Commission, and moved a resolution incorporating any recommendations the Council saw fit to propose—a process that was usually highly orchestrated, with the Mandates Section vetting (and sometimes writing) the 'rapporteur's' text, and the mandatory powers themselves negotiating over any recommendations.

Since only the 'C' mandates for South West Africa, Western Samoa, New Guinea, and the Japanese-mandated islands had been ratified when the Commission first met in October 1921, that session was only five days long. But the second session, in August 1922, took twice as long, and in 1923, for the third session, the Commission needed three weeks to review all Pacific and African territories and to deal with its first big scandal. From 1924, when it started reviewing the Middle East 'A' mandates, the Commission held two three-week sessions a year (except in 1932, when the League's austerity measures limited it to one marathon five-week session). There were also three special sessions: in February 1926 to discuss the Syrian Rising, in June 1930 on British responses to the Western Wall riots in Palestine, and in June 1937 to review British plans for the partition of Palestine. The Commission's 37th and last session was held in October 1939, and its 38th session was scheduled for spring 1940 when the German attack on Belgium and France made further meetings impossible.

All mandated territories were reviewed. The time spent on those reviews, however, varied widely. Some perfunctory reviews lasted a few hours; others absorbed almost a week. Based on a rough count of the proportion of its minutes devoted to each territory, presented in the table below (Table 3), we can estimate that the Commission spent well over half its time on five territories—Palestine, Syria, South West Africa, Tanganyika, and Rwanda-Burundi—and less than a fifth of its time on another five (British-mandated Togo, British-mandated Cameroon, French-mandated Togo, Nauru, and the Japanese Islands). French-mandated Cameroon, Iraq, New Guinea, and Western Samoa fell somewhere in between. That variation reflected patterns of interest and knowledge. The astonishingly little time devoted to the Japanese Islands, for example, says more about the Commission's ignorance and Japan's retentiveness than about the contentment of the native population. But the Commission also responded to internal rebellions or geopolitical tensions, spending a third of its time in the first six years on two territories—Syria and South West Africa—that saw serious disaffection. In the period of German membership, British plans to grant independence to Iraq and to create an administrative union involving Tanganyika absorbed much time (Germany using the Commission to oppose the latter), as did the worsening tensions in Palestine. Between 1933 and 1939, as Palestine became both a site of intense communal conflict and a focus of international attention, the Commission spent nearly a quarter of its time on that territory alone.

Table 3. Review of Different Territories by the PMC, 1921–39.

**Coverage of Different Territories in the Permanent Mandates Commission Minutes, 1921–1939 (37 Sessions)**

| Territory | Percentage |
|---|---|
| Palestine/Transjordan | 17.3 |
| Syria/Lebanon | 14.3 |
| South West Africa | 9.8 |
| Tanganyika | 8.0 |
| Ruanda/Urundi | 7.1 |
| Iraq | 6.3 |
| Cameroon (French) | 6.0 |
| Western Samoa | 5.9 |
| New Guinea | 5.6 |
| Togo (French) | 4.9 |
| Cameroon (British) | 4.8 |
| Togo (British) | 4.4 |
| Japanese Islands | 3.7 |
| Nauru | 2.0 |

Source: Minutes of the Permanent Mandates Commission, 1921–1939.

That pattern of attention drove a pattern of response. The early period was one of political learning, with the Commission teaching the more recalcitrant powers—France, South Africa—how to provide documentation and speak a language that would win approbation. (The South Africans never really learned this lesson.) Most mandatory powers came to understand how much store the Commission set on formal adherence to the system's procedures and on verbal deference to its stated aims. Reports mattered, and states used them to disguise weaknesses and accentuate strengths; indeed, in the manner of bureaucracies everywhere, the more they had to hide, the lengthier the submission. But personal contacts mattered too, as did the choice of whom to send as the 'accredited representative'.

Who was sent to Geneva to meet with the PMC? Colonial policy in France and Belgium was controlled by a very small group of officials who also arrogated the task of managing the Commission. Robert de Caix, the passionate imperialist who crafted France's interwar strategy in the Levant, not only compiled all reports on Syria and Lebanon but also attended every PMC session on those territories, although sometimes he brought a High Commissioner with him. Albert Duchêne, Director of Political Affairs at the French Colonial Ministry, and his colleague Maurice Besson, routinely handled the West African mandates. Halewyck de Heusch, Director General of Political and Administrative Affairs at the Belgian Colonial Ministry, wrote all reports on Rwanda and Burundi and attended every PMC session between 1924 and 1939. Belgian colonial archives show him giving much thought to how to explain bad news (mass famine, for example) or prepare the Commission for decisions—such as that to depose the Rwandan king, Yuhi Musinga—likely to arouse criticism.

Britain followed a somewhat different tack. Traditions of ministerial responsibility drove Under-Secretaries of State for the colonies and even Colonial Secretaries to Geneva, with their civil servants in tow. William Ormsby-Gore made that trek most often, appearing before his former colleagues six times while Under-Secretary in the 1920s and once while Colonial Secretary. Aware that the Commission liked to hear from 'the man on the spot', Britain sent Chief Secretaries from Iraq, Palestine, or Tanganyika; Deputy Commissioners from Gold Coast (for Togoland); and Nigerian Provincial Governors (for Cameroon). The distant Dominions, which had little choice but to send their London-based High Commissioners, were at a disadvantage. Most of these men knew far less than their interrogators and found the sessions (and the ridicule heaped on them afterwards by the press back home) excruciating. In the 1930s South Africa and Australia tried to compensate by sending the occasional government anthropologist or native commissioner. By contrast, although Japan also usually sent a diplomat posted in Paris or Geneva who could do little more than promise to forward the Commission's questions, the Japanese representatives were always treated with scrupulous courtesy—a sign less of the Commission's respect than of its discomfort when faced with a non-Western imperial power.

These were the usual suspects, but all mandatory powers occasionally tried to impress the Commission with the top man. (See Appendix 2 for a list of high administrators' appearances before the PMC.) Crises within the territory that spilled into the international press often catalyzed these visitations. South Africa sent its South West Africa Administrator, Gysbert Hofmeyr, to Geneva in 1924 after the Commission publicly condemned his handling of a local rising; France likewise sent its new High Commissioner, Henry de Jouvenel, at the height of the 1925–26 Syrian revolt. Alfred Marzorati, Belgian Governor of Rwanda-Burundi, met the Commission in 1926, following the territory's controversial administrative union with Belgian Congo, and again in November 1929, amid fierce public criticism of Belgium's handling of the Rwandan famine. Three Palestine High Commissioners were sent to soften PMC criticism of British policy there, while Sir Francis Humphrys, High Commissioner in Iraq between 1929 and 1932, was kept in Geneva for two sessions in 1931 when Britain's controversial proposal to grant independence for Iraq was up for debate. In 1932, as the Manchurian crisis exploded, even Japan took the precaution of posting off a recent Governor of its South Seas territory. That November 1932 session, indeed, resembled a kind of Concert of Empires, with the French High Commissioner for Syria, the British High Commissioner for Palestine, Britain's Governor of Nigeria, the French Commissioner for Cameroon, and the Japanese Governor of the South Seas Islands all rubbing elbows and awaiting interrogation. But 1932 was the height of the Commission's influence. In 1921 it was meeting for the first time.

## The Commission gets to work

That first meeting took place 4–9 October, towards the end of the Second Assembly session. All nine members were present, and precisely as Sarraut feared (but as anyone who has served on committees packed with old, powerful, and self-regarding men could predict), it asserted its authority and independence from the start. At Ormsby-Gore's suggestion, the group chose a member from a non-mandatory power—the Italian Theodoli—as Chairman, and later elected a second such—the Dutchman Van Rees—as Vice Chairman. Van Rees, stiff-necked and voluble, had argued the very first day that the Commission ought to have the right to modify the mandate texts, leading the Commission to point out that the phrase defining when forced labour was allowed in the French mandate texts (for 'travaux publics et services essentiels') was much less restrictive than the parallel English phrase ('essential public works'). By calling attention to this discrepancy, the Commission forced a textual revision (to 'travaux et services *publics* essentiels') that formally disallowed forced labour on any private enterprises.[67] Showing a fine disinterest in the sensitivities of mandatory powers, members also agreed that they had the right to examine *all* aspects of administration in the mandated territories and not simply those mentioned in the mandate texts, drew up a comprehensive list of questions they wished each mandatory power to address, agreed that mandatory powers should send copies of all legislation passed affecting the territory, and encouraged Rappard to pass along to them a protest about conditions in South West Africa received from the Anti-Slavery Society.[68]

Philip Baker, now watching from the sidelines, was delighted. The Mandates Commission, he told the editor of the *Daily News* (while sending him the Commission's report 'for your very confidential use'), 'is the most enlightened and most progressive body the council has yet created...the only Commission that has consistently tried to run faster than the Secretariat suggested that it should'.[69] Indeed, in its first two sessions, the Commission waded into three controversial questions, all of which worked to enhance its own authority and gave one or more mandatory powers pause. Not coincidentally, Ormsby-Gore was a catalyst for each.

The first tricky issue was nationality. What nationality did the population of a mandated territory have? An aggressive move by South Africa prompted the question. In all other mandated territories, the German population had been deported; for South Africa, however, all whites were brothers. 'The first requirements of success' in South West Africa, Smuts had told an assembly of German settlers in Windhoek in 1920, was a combination of 'whites and capital'. If the Germans agreed to accept South African authority— since a 'C' mandate was, Smuts tendentiously explained, 'annexation in all but name'—they were welcome to stay. Rappard, after reading the speech, wrote to ask Smuts for clarification; Smuts' reply, which laid out his plan to grant British nationality en masse to the territory's German population, was examined at that first session.[70] Ormsby-Gore expressed his discomfort, pointing out that jurists had ruled that the Samoans—also under 'C' mandate—were 'citizens of Samoa' and not British subjects; to consider them subjects was tantamount to claiming sovereignty over the territory.[71] Theodoli brought the Commission's concerns to the Council, which asked him to form a subcommittee and ascertain the views of all the mandatory powers.[72] On 17 November 1921, Theodoli, the Portuguese member Freire d'Andrade, and Rappard set off for Paris, London, and Brussels, where Beau, Ormsby-Gore, and Orts waited to help them.

Their investigation underscored their dependence on British support. In Paris they found most French officials mysteriously unavailable; in London,

by contrast, British officials had already met and agreed to consider populations under mandate as 'British protected persons'—a decision the New
Zealand and Australian High Commissioners supported as well.[73] Brussels
still preferred to consider such peoples Belgian subjects, but by the time
they returned to Paris, French officials had met and agreed to define them
as 'administrés français'; in the wake of that decision, Japan and Belgium too
came round. At their second session the Commission recommended that
inhabitants of both 'B' and 'C' mandates be given a national status distinct
from that of the mandatory power.[74]

The significance of this proposal was not hard to see. As Rappard said in
the Brussels meeting, should the League allow mandatory powers to treat
populations as nationals, those who claimed that mandates were nothing
more than a cloak for annexation would feel vindicated. A distinct national
status, by contrast, would preserve the territory's legal autonomy and imply
that, at some future point, it could become a state of its own. Yet, while the
mandatory powers reluctantly bowed to the Commission's recommendation, they resisted its logic. Nationality was a link between an individual and
a state, Belgium's colonial official Halewyck de Heusch had told the sub-
committee, and since there was no 'state' in a European sense in Rwanda-
Burundi, and the population was 'uncivilized', the inhabitants could hardly
be thought to possess any nationality at all. Halewyck had thought they
should be given the nationality of the mandatory power—not, he hastened
to add, in the sense of citizenship with political rights, but as subjects granted
protection[75]—but the Japanese minister they consulted in Paris thought the
mandates system's distinction between 'civilized and backward peoples' rendered such a plan impossible. While strengthening the barrier to annexation,
then, the Commission reinforced the 'civilizational' barrier as well, erasing
the possibility, dear to French ideology, that 'evolved' Africans could become
truly 'French'. In the Middle East, France and Britain would create local
'nationalities'—Iraqi, Syrian, Palestinian—on the understanding that such
populations were entitled to a legal status of their own; in Africa and the
Pacific, however, inhabitants remained minors, defined more by incapacity
than by nationality. In theory, the door to statehood was open, but since no
one imagined those populations would pass through it anytime soon, in
practice they were left with no real national status at all.[76]

The Council, moreover, allowed one 'exception' that made the racial
logic underlying civilizational language perfectly clear. The one mandatory
power that had continued to raise difficulties about 'nationality' was South

Africa, but hardly because it wished to grant the *indigenous* population any rights. South West Africa's black inhabitants were 'obviously unfit for self-government' and of course should be considered 'protected persons', High Commissioner Sir Edgar Walton had told the mandates subcommittee in London; but as the white South Africans flooding the territory were British subjects, surely the German settlers should become 'British'—in other words, South African—as well. Walton proved so obdurate on this point that the Council caved in,[77] allowing Smuts to negotiate an agreement with the German government that would offer British nationality to the whole of the German settler community.[78] British lawyers, Council members, and the PMC all realized the South African actions were entirely at odds with the 'spirit' of the Covenant, but no one wished to raise the deeper problem, which was that South Africa had created a unified rights-bearing white citizenry while dispossessing the indigenous African population. Already, South West Africa was a ticking bomb.

The second delicate question involved the border between Tanganyika and Rwanda—and, more generally, whether territorial arrangements had to take 'native interests' into account. When Lord Milner had agreed to let Belgium retain the two East African kingdoms, he nevertheless insisted that Gisaka, a strip of territory west of the Kagera River thought the only possible site for the proposed Cape-to-Cairo railway, be handed over to British control. But Rwanda's King Yuhi Musinga thought Gisaka's rich pasturelands, brought under subjection by his father, part of his domain, and made clear to the Belgian occupiers how much he resented their loss.[79] At the first PMC session, Pierre Orts mentioned that the transfer was causing local problems;[80] the following year, having received appeals from Monseigneur Léon Classe of the Catholic Society of Missionaries of Africa (the White Fathers) and Pastor Henri Anet of the Belgian Society of Protestant Missions, the Commission alerted the Council.[81] One year later, Britain and Belgium informed the League that they had agreed to move the boundary to midstream in the Kagera River.[82]

Belgium, Britain, and the Mandates Commission all drew praise for this decision. The colonial powers, it seemed, had put the interests of indigenous populations first, just as the Covenant demanded. Yet the Belgian archives tell a more complex story—one of Belgian colonial officials taking advantage of Musinga's distress, the willingness of Classe 'to remain at the disposal of the Belgian government', and Ormsby-Gore's genuine commitment to mandatory principles, to consolidate their territory.[83] At the first session, Orts had asked Ormsby-Gore privately to intercede with the British government, and Ormsby-Gore faithfully did so, but the Colonial Office, clearly feeling that the Belgians had been given quite enough (especially in light of wartime rape and pillage in Rwanda by ill-disciplined Belgian troops), turned his request down flat.[84] Orts then made sure that all members of the Commission received copies of the missionaries' appeals (one of which may have been written at his behest) and carefully explained the case to each member at the second session in August 1922. There, he wisely took a back seat, leaving the Spanish and Italian members to make the case.[85] Now backed by humanitarians and 'impartial' experts, it was an appeal the British could not turn down.

The Belgians, in other words, had learned to play the mandates game. Yet, with victory came constraint. By using the Commission to strengthen their case, they enhanced the Commission's authority; more troubling to Orts, they had also inadvertently enhanced the authority of the Rwandan king. Commission members were intrigued by the 'curiously feudal character' of these Central African kingdoms.[86] In the Tutsi's authority over the Hutu, described by the Belgians as ratified by custom and racial difference alike, the Belgians insisted they had found an indigenous hierarchy already well suited to their 'civilizing' ends. But with such well-established monarchies, Ormsby-Gore and Van Rees suggested, perhaps Rwanda and Burundi were really more like 'A' mandates, states almost able to govern themselves with Belgian advice? Orts swiftly denied this—'these little negro "states" had never been recognized as such'—but warned the Colonial Minister to be prepared to refute such arguments.[87] That refutation forced the Belgians back onto the language of race. Musinga could not be treated as a genuine head of state, the Belgian representative clarified the following year, since to do so 'would have called into question the rights of the white race to occupy the country as protector of the black races'.[88] Everywhere, mandatory administrations deployed the language of civilization to justify their presence. Occasionally, however, the realities of race and power shone through.

As they did in the third matter raised by the Commission, the peculiar administration of Nauru. A remote Pacific island of some eight square miles with scarcely two thousand inhabitants, Nauru was of interest to the imperial powers only because centuries of migrating seabirds had left its central plateau covered in as much as 112 million tons of guano, the source of the phosphate fertilizers that were raising crop yields across the commercialized world. In the German period, the concession for mining those deposits had been granted to the Pacific Phosphate Company, a British concern that shipped their product primarily to Germany but also to Australia and other areas. Now, however, Britain and the Dominions thought they could establish exclusive control. 'The enormous value of this small island is known only to experts, but there is no doubt whatever about it,' Lloyd George telegraphed Milner during the Peace Conference in April 1919, and since Australia, New Zealand, and Britain wanted to share the phosphate between them, the mandate should be granted to all three.[89] Milner dutifully made sure Nauru was categorized as a 'C' mandate assigned to the British Empire and negotiated the joint purchase of the company by the three governments for some £3.5 million. The resulting 'Tripartite Agreement' vested control in a 'British Phosphate Commission' directed by representatives of the three powers and turned over local government to an Administrator appointed by Australia for the first five years. All phosphate mined in Nauru was to be sold to Britain, Australia, and New Zealand at cost price; only after that demand had been met could any additional supplies be sold on world markets.[90]

Milner kept these negotiations secret, but when the bill ratifying the Agreement came before Parliament, League supporters raised an outcry. The House should reject a Bill 'which is in direct conflict with . . . the open door and the principles of trusteeship,' Ormsby-Gore stated on 16 June 1920. The mandatory power was supposed to be trustee for the native population; instead, it was planning 'to establish a Government monopoly of the raw material of the territory of which it is trustee'. How could it do that and then turn around and say that the French could not control all native produce in Cameroon, or conscript natives in Togo? Robert Cecil, Oswald Mosley, and the free-trading Liberal leader H. H. Asquith all supported Ormsby-Gore, with Cecil pointing out that in the German period Nauruan phosphate had been sold at market prices to all and Asquith insisting that since the agreement was in conflict with the Covenant, it was illegal anyway.[91] Given the crushing majority enjoyed by the Lloyd George coalition, the Nauru Islands Agreement Bill passed overwhelmingly, but even *The Times* admitted that the critics had the best arguments.[92]

Britain and the Dominions thus had Nauru's future neatly tied up before the mandate was even written, but Ormsby-Gore never lost his sense of outrage. The natives were supposed to be owners of the mandatory territory, but the contract with the British Phosphate Commission treated the three governments as owners, the Dutch member Van Rees told Australian High Commissioner Sir Joseph Cook at the Commission's second session in August 1922; if that was a violation of the Covenant, Ormsby-Gore added, the contract would have to be amended. In their public session, the Commission suggested that Britain was violating the mandate in two ways: by 'subordinat[ing] the interests of the people to the exploitation of the wealth', and by 'reserving the ownership and exclusive exploitation of the resources of this territory to itself', instead of making them available to the world. Cook, furious, retorted that the phosphate royalty meant Nauruans 'enjoyed affluence and prosperity beyond their fondest hopes', but Ormsby-Gore felt (as he reported to his mother) 'very impenitent'.[93] He was delighted that the British papers picked up the criticisms.[94]

Yet, the dispute over Nauru went no further, not only because Ormsby-Gore left the Commission soon after but also because the Commission had been confronted by a *fait accompli*. Nauru was far, far away; no one on the Commission knew anything about it; and Australia—which continued to furnish the Administrator after that initial five-year period—carefully suppressed any record of Nauruans' discontent.[95] That the Nauruans, having achieved independence in 1968, would haul Australia before the International Court of Justice over the environmental devastation of their tiny homeland was, in an era of empire, unimaginable.[96]

Through the nationalities question, the Rwandan border dispute, and the debate over Nauru, the Commission tried to uphold two key principles of the mandates regime: that the territories were to remain distinct entities in international law, and that the interests of its indigenous population were paramount. Tentative though their actions were, they forced the annexationist tide finally to turn. Without these early actions, the more explicit debates of the mid-1920s over sovereignty and the 'open door' could not have happened. Yet as the distinctiveness of the category of the 'mandated territory' emerged more clearly, so too did its central contradiction: that it was to be governed in its inhabitants' interests but not by the inhabitants themselves. According to the Covenant, it was the mandated populations' incapacity that required trusteeship. What the Belgians implicitly acknowledged, however, was that trusteeship in turn required—even constituted—that incapacity. Nothing would be more hotly disputed than that assumption of incapacity. And Ormsby-Gore's last contribution, before leaving the Mandates Commission, was to insist that those protests be heard.

# THREE

## A Whole World Talking

The first principle laid down by President Wilson was, applied to the German Colonies, that no people must be forced under a sovereignty under which it does not wish to live...We were expecting the League of Nations or the Peace Conference will send delegates out to ascertain our wishes but they have not done so. I therefore humbly beg you for mercy sake to ask the Peace Conference or the League of Nations to send delegates out to ascertain our wishes. The French Government is forcing us to live under his Government Administration but our country don't want French Government.

Joseph Bell, Cameroon, to the Anti-Slavery Society, 17 October 1919[1]

For the victorious imperial powers, the mandates system was a tool to legitimate the territorial settlement agreed in 1919. For internationalists and League officials, it was a mechanism for spreading common norms about trusteeship and the 'open door'. But for a politicized minority in those territories to which it was applied the mandates system was something simpler: a shameless betrayal of the promises of self-determination the allies had made in 1918 with their backs to the wall. Britain and France hadn't just called on indigenous voices and troops in their campaigns; they had also promised that any new dispensation—in Africa as well as the Middle East, if Lloyd George was to be believed—would be crafted in consultation with those populations themselves. Yet, once they had secured their conquests—and, of course, once the United States exited the room—those promises had been pushed aside.

Duala elites in Cameroon, anglophone traders in Togo, Samoan chiefs, the stubbornly independent Rehoboth Basters of South West Africa, and a host of Arab organizations and potentates mobilized in protest. Communities happy to voice their detestation of German or Ottoman rule now wrote to dispute the decisions reached in Paris and San Remo. Much of that epistolary wave came ashore in imperial capitals, where it was suppressed by local officials or quietly filed away. Yet, even though the League of Nations was, in 1919 and 1920, little more than a postbox, some appeals also made their way to the Secretariat's temporary quarters. And they left a surprising deposit in their wake: a petition process, through which populations living under mandatory rule learned to claim that they, too, were nations deserving to be heard.

This petition process was perhaps the most significant aspect of the mandates system, for it brought the voices of the system's subjects—albeit muted, ventriloquized, and distorted—into the rooms in which their fates were determined. But this process was entirely unplanned. Neither the Covenant nor the mandate texts made any provision for petitioning.[2] Indeed, when the Milner Commission had begun drafting those texts in the summer of 1919, all members save the American George Louis Beer were agreed that while it was appropriate to allow *governments* to appeal to the Permanent Court of International Justice, if inhabitants of the mandate themselves were given such rights, as the French Colonial Minister Henry Simon put it, 'all administration would be impossible'.[3] Yet a petition process arose despite those objections.

On a fundamental level, of course, the emergence of that process was the achievement of petitioners themselves—of those thousands of men and women who, often at considerable risk, raised their voices against the new dispensation. Some drew upon earlier political and discursive traditions: Ottoman subjects had petitioned Ottoman authorities before 1914; Samoan chiefs and Duala elites had sent appeals about administrative practices or land rights to the Wilhelmine government.[4] But those appeals were made to national states claiming sovereignty over those they ruled, not to an international body. To understand how petitioning moved into the international sphere, we must examine what happened to those appeals to Geneva in the years immediately following the Peace Conference. As we shall see, some familiar figures—especially William Rappard, J. H. Harris, and William Ormsby-Gore—exploited mounting outrage and Anglo-French antagonism to create the League's most truly 'global' structure for mobilization, protest, and claim-making.

## The struggle for petitions

The situation in West Africa was one catalyst. Although the British held much of Southern Cameroon (including the crucial port of Douala) until

1916 and most of Togo (including the port of Lomé) until 1919, Britain ceded the bulk of both territories to France in exchange for recognition of claims elsewhere. Those retrocessions were unpopular with local British officials, with the Liverpool-based Association of West African Merchants and with English-speaking or German-speaking Duala and Ewe elites who had worked for British or German firms before 1914 or during the wartime British occupation.[5] In 1918 British authorities in both territories reported that local people were resisting French pressure to sign testimonials in their favour, and appeals to the authorities soon followed. 'There can, I fear, be very little doubt that... French rule in West Africa is in even worse odour among the natives than was that of the Germans before August 1914,' Hugh Clifford, Governor of Gold Coast, wrote to the Colonial Secretary in December 1918. From Cameroon, the British consul warned that Duala elites might depart for Nigeria en masse.[6]

The Foreign Office warned local officials that if they encouraged African disaffection they might have a diplomatic incident on their hands.[7] But if officials had to watch their tongues, J. H. Harris of the Anti-Slavery Society did not. Harris had been outraged when Lloyd George reneged on his promise to consult African opinion, and he vented his anger (and his low opinion of French actions in West Africa) in a series of hard-hitting articles in *The Times*, *The Manchester Guardian*, the *Contemporary Review*, and other indisputable organs of 'public opinion'.[8] Harris's high profile and the Anti-Slavery Society's strong ties to West African churchmen and traders made him the obvious channel for African grievances too. Duala protests about partition and French occupation had arrived on his desk in 1919, and in 1920 and 1921 he received reports from several sources (including one J. T. Mensah, formerly a clerk in a British trading company) about conditions in French-mandated Togo. Through his ties to Liverpool merchant interests, Ormsby-Gore saw some of this material and grew convinced that inhabitants under mandate must have the right to petition the League.[9] In January 1921 a League of Nations Union committee under his chairmanship urged the Council to recognize that right.[10]

In Geneva, William Rappard had come to the same conclusion. A few West African petitions made their way to the Secretariat, but protests against the British and French dispensation in the Middle East were flooding the League. The San Remo decisions of April 1920, Faysal's subsequent expulsion from Syria, the establishment of 'greater Lebanon', and the publication (revealingly, first in *The Jewish Chronicle*, which had managed to secure a copy before *The Times*)[11] in February 1921 of the draft Palestine mandate incorporating the Balfour Declaration, unleashed protests from King Husayn of the Hedjaz and from Arab organizations around the world. The emphasis in those appeals could vary; most, however, would have agreed—as Faysal put it in a letter on behalf of his father in February 1921—that French and British actions violated not only the wartime allied pledges but also that 'provisional recognition' of Arab independence contained in Article 22 itself. If Britain and France intended to impose their own rule, he warned prophetically, they would 'have the effect of making permanent the present state of unrest throughout the Middle East'.[12]

Direct lobbying in Geneva accompanied those missives. After the French expelled Faysal's government from Damascus in July 1920, many of his former ministers and supporters had sought refuge in Cairo, where Michel Lutfallah, the son of a rich Lebanese Christian émigré, had started building an organization to coordinate the Arab nationalist movement. There were plenty of disagreements to overcome, for pan-Islamists like Rashid Rida and the Druze aristocrat and former Ottoman official Shakib Arslan did not share Lutfallah's loyalty to the Hashemite cause, while some Palestinian nationalists resented Syrian dominance and what they saw as a Hashemite willingness to compromise with Zionism. Nevertheless, at Lutfallah's invitation (and largely at his expense), in late August 1921, right before the opening of the second League Assembly, an impressive gathering of Arab nationalists from across these divides convened in Geneva and formed the Syro-Palestinian Congress. Lutfallah was elected President, Rida its Vice President, and Arslan—the man who would become Arab nationalism's most indefatigable interlocutor in Europe—its Secretary (Figure 3.1).[13]

The Congress intended to bring before the League their demands for independence, the termination of the mandates, and the withdrawal of the Balfour Declaration. Yet, just as King Husayn discovered that the Council would not entertain his appeals against the San Remo accords in 1920 (a decision strenuously protested by Philip Noel-Baker),[14] so too the Syro-Palestinian Congress found that neither the Council nor Sir Eric Drummond would receive them.[15] Only Rappard heard them out, emerging from those meetings with considerable sympathy for the exiled Arab nationalists and a good sense of their grievances.[16] But what was he to do with this information—or, for that matter with the mounting pile of appeals against the Middle East settlement? They should be circulated to the Council and to all

Figure 3.1 The Syro-Palestinian Congress, Geneva, August 1921. Seated, left to right: Suleiman Kanaan, Rashid Rida, Michel Lutfallah, Taan al-Imad, Tawfic Hammad, and Shakib Arslan. Standing, left to right: Ihsan al-Jabiri, Shibly al-Jamal, Amin al-Tamimi, and Najib Choucair.

League member states, Rappard told Drummond. Given the 'tremendous agitation' about the 'A' mandates all over the world, that seemed 'a minimal concession' to their authors' pleas for League intervention. Drummond flatly disagreed. The Council had decided that the allied powers, and not the League, were responsible for allocating the mandates, and he would prefer to keep documents full of 'absurd allegations' from travelling further. Most reluctantly, on Drummond's express orders Rappard withdrew all the protests from the dossier sent to delegates to the Second Assembly, save two which had been inadvertently promised circulation in a letter signed by Drummond himself—a decision that captures perfectly Drummond's punctilious adherence to the letter rather than the spirit of the law.[17]

That Arab populations strongly objected to the fate being planned for them was common knowledge anyway, but the Assembly did not take the question up. Rappard remained conscience-stricken about his part in pushing the Arab nationalists offstage. 'Personally, I cannot bring myself to feel that we are doing our full duty towards the inhabitants of these territories,' he wrote to Drummond on 11 October 1921, after the Assembly had closed. The Arab protests might have been 'often naïve and badly worded, but I do feel that they can make out a strong case against the way in which they have been and are being treated by France and Great Britain'.[18] Indeed, behind the scenes, Rappard had already taken steps to circumvent his obstructive chief, raising the matter of petitions at the PMC's very first session held immediately following that Second Assembly. There, Ormsby-Gore lent his support: as any resident in a British colony had a right to appeal to the Privy Council, surely an inhabitant of a mandated territory ought to be able to appeal to the League! By the end of that first session, it was clear that the Mandates Commission would make a bid to receive petitions.[19]

If Rappard had managed to keep the right of petition alive, however, Drummond's delays had given British and French statesmen what they needed—a chance to turn their Middle East dispensation into a *fait accompli* before the League's self-appointed guardians of 'international conscience' reconvened. The British especially needed to do this, for in 1921 opposition to Britain's support for the Zionist project, endemic in Palestine, had taken root in Britain itself. In May 1921 a Palestine Arab Congress had sent a delegation to England, and while months of talks proved fruitless, their presence had made a mark. By June 1922 the House of Lords had passed a motion opposing the Palestine mandate, and *The Times* had discovered that Palestine was 'not an empty land' and concluded that it should not be administered in the interests of a Zionist movement which 'takes little account of the desires and traditions of the indigenous population'.[20] Out of this ferment emerged the definitive White Paper of July 1922, which confirmed Britain's commitment to the Jewish 'national home' while also clarifying that Britain intended neither to create a Jewish state in Palestine nor to displace the existing population.[21] The government then moved swiftly to secure international approval. In mid-July 1922 A J. Balfour, now Lord President of Council and handling League relations for the Foreign Office, not only extracted approval of the 'B' mandates from the League Council at a meeting in London but also (together with French minister René Viviani) put great pressure on the Italian delegate to let the formal ratification of both the Palestine and Syrian mandates go ahead. Balfour then informed 'all parties'—that is, the Zionists who had wanted the mandate and the Arabs who did not—that the time for debate was over.[22] Chaim Weizmann of the Zionist Organization (who had worried that 'if the mandate doesn't go through this time, it never will')[23] telegraphed his effusive thanks to Churchill, Balfour, and Lloyd George. The Palestinian delegation, recalled by their Executive, headed home.

But the idea that the debate in Palestine was 'over'—or indeed that it was 'over' in Syria or Cameroon or Togo or Samoa or South West Africa—could not have been more delusional. Rappard, in Geneva, knew that. The appeals were still flooding in—613 about Syria and Palestine alone by the second session of the Mandates Commission in August 1922.[24] Ormsby-Gore in London knew that too, and worked with friends in the Colonial Office to draft a petition process. Unsurprisingly, those officials would not be bypassed. Any petition from an inhabitant of a mandated territory had to be submitted *through* the mandatory power, which would forward it with a comment; only petitions originating outside the territory could be sent directly to Geneva and then forwarded for comment to the mandatory power. After considering both petition and the comment, the Commission was to report to the Council about whether it considered any action necessary.[25]

Ormsby-Gore brought this proposal to the Commission's second session in August 1922, where it met with a straight veto from the French member. The PMC could not consider setting up a petition process unless explicitly requested to do so by the Council, Jean-Baptiste Paul Beau contended, and the Council, citing the 'delicacy' of the matter, declined to get involved.[26] Yet, once again, 'publicity' and the Assembly came to the rescue. The Third Assembly met in September 1922 amid news that South Africa had sent planes to bomb ostensibly rebellious tribesmen in their South West African mandated territory, and outrage over that act created a groundswell of support for the proposed petition process. Buffeted by publicity, and with the British and the Secretariat both in favour, in January 1923 the Council gave its grudging approval.[27] Thanks to the persistence of Rappard, Harris, and Ormsby-Gore, a mechanism now existed through which those protests arriving from the mandated territories could be considered by the Mandates Commission, circulated to all League states, and publicized throughout the world.

## Setting the rules

The mere establishment of a petition process, however, hardly assured its effectiveness. Recall that petitioners appealing from a mandated territory were required to send their missive *through* government channels—or, as

Dantès Bellegarde, the Assembly delegate from Haiti, sardonically put it, to 'communicate their grievances to the very persons of whom they complain'.[28] Some of those 'persons' made sure that complaints went no further. Togolese petitioners reported to the Anti-Slavery Society in 1924, for example, that the French Commissioner had threatened them with immediate deportation should they try to petition again (and backed up his threat by deporting one outspoken critic),[29] and his counterpart from French Cameroon, when asked at a PMC session in 1929 about a petition the Commission had heard was on its way, replied unblushingly that he had called the petitioner in and told him his grievance was not a matter for the League.[30] During the 1925–26 Syrian rising, when deluged by petitions from around the world, the Commission was astounded to be told by the Quai d'Orsay's Middle East expert Robert de Caix that neither the French High Commissioner in Syria nor the government in Paris had received any petitions at all.[31]

As these examples suggest, French mandatory administrations were perhaps most hostile to petitioning, but the Belgian and Dominions administrations were not far behind, and not even the normally rule-bound British could be counted on consistently to defend the process they had proposed. Indeed in 1925, when the Commission gingerly raised the question of hearing petitioners in person, British Foreign Secretary Austen Chamberlain galvanized all the mandatory powers to join in a premeditated and public attack (discussed in Chapter 7) on the PMC. Worse, a few members of the Commission found such behaviour untroubling. The French member, Martial Merlin, proclaimed that anyone with any experience of 'Orientals' knew of their 'taste for wrangling, for intrigue and for complaining', and, as Beau had before him, fought every effort to treat petitions as credible documents.[32] When the Commission's Italian Chairman, Marquis Theodoli, tried to persuade his colleagues in 1929 to ask the mandatory powers to make the local inhabitants aware of their right of petition, Merlin retorted that petitions were usually trivial complaints submitted by unscrupulous agitators or self-aggrandizing busybodies and that the PMC should not encourage their proliferation.[33]

Merlin was, however, the Commission's near-pariah. Most members came to see petitioning as an essential right and did what they could to uphold it. Theodoli, as chairman, played an especially important role. With Rappard aiding him, he established rules of procedure that granted him some key powers, including that of deciding whether a petition sent from outside the territory was 'receivable'.[34] There were guidelines, codified in 1925, on which he was to base his judgement. To be 'receivable' a petition could not stem from an anonymous source, call the terms of the mandate itself into question, cover ground already gone over by another petition, or—since the Commission was not a court nor the petition a legal document—ask for intervention into matters justiciable in law in the mandate itself.[35] Yet, driven by an itch to cause France and Britain as much trouble as possible, Theodoli deliberately erred on the side of leniency; nor would he agree that, as was the rule in the minorities regime, petitions expressed in 'violent language' must be rejected.[36] The vast majority of communications, memoranda, memorials, and appeals that crossed Theodoli's desk (including a great many that certainly *did* call the mandate into question) were thus ruled 'receivable', sent to the mandatory power for comment, and put through a procedure that would make the petitioner's grievance more widely known.

Theodoli also used his right to name the 'rapporteur'—the PMC member who would consider the petition and write an initial report—highly strategically. A small number of long-serving members with no apparent stakes in the Middle East handled the floods of Syrian and Palestinian petitions. Orts, Palacios, the Portuguese De Penha Garcia, and the Japanese Sakenobe each reported on between 130 and 150 petitions during their time on the Commission, while the analytical and efficient Rappard handled an astonishing 435 petitions. Beau, Merlin, and the other French members, by contrast, together reported on a mere thirteen over the whole of the Commission's life.[37] Theodoli also distributed particularly important missives to those most likely to sympathize, passing petitions from hard-pressed South West African communities to Lugard or later Valentine Dannevig (both of whom cordially detested South Africa's native policy), Samoan and Palestinian claims for self-determination to Palacios (the only member with much sympathy for them), and appeals from Iraq's ethnic and religious minorities to Rappard and Orts (both of whom were fearful about the likely fate of those communities if Iraq were granted independence).

Finally, Theodoli, Rappard, and the Secretariat officials who worked under them did what they could—little though it often was—to force mandatory powers to respect the right of petition. Although they dutifully returned petitions from inhabitants sent directly to the League with instructions to send them *through* mandatory authorities, they sometimes kept notes or copies of those petitions supposedly on their way or asked questions intended to shame the mandatory power into producing them.[38] By 1928 the petition process was routine enough for the Section to begin keeping a Register of Petitions. Over the next dozen years, some 1,500 petitions (or, occasionally, groups of petitions) would be listed in that register and their progress painstakingly tracked.[39] At points, to be sure, this system rather broke down. During the 'Wailing Wall' conflict in Jerusalem in 1929–30 and the turbulent 1936–39 period in Palestine and Syria, petitions arrived in such numbers that they were sometimes listed as a group; petitions on similar subjects were also routinely considered together in a single report. Nevertheless, between 1925 and 1939 the Commission submitted some 325 separate reports (many treating multiple petitions) to the League Council.

As the system expanded, moreover, its workings became more public and visible. True, petitions were discussed by the PMC in closed session and with the representative of the mandatory power alone. Yet, petitioners' grievances made their way into the public record anyway, for the minutes of those discussions were always published (if in sanitized form), the Commission's reports on petitions were usually published, and in especially important cases the full petition was printed as well. Moreover, while petitioners were told that the Commission itself would not formally receive them, they quickly learned that Theodoli, Rappard, members of the League Secretariat, and journalists out for a good story certainly would. True, only the well-financed petitioner could travel to Geneva to try to make their case in person, but Zionist, Syrian, and Palestinian organizations, and even the odd Samoan and Cameroonian individual, had either the private wealth or the organizational support to do so. Indeed, both the Zionist Organization and the Syro-Palestinian Congress took the precaution of establishing offices with a resident representative in Geneva, who kept the PMC well supplied with petitions and met regularly with any member who would see him. By the late 1920s petitioning had become a routine part of the mandates regime.

## The scope of petitioning

Who took advantage of that right? Let us begin with some numbers. Although it is impossible to know how many petitions were *sent* to the League (since some were suppressed along the way), through a painstaking study of the archives in the Mandates Section, the Dutch scholar Anique van Ginneken established that more than 3,000 appeals, charges, or communications of some kind *reached* the Secretariat in Geneva.[40] As the following chart shows (Table 4), those were very unevenly distributed across the fourteen mandated territories. The vast majority concerned Syria or Palestine. Some of these were individual appeals alleging violations of property rights or educational discrimination, but most articulated collective claims or grievances. Every detail of France's wretched record in Syria and Lebanon—from the arrest of local political leaders, to the bombing of Damascus, to the suppression of the Syrian Assembly, to the decision to cede Alexandretta to Turkey—was protested in petitions sent by civic and political organizations within Syria and (especially) by diasporic Syrian clubs and communities all over the world.[41] Palestine, unsurprisingly, produced similar numbers, especially after 1933, when the search for refuge for Central European Jews and Arab protests against increased Jewish immigration both

**Table 4.** Distribution of Petitions by Territory.

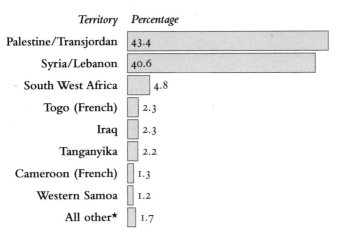

**Distribution of Petitions and Communications by Territory, as Received by the Permanent Mandates Commission**

| Territory | Percentage |
|---|---|
| Palestine/Transjordan | 43.4 |
| Syria/Lebanon | 40.6 |
| South West Africa | 4.8 |
| Togo (French) | 2.3 |
| Iraq | 2.3 |
| Tanganyika | 2.2 |
| Cameroon (French) | 1.3 |
| Western Samoa | 1.2 |
| All other* | 1.7 |

* This category includes general petitions, petitions about multiple territories, and petitions for New Guinea, Japanese islands, Ruanda/Urundi, Cameroon (British), Nauru, and Togo (British), each of which accounted for fewer than one percent of the total petitions sent.
Source: A. H. M. van Ginneken, 'Volkenbondsvoogdij: Het Toezicht van de Volkenbond op het Bestuur in Mandaatgebieden, 1919–1940' [The League of Nations as Guardian: The League's Oversight Machinery and the Administration of Mandated Territories 1919–1940]. Dissertation, University of Utrecht, the Netherlands, 1992, pages 211–217.

intensified. Zionists, in Palestine and abroad, alleged that British authorities were not fulfilling their obligation to promote 'close settlement' by Jews on the land and were too slow to crack down on Arab violence; Arab organizations, in Palestine and abroad, protested that the British allowed excessive Jewish immigration, were treating the Arab population brutally, and were not living up to their promise to set up representative institutions.[42] In both territories, petitions were also sent by groups who contested other petitioners' right to represent popular opinion. Revisionist Zionists determined to establish a Jewish state and religious Jews averse to secular politics protested the Zionist Organization's privileged status as the designated representative of Palestine's Jewish population. Lebanese Maronites asserted their loyalty to French mandate authorities and contested the claims of Damascene or exiled Syrian nationalists to speak for the whole population.

No Pacific or African territory produced anything like this volume of petitions. When one takes into account the size of the population, however, as Chapter 6 shows, it is clear that tiny Western Samoa surpassed even Palestine and Syria in the use made of petitioning. Appeals to the League—and to the King, the German Reichstag, and the American President—lay at the heart of the decade-long civil disobedience movement carried on by virtually the whole of the Samoan population. By contrast, while South West Africa generated quite a few petitions, a high proportion of these were from individual Germans seeking to recover lost property or stake new claims rather than from African communities. Indeed, the explosion in petitions from the territory in the early 1930s owed much to the monomaniacal activity of one Mr J. E. Lange, who bombarded the Commission with claims for lost cattle or appropriated land until even Theodoli wearied of him and ruled further communications 'not receivable'.

Several mandated territories generated very few petitions to Geneva. In some cases, however, this was more a matter of grievances being dealt with (or suppressed) at the local level than it was of inhabitants failing to petition at all. The well-organized Nauruans (like the Samoans) petitioned London and Canberra on several occasions, but those appeals were neither forwarded to nor mentioned at the League.[43] British authorities attempting to amalgamate chieftaincies in mandated Togo found themselves caught up in disputes between rival clans, some of whom petitioned local officials, but those conflicts were kept away from Genevan eyes.[44] Few complaints about conditions in British Cameroon reached the League either, and while

Belgium's repressive administration in Rwanda and Burundi aroused plenty of negative press comment (especially in Germany), Rwanda's king complained directly to Belgian officials, who carefully concealed his protests. Japan submitted fulsome reports about demographic, economic, and social conditions in its mandated territory, but no Micronesian comment reached the League, the few petitions being foreign claims about confiscated property or foreign protests about Japan's unwillingness to allow tourists into its island fastnesses.

But if the international petition became a popular form only in Syria, Palestine, and Western Samoa, in several other territories particular ethnic, religious, or political groups discovered and exploited this right. In South West Africa, for example, the Rehoboth Basters, a mixed-race group granted significant autonomy under the Germans, petitioned the League doggedly if unsuccessfully across the whole of the period for restoration of that status,[45] while in Tanganyika Indian traders petitioned against the efforts of white settlers to monopolize particular growing and trading rights. One 'Bund der Deutschen Togoländer', which was led largely by (Ewe) exiles from French Togo living in Accra but which claimed support across partitioned Eweland, irritated French authorities (and the deeply anti-German French and Belgian PMC members) with their persistent criticisms of French policy in Togo. Duala elites in Cameroon with allies in Germany and metropolitan France continued to protest land seizures that dated to the German period as well as French taxes on their trade.[46] Petitioning was also seized upon by vulnerable ethnic groups at moments of particular danger or stress. When Britain announced in 1929 that it would support Iraq's entry into the League as an independent state, petitions began bubbling up from Assyrian and Kurdish groups presciently fearful that they would be targets of what we would now call ethnic cleansing.

Petitioning was not, however, the monopoly of inhabitants of these territories; indeed the majority of petitions that made it to Geneva (about 60 per cent according to Van Ginneken's count) emanated from 'outside sources' and were thus sent directly to the League. True, the great majority of these came from individuals or groups—Syrian clubs, Zionist organizations—with close ties to the territory's inhabitants and a direct interest in their fate, or even indirectly from inhabitants using exile groups or sympathetic friends to bypass the obligation to send the petition through the mandatory power. Members of the Adjigo family, who carried on a long campaign against the French authorities in Togo for appointing a rival clan to a throne (or 'stool') they considered rightfully theirs (and for deporting them to a remote region when they protested) thus petitioned France directly. But they also garnered interest in their case from J. H. Harris and the prominent Gold Coast lawyer, newspaper proprietor, Legislative Council member, and early African nationalist J. E. Casely Hayford.[47] Telegrams about French troops firing on demonstrations by market women against tax increases in mandated Togo were sent from just over the border in Gold Coast, probably by exiles who had fled the violence; protests about comparable violence in Cameroon also arrived from contacts outside the territory.[48] Cameroonian and Syrian students in Paris dispatched petitions to Geneva that local authorities would doubtless have suppressed.

Some states, organizations, and individuals also tried to use petitions to pressure the imperial powers. German colonialist organizations made clear how dimly they viewed the prospect of Britain federating Tanganyika with its neighbouring East African colonies; Italian-dominated oil concerns challenged Britain's grip on Iraqi oil. Some vigilant humanitarian or political organizations—notably Harris's Anti-Slavery Society but also the League of Nations Union, the Bureau International pour la Défense des Indigènes, the Communist-influenced League Against Imperialism, the Ligue de Défense de la Race Nègre, and the Women's International League for Peace and Freedom—petitioned when they caught wind of labour abuses, religious bias, or political repression within a territory. Both the Second Pan-African Congress chaired by W. E. B. Du Bois in Paris in 1921 and Marcus Garvey's Universal Negro Improvement Association petitioned—Du Bois urging the appointment of a coloured member of the Commission and Garvey contesting the Pan-Africanist Congress's right to speak for Africans and to advance his own organization's qualifications as trustee for Germany's former African wards.[49] Finally, some businessmen, scholars, and simple tourists, stumbling across questionable practices or situations, unburdened themselves to the League only to discover, to their surprise, that they had submitted a 'petition'.

Petitioning, then, was a more widespread and complex practice than we might suppose. It became a recognized medium for complaint in some mandated territories, and even when it was repressed or little known, diasporic groups, humanitarian organizations, and even a few early anti-colonialists petitioned on behalf of inhabitants. But what 'work' did all that talking do? What difference did petitioning make?

# Impact and meaning

It is important, first, to be clear about what petitioning did not do. It did not normally win the petitioner redress. According to Van Ginneken, in the large majority of cases (some three-quarters of those for which full information is available), the PMC recommended that no action be taken. Only in 10 per cent of cases were complaints upheld, which did not in itself constrain the League Council or the mandatory power to remedy the situation, although the Commission did give some partial support—such as acknowledging the legitimacy of a petitioning group's concerns—to a greater number.[50] Why was petitioning so fruitless?

Part of the explanation lies in the PMC's own understanding of the nature of the mandates regime and in its own restrictive rules. Mandatory powers and the PMC agreed that the mandate was a contract between the mandatory power and the League, not between the League and the local population. Petitions were thus considered by the Commission to be sources of information and not juridical documents; indeed, it was because they were not considered justiciable that the Commission was able to justify its expansive definition of what was 'receivable'. Yet the flip side of this openness was that the petitioner was never considered (as a legal plaintiff would have been) to have any real rights before the PMC at all. The Commission's responsibility was not to petitioners but to the League Council: if a petition contained persuasive evidence of malfeasance within a mandated territory, the PMC was to alert the Council, not to 'decide' for a petitioner themselves. Indeed, the PMC's practice of transmitting their report on the petition not only to the Council but to the petitioners greatly irritated the mandatory powers, who tended to argue that the Commission should have no independent communication with petitioners at all.

Then there were the rules on petitioning, which further restricted the scope of the practice. Petitioners, remember, were not to turn to the League to remedy perceived injustices that could be addressed through the territory's own courts. Many did so anyway, to find that the Commission would not consider their case. Petitions also failed because the PMC had no capacity to conduct independent inquiries and little outside information with which to challenge the usually dismissive response of the mandatory power. The more independent-minded members found it frustrating (and petitioners no doubt enraging) that, when faced with diametrically opposing accounts, the Commission usually felt constrained to accept the mandatory power's word. 'In such cases, in fact, the mandatory Power was both judge and party,' Rappard complained in the discussion of the shooting of market women in Lomé. 'That was one of the fundamental defects' of the process.[51]

Yet the failure of most petitions was not really due to inadequate information. More failed because they challenged the fundamental premises of the system itself. Territories had been placed under mandate, after all, because the Covenant had stated that their populations were not yet able to 'stand by themselves'. When Syrian, Palestinian, Cameroonian, and Western Samoan petitioners insisted, as they were wont to do, that they could in fact stand alone, the Commission ruled those claims outside their competence. That logic might seem perverse and racist but it was *logical*, for, as the PMC repeated over and over, its duty was to see that the system's rules were observed, not to judge those rules themselves. Petitioners could claim protections due them under mandate; they could not slough off protection altogether. The PMC's restricted authority, its need to balance supervision with cooperation, and especially its 'textualism', led it to adopt what Balakrishnan Rajagopal has rightly called 'an attitude of containment', with the most radical petitions 'put off by bureaucratic techniques'.[52]

Those presumptions about the incapacity of indigenous peoples didn't just doom what we might call 'proto-nationalist' petitions, however. They also inevitably shaped how the Commission responded to indigenous petitioners *tout court*. 'It was the duty of the Mandates Commission to examine very conscientiously all the petitions that reached it,' Pierre Orts stated once when discussing the appeals of the Bund der Deutschen Togoländer, 'but, obviously, the value of a petition depended mainly on the standing of the persons who submitted it.'[53] Here, 'civilizational' thinking did its most pernicious work, for how could petitioners presumed to be 'backward' and 'primitive' have 'standing'? It was common knowledge, intoned the Council document that first outlined the petition process, that 'peoples of a less-advanced civilization' were prone to make complaints 'about the most insignificant matters for reasons which have little, if any, foundation',[54] while their 'simplicity' and 'gullibility' made them susceptible to manipulation. When petitions arrived from 'natives', both mandatory powers and PMC members were prone to detect, as Australian High Commissioner Joseph Cook put it, 'someone who is behind the natives for some ulterior purpose of his own'[55]—the agitator, the 'half-caste', the communist, the German, the

Turk. Educated and 'detribalized' natives were particularly suspect and routinely saw their petitions dismissed and their motives impugned. White
petitioners were not always treated respectfully (South West Africa's importunate German or Afrikaner settlers, for example, were roundly disliked by
the PMC for their rapacious and brutal attitude towards the native population), but they were never dismissed as corrupt, childlike, or incapable of
knowing their own minds.

Petitions from whites that partook of the system's racial and civilizational
logic fared very differently. All petitions from the Anti-Slavery Society and
the Bureau International pour la Défense des Indigènes were thoroughly
investigated, for both societies were seen as impartial humanitarian bodies
with natives' interests at heart. Allegations about forced labour or other
violations of the mandate made by well-placed white officials or respected
scholars (such as those found in Raymond Leslie Buell's *The Native Problem
in Africa*, discussed in Chapter 8) elicited painstaking point-by-point responses.
Similarly, although Syrian charges of torture by French forces were dismissed
(as we shall see in Chapter 5) on the grounds that civilized powers simply
didn't act in such ways, indigenous charges against 'native' officials or governments could receive a more sympathetic hearing. Petitioners who sought
the Commission's protection against majority nationalisms or who opposed
the lifting of mandatory protection—as did Iraq's Bahai, Assyrian, and Kurdish
communities—found the Commission very willing to publicize grievances
so in keeping with its assumptions.

So what did petitioning do? To a considerable degree, it worked to contain and delegitimize pressures and protests coming from below. Petitioners
appealed to the League for a wide array of reasons. The PMC, however,
could only endorse those appeals that acknowledged the mandatory power's
authority and the inhabitants' subjection. Yet, at the same time, the process
also instantiated—made visible and forced petitioners to comprehend—the
authoritarian structure and paternalistic logic of the mandates regime. The
question must thus be asked: Did the lesson take? Did petitioning act primarily as a kind of safety valve or decoy, as petitioners were drawn into
time-consuming contests they could not win?

The stories in this book suggest that it did not. True, many petitioners
first approached the League with faith in its ideals and a genuine hope of
redress, but they did not persist, sometimes for decades, in the deluded belief
that they could change the Commission's mind. They persisted, rather,
because of what petitioning offered: exposure, contacts, credibility, publicity,

voice. Martial Merlin's jaundiced observation that petitioners appealed to the League to set themselves up as 'somebodies' was not entirely wrong, for petitioners were often addressing their fellows, followers, and an international public quite as much as the PMC. Petitioning mobilized movements and built up mass support. There is no evidence at all that it somehow dissipated nationalist energies or channelled it along unproductive lines. To the contrary, the Samoan Mau, the Syrian nationalist movement, the Rehoboth Basters, the Bund der Deutschen Togoländer, and Kurdish politicians honed their organizational skills and built up international and publicity networks through petitioning. Moreover, since the justice of their claim was (in the eyes of such petitioners) beyond dispute, the fact that the Commission usually rejected it rarely damaged either the petitioner's credibility or the movement's popularity—indeed, petitioners eagerly publicized such rejections in the sure knowledge that abuse only enhanced their standing. Such actions show an astute awareness of the system's logic and a canny ability to exploit it to political advantage.

The significance of petitioning should be sought, then, not in the realm of law but of politics—and of global politics at that. Petitioning mattered not because it offered petitioners redress but because it allowed them to enter and speak in a multi-vocal, international arena. It was one of the key mechanisms (publicity being another) through which a previously binary relationship—colonizer, colonized—was triangulated. Suddenly, there was another location for confrontation, and new participants in the room. Moreover, as those dramas unfolded, they could have consequences beyond simply sustaining movements or reputations. Some of those effects were modest, as officials made concessions or stayed their hand to improve their international reputation, but in other cases the force field of Geneva fundamentally altered what the mandatory power not only *could* but also *wanted* to do.

The remaining nine chapters in this book trace the difference that 'internationalization' made not simply in different territories but to the unstable interwar order. Effects varied across the different territories. Where League oversight was perfunctory and international networks weak, imperial overseers in London, Paris, or Tokyo could carry on with only the occasional foray into the Genevan arena and the odd polite reference to mandatory ideals. Yet, where rival national and geopolitical interests were strongly engaged and either humanitarian lobbies or local populations mobilized and well connected, the League became both the prize and the stage in a symbolic drama that could not but affect those caught up in it. Increasingly, colonial subjects and imperial powers alike adjusted their strategies to amplify, exploit, or seek to avoid the 'noise' emanating from Geneva.

We shall turn shortly to three instances—in South West Africa, Syria, and Western Samoa—in which local risings or protest movements in the 1920s became global media events, leading all parties to reflect on how to manage the process of 'internationalization'. Yet the territory in which politics was most thoroughly 'internationalized' was none of these: it was Palestine. Politics in Palestine crossed borders from the start, not only because the British had insisted on an 'international guarantee' for the policy of the 'National Home', not only because both the Zionist movement and the Palestinian Arab movement sought to mobilize support across the globe, but also because, in this case alone, the Mandates Commission came down on the side of one party to the debate. Not all members of the PMC came to support the Zionist cause, but over time a majority did so—a development that placed both the Palestinian Arab movement and eventually the British government on the defensive, and that came to shape the way the PMC viewed Arab aspirations in Syria and Iraq as well. We shall discuss Syrian and Iraqi developments in Chapters 5 and 9, and the difference the mandatory structure made to the political transformation of Palestine in the last chapter, but because Zionist mobilization and Palestine's 'internationalization' were so significant for the mandates system as a whole, let us return to Geneva in 1924. As we shall see, once it became alert to the dangers and uses of 'Geneva', the Zionist movement mobilized swiftly to contain the challenge posed by Palestinian petitions and to build up durable ties to the Commission and the Secretariat.

## Competitive internationalization in Palestine

William Rappard, recall, was well aware of the depth of Arab unhappiness about the post-war territorial dispensation, but because the Syria and Palestine mandates were not approved until July 1922, and their 'start dates' further delayed until September 1923, the Commission did not review administration in Syria and Palestine until their fifth session, in late October and early November 1924. By that point, Palestine had been under Sir Herbert Samuel's civil administration for four years. Key steps to realize the Zionist project had been taken. Legislation to facilitate transfers of land

held by the state or by absentee landlords had been passed; Hebrew made
an official language alongside English and Arabic; the firm of a Russian
Jewish businessman, Pinhas Rutenberg, granted an exclusive concession
to generate electricity by water power through the whole of Palestine; the
Jewish proportion of the population doubled to just under a fifth.[56] Yet
Samuel, shaken by the anti-Jewish riots in Jaffa in 1921 and genuinely committed to the pledge made in the 1922 White Paper to foster representative
institutions, had also come up with one contrivance after another—for a
Legislative Council, for an expanded Advisory Council, even for an 'Arab
Agency' to balance the Jewish Agency—to give the Arab population some
voice in government.[57]

Since all those proposals stipulated that the policy of the 'National Home'
would be kept off the table, the Arabs rejected every one. Two further delegations from the Palestine Arab Congress in 1922 and 1923 tried but failed
to persuade the Conservative government to break with Zionism.[58] With
no progress visible in London, the Congress's Executive Committee turned
to the League, submitting a 'Report on the State of Palestine during Four
Years of Civil Administration'—a title clearly modelled on the government's own reports—for the Mandates Commission to consider. It is a mark
of Britain's propensity to play by the rules that this missive, sent as required
first to the mandatory power, was indeed forwarded to Geneva. The arguments advanced therein were hardly new. The petition protested the injustice of planting a Jewish National Home in a country that was 'the
well-established home of the Palestinian Arabs (Moslems and Christians)'
and insisted that that policy traduced promises of Arab independence made
to King Husayn and Article 22 of the League Covenant itself. Citing land
laws, tax policies, the Rutenberg concession, and government spending,
the report also charged that Samuel's administration was biased, costly,
inefficient, and violated the Palestinian population's basic rights.[59] What
was new was that the Mandates Commission was empowered to consider
these complaints.

Not only empowered but willing. In 1924 sympathies on the Commission
flowed in the Arab direction. True, few members had much knowledge of
the Middle East; with Ormsby-Gore gone, only the Chairman, Theodoli,
had spent much time there. Theodoli, however, was and would remain
anti-Zionist, not only because he was a papal count and protective of
both Italian and Catholic interests, but also because he had married into
the wealthy Lebanese clan of the Sursocks—a family, Chaim Weizmann

sourly remarked, that had sold the Jezreel valley privately to the Zionists while denouncing the Jewish National Home in public.[60] The newly appointed Spanish member, Leopoldo Palacios, also believed that all 'A' mandated territories should become independent as quickly as possible. But the most important sympathizer was Rappard, who had been receiving appeals from Arab nationalists and meeting with Arab delegations for four years. In 1922 Samuel had told Rappard privately that the Arabs had 'nothing to fear' since there was 'no chance of establishing a Jewish Kingdom or a Jewish State in Palestine for two or three generations at least', but Rappard understood that this would not reassure a majority Arab population that did not want its grandchildren to live in a Jewish state either.[61]

Under Theodoli's and Rappard's leadership, the Commission thus grilled Herbert Samuel about every charge the Palestinians had raised. Britain's failure to introduce those self-governing institutions promised in the Covenant and the White Paper came in for particular censure. True, Samuel explained that since 'the Arabs had declared that if they had a majority they would use it to oppose the establishment of a Jewish National Home, it was not possible to afford them an opportunity of acting in a way that was hostile to this requirement of the mandate'[62]—but if self-government had to be continuously postponed in this way, was the Zionist project really compatible with the obligation to promote the local population's 'well-being and development'? In June, Rappard had told Ormsby-Gore that the Arabs were worried that Jewish settlement would mean their own displacement, for even if individual Arabs sold their land to Jews voluntarily and for good prices, 'the Arabs as a whole looked askance at these individual purchases, which seemed to them to signify the gradual acquisition by a foreign race of their inheritance'.[63] Samuel was emollient and reassuring. There was no plan to displace the Arabs; indeed, the White Paper had clarified that Jews and Arabs were to work together on the development of their common 'home'. Moreover, since the influence of the Palestine Arab Congress was declining, he was certain that it would soon be possible to introduce representative government by stages. The British would thus be able to fulfil both obligations of the mandate—to foster the 'National Home' while also safeguarding Arab interests.

The Commission, however, was not convinced, and in the draft of their report to the Council all their ambivalence came out. That draft welcomed Samuel's statement repudiating the hopes of 'certain Zionist extremists' to supplant the Arabs in Palestine and accepted that his administration believed in, and conscientiously worked to achieve, the reconciliation of the two communities' interests. Yet, the report implicitly questioned whether that goal was realizable, pointing out that on many key issues—most notably Jewish immigration but also the need to build representative institutions—Zionist and Arab views and interests clashed. Finally, the report queried the Zionist project itself, suggesting that Eastern European Jews entering Palestine, however great their 'ardour and zeal', were unprepared for the kind of agricultural and manual work which the territory required. No one reading that document—which the *Daily News Bulletin* of the Jewish Telegraphic Agency managed to publish before it was released to the press—could fail to conclude that the Mandates Commission viewed the whole Zionist enterprise with scepticism.[64]

Chaim Weizmann was one of those readers, and he was horrified. Weizmann had travelled to Geneva for that November 1924 PMC session expecting that, as President of the World Zionist Organization, he would receive the same kind of privileged political access he enjoyed in Britain. To his chagrin, he discovered that the Commission would not officially hear him (since only representatives of the mandatory power could appear before it) and, worse, that Theodoli had ruled the Zionist Organization's lengthy report (which had been sent directly to the League, and not, as required, through the mandatory power) 'not receivable'. 'We have neglected Geneva,' Weizmann wrote to his allies in New York, 'and the Arabs have been hard at work there.' He thought he had had a 'very good *innings* privately' with many members of the Commission, but it had not been enough.[65] 'The Commission,' he reported to Samuel on 13 November, 'has simply endorsed the views expressed in the Arab protest.'[66]

Weizmann set himself swiftly to control the damage. In London he persuaded J. E. Shuckburgh, head of the Colonial Office's Middle East Department, to read him the PMC draft report in full and then wrote suggesting amendments. He reported on this meeting to Samuel, in the process rehearsing the arguments the High Commissioner could use to rebut calumnies about Jewish immigrants. The argument that Palestine was being handed over to a 'minority' was especially misplaced, he insisted, for the Balfour Declaration was 'not given to the Jews of Palestine, but to the Jews of the World', millions of whom would enter if given a chance. Weizmann then wrote to Lugard and to Rappard to protest the PMC's characterization of their work and his own dismissive treatment. He had come to Geneva, he told Rappard in that long 'unofficial' missive, 'not in order to register complaints and grievances, but to give information and present facts', only to find that a 'vociferous group of Arab propagandists' without an 'atom of truth' in their claims had been heard instead. Zionists had no quarrel with Arab peasants, Weizmann insisted—'poor wretches [who] have been bled white by the Effendis, the very agitators who write protests to the League'. In a separate letter to Drummond, he proposed that since the Commission was no doubt 'fair minded and wishes to describe Palestine accurately', the offending passage on Jewish immigrants be revised.[67]

Rappard was taken aback. As he told Drummond, he had drafted the report at the request of the Commission, which had approved it. It could hardly be amended at an outside organization's request.[68] The Commission's report was thus published with only slight revisions, and the Palestine Arab Congress had the gratification of seeing their appeal printed in full in the appendix to the minutes of that PMC session. But what particularly troubled Rappard was that the representative of the Jewish Telegraphic Agency had clearly managed to extract the *draft* report from someone inside the Secretariat. Drummond should try to find out who was leaking confidential information.[69] Yet Rappard never learned the identity of that source. On this, as on many occasions, the Zionist Organization proved able to lay its hands on secret League material before it reached even the British government.[70] In this case too, and not for the last time, the Zionist movement's rapid mobilization and Weizmann's adept lobbying had its effect. Weizmann had made sure that Alexander Cadogan at the Foreign Office as well as the sympathetic Belgian and Czech Council members had received memoranda refuting the PMC's criticisms.[71] When the Council met to review its report, Foreign Secretary Austen Chamberlain remarked that it 'hardly did full justice to the results achieved by Jewish immigration'.[72] The Zionist project, the Council implied, was not open to question by the PMC.

This incident reveals much about how the mandates system 'internationalized' both imperial and national projects. Years of protests and work by Arab organizations had finally born fruit, with the Mandates Commission submitting the only report they ever wrote sceptical of the Palestine mandate. The Zionist Organization, secure in British support, had (as Weizmann acknowledged) paid Geneva less mind. Yet, once alerted to the existence of pro-Arab sympathies on the PMC, the Zionists countered quickly and effectively, taking advantage of their contacts within the Colonial Office, the network of representatives across Europe, and confidants within the Secretariat itself to have the Commission's judgements overturned. They

then moved swiftly to establish a Permanent Office in Geneva, appointing
Victor Jacobson and then Nahum Goldmann to handle relations with the
League. Henceforth, Jacobson would keep the Commission, the Council, and
sympathetic journalists well supplied with the Zionist Organization's comprehensive memoranda and his own advice, apprise colleagues in London
and Palestine about upcoming meetings in Geneva, and induce the Secretariat
to treat him, if not exactly as the delegate of a member state, then at least as
the representative of an organization entitled to the League's benevolent
support. (When Jacobson died in 1934, there was a nice little to-do within
the Secretariat about whether his wife should be sent an 'official' condolence letter.)[73] But it was Weizmann above all who cultivated individual
PMC members. He recalled in his autobiography that while he did not
think it 'dignified or proper' to lobby the Commission in the hallways in
Geneva, he much enjoyed his 'regular visits' to Lugard's modest Surrey
home and the 'long evenings' he spent in Orts' study in his home in Brussels,
explaining the Zionist position and 'learning from [Orts'] wide experience
as a great administrator, statesman, and man of the world'. In the 1930s
Nahum Goldmann continued this adept diplomacy.[74]

Yet no relationship proved as useful and important as that Weizmann
forged with Rappard. After the 1924 debacle, Weizmann asked the Swiss
academic to come to Palestine to see the Zionists' work for himself, and
when Rappard worried that accepting Zionist hospitality was incompatible
with his duty to remain impartial, Weizmann had Herbert Samuel invite him
to the founding ceremony for the Hebrew University in his role as Vice
Rector of the Geneva law faculty (Figure 3.2). Rappard made the trip that
spring in the company of Weizmann and A. J. Balfour (who was given the
honour of declaring the university open), visited Tel Aviv and Jerusalem,
joined Balfour in climbing the Mount of Olives, and spent several days
touring Jewish settlements.[75] He enjoyed (and was a bit star-struck by) the
company and could not but be impressed by the commitment and spirit of
the Zionist pioneers. That they were 'unsuited' for this task, or that the suppressed mass of Arab peasants would not be helped by their progressive
ideals, or that the Arab nationalists who had hung out black flags to protest
Balfour's visit would be better state-builders, now seemed so much moonshine. Rappard returned an ardent Zionist. As he told his colleagues on the
PMC, the visit 'had entirely changed his point of view'.[76] For the next fifteen years Rappard would act as a reliable channel of information and advice
for the Zionist movement.

**Figure 3.2** Lord Balfour opening Hebrew University, 1 April 1925; behind him, on the right, Chaim Weizmann.

Palestine's Arab nationalist movement had no figure to rival Weizmann in political access and acumen, nor did Shakib Arslan's Geneva office of the Syro-Palestinian Congress ever enjoy the kind of friendly and confidential relations that Weizmann, Jacobson, and Goldmann built up with members of the Secretariat and the PMC. Its inability to wrest meaningful concessions from the British also told on the Arab movement within Palestine, which fell into factionalism in the mid-1920s.[77] Yet the Palestinian Arabs' political weakness was a consequence not only of Zionists' superior connections or even their own internal rivalries but even more of the Zionist cast of the mandate text, in which Arabs figured only as 'inhabitants' to be protected and not, as the Jews did, as a people represented by an official body with which the mandatory power was instructed to collaborate.[78] Rappard's initial sympathy for the Arab cause arose from his belief that those Syrian and Palestine mandate texts were *in themselves* unjust, being incompatible with the promises of the Covenant and the November 1918 Anglo-French declaration. His initial objection, in other words, was less to the British and French treatment of Arabs *under* the mandate than to the mandates themselves. Yet once the Palestine mandate had been confirmed, Rappard's own deep textualism made opposition to its Zionist pledges difficult to sustain. From this point, the advantage would go to the party best able to deploy the skills of legal argument and textual interpretation to make the mandate 'speak' on their behalf—and, as Natasha Wheatley has shown, the Zionist Organization's adept international lawyers in Geneva, Jerusalem, and England won this competition easily.[79]

The year 1924 thus proved to be the high point of sympathy for Palestinian Arab arguments on the PMC. Rebuked by Chamberlain and with Rappard's loyalties shifting, the Commission would never question the Balfour Declaration again. The obligation to facilitate Jewish immigration to the 'economic absorptive capacity' of the territory, enshrined in the 1922 White Paper, would be treated henceforth by the Commission as a given— as, in Weizmann's favourite phrase, '*chose jugée*'. Although the Executive Committee of the Palestine Arab Congress petitioned the League again in 1925, reiterating their claim that the Balfour Declaration and the adminis- tration's 'colonial system of government' violated both the Covenant and the Husayn-McMahon agreements, the PMC concluded that it could not consider petitions that called into question 'the very principle of the Palestine Mandate', which included that Palestine must accommodate the Jewish National Home.[80] Theodoli and Palacios would still insist on the need to protect Arab 'civil and religious' rights, and the Palestine Arab Congress would continue to petition, struggling to find arguments—that Jewish immigration was being encouraged *beyond* Palestine's 'absorptive capacity', for example, or that the 'local government' the mandatory power was intro- ducing was less democratic than the system that had existed in Ottoman times—which questioned less the mandate per se than Britain's fulfilment of its obligations to the non-Jewish population.[81] Palacios, noting in 1927 that such arguments were 'substantially more moderate', deludedly detected 'a genuine, if gradual, movement . . . in the direction of conciliation and con- cord'.[82] The other Commission members were happy to believe him.

Palestine was the case in which the policymaking process became most thoroughly internationalized. Unlike the French, the British had fostered that internationalization, deploying the League imprimatur to legitimate a policy unpopular with most local inhabitants and with the other allied powers. Yet internationalization, once embarked upon, proved difficult to curb. In the 1930s, when British governments concluded—as had many interested commentators at the time and indeed most historians since—that the 'dual obligations' were indeed incompatible and the mandate unworkable, the very internationalization they had promoted would constrain them. Not until 1929, however, did that crisis begin. In the late 1920s Palestine was relatively quiet and Britain the closest thing the League had to a model mandatory power. The first challenges erupted elsewhere: in South West Africa and Syria, where neither the mandatory power nor the mandated population had any attachment to the League regime. That regime would take shape, and some of those players learn their roles, through those risings in the mid-1920s.

# PART
# II

# Retreat from
# Self-Determination,
# 1923–30

# Preface: Allies and Rivals

In July 1923, Sir Frederick Lugard travelled to Geneva for his first Mandates Commission session. He took along his wife, the renowned journalist and African traveller Flora Shaw. He didn't like to be apart from her and in any case felt he would need her help with the French that was the Commission's lingua franca. But Lugard did fairly well with the mix of French and English that was spoken, and Flora found herself 'more of a luxury than a necessity'.[1] 'Fred is in his element on this Commission,' she wrote. He was deeply interested in the subjects discussed, and didn't mind the long working days—from 10 to 1 in the morning, 3:30 to anywhere from 6:00 to 8:00 in the evening, and then another three hours or more of reading and correcting proofs at night. He liked his new collaborators, finding Rappard zealous and uniformly helpful and the Belgian member Pierre Orts 'clear-headed, well-balanced, shrewd and just in his judgements and views'. They had had a nice dinner with Orts and the Marquis Alberto Theodoli, Flora reported, where they talked about the Ruhr crisis but also about how to defend 'the best results of western civilization from the attacks likely enough to be made by degenerate Europeans and inferior races'.[2]

No comment could capture more perfectly the atmosphere of the Mandates Commission as it found its feet in the early 1920s. Its members may have been hard-headed ex-colonial administrators in late middle age, but they were also, in their own way, idealists. They believed in their civilizing mission, in their right to rule. And for the next dozen years, no one better articulated their principles and honed their practices than Lugard. Lugard's authority owed something simply to his nationality, for as Ormsby-Gore told his successor privately, 'the whole Commission took anything from the British member largely because he was the British member'.[3] Lugard's personal qualities helped too, for his colleagues found the famous governor courteous, industrious, circumspect, and disarmingly modest. As late as 1933, with Germany attacking the League at every turn, the German member still paid tribute to Lugard's adherence to 'the spirit of absolute impartiality, equity and justice'.[4] But the most important basis for Lugard's authority was that he saw imperial administration primarily in *moral* terms, an approach that dovetailed nicely with the language of the Covenant, reassured those humanitarians and activists growing sceptical of empire, and provided the Commission with a coherent rationale and programme for their work. The essence of Lugard's approach was laid out most clearly in his masterwork, *The Dual Mandate in British Tropical Africa*, published one year earlier.[5]

*The Dual Mandate* is usually read as the classic statement of the doctrine of 'indirect rule' and as the blueprint for interwar British administrators throughout the empire. To read it that way is, however, to ignore the fraught international moment in which it was written and to overlook its very obvious political and international aims. For *The Dual Mandate* was more than a synopsis of Lugard's programmatic ideals. It was also a pitch for the extension of that programme across the British Empire and indeed throughout the globe, and—since Lugard was under consideration for appointment to the PMC when he wrote it—perhaps the longest job application in history. Many things about the book—its appropriation of the word 'mandate', the date of publication, its extensive discussion of the emergence of the League regime, and especially its persistent denigration of French colonial practices and elision of British and international ideals—show how it worked to establish British (and indeed Lugard's) leadership over the League project.[6]

Note, for example, that Lugard identified the 'dual mandate'—the principle that African administration could at once promote the happiness and well-being of the inhabitants (the first 'mandate') and develop the continent's natural resources for the 'mutual benefit of the people and mankind in general' (the second 'mandate')—as a 'European' and not specifically British concept, tracing its emergence to the international agreements on slavery and trade crafted at the Berlin Conference in 1884–85 and the Brussels Conference in 1890. The mandates system, he claimed, was the apotheosis of that concept.[7] Yet the international aspect of the mandates regime, Lugard made clear, was and should be limited to standard-setting and oversight. The actual work of government must be left in the capable hands of national administrations. And in this effort, the British would light the way. The system of 'indirect rule'—of administration through native chiefs and ostensibly along 'traditional' lines—that he had introduced in Nigeria was, Lugard insisted, the model best in line with the principles and obligations of the 'sacred trust'.[8]

Of course, part of the brilliance of the *Dual Mandate* rested on Lugard's elision of blueprint with practice, so that his carefully elaborated system of 'indirect rule' emerged as an accurate description of actually existing British colonial rule. In fact, as we know, even in Africa British administration was anything but uniform. Lugard's model was based on his own experiences grafting British administration onto the Ugandan monarchy and the emirates of northern Nigeria, but in Kenya and Rhodesia, for example, a very different type of settler-dominated rule had already evolved, complete with the massive land alienation, coercive labour laws, and restrictions on African movement also characteristic of South African rule. When 'indirect rule' was deployed, moreover, it was shaped less by any clear plan than by financial stringency and the minuscule size of most colonial administrations (a few hundred to govern Nigeria's tens of millions, for example). British administrators relied on African collaborators because they had no other choice. Indeed, when 'traditional authorities' weren't readily apparent, officials created them.[9]

To make this patchwork system into a model for internationally sanctioned imperial rule was a real feat, but Rappard, in Geneva, was already persuaded. *The Dual Mandate* had been 'the bible of the Mandates Section ever since its publication', he wrote to Lugard enthusiastically.[10] Rappard had been angling for Lugard's appointment since Ormsby-Gore's resignation, believing that nothing would boost the Commission's prestige like the famous governor's collaboration. This was correct, but if Lugard's presence enhanced the standing of the Mandates Commission, his particular interpretation of the 'sacred trust' also significantly affected—even shifted—its doctrines and direction. Three consequences of the move towards 'Lugardism' deserve mention.

First, that shift consolidated and legitimated a reaction against 'self-determination' that had been underway virtually from the moment those rash promises had been made. Lugard thought that language entirely premature for Africa anyway. The Versailles Treaty had recognized 'that the subject races of Africa are not yet able to stand alone', and experts were 'unanimous' in their view 'that the era of complete independence is not yet visible on the horizon of time'.[11] Lugard thus took it as given that the mandates system should aim to uphold humane principles of colonial rule, not to plan its supersession. This had not been the first British member's view. Ormsby-Gore had considered mandates a tool for state-building, telling Rappard that he thought it perfectly possible 'to make Tanganyika Territory into an independent African native State'.[12] Lugard, by contrast, insisted that 'the danger of going too fast with native races' was much greater 'than the danger of not going fast enough';[13] indeed, one of the advantages of 'indirect rule' was that it could slow down the pace of change. 'Character-building' and containment were the regime's goals.

With that shift came a heightened focus on cultural and racial difference, for a particular view of African culture and capacity underwrote Lugard's thought. Lugard was not 'racist' in the simplest sense. He was interested in African cultures, thought vernacular languages and traditions worth study and preservation, and vociferously condemned those who considered Africans only as tools for white exploitation. He helped found and guide the International Institute of African Languages and Cultures, which sought to coordinate information and research on African Studies.[14] Yet, like so many of his class and time, he did think races possessed distinct talents, characteristics, and cultures, and found anything that blurred those boundaries (non-vernacular education, contract labour, urbanization, racial mixing) dangerous or even abhorrent. In language that echoed that of Booker T. Washington and that sounded dated when he wrote, Lugard insisted that each race should develop along its own lines—although Africans, being 'backward', would require sympathetic white guidance for some time to come.[15] Ormsby-Gore, a generation younger, had not thought in such terms. 'I feel that in the coming century Europeans will have to alter very substantially their fundamental attitude towards the coloured peoples', he had told Rappard; white prejudices, not black aspirations, were the problem.[16] Yet, with Lugard at their head, members of the Commission need not start down this self-flagellating road. They could focus on 'protection' of Africans—in which sphere, admittedly, they found plenty to do.

But the appointment of Lugard, and the construction of what we might call the Rappard-Lugard axis, meant not only that the Commission as a whole became more 'Lugardian'. It also marginalized the French in the battle to shape the nature of trusteeship. This was not a foregone conclusion, for if Britain had the advantage of having engineered most of the rules of the League game, France's colonial establishment also made a strong bid for international leadership in the immediate post-war years. Colonial Minister Albert Sarraut's massive 1923 tome, *La Mise en Valeur des Colonies françaises*, laid out a comprehensive plan for colonial development that put the backward-looking pieties of *The Dual Mandate* to shame. Coloured and creole intellectuals in the 1920s found France's republican rhetoric and less segregationist practices appealing, although the government's seeming shift from a policy of 'assimilation' to one of 'association' in Africa appeared to signal a move in a more 'culturalist' or 'Lugardian' direction.[17]

Yet the French found themselves hamstrung not only by the post-war budget crisis and by serious colonial unrest but equally by their inability to use the Commission to good effect. Jean-Baptiste Paul Beau, the French member until 1925, was businesslike and affable, but as a career diplomat he could not rival Lugard's claims to expertise. His successor, the eminent African Governor Martial Henri Merlin, ought to have been able do so, but in fact Merlin proved too pompous, indolent, and transparently partisan to win any friends. No one on the Commission much liked him, and when in 1932 he faced a public trial for embezzlement, officials at the Quai d'Orsay squirmed with embarrassment.[18] Lugard's energy and probity formed a sharp contrast, and officials in London had the wit to understand that it was precisely his seeming impartiality and willingness to criticize British (or rather Dominion) practices as well that made him 'very valuable'. Of course, one wrote in 1926, he was self-referential, and tended 'like all ex-Governors...to forget that there were stout men *after* Agamemnon', but no one could represent Britain better.[19]

We can thus see the period between Lugard's appointment and German entry into the League as the mandates system's Lugardian moment—the period when Lugard's presence, French disarray, German absence, and relative allied harmony fostered a particularly 'Lugardian' interpretation of the theory and practice of the 'sacred trust'. But this interpretation, obviously, wasn't hammered out through a diligent reading of Lugard's tome—which, Margery Perham noted, sold a grand total of 2,242 copies over some fifteen years.[20] It was, rather, worked out in argument and practice, as the Commission reviewed the reports it received and especially as it scrambled to respond to three early scandals or risings: in South West Africa in 1922, in Syria in 1925–26, and in Western Samoa from 1927 until the mid-1930s. Through these conflicts, discussed in the next three chapters, the Commission, the mandatory powers, and the mandated populations struggled to shape the principles and character of the new mandates regime. The programme that emerged was at once paternalistic and authoritarian, rhetorically progressive and politically retrograde—a programme perfectly tailored to the task of rehabilitating the imperial order at its moment of greatest disarray.

# FOUR

## News from the Orange River

In the case of these natives one always has to bear in mind that one day
they tire of a white man about their necks all day long. Although we
imagine we are there for their benefit, they do not always think so, and
they like to remember the days when they were in possession of that part
of the country and roamed it at will.

Major Herbst, Secretary to the Administrator of South West Africa, 31 July 1923[1]

There were very few black delegates at the League Assemblies between
the wars. In the whole of sub-Saharan Africa, only Liberia and Abyssinia
were (precariously) independent member states not under white rule; in the
Caribbean, only Haiti and the Dominican Republic. So there was a stir of
interest in Geneva's Salle de la Reformation on 8 September 1922, when
Dantès Bellegarde, the handsome silver-tongued delegate for Haiti, rose to
draw the Third Assembly's attention to a massacre in South West Africa, a
mandated territory (Figure 4.1). The delegates might have noticed a mention of this in the press, Bellegarde said, and he was glad South Africa's
delegate Sir Edgar Walton had submitted a report on the incident a few days
ago. Still, he didn't think the Assembly had understood its full gravity.

What had happened, Bellegarde said, was this. The South West African
administration had imposed a tax on the dogs that the Bondelswarts—a poor
pastoral tribe—used to guard their flocks, taxation being 'the usual form
in which civilization makes its appearance to savages'. The Bondelswarts
couldn't pay but had not rebelled, yet the administration had sent 'all the
materials of modern warfare—machine-guns, artillery, and aeroplanes'
against them, with great loss of life. 'That women and children should have
been massacred in the name of the League of Nations and under its protection is an abominable outrage which we cannot suffer,' Bellegarde declared,

Figure 4.1 Dantès Bellegarde, Delegate of Haiti to the League of Nations.

to prolonged applause.[2] A galvanized Assembly agreed that the Mandates Commission needed to look into the whole sorry situation.[3]

The job of bringing South Africa into line with the principles of the 'sacred trust' had been laid at the door of the Mandates Commission. In the Secretariat, William Rappard worried it might not be up to the task. From J. H. Harris of the Anti-Slavery Society, already swinging into full campaign mode in defence of the Bondelswarts, Rappard understood how determined South Africa was to settle and annex the territory. He knew too that powerful voices in Geneva—Britain's Lord Robert Cecil, the League's Secretary General Sir Eric Drummond—were close to Smuts and disinclined to thwart him. Rappard's new Commission had only met twice and had no single view about 'trusteeship'. Would it be able to bring South Africa to heel?

The protracted, divisive, and high-profile inquiry by the Mandates Commission into the Bondelswarts' affair, its first real test, accomplished both less and far more than Rappard hoped. Certainly it did nothing to aid the beleaguered Bondelswarts or to weaken South Africa's determination to turn the territory into a 'white man's country'. Yet, paradoxically, it did more to crystallize the Commission's ideals, define its practice, enhance its reputation, and make League oversight a reality, than any other conflict. It is one of the nice ironies of our story that South Africa, which loathed the

Commission and consistently tried to flout it, was the instrument for establishing its authority. Circumstances and personalities mattered too, but it is impossible to discount the genuine revulsion some members felt when they examined South West African practices. Let us turn to the policies that provoked what humanitarians called the 'Bondelswarts affair' and white South African officials then—and, proudly, Namibians today—the 'Bondelswarts rebellion'.

## Colonial continuity and African dissent

When South African forces crossed the Orange River to occupy German South West Africa in the spring of 1915, African 'scouts' guided them through the territory's unfamiliar landscape. One of these was Abraham Morris, a deeply religious man and an experienced fighter, for whom the white officers came to have a great deal of respect. Although living in exile in the Cape Colony, Morris was from the South West African tribe of the Bondelswarts, a Nama community established in the area around Warmbad in the extreme south of the territory. The Bondelswarts, 'men of men' in their own estimation, had risen against the Germans in the Nama War in 1903–6, and had been brutally repressed. Morris had been one of the main commanders in that war and in 1915 was happy to do all he could to help drive these oppressors out.

   The Bondelswarts were not the only African community to imagine that a German defeat might restore their lands and livelihoods. All had deep reasons for resentment, for German rule in South West Africa had been unrelievedly harsh. Following the declaration of German sovereignty in 1884 and the brutal war against the Herero in 1904–6, a legal and penal framework had been created to prevent any future rebellions and to place Africans at the disposal of German settlers. With the exception of a few groups who had allied with the Germans in that war (notably the Rehoboth Basters), existing tribal structures had been 'broken', African lands and stock expropriated, African ownership of property forbidden, and a dense network of manned police posts established to control movement throughout the southern two-thirds of the country—the so-called 'Police Zone'. Male Africans over the age of seven had carried metal identification tags and 'service books' recording their labour contracts; they had also been required to work and subjected to 'paternal chastisement' (or flogging) at their master's will.[4] Small wonder

Africans had welcomed the invaders from the South. Even the mixed-race Rehoboth Basters had lent their support and in 1917 petitioned the British crown for recognition of their independence.[5]

These hopes would be dashed. South Africa had long coveted the vast territory to the north, intending to use it to settle its own troublesome 'poor whites'. Yet, with Wilsonian sentiment sweeping the globe, Smuts and the new military administration understood that they would need to make a moral case to retain this prize. The territory's Administrator, Sir E. H. L. Gorges, thus repealed the most draconian of the German measures while leaving the kinds of controls operative in South Africa intact. The ban on African stock-holding was lifted, corporal punishment for breach of contract (but not for stock theft) outlawed, and the hated metal tags replaced with a written pass. To the disgust of the remaining German farmers, Gorges also outlawed 'paternal chastisement' and insisted that magistrates prosecute white settlers who committed such assaults: over 300 such prosecutions were undertaken under his watch. Nothing, however, so offended the German population as the 220-page indictment Gorges compiled of German rule. Stuffed with incriminating archival records, gruesome photographs, and the testimony of Africans eager to denounce their former oppressors, it offered, he wrote, 'irrefutable proofs of the gross ineptitude with which Germany entered upon her scheme of colonizing this territory, of the callous indifference with which she treated the guaranteed rights of the native peoples established here, and of the cruelties to which she subjected those peoples when the burden became too heavy and they attempted to assert their rights'.[6] 'Native opinion,' he insisted, 'is unanimously against any idea of ever being handed back to the tender mercies of Germany.'[7]

Released in January 1918 and printed as a Parliamentary Blue Book that August, the revelations solidified sentiment against any return of Germany's colonies. In his office in Windhoek, however, Gorges was already suffering pangs of conscience. He had compiled the Blue Book 'in order to shew the world the state of affairs that existed here prior to our occupation'. Now he found, as he wrote to Colonel de Jager, the officer in charge of the military constabulary, 'to my amazement and dismay ... our own people dropping into the same reprehensible ways'.[8] He had been 'living in a fool's paradise for the last twelve months,' he told Pretoria, having discovered that his own officers also thought that 'occasional corporal punishment is what all natives require', and that the men under their command—Afrikaner farm boys recruited with promises of adventure—were 'not averse to doing a little sjambokking'.[9] Much use was being made in Paris of his Blue Book, he wrote in despair in April 1919, but what would happen if it were discovered that South Africa too was governing through 'chains and the liberal use of the sjambok'?[10]

By this point, however, the squeamish Gorges had served his purpose. Once the Peace Conference confirmed South African control, Gysbert Hofmeyr, a close friend of Smuts (Figure 4.2), replaced him as Administrator. Hofmeyr (Figure 4.3) shared Smuts' commitment to white supremacy. 'We presume in South Africa that white civilisation must be the guiding influence,' Hofmeyr would tell the Mandates Commission in 1924. White South Africans were 'preeminently fitted, while ensuring just and fair treatment for the native, to inspire him with that measure of respect for the supremacy of the white man which is essential in a land the vast majority of whose inhabitants are as yet uncivilised'.[11] In full retreat from Gorges' modest reforms, Hofmeyr's administration swiftly began demarcating landholdings, arranging loans, and advertising for South African settlers; in 1921 between 800 and 900 applications rolled in for the first seventy-six farms.[12] At the same time, again taking a cue from Smuts, Hofmeyr approached the German population conciliatorily, subsidizing German schools and allowing German as a medium for official communications (if not as a formally official language), while also carrying through the naturalization reform that—he hoped—would assimilate the embittered ex-enemy population into a unified white ruling class. That plan was only partially successful, for the German population remained persuaded of its cultural superiority and opposed to the territory's incorporation into South Africa; when a whites-only Legislative Assembly was set up in 1925, political parties reflected that national divide.[13] Yet the Germans and the South Africans were united in their commitment to white supremacy. A year after confirmation of the mandate, millions of hectares of land had been handed over on generous terms, and a white population estimated at 15,000 in 1913 had grown to 20,000, or nearly 10 per cent of a total population around 228,000.[14]

White farmers, desperate for labour, were soon clamouring for a return to 'German' methods. If able to survive by stock-raising and hunting, most Herero and Nama pastoralists flatly refused to work on white (and especially German) farms. Hofmeyr agreed that they should be made to do so, and constructed a mesh of legal, financial, and bodily controls to leave them no other option. Although 'native reserves' were set aside as the grazing lands of Africans disappeared under white title, those reserves were often

**Figure 4.2** Smuts arriving in Windhoek, probably 1920.

**Figure 4.3** Gysbert Hofmeyr (front, third from left) with officials of the mandate government, early 1920s.

too small and too arid to support pastoralists and their flocks. In 1921 Africans' ability to live off the land was also curtailed by a prohibitive, more than fourfold, increase in the tax on dogs, used for herding and hunting. Henceforth, Africans would have to pay a pound in cash—more than a man could earn in a month and sixteen times the tax rate prevailing in the Union itself—for a single dog, and the rate rose rapidly for each additional animal.[15] Yet, when Africans did accept labour contracts, they found cash-strapped farmers very unwilling (and sometimes unable) to pay their wages at all. If they deserted, they could be arrested for breach of contract or vagrancy (both criminal offences) and ordered to serve out their sentences in unpaid labour on government projects or white farms.

By 1922 such controls had left the fifteen hundred or so Bondelswarts desperately poor and resentful. They remembered the era before the Germans, when they had controlled large herds and called no man master. Now their lands were being turned over to whites; the administration had insisted that they begin branding their stock; they were locked in a dispute over its refusal to acknowledge the hereditary leader Jacobus Christian as their headman; and more than a hundred members of the tribe had been sentenced to fines or imprisonment for failing to pay the dog tax. The immediate catalyst to the revolt, however, was Abraham Morris's return from the Cape Colony with some companions and a few rifles in April 1922 (Figure 4.4). Hofmeyr, aware of Morris's reputation as the doughtiest living Bondelswarts commander (he had fought against the Germans in the Nama war and then again as a scout during the South African invasion), sent police to arrest and disarm him. When his tribe refused to give him up, Hofmeyr concluded that they were bent on rebellion. He then assembled a force of some four hundred police and settler volunteers and in late May rode out to force submission. In a move designed to foster terror and break the Bondelswarts' will (and which catalyzed international protest), airplanes sent up from South Africa bombed their encampment, killing some women and children and maddening the corralled animals. The next morning, most of the population surrendered, and Hofmeyr's men burned their huts to the ground. Under cover of darkness, however, Morris and perhaps 250 men with some dozens of rifles set off for the Orange River. Not without difficulty, they were tracked down and defeated. Morris and some hundred other Bondelswarts fighters lost their lives. Jacobus Christian was wounded and captured. Two were killed on the government side.[16]

**Figure 4.4** Abraham Morris, leader of the Bondelswarts, in uniform during the First World War.

Southern Namibia was a thinly populated frontier landscape of isolated farmsteads and scattered native settlements, but when South Africa dropped those bombs, the explosions were heard around the world. The London *Times* printed a brief article on the bombing sent by their correspondent in Cape Town on 31 May, and newspapers from Ireland to India would soon pick up the story.[17] Smuts found himself facing sharp questions in the South African parliament, and while he refused to allow discussion, he realized trouble was brewing. He warned Hofmeyr not to follow up his victory by (as he had intended) seizing the Bondelswarts' land, since this would 'raise a storm in Union among natives & whites who favour native interests & in League of Nations',[18] and on 5 July informed his old friend that he would have to ask South Africa's Native Affairs Commission to look into the incident.[19] By August a three-mem-

ber Commission of Inquiry was in Windhoek interviewing witnesses. Its
minutes of evidence would run to some 1,200 pages.

Smuts' quick response bought the South Africans some time, allowing
the South African High Commissioner in London, Sir Edgar Walton, to tell
Bellegarde at that third League Assembly that the incident was under investigation. The Anti-Slavery Society, however, had no intention of waiting
quietly for the South African report. J. H. Harris had heard about Hofmeyr's
actions from South African friends in July and had swiftly arranged for a
question in Parliament, a deputation to Walton, a blistering article in the
*New Statesman*, and a formal letter to Sir Eric Drummond requesting that
the League investigate an incident in such 'violent conflict with the principles of the Mandatory system'.[20] He and his fellow humanitarians were
outraged—but it is also true that this was the sort of emotionally charged
and morally unambiguous cause with which they were most comfortable.
Indeed, in their rendering of the incident, the Society consistently accen-
tuated the Bondelswarts' helplessness and the Administrator's wanton cruelty. That Morris and his followers, reputed to be proud and courageous
men, might have chosen to make a (however hopeless) stand did not fit
that framework.[21]

For more than a year, the Society's speakers and publications harped on
the scandal of the bombing of the Bondelswarts. 'I think we can fairly say
that it is due to this Society that attention was drawn to this matter,' its
President Charles Roberts said at the Society's annual meeting in 1923.[22]
They brought other British internationalists—the historian Arnold Toynbee,
the classicist Gilbert Murray (who thought the incident 'like Amritsar,
but with less justification')[23]—onto the bandwagon. Progressive African
American intellectuals paid attention; so too did those American internationalists and academics who were finding the League such a fruitful vehicle
for career advancement. The global web of 'talk' discussed in the last chapter
was expanding fast, but not all speakers shared Harris' belief in the progressive potential of 'trusteeship'. If anything, Johannesburg's communist paper,
*The International*, editorialized that May, South Africa's handling of the
Bondelswarts had proven that 'the views of the idealistic missionary—the
sacred trust—are irreconcilable with the "realism" of the colonist'.
Imperialists, driven into a corner, would always 'drop that cant altogether'
and bring out the guns.[24] Many eyes would be on the Commission when it
finally convened in Geneva on 20 July 1923, its third session, to deal with
the Bondelswarts question.

# Settler colonialism at the bar of the League of Nations

That third session had a packed agenda. The Commission was scheduled to review reports on all the African and Pacific mandates. Members had also prepared special overviews on liquor regulation, education, land tenure, and other questions, and were eager to present them. The Commission thus kept hard at it for three straight weeks; the minutes took up 212 closely printed pages. Yet, no doubt to the relief of the representatives of other mandated administrations hanging about the corridors, the Bondelswarts question absorbed fully twelve of the Commission's thirty-three sessions.

Very quickly, members identified what they felt was a serious problem. The South African government had sent them no clear statement of its views. They had the appeal from the Anti-Slavery Society (what one might call a statement for the prosecution), Hofmeyr's various reports (statements for the defence), even the recently published report of the three-member South African Commission appointed to inquire into the rebellion. That Commission's majority had been highly critical of Hofmeyr's handling of the Bondelswarts and indeed of his whole administration,[25] but the South African government had not told the PMC that it accepted those conclusions. Indeed, in the House of Assembly, Smuts had vigorously defended Hofmeyr, insisting that his decisive actions had warded off a rebellion.[26] Moreover, even when pressed by the Commission, High Commissioner Walton refused to clarify the government's stance. One could infer that Smuts did not agree with the Report's majority, Walton stated, but he had not been authorized to say this was government policy. Did the South African government then share the views of General Lemmer, the inquiry's single Afrikaner member, who had disputed every criticism of the Administrator? Walton had no instructions about that either.[27]

Why did this matter? Why couldn't the Commission look at the evidence and come to its own conclusions? In the end, it had to, but the procedural qualms of its members reveal their emerging sense of the nature, and especially the limits, of their authority. They could not act as a court of inquiry, the new (but already vocal) member Sir Frederick Lugard insisted, for an adequate understanding of any disputed incident could only emerge through careful study on the ground. Nor could they act as a court of law and put the mandatory power in the dock. Thus, although the Anti-Slavery

Society was welcome to submit written materials, its request to offer oral evidence—which would place the Society in the same position as the man-datory power—must be (and was) turned down.[28] Yet, if the PMC was neither a Commission of Inquiry nor a court of law, nor was it a kind of superior Administrative Council, empowered to define policy. Its obliga-tion, rather, was only to judge whether the mandatory power's policy con-formed to the Covenant and the mandate text. To do that, however, it needed to know what that policy actually was. Hence the question: Did the South African government approve Hofmeyr's actions?

It was obvious that Smuts, at least, did so. But it was also clear that he had no intention of saying something that would make South Africa's name, as one of his parliamentary opponents pungently put it, 'stink in the nostrils of countries of the world'.[29] The Mandates Commission thus had to decide itself whether those actions could be reconciled with the 'sacred trust'. The Commission's Vice Chairman D. F. W. Van Rees and Lugard came up with a list of questions. On 31 July and 1 August, Walton and Major Herbst, the Secretary of the South West African administration, who had taken part in the expedition and who the Anti-Slavery Society thus thought should not be there at all, were subjected to a comprehensive grilling. The details of the expedition were gone into, with Hofmeyr's decision to call in airplanes sharply questioned. Britain had been bombing tribesmen in Mesopotamia too, Herbst pointed out.[30]

Lugard also worked to elicit a detailed portrait of the administration's native policy. All of it came out: the pass laws, the dog tax, settlers' steady encroachment on African land, the lack of any educational facilities, the avidity with which farmers hung around magistrates' offices hoping to pick up convict labour, the 'general feeling of the ignorant farmers...that the natives were there chiefly as labourers for themselves'. ('It was not only the ignorant farmers, it was also the educated farmers who thought that,' Major Herbst corrected.)[31] Careful questioning on the subjects the League Assembly had asked the PMC to scrutinize—the steps taken to aid the suffering and to restore the life of the tribe—revealed that, beyond giving back stock that had not been killed or starved in the conflict and telling the surviving men to seek work, nothing had been done.[32] The key recom-mendations made by the majority of the Commission of Inquiry—that some autonomous tribal institutions be reconstituted, and that the local officials involved in the repression be transferred out of the district—were, Herbst stated, impossible. It was settled policy since German times that all tribes in the Police Zone be 'broken', and public opinion would stand no censure of local officials.[33]

And here we get to the heart of the matter. Humanitarians were shocked by Hofmeyr's actions. What the minutes reveal, however, is the extent to which Hofmeyr was responding to, even constrained by, white settler opinion. He could not have approached Morris in a conciliatory manner, Herbst clarified, without losing face with the white community. 'Public opinion' would not stand for any leniency towards the tribe. The petitions that Herbst provided in Afrikaans, German, and English from white farmers and residents in the Warmbad region certainly supported his claims about white feelings. Those warmly applauded the Administrator's actions, dismissed the Bondelswarts as 'a horde of savage marauders and stock thieves', and insisted that, now they were finally crushed, nothing be done to aid them. Their chieftaincy should be permanently abolished, no water holes should be bored on their reserve, no reduction of the dog tax introduced, and no education offered to them save teaching them 'a love for work'.[34] Here we find the authentic voice of settler colonialism. The native should work or starve.

When the South African representatives left the room, the Commission began to discuss what to make of it all. Quickly, however, divisions emerged. Theodoli and the Belgian member Pierre Orts had drawn up provisional conclusions. Those stated that there had been no mass insurrection, that the causes of the rising were 'various and remote', that it could have probably been prevented by timely personal action by the Administrator, and that the repression was carried out with 'excessive severity'. But the Portuguese member, Alberto Freire d'Andrade, objected. The territory had a small white population and a large black population that, deprived of its ancient rights and lands, wanted to throw the white population in the sea; unquestionably, the Administrator had had to take prompt and effective action.[35] The divided Commission agreed that each member should write up their opinions and the group would pause for a few days of other business. Yet someone—possibly Freire d'Andrade—showed Walton and Herbst the draft, for on 7 August the Commission was treated to Herbst's strenuous defence of the Administrator's actions and a passionate appeal not to make his work more difficult by censuring him.[36] The next day Freire d'Andrade announced he was needed back in Lisbon and, having submitted a brief statement exonerating Hofmeyr, left Geneva.[37]

With the Portuguese member out of the way, those left could agree that the South West African administration had behaved deplorably. Yet they were still divided about the broader lessons to be drawn. Had Hofmeyr and his associates erred *because they had treated the territory as a colony* when, as a mandated territory, it was to be governed on entirely different lines? Or, alternatively, had they erred because they had fallen below the colonial 'best practices' to which mandatory powers were pledged to adhere? Was mandatory administration, in other words, different *in kind* from colonial administration, and was it the job of the Commission to define and defend that difference? These were serious questions, for if the Commissioners answered them in the affirmative, they implied that the Mandates System was something more than a mechanism for collaboration and standard-setting *among* the imperial powers, even that it constituted a critique of imperialism itself.

Unsurprisingly, men who had spent their whole lives in imperial service had some trouble embracing such a doctrine. They were happy to condemn Hofmeyr's errors but not to impugn colonial rule itself. To the surprise of his fellow members, however, the Commission's Chairman, the Marquis Theodoli, intended to do so. On the morning of 9 August, following another day of fruitless wrangling, Theodoli announced that he was too exhausted to participate further but had written up his own views, which he would read out publicly and which must be part of any report sent to the Council.[38] That statement was an uncompromising articulation of the doctrine of mandatory 'difference'. In a colony, Theodoli stated, the administration could seek to promote particular colonial aims and balance various interests. In a mandated territory, however, the Covenant of the League 'has profoundly and substantially altered colonial law and colonial administration', laying down the principle that 'the well-being and development of less advanced peoples forms a sacred mission for civilization'. That principle required a different attitude towards the competing interests within the territory. '*First in importance come the interests of the natives, secondly the interests of the whites. The interests of the whites should only be considered in relation to the direct or indirect exercise of protection over the natives*' (emphasis mine). The Commission must thus judge the handling of the Bondelswarts affair in light of this doctrine, and doing so, they could only conclude that South Africa had violated the system's core ideals. Mandate doctrine directed the administration to implement 'a policy and an administrative practice calculated to lessen the racial prejudice', which was 'the fundamental cause of the hostility ... between the native population and the whites', but Hofmeyr had done the opposite. The administration, Theodoli charged, 'has pursued a policy of force rather than of persuasion . . . conceived and applied in the interests of the colonists rather than in the interests of the natives'.[39]

Theodoli's statement, and his decision to withdraw, caused consternation. Beau, Orts, Lugard, and Van Rees all urged him to reconsider. They should work for agreement and present a united view. But Orts himself admitted that he was 'greatly averse' to approving the sentence about the primacy of native interests, and Lugard, too, made clear that he could not accept some of Theodoli's formulations. Significantly, it was not Theodoli's condemnation of South West African policy to which Lugard objected. He too thought that the root cause of the affair was 'the practically universal feeling of the white population that the natives were to be regarded as their serfs and helots' and thought Hofmeyr ought to have responded sympathetically to the Bondelswarts' grievances.[40] What Lugard objected to (verbally, but also in writing), rather, was Theodoli's claims, first, that incidents like the repression of the Bondelswarts had always occurred and would always occur in colonies—a statement that 'constituted a charge against every nation possessing colonies'—and, second, that the mandates system was based on a new principle. Lugard disagreed, insisting that the requirement to protect the native population was one to which many colonial empires, and notably the British Empire, subscribed.[41] Lugard was intensely proud of Britain's colonial policy and colonial record; he tended to think of the mandates system as a mechanism for generalizing ideals he routinely conflated with British imperial practices. That it might be, instead, a superior and different system could not be contemplated.

Theodoli, however, would not change his views. It was inconceivable, he stated, that the policy laid out in Article 22 was not 'an entire departure from precedent'. His statement must appear exactly as he wrote it in the Commission's published report; he would not give way.[42] His adamancy is remarkable, for Theodoli would play many less principled roles within the Commission in future years. He would connive with the later Director of the Mandates Section, Vito Catastini, to try to enhance Italian influence; he would grow inured to the brutality of South West African policies; he would defend Italy's conquest of Abyssinia. In 1923, however, something—what he, a papal count, called his conscience—drove him to articulate the strongest condemnation of white-settler colonialism, and the clearest definition of the 'sacred trust', that ever appeared in a Commission report.

With Theodoli gone, Van Rees and Lugard marshalled the rump of the Commission and got the majority report written. Although less concerned with core principles, it too amounted to a near-censure of the South West African regime. True, the Commission declined to implicate Smuts' government (as opposed to the local administration), insisting that South Africa, 'under the guidance of so distinguished and enlightened a statesman as General Smuts', would of course share their interpretation of the sacred trust. Yet, while stressing that they had neither the authority nor the capacity to conduct a full inquiry into the conflict and declining to criticize the measures taken to suppress it, the Commission stated that the majority too had 'been unable to convince itself' that any local circumstances or difficulties 'justified in a territory under mandate the treatment of the natives' disclosed in the evidence. In answer to the Assembly's specific queries about measures taken to aid and restore the tribe, the report included two pages of verbatim testimony in which Herbst had disclosed that 'nothing special had been done'.[43]

However temperately phrased, the report's implicit acknowledgement of a conflict of interest between white settlers and African interests outraged the South African government. The maintenance of law and order and the process of white settlement were not inimical to native interests but were rather the means by which 'the native is being gradually civilised', Walton wrote in a bitter response. The Commission's criticisms would 'be resented by the whole of the white population' and might well make the natives 'more difficult to manage and less amenable to civilising influences'.[44] South Africa, clearly, did not intend to change course—provoking Lugard to write an astute letter to Rappard predicting how the League Council would handle the whole thing. Most likely it would simply refer the report back to South Africa, which would express itself mystified by the criticisms and retort that the Commission had not understood the local conditions and that Hofmeyr had done his best. Since the reference back would have postponed the whole question for a year, when it came up again the Council 'will thank General Smuts for his promises and express complete confidence in his high ideals. And pigeon-hole the papers.' The result would be a 'victory for Smuts who retains in office all those connected with the affair', and who would be even more determined to shake off mandatory oversight as quickly as possible. Perhaps some of the statesmen on the Council, who were 'not as well informed as we necessarily are... (Lord R. Cecil for instance)' might want to visualize this outcome and ask themselves whether it was really what they would wish?[45] Rappard privately sent the letter to Drummond and Cecil, the first of many times when he and Lugard would try to sway matters behind the scenes.

It had no effect. The Fourth Assembly, in September 1923, once again passed a critical resolution,[46] but just as Lugard had predicted, when considering the report in December the Council took a much more conservative line. Drummond had already told Rappard that he didn't think the Council needed to express an opinion anyway,[47] and when Hjalmar Branting, the Swedish Social Democrat and former Prime Minister who was the rapporteur on the question, suggested mildly that South Africa do something to aid the Bondelswarts, he found the British Empire standing solidly in the way. Walton, who was present to represent South Africa, vociferously objected that South Africa had already made 'great efforts' to improve their conditions, prompting Branting to point out stiffly that Herbst had specifically stated that nothing at all had been done. Perhaps, Robert Cecil silkily suggested, the Council could just 'note with satisfaction' Walton's assurances that South Africa *desired* to take 'all practical steps to restore the prosperity of the Bondelzwart people'? Walton, happy to lie for his country, said that would do.[48] For the Council, that was the end of the Bondelswarts question.

# Ripples in all directions

But not for the Mandates Commission, South Africa, the Anti-Slavery Society, or the mandates system in general. Like a stone dropped into a pond, the Bondelswarts affair sent ripples in every direction. It influenced South Africa's attitude towards the League and reputation in the world; it drove the Commission to define its doctrine and practice; it shaped how the Commission viewed all other mandatory powers and how those powers responded. Let us take these issues in turn.

## A rogue state in the making

First, the incident damaged South Africa's international standing, revealing a rift between South African principles and internationalist sentiment that would only deepen. There is no question but that the South African government, the South West African administration, and the territory's white settlers all found the League's condemnation outrageous and indeed

**Figure 4.5** The Permanent Mandates Commission, with British Empire accredited representatives, in session, 1924. Seated from left: Accredited representatives from mandatory powers: James Allen (New Zealand), William Ormsby-Gore (Britain), Gysbert Hofmeyr (South Africa); followed by PMC members: Leopoldo Palacios, Alfredo Freire d'Andrade, Pierre Orts, D. F. W. Van Rees, Alberto Theodoli, William Rappard, Jean-Baptiste Beau, Anna Bugge-Wicksell, Harold Grimshaw, and Frederick Lugard. Note large wall maps of South West Africa.

immoral.[49] They believed that white supremacy and strict control of Africans was proper and right. One could not, Walton told the League Assembly, deal with natives who had been 'sunk in barbarism for untold centuries', in any other way.[50] True, the administration made a few conciliatory gestures. Hofmeyr commuted Jacobus Christian's sentence and, in exchange for a promise of good behaviour, recognized that he acted as 'Headman' (not Chief) for his tribe;[51] the dog tax was lowered and the charge for branding irons abolished. Hofmeyr also tried 'to disarm the would-be executioners' (as he put it) by attending the Commission's 1924 session himself—a gesture that his Chief Secretary was certain had done 'an incalculable amount of good' (Figure 4.5).[52] The administration learned caution. Although airplanes were sent over the 'Gebiet' of the Rehoboth Basters in the mid-1920s in an effort to intimidate them into abandoning their claims to self-government and appeals to the League, they did not drop bombs.[53]

Yet League condemnation could not shift the balance of forces between the antagonists in South West Africa and had no impact on the administration's core aims. Throughout the mandate period, the steady work of building up white property and power continued. By 1936, fully 55 per cent of non-desert land in the 'Police Zone' was held by whites, twice as much as in the German period.[54] From 1925 the whites-only Legislative Assembly ensured the domination of settler interests not only over those of Africans but also over those of the diamond-mining companies on whose profits the territory often relied.[55] The need to deprive Africans of any alternative to farm labour, and to check their insubordination, sounded as a leitmotif through that Assembly, and indeed—when far from Geneva—through the pronouncements of officials. 'White women and children were doing Kaffir work' because 'the Kaffirs had been permitted to become stockowners,' Hofmeyr's successor A. J. Werth told farmers in a speech in Warmbad in 1926, but 'the Kaffirs should not be allowed to realize their dreams'. Reserves should be closed, the master-and-servant laws enforced with fines, corporal punishment given on a second offence, the dog tax again raised. The Administration would have to be careful, Werth cautioned, since they were watched by many eyes, but he left no doubt about where his sympathies lay.[56]

The members of the Mandates Commission most exercised about South African policy chafed at such defiance of the Covenant's ideals and of their own authority. Unable to check South Africa, they sought at least to deprive it of international legitimacy. The Commission spent more time on South West Africa than any other territory save Palestine and Syria, and those sessions—usually with South Africa's London-based High Commissioner, but in 1924, 1928, and 1935 with the territory's Administrator himself—were often acrimonious. Thus in 1928, when Administrator Werth came to meet with the PMC, he was asked, among other things, why the dog tax had again been doubled; why the administration spent perhaps one hundred times as much on the education of a white child as an African child (but natives don't want their children educated, Werth replied); why the administration deplored the increase in the numbers of goats owned by Africans when those animals were the staple of their diet; why it had drastically increased fines and prison terms for breach of contract and reintroduced whipping; why of the 229 new water holes the administration had bored that year, only fifteen were on the native reserves rather than private farms; why missions working in Ovamboland were required to promise in writing that they would encourage Africans to take up employment in the Police Zone.[57] Was it true, the Commission asked in 1930, that a group of farmers had rounded up some fifty Bushmen and sold them as labourers at a pound per head? (It was.)[58] And given that the territory was suffering in the early 1930s from an economic downturn, drought, and malaria, couldn't the administration at least maintain the tiny sums devoted to native welfare? It couldn't: the whites were the taxpayers, and would not countenance spending on Africans. The Commission was unimpressed, for they knew that more than half of the government's revenue came from mining royalties—a windfall earned by the hard labour of six to eight thousand African workers, half of them Ovambos shipped in from the north who suffered a death rate of 110 per 1,000.[59] Yet efforts to shame officials had little effect. Indeed, in 1938 the administration reported that, having decided that 'it would be unwise to accelerate the development of the native races unduly' and wishing to 'convey . . . the lesson that their improvement must depend on their own exertions,' it would no longer devote any tax revenues to the native reserves at all.[60]

The Commissioners found it hard to contain their frustration. Rappard did not know of 'any more depressing reading' than the administration's report, he told Werth in 1928; its authors seemed to be entirely lacking in 'human sympathy' for their charges. Since the territory had proven fit for whites to live in, 'it was inevitable that the whites should come to regard the natives as being in their way', but the administration was supposed to resist this view, not share it![61] Instead, he told Werth, South Africa had, in violation of the mandate, delivered the natives over to the whites. South West Africa was a settler state, a 'white man's country'—and, Rappard concluded, 'history . . . showed that it was a misfortune for natives to inhabit a white man's country'.[62] Not all of the Commission agreed with Rappard's harsh judgement, and the Commission's reports to the Council were always more restrained. But even if the South Africans declined to change course and the Council (usually) preferred not to get involved, we can see in the PMC's dogged interrogations a foreshadowing of the international censure that would later descend on the apartheid state. In the eyes of the Commission, South Africa's administration of South West Africa had already become, as it would be labelled after 1945, 'a mandate betrayed'.[63]

## Defining 'well-being and development'

If the controversy poisoned the Commission's relations with South Africa, it greatly enhanced the standing and coherence of the PMC itself. Those who had feared it would be the tame lapdog of the Council were proven wrong. Most of the League's liberal supporters agreed (with the Assembly) that it had demonstrated 'zeal' and 'impartiality'.[64] While the debates had allowed internal divisions to emerge, they had also fostered a feeling of common purpose and created a kind of ideological middle ground. That 'ground' was marked out and defended especially by Lugard, who over the next few years challenged and then isolated the Portuguese member Freire d'Andrade, hitherto the Commission's dominant voice on African questions and the only member sympathetic to Herbst and Hofmeyr during the Bondelswarts conflict.

From the Commission's founding, the Portuguese member had insisted that unfettered economic development was the best way to fulfil the 'sacred trust'. In the interests of the territory as a whole, he told the first PMC session, Africans must be made to work—for surely the Covenant's prohibition on forced labour was not intended to undermine 'the obligation of labour, which is the foundation of all civilised society'.[65] Even after the Council confirmed that forced labour for private enterprises was indeed forbidden, Freire d'Andrade continued to carp about the need for 'realism' and to support the web of taxes and controls the South West African administration had devised to drive Africans to work on white farms.[66] His views alarmed his colleagues, but as he was the only ex-African governor on the Commission in the first two years (a qualification of which he boasted), the other members found it hard to challenge him.

Lugard's appointment shifted the balance of power, for with his string of colonial governorships and the prestige of the world's largest and richest empire behind him, he easily outranked Freire d'Andrade. Lugard also had the lowest possible opinion of Portugal's colonial record and little patience for his Portuguese colleague's views. At PMC sessions in 1924 and 1925, the two men clashed sharply over whether Africans should be given 'as large a share as possible in the control of their own affairs' through native councils and courts (Freire d'Andrade thought not), whether ambitious development projects should be restricted if the burden they imposed on African population was too great (Freire d'Andrade thought not), and, of course, whether Africans were, in Lugard's words, on the whole 'industrious and hard-working' (Freire d'Andrade most emphatically thought not).[67] In the summer of 1925, perhaps wearying of the wrangling, Theodoli asked both men to put in writing their understanding of that crucial passage of Article 22 enjoining mandatory powers to promote the 'well-being and development' of the population. Four memoranda—two initial statements and two responses—resulted.[68]

That there was a tension between 'well-being' and 'development' (or between what Lugard termed the 'philanthropic' and the 'utilitarian' approaches to policy), the two men could agree. In other respects, however, they were far apart. It wasn't just that Lugard thought 'well-being' should take precedence over 'development' and Freire d'Andrade thought the reverse. It was also that they had very different ideas of just *whose* 'well-being and development' they were charged to protect. Lugard assumed that those defined as 'not yet able to stand alone' were non-white natives, whose protection was the mandatory power's first charge. As a result, while he agreed that public infrastructural projects (railways, harbours) and private enterprises were necessary to develop markets and spur local economic growth, he thought governments should keep tight control over concessions and contracts to make sure they didn't overtax either the individual native labourer or the indigenous population as a whole. He also insisted that native labour should remain 'free'. If work was adequately remunerated and conditions 'sufficiently attractive', workers would present themselves. Yet Lugard also thought that the government should not consider policy exclusively from the 'utilitarian' standpoint but also in light of the promise that African populations would someday (even if that day 'may not yet be visible on the horizon') 'stand alone in the strenuous conditions of the modern world'. Education and services should aim not simply at providing better workers but also at fostering community feeling and civic consciousness.[69]

Freire d'Andrade favoured very different policies, but, crucially, he also began from very different assumptions. The first was that the population whose 'well-being and development' was to be fostered was the territory's *whole* population, whether native, settler, or indeed shipped in yesterday. The second was that Africans—or at least African men—would, if not compelled to work, spend their time 'talking, singing and drinking' while their wives laboured. For Freire d'Andrade, the fact that the Covenant had laid stress on 'development' was clear evidence both that Africans could legitimately be compelled and that any restriction on white settlement and capital was out of the question. Indeed, given African laziness and the need for labour, if the mandatory power failed to take on the duty of organizing work, white settlers and employers might well—and, in his view, legitimately—resort to compulsion, for 'it is only natural that those who invest their capital and their work in African enterprises will not passively sacrifice the results they are entitled to expect because the natives refuse to work'. Finally, he reasoned, if African populations declined as a result of such pressures (and indeed, he thought they were already declining), this was not in itself to be deplored, since 'the slow enforced assimilation of weaker or inferior communities by stronger and more highly developed ones' was both the 'ideal' and a kind of natural law. Freire d'Andrade, unlike Lugard, had nothing against racial mixing (or, rather, against unions between native women and white men), anticipating that—as in Brazil—a robust, creole race would arise and supplant both natives and whites.[70]

For Lugard, this was a nightmare vision and one that paternalistic administration should work to prevent. The two men's second memoranda thus clarified their disagreements. Lugard did not deny that the mandatory power—and, by extension, the PMC—had authority over *all* inhabitants but insisted that the drafters of the Covenant had quite obviously had in mind the native population when penning the trustee's charge. Native interests—and, in particular, the natives' right to be spared the kind of exploitation that Freire d'Andrade considered essential—must determine policy. Lugard believed that African communities might become ever more prosperous and autonomous, but only if their indigenous authorities and institutions were preserved, if they were shielded from the exploitative demands of European settlers and companies, and if they were carefully guided by sympathetic European administrators. Freire d'Andrade disagreed, not only because he thought African institutions incapable of political evolution ('history, which is a good teacher, furnishes me with no instances to show that the system of maintaining native institutions has…led the natives up to self-government'), but also, interestingly, because he thought that paternalistic oversight might simply entrench 'two classes—one the supervised and the other the supervisors—who will send out punitive expeditions if their orders are not obeyed'. Freire d'Andrade, in other words, was happy to imagine race-blind administration, but only because he was so certain that in any level playing field Africans would be—culturally, economically, biologically—swiftly submerged. Lugard, by contrast, wanted to see African societies preserved and protected, but assumed that required racial separation and administration by a benevolent, superior, alien caste.[71] That Africans might flourish under a regime of equal rights was, to both men, unthinkable.

There is no question but that Lugardian paternalism was more attractive to the Commission than Freire d'Andrade's Darwinian fantasies. The more 'independent' and internationalist members—Theodoli, after his appointment Rappard, the Swedish member Mme Bugge-Wicksell, the Dutchman Van Rees—rallied to the kind of attentive scrutiny of native conditions, sym-

pathy for 'traditional' authority, and scepticism of aggressive plans for settlement or investment that Lugard favoured. Such paternalistic oversight went
down well with the Assembly and won commendation from humanitarian
organizations. As we shall see, it also sometimes drove mandatory administrations to weigh the risks of the Commission's (and especially Lugard's) reaction
when considering local policies.

Yet it is important to recognize just how culturally conservative this paternalistic vision was. Take, for example, the Commission's treatment of educational questions. Each African and Pacific mandate required the mandatory
'promote to the utmost the material and moral well-being and the social
progress of the inhabitants', and from the outset the Commission urged
authorities to expand educational provision. The women members (Bugge-
Wicksell and then the Norwegian Valentine Dannevig) proved especially
vigilant in this regard, drafting the Commission's reports on schooling, tire-
lessly questioning mandatory representatives at each session, and stressing the
need to educate (usually overlooked) girls as well as boys. Revealingly, however, when Bugge-Wicksell sought to specify just what *kind* of education
might be 'particularly suitable to the conditions of life of backward peoples',
she turned not to European precedents, nor even to more expansive French
colonial efforts, but rather back to Lugard. In the *Dual Mandate*, Lugard had
argued that colonial schools should concentrate on 'the formation of character and habits of discipline' rather than mere 'book-learning', and should take
care to uphold 'native customs' so that pupils would not become 'denation-
alised or consider themselves a class apart'.[72] Bugge-Wicksell echoed these
views. Education should be practical and not theoretical, concentrating on
'character training and discipline' and on 'the teaching of agriculture, animal
husbandry, arts and crafts, and elementary hygiene'—a programme that was to
promote the native population's 'gradual civilization' but that unquestionably
would also make them good workers[73] Assumed racial hierarchies, and typi-
cally Lugardian anxieties about the destabilizing influence of a 'Europeanized'
class, structured the Commission's thought, persuading even Bugge-Wicksell
that institutions of higher education would be unnecessary for a long time to
come.[74] Proposals like these did little to meet the ambitions of that small but
growing elite chafing at European and 'chiefly' rule alike.

## Grading on the Lugardian curve

Finally, the PMC began consciously to evaluate other African and Pacific
mandatory administrations from a 'Lugardian' standpoint and with the

negative example of South West Africa in mind. That turn to comparative evaluation had a real impact, shaping how the Commission—and, crucially, the newspaper-reading European public—viewed and ranked not only the different mandate regimes but also, importantly, the imperial powers governing them. The result was a quite undeserved reputational bonanza for Britain. Because Lugard insisted so strenuously that his administrative ideas were superior and reflected actual British practice, the fact that the colonial state in much of British Africa relied on just that settler-driven combination of pass laws, land seizure, and labour coercion that marked Hofmeyr's regime was lost to view. Instead, the Dominions bore the burden of criticism from internationalists and humanitarians, while quiet Tanganyika was extolled both as representatively British and the model for mandate rule. This was a propaganda coup the French, quite understandably, found enraging.

That the Commission would view Mandated New Guinea through a 'South West African' lens is not surprising, for the two territories shared some similarities. Although much of the territory was still unexplored, Germany had established a settler agricultural sector (in this case, copra plantations on the islands and the coasts) and a harsh indentured labour regime. Australia shared some of South Africa's racial and economic ambitions for its new possession as well. It too saw itself as a beacon of white civilization in a coloured sea; it too wanted to use its new territory to settle troublesome and landless whites. Indeed, so certain was Australia of its rights and aims that it initially made little effort to appropriate the language of trusteeship, with Australian Prime Minister William Hughes insisting at the Peace Conference that Australia was owed New Guinea because of its war sacrifices alone. Whether natives would be better treated had nothing to do with it.

The Australian military administration thus did not bother to break with 'German' methods, relying on flogging and brutal recruitment practices to keep the copra plantations going. (Indeed, both copra production and the numbers of workers under indenture rose substantially during the occupation period.)[75] The Hughes government also declined to merge the territory's administration with the neighbouring Australian colony of Papua (as was allowed under its 'C' mandate), not because it had any reservations about annexation but rather because it did not wish to see the paternalistic methods favoured by Sir Hubert Murray, Papua's long-serving Lieutenant Governor, extended to the mandated territory.[76]

Yet even before the mandatory system came into effect, the Australian administration—unlike the South African—began to change course. Although the wartime military administrators S. A. Pethebridge and G. J. Johnston strenuously insisted that the territory's 'primitive beings' could only be controlled through flogging,[77] the Cabinet disagreed, and when a civilian administrator was brought in, he was told firmly 'that not only the dictates of humanity but the obligations which the Commonwealth Government has undertaken to the League of Nations' required that cruelty towards natives be prevented and punished.[78] Harsh labour recruitment methods continued, and labourers' pay was kept *below* the rates enforced in Murray's Papua, but the end to military administration, the appointment of the reform-minded E. L. Piesse as Director of the Pacific Branch of the Prime Minister's department, and worries about exposure in Melbourne and Geneva did have an effect. Archival records thus reveal both a widespread white culture of casual violence towards New Guineans, with repeated instances of 'selling' labourers, flogging or even murder, and the capture and 'use' of local women (a practice known as 'pulling marys'), *and* administrators' persistent efforts at reform. Egregious offenders were disciplined, tried, or simply sent 'home'. Slowly, the statistics on whites punished for violence against natives inched upwards.[79] New Guinea remained a hard-scrabble, uncertain place, a magnet for disaffected ex-soldiers and adventurers down on their luck. But while the Mandates Commission's sessions with Australian representatives were often plain-spoken, when scandals about brutality towards natives erupted (as they regularly did), the administration tried to respond. And in Geneva, one Australian representative noted with relief, at least they shone when placed against the South Africans.[80]

Tanganyika needed no such comparative leg up. Until the Conservative Colonial Secretary Leo Amery destroyed the Commission's goodwill with his efforts in the late 1920s to bring the territory into an East African union with neighbouring Kenya and Uganda, Tanganyika was—as British colonial officials smugly recognized—the standard against which other territories were measured and found wanting. Certainly the policy pursued was in sharp conflict with Smuts's ideals. Unlike in South West Africa, the territory's German population was repatriated, and initially at least the administration made little effort to attract white settlement, concentrating instead on rebuilding the economy and a population devastated by wartime epidemics and forced labour. The plantation sector was maintained, with the government regulating transport and labour contracts, but the strong-minded, Labour-appointed governor Sir Donald Cameron, who ran Tanganyika from the mid-1920s until the early 1930s, resisted raising taxation to drive

Africans into the plantation sector and pursued instead a vigorous policy of 'peasantization'.[81] Thus, even though additional land was alienated to whites in the mandate period, and the Germans were allowed to return once Germany entered the League, by 1938 only slightly more than 1 per cent of land was held by Europeans.[82] Cameron also imposed a system of 'indirect rule' by identifying appropriate 'native chiefs', replacing their right to tribute with a regular income paid from tax revenues, and granting them some authority over land allocation and the administration of justice. He intended, as he put it, 'to develop the native on lines which will not Westernise him and turn him into a bad imitation of a European'.[83]

Unsurprisingly, urban and educated Africans came to resent a system that enforced the authority of often backwards-looking 'native chiefs', but the Mandates Commission found much to laud in these efforts. Meetings ostensibly spent reviewing Tanganyika's administration resounded with mutual congratulations. Members praised the administration's restrictive policies on land transfer in 1923, its efforts at agricultural instruction in 1924, its creation of a new Labour Department in 1925, its regulations on forced labour in 1928, and its efforts to improve labour conditions in 1929.[84] They were delighted when Cameron appeared in person at their session in July 1927, professing themselves 'greatly impressed' by his efforts to build up 'a system of administration which makes use, as far as possible, of traditional tribal organization', and reassured by his pledge that Tanganyika 'would always remain a predominantly native country, like Uganda'.[85] Tanganyika, the Commission clearly felt, was the diametric opposite of South West Africa, and the territory in which the 'spirit' of the sacred trust was amply fulfilled.

British policy in Tanganyika, at once autocratic and paternalistic, certainly dovetailed nicely with the assumptions underlying the mandates system. Yet that affinity was the result less of Tanganyika's adoption of League precepts than of colonial officials' adroit use of the mandates regime. 'Trusteeship' did not mirror British colonial practice *tout court*, which was anything but uniform and in many territories (notably Kenya) submissive to settler interests. It did, however, express ideals to which a slice of the British colonial establishment was committed. A sharp battle between a policy of deference to settler interests and a policy of 'native paramountcy' raged in the 1920s, both within the Colonial Office and across the African colonies, and partisans of trusteeship worried that they were losing. 'The only part of British tropical Africa where things are on a satisfactory basis is Nigeria', the

Colonial Office's Sir Charles Strachey remarked sourly in 1919. Elsewhere, 'when we object to handing over huge areas for ranching and other purposes (which areas do not belong to us) we are accused of unbusinesslike methods and fettering legitimate enterprise'.[86]

For Strachey and his allies, the establishment of the mandates system was a godsend. A much-disputed policy of 'native paramountcy' now had international sanction, and Lugard's presence in Geneva enabled officials to present it (no doubt to the irritation of often pro-settler politicians back home) as the British way of empire. The fact that the Anti-Slavery Society was paying ever more attention to the question of African land rights helped too. In 1919 the Society had argued that all 'B' mandated territories be considered 'generally unsuited to European Colonization' and their land be declared inalienable native land,[87] and while in the end the 'B' mandate texts enjoined the administering powers only to 'respect the rights and safeguard the interests of the native population' when framing land laws, the Society wrote to the Commission urging strict prohibitions against land alienation.[88] A sympathetic Commission published their letter as an annex to the minutes of the second session, and the obsessive Van Rees immediately began working through land laws.[89] Tanganyika's stringent Land Law of 1923, drafted by Strachey in consultation with Ormsby-Gore, which declared all land the property of the territory itself and barred all transfer except with the governor's consent, was thus treated by the Commission as a 'model' measure.[90] For Strachey, Harris, Lugard, Cameron, and other British architects of the 'West African' school of colonial administration, the Mandates Commission was an ally against the settler lobby. And for Lugard especially, the affinity between the Tanganyika project and the Commission's evolving doctrine had another added benefit. It kept the French on the defensive.

The Commission treated the French representatives who appeared before it with caution. At least some members were aware that France had resisted placing Togo and Cameroon under mandate at all. Ormsby-Gore, Rappard, and later Lugard also knew that disaffected or exiled Togolese had appealed against French rule. Yet, as Michael Callahan's careful study has shown, the French made a serious effort in the early 1920s to conform to norms and principles devised to suit *British* ideals. First, although the French had pressed for that clause allowing their portions of Togo and Cameroon to be administratively incorporated into neighbouring colonies, in fact it was Britain that took advantage of that stipulation, subdividing its (admittedly much smaller) portions of Togo and Cameroon and then placing the fragments under the administrations of neighbouring Gold Coast and Nigerian provinces—a clever move that made it difficult for the Commission to oversee those territories at all.[91] France, by contrast, established Togo and Cameroon as distinct administrations, headed by separate 'Commissioners of the French Republic' reporting directly to the Colonial Ministry. Those local administrations dutifully refrained from recruiting soldiers in the mandated territories, a decision that prevented 'militarization' but also deprived some Africans of a type of employment on which they had come to rely.[92]

Yet the French won little credit for these steps, for they were wrong-footed by the early debates over land laws. The Anti-Slavery Society immediately pounced on French legislation that declared all 'vacant' land in French Cameroon to be the 'private domain of the state'—thus, so the Society charged, appropriating 'those large areas of tropical lands upon which are found to-day sylvan products, normally gathered by the natives and forming the basis of their physical, social and economic existence'.[93] Van Rees agreed, and at the 1922 session told Albert Duchêne, Director of the Political Affairs Department at the French Colonial Ministry, that France should make clear that it was not claiming ownership of the territory.[94] As Rappard reported privately to J. H. Harris, however, Beau and Orts 'showed such bitter resentment concerning the initiative of the British Anti-Slavery Society to which they seemed to attribute nationalistic motives' that the Commission had asked Van Rees to look into land laws in *all* mandated territories and not in Cameroon alone.[95]

Already irritated by what they perceived, not wrongly, to be a pro-British bias, the French made their position still worse by alternately aggressive and defensive behaviour. When the Commission questioned both Duchêne and Ormsby-Gore (now appearing before his former colleagues as Britain's 'accredited representative') about the government's land policy, Duchêne's prevaricating response looked particularly bad when placed against Ormsby-Gore's flat declaration that the British government had employed the term 'public land' in preference to 'Crown lands' specifically to acknowledge that 'the community of Tanganyika'— and not the British Crown or the British Empire—'was the owner of the land'.[96] The following year, the Commission resolved that any legislation implying ownership of land by the mandatory power be amended.[97] The Commission was seeking simply to limit land alienation and establish the 'non-sovereignty' of the mandatory power, but their interrogation highlighted the differences, rather than the broad similarities, between British and French administration. The portrait that emerged was idealized and far from accurate. Even Donald Cameron allowed the sale of significant tracts of Tanganyika's fertile land to white settlers, while the French practice of allowing Africans to own land individually in Cameroon (rather than, as in Tanganyika, granting 'natives' only customary or use-rights) at least did something to erode the pernicious link between race and property rights. Nevertheless, that imagined opposition between the paternalist British and the *dirigiste* French anchored the Commission's thought.

This was the case, as Véronique Dimier has argued, because Lugard especially seemed determined to accentuate those supposed differences and to catch the French out.[98] In discussions in 1925 with Paul Bonnecarrère, who had come to Geneva to impress the Commission with his progressive Togoland administration, Lugard went out of his way to disparage not only Bonnecarrère's use of labour levies but equally his educational and cultural policies. Even though Bonnecarrère insisted that he intended neither to introduce a European-style electoral system nor to 'turn natives into Europeans', his insistence that one could 'convert [the native] into a civilized man' clearly raised Lugard's hackles. Educated natives, Lugard retorted, were 'imbued with foreign ideas and did not in any way represent' the native population as a whole, and he questioned Bonnecarrère's policy of teaching even 'bush' natives French.[99] Chastised for policies that seemed directly in line with the principles of Article 22, the French must have felt they could do nothing right.

★ ★ ★

By 1925, through the medium of the Bondelswarts affair, the Commission had defined its ideals and practices. Those ideals were heavily Lugardian. Mandatory administrations should protect native populations from economic exploitation and settler violence; they should seek to preserve 'native practices' and limit racial contact and cultural 'hybridization'; they should bolster 'traditional authorities' but keep political rights and the prospect of self-determination off the table. This was a vision that took civilizational and racial hierarchy for granted, one that could appear 'progressive' only when held up against South African or Kenyan ideals. In that sense, the Commission was lucky to have faced their first challenge in South West Africa.

Yet claims for national self-determination had a way of rearing their heads. By repeatedly postponing ratification of the Middle East mandates, France and Britain had kept their fractious and highly contested rule in Iraq, Syria, and Palestine away from the Commission's scrutiny. Beginning in 1924, however, those administrations would also have to answer the Commission's questions. Unlike the African and Pacific populations, moreover, 'certain communities formerly belonging to the Turkish Empire' had had their status as 'independent nations' confirmed by the Covenant. The question of political rights thus could not be swept under the rug. And, as French luck would have it, the very next year Druze militants rose against the French occupation in Syria, determined to make that promise of independence real. The Mandates Commission was about to confront its second test.

# FIVE
## Bombing Damascus

The Syrians, as you doubtless know, have little, if any, confidence in the
League or in the whole of western civilization for that matter. France cannot bolster herself up by showing that western civilization is behind her,
rather she must create confidence in western civilization by her conduct.

Quincy Wright to Huntington Gilchrist, 5 April 1926[1]

Officially, the French insisted that the Syrian revolt of 1925 had no deep
causes. It was just the work of brigands and agitators who took advantage
of a rising in the ever-volatile Jabal Druze to prey on vulnerable villagers and
harry the French forces. Most observers at the time, however, not to mention
virtually all historians since, saw early mandate Syria as a tinderbox of dis-
contents, which even the slightest spark could burst into flame.[2] Except
among the Christian population of Mount Lebanon, resentment against the
French presence was near-universal, and in Syria feelings against the creation
of 'Greater Lebanon' and the division of the rest of the country into four
separate statelets ran high. Syrian notables educated in the West or at Ottoman
schools and accustomed to running their local administrations deeply
resented orders that made the actions of every local official subject to French
approval; Syrian military officers were offended when forced to accept commissions far below their Ottoman ranks. French economic policy also hit the
population hard, for France pegged the new Syrian pound to the unstable
franc, creating serious inflation. Finally, as luck would have it, 1924 was a year
of drought and bad harvests, sowing hardship and anxiety among populations
for whom the memory of the wartime famine was still very real.

But there were immediate causes too, especially in the Jabal Druze, where
the tinder found the match. One spark was provided by Gabriel Carbillet, a
French officer with experience in West Africa who had been appointed as
local governor in 1923. An authoritarian, active fellow and possibly slightly

**Figure 5.1** Captain Gabriel Carbillet with Druze leaders, c. 1925.

deranged, Carbillet saw the Jabal Druze through a framework of medieval feudalism and took it upon himself to emancipate its 'serfs' through an ambitious programme of road construction, school-building, and land reform (Figure 5.1). Unable to persuade peasants of the usefulness of his plans, and without the money to hire them, he made extensive and unlawful use of forced labour. When individuals protested, they received summary chastisement; minor acts of resistance—including, in a case that became famous, the disappearance of one officer's cat—elicited collective punishments and fines. Druze sheikhs who remonstrated were set to road-breaking or locked up. By the spring of 1925 unrest had reached such a pitch that the High Commissioner sent this Kurtz-like figure off to France for a holiday. Druze notables and the intelligence officers of the Service de Renseignements advised his permanent removal.

Unfortunately, the man who would consider their appeals—General Maurice Sarrail, the new High Commissioner—was inclined to fan the flames. Sarrail was an unusual figure within the French Army: anti-clerical, a freemason, and a war hero to boot, he was self-consciously a man of the left. He had been appointed by the new Cartel des Gauches government in late 1924 to replace the Catholic Maxime Weygand, an act roundly criticized by the French right as driven only by 'party' considerations—and indeed, within days of his arrival in Beirut, Sarrail had alienated Lebanese Christians.

Determined to follow a policy of 'impartiality' (which was read on the right as pro-Muslim), Sarrail promised free elections and allowed parties to form, leading to the swift emergence of a Syrian People's Party under the leadership of 'Abd al-Rahman Shahbandar, former Foreign Minister in the Faysali government. Yet, as both the Druze sheikhs and the Damascene nationalists quickly discovered, the seventy-year-old Sarrail had no intention of tolerating any real challenge to his authority. Initially inclined to ignore intelligence warnings about the depth of discontent, in early July Sarrail instructed officials in Damascus to lure the Druze chiefs there on the pretext of hearing their complaints, and then to arrest and exile them forthwith.

For Sultan al-Atrash, the most militantly anti-French local leader in the Jabal Druze, this was the last straw. Al-Atrash had long been the French authorities' most implacable foe. He had opposed the administration's 1921 concordat with the Druze, carrying on a guerrilla war from bases in Transjordan throughout 1922; not until the British forced him out in 1923 did he submit to French authority. But when his compatriots and kinsmen were arrested after an invitation he had wisely declined to accept, he resolved to throw these ill-mannered interlopers out. On 18 July 1925 Druze highlanders brought a French airplane down, and four days later a band under al-Atrash's command engaged a column of between 150 and 250 French colonial troops, killing most of them. Al-Atrash's forces suffered losses as well, but this early success brought men flocking to his ranks.[3] By the end of July, his troops had the main Druze town of Suwayda under siege, and when the French dispatched a column of 3,000 men under General Roger Michaud to relieve it, that column too was cut to pieces. Overnight, Damascus knew of al-Atrash's victory.

Over the next three months, a Druze revolt became a national rising. It did so, as Michael Provence has shown, less because Damascus's nationalist notables rallied to the cause (although some, including Shahbandar, quickly did so) than because a lesser-known collection of men, usually from socially modest backgrounds and often educated in Ottoman military schools, took up arms and recruited a following. As the French never quite understood, al-Atrash was a Syrian nationalist and not simply a local warlord. He had been a young Ottoman army conscript in the Balkans before the First World War, had later joined the Arab Revolt, and had supported the Faysali state. By mid-August 1925 he was in touch with Shahbandar and the Peoples' Party in Damascus, and on 23 August, as the 'Commander of the Syrian Revolutionary Armies', he issued a general call to arms. Appealing to all

Syrians to 'remember your forefathers, your history, your heroes, your mar-
tyrs, and your national honour...remember that civilized nations that are
united cannot be destroyed', al-Atrash called for the complete independence of Syria, the institution of free elections and a popular government, the
expulsion of foreign armies from Syrian soil, and—an interesting touch—
'the application of the principles of the French Revolution and the Rights
of Man' (Figure 5.2 and 5.3).[4]

Exploiting the long-standing alliances between the grain-producing villages of southern Syria and Damascene merchants, the revolt spread; friendships forged in Ottoman military schools drove it northwards. In August
and September 1925 insurgent bands penetrated the garden district around
Damascus; in early October, Fawzi al-Qawuqji, a former Ottoman army
officer who was now a captain in the French Legion, mutinied together
with his men and joined with Bedouin bands to seize Hama, 200 kilometres
north of Damascus. The French—rattled, short of men, and facing an enemy
they couldn't clearly see—turned to Circassian, Kurdish, and Armenian
irregulars to do the work of sweeping into villages and routing suspected
rebels; tales soon spread of the rampant violence and rapacity of those troops,

**Figure 5.2** Sultan al-Atrash in exile in Arabia following the revolt.

**Figure 5.3** Al-Atrash with Druze and Bedouin fighters at a prisoner exchange, 1925.

who openly hawked their looted goods in Damascus. Heavy use was also made of aerial bombardment, including in Hama, where notables forced the insurgents to withdraw following a prolonged bombardment that cost several hundred lives.

This was a vicious, ugly, war. One morning in early October, Damascenes woke to find French troops parading the corpses of a few dozen ostensible rebels through their streets and then stringing them up for public view in Marghul Square. Three days later, insurgents dumped the bodies of twelve Circassians outside the city's Eastern gate. With both insurgents and irregulars active in the city, on 18 October the French sent tanks careening through its narrow streets and that evening began a bombardment.[5] Next day all troops were withdrawn and for the next two days Damascus was under fire from live shells and airplanes. It was at this point that the real international outcry began.

## From humanitarian protest to legitimation crisis

Unease over Sarrail's handling of the Syrian revolt had been growing at the Quai d'Orsay for some time, but only the bombing of Damascus and the explosion of publicity that followed transformed that unease into a full-blown crisis of legitimacy for French rule and for the mandates system in general.[6] No other controversy so rocked the system's very foundations. This was the case not only because the Syrian revolt was the most serious rebellion to take place in a mandated territory, but also because, unlike the scandal over the repression of the Bondelswarts, it could not be contained within the framework of civilizational uplift and tutelage that underpinned mandatory rule. Instead, for a number of specific and contingent reasons, not least the presence of an articulate Syrian nationalist lobby within Geneva itself, even some within the West came to see the conflict not as brigandage and overreaction but rather as a war of national liberation against an occupying power. How did this shift in frameworks become possible?

We can begin to answer that question by tracing the treatment of the conflict in the pages of the London *Times*. The newspaper had begun covering Syrian disorders on 4 August 1925, two days after the destruction of Michaud's column, and printed almost daily reports thereafter. Since Sarrail kept official information tightly censored, both the British public and (to the French authorities' irritation) the French public turned for information to the independently sourced *Times*.[7] There, the Syrian unrest was first portrayed as just one of those 'disagreeable Oriental problems' that erupt when 'bold warriors' like the Druze are 'tactlessly handled'.[8] The Druze, in other words, were another honour-obsessed martial race, brave and admirable in their own way no doubt, but primitive and irrational. Their rebellion was local and evanescent; there was no reason to think that al-Atrash would turn into 'a second Abd-el-Krim'.[9] This argument mirrored that retailed by French colonial lobbyists in their publication, *L'Asie française*,[10] and persisted even as the revolt spread, with the *Times* ascribing the troubles to Syria's intractably polyglot character—the 'juxtaposition of comparatively civilized and extremely primitive and predatory communities'—as well as to the unrealistic aspiration for complete independence which the 'Sharifian experiment' had aroused in a 'vain and fanatical people'.[11]

Those easy assumptions about civilizational hierarchies and Arab fanaticism could not, however, accommodate the eyewitness account of the bombardment of Damascus that the *Times* ran on 27 October (Figure 5.4). There, readers learned for the first time of the French army's burning of villages, its display of the rebel corpses in Damascus, and its use of tanks in the city's narrow streets. But it was the bombardment—the wanton destruction of an ancient and beautiful city and the subjection of its civilian inhabitants to

**Figure 5.4** A widely distributed photograph of the destruction of the Azm Palace by the bombardment of October 1925.

terror and fire—that really turned civilizational assumptions on their heads. Readers knew nothing about Druze villagers and placed them easily in the category of the primitive, but every biblically literate child had heard of Damascus and the now-blasted Street Called Straight. Readers learned, further, that Europeans in the city had escaped harm from rival bands only because Muslim notables had defended the Christian quarter and protected its inhabitants from molestation. Those Westerners, *The Times* reported, felt 'unable adequately to express their gratitude to the Muslims' but 'considerable resentment' at the French for bombarding 'an open town like Damascus, including areas which are officially known as European...without the slightest warning'.[12] Perhaps France's monopoly on 'civilization' was not so secure after all.

Syrian nationalists, of course, had been saying this all along. Syrian elites who had remained loyal to the Ottoman administration or who had served the Faysali government had been ousted and often exiled by the early 1920s, but they were not silenced. From its formation in Cairo in 1921, the Syro-Palestinian Congress—along with other diasporic groups—ceaselessly protested that the French presence violated both the specific pledges made to the Arabs during the war and the recognition of the right of Middle East populations to self-determination contained in the League Covenant. Those appeals to the League didn't so much repudiate 'civilizational' language as seek to appropriate it. An ancient land, home of a civilization as cultivated as any in the West, Syria could not be placed 'alongside Cameroon, Togo and other savage countries' needing Western uplift and instruction.[13] After all, alone among mandated populations, the Syrians had already demonstrated their capacity for modern state-building. The Faysali regime may have been fragile and short-lived, but the fact that the French mandate could be imposed only after its military defeat made it impossible to paint French rule as anything but an occupation. France could hardly claim to be bringing 'self-determination' to Syria when it had ousted the only national government Syrians had ever had.

In September, as the revolt spread, Shakib Arslan, the Druze aristocrat who acted as the Congress's Secretary, hurried back to Switzerland to rent a house and organize its appeal to the League. A comprehensive indictment of French policy sent to the Assembly on 29 September—well before the bombing of Damascus—made the case. Mandatory rule, far from guiding Syria's population towards the independence promised in the Covenant, had led only 'to their political and economic retrogression'; the revolution underway was the Syrian nation's understandable response.[14] The bombardment turned that protest into a global mobilization. From Buenos Aires to Detroit, Jerusalem to Bombay, the clubs and associations of the Syrian diaspora met to draft memoranda and send telegrams; in Geneva the Secretariat duly logged them and forwarded them to Paris for a response.[15] Most of these appeals urged League intervention and made the case for Syrian independence—or, at least, for the transfer of the mandate. Syrian-Americans, citing Woodrow Wilson's promise of self-determination and the disregarded King-Crane report, called on the US to assume it;[16] others urged that France follow the British example in Iraq, where Faysal had been installed as king and an Anglo-Iraq treaty negotiated to replace the detested mandate.

It is a sign of the depth of the crisis that at least some of the influential, internationally minded Anglo-American scholars and writers whom the League founders had always had in mind when they spoke of 'public opinion' now found the Syrian nationalists' arguments more persuasive than the language of tutelage. Take, for example, the response of Quincy Wright, Professor of International Law at the University of Chicago, only thirty-five years old but swiftly emerging as the world's foremost legal expert on the mandates system. Wright had received funding from the Guggenheim

Foundation and a sabbatical from his university in the autumn semester of
1925 to travel to London, Paris, Geneva, and the Middle East to conduct
interviews and gather material for what would become his authoritative
1930 study, *Mandates under the League of Nations*. As luck would have it, he
and his wife arrived in Beirut on 30 October 1925, less than two weeks after
the bombardment of Damascus, and while they rearranged their schedules
to take a trip to Baghdad first, they nevertheless made their way to Damascus
in mid-November, where they saw the damage first-hand.[17] That bombardment (as well as the fact that the French officials in Syria refused to speak
with him with any frankness about their policy) affected Wright, and on his
return to the United States he immediately wrote a note about its implications for the *American Journal of International Law*. Let us follow his careful
argument.

Wright admitted at the outset that legal authorities often held that civilized states were not bound by international law in their relations with
'savage' and 'barbarous' peoples, on the grounds that such peoples could not
be counted upon to keep contracts and thus could legitimately be 'policed'
through more forceful methods. Yet he rejected the French view that one
could cast the Syrian conflict in such terms. France was not Syria's imperial
overlord, nor was Syria 'barbarous'; indeed, the Covenant had already 'provisionally recognized' the right to self-determination of the populations
formerly under Ottoman rule. Given that civilizational status, it was necessary to ask whether the current unrest might be not primitive 'brigandage'
(as France claimed) but rather a rising aimed at making nominal independence real. That was 'a question of fact': one simply needed to know whether
the rebels had constituted a government, were masters of a portion of the
territory, and aimed at independence. If those conditions held, and Wright
insisted that they did, then the Syrian rebels were a state in the making,
entitled to treatment according to the laws of war. And in that case, the
bombardment of Damascus—a city without modern fortifications, offering
no resistance, and inhabited by a civilian population and foreigners given no
notice of the attack—was indeed a war crime. France, unable to hold the
country against 'a determined native rising', had fallen back on 'a policy of
terrorism'.[18]

A progressive American might hold such views. But the crisis was made
more severe because forces who might have been expected to rally to the
French administration—officials at the Quai d'Orsay, the British holding
the mandates for neighbouring Palestine, Transjordan and Iraq, the patriotic

French right—were either caught off guard by Sarrail's actions or willing to exploit them for their own political ends. Party-political machinations in France played a major role in escalating the crisis. Beginning in August, the right-wing *Echo de Paris* had begun a campaign of vilification against Sarrail stoked by documents leaked from disaffected intelligence officers in Syria; that December, conservative deputies would read the most incriminating of that material into the parliamentary record.[19] The British also found Sarrail's actions hard to stomach. Austen Chamberlain at the Foreign Office, although committed to the policy of entente with the French, was shocked by the accounts of the bombardment he received from W. A. Smart, the British Consul in Damascus, and commended Smart's vigorous efforts to protect British subjects and to secure compensation for damage to their property.[20] The French ambassador was called in to be read excerpts from Smart's reports, and the British ambassador in Paris likewise carried Chamberlain's protests about French treatment of British subjects to the Quai d'Orsay.[21] The Cartel government—preoccupied with economic and European questions, running through three Prime Ministers in 1925 alone, and unable to extract anything but platitudinous assurances from the laconic Sarrail— found it hard to respond. It was a perfect storm.

France rode out the rebellion in Syria with a policy of force, shipping in troops from North Africa and fighting a counter-insurgency campaign through 1925 and 1926 both from the air and, village by village, throughout southern Syria. But the international crisis required a different response, driving France, really for the first time, to answer to, and then to enlist the support of, the League. This 'Geneva strategy' was crafted by Foreign Minister Aristide Briand, architect of the recently signed Locarno accords, and by his close ally at the Quai d'Orsay, Philippe Berthelot (who was, the British ambassador in Paris reported, 'thoroughly ashamed of the bombardment')[22]. But it was carried out by Robert de Caix, who had first devised the plan to fragment Syria into multiple states and who would remain at the helm of French policy in the Levant through the whole of the interwar period. De Caix mistrusted the League, seeing it as a stalking horse for British interests, and had, thus far, done all he could to evade and diminish its powers. Between 1925 and 1927, however, he came reluctantly to realize that if France were to surmount the crisis, it needed the Permanent Mandates Commission on its side. The problem was that, in October of 1925, many on the Commission were also shocked by France's behaviour and not eager to come to its aid.

Over the next year, they would overcome those reservations, but their assistance came at a price. It is important to be clear about just what that price was. The PMC did not ask France to treat with the rebels, change its military tactics, or abjure its efforts to promote regional and religious loyalties as a bulwark against nationalism. It insisted, rather, that it comply with the rules of the mandatory game—that is, that it send comprehensive reports to Geneva, respond to petitions, and pay lip service equally to the Commission's authority and to the system's stated ideals. In return, the PMC would uphold French authority, undercut the standing and claims of Syrian nationalists, sanction the methods with which France sought to restore order (including bombardment of undefended towns), and, crucially, work to encode a distinction between the 'civilizing' tutor and the Syrian 'ward'. The Commission did not do this as promptly and fulsomely as the French would have liked, but its members did it—and not because they were coerced or cynical about their task, but rather because they were convinced that order and civilization depended on upholding French authority. Let us turn, now, to that process of legitimation.

## The Mandates Commission at work

As luck would have it, the Mandates Commission convened in Geneva for its seventh session on the morning of 19 October 1925, the very day French artillery opened fire on Damascus. The Syrian mandate was even on the agenda. Yet, because members of the Commission routinely based their discussions on the written report of the mandatory power, which in this case was for 1924 and had nothing to say about the rising, they felt themselves in a sticky situation. They could, of course, proceed to discuss that 1924 report, but as the Commission's president, Marquis Theodoli, put it, public opinion might quite understandably protest against such 'excessive detachment'. But what could they conclude about the unrest in Syria when they had not a word from France? There were press reports, the protests of the Syro-Palestinian Congress, a mounting pile of telegrams from all corners of the globe, but nothing from the French government. Perhaps, Theodoli suggested on that first day, they should postpone consideration to a special session to be held in Rome?[23]

Most of the Commission, as well as the French officials in Geneva, gratefully rallied to this proposal.[24] Sir Frederick Lugard, however, was unhappy.

He felt that the Commission had both the duty and the right to inquire into a conflict in progress, and on 28 October—not coincidentally the day after the explosive *Times* report on the bombardment, which he had undoubtedly read over breakfast—he told his colleagues (still in session) so. Just that August, the Council had intervened to prevent a border conflict between Greece and Bulgaria from escalating into war, and the Syro-Palestinian Congress was asking the Council to intervene in the same manner here. The Commission's silence, Lugard said, was being taken for disinterest in or approbation of French behaviour. At the very least they should forward the Syrian requests for action to the Council.[25]

Members of the Commission, however, declined to do this—a refusal that was significant for two reasons. First, they signalled thereby that they were not willing to press at the boundaries of their authority. That is, they would *review* the mandatory power's handling of a crisis, but would not intervene in any conflict themselves. Second, and equally importantly, they would uphold the privileged standing of the mandatory power. However much information was available to them, they would await a statement by the mandatory power itself. In a sense, this was hardly surprising. The Commission had been appointed to uphold the territorial dispensation arrived at in Versailles and thus could scarcely entertain protests that called that into question. But the Syrian nationalists, in consequence, remained 'petitioners', without the standing of a member state and unable to speak internationally in their own right.

The decision to postpone also bought the French time, enabling Briand to begin to cobble together a response. On 30 October Sarrail was finally recalled, and in November the government broke with the tradition of military men and chose a civilian to replace him, settling on Henry de Jouvenel, a senator and literary figure once married to Colette who had been part of the French delegation to the League Assembly. Jouvenel, in another unprecedented gesture, met with Shakib Arslan of the Syro-Palestinian Congress before setting out for Syria—a dialogue that revealed to Jouvenel the impassable gulf between French and Syrian nationalist positions and that both elevated Arslan's standing and exposed him to sharp attacks from fellow nationalists who had not authorized him to speak (much less to offer concessions) on their behalf.[26] Briand, Berthelot, and de Caix also went so far as to ask the advice of France's old bête noire, now King Faysal of Iraq. Faysal told them to stop catering to Syria's religious minorities, to reunite the country, and to look for a native leader with whom they could come to a treaty agreement and end the mandate—essentially, the strategy the British were pursuing in Iraq.[27] The Quai d'Orsay also took advice from League officials about how best to prepare for the session with the PMC and were told how much weight the Commission placed on receiving full documentation.[28]

Briand also began working behind the scenes to repair relations with the British and craft a common Anglo-French stance. This was much to Austen Chamberlain's liking. True, the Foreign Office had been privately very critical of Sarrail's anti-British attitudes and ham-fisted behaviour;[29] both Smart in Damascus and the Acting Consul General in Beirut worried that he had brought the whole mandatory system into disrepute.[30] Yet even Smart, who considered the 'bitterness of the British Colony' over the bombardment 'entirely justified', thought that 'our own vital interests and the prevention of anarchy in all Arabian Mandated Territories demand a complete Anglo-French solidarity'. Although the British government should try to obtain compensation for damages suffered by British nationals—especially since most were 'Asiatics' on whose loyalty the empire relied[31]—when it came to French actions, 'everything possible should be done to consign this painful story to oblivion'.[32] Chamberlain entirely agreed. Sir Eric Phipps at the British Embassy in Paris was sent to tell Jouvenel of Chamberlain's commitment to Anglo-French cooperation in the Middle East and to invite him to meet with Chamberlain and Colonial Secretary Leo Amery in London.[33]

But Briand and Berthelot wanted something more: British help muzzling Lugard at the forthcoming meeting of the PMC. The request caused much hand-wringing in the Foreign Office, for Lugard, as an 'expert' appointed directly by the League Council, wasn't formally under their control. Perhaps someone could have a private word? Chamberlain shut down the debate by saying that he would see Lugard himself.[34] This was very much the British style, and when Briand complained again about Lugard's 'really unfriendly and impassioned' attitude on the PMC,[35] Chamberlain insisted that he be told that, whatever other nations might do, it was alien to the 'traditions of English public life and service' and 'injurious and derogatory to the League' to seek to influence Sir Frederick in any way. Yet he also let Briand know that he had met Lugard for lunch, 'as a personal friend and not in any sense as a Minister', and had there spoken of French sensitivities.[36] Lugard, unsurprisingly, experienced this as pressure, especially when Leo Amery called him in to repeat the lesson. He became thoroughly uneasy—he left the Colonial Office, his wife Flora Shaw told Amery, 'murmuring to himself,

"Thou shalt not muzzle the ass that treadeth out the French!" '³⁷—and was tempted to plead illness and skip the Rome session entirely. Flora's convictions and Lugard's own sense of duty made shirking impossible. 'Of course he realizes,' Flora wrote, 'that higher issues must take precedence over lower'—one might say, great-power comity over Syrian rights—'and he determined with your warnings in his mind to go and do his best'.³⁸

Theodoli, too, came under pressure to be 'helpful', but here his own inclinations and French interests coincided. Theodoli had, to this point, been the Syrian nationalists' most receptive ear, for ties of family and friendship bound him to the Levant. His main aim was, however, to increase Italian influence in the region; when a breach opened between the British and the French, he immediately sought to widen it. Theodoli thus went out of his way to tell the French ambassador in Rome that they could count on him to help contain Lugard, leading Briand to thank Mussolini for his support.³⁹ De Caix remained mistrustful, worrying that the French ambassador had been too easily taken in by 'our subtle Italian'; he also knew he would likely face sharp questioning from the liberal Swiss member William Rappard and the other 'independents' on the PMC.⁴⁰ Yet, to a considerable degree, Briand's behind-the-scenes manoeuvres had eased de Caix's situation before the session even began.

But might Anglo-French collusion carry risks of its own? Smart in Damascus, much the most acute observer of the whole affair, worried that it might. It was obviously in Britain's interest for France, somehow or other, to hold Syria, he wrote to Chamberlain, but too close an identification with France's anti-nationalist and pro-Christian policy could seriously jeopardize Britain's standing in the Muslim world. Nor could the crisis be ducked, for 'clouds of journalists' had descended on Damascus. 'What has happened, and is happening, in Syria, is no longer a secret.' Indeed, aware they had a global public's attention, the Syrians were determined to challenge France at the forthcoming meeting of the PMC, and while Smart had no doubt that their efforts would fail, he also warned that too great a rout would bring discredit on Britain and the League alike. If the Commission was simply forced to accept the kinds of statements French ministers had made in the Chamber of Deputies—where Poincaré blamed the damage to Damascus on the insurgents and Briand had defended France's presence in Syria as a 'civilizing' duty—'then it is not difficult to imagine what murmurs will pass through the watching Moslem world'. Nothing less than the credibility of the international order was at stake, for 'if it is desired that the League of Nations should gradually acquire a universal character, and not appear as an association of the West against the East, then the prolongation of situations such as that of Syria to-day under French mandate can only be regarded as morally damaging to the League's cause'.[41] Smart thus hoped, but with ever-diminishing confidence, that the PMC might find a way to uphold French authority while also making the French genuinely change their ways. But could Lugard and his fellows accomplish that tricky task?

The eighth session of the Permanent Mandates Commission, which met in Rome from 16 February until 6 March 1926, was 'extraordinary' in several respects. It was the first session, and would remain one of only three sessions, held to discuss conditions in a single territory (the other two would concern Palestine). It was also the only session ever held away from Geneva. That location made it a logistical nightmare, for a staff of twenty-six—five officials from the Mandates Section (including Catastini and Gilchrist), two interpreters, two English and two French précis-writers, six English and six French typists, and three duplicators—had to be transported, with their equipment, to Rome and then brought back in time to staff the Council session immediately afterwards.[42] From various corners of Europe came the ten Commission members, including for this session only Ernest Roume, pre-war Governor General of French West Africa, hastily appointed to replace the ailing Jean-Baptiste Beau, who would die in the course of the session. De Caix and Count Gaston Clauzel attended as 'accredited representatives' to defend French policy; Arslan, Michel Lutfallah, and Ihsan al-Jabiri of the Executive Committee of the Syro-Palestinian Congress arrived to challenge it; press correspondents speculated about what was happening behind the closed doors.

We have some sense of those secret discussions from the printed minutes of the session, but that account was (as de Caix noted thankfully) much 'softened' by Roume's last-minute editorial corrections; in the process, some of the bluntest exchanges disappeared.[43] More revealing are the letters de Caix sent to Berthelot and Briand in Paris, those that Lugard sent to his wife (who shared them, with his consent, with Amery), and those that Huntington Gilchrist wrote after the session to internationalist friends in the United States, among them Quincy Wright. Taken together, these sources show how the Commission and the Quai d'Orsay came to terms on a project of mutual legitimation—but one that, as Smart feared, did little to reconcile 'West' and 'East'.

The session opened in an atmosphere of tension. According to Lugard, the PMC members were 'imbued with a sense of the great gravity of the position' and very subdued; de Caix looked tired and on edge. No one was certain quite how to proceed, and in the absence of a clear plan Roume took charge, insisting that it would be most proper and dignified if the Commission began by discussing the overall condition of the territory as revealed in the 1924 French report.[44] On some level, this was ridiculous. As the Dutch member D. F.W.Van Rees assertively pointed out, the session had been organized to discuss the rising, and should start with that. But the Commission was so eager to be seen as impartial that it agreed with Roume's suggestion—a decision that both cut into the time it had to rake over the revolt itself and that implicitly reduced the rising to, as Roume put it, 'only an incident', and one involving a population—the Druze—'which at all times had revolted under every regime which had been imposed on it'.[45] The PMC thus whiled away the first four days discussing France's fiscal regime in Syria, its provisions for schools, its attitude towards refugees— anything and everything but its handling of the rising.

Lugard spent that first week feeling distinctly uncomfortable. He tried to bear in mind Flora's words—'that "the peace of Europe is more important than criticism however well founded of French action in Syria"'—but Theodoli's jibes about his silence chafed, and when Lugard learned that the Belgian government had left his colleague Pierre Orts perfectly free to fol- low his conscience, he 'felt very guilty for my Government'.[46] Lugard dis- liked 'pompous Roume', thought de Caix 'possibly a little unscrupulous', and hated the idea of identifying Britain with French actions.[47] Yet, as the session proceeded, he too came round to a conciliatory stance, not because he came to trust de Caix, but rather because he, like Smart, had concluded— and meeting with the Syrian petitioners did nothing to change that view— that 'there is no alternative to the French mandate'. Lugard took it as axiomatic that Syria could not govern herself, which meant that some other country would have to do so. And, as he told Flora: 'We do not want it and we do not want to see the Turks back again. I would like to see Italy burn her fingers over it but there is no possibility of that.' The French must there- fore stay—and that meant that 'we must not make [their] position impossi- ble'.[48] Orts, he had discovered, felt exactly the same way. Both thought the PMC must avoid doing anything that would further undermine French authority, while also making de Caix realize 'that there must be a radical change'.[49]

The minutes of the sessions, and especially their eloquent lacunae, are a monument to that work of rehabilitation. Together, de Caix and the Commission worked to overcome two challenges. First, they searched for a formula that would enable them to say that France's autocratic administration did not violate Article 22's pledge that the independence of the Middle East populations was 'provisionally recognized'. De Caix found what he needed in the language of tutelage, proclaiming that while France fully understood that the mandates system was 'a provisional system designed to enable populations which, politically speaking, are still minors to educate themselves so as to arrive one day at full self-government', until those minors arrived at 'maturity' political control must necessarily remain in French hands.[50] It was thus for France to decide when and how powers should be devolved—and indeed, de Caix implied, if anything France had been guilty of trying to force the pace, for the revolt showed that a population accustomed to Ottoman oppression was not ready to participate responsibly in politics.[51] Again and again, de Caix evoked the trope of Ottoman backwardness, using it to explain why Syrians could not govern themselves and why the French were driven to use the kinds of forceful methods these 'minors' could understand—an explanation profoundly offensive to Syrian nationalists who had often held political posts within the Ottoman state.[52]

The Commission, deeply relieved that de Caix was willing to acknowledge the system's rhetorical aims (and thus its own authority), happily echoed this language of tutelage. The Swiss member Rappard, for example, expressed his 'very great satisfaction' at de Caix's remarks, both because they would 'allay the disquiet of those Syrian patriots who...only desired the independence of their country' and because 'they asked the League of Nations for effective cooperation'.[53] In fact, Syrian patriots' 'disquiet' was far from allayed, for they neither considered themselves 'minors' nor accepted that the Covenant left the right to determine the character, structure, and timetable of 'independence' entirely in French hands. The Commission, however, was willing to treat the mandate text (which the French themselves had drafted, and which granted them wide administrative powers) rather than the Covenant as authoritative. From here, it was a short step to the decision to deny a formal audience to the three representatives of the Syro-Palestinian Congress who had travelled to Rome,[54] and a further short step to declare that while the mandate text directed France to facilitate the progressive development of Syria and Lebanon as independent states, since it had not specified the *number* of such states to be created, the mandatory power could set up a multiplicity of smaller, federated states if it so chose. For Syrian nationalists, this was a major defeat, for they understood that France, first by founding an expanded 'Greater Lebanon' and then by creating a set of discrete native states, hoped to undermine shared bonds and sentiments among Syria's various regions and peoples and make a unitary Syrian state impossible. By failing to challenge these plans, the PMC had turned its back on the Covenant's implicit recognition of Syrian nationalism.[55]

Second, de Caix and the Commission managed, not without difficulty, to contain the humanitarian crisis. By February, evidence of French atrocities had mounted well beyond that available at the October session, with Lugard reporting telegrams pouring in 'from Cairo especially but also from every quarter of the earth, South American states, every capital of Europe and Asia' alleging that 'prisoners are being tortured and villages burnt and women outraged'. Some were quite explicit, naming names of specific officers who had condoned or conducted atrocities, and Lutfallah, al-Jabiri, and Arslan, who met with almost all the commissioners individually, amplified those charges. Lugard, for one, thought them credible, 'because I know what [the French] have done in similar circumstances in Africa', and it seems clear that others did as well[56]—and had they been able to read the confidential dispatches coming in from Smart in Damascus, they would have had many of their suspicions confirmed.[57] Yet the published minutes of the session contained few traces of the charges and even fewer of the credence members placed in them. This was deliberate, for once Orts and Lugard had decided that there was no alternative to French control, they also agreed—again, as Smart had in Damascus—that as little as possible should be said about specific charges and that pressures for an independent League inquiry (for which the Syrians were pressing) must be resisted. Such an inquiry would destroy France's prestige and make its position impossible.[58]

Yet Lugard and Orts also realized that if the League was to retain any legitimacy, those charges must be answered. Simply approving French actions, with its brutal record publicly available and the eyes of the world upon them, would damage their own credibility beyond repair. The PMC thus used the threat of a public inquiry to force the French to play the legitimation game. On 19 February 1926 de Caix telegraphed Briand for permission to announce that Jouvenel had *already* decided to conduct just such an inquiry into French actions—a flat lie, but one that de Caix rightly judged he had to tell to quiet the Commission.[59] Berthelot and Briand then instructed Jouvenel to undertake investigations that, as Berthelot put it, 'would undoubtedly lead in most cases to the embarrassment of the libelers and petitioners'.[60] It is important to note the phrasing of the charge. The order to conduct the inquiry and the order to exonerate French authorities were never uncoupled. De Caix's telegram to Briand, Berthelot's telegram to Jouvenel, and Briand's more extensive letter to Jouvenel all stipulated not only the scope of the inquiry but also *what it must find*. The inquiry need not deal directly with acts of war, Briand explained, since the PMC had accepted that these were not its concern, but it must refute charges of cruelty, pillage, and excessive punishment, and must challenge the 'exaggerated' claims made of the numbers of civilians killed and villages destroyed. A more forthright invitation to a cover-up can scarcely be imagined.[61]

Having secured de Caix's promise of full documentation, the PMC wrote its report. Orts was the chief draftsman, but Rappard, Van Rees, and (especially) Lugard guided his hand.[62] Embedded in the report, certainly, were criticisms of French policy and of the harsh treatment of the Druze, yet the report ranged the Commission firmly on the side of the mandatory power. Syria's inclusion in the mandates system, and the attribution of its mandate to France, were both ruled per se outside the PMC's competence, and the Commission for the first time stated that its duty to 'cooperate' with the mandatory power was as important as its duty to supervise it. Precisely because of that alliance, the Commission reserved its strongest criticism for the French failure to provide it with full documentation, yet that lack of information also enabled the PMC to 'reserve judgment' about atrocity charges. By contrast, the report praised both de Caix's verbal commitment to mandatory ideals and Jouvenel's ostensible policy of conciliation, and Syrian patriots were told firmly that since 'France proclaims that she is not pursuing in Syria and the Lebanon any other aim beyond that of assisting nations which from henceforth are recognized as sovereign to acquire the capacity to exercise this sovereignty themselves . . . a refusal to collaborate in carrying out the mandate, far from hastening the day of complete emancipation, can only postpone it'.[63] France had verbally proclaimed its commitment to League ideals; in return, the PMC was willing to accept the legitimacy of its rule (Figure 5.5).

After the session was over, de Caix sat down and wrote a summary for the Quai d'Orsay. It had been a taxing marathon, with seventeen of twenty-one sessions devoted to questioning him. He admitted it had begun badly. The

**Figure 5.5** Show of solidarity: Palestine High Commissioner Viscount Plumer and Syria High Commissioner Henry de Jouvenel, with Plumer's grandson, April 1926.

Commission had been inquisitorial and suspicious, and those who accused the French of misgovernment had been able to cite press reports, parliamentary statements, and even leaked High Commission documents; given the heaps of dirty linen French politicians had flung about in public, that criticism was inevitable. Yet, remarkably, it had ended well. The Syrian petitioners, who had thought to profit from the crisis, had received no support and some criticism; they had been told, 'in measured but perfectly clear language, that neither the mandate nor the choice of mandatory was up for discussion, and that the shortest route towards independence was, for the political minor placed under mandate, sincere collaboration with the tutor given him by the League of Nations'. This 'declaration of solidarity between

the League and the mandatory power' was, de Caix wrote, 'the happy conclusion' to a chapter that they all wanted to close.[64] A week after the session
ended, the League Council accepted the Commission's report and appealed
to the rebels to lay down their arms.[65]

## The return of 'civilization'

If de Caix left Rome feeling that he had survived the ordeal rather well, the
PMC and the Mandates Section officials also felt proud of their work. On his
return to England, Lugard met with the League of Nations Union's Mandates
Committee to justify their actions.[66] In Geneva, Huntington Gilchrist likewise undertook to calm the Americans. In a circular letter sent to several
dozen prominent American internationalists, Gilchrist painted the Rome
session as a landmark in international politics, the first time a great power had
'quite automatically been subjected to an international enquiry into its
alleged mal-administration of backwards peoples'. True, the PMC had not
done the things 'our radical friends' had clamoured for, such as taking away
the mandate, but every criticism had been examined, France sharply criticized for its 'failure... to supply full documentation', and a new policy of
conciliation approved.[67] His account won praise from Sir Eric Drummond,
as well as from Raymond Fosdick, for whom he had acted as Secretary at the
peace conference. Gilchrist also posted a copy to Quincy Wright, sure that
Wright would be interested 'in the satisfactory way in which the League
responsibilities over the former enemy territories... are being discharged'.[68]

Wright was indeed interested, but—unusually for a Western observer—
he considered the PMC's work anything but satisfactory. The PMC's
emphasis on cooperation with the mandatory power, he told Gilchrist, was
misguided, for if the system aimed to safeguard the interests of the inhabitants, 'I cannot see that the Commission or League has any duty to cooperate
with a mandatory whose policy is contrary to the spirit of the mandates.'
And France's policy *was* contrary to that spirit, not only because of the brutality of its occupation but more precisely because in promising to 'create
native governments' in Syria (rather than help Syrians create whatever government they desired), France was arrogating rights that the Covenant had
agreed belonged to the mandated population itself. Syrians understandably
felt those rights had been trampled, and the League needed to investigate
their complaints impartially, for 'if it is indeed true that French administra-

tion is in such a state that it cannot stand investigation, the question might well be raised whether she ought to continue there.' If, by contrast, the League simply endorsed French policy, Syrians would just say 'so much the worse for the League', for they knew from their own experience that this policy has meant 'economic depression, administrative abuses, military barbarities and a violation of specific political pledges'.[69] Gilchrist, shocked, retorted that the PMC had endorsed not past French policy but the new Jouvenel approach, that the English press had applauded their action, and that while they would have been happy to hear from inhabitants themselves, they had received no petitions from within the territory.[70] Wright bluntly told him what Gilchrist surely knew but would not admit: that Syrians inside the country couldn't approach the League because the French examined the mail and jailed or expelled anyone complaining of the internal situation. Wright's friends only mailed letters from outside Syria, and they told him that things were getting worse.[71]

Other information trickling into Geneva said much the same thing. Jouvenel's 'liberal policy' hadn't amounted to very much. Although he had met with the exiled nationalists in Cairo on his way to Beirut, there was no common ground; attempts at negotiations in Syria had also swiftly broken down. He had attempted to hold elections anyway, but they were boycotted in Damascus, Aleppo, and several other towns. He had managed to appoint a new government in Damascus, but soon arrested and jailed the three nationalist ministers who had agreed to take part in it.[72] Smart, reporting on the continued loss of French 'moral authority' in Damascus (where the insurgents were operating freely in some parts of the town), concluded by January that the High Commissioner's 'vague peace professions' had been intended merely to win League support before embarking on a policy of repression[73]—and indeed, that spring, with more troops in the country, the French counter-attack began. Air bombardment was used extensively and (according to Smart) always without warning, while ground troops and irregulars swooped down on villages suspected of harbouring rebels.[74] By August 1926 the rebellion in the Damascus region (but not in the Jabal Druze) had been crushed, but as one Swiss traveller reported to Fritjof Nansen, the 'mutual hatred' was terrible, with the whole population in a state of 'violent exasperation' with the French authorities.[75]

But if Syria was still ablaze, European press and political interest had subsided, making it possible for the PMC to cling to the path of 'cooperation'. Jouvenel travelled back to Geneva to deliver what one Colonial

Office observer thought a 'more optimistic than realistic' account of his progress at the Commission's June 1926 session,[76] and although the PMC was annoyed when he resigned soon after (leaving, de Caix commented sourly, the territory in a more chaotic condition than he found it)[77], the November PMC session with de Caix passed off amid an atmosphere of mutual good will.[78] That calm was not caused by improvements in Syria, where al-Atrash was still at large and the Jabal Druze 'unpacified'; nor was it shared by Syrian nationalists, who sent in 129 separate petitions. Instead, as de Caix cleverly understood, it was possible because public attention had shifted elsewhere and, still more, because France had finally provided the 'full documentation' on their actions during the rising that the PMC had long requested.[79]

Thus, although French behaviour in Syria had scarcely changed, and Syrian protests were if anything more vehement, the PMC's response was very different. Take, first, the treatment of the exiled Syrian nationalists. In Rome the Commission had urged them to collaborate with the French authorities, but when Arslan and al-Jabiri asked to see Briand, he refused to receive them.[80] Together with Lutfallah, the two then attended the public opening meeting of the PMC's June 1926 session only to hear Jouvenel denounce them as trouble-makers; Arslan shouted 'Je proteste!' and sat through the rest of the meeting with a Swiss policeman at his shoulder.[81] The Congress then flooded the PMC with petitions, but that proved counter-productive. Indeed, the members took it as a good joke when the overworked secretaries at the November session vengefully placed a different Congress petition on each seat at that public meeting.[82] Familiarity had bred contempt: although Arslan would remain in Geneva for more than a dozen years, a central link in the continent's vibrant networks of exiled Arab nationalists and a ubiquitous and eloquent petitioner, the Commission would never again take him entirely seriously.

Nor would the PMC show much concern henceforth about allegations of French brutality. They had asked the French to inquire into such charges and now willingly accepted the French response as authoritative. He was very glad that the Commission had not taken the petitioners at their word, Pierre Orts said at the November 1926 session, at which those reports were finally available, for they now knew that 'no atrocities had been committed'. Of course there had been regrettable casualties involving innocent people, but that was inevitable in war; he now regarded the case as settled.[83] Their consciences clear, the PMC briskly dismissed the new petitions too.

Reporting on accusations that French officers had ordered pillaging, the Portuguese member Freire d'Andrade stated that he 'was entirely convinced that no French officer would be capable of protecting thieves and pillagers'; rejecting charges that French officers had ordered suspects killed or young girls raped, the Spanish member Leopoldo Palacios stated that the French nation had shown such 'glory and prestige in the history of civilization' that it was impossible she could have used 'methods such as murder, burning, pillage and rape'.[84] This was the return of civilizational discourse with a vengeance, with the French, simply by virtue of being French, judged incapable of brutal acts. The PMC now assumed that allegations coming from Syrian nationalists were calumnies—so much so, de Caix reported with some surprise to Paris, that its members had not even noticed that the evidence for the pillage of one village by Moroccan troops actually came from a French officer's letter which had fallen into the insurgents' hands. Henceforth, de Caix concluded, they should inundate the PMC with documentation but never again agree to an extraordinary session.[85] Awash in paper and no longer interested in tales of repression, Commission members worked hard to keep their fingers in their ears.

Note, in consequence, the illuminating fate of the reports sent to the League in early summer 1926 by an American journalist, B. F. Dawson, about the French counter-insurgency campaign in the Jabal Druze. He had been an eyewitness to aerial attacks on 'absolutely undefended villages,' he wrote, which had killed women and children and created havoc, and which were even more appalling because the Druze had neither anti-aircraft guns nor cellars in which inhabitants could take refuge. The victims had asked him to tell the League of their plight, so he was now doing so—although he had warned them that the League, having permitted 'every form of treachery, incompetence, and brutality on the part of the mandatory power in Syria', was unlikely to take much notice.[86] And indeed, while Vito Catastini from the Mandates Section passed a first telegram along to the Quai d'Orsay, when he showed Dawson's second and fuller letter to Sir Eric Drummond, the Secretary General said he had 'grave doubts' about the wisdom of transmitting communications from 'irresponsible persons' that consisted 'chiefly of abuse'.[87] Catastini thus informed Dawson that, since his communications were 'violent' and contained 'no definite information', they could not be passed along. Dawson, clearly astounded, replied that it was 'almost impossible for anyone with human feelings and ordinary standards of decency to discuss the topic in question without indignation', but sent the details—date, time, name of village—of one particular attack.[88] Yet this letter, too, was judged not receivable.[89]

It is important to be precise about what was produced through bureaucratic tussles of this kind. Aerial bombardment of undefended villages, the practice that had evoked the PMC's outrage in South West Africa, that the PMC told de Caix in Rome was unacceptable (the British did it in Iraq too, de Caix retorted)[90], and that Berthelot himself thought illegal under the 1907 Hague agreement,[91] was being gradually normalized. International oversight, which was to guarantee more humane treatment of 'backwards peoples', had done the exact opposite, instead sanctioning new and more extreme forms of killing. Only Dawson's first telegram was ever forwarded to the French. When the PMC finally replied to the telegram almost a year later, it blandly stated that it 'considers that the mandatory Authorities should have recourse to such extreme measures as air bombardment, burning, destruction of villages and collective fines only in cases of absolute necessity and then only under the direct supervision of French officers', and that de Caix had assured the Commission that, 'so far as he is aware', the French were operating on such lines.[92] The French and the PMC, clearly, were now fully 'cooperating', so that even eyewitness accounts of bombings sent by Western witnesses—the kind of information that had caused the legitimation crisis a year earlier—could not penetrate the system's rhetorical defences.

★ ★ ★

On 12 October 1926, Henri Ponsot, a diplomat and official in the Quai d'Orsay, replaced Jouvenel as High Commissioner in Syria. Ponsot would remain in the job for six years, a sign if not of the 'radical change' that Lugard and Orts wanted, then at least of the Quai's determination to end the lurches and about-faces that had marked the past six years. When he left for Beirut, Ponsot took with him a memorandum by de Caix of some dozens of pages laying out the organization of Syria and Lebanon, the causes of the revolt, and the best lines of future policy. The document is remarkable for its contempt for Jouvenel's 'torrents of eloquence' and political 'twists and turns', for its absolute repudiation of Syrian nationalism, and for its bitter anglophobia. Britain's help restraining Lugard notwithstanding, de Caix insisted that Britain had created Arab nationalism 'as a pretext and means to oust us from Syria' and had 'infected' Syrian soil with the nationalist virus ever after. No compromise was possible with that nationalism.

Instead, the French would have to contain it by bolstering regional and 'minority' loyalties more strongly and by staying in Syria long enough—'which might be very long'—to actually create the mores (*moeurs*) and collaborators to whom they would cede control. De Caix could not pretend that would be easy, and French Republican traditions if anything would make it harder, since it would force the High Commission to spend much time and trouble making sure that elections—which could not be 'free' but must be seen to be 'free'—delivered the right outcomes.

Yet de Caix did not rule out another possibility, suggesting that once Maronite control of Lebanon was secure, the French might be able to live with a strong indigenous government in Syria. This would be the case, however, only if that government were monarchical or authoritarian rather than democratic—were the kind of government, in other words, that the British were building in Iraq. It clearly irritated de Caix enormously that Syrian nationalists held up the example of Iraq as a progressive alternative when the reality, he insisted, was much different. Britain had imposed Faysal, not without difficulty, on Iraq, and used their planes and machine guns to keep themselves in control and him in power. It might not be possible to create something similar in Syria, given its more cosmopolitan and less easily dominated population, but it might be worthwhile to try. Self-determination, then, was dangerous if democratic—recall al-Atrash's appeal to the principles of the French Revolution and the rights of man—but if delivered by a friendly autocrat, it lost much of its terror. But in any case it was important to remember that the Syrian and Iraqi models were less different than often supposed. The basis for control was the same: 'le fond, c'est la force'.[93]

Ponsot understood this. Under his watch, French forces mopped up the last pockets of resistance, driving Fawzi al-Qawuqji into exile in Iraq and the remnants of Sultan al-Atrash's army into refugee camps in Arabia. The Lebanese state was further consolidated with its much-disputed borders confirmed; the Alawite state, Alexandretta, and the Jabal Druze retained their autonomy. But Ponsot, a far more pragmatic thinker than any High Commissioner thus far, also moved cautiously to seek out collaborators in Damascus, Aleppo, and within the now-divided exile community in order to craft a constitution that Syrian notables might accept but that would also safeguard French interests. That task was difficult. The 'minorities policy' France had fostered took on a life of its own, nor did France ever find another Faysal with whom to reconcile French interests and Syrian nationalism. ('Alas, we have lost *you!*' Berthelot had whispered to Faysal at that 1925 meeting.)[94]

France could, however, usually count on the support of the PMC, which over time grew steadily *less* rather than more persuaded of the wisdom of any swift movement towards independence. The Syrian rising of 1925 was the Commission's chance to make that leap in the dark, and having drawn back, it would be in retreat from self-determination ever after. That move, as Quincy Wright and W. A. Smart had predicted, cost the Commission what little credibility it had among Arab nationalists. Yet what those perceptive observers never quite realized was that, with America outside the League and the great powers back in the saddle, the mandates system was no longer principally absorbed in the hopeless task of persuading populations under mandate (now defined in any case as 'minors') of the justice of their subjection. Rather, as Lugard rightly understood, the aim was to enlist the great powers in a drama of public accountability that would legitimate this form of alien rule before a sometimes critical, newspaper-reading, *Western* public. Through the crucible of the Syrian revolt, France, Britain, and the PMC all grew to understand their roles better.

# SIX

## A Pacific People Says No

The Mau is like a ship with the cargo in it. When the ship reaches the land then the cargo will be discharged. Now you said to end the Mau, but what about the objects of the Mau? You have beaten the Mau and disturbed the Mau and treated the Mau improperly, and now you ask to end it. How about the Mau belongings? . . . You only urged the Mau to give up, and you have nothing to give to satisfy us. The Mau will not say 'Yes', until you have put a Crown on the Mau.

High Chief Tuimaleali'ifano speaking to Colonel Allen, 5 March 1930[1]

Next to Nauru, Western Samoa was the tiniest mandated territory. With some 2,950 square kilometres of land spread across two islands, it was slightly larger than Luxembourg and had a population of just over 30,000. Unlike Nauru, however, the Samoan islands had no great economic importance and were of strategic interest only to the United States Navy, which administered American Samoa next door. Yet tiny Samoa mounted what was probably the most protracted, well-organized, and impressive campaign for self-determination of any mandated territory. The Samoan 'Mau' movement did not have the kind of profound repercussions on the mandates system that the Bondelswarts rebellion and the Syrian revolt had, but no conflict better illuminates the ideals and practices underlying League oversight.

The Mandates Section first learned that all was not well in Western Samoa in May of 1927, when Vito Catastini was passed a letter from one Newton Rowe, a disgruntled former official in that administration now resident in London, charging his former superiors with corruption and incompetence.[2] Catastini must have found the letter rather startling. Up to that point, the Mandates Commission had judged Western Samoa a model mandated territory. Every year Sir James Allen or Sir James Parr, successive

New Zealand High Commissioners in London, had travelled to Geneva to assure them that it was peaceful and prosperous; every year an admirable report had appeared detailing the administrator's efforts to improve public services and to cement structures of indirect rule. Given their preoccupation with South Africa's brutal practices in South West Africa and the smoldering ruin of the French mandate in Syria, the PMC had viewed Western Samoa with a benevolent, if not very searching, eye.

Now evidence of trouble was mounting. Hot on the heels of Rowe's communication—now resubmitted as a petition, and with its substance printed in the British press[3]—came a missive from one of the European elected members of the Samoan Legislative Council, claiming that 90 per cent of Samoa's inhabitants opposed the New Zealand administration.[4] A civil disobedience movement known as the 'Mau' (or 'Our Opinion') had arisen, and one month later Travers Buxton of the Anti-Slavery Society wrote to say that the Society had heard that New Zealand had been deporting Samoan chiefs who had taken part in it.[5] The Commission also learned that the Samoans had petitioned King George in 1921 asking him to remove the mandate from New Zealand—a communication unmentioned in five years of New Zealand's official reports.[6] The PMC had been broadly positive about Western Samoa. Now, faced with evidence of long-standing grievances, widespread civil disobedience, and an administration that had resorted to banishment and repression, they felt they had been made fools of. When Parr showed up in Geneva for his annual grilling in the autumn of 1927, he was in for a rough ride.

But Parr gave as good as he got, categorically denying that Samoans had any legitimate complaints and articulating the framework that would govern New Zealand's handling of the crisis until 1935. The Mau was simply the creature of one merchant, 'a half-caste called Nelson, who had no British blood in his veins', who had felt his prosperity threatened by the Administrator's plan to bypass merchants and buy high-quality copra—Western Samoa's major export crop—directly. Nelson had first mobilized a European population aggrieved by New Zealand's prohibition of liquor, and then 'manipulate[d] with consummate skill' the native Samoan population—in Parr's words, 'a simple and loveable race', but 'ready to listen to any tale, and hence...most susceptible to the wiles of the agitator'. Nelson's platform of manhood suffrage and the admission of natives to the Legislative Council was really just a bid for power, Parr explained, for since the natives were immature and easily led, such 'democracy' would make Nelson 'a sort of uncrowned king of Samoa'. New Zealand could not allow this, but it took the unrest seriously and had appointed a Royal Commission to investigate.[7] Outmanoeuvred, the PMC agreed to await its report.[8]

Parr went back to London, and the PMC members returned to their homes as well—where, early in 1928, a Royal Commission report entirely exonerating the Administrator reached them. By the time they reconvened in Geneva that June, yet more material had accumulated—an ordinance allowing the Administrator to deport agitators and forbid meetings, press reports about the continued activities of the Mau, and pamphlets denouncing New Zealand's policy from a new 'Samoan New Zealand Defence League' based in Auckland, where the deported Nelson was now living. The PMC also learned that New Zealand had dispatched General Richardson, the territory's ill-fated (and now retired) Administrator, to join Parr at the session, and that Nelson and his London solicitor were on their way to Geneva as well. There were also three more petitions: one from the Anti-Slavery Society enclosing evidence of government attempts to deter Samoans from petitioning the League, one from Nelson himself, and an ornately lettered formal appeal against New Zealand's rule bearing the signatures of 7,982 male Samoan taxpayers of an adult male population estimated at 8,500.[9] We can learn much about the mandates system—and especially how central racial hierarchy was to its logic and legitimation—from the incomprehension and hostility with which the two latter appeals were met. First, however, let us turn to Samoa to discover just what it was about Samoan society—or, perhaps, about Richardson's administration—that had led to such an impasse.

## The emergence of the Mau

Throughout their decade-long conflict with the Mau, the New Zealand administration and the Mandates Commission professed themselves unable to understand quite what the 'natives' were so stirred up about. But the naval officers who governed neighbouring American Samoa in the late 1920s, and who had had to deal with their own local 'Mau', thought the disaffection easy to understand.[10] New Zealand's administration of Western Samoa 'will never be successful,' Governor Stephen V. Graham wrote confidentially to his superiors in Washington at the height of the conflict, for the simple reason that 'after centuries of self-government the Samoan race has acquired a very great degree of pride in its ability to administer its own affairs'. The League had 'seriously injured' that pride by including Western Samoa in the list of 'backward nations' requiring alien administration and international oversight.[11] Concerned to keep American Samoa uninfected by the troubles, Graham sought to maintain cordial relations with both Richardson's successor and the high-ranking Western Samoans supporting the Mau, many of whom had kin on the American islands.

Graham's perceptive comments capture something crucial about Samoa: that it was one of the few mandated territories whose population had managed to live through an encounter with the European powers with its governance structures and ornate cultural systems still in its own hands. Through the nineteenth century and indeed during the German period, Samoans retained a complex rank-based social structure and effective representative institutions. Although ordered and hierarchical, Samoan society was also deliberative and inclusive, with land held collectively and the *matai* (heads of families) meeting in village *fonos* (assemblies) to decide business and organize tasks. There was a great deal of travel and ceremonial exchange between villages, however, and men holding higher titles met in *fonos* as well, to deal with larger, we might say national, questions. Consensual, negotiated, decentralized, and quite formal, Samoan society possessed, in Malama Meleisea's apt phrase, a 'unitary system of dispersed power'.[12]

Europeans, as they washed ashore in Samoa in increasing numbers over the course of the late eighteenth and nineteenth centuries, disturbed these social structures but did not destroy them. Instead, competing Europeans allied with competing Samoan dynasties, leading to a period in mid-century of considerable civic strife and land-grabbing. That ended with a classic great-power horse-trade, the Tripartite Agreement of 1899, through which Germany was recognized (by the powers) as controlling the western Samoan islands, the United States the much smaller eastern Samoan islands, and the British withdrawing their claims in exchange for German concessions elsewhere. The powers also established a Land Commission, which confirmed European ownership of about 8 per cent of Samoan land (and 35 per cent of cultivable land) but forbade further transfers of land to Europeans.[13] Thus, while a copra-plantation sector developed in Western Samoa, the territory never became a classic settler colony, for Samoans retained most of the land and avoided plantation labour, such work being done mostly by indentured Chinese. Moreover, in sharp contrast to their compatriots' rapacious behaviour in South West Africa, Western Samoa's German administrators, many of them enthusiastic ethnographers, never tried to force the Samoans to work, considering it their mission rather to preserve the unique culture and way of life of the natives.[14] The Samoans, dealing with that administration through their vibrant representative structures (and especially through the *Fono* of *Faipules*, a kind of national assembly) considered themselves to be under German protection but not under German rule.

The fly in this paternalistic ointment was the so-called 'European' population, and it isn't surprising that it became a flashpoint for discontent. Paternalistic colonial administrations often view white settlers with ambivalence, worrying that they will exploit vulnerable native populations. Yet, as the Germans discovered and as the New Zealanders would learn as well, Western Samoa's 'European' population constituted a threat precisely because it did not conform to that mould. European traders and settlers had long intermarried with Samoan women, and the children of those unions, while usually classed as 'Europeans', were accepted in Samoan society; there, they acted as the agents of a commercialization and cultural transformation that paternalistic German officials abhorred. By the end of the German period, that disapproval had reached such a pitch that 'mixed marriages' were outlawed. The so-called 'European' population had, however, already acquired its distinctive shape. This population—bi-cultural, often mixed-race, worldly, economically important—would play a critical role in the Samoan rebellion.[15]

New Zealand's bloodless occupation of the islands in the Great War initially brought little change. German officials were replaced and plantations confiscated, but the caretaker military administration made few further incursions into local life.[16] What traumatized and then mobilized the local population was something quite different: the devastating consequences of the global flu epidemic of 1918. In November 1918 a ship carrying infected passengers was allowed to dock at Apia, Western Samoa's principal town, although the government of American Samoa had wisely turned it away. Immediately, and terrifyingly, the disease swept the islands, killing some 7,500 people, or about a fifth of the population. Samoan elites and the mixed-race population clustered around Apia were particularly hard hit. To give just two examples, twenty-four of thirty members of the *Fono* of *Faipules* died, and the trader Nelson, later the subject of such controversy, lost his mother, his only son, and several other members of his family.[17] The epidemic destroyed any confidence the local population might have had in New Zealand's administrative capacity. When Colonel R. W. Tate arrived some two months later to take over the administration, a group of Samoan leaders immediately asked him to transfer the islands to American—or, failing that, direct British—rule.[18]

Tate succeeded in getting that petition withdrawn, but Samoan unhappiness with the new dispensation remained. All sections were discontented, Quincy Roberts, the American Consul in Apia, reported to the State Department some two years later, with white and 'half-caste' traders deploring the government's high tax rates, the Samoans its failure to consult them, and both the cost and incompetence of the New Zealand officials flooding the territory.[19] Since Britain had fought the last war to defend the rights of small nations, the Fono of Faipules wrote to George V that July, 'may it please Your Majesty to consider favourably a petition of the smallest of countries now under Your protection'. They had been a protectorate of Germany but New Zealand was treating them as a colony, governing through highly paid white officials who had little respect for the Samoans. This was wasteful and unnecessary. 'We and our children who have been educated are quite sufficient to perform the various duties of our Administration.'[20] At the Samoans' insistence, Tate transmitted this petition to London but added that the protest had been fomented by whites, that 'no real Native dissatisfaction exists', and that the idea that the Samoans could govern themselves 'need not be considered seriously'. The best thing to do, the New Zealand government advised, was for the King to inform the Samoans clearly and finally that New Zealand had been granted the mandate for Samoa. Winston Churchill, now Colonial Secretary, complied.[21]

Having, they imagined, overcome these early challenges to their authority, the New Zealanders got down to governing. Much of the German system was preserved. The sharp distinction between 'Europeans' and 'natives' was retained, with Europeans granted a property franchise and representation on a new Legislative Council and Samoans holding land communally and represented through native advisors and the Fono. Yet New Zealand was determined to take its responsibility for 'trusteeship' seriously, banning the sale of alcohol and developing programmes to 'uplift' Samoans, a process accelerated in 1923 with the appointment of Brigadier General Sir George Richardson to replace Tate as Administrator. This former gunnery instructor might have seemed a peculiar choice, but Richardson was nothing if not dogged, and—having read his Lugard and learned some Samoan—began drawing up plans to improve the islanders' health, education, and productivity. A carefully composed photograph of Richardson with two

Samoan children, reproduced here, perfectly captures how the new Administrator wished to be seen (Figure 6.1). Note the children's upturned gaze and the hand trustingly placed in the hand of the benevolent and far-seeing father.

But things did not go quite as intended. At first Richardson was welcomed, but as his officials penetrated further into village life, they aroused a feeling of unease. Richardson meddled in too many matters that were not his concern and, when his directives were ignored, could turn ugly. In one particularly silly but revealing confrontation, Richardson banished Tupua Tamasese Lealofi III, a Samoan high chief, to another part of the islands for failing to comply with a 'village beautification' directive to remove a hibiscus hedge on Tamasese's own land. Richardson's pompous processions around the islands began to be resented; his pidgin Samoan was laughed at; his insistence on appointing the hitherto elected members of the Fono of Faipules discredited those appointees and left him further out of touch.[22]

The disaffection of the 'European' community grew as well. Already irritated by prohibition, tax-paying traders resented the cost of Richardson's administration, his challenge to their pivotal place in the islands' economic life, and the fact that, given the government's automatic majority on the Legislative Council, they were powerless to block his plans. What particularly annoyed them, though, was Richardson's insistence that they could not speak for, and should not have anything to do with, the native population. 'Europeans' who were themselves married to Samoan or part-Samoan women must have found such paternalistic directives absurd, but to a man like Olaf Nelson they were deeply offensive. The son of a Swedish trader and a high-ranking Samoan woman, Nelson had inherited a thriving business from his father and then built it up further. Educated, trilingual, well-travelled, and elected in 1924 to serve as one of three 'European' members on the Legislative Council, he was the islands' most important copra trader and richest man. Yet he remained close to his Samoan family and held a Samoan title. In brief, he confounded the categories of 'trusteeship' in every way (Figure 6.2).

By 1926 Nelson not only shared the grievances of his European colleagues but had become a conduit for Samoan grievances as well. That spring he travelled to Wellington to present their united case to William Nosworthy, New Zealand's Minister of External Affairs, and thought he secured the minister's promise to investigate. But that visit was postponed, and in October the Samoans began to hold mass meetings in Apia—ironically, the

**Figure 6.1** Brigadier General George Richardson as he saw himself, with Samoan children.

**Figure 6.2** Olaf Nelson (in tan suit), with his daughters and Mau leaders, in 1933.

very month when Gordon Coates, New Zealand's Prime Minister, would tell the Imperial Conference in London that his government was doing a splendid job of governing the Samoans and that any disaffection had entirely disappeared.[23] In fact, disaffection was crossing over into defiance. When Richardson made clear his disapproval of any cross-race political discussion, 'as its tendency must be to disturb the peace, order, and good government of the Natives', those 'Natives' and 'Europeans' voted overwhelmingly to continue their collaboration.[24] The racial categories on which the New Zealand administration relied were unravelling.

In March 1927 they eroded further, when the parallel organizations of the European 'Citizens Committee' and the Samoan mobilization came together in a new 'Samoan League'—the 'Mau'. The Mau soon had its own newspaper—the *Samoa Guardian*, bankrolled by Nelson; in Nelson's trading stations, it had a ready-made propaganda network. But the real strength of the movement lay in the thousands of ordinary Samoans who descended on Apia to show their support when Nosworthy finally arrived that June. That visit proved disastrous, for when the Minister declared his government's firm support for Richardson and ordered the natives back home, Samoans simply stopped recognizing New Zealand's authority. When Richardson arrested several hundred Mau leaders, some additional hundreds asked to be arrested as well; when he insisted that they pay their taxes, they paid them to the Mau. Over the next few months, the Mau distributed uniforms, organized its own police force, began a boycott of government services and certain white businesses, and refused all requests to meet with the Administrator. 'The Administration of Western Samoa,' the American Consul in Apia reported that August, 'is ignored by 95 percent of the population.' He thought there was no danger of violence, for the Administrator had not resorted to further banishment; instead, the population was simply waiting patiently for New Zealand's Royal Commission—which had just spent five weeks in Samoa hearing witnesses—to report.[25]

That report, issued at the end of 1927, upheld the legality of the Administrator's repressive actions (including banishment), but the Mau refused to accept it.[26] Angry, humiliated, and aware that his small native police force could no longer be relied upon, Richardson asked for reinforcements and in February 1928 was sent military police and two naval destroyers. He then forced a bill allowing deportation through the Legislative Council and used the military police to clear Apia; it is at this point that the Mau leadership wrote their petition to the League and gathered those near-8,000 signatures. By this point, however, the Wellington government, concerned to avoid bloodshed, no longer trusted Richardson to keep his head. His term was about to run out, and he was not asked to stay on. When he left the islands Nelson was gone as well, having been sentenced to five years deportation under Richardson's new law. Nelson, however, left promising to take the Mau's case to the League and return in victory. Two months later, Richardson, Nelson, and the petitions were all on their way to Geneva.[27]

## Geneva and the work of legitimation

The conflict in Western Samoa would dominate the Mandates Commission's thirteenth session, held in June 1928. This was itself unusual, for the Pacific mandated territories had occupied a relatively small share of the Commission's time. Few of its members knew much about them. Only Kunio Yanagita, the unusual first Japanese member, had ever been to the South Sea Islands, and he had left the Commission in 1924. The Dominions had no members on the Commission and tended to resent—and, when they could, ignore—its distant scrutiny; the great powers rarely paid these territories much mind. Only the United States kept a careful eye on Samoa, but it did not share its excellent intelligence with Geneva. Nor could the Secretariat tap the kind of diasporic networks or humanitarian lobbies well informed about Middle Eastern or African affairs. In time, liberal New Zealanders would convey their distress about their government's Samoan policies to the League, but when the Commission first assembled it found itself largely on its own.

That isolation and relative ignorance led the Commission to make embarrassing misjudgements, but those errors also reveal much about its members' world view. Absent good information, and free from the kind of official back-chat and lobbying that often influenced their work, the Commission fell back on what advice the Secretariat could offer and its evolving views about administrative 'best practice'. In the Secretariat, the American Huntington Gilchrist again took the lead; within the Commission, Lugard was again influential. Through these deliberations, we can see how protective ideals and civilizational distinctions were again mobilized to render claims to self-determination inadmissible.

As the situation in Samoa deteriorated and the June session approached, Gilchrist wrote a memo for Sir Eric Drummond trying to make sense of the whole mess. There seemed to be a struggle between the Administrator and the European population for authority over the Samoans, he wrote, but why couldn't the Administrator keep the upper hand? Perhaps, Gilchrist suggested, New Zealand had paid too little attention to 'native psychology'? It was 'well known that peoples of the primitive and sentimental type' were greatly impressed by distant kingly authority, yet New Zealand had consistently shut out London and Geneva and acted on its own. Now, however, the League could help, for support from the Mandates Commission could restore the Administrator's prestige and power. 'It seems to me very unfortunate that ... the mandatory Powers and their representatives in the mandated territories appear to regard their responsibility to the League of Nations as a handicap whose existence ought to be ignored as much as possible rather than as an asset which could be used to advantage in handling local problems,' Gilchrist wrote. Drummond agreed, and promised to try to make some suggestions along these lines.[28]

Did Drummond have a quiet word with the members of the PMC? Certainly the Commission made its support for the mandatory power perfectly clear. Nelson—his ten-thousand-mile journey notwithstanding—was not received, although one or two Commissioners saw him privately.[29] The Commission spent four days, by contrast, with Richardson and Parr, and while those conversations were sometimes acrimonious, by the end all eleven PMC members save Palacios had lined up behind Richardson's point of view. That view had not shifted. The Mau movement, the general insisted, had no real support, being just the creation of a few ambitious men who had intimidated the white population and misled the gullible natives. When an irritated Rappard pointed out that ambitious men existed in many countries but did not succeed in bringing civil order to a standstill,[30] Parr and Richardson cited three factors peculiar to Samoa. Much was made, first, of Nelson's wealth and cunning—of his persuasiveness, his monopoly of information channels, his business ties, and the fact that European merchants were loath to cross him. Stress was placed too on the practical limits to the authorities' power. When the troubles began, Richardson pointed out, Samoa had no prison and no reliable police. Although he issued banishment orders, he could not enforce them; arrested men could only be kept for a short time in a rudimentary jail. Now that the new Administrator had some military police at his command, however, the whole problem was likely to go away. This was because of the third and most important factor—the 'extraordinary nature' of this 'most fickle of people'. Richardson didn't hold the Samoans responsible for the Mau, for he thought of them simply 'as children', who hadn't much to do and had been attracted by the movement's festive character. But with the Mau now boycotting the schools and Richardson's improving social programmes, matters had gone too far. However charming and picturesque, the natives had to be brought to heel.[31]

The Mandates Commission agreed. Indeed, Lugard made clear that he thought such firmness long overdue. Richardson, after all, had taken his ideas 'from a study of Lord Lugard's works';[32] the principles he espoused— those of separating 'native' and 'European' political institutions, and of shielding those natives from 'European' subversion—were Lugardian to the core. Indeed, in 1924, when Parr first explained the Administrator's decision to exclude natives from the Legislative Council but to preserve (on an advisory basis) the Fono of Faipules, Lugard warmly agreed that 'the development of the executive power of the local chiefs and of the village council was of greater benefit to the native than the other course'.[33] Nosworthy, the Minister for External Affairs, thus gratefully cited 'one of the greatest living authorities on British colonial administration, Sir Frederick Lugard', when telling the Samoans on his fateful visit to Apia that there was 'no justification whatever for the appointment of Native members to a Legislative Council having a majority of European members'.[34] Concerned as he was to bolster 'traditional' authority, and with his almost instinctive dislike of the 'half-caste' and detribalized, Lugard also concurred in Richardson and Parr's judgement that Nelson's interracial mobilization breached colonial administration's 'unwritten law'.[35] Setting down his views in a draft report at the end of the session, Lugard judged that none of the charges against Richardson's administration could be upheld; to the contrary, the Administrator had 'made praiseworthy efforts to improve the conditions of life of the native population'. The Samoans had been misled, but since neither they nor the 'Europeans, as distinct from the half-caste population' were truly disaffected, with Nelson deported and the Administrator finally allowed to take a strong hand, the unrest would surely die away.[36]

But Lugard was not Richardson's only ally. In sharp contrast to their stance during the Bondelswarts affair, Theodoli and Rappard also (in Theodoli's words) 'wished the New Zealand Government to know that it was strongly supported by the Commission in its efforts to maintain order and respect for the authorities'. Here, concern for the reputation of the League itself played a part. In a colony, Rappard told Richardson and Parr, 'the mother-country could do what it liked; it could encourage anarchy if it desired to do so'. In a mandated territory, however, the mandatory power's 'first duty' was to keep order, supplying the 'police, gaols and other things that were necessary'.[37] Their dismay at New Zealand's laxity is most illuminating, for Theodoli and Rappard were devoted to ideals of protection; both deplored South Africa's many violations of the principles of the 'sacred trust'. Yet, precisely because of, and not in spite of that dedication, they insisted that the mandatory power's authority must be upheld. The Samoans were to be governed in their best interest; if it was necessary for them to be locked up or held down to take their medicine, New Zealand should hold them down. Questions of self-determination were irrelevant, since inhabitants of the mandates had been defined by the Covenant as per se politically immature. Inevitably, the analogy of the schoolroom followed. 'The mandatory power was in the position of a tutor,' Rappard lectured. 'A tutor who did not punish his ward when the ward was obviously insubordinate . . . was a bad tutor; he was not doing his duty.'[38] Only Palacios questioned this paternalistic framework, drily pointing out that movements thought to be weak and artificial had an uncanny habit of suddenly triumphing, with individuals banished today coming to power tomorrow. The Mau movement might well be just such a genuine national movement, and it was surely contrary to everything for which the League stood for such a movement to be more harshly repressed by a mandatory power than it was by the United States in American Samoa next door.[39] His reservations were brushed aside, and in its report to the Council, drafted largely by Lugard and Rappard, the Commission blamed the unrest exclusively on the personal ambition and manipulative skill of Nelson and his associates, and deplored the fact that New Zealand had left Richardson with a 'lamentable absence of sufficient means to enforce the law'. Since New Zealand had now dispatched such means, the Commission felt certain that the Samoans would again place their trust in the mandatory power, which would re-establish peace and prosperity 'by a policy both firm and liberal'.[40]

This exhortation to 'firm government' would have, as we shall see, most unfortunate consequences, but the PMC did not stop there. The Commission also used their reports on the Samoan petitions to make clear their support for New Zealand's authority. Note, to begin with, the striking variation in their treatment of the different petitions. If one were to think of the mandates system as a mechanism for training peoples in self-government, one would certainly find the lengthy, detailed, and formal petition from the 8,000 Samoans claiming membership in the Mau much the most important. Carefully moderate in its language but adamant about Samoans' rights, the petition is a physical incarnation of that collective identity and political capacity on which successful nation-building depends. Not even Nelson's petition, thorough and persuasive as it was, is so impressive, and the Rowe and Anti-Slavery Society petitions—the former being a catalogue of personal accusations about specific administrators and the latter being queries into particular administrative acts—were much less important.

The Mandates Commission, however, exactly reversed that valuation. The protest of the Anti-Slavery Society was treated most seriously. In one of his more ham-fisted acts, Richardson had induced a schoolmaster to compose a 'catechism' for schools that explained that the League of Nations had been set up to promote international cooperation, that it had no authority in the mandate territories, and that any complaints would simply be sent back to the country from whence they came. Such claims, the Anti-Slavery Society wrote to the Commission, were 'inaccurate and misleading' and if upheld would 'deprive the natives of mandated territories of a recognized right'.[41] The Commission, always vigilant about formal rules, agreed, but the New Zealand government adroitly backpedalled, disclaiming all

knowledge of the circular and assuring the League they felt 'bound to forward . . . any petition that may be received'.[42] Quite content with this formal
acknowledgement of its authority, the Commission reported that the catechism was 'not an official circular but a document used by a European
schoolmaster for the information of his pupils'—a description that entirely
suppressed Richardson's instigating role—and stated that New Zealand had
promised 'to give full and proper knowledge to the inhabitants of Western
Samoa of their recognised rights'.[43] Just how that 'full knowledge' was to be
transmitted to the misled schoolchildren, given that Samoan schools were
under boycott, was left unclear.

The PMC's consideration of the Anti-Slavery Society petition thus
served above all to assert the League's own authority and to repair relations
between the Commission and the mandatory power. Also notable was the
courtesy with which the petitioners—the well-connected humanitarians of
the Anti-Slavery Society—were treated. Very different was the response
accorded both the former official Newton Rowe and the Mau leader Olaf
Nelson. Even in the League Secretariat, the Rowe petition—which named
names of allegedly incompetent or corrupt officials, and fingered one (who
had subsequently committed suicide) as a paedophile who preyed on
Samoan boys—was considered so inflammatory that Sir Eric Drummond
considered suppressing parts of it.[44] When the petition went forward, the
New Zealand government extracted a voluminous report from Richardson
answering every single charge and besmirching Rowe's own name.[45] Those
efforts paid off, for the puritanical Lugard felt 'it was beneath the dignity of
the Commission to examine in detail a petition of this nature' and persuaded the PMC to issue only a brief and dismissive report. A year later the
Commission would be embarrassed to learn that an inquiry by three senior
New Zealand civil servants had found the Samoan administration a nest of
incompetence, corruption, and extravagance, but for Rowe the damage had
been done.[46] Libelled in the Commission's published minutes as a man of
doubtful morality, 'dismissed from his office on account of incapacity', he
must have been sorry he had ever contacted the PMC. League files show
him, in 1928, collecting affidavits about his work and character in a fruitless
effort to clear his name.[47]

Rowe's petition was at least taken seriously. Nelson was denied even that
backhanded compliment. Lugard was not the only member to reveal a vis-
ceral dislike for the disturbingly cosmopolitan and modern persona this
educated 'half-caste' projected, or to find his lawyerly submissions (not to

mention his ability to put up at Geneva's most expensive hotel) an offence against the natural order. Certainly the Commission did all it could to put Nelson in his place. Not only was his petition—which combined a meticulous catalogue of Richardson's repressive acts with an appeal to 'great ideals of freedom and justice' for which the British flag stood[48]—dismissed virtually without discussion, but the Commission also impugned his motives and smeared his name. Nelson, Rappard insisted, 'had deliberately and almost treacherously stirred up native discontent'; the Commission should thus approve his deportation and 'do what it could to deprive him of the prestige which he had apparently enjoyed'.[49] Lugard entirely agreed. Nelson and his associates were 'inspired less by a desire for the public welfare than by personal ambition and interests'; they had '[b]y unworthy means... worked upon the minds of an impressionable and fickle people who prior to their propaganda were contented and prosperous'.[50] This vindictive and personal language survived into the Commission's published report. Only Palacios abstained.[51]

But if Rowe and Nelson were both subjected to character assassination, no response could have been as dismissive as that accorded the Samoan petition. That petition directly challenged the racial presumptions and undemocratic nature of New Zealand's rule, protesting the treatment of Samoans 'as a subjugated race' and the concentration of power in the Administrator's hands. Richardson's autocratic acts were carefully enumerated. He had suppressed cherished customs, appropriated the right to appoint the hitherto-elected *Faipules*, abolished some chiefly titles, individualized collectively owned land, perverted the rarely used custom of banishment into a tool with which to punish political dissenters, and, most offensively, attributed their protests entirely to European instigation. That latter claim, the petition insisted, was 'an insult to your Petitioners' and to their 'justifiable and creditable national aspirations'.[52] Yet, on the questionable authority of Richardson, the New Zealand government repeated that insult, insisting that the petition had been 'instigated and carried to completion by persons other than natives' and especially by the Mau's solicitor Thomas Slipper, who paid for his part in the matter by a sedition trial shortly afterwards. The 8,000 signatures were dismissed with the claim that it was 'a recognized fact that numerous signatures of Samoans may readily be obtained to petitions on almost any subject', and the Mandates Commission most shamefully colluded in that devaluation by referring to the signatories merely as 'certain natives'—a formulation that suggested a minor communication from a few disgruntled persons (three perhaps, or five), not a plea from virtually the entire male population of the territory.[53] In a brief report on the petitions from Nelson and 'certain natives' together, the Commission stated that none of the charges had been substantiated and that the petitions contained 'no evidence of policy or action contrary to the mandate'.[54] In a sense, of course, that was right. The Samoans' principal complaint was that they were being governed autocratically and wished to govern themselves, but since they were defined by the Covenant as not yet capable of self-government their complaint fell outside the Commission's jurisdiction. Alien administration was the essence, and not a violation, of the mandates system. It was the claim to capacity that was inadmissible.

## Punishing the disobedient ward

The Mandates Commission's dismissal of Samoan grievances was based on three assumptions, all firmly defended by Richardson: first, that Samoans' involvement in the Mau was based on their suggestible and wilful character and if deprived of Nelson's leadership would vanish overnight; second, that Nelson was seeking power and personal gain and had no deep convictions; and third, that the Administration could, by a policy of 'firmness', defeat the protest movement. Over the course of the next few years, to the bewilderment of the Mandates Commission and the New Zealand government, every single one of those assumptions was proven wrong.

First, the removal of Nelson did nothing to weaken the Mau. To the contrary, it simply shifted leadership of a movement hitherto heavily dependent on his support into chiefly Samoan hands. The boycott of official services and of personal contact with the Administrator continued, and the Mau took over much of the running of the local economy. Perhaps 80 per cent of taxes went unpaid (or were, sometimes, paid to the Mau); the Mau also kept the copra trade going and set up its own police force to maintain good order at demonstrations and in the towns. Although the Mau committee kept in close touch with the exiled Nelson, leadership passed to important titled Samoans, especially Tupua Tamasese Lealofi III (he of the hibiscus hedge fame) and Tuimaleali'ifano Si'u, who as an appointed government advisor had initially held aloof from the movement but who later became a prominent supporter. At the end of 1929 the Mau chiefs again petitioned the League; once again, their petition was dismissed as groundless. The

administration in Samoa, at a loss about how to deal with a movement that
behaved as if it simply didn't exist, had no choice but to abolish the Fono of
Faipules, which had lost its representative character and hence its credibility.
It also replaced the uncollectible poll tax with an export duty on copra—a
move that further alienated the European community, on whose businesses
that duty would fall.[55]

Nor were the Commission's assumptions about Nelson borne out.
Castigated as a power-hungry schemer eager only to build up his financial
holdings, Nelson endured two consecutive periods of exile, compromised
and nearly bankrupted his business, and spent much of his personal fortune
supporting the Mau. In exile with his daughters in Auckland from 1928, he
founded the 'New Zealand Samoa Defence League', which drew support
from local clergymen and university professors, wrote yet more pamphlets
(including one accurately entitled *Samoa at Geneva: Misleading the League of
Nations*), appealed to the Privy Council against his second deportation, and
continued to petition the League.[56] Those later petitions were written with
few illusions about their likely reception (and they were, indeed, dismissed)[57]
but with a sharp awareness of their propaganda value. Intelligently, but probably also out of his profound sense of disappointment with his treatment
under European law, Nelson also began sometimes writing under his
Samoan title of 'Taisi' rather than his paternal name.[58] In this sense as in so
many, he was a harbinger of a world to come. To this point, most Samoans
of mixed parentage had identified as 'Europeans', a status that allowed them
to hold land, contract individually, and vote for Legislative Council representatives. But as the Mau grew in strength, a trickle—and in the 1950s it
became more than a trickle—renounced that 'European' status to be classed
officially as 'natives'. A good number of independent Samoa's political leaders have had some family tie to that once-'European' population and not a
few to Nelson.[59]

Of all the Commission's assumptions, however, none proved as groundless, or had such damaging consequences, as its claim that New Zealand
could, with 'firm government', defeat the Mau. This claim, of course, rested
on the perception that the Samoans were children, certain to respond to the
wise but firm hand. Whenever Rappard or the Norwegian school director
Valentine Dannevig (the Commission's sole woman member) spoke, the
analogy of the schoolroom surfaced.[60] Indeed, the incomprehension and at
times anger expressed by virtually all members of the Commission (save
Palacios) when the Mau failed to learn their lesson is striking testimony to

how profoundly 'civilizational' and racial assumptions structured their thought. Revealing, too, is the fact that the mandates system's most stalwart British supporters—John Harris at the Anti-Slavery Society, A. J. Toynbee at Chatham House, Lugard's friend and protégée Margery Perham at Oxford— entirely shared that bafflement.[61] Perham, indeed, found the conflict so incomprehensible that she decided to investigate it for herself, spending three weeks in Samoa as part of a Pacific tour in the summer of 1929. She did not like what she found. The 'natives'—all clad in the blue and white Mau colours—were 'near insolent', Richardson's successor Colonel Allen was 'detached', 'prim', and 'without a genuine, human liking for his people', his officials were 'men without culture ... with no inkling of their own igno-rance about native administration', and Nelson (whom she met in Auckland) was a pitiable anomaly whose 'half-blood' had given him aspirations 'beyond his skill and character'.[62] Hierarchies of race and status, in other words, had become disordered. The upstart New Zealanders were clearly 'unfitted ... to undertake the supremely delicate task of educating a primitive people', but that the 'difficult' Samoans needed such tutelage was (to her) obvious as well.[63] Predictably, she could only wish vainly that 'the expert, England' could add this little venture to her 'great work' of imperial government.[64] Perham's mentor Lugard agreed, and he deeply offended New Zealand rep-resentatives over the next few years by urging them to hire Englishmen.[65]

New Zealand, however, had always insisted its experience with the Maoris and the Cook Islands made it especially suited to govern Western Samoa. It was left to the new Administrator, Colonel Allen, to demonstrate that capacity. Determined, like Richardson, to assert his authority and pos-sessed (unlike Richardson) of the means to do so, in December of 1929 Allen decided to use the opportunity of a Mau demonstration to seize a number of supporters who had been charged with non-payment of taxes or other offences. An armed group of military police was sent to make the arrests on 28 December; they were met by a large demonstration of Mau; a scuffle ensued; and in the resulting fracas the police opened fire. One police-man and eleven Samoans died, including Tamasese, at that point the Mau's most prominent leader. A coroner's report predictably cleared the police of deliberate murder and explained the chief's death as an unfortunate acci-dent, but since he had been wearing distinctive dress and was shot while trying to quell the crowd, no Samoan believed it. 'Black Saturday' is Samoa's equivalent of the 1919 Amritsar Massacre (Figure 6.3). The grave of Tamasese became a site of pilgrimage and commemoration.[66]

**Figure 6.3** The lying in state of Tamasese, 29 December 1929.

The Cabinet in Wellington, rattled by the deaths, agreed that Allen must be backed up. Any reinforcements he needed would be sent, and law and order maintained 'by whatever means might be found necessary'.[67] As Gilchrist and Drummond would have hoped, however, the government also looked to the League for legitimation. Immediately after the incident, New Zealand's Prime Minister Joseph Ward telegraphed the Secretary General with a (highly selective) official account; at his request, that telegram was circulated to the full League Council. Subsequent telegrams assured the Council of New Zealand's intention 'to stamp out the whole subversive movement' and passed along the coroner's verdict that the police actions on 28 December had been 'reasonable and proper'.[68] At this critical moment, Wellington was happy to enlist the League in its effort to stabilize its rule.

Over the next few years, with Wellington's anxious backing and the tolerance of the League, Allen and his successor pursued his policy of firmness. The Mau was outlawed as a seditious organization, and its members were harassed and arrested (Figure 6.4). Male supporters went into hiding and a 'women's Mau' emerged—by no means the only instance in which the

**Figure 6.4** Sailors removing Mau insignia from lava-lavas.

League inadvertently fostered a specifically female militancy (Figure 6.5). That women's mobilization became transnational too, for Allen's dismissal of its members as 'many old women and all known prostitutes' aroused the sympathetic outrage of the Auckland chapter of the Women's International League for Peace and Freedom and generated a petition of its own.[69] University professors and clergymen in Auckland sent petitions as well, and the New Zealand Labour Party publicly dissociated itself from Allen's harsh stance.[70] The Mau, disappointed in the League but not inclined to abandon petitioning (which had such a nice affinity with Samoan deliberative practices), appealed to the British Foreign Secretary, the German Chancellor, and the American Secretary of State for reversion to the autonomy enjoyed under the settlements of 1889 and 1899.[71] All of these communications were duly noted in Geneva (as well as in London, Berlin and Washington)[72], but none elicited any action. As Mary Sheepshanks of the Women's International League wrote to Rappard in some frustration, there appeared to be no way to get the Samoans' case heard.[73] And apart from a flurry of activity following Nelson's first return from exile in 1933 (he was swiftly rearrested, tried, and again deported), the islands were quiet. Allen and his successor, sending their dispatches to Wellington, insisted that the Mau was beaten.

They were deluded. When the Labour Party won the 1935 election in New Zealand and dispatched a 'goodwill mission' to Samoa, it became clear that the Mau had permeated—indeed to a considerable extent was—the

**Figure 6.5** Leaders and the committee of the Women's Mau, 1930. Seated on chairs, left to right, Mrs Tuimaliifano, Mrs Tamasese, Mrs Nelson, and Mrs Fauimuina.

local government. On the advice of that mission, the Mau's immediate demands were met. Legislation allowing the Administrator to banish offenders and cancel Samoan titles was repealed; restrictions on free movement were lifted; arrears in tax payments were cancelled; Nelson's second sentence was revoked and he returned to an official welcome. The Mau was recognized, and the government promised—as the Mau had requested in that petition of 1928—to restore the representative character of the Fono of Faipules, to submit all spending plans to review by the legislative council, and to publish all financial accounts in Samoan. Henceforth, Samoa would be governed in partnership with the Mau.[74]

In Geneva the majority of the Mandates Commission viewed with consternation this last twist in New Zealand's policy. Once again, they had been caught wrong-footed. After all, just the previous year, Parr had assured them that the Mau was 'moribund' and that there was no 'real Samoan desire for self-government'.[75] Now C. A. Berendsen, the new accredited representative, informed them that the government considered Nelson a wronged man and the Mau a legitimate and fully representative movement. Except for Palacios, who did not scruple to tell his fellows that this was what he had been saying all along, the members flatly refused to believe it. Themselves utterly implicated in efforts to attribute the movement to the Samoans' 'childlike' character and Nelson's unscrupulous manipulation, not to mention Allen's application of 'firm government', most thought the new policy driven only by the short-sighted political calculations of the new left-wing government in Wellington.[76] In their report to the Council in November 1936, they 'reserved judgement' about Labour's actions—although anyone reading through the minutes could sense their deep disapproval. By this point, however, the Council had much larger matters on its mind, and neither the New Zealand government nor the Mau felt much inclined to listen to them.

★ ★ ★

The mandates system was founded under the sign of self-determination. Although the populations to which it was applied were, so Article 22 went, 'not yet ready to stand by themselves under the strenuous conditions of the modern world', Wilsonian rhetoric, wartime promises, and the Covenant implied they would someday do so. Syria and Western Samoa witnessed the two best-organized movements for self-determination in any mandated territory in the 1920s, but other communities also took this language seriously. Petitions languishing in the League archives show how, at particular moments of distress or crisis, Duala in Cameroon, Ewe in Togo, Kurds in Iraq, the Rehoboth Basters in South West Africa, and all manner of communities in Palestine declared their faith in Wilsonian ideals, their collective purpose and capacity, and their readiness to start down the road to self-rule.

The mandatory powers were supposed to help them embark on that journey. As the cases discussed here make clear, however, they more often acted as border guards or brakesmen, and their ostensible charges often felt they were going the wrong way. Arabs, Africans, and Pacific Islanders alike complained that they had if anything less scope for political expression than under the Germans or Ottomans, for—as Jacobus Christian, 'Abd al-Rahman Shahbandar, or Olaf Nelson could all attest—mandate officials were quick to replace or exile local leaders who took an independent line. In every mandated territory save Iraq during these years, nationalist movements were forced on the defensive.

The Mandates Commission played a crucial part in that work of containment. Although South Africa, France, and New Zealand all complained bitterly about the Commission's meddling, in all three cases League scrutiny offered those powers a means of rehabilitation. South Africa mostly failed to capitalize on those opportunities, but both France and New Zealand were able to justify repressive acts through the language of tutelage, with authorities explaining that they were protecting their 'primitive' or still-childish charges from the evil influences of agitators or the consequences of their own immaturity.

The first half-dozen years of the mandates system were thus a period of considerable ideological creativity and shift, as the 'civilizational' and often overtly racial framework of trusteeship elbowed 'self-determination' off the liberal-international stage. They were also years of intense political learning, not only for local petitioners but also for the mandatory powers themselves. For many reasons, including that the system had been crafted with British colonial practices in mind and that Britain's most respected colonial authority was the Commission's dominant member, Britain was the system's star pupil. Yet Britain also had the good fortune to have faced its most serious rebellion in a mandated territory (that is, in Iraq) before oversight began; in the mid-1920s the British territories were fairly quiet. A dozen years later, having chafed under Lugard's obvious disapproval, French officials would enjoy watching British ministers squirm under the Commission's sharp criticism of their handling of the Arab Revolt in Palestine.

Long before then, however, Britain's easy hegemony over this international regime had come to an end. The reason for that was simple. In 1926 Germany entered the League. Henceforth, the Commission would have to do more than urge mandatory powers to adhere to humanitarian norms; it would have to see whether the regime could be made at least minimally acceptable to its main (and still unreconciled) loser. In 1919 the allied powers had turned to internationalism to give their empires a new lease on life; Germany, however, wanted to use that internationalism to reclaim a global role. Germany would challenge the mandatory powers to make international control real.

# PART
# III

# New Times,
# New Norms, 1927–33

# Preface: Enter the Germans

Whatever their quarrels, the mandatory powers could agree on one thing: there must be no German on the Mandates Commission. France felt strongly on this point, the French ambassador in Brussels told the Belgian Foreign Minister Paul Hymans in September of 1924, for how could any German exercise the 'entire impartiality' needed for the role?[1] The Belgian government concurred, but thought it might be best not to raise the question openly in the League Council, since a discussion based on principle might favour the German case.[2] For the moment, they would hold their fire.

They had reason to be worried, for Germany was seeking to join the League. After watching the economic chaos unleashed by the French occupation of the Ruhr and the subsequent inflation, Foreign Minister Gustav Stresemann had concluded that Germany would only rebuild its economy and recover its international standing if it shed its pariah status. He knew, however, that entry into the 'victors' club' was far from popular among the right-wing parties still chafing at Germany's shrunken borders and vanished empire. The German note of 29 September 1924 clarifying the conditions and reservations governing Germany's application stipulated that it expected to play a part in the work of administering mandates.[3] During the Locarno negotiations in autumn 1925, Stresemann repeated Germany's claim.

How serious was Stresemann's colonial revisionism? There is some evidence that he was trying to play both sides of the fence. When told by British Foreign Secretary Austen Chamberlain and French Foreign Minister Aristide Briand that no mandatory power was inclined to resign their mandates and that the best Germany could do was to offer its services should one become available (roughly what the British tended to tell Italy), Stresemann seemed unperturbed. He dismissed British and French anxieties about the ferocity of German colonial propaganda, explaining that it was prudent to let extremists 'let off steam'.[4] Certainly he had plenty of 'steam' to contend with, for the 30,000-strong German Colonial Association, led by the vociferous Heinrich Schnee and the only slightly less vociferous Theodor Seitz (former governors of German East Africa and German South West Africa, respectively) thought Germany should use the moment of League entry to insist on a new division of the pie. In a barrage of pamphlets, news-paper articles, public meetings, Reichstag debates, and even petitions to the League, they and their supporters protested Germany's expulsion from the imperial club, contested claims of German colonial atrocities (or what they called the 'Kolonialschuldlüge'), painted dire portraits of the neglect of Germany's former territories under mandatory administration, and urged that some territorial transfer be made the condition of Germany's entry into the League.[5]

The Foreign Ministry had the good sense to ignore much of this noise. 'The demand that Germany should make its entry into the League condi-tional on receiving mandates is really not to be taken seriously and unreal-izable anyway,' wrote Bernhard Wilhelm von Bülow, head of the Ministry's League of Nations section, adding grumpily that the government, and not the Colonial Association, set Germany's foreign policy.[6] Yet if the manda-tory powers had been able to listen in on the discussions going on in the Wilhelmstrasse, they would not have been reassured. The colonial lobby wanted their territories back, but the Foreign Ministry's goal was rather different: to rebuild Germany's position as a great power in a globalizing world. In the past, colonies had been essential to that effort, but if colonial restitution was not possible, they would find another path. Between 1924 and 1926, sometimes in consultation with the ex-colonial governors but also without them, officials hammered out their strategy.

That strategy was based, in the first instance, on the intelligent and dev-astatingly pragmatic assessment of Germany's colonial opportunities pro-duced by Edmund von Brückner, former Governor of Togo and from 1924 until 1935 head of the Ministry's Colonial Department. Brückner thought any return of German territory most unlikely. The Pacific mandates were certainly gone for good, for the Japanese were sending large numbers of settlers into their mandated islands, while New Zealand and Australia viewed their territories as buffers against the Japanese threat to the north. Nor were African prospects very bright, as Britain had always craved Tanganyika in order to complete its Cape-to-Cairo domination, and South Africa had always hoped to absorb the German and British protectorates to the north. True, Britain might like to have the Germans back in West Africa (at least as a buffer against the French), but its slices of Cameroon and Togo were too small to be much use without the much larger French portions, and the French (not to mention the Belgians) were never going to return anything.

But for all that, Brückner was not unhopeful. Even before Germany joined the League, he had been able to engineer repurchase of almost all the German plantations in Britain's sector of Cameroon and by 1925 was setting up a development company to underwrite similar acquisitions in Tanganyika.[7] Moreover, once in the League and entitled to do business in the mandated territories under the principle of the 'open door', Germany might well be able 'in short order to so economically penetrate [durchdringen] our unreturned former protectorates... that their later return to Germany would not be out of the question'.[8] In South West Africa too, Germany could support the existing German minority with further immigrants and economic aid, so that the territory would become, even under South African protection, 'an essentially German land'.[9]

Theodor Seitz, President of the Colonial Association, then weighed in, and to the Foreign Ministry's surprise, was also more pragmatic than expected. True, he set great store by the propaganda that was causing the Ministry so much trouble and was less sanguine than Brückner about the benefits of League membership, pointing out that Britain allowed German trade in their territories anyway, while France would certainly—whatever the obligations of the 'open door'—find some way to keep the Germans out. Yet Seitz too found grounds for optimism, especially in the outspoken discontent with French rule in Togo. Remarkably, he thought that Germany should support those African aspirations for self-government—for surely the Togolese could govern themselves as well as the Liberians, and, if granted autonomy, would turn to Germany for economic and political guidance. In South West Africa too, Germany could send immigrants to strengthen white rule and, over time, seek to move the territory towards greater independence. By supporting the principle of self-determination, in other words, rather than simply claiming a share of the colonial pie, Germany could regain its influence over its lost colonies.[10]

Brückner's and Seitz's memoranda made the rounds in the Foreign Ministry, leaving a trail of commentary in their wake.[11] Not all of Seitz's assessments were thought well founded, but officials appreciated his realism about the likelihood of any territorial transfers and both men's insistence on the need for an aggressive economic policy. Most also agreed that Germany's road to global power lay through Geneva. As the only great power on the Council without an empire, it was in Germany's interest to insist that putative League norms promoting equal economic access and limiting imperial sovereignty be made ever more stringent and real. If the benefits of territorial control were limited, Germany's disadvantages would diminish. After years of frustrated criticism from without, Germany must become the most vigilant guardian of the mandates system.

During Germany's years of League membership, its officials would adopt a four-part imperial strategy. First, they would unhesitatingly defend Germany's colonial claims and colonial record, at no point admitting publicly that its colonies were gone for good. Second, they would support German participation in the scientific, technical, public health, and cultural efforts undertaken by the League in the colonial arena, in order to rebuild Germany's reputation as a leader in these fields. Third and most critically, they would work hard, taking advantage of the League's 'open door' requirements and in concert with trading interests, to reclaim Germany's strong position in East and West Africa and would try to force open the New Guinea market as well. Finally and equally importantly, they would combat tooth and nail any moves on the part of the mandatory powers to bind the mandated territories more closely to their colonial empires, insisting on their status as autonomous territories under collective League control and slated ultimately for independence.

To carry out these goals, however, Germany had to be firmly within the League—and especially within the Mandates Commission. Having watched the Commission at work, and especially the roasting given the French during the special session on Syria, the Wilhelmstrasse had concluded that the Commission was the key to the whole system. The Council was too busy, and the Assembly simply too big, to pay the mandates system much mind, but Commission members—and especially the 'neutrals' Theodoli, Rappard, and Van Rees—had shown themselves willing to turn over every rock and expose every flaw. League supervision, which Germany had dismissed as a cloak for annexation, was becoming real. The implication was obvious. 'If we wish to win some real influence over the oversight of mandatory administration, we must work from here on out to obtain a seat on the Permanent Mandates Commission.'[12]

In September 1926, at the annual assembly in Geneva, Germany was admitted to the League of Nations and immediately asked for a seat on the

PMC. That appeal was rebuffed, for France and Belgium were entirely opposed, and the Dominions—which themselves had no members—found the prospect of answering to a German repellent. But British opinion was already shifting. Germany was 'likely to be less dangerous if represented on the Mandates Commission than if excluded from all participation'; on balance, the Colonial Office was cautiously in favour.[13] Austen Chamberlain was not, but he did agree that the question should be decided in the way most likely to promote European conciliation.[14]

Sir Eric Drummond, caught as ever in the middle, tried to mediate. He understood how important this question was to the Germans.[15] Britain would be making a great mistake if it tried to postpone the addition of a German member, Drummond told William Ormsby-Gore (now Colonial Under-Secretary) in Geneva.[16] He then travelled to London to repeat his warnings to Chamberlain. Not only would it be easier for Stresemann to resist his extremists with a member on the PMC, Drummond argued, but he would also willingly compromise on the person appointed; a later German government might be less accommodating.[17] Chamberlain was unconvinced, but when the British ambassador in Berlin called at the Foreign Ministry to ask Germany not to pursue the question in light of the strong feelings of the Dominions, he was told in no uncertain terms how very unfriendly Germany thought that request.[18] Stresemann would postpone (briefly), but did not intend to back down.

In the spring, with pressure from the colonial lobby intensifying, German ambassadors in London, Paris, Brussels, and Tokyo were instructed to raise the matter again.[19] All but the Japanese government remained recalcitrant,[20] but Stresemann, now playing a major role in the League Council, promised to raise the question at the Council's June meeting (Figure III.1).[21] The prospect of a public altercation, Drummond's steady pressure, and Stresemann's private promise that the German member would not be an outspoken revisionist like Heinrich Schnee (whom the Foreign Ministry also found quite impossible), wore Austen Chamberlain down.[22] Under Drummond's subtle management, the issue was presented to the Council as a minor budgetary matter, with the Council merely asked to approve an appointment for which the Assembly had already voted funds. As a courtesy, the Commission was asked for its view, with Chamberlain expressing the hope 'that it would welcome the contemplated addition'. No one reading these bland minutes could have detected the passions roiling underneath.[23]

**Figure III.1** 44th session of the League Council, Stresemann presiding, March 1927. At the head of the table: Aristide Briand, Gustav Stresemann, Eric Drummond, and Austen Chamberlain.

But the French and the Belgians were furious, especially when Stresemann returned from Geneva to give a rousing Reichstag speech proclaiming victory.[24] The British attitude was 'incomprehensible, inexplicable,' Philippe Berthelot at the Quai d'Orsay told the Belgian ambassador. Chamberlain had opposed appointing a German; now he had reversed himself without letting anyone know his intentions in advance.[25] The Commission, which Drummond and indeed Theodoli had expected to welcome a German member, also proved touchy, for the French and Belgian representatives categorically refused to play along. They were a technical body and the matter was a political one, Pierre Orts insisted at their summer 1927 session; they could have nothing to say. When his colleagues disagreed—or, worse, suggested that a German might have something valuable to contribute— Orts said bluntly that Germany's colonial experience was, if anything, a disqualification. 'Was the eagerness which Germany showed to obtain a seat on the Commission due to any particular solicitude for the mandates system and to the wish to contribute to the maintenance of the colonial regime set up by the Treaty of Versailles?' Hardly, for the names it first proposed for membership—he had in mind Schnee—were precisely those 'who personified the German protest against the colonial machinery of which the Commission formed the main wheel'. If the Council wished to destroy the mandates system, that was their business. The Commission should refuse to comment and, for good measure, delete from the minutes 'all trace of this deplorable discussion'. Hours of persuasion by Rappard, Van Rees, and Palacios entirely failed to bring Orts and Merlin round, and the Commission could only record that, while the majority saw 'no technical objection to the appointment of a new member', a minority would express no view 'on account of the political character of the question'.[26]

Taking this for consent, the League Secretariat handled the tricky negotiation over whom to appoint to the job.[27] The man chosen, on Stresemann's recommendation, was Ludwig Kastl, forty-nine years old, a lawyer, and the salaried Managing Director of the National Federation of German Industries (Figure III.2). Kastl had enough colonial experience to qualify as an expert—he been Assistant Treasurer in the German South West Africa administration, remaining there until 1920 to handle negotiations with the occupying authorities over German property and interests—but he was essentially an industrial lobbyist and financial expert. He had headed the reparations section in the German Finance Ministry after the war and been involved in negotiating the Dawes Plan, and allied officials who worked

**Figure III.2** Ludwig Kastl.

with him found him pragmatic, businesslike, and astute.[28] When Kastl
stepped down in 1930, unable any longer to leave his work at the Federation
for the two annual sessions, another man rather like him—Julius Ruppel,
who had served before the war in the Cameroon administration but who
spent six years after 1924 at the Reparations Commission—seamlessly
replaced him.[29] Revealingly, a secretary from the Federation of German
Industries handled both men's correspondence with the League Secretariat.

Kastl's appointment was not popular with the colonial lobby.[30] They had
wanted to balance Lugard with one of their own ex-governors and had
particularly relished the prospect of Schnee facing the enemy head-on.
(Schnee had unabashedly lobbied for the appointment as well.)[31] The
Foreign Ministry, however, found Kastl excellent, and rightly so. Although
intensely busy, Kastl prepared scrupulously for each session, challenged any
aspersions on Germany's colonial record (the Governor of Tanganyika
should be given a hint to avoid such statements in the future, the British
Colonial Office noted),[32] fought to get German doctors into Rwanda and
German archaeologists into Iraq, scrutinized trade agreements and concessions to make sure they didn't exclude Germany or offend the principle of
the 'open door', and met regularly with Foreign Ministry officials and the
ex-governors in Berlin to coordinate responses to any annexationist moves.
Kastl's correct manner, entirely conventional views on 'native policy', and
air of impartiality shielded him from open attack. At the same time, as the
Foreign Ministry noted, his presence strengthened the hand of the
Commission's 'neutrals' and helped it move in a more critical and independent direction.[33] The divide between Britain and France began to look
less deep than that between the mandatory and the non-mandatory
powers—or even between the principles of imperial and international control. In the future, not only South African and French representatives, but
the British and Belgians as well, would be forced on the defensive.

We can thus see 1927 until 1933 as the mandate system's most innovative
period, the era when German entry, Italian revisionism, intense great-power
diplomacy, and deepening economic and political uncertainty blasted open
an institution that had hitherto operated very largely to reconcile and legitimate British and French geopolitical aims. Suddenly imperatives shifted, for
the mandates system needed now to win the support of imperial 'have-nots'
hitherto excluded from a share of the pie. Pressed by its German, Italian, and
'neutral' members, the Commission would move beyond Lugardian ideals
to attempt to enforce the two core principles on which the system had been

founded: that mandatory powers were not sovereign in the mandated territories, and that trade and labour must be 'free'. German consent in particular would turn on the degree to which the League could force acceptance
of these norms.

These efforts met with mixed success. As Chapter 7 shows, the PMC did
successfully combat Belgian, South African, and British annexationist moves,
forcing the Council to uphold the principle that the imperial powers were
*not sovereign* in the mandated territories. Or, to be precise, they were not legally
or politically sovereign; what we might call their economic sovereignty mush-
roomed unchecked. Indeed, as the case of interwar Rwanda—discussed in
Chapter 8—shows, intense international scrutiny led the Belgians if anything to
tighten economic control, as they passed off increasingly coercive and extractive
labour practices as 'native custom'. That decoupling of legal sovereignty and
economic control implicitly posed a question: what sort of 'independence'
might be envisaged for the mandated territories—and, implicitly, for colonies—anyway? As we see in Chapter 9, in 1929 Britain offered one answer
to that question. By seeking League recognition for Iraq as an 'independent'
state, even though Iraq's oilfields and airfields would remain largely under
British control, Britain sought to win international consent for a form of
independence that would safeguard geopolitical interests even after formal
empire was gone. In this protean period, under pressure from the revisionist
powers, we begin to glimpse some of the outlines of the world of normative
state sovereignty, even when accompanied by diminished state capacity, that
would emerge after 1945.

On 24 October 1927 Ludwig Kastl took his seat for the opening of the
twelfth session of the Mandates Commission. Since the 'deplorable discussion' of the summer had appeared in the printed minutes after all, Kastl
knew perfectly well how some of his new colleagues, especially Orts and
Merlin, felt about his presence. 'You are the first German I have spoken with
since 1914,' Orts told Kastl straightforwardly. 'It is a fortunate thing that I am
a good-natured man,' Kastl replied. 'I would recommend you to be careful
in future to whom you address such a remark.' Orts was studiously cordial
for the rest of the session.[34] It was a new world.

# SEVEN

## The Struggle over Sovereignty

Hide-bound as we are by the traditions of the sovereign state demanding from its citizens supreme and undivided dedication, the world does not yet realize the possibility of new forms of political organization...

George Louis Beer, *The English-Speaking Peoples*, ix[1]

No question raised by the mandates system was more disputed than that of sovereignty. The system purported to be an alternative and a barrier to annexation—that is, to deny the conquering powers full sovereignty—but neither the Covenant nor the crucial Hymans Report of August 1920 defining its character specified just where sovereignty then lay.[2] The problem wasn't simply that the legal question was complicated, although it was. It was also that the mandatory powers *preferred* to leave it unresolved. True, Britain and France acknowledged that they exercised but did not possess sovereignty in the Middle East, but no mandatory power said anything so unequivocal about the ex-German territories. Official statements ranged from aggressive to evasive to contradictory. Only South Africa would publicly claim sovereignty in South West Africa, but since at least some of the other mandatory powers also hoped to absorb the territories into their formal empire, they had no wish to explore legal impediments. Not even the British spoke with a single voice. Thus, while one junior official in the Lloyd George government confirmed publicly in 1922 that mandated territories were 'no...part of His Majesty's Dominions'[3] (a statement noted carefully by the German Foreign Ministry), A. J. Balfour that same year told the Council that mandates were only 'a self-imposed limitation by the conquerors on the sovereignty which they exercised over the conquered territory'—a far less restrictive formulation.[4] Until Germany entered the League, the Council did its best simply to avoid the question.

Absent political clarity, the jurists went to work. By 1930, when the University of Chicago Law Professor Quincy Wright published his classic study, *Mandates under the League of Nations*, he was able to claim that ten separate theories had been advanced. Most, he admitted, were variants or combinations of four claims: that sovereignty was held by the associated and allied powers, to whom Germany had surrendered its colonies; that it was held by the mandatory powers; that it was held by the League as the oversight body; and that it was held, albeit only in a latent form, by the population of the mandated territory itself. Different experts argued each of these views, with a noticeable correlation between national interest and legal reasoning. Thus, while many British and American scholars claimed that sovereignty was held by the allied and associated powers, sometimes in conjunction with the League (both of which they had dominated), French experts leaned towards the view that it was shared between the mandatory power and the mandated population. German and Austrian jurists usually preferred to argue for League sovereignty, the only formula under which Germany could aspire to a share in their rule. No one referred the question to the Permanent Court, so the theories could keep coming.[5]

Unlike the Council, the Mandates Commission could not avoid thinking through foundational questions, and by the mid-1920s had effectively agreed that, wherever sovereignty might lie, it was not with the mandatory powers. That a body composed largely of European ex-colonial officials of conservative views would come to take such a firm stand on this question needs some explaining, for the private convictions of some of them were anything but anti-imperial and in most cases hardly even internationalist. Orts, for example, had told Lugard in 1926 that although he would loyally do his best so long as he was on the PMC, he actually did not believe in the mandates system and thought the ex-German territories best annexed—and one can surmise that Martial Merlin felt the same.[6] Lugard too strongly dissented from Theodoli's oft-stated claim that the mandates system was something entirely new under international law, preferring to see it as merely the extension of British 'best practices'.[7] These were not men out to bring the European empires down.

Yet the Commission was constrained—even its most conservative members were constrained—by its deep textualism. It was charged to uphold the authority of the Covenant and the mandates; indeed, its own authority was rooted in those texts. When examining reports, petitions, and problems, the Commission thus turned to exegesis, always holding real-world information up against original intent. Slowly, a kind of case law evolved, as determinations were made on one sticky question after another. By ruling that the territories' inhabitants must be given a distinct national status, that the mandatory powers be obliged to keep entirely separate territorial accounts, and, especially, that the mandatory power could not claim ownership of the land, slowly but surely the Commission elaborated a distinct and separate status for mandates under international law. And one man pushed that argument further—the Commission's Dutch member, Daniel François Willem Van Rees.

Pedantic, socially inept, and with apparently few other obligations or ties, Van Rees was by some distance the Commission's wordiest, and also most hard-working, member. Many of his fellows complained about the amount of work and travel the Commission required. Not Van Rees. When appointed in 1921, he promptly rented rooms in nearby Montreux, telling Rappard at the Secretariat that he intended to devote a good deal of time to his new duties.[8] When the PMC divided up responsibility for various special topics at their early sessions, Van Rees eagerly took on the most complex topics— general administration, land law—and, unlike some of his fellows, spent what were clearly for him many happy hours poring over legal texts and writing long and intricate memoranda in his almost illegible hand.[9] It was Van Rees who insisted that Rappard begin compiling monthly dossiers of important articles about the mandates and sending them to all members (don't bother to send them to me, said Merlin),[10] and Van Rees who rebutted any challenge to the PMC's authority. Van Rees treated the staff of the Mandates Section like personal secretaries, constantly ringing them up to ask for particular documents. He thought nothing of taking up whole hours of the Commission's time with his reports, and browbeat his fellows into approving them.[11] He was a great nuisance and no doubt a great bore, but no one did more to establish the principle that mandatory powers were 'not sovereign' in the mandated territories.

Internationalist convictions had little to do with his persistence. Van Rees was a card-carrying 'colonial', born in Indonesia, son of a Governor General of the Dutch East Indies, and in that service himself until his retirement in 1914. Indeed, the fact that he was so transparently unsympathetic to self-determination, and so distant from great-power machinations, lent his ruminations added weight. Lugard, for example, thought Theodoli a manipulative schemer out only for Italian interests (not entirely without reason) but considered Van Rees trustworthy and impartial, recommending the Dutchman's two-volume study completed in 1928 as the authoritative text on mandate law.[12] And Van Rees, after reading through various legal opinions and the relevant articles of the Treaty of Versailles, had already concluded by December 1922, when he wrote that first crucial memorandum on the legal status of the transferred territories' lands, that mandatory powers were not sovereign. They possessed only a trustee's right, the right of administration.[13] Van Rees did not claim that sovereignty rested with the League, 'a thorny question, on which opinions will always differ',[14] but insisted that the passages in the Versailles Treaty stipulating that the property of each territory 'shall pass' to a designated mandatory power 'in its capacity *as such*' (that is, *as mandatory*) could only be understood to mean that the territory was being transferred not into the mandatory power's sovereignty but into its trust.[15] The following year, the Commission approved this argument—and, importantly, asked the mandatory powers to amend any land legislation that claimed sovereignty.[16] Britain and France were willing to concur, but by 1925 Belgium, Japan, Australia, South Africa, and New Zealand (all but the last of which intended to settle their nationals in the territory) had not responded to the PMC's request.[17] Van Rees may have been too politically naive to realize it, but he had put the PMC on a collision course with the mandatory powers.

It was at this moment that Germany sought entry into the League. Inevitably, that prospect revived the annexationist desires of the allied powers. Precedent and legalism, quite as much as conviction, would drive the PMC to resist those developments, and the openness created by German entry strengthened its ability to do so. Between 1925 and 1931, the Commission confronted three annexationist challenges—a Belgian law tying Rwanda and Burundi more tightly to its colony of Congo, a direct South African claim of sovereignty over South West Africa, and British plans to federate Tanganyika with its neighbouring colonies of Kenya and Uganda—as well as a public, coordinated, and premeditated attack, led by Britain, on its authority. That the Commission emerged from this time of trial more united, and with the norm of non-sovereignty strengthened, is due to a confluence of factors, not least the tenacity of D. F. W. Van Rees.

## The Belgian law of 21 August 1925

Belgium's hold on its mandated territories was weak. Perhaps for that reason, it was particularly touchy about its rights. In 1917 Pierre Orts made clear that Belgium wished to hold any territories granted to it in full sovereignty, and the Colonial Ministry only reluctantly conceded their inhabitants should not be considered Belgian subjects. Recall, too, how Belgium took advantage of early uncertainty over the fate of the mandates system to insert that clause allowing them to bring Rwanda and Burundi into an administrative union with neighbouring colonial possessions.[18] In 1924, when the mandate was finally fully in effect, officials in Brussels and Usumbura moved swiftly to strengthen their hold.

Fear of German demands and mistrust of the British drove them. The Belgian Foreign Ministry monitored the German press closely and in late 1924 concluded that the colonial lobby's agitations were having some effect. Even before 1914 Britain had been inclined to try to appease Germany at the expense of smaller states (especially Portugal); ten years later the argument that a nation of 60 million needed outlets for its population and its products was again winning sympathetic ears. 'Little by little, across the world,' warned one civil servant, 'opinion was growing favourable to German colonial aspirations.'[19] In Usumbura, Alfred Marzorati, Belgium's Royal Commissioner for Rwanda and Burundi, grew worried. The two territories had much to offer Belgian Congo—a supplementary food supply, labour for the Katanga mines—but the press seemed to think their return to Germany imminent. Everything possible should be done to incorporate the territories into Belgian Congo, Marzorati advised, but if their retrocession was inevitable, at least care should be taken to ensure acceptable boundaries.[20]

The Colonial Minister wrote quickly to check Marzorati's defeatism. Under no circumstances would Belgium renounce the mandate.[21] Halewyck de Heusch, Director General at the Colonial Ministry and the man who represented Belgium before the PMC during the whole of its existence, got to work on a lasting solution. At his urging, the Belgian Colonial Minister asked Marzorati and the Governor General of the Congo to consider amalgamating their administrations. Did it really make sense to maintain a separate regime in the small and relatively under-developed mandated territories when they could take advantage of the existing legislation, institutions, and experience possessed by Belgian Congo?[22]

Marzorati found this a fine idea. Much was to be done in the new territories: the penal system was in bad shape, education was rudimentary, public works were minimal, and authority over the native population was weak. The administration had the personnel and resources it needed to keep the peace, but to really 'impregnate its population with our work of civilization'

THE STRUGGLE OVER SOVEREIGNTY          209

it would need to build up its economic capacity. Administrative union was essential, for the territory could then be 'settled by our nationals and so saturated by Belgian capital and business as to be effectively welded to the Congo'.[23] Halewyck agreed entirely, so much so that when Pierre Ryckmans, Royal Commissioner in Burundi (and Marzorati's direct subordinate), questioned the benefits of the plan, he was told firmly to shut up. Belgium needed to bind the mandated territories to Congo in light of Germany's return to the European stage, but it would be dangerous to divulge those reasons in public.[24] In early 1925 the Belgian government thus introduced legislation placing the territories under the Congo administration. The Royal Commissioner of Rwanda and Burundi would henceforth be a provincial Governor answerable to the Governor General of the Congo.

Germany interpreted these moves, rightly, as a step towards annexation. On 28 March 1925 its Foreign Ministry sent a protest to the Belgian government alleging that the proposed law violated Article 22 of the Covenant, and hence the Treaty of Versailles, of which Germany was a signatory.[25] The Belgian government refused to receive the communication. Having surrendered its colonies to the allied powers, the Belgian Foreign Minister Paul Hymans told the German ambassador in a blistering dressing down, Germany had no right even to open such a discussion.[26] Humiliated, the German ambassador withdrew the protest,[27] and the Belgian government rushed the new law through parliament—only to discover, two months later, that Germany had not been silenced. It had just redirected its complaints to Geneva.

Dispatched on the eve of the Locarno Conference (a sensitive moment, when all parties were eager to appear conciliatory), the German note of 16 September 1925 was carefully calibrated to the sensitivities and concerns of the Mandates Commission. No mention was made of Germany's colonial claims; instead, the note stressed the Belgian law's incompatibility with the Covenant. Rwanda-Burundi would cease to be 'a *person* in the sense of international law' and become a mere province, the note charged, and its inhabitants would effectively become Belgian subjects. True, the mandate itself allowed administrative federation, but the proposed law went much further, subsuming the mandated territory within a much larger colonial possession. The League, Germany stated, must protect the mandates regime from legal moves 'which suggest covert annexation'.[28] Drummond duly circulated the German note to all members of the Council—but then, when Belgium protested that Germany had no *locus standi* in the matter, promised that the PMC would not discuss it without the Council's request.[29]

The Mandates Commission, still without a German member, thus found itself on sensitive ground. It was scheduled to review Belgium's report on Rwanda and Burundi at its seventh session, which had just opened on 19 October 1925 in Geneva. Its members were well aware of the controversy over the new Belgian law. Yet the Council had not asked the Commission to review the German note, and the Belgians themselves insisted it was inadmissible. Thus, while the PMC could question the Belgian representative about the new law, members—with the exception of the Italian Theodoli, who usually felt free to say whatever he liked—felt constrained to avoid mentioning German contentions.

Yet the German charge that Belgium was attempting a 'veiled annexation' dominated the discussion anyway, with the Commission raking over every questionable phrase in the law. In order to explain these away, Halewyck de Heusch conceded point after point. Belgium had no intention of annexing these territories; it would preserve their distinct 'legal personality'; it did not consider their inhabitants to be Belgian subjects; it would keep entirely separate financial accounts and legislative records; it would transmit those to the PMC. The League's diligent stenographers recorded every pledge, and the Commission told the Council that those assurances must now be regarded 'as an authorized interpretation of the [law's] text'.[30] Sweden's Foreign Minister Östen Undén then read Halewyck's promises into the record at the next Council session, concluding that they had dissipated fears of a 'possible covert annexation'.[31] Everyone in the room understood that Belgium did wish to annex the territories but had been outwitted.

Pressed by the PMC, the Council thus forced Belgium to concede that mandated territories had a distinct status under international law. The German Foreign Ministry, kept informed of the Commission's private discussions by their Consul in Geneva (a man clearly with cooperative friends in the League secretarial pool), could congratulate itself on its success.[32] Impressed by the conscientiousness and independence of the Commission, it grew more determined to add a German member to its ranks.

## The powers of the Mandates Commission, 1926

But would a seat on the PMC still be worth having? One year after the controversy over the Belgian law and six months before the Council granted Stresemann his wish, the Mandates Commission found itself under attack by the very body it served. In September 1926 the Foreign Ministers of the mandatory powers banded together to accuse the PMC of inquisitorial tendencies and to seek to reduce its sphere. This was the most serious attack on its rights that the PMC would face over its twenty-year existence, and it was all the more troubling for being led and organized by Britain, usually the Commission's most stalwart friend. Against expectation, however, the conflict—if formally won by the mandatory powers—enhanced the credit and legitimacy of the Commission, which would never be so challenged again. How did this fight come about, and what did it mean?

The German Foreign Ministry, watching the conflict throughout 1926, thought that the mandatory powers wished to reduce the Commission's influence before allowing a German member to join, but that was only part of the matter.[33] Resentments against the PMC had been simmering for a long time. Already in a Council meeting in December 1923 the French representative Gabriel Hanotaux said the Commission was prone to exceed its powers (Van Rees responded with a lengthy memo citing the textual basis for every part of its work),[34] and the London-based High Commissioners of the remote Dominions governments agreed.[35] The Council responded by inviting all mandatory powers to be represented whenever the work of the PMC was discussed, but until 1925 the steady support of the British kept grumbling in check.

In 1925 that changed, when Britain's new Conservative Prime Minister Stanley Baldwin appointed Austen Chamberlain as Foreign Secretary. Ironically, Chamberlain, the man who did more than any other interwar Foreign Secretary to rebuild European comity and enhance the authority of the League, would give the Commission their worst few months. Chamberlain took over the job (previously often handled by Lord Robert Cecil) of attending Council and Assembly meetings himself, but he did so because he considered the League an updated Concert of Europe, not a courtroom in which representatives of small states, do-gooders, and agitators of all kinds could call the great powers to account. Unsurprisingly, he found the activism of the Mandates Commission very alarming. He was astounded when Theodoli mentioned in December 1925 that some members of the Commission wanted to conduct a 'visit of inspection' to Palestine and immediately shut the possibility down,[36] and he was horrified to learn that the PMC sent their reports on petitions to the petitioners themselves. (The Council, when handling complaints under the minorities regime, dealt only with the state concerned and never responded to the petitioner

at all.)[37] When, later that summer, the PMC forwarded to the Council a
new questionnaire for the mandatory powers to use when writing reports
and also raised the question of whether they ought to hear petitioners in
person, he thought things had gone quite far enough.[38]

The Council meeting of 3 September 1926, which was conducted in public,
thus witnessed one of those moments of political drama so cherished by the
Geneva press corps. The proposed questionnaire, Chamberlain charged, was
'infinitely more detailed, infinitely more inquisitorial' than the one used previously, and he saw 'great objection' to adopting it. It seemed to him, 'and he knew
that this feeling was shared by other Members of the League', that the
Commission was trying 'to extend its authority to a point where the government would no longer be vested in the mandatory power but in the Mandates
Commission'—a move that was 'not the intention of the Covenant'. Even
worse was the 'very extreme proposal' that the Commission hear petitioners—a
prospect he thought 'unwise, imprudent and even dangerous'. Representatives
of the other powers, alerted beforehand to Chamberlain's attack, eagerly jumped
on the bandwagon. One by one, Aristide Briand for France, Viscount Ishii for
Japan, Emile Vandervelde for Belgium, Sir Frances Bell for New Zealand, and
J. S. Smit for South Africa praised Chamberlain's 'wise remarks', warned against
the possible abuse of the right of petition by 'discontented' or 'unrespectable'
elements, and voiced their frustration with the Commission's penchant for
'minute investigation'. Van Rees, attending for the Commission, was stunned by
the wave of vitriol. The Commission had not gone beyond the duties entrusted
to it, he retorted. It had always worked 'in a very cordial spirit of co-operation'
with the mandatory powers. Chamberlain's rebuke was 'not at all deserved' and
'could not but have a painful effect on all the members of the Commission'.[39]

Once back in London, Chamberlain pressed on. The whole mandates
system, he wrote in a private minute, seemed to be headed down the wrong
path. The allies had never intended 'to create a superior Council of
Administration' over the European empires, but rather 'to assure the world
that the abuses of King Leopold II's personal exploitation of the Congo are
not being repeated elsewhere'—a narrow description of their duties that
would certainly have shocked the PMC.[40] The Legal Advisor to the Foreign
Office, Sir Cecil Hurst, then drafted a memorandum for Chamberlain to
take to the Dominions' premiers at the 1926 Imperial Conference. That
document, which became the British note to the League of 8 November,
returned to the Covenant text (which Hurst had helped to draft) and to
Hymans' landmark 1920 Report to point out that mandatory powers were

to enjoy 'a full exercise of sovereignty' in their territory. While the Council was indeed to oversee their work, it was 'not called upon to check and examine every minute detail of administration, nor can it have the means to discharge such a Herculean task'.[41] The Dominions' premiers, who had helped set up Chamberlain's attack, entirely agreed.[42] So did the French and the Belgians, De Caix even hoping that it might now be possible to stop publishing the PMC's proceedings.[43] Every mandatory power reported that they found the questionnaire and the proposal to hear petitioners mischievous and unnecessary.[44]

The Council bowed before this onslaught. At the next session it would confirm that there was no need for the PMC to modify the petitions process.[45] The questionnaire, too, was referred back, and the Commission agreed that the mandatory powers need not use it.[46] But if these two innovations were rejected, it would be wrong to conclude that the PMC was tamed; to the contrary, this controversy enhanced its cohesion and standing. Like a pebble dislodged on a hillside, Chamberlain's intervention let loose an avalanche of talk among well-placed British supporters, the Commission itself, and a wider international public. The PMC emerged more united, less reliant on British patronage, and if anything with a higher public reputation—an outcome Chamberlain could have foreseen, if he had paid any attention to the history of the practices he attacked.

For the two processes that aroused his ire—the questionnaire and the petition—were largely British creations. Ormsby-Gore, now Chamberlain's colleague as Colonial Under-Secretary, had pushed for the petition process; Lugard, Orts, and Van Rees had compiled the new questionnaire (Lugard even writing the preface);[47] and the fateful query about hearing petitioners was Lugard's as well. True, that last proposal had arisen at regular intervals, with Rappard, Orts, and Theodoli all at some point expressing cautious support,[48] but it was Lugard who, over Martial Merlin's vociferous opposition, had forced the question. Lugard had a reasonable sense of fair play and the wit to know when he was being lied to, and the Commission's decision not to hear the Syrian delegation at the special Rome session had troubled him.[49] He had no wish to turn the mandated territories into 'centres of agitation against constituted authority and possibly of racial antagonism,' he told his colleagues soon afterwards, but he found it 'difficult to reconcile an attitude of complete impartiality with a denial of audience to a petitioner, while hearing the Representative of the Mandatory'.[50] Confident of his own judgement, Lugard also disliked the anxious, not to say craven, spirit shown by some of his fellow members towards the Council. The Commission needn't 'implore the Council to grant it the right to hear certain petitioners,' he told them irritably at the summer 1926 session, but rather simply needed to ascertain whether the Council wished them to hear petitioners if they couldn't do their duty otherwise. Personally, he stated, 'in any case regarding which his conscience did not permit him to give his opinion without having heard the petitioners, he would refuse to give that opinion'.[51]

In attacking the PMC, Chamberlain thus attacked Lugard—and, by extension, undermined Britain's cherished reputation as the model mandatory power of the League. Until Chamberlain got involved, the British Colonial Office had always tried to align itself with the League; indeed, its officials had even been ready to contemplate granting the PMC the right to hear petitioners.[52] Now Britain had revealed itself to be just another imperialist power—a Mr. Hyde-like transformation that struck many observers of British imperial rule as no revelation at all. For newspapers across the globe covered the quarrel, and if some Conservative papers in Britain, France, and Belgium defended Chamberlain, writers for the *Washington Post*, *L'Humanité*, the *Deutsche Allgemeine Zeitung*, and the *Indian Social Reformer* agreed that it exposed the annexationist desires of the imperialist powers.[53] British liberals and internationalists were appalled. J. H. Harris, in Geneva for the Assembly that opened days after that Council session, met immediately with Rappard and the Swedish representative Anna Bugge Wicksell, and found both 'burning with indignation'.[54] The Anti-Slavery Society, he reported to Sidney Olivier, 'simply cannot sit down under this censure of the Permanent Mandates Commission'.[55]

The whole apparatus of liberal opinion-formation mobilized. The Mandates Committee of the League of Nations Union met four times on the question (once with Lugard), called at the Foreign Office, and—once the Foreign Office note was published—issued a defence of the Commission. The Union of Democratic Control did the same. Letters were sent to the papers. The controversy reached both Houses of Parliament.[56] Revealingly, British critics deplored Chamberlain's behaviour not only because they wished to defend the League but also because they took for granted that Britain should 'set the standard' for exemplary colonial practice and 'show the way' to more 'backward' or 'hesitating' powers.[57] Domestic criticism on this scale forced a retreat. Lord Robert Cecil in the House of Lords and William Ormsby-Gore in the Commons were authorized to proclaim, as good League men, 'that the British Government have no desire in the world to hamper, or interfere with, or do other than support to the utmost of their power, the work of the Permanent Mandates Commission'.[58]

But the damage—or, from the standpoint of internationalism, the good—had already been done. In Geneva, Huntington Gilchrist from the Mandates Section had reviewed the British note and concluded that its arguments were based on a biased and partial reading of the documentary record. The Commission had quite clearly been charged to oversee the execution of *all* the obligations laid out in the mandate texts, and, having pursued that work with 'much good judgment and wise discretion', deserved the Council's full confidence.[59] The PMC—'distinctly sore' over Chamberlain's attack, Ormsby-Gore reported from Geneva[60]—also thought itself blameless, and even the cautious Drummond agreed. Ormsby-Gore would do his emollient best to mend relations, but the Commission would never be so deferential to the British again.

Instead, it developed a new sense of solidarity and power. The Commission had always stressed its independence of national ties. Now, it began to believe its own claims. At the opening public meeting of the PMC's tenth session, 4 November 1926, Van Rees was warmly applauded by his colleagues for his repudiation of the Council's criticisms—applause in which, the watching journalists perceptively noticed, the British and French members joined. Rappard then delivered a long speech on the PMC's obligation to discharge its duty, however 'disagreeable' the great powers might find that, and Theodoli thanked public opinion and the press for their 'assiduity and interest'.[61] Of course, all was not utter harmony. Orts still hated the idea of a German member; Merlin still defended France no matter what it did. Yet the PMC had come to feel that it represented, collectively, something more than an assemblage of individuals, still less of national representatives. Instead, it stood for the principle of international control. With that self-consciousness, and soon with a German member, the PMC would be willing to take the anti-annexationist argument further.

## South West Africa's harbours and railways, 1926–30

This time it would face South Africa, with whom its relations were already fraught. Many Commission members found South African 'native policy' deplorable, but the South Africans often behaved as if their territory were not under mandate at all. Through their actions in the early 1920s—shipping in settlers, granting British nationality en bloc to the territory's German population, and setting up a whites-only legislative assembly—South Africa made clear that it thought South West Africa's incorporation into the Union inevitable. As we have seen, the Mandates Commission disapproved equally of the specific policies and the overall plan, but that disapproval had no effect. South Africa did not intend to let the Mandates Commission stand in the way of its manifest destiny.

Most galling was South Africa's propensity to pass legislation that included a claim to sovereignty. A first challenge emerged as early as 1922, with an act vesting the territory's railways and ports in the Union in 'full dominion'. In 1923 and again in 1925 the PMC asked the South African representative to clarify precisely what was meant by 'full dominion', but although South Africa made placatory statements about its loyalty to the mandate, it would not change the wording of the law.[62] By 1926 Van Rees had become quite testy about such prevarication. The term 'full dominion' implied ownership, he told the South African High Commissioner J. S. Smit at the ninth session that June, but the former German railways had been transferred to South Africa only in its role as trustee. Thus, 'it was not the full dominium which had been transferred but the right of management or of administration'. All other mandatory powers accepted that state lands and formerly German property were now held by the mandated territory. None thought it necessary to insist—as Smit seemed to do—that such property could only be managed if it was held in full ownership.[63] South Africa should thus revise its Railways and Harbours legislation to acknowledge that it was not sovereign in the territory.[64]

Unfortunately for the PMC, and especially for Van Rees, that request came before the very Council session at which Chamberlain let loose about the meddlesomeness of the PMC—a brouhaha that gave Smit a perfect opportunity to go on the attack. A territory under 'C' mandate was 'an integral part of the mandatory's own territory,' he told the Council. The PMC really had no business conducting 'an investigation of the policy of the Mandatory in its own territory'.[65] Actually, of course, the Covenant had stipulated that 'C' territories could be *administered as* an integral part of the mandatory power's territory, not that they *were* an integral part, but no Council member called Smit's bluff. That same month Smit told the League Assembly that South West Africa was, for all practical purposes, part of the Dominion of South Africa—although in this case the Italian delegate intervened to insist on the crucial importance of that little word, 'as'.[66] And in a border agreement with Angola negotiated around the same time, South Africa bluntly stated that, 'subject to the terms of the...mandate', it 'possess[ed] sovereignty over the Territory of South-West Africa'.[67]

If the South African government thought the PMC would let language like this pass, however, it was deluded. Instead, the Commission rallied around Van Rees and his stiff-necked conception of duty. Although South West Africa was not scheduled for review at the PMC's tenth session that November, the Commission examined the South Africa-Angola treaty anyway, telling the Council that it doubted 'whether such an expression as "possesses sovereignty"...can be held to define correctly...the relations existing between the mandatory Power and the territory placed under its mandate'.[68] Van Rees showed up at the next Council session, according to F. T. B. Friis from the Mandates Section, 'armed to the teeth' and itching 'to deliver a speech loaded with strong arguments in favour of the view expressed by the Commission'; if anything, he was disappointed to learn that the Council had agreed privately just to forward the PMC's statement. Catastini and Friis assured Van Rees that the South Africans would take the hint anyway.[69] But they did not, observing that as the Council had refrained from commenting, they would refrain as well.

Van Rees, undaunted, returned to the attack. No sooner had Smit been politely welcomed to the table for the PMC's eleventh session in June 1927 than he started in. He was very sorry that South Africa had declined to make its own views on sovereignty clear, for this was not a question of secondary importance. Instead, what was at stake was 'a fundamental principle', one that 'formed the basis of the mandates system': the principle of 'non-annexation'. True, mandates conferred full rights of legislation and administration on the mandatory powers, but they did not confer sovereignty. Those who held that the mandates system was nothing more than 'a special convention comprising certain restrictions on the sovereignty held by the Power invested with the mandate' were wrong. In what was probably the clearest exposition of the League-centred theory of sovereignty, Van Rees stated:

> The mandates system, on the contrary, implied the exclusion of the right of sovereignty of the mandatory Power over the territory which it administered, and implied restrictions only with regard to the *application* of that administration. In other words, according to this system, the mandatory Power held its powers of administration and legislation, which were necessary for the

accomplishment of its duties as a guardian, not in virtue of its sovereignty over
the administered territory but in virtue of the mandate conferred upon it.

Smit, chafing, interrupted to ask the Chairman whether Van Rees was even
in order. He had had no notice that the PMC would wish to discuss this
question and had no instructions from his government. When Theodoli
happily quoted passages from the Rules of Procedure authorizing the PMC
to deal with 'all matters relating to the observance of the mandates', Van
Rees carried on with his lecture. Smit, he concluded, would surely be happy
to dispel the Commission's doubts and to confirm that South Africa was not
sovereign in South West Africa.[70]

Smit was happy to do no such thing. He would pass along the PMC's
request for clarification but would not advise his government to answer
their impertinent questions. He took comfort from the fact that Lugard and
Freire d'Andrade also found Van Rees's persistence excessive; on this issue,
however, the majority—including even Orts and Merlin—sided with Van
Rees. Indeed, when Smit tried to appeal to mandatory-power solidarity,
Orts piously if mendaciously retorted that if other mandatory powers had
not been grilled the way Smit had been, it was because South Africa was the
only power whose behaviour had called forth such questioning. Reporting
to the Council, the PMC noted that Prime Minister J. B. M. Hertzog himself had endorsed the South African Supreme Court's view that 'the majes-
tas or sovereignty over South-West Africa resides neither in the Principal
Allied and Associated Powers, nor in the League of Nations, nor in the
British Empire, but in the Government of the Union of South Africa'. Such
a statement, the PMC insisted, required clarification. Did the South African
government think the phrase 'possesses sovereignty' meant only that it had
the right 'to exercise full powers of administration and legislation in the
territory of South-West Africa' under the mandate and the Covenant, or did
it mean 'that the Government of the Union regards itself as being sovereign
over the territory itself'? Having repeatedly and unavailingly asked the
South African representative this question, the Commission was 'obliged' to
bring the matter to the Council itself.[71]

When Catastini told Sir Eric Drummond's kitchen cabinet of top League
officials on 29 June 1927 that the PMC intended to press the question
(a move the new German Under-Secretary supported), Drummond coun-
selled caution. The Council, he feared, might well tell the Commission that
'as it was not a body of jurists and as the question which it raised was a legal
one', it did not want its advice.[72] But Drummond was wrong. With Germany

now represented on the Council, the British and French declined to defend South Africa. Thus, while the Council refrained from ruling on sovereignty, it forwarded the Commission's observations to South Africa—a move that Huntington Gilchrist and Quincy Wright, among others, took as evidence that the Council was moving behind the Commission's view.[73]

Spared open censure, South Africa still refused to submit. Instead, it dispatched the new administrator A. J. Werth to Geneva for the PMC's next session. The mandatory powers knew the Commission tended to turn deferential when confronted by the man on the spot. Yet while the discussions that October were more courteous than the bare-knuckled bust-ups with Smit, the question of South Africa's annexationist ambitions once again reared its head. Werth insisted that the words 'full dominion' were simply employed as a convenience, since under Roman-Dutch law a trustee could only manage property if ownership were transferred as well,[74] but Van Rees, Orts, and Rappard clearly thought that some other formulation wasn't beyond the genius of the legal mind. There had long been 'a certain cloud' over the relations between the Commission and South Africa, Theodoli told Werth at the conclusion of the session—a cloud formed not only by persistent official statements that seemed in conflict with the mandate but also by the fact that 'very proper requests from the Commission had too often been answered in an evasive or dilatory manner'. In their Report to the Council, the PMC hoped that South Africa would now finally find it possible to amend the Railways and Harbours legislation.[75]

By now, even the Council shared these hopes. Given the clear statements made by Werth about the ownership of these domains, the Council rapporteur stated, 'I trust that there will now be no difficulty in meeting the Mandates Commission's wishes by bringing the legislative acts of the Union into line with its representative's statements.'[76] When, at the 15th session in July 1929, the South African representatives still prevaricated, Van Rees and Rappard lost their tempers. The Commission was not asking for clarification because it was itself confused about the location of sovereignty but because they needed to know South Africa's views, Van Rees told the new High Commissioner Eric Louw bluntly. It was a thankless task to have to repeat the same questions year after year, Rappard added, but Louw should not think the Commission's 'curiosity could be killed by prescription'.[77] 'In spite of all its previous discussions on this subject,' the PMC reported in exasperation, they still had not been able to get South Africa to give 'an explicit answer to its repeated question on the meaning attached by that

Government to the term "full sovereignty." ' Until it answered this question, 'a regrettable misunderstanding' would continue. Would the Council then please clear up this question once and for all?[78]

Asked so bluntly for its support, with Stresemann in the room and its own credibility on the line, the Council finally unambiguously backed the Commission up. It was quite clear *that sovereignty, in the traditional sense of the word, does not reside in the mandatory power*' (my emphasis), the Council's rapporteur stated in September 1929, and in view of the confusion over this question, the South African government's attention should be drawn to that ruling.[79] The South Africans still stonewalled and were granted a brief deferral,[80] but through the initiative of a South African Secretariat member they were finally brought around.[81] Their agreement might not denote any real change of heart, the German Under-Secretary at the League reported to the Wilhelmstrasse,[82] but after nearly a decade of resistance South Africa grudgingly gave in, telegraphing the Secretary General that it 'would not oppose' the Council's interpretation.[83] In January 1930 the government overcame those ostensible rigidities of 'Roman-Dutch' law and amended the Railways and Harbours legislation.[84]

This change was meaningless, Hertzog assured members of the South African House of Assembly. Not through annexation but rather through the population's free choice, South West Africa would certainly be incorporated.[85] But both Hertzog's analysis and his foresight were faulty. For if this ten-year struggle to bring South Africa to heel changed neither South Africa's aims nor its administrative practices, it did make clear to all concerned—mandatory powers, international lawyers, League officials, and the local population alike—that no change could be made to the status of any mandated territory without international consent. The implications were serious, for while Hertzog took comfort in the knowledge that the white population of South West Africa would surely wish to join the Union, it never occurred to him that the territory's natives might become, in international eyes, 'people' as well, and thus need to be taken into account. But this, Rappard told Smit bluntly in an early exchange, was precisely what the system was designed to accomplish. 'There might certainly be autonomy for a mandated country as soon as the inhabitants were recognised to be able to stand by themselves', but there was 'no justification for terminating the mandate merely because a small white minority of the population declared that they were ready to assume responsibility'.[86] On sovereignty, the views of the inhabitants—that is, the *native* inhabitants—must ultimately prevail.

Hertzog, Werth, and Smit clearly all thought such a prospect unimaginable. South Africa's future as the international community's favourite 'rogue state' is prefigured in their incomprehension.

German officials, legal scholars, and colonial activists followed these debates, with the *Koloniale Rundschau* devoting several articles to the issue of sovereignty in 1928. The Foreign Ministry's stance was clear: since Germany no longer held colonies and wanted to level the playing field, it was in Germany's interest, 'at least at the current moment', to support the view that sovereignty rested with the League and not with the individual mandatory powers.[87] Yet Germany also wished to avoid antagonizing South Africa, an important trading partner and the only mandatory power that had allowed a sizable, culturally distinctive German settler population to stay on. Ludwig Kastl, on entering the Commission, thus prudently let Van Rees take the lead in the struggle to bring the South Africans to heel; only when he and Van Rees disagreed—for example, over the legality of the 1927 South African law extending Union citizenship en bloc to all white settlers who did not yet hold it, an act that Germany saw as compromising the autonomy guaranteed that population—did Kastl lead the attack.[88] Kastl also declined to join in Rappard's sharp criticisms of the administration's harsh labour policies, clearly agreeing with Werth that the territory's uncivilized natives should be forced to work. Germany did not want South West Africa absorbed in the Union, but—provided its own settlers were welcomed—it had no problem with settler rule.

It should thus come as no surprise to learn that before attending the PMC session in Geneva in 1928, South West Africa's Administrator A. J. Werth went not to London, ostensibly his empire's beating heart, but rather—as his predecessor had before him—to Germany. After meeting with the Commission in 1924, Hofmeyr had gone to Hamburg to discuss refrigerated shipping of the territory's meat; Werth pushed those contacts further. He met with Foreign Ministry officials, saw Kastl and his business friends, and visited fur dealers in Leipzig; in Hamburg the Deutsche-Ost-Afrika shipping line held a banquet in his honour. Most remarkably, he saw the German ex-governors as well, writing fulsomely to Theodor Seitz of how happy he was to have got to know 'the exceptional men who had laid the foundations for this beautiful and promising [*zukunftsreich*] land'.[89] Germany and South Africa could do business—and in any case, Germany was saving its ammunition for a more important fight.

# Tanganyika and the dream of an East African Dominion, 1927–31

This was the fight over the British plan to draw Tanganyika into a federation with its other East African dependencies, a project known as 'Closer Union'. Of all the controversies over sovereignty that preoccupied the Mandates Commission, none was more critical; not even preserving South West Africa's autonomy mattered so much. Tanganyika's importance stemmed in part from its size as the largest mandated territory in both area and population but even more from the fact that it was the poster child for mandatory, and to a degree for British imperial, rule. Seemingly governed on good Lugardian lines and causing the PMC no trouble at all, Tanganyika's status as a 'model mandate' had become critical to the legitimacy of the mandates system itself. Exceptional but extolled as normative, Tanganyika worked to legitimize both British and mandatory rule.

Yet Tanganyika's mandatory status was vulnerable. Before 1914 only Germany had stood in the way of a Cape-to-Cairo domination of Eastern Africa that was the ideal of many British imperialists, among them those architects of the mandates system, Alfred Milner and Jan Smuts. In Kenya, too, the white-settler population was eager to capture Tanganyika's fertile highlands and create a new dominion along white supremacist lines. True, the Colonial Office and Tanganyika Governor Sir Donald Cameron seemed determined to hold them at bay. But that resistance could weaken if priorities or personnel changed, for Milner, prophetically at the urging of his then Under-Secretary Leo Amery, had taken the precaution of inserting a clause into the mandate allowing Britain 'to constitute the territory into a customs, fiscal and administrative union or federation with the adjacent territories under its own sovereignty or control'.[90]

Even before Germany entered the League, Berlin watched anxiously for any steps towards such an amalgamation. For several reasons—because it was under Britain rather than under the friendlier South Africans, because it had been the jewel in Imperial Germany's sparsely bedizened crown, and especially because it had been governed by Heinrich Schnee, now Germany's most aggressive colonial propagandist—Germany paid more attention to Tanganyika than it did to any other ex-colony. As early as 1924 the German ambassador to London was instructed to tell Labour Prime Minister Ramsay MacDonald how strongly Germany would resent any move to limit Tanganyika's autonomy.[91] When that government fell in late 1924, and Leo

**Figure 7.1** Leo Amery as Colonial Secretary.

Amery (Figure 7.1) was appointed Colonial Secretary in Baldwin's new Conservative administration, Berlin—and Schnee—understood that the citadel was nearly in the enemy's hands.

For Leo Amery was the front-rank politician most firmly committed to the project of East African federation in its most ambitious, 'Kenyan' incarnation. That is, Amery wished to see not only closer economic collaboration between Kenya, Uganda, and Tanganyika—a goal also supported by Ormsby-Gore, now Amery's Under-Secretary—but also the gradual extension of 'responsible government' to the white-settler population. South Africa was, obviously, the model for such a plan, but two prior pledges stood in the way. The first was the famous memorandum issued by the Duke of Devonshire in 1923, which had laid down that Kenya was primarily 'an African territory', one in which 'the interests of the African natives must be paramount'.[92] The second was Tanganyika's status as a mandated territory.

Amery was determined to knock over both hurdles. Britain had imposed the doctrine of 'native paramountcy' upon itself and thus could amend or repudiate it at will, but Amery also insisted that the mandate was no bar. As early as 1919 he had dismissed the argument that the League exercised any sovereign rights. To the contrary, it should be clear from the language about stages of civilization that 'the real sovereignty is vested in the local population in so far as they are capable of exercising it, and otherwise vested in the man-datory power, subject only to such 'servitudes' as may be imposed in the terms of the mandate'.[93] Now in office, Amery reiterated that view (albeit without using the tricky term 'sovereignty') at an 'East Africa' dinner held at the Savoy on 11 June 1926. 'Our mandate for Tanganyika,' he told a cheering crowd:

> was in no sense a temporary tenure or lease from the League of Nations. It was rather what might be called in lawyers' language 'a servitude', that was to say, an obligation to observe certain rules of conduct with regard to our adminis-tration in that territory . . . We held Tanganyika under our obligations to the League of Nations, but we held it in our own right under the Treaty of Versailles. The foundations of the East Africa of the future were as sure and as permanent in Tanganyika as they were in any other East African territory.

British rule in Tanganyika was not 'based on Indian or West African princi-ples' of native administration but rather on that same 'dual policy' applied in Kenya. In other words, while Britain might be responsible for African well-being, the empire was also responsible to the whole world 'for the fullest development of those territories' and especially to 'those in particular of our own race who had undertaken the task of helping that develop-ment'.[94] As plainly as possible, Amery signalled his support for white-settler rule. Lord Delamere, in England to represent the Kenyan settlers' point of view, was delighted.

Heinrich Schnee was not. Taking issue with Amery in the *Deutsche Allgemeine Zeitung* one week later, Schnee insisted that Britain held Tanganyika Territory only in trust—and, indeed, that when Germany entered the League, Britain might have been expected 'to return the terri-tory for which she was trustee to its original owner'. Was Amery speaking for the Cabinet as a whole? If so, 'Great Britain, while talking about a peace-ful League of Nations policy, would actually be pursuing a policy of annex-ation.' Amery was happy to stand by his imperialist guns. At a dinner on 23 June 1926 he repeated 'what Joseph Chamberlain once said in answer to somewhat similar criticism from the same quarter: "What I have said I have said." '[95] The following summer he called the East Africa governors to

London to discuss Closer Union, and appointed a new Commission headed by Hilton Young, a loyal ally, to examine the question. A White Paper issued at the same time reiterated Amery's own views. The claim of the settler communities 'to share progressively in the responsibilities of government' could no longer be ignored. Indeed, 'if clashes between these interests and those of the vast native populations are to be avoided, *their* [that is, white settlers'] *share in the trusteeship for the progress and welfare of the natives must be developed*' (my emphasis). Political control over Africans should be placed in the hands of white settlers. No international obligations stood in the way. 'The fact that we have undertaken mandatory responsibilities in respect of Tanganyika creates no difficulty or complication.'[96]

The controversy over Closer Union in East Africa, which lasted as a live issue from Amery's appointment in late 1924 until a Parliamentary Joint Select Committee decided against it in October 1931, was one of the greatest and most significant stories in interwar British imperial history. No imperial question save the six-year argument over Indian constitutional reform so dominated parliament, exercised public opinion, or did more to shape the character and trajectory of British imperial rule. The status of Tanganyika was not the only issue at stake in this long conflict. The real question was whether white settlers would be given the freedom to run East Africa as they wished (and, all assumed, to keep the African population in subjection), or whether the Colonial Office would retain direct control in the interests of 'native paramountcy'. British politicians, officials, and the public were divided on this question, with Amery, much of the Conservative Party, the Governor of Kenya Sir Edward Grigg, and the Kenyan settlers largely in favour of Closer Union. The following institutions and individuals were all opposed: the Labour Party; Amery's own Under-Secretary Ormsby-Gore; Lugard; a colonial office largely loyal to his ideals; Tanganyika's Sir Donald Cameron; East Africa's large and politically active Indian community; the African populations of all three territories (to the very limited extent that they were allowed to express their views); and the various humanitarians associated with the League of Nations Union and the Anti-Slavery Society.[97]

The Mandates Commission was of course opposed as well. Committed as it was both to racial paternalism and to anti-annexationism, the Commission would come down very much on one side. Yet, because this was a fight *within* the mandatory power, rather than—as with Belgium and South Africa—between the mandatory power and the League, the PMC

sessions remained, for a time, cordial. Indeed, so long as much of the colonial establishment itself was opposed to Closer Union, the mandate acted
less as a constraint on the Tanganyika administration than as a resource that
Cameron, Lugard, and their allies could mobilize against Amery, Governor
Grigg, and the settler lobby to the north.[98] Grigg wanted Kenya to become
'a great European state' and to force Tanganyika to follow suit, Cameron
told Lugard, but he intended to 'use every power at my command to frustrate
[his] most dangerous proposals'.[99] Cameron thus assured the Commission in
June 1927 that Tanganyika 'will always remain a predominantly native country, like Uganda' and could be considered part of the British Empire only in
the sense that it was within the empire's administrative framework, for it was
not actually a British possession nor were its inhabitants British subjects.[100]
Amery, assuredly, would not have said anything of the kind, but Cameron
had already shown himself willing to cross swords with London. 'I care little,'
he wrote to Lugard, 'as I am prepared *at any moment* to resign from Tanganyika
if I consider that the interests of the natives are being made a pawn in any
political game.'[101]

The PMC welcomed such statements. For the next few years, they would
pay tribute to Cameron's 'unique and most successful experiment' and ask
for assurances that the territory would still be governed on his lines.[102] Yet,
as the PMC and (still more) the German Foreign Ministry came to realize,
Lugardian principles alone would not necessarily keep Closer Union off the
table. For many in Britain who opposed Amery's vision did so primarily
because they feared African interests would be subjected to those of Kenya's
white settlers and only secondarily to defend the authority of the League. If
a form of 'closer union' could be devised that would constrain the power of
Kenyan settlers rather than expand it, some of that opposition might vanish.
And in fact, when the Hilton Young Commission returned from East Africa
at the end of 1928, the majority—including Lugard's ally, J. H. Oldham of
the Church Missionary Society—declared itself opposed to the kind of
political union desired by the Kenyan settlers but still favourable to administrative union for all three territories. Such union, the report insisted, was
reconcilable with League oversight and specifically allowed by Article 10 of
the mandate text.[103]

The German Foreign Ministry disagreed. Germany wanted to prevent
*any* move that would bind Tanganyika more closely to British possessions;
whether it was governed in the interests of settlers or natives was a distinctly
secondary concern. Indeed, insofar as former German settlers were now

returning under League sanction, sympathies lay rather with the settlers. True, Article 10 of the mandate text explicitly allowed administrative union, but the German government contended that that article was itself illegal, since the Covenant had allowed administrative union only for 'C' and not 'B' mandates.[104] Germany's Colonial Association mobilized to combat British plans, and Heinrich Schnee told Kastl to his face that he needed to be more outspoken on the PMC.[105] In February 1929 Stresemann thus informed the British ambassador that the Foreign Ministry was being besieged by communications about Closer Union, which the public viewed as an affront to the mandates system and as veiled annexation. Yet while Stresemann promised the Reichstag that the government would resist Closer Union by all means available,[106] in his conversations with the British he stressed not German resentments but rather League ideals, telling the ambassador that German colonial claims were not the issue here. What was at stake was the integrity of the mandates system itself.[107] The ambassador responded that Britain too was committed to uphold the mandate and was submitting the Hilton Young Report to the PMC to see whether it conflicted with its requirements—a move that Britain, as the League's most committed member, was constrained to make, but that played nicely into German hands.[108]

For the whole of the PMC, Kastl had assured the Foreign Ministry more than a year earlier, were agreed that the mandatory powers were 'not sovereign' and could be brought to oppose Closer Union.[109] Through the spring of 1929, Kastl diligently worked up his case, and Theodoli privately told the new German Under-Secretary to the League, Albert Dufour-Feronce, that a majority of the Commission's members would back him.[110] At the July session Kastl's claim that the plan to appoint an East African Governor General was 'fundamentally incompatible with the character of the mandates system' was thus read into the record. Lugard, although involved in efforts in Britain to slow Amery down, disagreed. As long as Closer Union would not 'deprive Tanganyika of its status as a constitutional unit' or deprive it of the PMC's supervision, there could be no objection; indeed, Closer Union might serve as a vehicle 'to extend the principles of the mandates system' to the adjoining territories. Yet the Commission's vocal 'independents', including Theodoli, Van Rees, Rappard, and Palacios, thought Kastl was right to be vigilant. Innovations that were technically allowed but might compromise Tanganyika's independence in the future should surely also be deplored.[111]

After the PMC session, Kastl met with the colonial lobbyists and officials at the Foreign Ministry to plan the next step. Seitz urged a formal German protest and a strong stand, but once again Kastl demurred. The PMC was likely to oppose the project in the end, and rather than face censure, the British might choose to retreat. Early and open German opposition, by contrast, might make them dig in.[112] At the League Council that September, Stresemann thus contented himself with defending the PMC's scrutiny of the British plan, noting that since the mandated territories were 'international and independent units for the administration of which the mandatory Powers were responsible to the League', any development that would damage that independence was of course inadmissible. 'For the moment,' he concluded rather ominously, 'he would say no more.'[113]

By this point, the Conservative government had been replaced by a second Labour Cabinet—a move that placed the Fabian socialist Sidney Webb, now Lord Passfield, at the Colonial Office. That government endorsed the principle of 'native paramountcy' and reiterated that there would be no move towards settler self-rule, but in a White Paper issued in June 1930 it also proposed to appoint an East African High Commissioner and unify key services—a move that would not 'involve any change in the status of the mandated area or of its inhabitants'.[114] Few felt much enthusiasm for this plan. Kenya's settlers were interested in Closer Union only if it put East Africa's lands and peoples at their disposal; Cameron and Grigg, both in the last days of their governorships, disliked one another and had no desire to collaborate anyway. Passfield thus submitted that proposal—and indeed the whole question of closer union—to a joint committee of both houses of Parliament that included Lugard, Amery, Orsmby-Gore, and virtually everyone else who had had anything to say on the question over the past four years.[115] In light of that move members of the Mandates Commission deferred discussion at their July 1930 session—although they did extract a promise that Britain would make no final decisions without consulting them.[116]

Labour's decision to keep Closer Union on the table may have caught Germany by surprise; in any case, it met with an immediate response. Passfield's White Paper was denounced strenuously in debates in the Reichstag and the German press.[117] That September the German ambassador delivered a formal note to the Foreign Office opposing the plan, and Stresemann's successor as Foreign Minister, Julius Curtius, reiterated those concerns in the Council.[118] Heinrich Schnee worried this was not enough.

'It was the English method to keep us quiet,' he warned the Foreign Ministry on 19 January 1931, 'until they've worked out a fait accompli.'[119] German international lawyers thought Article 10 of the Tanganyika mandate allowing administrative union was itself in violation of the Covenant, Schnee told Drummond, warning that any threat to the mandates system would be strongly resisted. Two massive memorials sent to Geneva—one signed by economic and colonial associations across Germany, the other by some seventy-four German women's organizations—underscored his point.[120]

While Schnee harangued, Kastl carried on behind the scenes. The November 1929 session of the PMC had been Kastl's last, but the following spring he wrote privately to Lugard, with whom he had been on good terms. Unifying administrative services under a High Commissioner necessarily would compromise Tanganyika's autonomy and thus mandate principles, he argued, but damage was being done to Anglo-German relations as well. Lugard replied politely that while he entirely agreed that Tanganyika's separate identity must be preserved, he thought the safeguards built into the White Paper did ensure that autonomy; both men reiterated arguments they had made in Geneva.[121] Yet Kastl had struck a nerve. Lugard was an administrator and not a lawyer. He found the debate over the location of sovereignty, he told one correspondent in 1937, 'a matter of purely academic interest of no practical importance', and had 'never thought it worthwhile' to read the many essays on the subject.[122] He had thus simply accepted the claim, insisted upon by Amery and repeated rather unthinkingly by Labour, that Closer Union would not violate the mandate. But Kastl's conviction that he had international law on its side unsettled Lugard, for surely Britain would not wish to face a German challenge before the Permanent Court of International Justice. First privately, and then on behalf of the Joint Committee, Lugard drafted a series of pointed questions for the Foreign Office about the legality of the plan.[123]

The answers that came back in early 1931—albeit from the Colonial Office's own law officers rather than from the Foreign Office—shocked Lugard, Passfield, Ormsby-Gore, and the Joint Committee alike. A High Commissioner who exercised any legislative authority would be in breach of the mandate, and Germany would be within its rights to bring the issue to the Permanent Court.[124] Michael Callahan, who first followed the trail of Lugard's international ties and established the importance of the law officers' decision, thus concludes—rightly—that Closer Union in its political form was dead by 1931: Passfield could not introduce a High Commissioner over his own department's legal ruling. Yet it is also true that the Colonial Office declined to publicize that judgement, allowing the Joint Committee to carry on, and leaving the PMC and the Germans on tenterhooks, for another nine months. Moreover, when that Committee finally reported, it went out of its way to repeat that Britain's mandate over Tanganyika was 'absolute and not revocable', that the formation of a 'customs, fiscal and administrative union or federation with the adjacent territories' was explicitly allowed, and that cooperation and coordination of economic and scientific services should be enhanced. True, the Committee also reported against political union, which the members now knew was open to legal challenge, but the form in which they made that recommendation—'this is not the time for taking any far-reaching step in the direction of formal union'—did not acknowledge that it was off the table forever.[125]

Indeed, the fact that a new Conservative government went ahead with the more modest administrative collaborations, institutionalizing a regular governors' conference and introducing a common postage stamp and a customs union among the East African territories without waiting for the PMC's consent, convinced some on the Commission—not to mention the apoplectic Schnee and the Tanganyika Indian Association as well—that the British were inching towards Closer Union by stealth.[126] The Commission had been assured, Rappard told Lord Plymouth at the 1932 session, that no changes would be made without consulting them. When Plymouth responded that he had understood British assurances to apply only to political and constitutional union and not to such purely administrative changes as postal unification, Rappard retorted that that had not been the Commission's understanding. 'Closer political and constitutional union would always strike the Commission as not even debatable,' he told Plymouth bluntly. 'It would upset the mandate which it was the Commission's business to defend.'[127] The danger, the Spanish member Leopoldo Palacios told the new Governor, Stewart Symes, the next year, was that even minor administrative reforms might lead to Closer Union by degrees and hence endanger the sovereignty or economic well-being of the territory.[128]

Lugard, still in the room and well aware that Closer Union had been shelved, thought such fears exaggerated and politically motivated. Bitter debate ensued, and in one of their rare acts of public discord, Lugard, Orts, and Merlin (not coincidentally the three members from states holding mandates in Africa), as well as Van Rees, all dissented from the condemnation of the majority.[129] As Orts privately warned the Belgian Colonial Minister, it was the German and Italian members who had led the attack, and if the Council supported that majority view, the decisions through which Rwanda, Burundi, and the French and British portions of Cameroon and Togo had been united administratively with neighbouring colonies might also come into question.[130] Germany's exit from the League that October took that possibility off the table, but the 'independent' members of the Commission kept a beady eye on any contacts between Tanganyika and neighbouring British administrations. In 1937 Rappard was still interrogating mandate officials about the possible pernicious effects of the common postage stamp.[131]

The story of the PMC's involvement in the Closer Union debate is thus replete with ironies, for while the proscription on annexation was upheld and indeed strengthened, the resentment generated by the controversy persisted as well. The vigilance of the PMC and the German Foreign Ministry as well as Kastl's adept personal diplomacy were crucial to bringing the proposal down. But since the British never publicly conceded, as the PMC put it, 'that the mandate in itself, so long as it exists, may constitute an insuperable legal obstacle',[132] those forces never knew they had won. Privately, British officials admitted as much, but saw no need to humble themselves before the PMC. They were accustomed to view international institutions as mechanisms devised to force lesser nations to live up to British standards and would not acknowledge that those 'lesser nations' had kept them from placing Tanganyika under the thumb of a Kenyan white-settler class. Much goodwill was lost thereby; that common postage stamp came at a high price. Amery may not have created an East African Union, but the movement he unleashed seriously weakened Britain's standing within the PMC and lowered Germany's already shaky confidence in the robustness of the mandates regime. The proscription of annexation had been strengthened, but not in a way that strengthened the League.

★ ★ ★

Establishing that mandatory powers were not sovereign in the mandated territories, and forcing those powers to accept, however grudgingly, that norm, was the most significant achievement of the mandates system. It is easy to see why this was so important. For if the mandatory power was not sovereign, not only could it not annex or otherwise dispose of the territory, but it also could not deny sovereignty to its wards forever. Except in relation to the Middle East, neither the mandatory powers nor the League worried about this very much. Europeans expected to govern Africa for generations. When that timeframe suddenly contracted, however, the South African regime in particular would discover that it could retain South West Africa, and govern it as it wished, only as an international pariah. South Africa, a regional and not a global power, was willing to go down that road, but other states could not bear the cost of such international disapproval.

One might argue that this norm was established by the Covenant itself—that that text, and not the controversies I have detailed here, truly mattered. I think that misses something crucial about how such norms work. Many international agreements exist on paper only. They become meaningful, and gain force, through iteration and concession, when states, against a narrow conception of their interest but in order to gain legitimacy and repute, profess their allegiance and change course. This is what happened here. For a variety of reasons—to keep their allies happy, to burnish their international reputation, to conciliate a hypersensitive ex-enemy, even to live up to their own cherished image of themselves—imperial powers decided to submit to a probably unenforceable norm. Publicity provided the context, German entry into the League the catalyst, and the PMC's dogged persistence the fuel, for that change. In a formal and semi-public setting, face to face with the unreconciled Germans, with legal scholars watching and the Geneva press corps waiting at the door, the mandatory powers were constrained to reiterate their own promises. They did not want to do this. The Council postponed and prevaricated, ducked and weaved. But with the question now an 'international' one, the imperial powers could not but submit.

They were not, then, sovereign—and yet, there is a sting in the tail. For if the mandates system established clearly that mandatory powers were not sovereign, it could not say just where that sovereignty lay. Some said with the League and some said with the allied powers, but neither of these bodies actually exercised it; those who held that the inhabitants were themselves sovereign were forced to admit that their powers were latent at best. As a result, what the mandates system did was less to deprive the mandatory powers of sovereignty than to create spaces from which sovereignty was banished altogether. If sovereignty and 'full powers of administration' could be so decisively severed; if the population that was to inherit sovereignty could neither claim nor exercise it; and if, moreover, the territory itself was to be held open to the free entry and exploitation of all League states, what remained to the 'sovereignty' that these populations would inherit? *Who rules when sovereignty is held in abeyance?* The British, the Germans, and the Dutch, great trading nations all, had always had a common answer to that question. Markets do.

# EIGHT

## Market Economies or Command Economies?

Forced labour was as hateful if required for private individuals as it was commendable when imposed on the natives to remedy their lack of foresight and induce them to produce the foodstuffs indispensable for their elementary needs.

Halewyck de Heusch, Director General of Political and Administrative Affairs
at the Belgian Colonial Ministry, 22 October 1925[1]

If sovereignty was the most contested issue with which the Mandates Commission had to deal, the question of economic rights—for the mandatory power, other League states, and the local population alike—ran a close second. Two economic principles marked the mandates regime from the start. The first, imposed on all Middle East and African mandate territories save South West Africa, was the principle of the 'open door'. Nationals of all League member states were to have an equal right to work, travel, reside, and hold property; 'complete economic, commercial and industrial equality' was to prevail; and concessions for the economic development of the territory were to be granted 'without distinction on grounds of nationality'[2] The second (albeit qualified) principle was that labour should be 'free'. All signatories to the 1919 Saint-Germain Convention which replaced the abrogated Berlin and Brussels Acts were 'to endeavor to secure the complete suppression of slavery in all its forms', and clauses obliging mandatory powers to suppress slavery and to allow (paid) forced labour only for 'essential public works and services' were included in every African and Pacific mandate text. From the outset, the Commission spent much time debating what was meant by both stipulations.

# The problem of the 'open door'

Long-standing British assumptions about the role of free trade in easing global tensions underwrote that 'open door' obligation. If tariff walls had fuelled the fin-de-siècle imperialist scramble, then surely the best guarantee of peace would be to divorce economic interest from territorial control. The fact that Germany had applied the 'open door' in its pre-war colonies made compliance with this norm especially important, for how else could the new mandatory powers demonstrate that they had no selfish or annexationist designs? Only if markets were open to all, the theory went, could the mandated territories become engines of peaceful development and economic cooperation—and, if that competition drove up wages, of native well-being as well.

In 1919, with credit cheap and internationalism ascendant, this rosy future seemed on the horizon. Three years later it had vanished. Economic downturns and deflationary budgets across Europe meant there was little surplus capital, and even had it been available, the mandated territories offered few enticing opportunities. True, a few had extraordinary natural resources—Iraq's oil, Nauru's phosphates, South West Africa's diamonds—but the allied powers had neatly sewn these up before the mandates were even agreed. Other opportunities—say, to take over German plantations in Cameroon and Tanganyika—seemed less appealing, particularly once cocoa and copra prices began falling. Those German holdings were to have been quickly sold and the proceeds paid into the reparations account (the German government taking on the job of indemnifying their private owners), but in 1922 many were still in limbo. When Britain put the German plantations in its sector of Cameroon up for auction in London, few found any takers.[3]

The Mandates Commission wanted its territories to be flagships, not backwaters, and found that economic sluggishness very worrying. Largely at the urging of Lugard, who as the former Governor General of Nigeria had been well informed about the failed Cameroon auction, between 1923 and 1925 it spent much time discussing how to encourage investment.[4] The problem, as the Commission saw it, was the following. The mandated territories needed capital for infrastructural development and commercial enterprises, but who would wish to put their money in a territory that could be transferred at any moment to another power? On the Commission's recommendation, the Council thus ruled in September 1925, first, that contracts and titles acquired in a mandated territory were as valid as if the territory were held in full sovereignty, and, second, 'that the cessation or transfer of a mandate cannot take place unless the Council has been assured in advance that the financial obligations regularly assumed by the former mandatory Power will be carried out and that all rights regularly acquired under the administration of the former mandatory Power shall be respected'.[5] Property rights and contracts would hold beyond the mandate's end.

What lay behind this action? From one perspective, one might say that the Commission was trying to secure investments crucial to these mostly resource-poor and fragile territories; from another, that it was laying the foundations of a neo-colonial order that would claw back through economic entanglements the sovereignty conceded at independence. Some members were aware of such dangers. Lugard thought that if mandatory powers were allowed to pledge infrastructural works—railroads, harbours—as security on public loans, 'the mandatory would have obtained such a hold upon the country as would amount to annexation, contrary to the principles of the Covenant'.[6] The Swedish member, Anna Bugge-Wicksell, held that if a mandated territory found such debts compromised its autonomy after independence, it ought to be allowed to negotiate their early liquidation.[7] The majority of the PMC, however, wanted only to improve the climate for investment, and by the time the issue reached the Council, such caveats had disappeared.

The Council's ruling that successor states must honour economic agreements made by their imperial overlords was of considerable significance for emerging international norms. Mandatory powers were, strictly speaking, *not sovereign*, but the League had accepted that they had the right to alienate their charges' resources and land virtually in perpetuity. Yet, however significant theoretically, that ruling did little to spur development in the African territories the Commission had had in mind. No European power spent much on colonial development in the early 1920s (indeed, of the mandatory powers, only Japan did so), nor were private companies or foreign investors beating at the doors of those mandatory administrations. With one exception, that is: German companies and owners swiftly sought to reclaim their African properties and trade. Already in July 1920 the French consul in Hamburg warned the Quai d'Orsay that the directors of the powerful Woermann line were colluding with rival German firms to mount a concerted assault. That summer, French officials throughout West Africa reported German ships seeking entry.[8]

Britain and France responded to the German commercial onslaught very differently, their reactions expressive of that Anglo-French divergence over how to handle Germany that was such a feature of the 1920s. Britain, historically a free-trading power, quickly reopened its African ports to German trade. Having failed to find non-German buyers, the Treasury also sold the vast majority of those Cameroon plantations back to their original German owners and soon allowed German investors into Tanganyika as well (Figure 8.1). The French, by contrast, saw German trade as a Trojan horse for colonial revisionism (not unreasonably, since the Wilhelmstrasse saw it that way as well) and kept Togo and Cameroon closed to German merchant shipping even *after* other French colonial ports reopened. Once Germany entered the League, France was forced to lift its ban, by which point Germany had re-established its pre-war position in merchant shipping along the African coast.[9] German firms then built warehouses and landed cargo in Douala and Lomé, but mandate authorities kept these companies under close supervision and successfully prevented Germans from acquiring concessions or land.[10] Since the mandate texts allowed deviations from the open-door principle to protect 'public order' or the territory's 'best

**Figure 8.1** Bananas from German plantations on the Afrikanische Fruchtkompagnie landing stage at Tiko, Cameroon, for transport to Hamburg.

interests', the PMC's German members Ludwig Kastl and Julius Ruppel could never persuade the Commission to condemn such restrictions.[11]

French resistance to German economic permeation in Togo and Cameroon came at a high cost, however, particularly since their British neighbour refused to share it. For France, the problem wasn't just that the gullible British allowed German agents to operate in their zone unchecked; it was also that the thriving Gold Coast economy and the higher wages offered by German-financed plantations and port works in southern Cameroon leached people and commerce out of the French zones.[12] French Cameroon and Togoland were backwaters in the 1920s, their infrastructure poor, their wage levels low, and their security-obsessed administrations quick to crack down on any sign of disaffection—and local populations voted with their feet and walked over their borders. French decisions meant that those territories were spared the irredentist movements that erupted among the German populations in British Cameroon, Tanganyika, and South West Africa in the Nazi period. But for a dozen years—that is, until German revisionism finally forced closer collaboration—French mandate authorities struggled to build infrastructure and expand production in the face of fiscal austerity and what seemed a perverse British willingness to let German firms and settlers do the work for them. Unsurprisingly, the French fell back on the one resource on which cash-strapped colonial regimes had always relied: the labour—and especially the forced labour—of the colonial populations themselves. As they did so, however, they ran afoul of the mandates system's second economic norm.

## The problem of 'free labour'

It was an open secret in the interwar years that *all* colonial powers used forced labour on infrastructural projects like road-building and that some (notably the Portuguese) compelled it for private plantations as well, but the mandate texts had laid out a higher standard. Compulsory labour was allowed *only* for public works and was in all instances to be *paid*. This was hardly a 'free labour' position, but nonetheless one far from the reality of many African colonies, and in the mid-1920s the Anti-Slavery Society, the League, and the International Labour Organization (ILO) began to seek its universalization through an international convention. To the disgust of the other colonial powers, the British delegates (notably Lugard) treated those international gatherings as an opportunity to establish Britain's moral leadership, leaving France, Belgium, and (especially) Portugal scrambling to defend compulsion.[13]

A stream of exposés penned by that new breed of African expert—the well-financed, liberal, and usually anglophile American academic—made that task harder. A damning 1925 study of the brutal labour regimes in Angola and Mozambique, for example, written by the sociologist E. A. Ross from the University of Wisconsin, placed Portugal in the spotlight just when the League's Temporary Slavery Commission was meeting. Yet no publication aroused quite as much imperial ire, or so directly affected the PMC, as Raymond Leslie Buell's *The Native Problem in Africa*, published by Macmillan in two massive volumes in 1928.[14] Buell, Instructor in Government at Harvard and an academic entrepreneur of the first order, was only in his late twenties when he persuaded the Foreign Policy Association to fund a year of travel in Geneva, London, Paris, and more than a dozen African countries— including, of course, most of the mandated territories. Dispatches from Dar es Salaam and Yaoundé soon noted the arrival of the 'dreadful young American pup' who thought he could rifle their files and question their natives (in Lomé those 'natives' obliged by deluging Buell with petitions and complaints); apprehensive colonial ministries braced themselves for his find-ings.[15] When Buell's manuscript reached Paris in 1927, French colonial offi-cials were so outraged by its contents that they tried unsuccessfully to get Harvard's President Lowell to suppress its publication.[16]

What caused this consternation? Buell thought he had been scrupulously impartial and professed himself mystified.[17] Yet he had begun his travels persuaded of the superiority of Lugardian ideals of 'separate development' and 'indirect rule', and an implicit Anglo-French comparison structured the book. He had been pleased to learn that the French were jettisoning a pol-icy of 'assimilation' for one of 'association', hoping that this meant that they too were adopting 'native-centered' policies, but his visit to Cameroon shat-tered those illusions. The French had indeed set up a structure of 'chiefly' rule, Buell wrote to Huntington Gilchrist in indignation, but those 'chiefs' weren't traditional authorities at all. They were just loyal henchmen, whose chiefly titles denoted nothing more than their willingness to collect the taxes and compel the labour on which the financially desperate administra-tion relied. Local despots were springing up, as 'chiefs' used private police forces to recruit labour not only for government work but also for their own plantations.[18] Mandatory authorities, in other words, weren't devolving authority on 'traditional' structures. They were *creating* tribalism as a blind for a forced labour regime.

French-mandated Cameroon was not the only territory relying on compulsion. Buell found forced labour in Belgian Congo, the Portuguese colonies, and even Tanganyika as well. But Cameroon and Tanganyika were supposed to set the standard for colonial 'best practice' and were also subject to international correction if they fell short. Buell knew this, and even before his book was published he was plotting with Gilchrist to have his charges considered by the PMC—although, given French sensitivities, in the end Henri Junod's Bureau international pour la défence des indigènes submitted a petition about Buell's findings instead. The Mandates Commission might have been expected to take this evidence very seriously, not only because of those restrictions on forced labour in the mandate texts but also because fully half of its members in the late 1920s—including Lugard, Merlin, Van Rees, Freire d'Andrade, and Grimshaw—served on those League and ILO expert committees working to frame international forced labour conventions.

Yet the Mandates Commission proved no more willing to take a strong stand on forced labour than it had on the open-door principle. This was not only because French representatives adamantly refused to respond to, or even discuss, Buell's charges.[19] More important was the fact that members' attitudes towards forced colonial labour were transformed during the late 1920s by their close review of Belgium's policy in Rwanda and Burundi. Until the mid-1920s, the Belgian territories had attracted little attention—so little, indeed, that Gilchrist had confessed to Buell that he had no 'very clear idea of native life and native tribal organisation' there and hoped that Buell might include them in his itinerary. But Buell hadn't been willing to wait a week in Kigoma for a boat to Usumbura; by the time Gilchrist's letter caught up with him, he was already in West Africa.[20] Rwanda and Burundi, in other words, were so remote that not even the intrepid Buell ventured into them, and just what the Belgians were doing there was hardly known. But if we want to understand how 'development' could intensify compulsion, and then win the League's approval, it is to Rwanda and Burundi that we must turn.

## Building 'indirect rule' in Rwanda and Burundi

Belgium's plans for its mandated territories were crafted with its Congo colony in mind. Rwanda and Burundi, densely populated and intensively farmed, could serve as the bread basket and labour reserve for Katanga's rich copper mines over the border. Under the Germans, the two kingdoms had been oriented towards Tanganyika and the port at Dar es Salaam; under Belgium, they pivoted westward. Usumbura (Bujumbura) on the western border became the administrative capital, and even before the formal link in 1925 the Belgians made communications and transport to Congo their first priority. Yet if they hoped to direct 'development' in a new direction, like the Germans before them they turned to indigenous political and social hierarchies (as they understood or misunderstood them) to do the work. The administration, Colonial Minister Louis Franck laid out in a key confidential memorandum in 1920, 'will from the outset consistently associate the native princes with our plans and bring the indigenous ruling class into our own service'.[21]

Several factors drove that decision. A desire to be seen as applying a version of 'indirect rule' was part of it, but so too was its appealing cheapness. Belgium, struggling to recover economically from the devastation of the German occupation, had neither cash nor personnel to spare and grasped eagerly at practices that would wring both from the local population. And indeed, the Belgian apparatus in Rwanda and Burundi was minuscule and amazingly stingy. There was a Royal Commissioner (from 1925, Governor) to oversee both territories in Usumbura, Residents responsible for each specific territory at Kitega and Kigali, a Belgian delegate at the court of the Rwandan King Musinga in Nyanza, Belgian officers in command of a small military force in each territory, and some dozens of officials scattered across departments responsible for territorial administration, finance, health, agriculture, and public works. Most of those services were skeletal. As the PMC noted critically in the mid-1920s, how could four doctors protect the health of perhaps five million people?[22] Yet salaries for white officials were a major charge on the budget—an African clerk would earn about a twentieth of the salary paid to his white superior[23]—which was funded through a steadily rising head tax, supplemented by loans from the Belgian state when international criticism grew acute.

But cheapness was only part of the appeal. Equally important was that officials 'saw' Rwanda and Burundi's complex and distinct social landscapes through the lens of a 'Hamitic' hypothesis that identified the stereotypically taller and predominantly pastoralist Tutsis, who made up some 15 per cent of the total population (but were often assumed to be a much smaller and exclusively 'chiefly' group), as a racially distinct and available ruling caste.

Léon Classe, the influential Catholic 'White Fathers' missionary active in Rwanda and Burundi from 1907, thought the kingdoms resembled nothing so much as a pre-Reformation European feudal society and looked forward to the day when mass conversion would make that resemblance yet more perfect.[24] Conservative officials and missionaries rejoiced that Rwanda and Burundi's two main 'races' were bound, so it seemed, by ties of protection and service rather than the monetized relations of the market, and Franck was quick to insist that the administration, while also upholding the 'customary' authority of Rwandan and Burundian kings (or *mwamis*), would preserve the privileges of that Tutsi caste. Obviously the administration must also protect the lives and property of the Hutu majority, but those obligations came distinctly second. '*There is no question, on the pretext of equality, of interfering with the basis of the political regime,*' Franck insisted. 'The Tutsis ["Watuzi"] are long-established, intelligent and capable; we will respect that situation.'[25] Accounts sent to the Mandates Commission elaborated those stereotypes. The majority Hutu were 'typical Bantus', 'expansive, noisy, cheerful and without guile', but the Tutsi—'proud', 'distant', 'pitiless', and 'polite', 'using the lance against the weak and poison against the strong'—were 'destined to rule'.[26]

What this meant in practice was that the Belgians codified privileges and tributes that monarchs and chiefs told them were 'customary' and then sought to make those privileges dependent on exactions and orders designed to serve Belgian aims. Chiefs were recognized, fiefdoms (*chefferies*) assigned, and laws issued in the names of the *mwamis*, for those traditional kings possessed, as Resident Pierre Ryckmans wrote in an article published in 1925, 'an unchallenged power which we will never have—that of conferring legitimacy'.[27] Yet as Ryckmans and Alfred Marzorati, the Belgian Royal Commissioner, quickly discovered, in neither kingdom could they govern through the monarch alone. In Burundi, King Mwambutsa Bangiricenge had been a young child at the time of the conquest, and power was in any case highly dispersed among regional notables of the princely (*ganwa*) lineages. In more centralized Rwanda, by contrast, Yuhi V Musinga, who had come to the throne in a palace coup engineered by his powerful mother and her brothers in 1896, resented the high-handed Belgian directives and did what he could to thwart them.[28] A 'School for the Sons of Chiefs' established in Astrida worked to ensure that the next generation would be more cooperative, but officials also concluded that they needed an 'effective and complete occupation'.[29] Much the most important part of the administration was thus the 'service territorial', some dozens of officials dispersed throughout each territory who made sure that Belgian directives were carried out by the 'chiefs' and 'sub-chiefs' (or 'hill-chiefs'—*chefs du colline*) who held fiefdoms under them. All administration—allocation of land, tax collection, recruitment of labour for portage and public works, administration of justice—was devolved on those chiefs, who were entitled to claim 'customary' days of labour and payments in kind, as well as a percentage cut of the tax revenues, from those they administered.

This coercive system enabled Belgium to begin building roads (to Congo) and shipping labour (to Congo), but was it not in violation of that proscription on forced labour central to the principles of the 'sacred trust'? At the October 1925 PMC session, a sharp debate on this question erupted. The Belgian representative Halewyck de Heusch robustly defended compulsion. Labour levies were 'traditional', had existed for 'time immemorial', and were 'commendable when imposed on the natives to remedy their lack of foresight'—opinions the Portuguese member Freire d'Andrade eagerly supported. Van Rees, however, insisted that the issue was not whether useful work was being done but simply whether forced labour as it was deployed in Rwanda and Burundi was legally admissible. Through an ordinance of November 1924, officials in Rwanda and Burundi had been granted the right to levy labour not only for public works but also for cultivation of food and 'exportable products' on private plantations, but the mandate, Van Rees pointed out, explicitly prohibited 'all forced or compulsory labour except labour for essential public works and services, and even in this case a just remuneration should be provided'. But the Belgians were not *themselves* imposing labour taxes, Halewyck protested. They simply made arrangements with the local 'native chief', who then took 'the necessary steps to carry out the scheme'.[30] This did not satisfy Lugard, who insisted that if chiefs were put on salary, and taxes used to support wages, it was perfectly possible to do without compulsion.[31] The labour obligations owed chiefs were far too heavy, the Commission reported to the Council, and it was not at all clear whether any of this labour was paid.[32]

This argument was not over the merits of preserving the 'traditional' order, which all on the Commission approved. What worried members was, rather, the fact that such compulsion was in clear violation not only of the mandate text but also of the principles articulated some three months earlier by the League's Temporary Slavery Commission, on which Lugard, Grimshaw, Van Rees, and Freire d'Andrade had all sat. Not that all those

" Church Missionary Society „. — L'Œuvre de la goutte de lait.

**Figure 8.2** Church Missionary Society famine relief, Rwanda, 1928.

they could. 'One finds women and children lying helpless in the road at night, perhaps to be eaten by hyenas before death comes to them,' Church wrote in April 1929.'It is a land of skeletons, living and dead.'[41] An estimated 35,000–40,000 people died. A whole social world died with them.[42]

The Belgian response was tardy and utterly inadequate to the scale of the disaster. In January 1928 the Belgian government granted the mandate authorities a small credit of 50,000 francs to purchase food; distribution centres were then opened (usually at mission stations); food exports were prohibited. But supplies to the famine areas had to be portaged in, and even though vast numbers were forced into service (the government used some four million days of portage labour in fiscal 1928–29, ten times the annual amount five years before or after),[43] as Ryckmans insisted in an article in June 1929, it was '*impossible*, humanly impossible' to feed a starving population of three hundred thousand with no other means of transport save portage.[44] Forcible cultivation thus began in earnest, with officials distributing non-seasonal plants, like manioc or sweet potatoes, and insisting that pastoralists turn over for cultivation the marshlands they used as winter pasture, which alone retained enough moisture for growth. Under the supervision of officials, missionaries, and the 'chiefs' who were to carry out these plans, the famished worked in exchange for food; amazingly, not only cultivation but also road-building proceeded. By mid-1928, if government maps are to be believed, the key road linking Kigali and Nyanza in mid-Rwanda to Burundi was complete, although the road from Kigali to the heart of the affected famine areas did not appear on maps until two years later.[45] Stricken populations built the roads to their salvation.

This action was directed by regional officials and notables. In early 1929, however, as suffering reached its apex, news of the cataclysm finally reached the outside world. The refugees tottering into Uganda were visual evidence of just how bad things were, and while the administration could usually rely on the Catholic 'White Fathers' to keep their reflections out of the international press, English Protestant missionaries proved less reliable. In March 1929 Reverend Church published an appeal for aid in an English-language Ugandan daily, and while he was careful to say that the Belgians were doing all they could, his horror and distress were evident in his portrait of a blighted landscape, its starving and diseased population preyed on by bloated hyenas, emboldened lions, and the vultures that circled overhead. Within days, that vivid account was picked up by English-language papers from Edinburgh to New York; Church's reports also drew J. J. Willis, the Anglican Bishop of Uganda, to tour the famine regions himself. On 16 April, soon after Willis's visit, a long special report on the famine written by Church appeared in the London *Times*.[46]

Belgian officials were dismayed by that attention. English humanitarian inquiries into Africans suffering under Belgian rule were uncomfortably reminiscent of the British-led exposé of Leopold's Congo regime; according to one English district officer working in southern Uganda, the mandatory officials were terrified that Willis would write to Geneva.[47] Through its careful monitoring of the British and German press, the Belgian government knew that many in Britain thought tiny Belgium and Portugal had larger colonial empires than they could responsibly manage anyway and would be happy to meet Germany's colonial ambitions at Belgium's expense.[48] And as the Belgian government feared, the debate over the famine quickly became enmeshed in the bitter politics of German colonial revanchism. On the Mandates Commission, Kastl had repeatedly criticized the mandate administration's scant medical service, and it was easy to argue the Rwandan crisis had been worsened by that neglect.[49] By late April the Belgian ambassador in Berlin reported that articles about the famine had appeared in the German press, their sympathy for its African sufferers insidiously feeding the conclusion that Belgium should be deprived of the territory.[50] Ryckmans, the Belgian Colonial Minister Henri Jaspar, and others retorted that famine was endemic in the region (including under the Germans) and extolled the Belgian response—a *tu quoque* reply that merely fanned the flames. In the *Koloniale Rundschau*, the territory's last German governor Heinrich Schnee correctly identified Rwanda's *Drang nach Westen* and the cancellation of the projected railroad linking northeast Rwanda to Tanganyikan markets as a major reason why the famine proved so hard to combat, while also mendaciously insisting that there had been no famine under the Germans. The expropriation of Germany's colonies had harmed African populations, Schnee charged. In their interests, the League now needed to free them from Belgium's inept rule.[51]

Arguments like this galvanized a Belgian response that the famine itself had failed to provoke. Some eighteen months after the first failed rains, but days after articles began appearing in the international press, the Belgian parliament voted a credit of 50 million francs, fear of international censure having multiplied the sum available a thousandfold. The Governor General of Congo was ordered to take charge of famine relief himself; he and Louis-Joseph Postiaux, appointed acting Governor of Rwanda and Burundi while Marzorati was home on sick-leave, then toured the famine regions, astounding the local missionaries with their ignorance.[52] Trucks and construction equipment bought on credit accelerated the work of road-building, finally making it possible to bring some of the 1,760 tons of food sent to the famine areas in 1929—up from 979 tons in 1928—by road (Figure 8.3). Some ten thousand hoes were handed out, and all families were made responsible for cultivating fixed plots of land with non-seasonal crops such as manioc or sweet potatoes as well as with seasonal peas, beans, and sorghum. Granaries with stockpiled foods were established in each district.[53] By November 1929, when Marzorati was sent to meet with the PMC for what everyone assumed would be a stormy session, if the situation was far from normal it was at least possible to imagine that an adequately fed peasant population would once again till the fields.

That society would emerge much changed. As Anne Cornet argues, the famine crises, and especially the international publicity they attracted, accelerated a fundamental shift in Belgian policy. Between 1928 and 1930 a reform programme was put in place which, while surely expanding infrastructure and resources, exacerbated ethnic and social inequalities. Aspects of those reforms, and especially the persistent heavy reliance on labour taxes,

Ruanda. — Construction d'une route carrossable.

**Figure 8.3** Building a road for motor traffic, Rwanda, 1929.

were in clear violation of mandate principles, but the spectre of famine silenced the objections of the Mandates Commission. First behind the scenes, and then at the PMC sessions, Belgian officials laid out the essentials of that transformation—and, importantly, *led the Mandates Commission to approve it.*

## The 'indirect' command economy

The new Belgian policy was summarized in a memorandum, 'Main Lines of General Policy to be followed in Ruanda-Urundi', which the new Governor Charles Voisin sent to all Belgian staff in the territory in September 1930. Putting an end to dearth and periodic famine was the first goal listed.[54] Yet one can detect the conceptual foundations of that new orientation in Halewyck de Heusch's attempts at the 1928 and 1929 PMC sessions to shift responsibility for the famine onto the shoulders of the native population itself. That the Belgians would blame Hutu peasants' 'fatalism', 'passivity', and 'inherent lack of foresight' should not surprise, for this racial rhetoric had been a fixture of Belgian reports from the outset.[55] What was striking was that that condemnation of native culture now encompassed the Tutsis as well. Already in 1926 Marzorati had attributed much of the suffering of the 'Gakwege' famine to the 'complete indifference of the native chiefs' who had failed to ensure that the manioc distributed to them was planted and allowed their cattle to trample the prepared fields.[56] Now, those criticisms became much more pointed. Although there were a few enlightened chiefs, Ryckmans wrote in a long, defensive article about Belgian famine policy in 1929, 'inertia, incomprehension, stupidity and bad faith' were the rule. 'It is without them, even in spite of them, that one saves the natives,' he insisted. 'The struggle against the famine is the work of whites, and of whites alone.'[57] What was the purpose of such rhetoric? Officials were preparing the Commission for a revolution. The ostensibly 'traditional' social order, which Franck had insisted in 1920 that the Belgians would accept, was about to be taken forcibly in hand.

The Belgian reforms of 1930 had four key aspects. First, chiefly authority was rationalized. Concluding that fiefdoms were too small and authority was too dispersed, officials began aggressively to consolidate fiefdoms—in Jean-Pierre Chrétien's formulation, forcibly 'feudalizing' societies they had wrongly thought 'feudal' already.[58] The number of regional 'chiefs' declined rapidly, falling in Burundi, for example, from 133 in 1929 to 46 in 1933, and the layer of 'sub-chiefs' below them came in for pruning as well.[59] Fewer in number and more territorially defined, chiefs and sub-chiefs would henceforth be more strictly supervised. During the famine, officials began deposing any who resisted Belgian directives to expand cultivation, extend roads, and drain marshes, and they never looked back. Throughout the 1930s, PMC members would express astonishment and some anxiety about the number of ostensibly 'traditional' authorities who were deposed each year—those wholesale depositions being, as the PMC perhaps dimly realized, evidence that faithful execution of Belgian directives had now become the main qualification for chiefly power.[60]

Second, that revamped structure would be directed above all towards extracting the labour needed for rapid development. The ambitious road-building, cultivation, land reclamation, and reforestation programmes introduced in the wake of the famines, Catharine Newbury writes, 'required vastly increased demands on rural manpower', and provided that labour was forthcoming, officials did not concern themselves greatly with how it was obtained. That was the chief's responsibility, and few who recalled the exac-

tions of those times had any recollection of being paid.[61] The mandatory
administration, in other words, not only declined to wean itself from just
that sort of unpaid forced labour that the Slavery Convention had condemned, but was actually rationalizing and extending these practices. Those
members of the Mandates Commission understood perfectly well that this
transgressed the letter of the law, but with the horrors of the famine crisis
fresh in their minds, they proved very reluctant to criticize compulsion.
Even the ILO's Harold Grimshaw had agreed in 1926 that compelling an
individual to work for his own benefit should not fall within the definition
of forced labour, and forced cultivation seemed to fall under this rubric.[62]
No one thought it worth noting that chiefs and officials were allowed to
compel labour for their own or other purposes as well.

Yet it mattered that forced labour was mediated through chieftainship,
especially since those coercive relations mirrored ever more clearly the
territories' ethnic divides. Indeed, strengthening ethnic hierarchies was a
third—and strikingly uncontroversial—aspect of Belgian reforms. Tutsi
privilege pre-dated the Belgian regime, but in the pre-colonial period, those
ethnic divisions had been moderated by other cleavages—by lineages,
patron-client relations, court politics, and the fact that some chiefs were
Hutu. Once chiefdoms were consolidated, however, these other affiliations
declined in importance, and education at the 'School for Sons of Chiefs',
which catered overwhelmingly to Tutsis, became the surest ticket into the
officialdom. This is not to say that all Tutsis were chiefs or sub-chiefs, far
from it—but henceforth virtually no chiefs were Hutu. In Burundi princely
lineages dominated chieftaincies and moderated those ethnic divisions—
but even here, as in Rwanda, the Hutu chiefly presence died out. The explosion in conversions that began among the Tutsi elites in both territories in
the years following the famine further entrenched those hierarchies, so that
by 1934, 90 per cent of chiefs were Catholic, compared to a mere 10 per
cent of the population.[63] Set apart by education, religion, privilege, and (it
was thought) their 'Hamitic' race, owed service by their subordinates and
constantly assured of their superiority, how could chiefs not come to be
resented by those they administered? When asked this question at the 1933
Commission session, however, Halewyck de Heusch insisted that 'race hostility' had no place in the social order. 'The lower race recognized all the
qualities of the higher race,' he insisted; the Hutu masses 'showed real ven-
eration for the Watutsi nobles'.[64] In this terrible claim we can detect the
spectre of much future suffering.

Rencontre des Mwami Musinga (I) et Mwambutsa (II).

**Figure 8.4** Mwambutsa IV Bangiricenge of Burundi (II) and Yuhi V Musinga of Rwanda (I), 1929.

But what of the Rwandan and Burundian kings (Figure 8.4), those 'traditional' authorities whose imprimatur had been thought necessary before the people would accept 'progressive' government? As the Belgian grip on the chiefly strata tightened, those collaborators began to look both anachronistic and dispensable, and bringing them to heel emerged as the fourth leg of Belgian policy. In practice, this battle was fought over the authority of King Musinga, for while officials thought the malleable King Mwambutsa of Burundi could be deposed without consequences, they could see no need for such an act, since the Belgian Resident 'is and will remain the real Mwami'.[65] King Yuhi V Musinga, already on the throne for two decades when the Belgians invaded, was a more formidable figure. Belgian authority over the court was much too weak, Marzorati had complained in 1924,[66] and through the decade the king fought to maintain his prerogatives. A litany of complaints about his intractability made its way from Kigali to Brussels. Musinga resisted Western influences, had no interest in Christianity, and scrupulously upheld established rituals and court practice. He declined to appoint Belgian favourites and promoted his own clients, ignored Belgian directives about cattle quarantines or inoculations, shunned those sons and pages who attended the Belgian school, and made sure he was kept informed about chiefs whose loyalty seemed to be shifting towards the whites. After 1929, as relations worsened, Belgian reports grew still more defamatory. Musinga was greedy and had no conception of his public duties; he was superstitious and consulted sorcerers; he was sexually perverse and thought to have had incestuous relations with his children of both sexes. Underlying— possibly driving—those scandalous accusations was a charge so explosive that officials declined to mention it publicly at all. Musinga, Marzorati informed the Colonial Ministry confidentially in January 1929, had approached the British authorities, asking them to take over the mandate for Rwanda.[67] Belgian administrators were now treating Musinga 'like a degenerate and a vagabond', one well-informed British officer in Uganda reported. 'They will probably try and substitute a young pawn as sultan before long.'[68]

Musinga's actions lie across a chasm of culture and time, but his resistance to Belgian directives seems easy to comprehend. He had been a dynastic monarch, with power 'to kill and to enrich', Rwanda's famous 'king lists' tracing his line back through more than a dozen generations.[69] Now he was expected to act as the figurehead for an occupying power. His rights to tribute were steadily chipped away and his authority over his subjects undermined. His clients were punished or deposed; converts and interlopers were given position and land. Sweating, uniformed Belgians muttering of cattle plague decimated his herds; when drought threatened, they forbade him to fulfil his ritual obligation to make rain. His sons had been sent to a Belgian school, where they turned into strangers; once the rumours of incest had spread, his younger children were not allowed in his quarters at night. Officials gave him shiny Western toys—most recently, a motorcar— and then complained when he didn't play with them. Small wonder he became (as the Belgians saw it) depressed and disloyal, casting his eyes across the border in search of new allies.[70]

In 1929, when those allegations of incest and treason first reached Brussels, Halewyck de Heusch insisted on calm. Neither the native population, nor the British, nor the ousted Germans, nor the Mandates Commission in Geneva (he thought) would easily tolerate Musinga's removal.[71] Governor Voisin thus contented himself with some blunt conversations, through which Musinga was constrained to accept Belgian choices for chiefdoms and to tour the country promoting intensive cultivation. But officials were certain that he was still scheming (as he surely should have been), and two years later, when Monsignor Classe reported that the *mwami* remained irredeemably hostile to progress and Christianization alike, the Colonial Ministry gave the green light.[72] In Kigali and Usumbura, careful plans were laid for Musinga's ouster. In Geneva, however, Halewyck de Heusch saw no reason to share that information with the PMC. Instead, he prepared the members' minds by dwelling on Musinga's egoism, avarice, perversity, and dereliction of duty. The *mwami*, he said, cared for nothing but tribute. When his people were dying of hunger, he had asked the Belgians to enforce his customary exactions. How could Belgium collaborate with such a man, members asked? They were considering various alternatives, he replied.[73] In fact, Musinga would be ousted while the Commission was still meeting, but—a world away—its members would hear nothing of it.

Thus on 12 November 1931, having decoyed the most prominent notables away from the court city of Nyanza to the administrative capital of Kigali, Governor Voisin informed Musinga that he was being replaced by his more docile, administration-educated son, Rudahigwa. Musinga took the news quietly; he had expected it for some time. Two days later, together with his mother, seven of his wives, and several hundreds of his most loyal clients, he left Nyanza for exile in the south. He travelled, as he preferred, in a hammock carried by Twa porters, leaving that automobile—and, presumably, the sky-blue uniform with gold braid—for Rudahigwa's use.[74] Musinga's deposition was received by the old with stupefaction—Rudahigwa, they said, was 'l'homme des Blancs' and knew nothing of their customs—but by young Belgian-educated chiefs with enthusiasm.[75] The administration, too, professed itself content. Although Rudahigwa and his young, Catholic wife seemed to an American woman who stumbled into Nyanza soon after like 'two very clean, well-dressed, polite children playing at keeping house' in the cold, modern villa the Belgians had built for them,[76] officials reported that the new *mwami* was taking their advice and had dutifully toured the country to promote swamp drainage and the cultivation of manioc and commercial coffee. Rudahigwa had a deplorable soft spot for his father, providing him with ample herds and pleading against his deportation, but otherwise was giving complete satisfaction.[77]

Belgium's action could have been an international incident. No mandatory power had relied more on the language of trusteeship and indirect rule. Belgian officials had won Gisaka from the British by proclaiming their solicitude for Musinga's authority; when defending Rwanda and Burundi's administrative union with Belgian Congo, they had promised to sustain the native order. Yet when the Mandates Commission heard about the ouster of Musinga—one year later, in November 1932—the members gave Halewyck de Heusch no trouble at all. Enough had been said about Musinga's cruelty and immorality to convince the Commission that—as Pierre Orts helpfully interjected—the administration had perhaps been too lenient in not deposing him sooner. The fact that the monarchy itself had been retained also placated Lugard, who worried only that the new *mwami* might have been Europeanized by his education at the 'chiefs' school', but he was reassured to be told that 'native customs' would henceforth be taught there.[78] Denuded of its power, the patina of tradition would remain.

From the Belgian standpoint, the fourfold reforms of 1928–32 were a thoroughgoing success, producing an astonishingly dense road network, food surpluses, and the beginnings of an export economy by the mid-1930s. Another famine was 'out of the question', Pierre Ryckmans, now Governor General of Congo, reported to the Mandates Commission in 1936, for even if local shortages occurred, food could be rushed swiftly to that region. Ryckmans stressed, however, that the cultural transformation had been just as profound. The new *mwami* was cooperating on all fronts with the Belgian regime, and rapid Christianization had inclined Tutsi chiefs to accept European advice on economic questions as well. Coffee cultivation was proceeding, and the balance of payments, once radically against the mandated territory, had swung in its favour.[79]

The Belgians insisted that the regime which had produced this happy result remained one of 'indirect rule'. Privately, some officials admitted that that was nonsense. Not only was their regime not 'indirect', the district officer for Nyanza commented in 1930, but it was 'the most direct rule possible', for wasn't the administrator involved 'in the smallest details of policy?' Weren't 'the tiniest quarrels brought to him for resolution?' Wasn't he 'in constant contact not only with "sub-chiefs" but even with all the people under them?'[80] On the Mandates Commission, too, Lugard and his successor Malcolm Hailey said that chiefs had too little authority, and were deposed too readily, for the system to be considered 'indirect'. It was, Hailey insisted in 1938, simply a bureaucratic structure, albeit one employing native officials instead of whites.[81]

Hailey was correct, but only to a point. For, however bureaucratized, the apparatus built up in Rwanda and Burundi was also structured along ethnic lines and continued to rely on such 'feudal' forms of service as the unpaid labour levies that Lugard found so objectionable. Halewyck de Heusch insisted that such practices, being 'traditional', were essential to the regime's legitimacy. Any 'slackening of the feudal bonds' uniting the native society would 'throw the whole social structure into confusion'.[82] That forced labour fostered ethnic harmony seems far-fetched—and yet Halewyck was not wrong to see such practices as a crucial tool of legitimation. The point is that they legitimated Belgian rule in the eyes of (many) Europeans, not in the eyes of the native majority.

In a recent book Karuna Mantena has argued that the ideology of 'indirect rule', elaborated by Henry Maine in India and above all by Lugard in Africa, functioned as an 'alibi of empire'. By constructing an image of native society as at once culturally coherent and vulnerable, and hence as intrinsically 'different', such theories could then deploy that 'difference' as a justification for protective imperial rule.[83] This certainly describes the dynamic of Belgian rule in Rwanda and Burundi, where coercive practices were reconstructed and adapted to new ends, and then identified as too integral to native custom to be discarded. Forced labour thus appeared not as a pillar of on-the-cheap colonial development but as a time-sanctioned 'native' form. Practices that were explicitly forbidden under mandate, indeed that aroused strenuous condemnation when indulged in by white settlers in South West Africa, were considered benign when deployed by (or, more accurately, required of) 'primitive' Africans.

Benign, but not modern. If the language of 'indirect rule' rationalized forced labour as a 'native custom', shifting responsibility for this key colonial practice onto Africans themselves, that sleight of hand also reinscribed 'natives' as ineluctably backward. Rwandan and Burundian peasants had to work for chiefs without pay because such was their 'tradition', but such traditions were also the mark of how primitive they were. In 1938 the Norwegian member Valentine Dannevig noted in some bewilderment the paradox that intense involvement in Belgian rule seemingly had not raised up the population. To the contrary, while Tutsi elites had in the past often been described as more advanced, 'they were now constantly spoken of as very backward'. Halewyck de Heusch could only reply that all Africans were, indeed, sadly backwards.[84] Belgium would have to stay in control for a long, long time.

★ ★ ★

Rwanda and Burundi were what we might call the mandates system's 'limit case' of economic development pursued through an ostensibly traditional structure of indirect rule. In no other mandated territory were ethnic hierarchy and economic coercion bound so tightly and perniciously together. Yet the dynamic at the heart of the Belgian system—the refashioning of indigenous authorities into an officer corps for a command economy—was common enough. This was the dynamic that Buell found officials operating in French Cameroon, that Donald Cameron set up in Tanganyika, and that the Belgians sought to recreate in Congo as well. The ostensible aim was to steer Africa towards 'progress' without dislocating local cultures or planting seeds of rebellion. Yet, as Buell noticed and a generation of African historians have confirmed, colonial officials and local notables or clients transformed or even invented tribal structures in the process, sometimes producing, in Mahmood Mamdani's apt phrase, a 'decentralized despotism' of unelected authorities exercising arbitrary power.[85]

It may seem paradoxical that these labour regimes were being refined and elaborated just as conventions restricting forced labour appeared. Yet, as the Rwandan case makes clear, that coincidence was not paradoxical at all. Imperialism, by the interwar years, was to justify itself through 'development'. By vanquishing famine—even if famine had been caused in part by its own exactions—the mandatory regime would prove its worth. But how could a cash-strapped small state like Belgium find the resources for such a project? It found them—not only the physical bodies to do the work but also the ostensibly traditional ethnic hierarchies to command them—within the local population itself.

Members of the Mandates Commission, in their roles as overseers of mandatory administration and advisors to the League and the ILO, struggled to reconcile the dual imperatives to restrict forced labour and promote development. Inscribing force under the banner of 'custom' helped them to do so. True, the severity of the Rwandan famine also inclined them to accept practices—forcible cultivation, *corvée* labour for portage and roadwork—that might otherwise have been condemned. Yet, as we have seen, coercion also became palatable when it was seen to be intrinsic to 'indirect rule'. This appropriation of his conceptual apparatus greatly irritated Lugard, who wanted mandatory administrations to replace unpaid *corvées* and chiefly exactions with fees and salaries, but his hectoring fell on deaf ears. If they paid lip service to 'traditional' rule, officials reasoned, they would be left free to implement it as they saw fit.

This was the case. The fact that the Mandates Commission refrained from condemning 'traditional' chiefly prerogatives is one sign; that the Commission in essence dismissed Buell's allegations a second one; and the fate of the ILO's Forced Labour Convention a third. On the ILO's Committee of Experts on Native Labour, France's Martial Merlin and several other colonial representatives fought hard to insert language that would safeguard their states' prerogatives, and the Convention showed the fruits of that work. While all signatories were to move towards abolition of forced labour, a set of ostensibly 'traditional' practices—'minor communal services', work customarily done collectively, and compulsory cultivation imposed as a precaution against famine—were all excluded from that category, and the right of 'duly recognized chiefs' to levy 'personal services' was explicitly allowed. Yet, moderate though the convention was, of the major imperial powers only Britain, Japan, and the Netherlands ratified it immediately, Italy waiting until 1934, France until 1937, Belgium until 1944, and Portugal until 1956.[86]

While restricting some forms of forced labour, then, international oversight legitimated other forms. Those colonial and mandatory powers who wished to use indirect rule as a mechanism of labour control would have little difficulty doing so in the 1930s. And most did wish to do so, not only because forced labour allowed them to pursue development on-the-cheap but also because, at a time when the mandatory powers faced increased pressure from revisionist states for a redistribution of colonial spoils, it kept the work of development securely in their own hands. This response dovetailed nicely too with a wider shift towards tariffs, preferences, and the construction of trading blocs in the wake of the 1929–31 recession. When global trade revived in the mid-1930s, it would be along those imperial and regional lines.

If the Mandates Commission defeated attempts by the mandatory powers to claim legal sovereignty, then, its record in the realm of economic regulation was far more mixed. Formally, the mandates enshrined the 'open door' principle, but while international trade to territories under mandate was kept 'freer' than to other territories—enabling Japanese silk manufacturers, for example, to swamp and destroy the Syrian silk industry in the 1930s[87]—those territories could not be immune from protectionist trends. Rather than serving to 'liberalize' global trade as a whole, they were drawn everywhere into their guardian's imperial economic network. Whether greater liberalization would have raised local living standards is, in any case, highly debatable. The 'open door' was imposed to ease great-power rivalries and grant a level playing field, not to benefit local populations. What is clear, however, is that the drive for 'development' in the absence of either resources or investment drove mandate administrations to extend the use of compulsion under the sign of 'custom'. 'Free labour' proved as elusive a goal as 'free trade'.

What then do we find under the mandates regime? We find former Ottoman and German territories knit into imperial networks through administrative and economic means and outside the legal umbrella of sovereignty. Those forms of control were not less intense, they were merely different, implicitly posing the question of whether great powers might be able to do without formal sovereignty altogether. Might economic dependence and political alliance be an attractive alternative not only to formal rule but also to the irritating oversight of Geneva? In the 1970s and 1980s scholars would craft new names and theories—dependency, neo-imperialism—to try to understand why legal sovereignty and economic sovereignty seemed farther apart than ever, but as historians of 'informal empire' have shown, such arrangements have a long history. The mandates system was not doing something new, then, when it drove a wedge between political and economic sovereignty. What was new was that it explicitly posed the question of whether such forms of governance would become normative.

Once again, Britain forced the question. In 1929 the British Foreign Office informed Geneva that it intended to support Iraq's candidacy for League membership in 1932. But Britain still controlled Iraq's airbases and oilfields; how then could Iraq be considered 'independent'? As political tensions and the global economic crisis worsened, a new definition of 'independence' was emerging.

# NINE

## An Independence Safe
## for Empire

I hold the view that, as regards the A-mandates the mandatory relationship should only be maintained as long as is absolutely necessary, for it is only desirable, and especially on the part of those powers who have no mandates, that the A-mandates should become independent as soon as possible. Independence, however...cannot consist in the mandatory relationship being abandoned in favour of a single power, with which the former mandated territory enters into a new and indeed uncontrollable relation of dependence.

Ludwig Kastl to Vito Catastini, 8 December 1928[1]

It would be wrong to suppose that, *a priori*, the emancipation of a country would result in its happiness. It was a great thing for the countries under 'A' mandate, which had not been prepared by their past history to govern themselves, to be guided in the exercise of liberty by States of a high civilization. The League of Nations should, in the interests of those countries, object to their emancipation if it was not justified by their standard of evolution and was only in the interests of the mandatory Power. Premature emancipation before the country under mandate had become capable of governing itself 'under the strenuous conditions of the modern world' would be a marked failure of the mandate...

Pierre Orts, 19 November 1929[2]

In the late 1920s, with Germany in the League and the world economy not yet in crisis, the effort to subject imperial authority to international norms was ascendant. Yet, 'internationalized' empire was still empire: League oversight did not bring self-determination any nearer. For, if the Mandates Commission sought to deprive imperial powers of exclusive economic and political sovereignty, this was because they insisted that such rights must be shared by 'civilization' as a whole. Most battles in Geneva in this period were over the extent of international authority, not over the rights of indigenous populations.

But in 1929 Britain broke ranks with its fellow mandatory states. On 4 November the Foreign Office informed Sir Eric Drummond that Britain would support Iraq's entry into the League as an independent state in 1932.[3] This communication sent shock waves through the Secretariat, the Foreign Ministries of the major European powers, and nationalist movements in Syria and Palestine alike. Although the Anglo-French Declaration of 1918 and Article 22 of the League Covenant had both acknowledged the national aspirations of the Middle Eastern populations, no text and no power had put forward a roadmap for their realization. Indeed, by the late 1920s most had made clear that they thought independence unimaginable or had opened fire on inhabitants who claimed it. And while the Mandates Commission had sometimes objected to such repression, it too thought oversight would last a very long time. There was no precedent for what Britain was doing.

Or was there? Plenty of British advisors and statesmen during the First World War had thought 'self-determination' could serve their ends; they could cite many instances where Britain guaranteed the 'independence' of various 'native states' in exchange for exclusive commercial privileges or military alliances. Indeed, Britain had made such an agreement with Faysal's brother Abdullah in Transjordan in 1928, brushing off the reservations of the Mandates Commission by pointing out that the Covenant's promises to communities under 'A' mandate would be 'meaningless if no delegation of administrative powers is to be permitted', and that Britain was retaining overall control anyway.[4] Yet the plan for Iraq went beyond such precedents for the simple reason that it was more than a bilateral arrangement. Faysal's Iraq, unlike Abdullah's Transjordan, was to become 'sovereign' not merely over its own territory and subjects but in the international arena—to become, in other words, a state among states. But this would take more than a British declaration: it would require a unanimous vote in the League Assembly, the closest thing to a global government that the world had yet known.

Iraq would be the only mandated territory to go through this process of 'emancipation'. But no one at the time knew that. The British, the Iraqis, the Mandates Commission, the jittery French, and indeed people living under mandate in Syria and Palestine next door hoped or feared that this was a precedent in the making. And if we think of today's world, in which

United Nations recognition has to a considerable degree displaced state capacity as the gateway to independence, who is to say they were wrong? Iraq was the first case in which the pre-eminent global institution changed the international standing of a territory—from 'dependent' to 'independent'— without war and through member vote: that is why it mattered so much. And that was why, when the British announced their plan, people around the world felt the tectonic plates shifting.[5]

## The evolution of British strategy in Iraq

Why did Britain make this daring move? It was the culmination of the plan, hammered out in 1921, to lower the dreadful military and financial costs of the Mesopotamian occupation by establishing a loyal Arab government in Baghdad. By the time British officials had engineered Faysal's coronation as King of Iraq, however, the territory had already been declared a League of Nations mandate—a status Faysal and Iraq's emerging nationalist movement found unacceptable.[6] Thus while Britain publicly promised the League Council that it would remain accountable for Iraq's administration,[7] as early as 1922 Colonial Under-Secretary William Ormsby-Gore privately explored the possibility of replacing the mandate with a bilateral treaty between Britain and Iraq. In Geneva, William Rappard warned him off. Such a course of action would be 'very strongly resented' not only by the French for its disruptive influence on Syria, but also—should that treaty include any special privileges for Britain in Iraq—by other Council members. The mandates system was to spread the advantages of imperial rule across the Western powers. If Britain withdrew Iraq from that system while incorporating it into its own sphere, those advantages would henceforth become a monopoly of Britain alone.[8]

Putting their strategic alliances above League solidarity, British officials had cautiously proceeded anyway, crafting a treaty with their Iraqi collaborators that recognized the new state's 'national sovereignty' while binding King Faysal to be guided by British advice 'on all important matters'. Financial, military, and judicial agreements were painstakingly worked out, through which Iraq ceded defence of the country to the Royal Air Force, agreed to maintain a number of British judges, and accepted a British advisor in each Iraqi ministry.[9] Those negotiations were anything but easy. The treaty was finalized in October 1922 only after High Commissioner Percy

Cox shut down nationalist newspapers and deported key opposition leaders, and not until 1924 was it finally forced through the Constituent Assembly. Yet, however unequal, the treaty was less humiliating than the mandate, and in the course of its negotiation Britain made several key concessions, reducing its duration from twenty years to a mere four, and promising to try to secure the disputed and oil-rich province of Mosul for Iraq and then to consider the country's candidacy for League entry at specified four-year intervals.[10] In 1924 Britain persuaded the League Council that the treaty, and not the still-unratified 1920 draft mandate, would govern British obligations to both Iraq and the League.[11]

Attention then turned to Mosul, but while resolution of this territorial dispute secured the new state's borders, it also brought the League further into the game. Turkey had refused to cede Mosul in the Treaty of Lausanne so the matter had been referred to Geneva, which in 1925 dispatched three commissioners to determine the will of the local population, about 60 per cent of which was Kurdish. British political officers, who were still administering the province, were instructed secretly to organize support for the Iraqi case, but it was a close-run thing, for Kurdish notables plumped for Iraq mostly in the hope that the British would protect Kurdish autonomy. When the commissioners recommended that Mosul be awarded to Iraq, they stipulated that the mandate continue for a considerable time—perhaps twenty-five years—and that Kurdish areas be administered by the Kurds themselves. Formally, Britain and Iraq both welcomed the decision—they had, after all, won—but the treaty they concluded in January 1926, while dutifully extending the mandate for twenty-five years, qualified this with the proviso that it would of course lapse if Iraq were admitted to the League at an earlier date.[12]

Indeed, in the eyes of Faysal and his ministers, the way was now clear for Britain to concede independence. A serious campaign in favour of League entry was in the offing, High Commissioner Henry Dobbs warned London in late 1926—and, to protect its own strategic interests and alliances, Britain should acquiesce.[13] Neither the Colonial Office nor key members of Baldwin's Conservative government were persuaded. The measure would be popular in Baghdad, one official minuted, but since Iraq was a 'mere geographical expression' and not a state, how could it be ready for self-government? He wished Britain could support Iraq's case and manoeuvre some other power—ideally the French—into turning it down, but such a plan 'would, in order to be successful, demand on the part of the British representatives concerned, a skill in dissimulation and deceit which is happily foreign to our national character, and on the part of other members of the League a degree of benevolent discretion for which it would be extremely unwise to look'.[14] Sir Hugh Trenchard, the Air Marshal who had found Iraq such a wonderful arena in which to try out his ideas about 'air policing' (that is, bombing local tribes into submission), blustered into the Colonial Office to tell one nonplussed civil servant that Britain should simply tell Faysal and his henchmen to shut up. 'It was time that this play-acting ceased,' Trenchard insisted, and anyway 'in dealing with Arabs, it was necessary to take a firm line'.[15] Colonial Secretary Leo Amery agreed: to propose Iraq for immediate League membership would be seen in Geneva as 'sharp practice' and open Britain to the charge that they had secured Mosul by making promises they had no real intention of keeping.[16] They would support Iraq's entry in 1932, the Cabinet decided, and Amery blithely told Baghdad that Britain would welcome another League Travelling Commission to ascertain whether such a serious step was justified.[17]

Amery was probably right to think that Geneva would have been astounded by a British proposal for Iraqi independence as early as 1928, although he was also clearly looking for an excuse not to go forward. (He was rarely so solicitous of the League's feelings.) For Faysal and the Iraqi nationalists, however, his decision came as a betrayal. After months of intense negotiations a new treaty recognizing Iraq 'as an independent sovereign State' and removing many of the more humiliating constraints on the Iraqi government was agreed, but since this treaty modified Britain's pledge to support Iraq's entry in 1932 with the fateful words 'provided the present rate of progress . . . is maintained and all goes well', Iraqi nationalists mobilized against it.[18] Nearly two years of political stalemate followed, with disagreement, predictably, crystallizing around Britain's military rights after independence. Yet, both Dobbs and his successor Gilbert Clayton (another old Arab Bureau hand) believed agreement was possible. Iraq's nationalist politicians, although eager to build their army, did not relish the prospect of keeping control of restive tribes without the RAF either. On their advice, and with a new Labour government in London, the stalemate was finally broken. In September 1929 Britain told Iraq that it would unconditionally support its entry into the League in 1932, that the unratified 1927 treaty would be dropped, and that a new treaty resolving all outstanding questions would be negotiated. The Colonial Office now had to bring the League round.

## The Colonial Office and the Mandates Commission square off

That the Colonial Office would face an uphill battle became clear immediately, for the British announcement reached Geneva just as the members of the Mandates Commission arrived for their sixteenth session. Anyone who might think that the mandates system existed to bring dependent territories swiftly to statehood need only listen to their reaction to be disabused. Only the Spaniard Leopoldo Palacios and the German Ludwig Kastl said forthrightly that 'the emancipation of the territories under mandate was, or ought to be, the normal goal of their development'.[19] Other members were horrified by Britain's unilateral action. They voiced 'a good deal of well-bred surprise, and even incredulity at the sincerity of His Majesty's Government's conviction that Iraq would be fit to enter the League in 1932', the Colonial Office's Gerald Clauson reported back to London, and they had peppered Sir Bernard Bourdillon, the acting High Commissioner following Clayton's sudden death, with hostile questions.[20] Why did Britain think Iraq could govern itself? If it was making progress, was that not because British advisors controlled every ministry? The Commission had seen little evidence of the Iraqi government's ability to function on its own, but enough to question its probity. Remember, Orts and Rappard pointed out, the petition the previous year from Baghdad's Bahai community over the wrongful seizure of a house sacred to them which bordered on a Shi'i site. The Commission had upheld the Bahai claim, but the Iraqi government, anxious of Shi'i loyalties, had not seen justice done. 'In a country... where religious fanaticism pursues minorities and controls power,' Orts lectured, 'a state of affairs prevails which is not calculated to ensure the development and well-being of the inhabitants.'[21]

Bourdillon handled the Commission well, pointing out that whatever Iraq's defects, it was as capable and indeed as 'independent' as some other League states. Yet the PMC's majority remained sceptical. Caution was appropriate, Orts insisted, for independence was not invariably a good thing:

It was possible to imagine the case of a mandatory Power which might wrongfully deny to a territory under mandate the right to govern itself because it wished to maintain that country under its authority. It was possible also that a mandatory Power, overburdened by the charges involved in the exercise of the mandate, or forced by considerations of a political nature, either domestic or external, might declare that a territory was ready to be emancipated when this was not so.

In the latter case (and it was clear Orts thought Iraq was just such a case), the League would be entirely justified in refusing to end the mandate.[22] Over the reservations of Kastl and Palacios, the majority concluded that it would welcome Iraq's entry only 'if and when' it became clear that the territory was able to 'stand alone' and effective safeguards could be secured for its religious and racial minorities and for League member states.[23]

Britain, stunned by the Commission's reaction, tried to bypass it entirely. Setting conditions for League entry was not the Commission's job, protested Labour's Foreign Secretary, Arthur Henderson; if anything, this was the prerogative of the Assembly—which, dominated by small states, was certain to welcome a new member. It is a sign of how anxious the imperial powers were about Britain's proposal that the Council instead elevated the Commission's standing, first requesting its advice about when a mandated territory might be considered ripe for emancipation, and then, eighteen months later, about whether Iraq had met the conditions laid out.[24] Those decisions meant that the Commission became the target of some two years of public appeals and private lobbying, as not only Britain and Iraq but also Iraq's minority communities and various interested League states tried to promote, shape, or halt the process of Iraqi independence.

But what did 'independence' mean? When and how might a territory achieve statehood? In late 1930 and early 1931 the Commission—well aware that it was making international law—began hammering out a doctrine.[25] That a mandate *could* end was clear from the League Covenant, for if the system had been constructed to protect peoples 'not yet able to stand by themselves', the implication must be that they might one day do so. But it was not for the inhabitants to decide when this day had come, the Commission's legal expert D. F. W. Van Rees insisted, and 'in the case of the African and South Pacific territories, this goal is beyond dispute still so remote that it would be safe to say that it is really no more than of theoretical interest'.[26] Instead, whether the stage had been reached was a question of fact, of the empirical and observable condition of the territory's institutions. In June 1931 the Commission thus laid out the minimal requirements a territory must have to be considered 'ready' for independence: a settled administration, the capacity to maintain its territorial integrity, the ability to keep internal order, adequate financial resources, and a judicial apparatus that would afford equal justice to all.[27] It need not be able to repel any possible attack entirely on its own, Lugard added, for that was a standard few small states could meet; internally, however, it had to have the rudimentary capacities of the modern bureaucratic state.[28]

This was a list of conditions many European political theorists of the day would have endorsed, but the Commission did not stop there. For the state in question was not being freed to act like an unbound captive in a Hobbesian war of all against all but rather to join a League community bound by norms to which it should conform. The mandates system had been set up as part of a peace settlement, Portugal's Count de Penha Garcia pointed out, and it was reasonable to insist that Iraq's emancipation not disrupt that peace.[29] The new state must thus honour commitments made by the mandatory government, accede to League conventions, and, most important, offer specific guarantees to alleviate the international community's doubts on particular points. After months of pressure and lobbying, the Commission knew just what those sticking points would be. League member states would insist that the new state guarantee equal economic privileges to fellow members; the Commission would insist that it safeguard minority rights.[30]

British colonial officials in London and Baghdad thus faced a difficult task. They knew that the Commission was 'distinctly hostile' to their plans, yet, concerned about their reputation in Geneva, they felt constrained to gain its consent.[31] They thus embarked on a painstaking, multi-pronged campaign less to persuade the PMC that Iraq had met its conditions than to make it impossible for the Commission to say it had not. First, they restricted the Commission's independent access to information, successfully preventing the League from sending out a fact-finding mission. (Such a prospect, cheerfully contemplated by Amery when the aim had been to slow down independence, was now out of the question.)[32] Second, they inundated the Commission with their own information, providing detailed observations on all petitions and writing a highly selective (one might say, 'sexed-up') survey of the expanding capacity of the Iraqi government under Britain's eleven-year tutelage.[33] Third, they dispatched the imposing new High Commissioner, Sir Francis Humphrys, to Geneva for the June 1931 and November 1931 PMC sessions. There, Humphrys stayed relentlessly on message, lobbying members individually and hosting luncheon parties featuring Iraqi ministers Nuri al-Sa'id and Ja'far al-'Askari.[34] Finally, they negotiated intensely behind the scenes to reconcile key states to the British plan.

That plan was carried out over the inward reservations of much of the officialdom itself. 'We are very doubtful of the truth of our own opinion that Iraq is fit for admission,' J. E. W. Flood at the Colonial Office admitted privately in October 1930,[35] and British staff in Iraq were if possible even less sanguine. Sir Kinahan Cornwallis, advisor to the Interior Ministry and in Iraq continuously since 1920, for example, doubted that there was a single British official who would agree with British statements about the steady progress of the Iraqi government. He himself thought that British withdrawal would lead to a period of near-anarchy followed by British reoccupation or the emergence of a dictator.[36] Reading these blunt comments, Elie Kedourie's old charge—that British officials supported Iraqi independence out of an excess of liberal idealism and self-delusion—falls to the ground.[37] Pragmatic calculations drove them. If Britain wished to retain control of Iraq's airfields and oilfields but was not willing to spend money and lives reoccupying the country (and it was not), there was no other choice. 'His Majesty's Government are committed lock stock and barrel to the opinion that Iraq will be fit for admission to the League by 1932,' Flood stated baldly, 'and whatever happens we must stand by that.'[38]

That strategy was successful, enabling Britain to secure its privileged position in Iraq for another quarter-century. But we must look more closely at the nature of that victory. For the 'emancipation' of Iraq required *international* approval, and to secure that approval two consequential bargains were struck—one over the extent of Iraq's economic and military sovereignty, the second over its internal authority. The great powers negotiating behind the scenes cared most about the first issue; the public debate in London and Geneva focused more around the second. But it is in the relationship between those two bargains—that is, in the way internal domination was traded for external concessions—that we begin to see a new definition of 'independence' emerging.

## Conditions for independence I: sharing the spoils

If we want to understand the emergence of the first of those bargains, we could do worse than to eavesdrop on the conversations about Iraq going on in the German Foreign Ministry. Ostensibly, Weimar Germany had no real interest in Iraq—no significant investments, no military ties—but that was, in a sense, the problem. Before 1914 German firms had won Ottoman concessions for oil exploration and railway construction in the Mosul region, and they were eager to re-establish their presence. But how, given British and French mandatory control in the region, could they do so? Or, to put the matter more generally, how could Germany regain 'great-power' status in the absence of formal empire? Gustav Stresemann hoped that League membership could widen Germany's opportunities, but as we have seen in the last chapter, in Africa at least that had yielded rather modest returns. How, then, might British moves in the Middle East affect Germany? For the Foreign Ministry, that was the question.

The person assigned to answer it was Fritz Grobba, the talented Arabist, former consul in Kabul, and later ambassador to Baghdad during the Nazi era, who headed the Ministry's Middle East and South Asia section in the late 1920s. Grobba followed debates over Iraq within the PMC and the Council closely, gaining a sophisticated understanding of just what the British were doing. Britain wished to retain its military and economic advantages in Iraq, he concluded—but at a low cost, with Arab collaboration, and free from harassing international oversight. This strategy confronted Germany with a dilemma. As a power without an empire, Germany too wished to see the Middle East mandates move rapidly to independence; unlike Britain, however, Germany needed that independence to be real. Thus, while Britain would make special military rights the condition of its withdrawal and other imperial powers would likely demand economic concessions, Germany should not do the same. Having had its own economic sovereignty constrained by the Versailles Treaty, Grobba advised, 'we must reject the imposition of such economic restrictions on another land on moral grounds'.[39] Yet, if morally right, this policy was also reassuringly pragmatic, for if Germany won the new state's friendship, economic concessions would likely follow.[40] At the League Council in January 1930, German State Secretary Carl von Schubert announced that Germany supported Iraqi independence free from harassing conditions—a statement that, Grobba noted, made a great impression in Iraq.[41]

Ludwig Kastl, the German member, capably represented the Foreign Ministry's views on the PMC. Well before Britain had announced its plan Kastl had made it clear that he supported independent statehood for the Middle East territories, provided such independence did not 'consist in the mandatory relationship being abandoned in favour of a single power, with which the former mandated territory enters into a new and indeed uncontrollable relation of dependence'.[42] While Kastl thus welcomed the British plan, he also insisted that the Commission scrutinize Iraq's treaty arrangements and economic concessions so as to gauge the true extent of its future independence. Just who would control Iraq's airfields and oilfields?

The Anglo-Iraq Treaty signed in June 1930 made it clear that defence at least would remain in British hands. Britain did recognize Iraqi sovereignty, but at a considerable price—including the right to move troops over Iraqi soil, the continued presence of the RAF, British ownership of two airbases, the right to train and equip the Iraqi Army, the continued employment of some British judges, and a phased diminution of other British staff.[43] Such provisions hardly seemed compatible with Iraq's 'complete independence', and as the Mandates Commission reviewed British policy and then the treaty across three separate sessions in 1930 and 1931, the German argument that Britain was effectively constructing a 'protectorate in disguise' came to be echoed by other members, notably Palacios, Theodoli, and Rappard. The question, Palacios told acting High Commissioner H. W. Young at the November 1930 session, was whether a new and genuinely international institution—the mandates system, under supervision of the League—was being done away with in favour of a bilateral system of protection removed from international oversight.[44] Whether such a change was genuinely to Iraq's advantage remained an open question, Rappard added a year later, for when a territory had to sue for its independence while under mandate, the mandatory power could easily 'compel the territory . . . to accept conditions contrary to its interests'.[45]

When it came to those airbases, however, the PMC proved reluctant to condemn Britain's continued hold. This was the case not only because no other power had strong strategic interests in Iraq, but also because the majority of the Commission, awash in petitions from anxious Assyrians and Kurds, also wanted to keep the RAF's bombers and bases out of Iraqi hands. The possibility that the RAF might be used against minority populations was raised repeatedly in the British press in the spring of 1931, provoking anxious questions from Lugard and Rappard at the June PMC session. Since Kurdish rebels had been bombed on British command in the mid-1920s, it is hard to see why (beyond simple racism) the Commission found the prospect of their being bombed on Iraqi command so disturbing. Nevertheless, the PMC did so, and Humphrys' assurance that the treaty 'contained no obligation to assist the Iraq Government to suppress internal disorder' only partly calmed its nerves.[46] That the treaty deprived the Iraqi government of the 'monopoly of the legitimate use of force' that Max Weber thought the essence of statehood was thus to be welcomed. As one British official noted, although most members of the PMC found it 'difficult to say' that the treaty 'did not in some measure impair the independence' of Iraq, they nevertheless thought it 'quite clearly in Iraq's best interest' to be so hampered.[47] Thus was the client state justified.

Oilfields were another matter. All major powers had an interest in their fate. All were aware that Mosul was 'a veritable "lake of petroleum" of almost inexhaustible supply', as a German technical commission had put it in 1901.[48] The decision of Lloyd George's government to remain in Iraq and to claim Mosul was based on the understanding that, as Cabinet Secretary Sir Maurice Hankey instructed Balfour in 1918, 'oil in the future would be as important as coal is now': hard bargaining over oil took place behind the scenes when the Middle East territories were parcelled out at San Remo and through the 1920s.[49] Those negotiations followed many twists and turns; by 1928, however, control of oil exploration and production within a 'red line' drawn around the whole of Anatolia, Arabia, and the mandated Middle East was essentially in the hands of four conglomerates representing largely British, American, Dutch, and French interests, and the exclusive concession to explore in Iraq was in the hands of the 'Iraq Petroleum Company' (IPC), at this stage largely a subsidiary of Anglo-Persian Oil. For our purposes, three things about this emerging producer's cartel stand out: first, that neither Germany nor Italy held any share; second, that the Iraqi government, while owed (and desperately in need of) royalties to be paid on production, also had no share in or control of the concession it had been forced—as the price of British support for its bid to retain Mosul—to grant; and third, that the majority of the companies involved—that is, the British, Dutch, and American concerns—had other oil interests and, given surplus supply in the peaceful 1920s, wished to boost world prices by *delaying* drilling in Iraq. The IPC had exclusive control of Iraqi oil, but its major shareholders—except the French, who had no other major oil interests—had little incentive to find and pump it.[50]

In this situation, the Mandates Commission emerged as an arena for publicly contesting not only great-power strategic interests but oil claims as well. The grounds for that contestation were precisely those 'open-door' requirements of the mandate, and the mechanism was, unsurprisingly, the Commission's right to review mandatory administration and consider petitions alleging violations. In 1927 Kastl had already argued that the Commission should review the 1925 IPC contract extension to see whether it was compatible with the economic equality requirements, and while the Commission did not agree that there was any violation (since contracts did not have to be put out to public tender), Kastl's argument that Iraq's interests might have been better served through open competition clearly struck a nerve.[51] At the November 1929 session, not only Theodoli and Kastl (that is, PMC members from states excluded from the concession) but also Rappard and the French member Martial Merlin subjected Bourdillon to a sharp cross-examination about the IPC's behaviour. The government of Iraq appeared to have agreed to a policy of monopolization, Rappard, Theodoli, and Kastl all pointed out, but how could it 'hope to exploit the country's oil resources to the utmost if it suppressed all competition'? Merlin, expressing French dislike not of cartelization but rather of the IPC's dilatory progress, also stated that the company should have started drilling much sooner.[52] Pressure for a repartition of the spoils was building.

Six months later, with Iraqi independence on the horizon, that battle was out in the open. In 1928 an under-capitalized company misleadingly registered in London as the 'British Oil Development Company' (BOD) had approached the Iraqi government with an offer to drill and transport Mosul's oil, and while it seemed clear the company didn't have the capital to do so, the Iraqis were able to use the bid to put pressure on the IPC. In 1929 and 1930 the BOD also petitioned, arguing not only that the IPC's concession violated the principle of the 'open door' but also that the concession was void since the IPC had failed to complete its explorations within the contracted time. Its name notwithstanding, the BOD acted in part as a vehicle for the interests of states excluded from a share of Iraqi oil (notably Italy, for an Italian company, the Azienda Generale Italiana Petroli, purchased 40 per cent of the shares in 1929); the Iraqi government, desperate for the revenues that would arrive when the oil started flowing, also backed the BOD behind the scenes.[53] The June 1930 and November 1930 sessions at which those petitions were discussed thus revealed a sharp division among PMC members. Van Rees (Dutch) and Merlin (French) insisted that since the Iraqi government had agreed the IPC concession, the Commission could hardly contest their decision, while Theodoli, Rappard, and others retorted that since Iraq was still under mandate, it could well have been unable to defend its interest. The Colonial Office argued that the matter was outside the Commission's jurisdiction anyway since the BOD could pursue its claim in court (no Iraqi court would *take* such a case, the High Commissioner privately admitted, but the Colonial Office could still tell the PMC that the company could *pursue* one), but the majority of the Commission was nonetheless openly critical of what it rightly saw as the IPC's attempt at price-fixing by holding back Iraqi oil—a policy that left the Iraqi government mired in deficits.[54] Revealingly (and atypically), the Commission published the BOD's petitions and rival reports from various members in full as annexes to their *Minutes*.[55]

International pressure, and an awareness that Iraqi independence was fast approaching, finally lit a fire under the IPC. The period from 1930 to early 1931 was marked by intense negotiations between the company and the Iraqi government over both the level of royalty that the IPC would pay and the route of its proposed pipeline to the Mediterranean, which the Iraqi government and the British wanted to run exclusively through British-controlled territory and the French wished to route through Syria. Here, the French won out. They were able to take advantage of the British vulnerability to international criticism and the threat to install rivals to the Hashemites on the Syrian throne to persuade King Faysal to support a bifurcated pipeline, with separate trunks debouching in Tripoli and Haifa.[56] Construction finally began, and the Iraqi government, borrowing against future revenues, averted financial disaster. It did not escape the PMC's notice, however, that Iraq still held no share in the management of the nation's most valuable asset, nor that the Palestine and Syrian mandatory administrations had neither put the pipeline contracts out to tender nor even set conditions which would guarantee some benefit to those territories. At the 20th session in June 1931, Orts, Julius Ruppel (replacing Kastl), Rappard, and the Portuguese de Penha Garcia all roundly denounced the pipeline agreement. Britain, Rappard stated, 'had subordinated the interests of the country under its mandate to the interests of a company of its own nationality'.[57] As Fritz Grobba in the German Foreign Ministry noted, had the two sides been forced to a vote, the Commission would have (narrowly) condemned the British government.[58]

One of those critics, however, was motivated less by any desire to maximize Iraq's autonomy than by his government's determination to seize the main chance. In the growing criticism of British hegemony, Italy found its opportunity. The Colonial Office became seriously concerned about the possibility of Italian obstruction right after that spring 1931 PMC session, when the Italian ambassador informed the British Foreign Secretary, Arthur Henderson, that his government felt the question of Iraq's readiness for self-government should be turned over to a League Commission, 'as representative of all the allied Powers who share an equal right of Sovereignty on the territories under Mandate'.[59] But the Italians had no interests in Iraq, the Colonial Office insisted. What on earth were they after? In late July,

Humphrys met the ambassador and got an answer: a share of Iraqi oil.[60] 'It is unpleasant to have to submit to blackmail,' J. E. Hall at the Colonial Office minuted, but the BOD should probably be given a concession after all.[61] Faysal thought so as well, and by January 1932 negotiations were underway in Baghdad for a concession—granted in May—to the BOD.[62]

Italy was also concerned that the Iraq proposals not be seen as a precedent, Italian Foreign Minister Dino Grandi added, for while Italy did not object to Britain's plan 'to transform a mandate into a protectorate' (as he bluntly put it), it would not accept a similar French proposal for Syria, on which Italy had always had designs.[63] The mandates system, Grandi opined at the League Council in September 1931, had not been devised to create 'a system of permanent and special relations between the mandatory Power and the territory under mandate'; to the contrary, the clauses prohibiting fortifications and requiring an economic 'open door' had been written expressly to prevent such an outcome.[64] Largely to deter the French from following the British lead, Grandi then ordered Theodoli to cause as much trouble as possible for Britain at the November 1931 PMC session. His position, Theodoli didn't mind telling High Commissioner Humphrys privately, would 'be greatly eased' if the British could find some argument that would justify their treaty with Iraq but 'could not be used to defend a similar Treaty between France and Syria'. This took a little ingenuity, but Humphrys obliged, cooking up an argument about how Iraq's near-landlocked status meant that its defence required a degree of air support from Britain that Syria would not require from France.[65]

It is worth noting that while German officials had crafted the initial critique of British strategy, they did not engage in open blackmail of this kind. German and Italian policies were both based on a strict calculation of national interest, but while the Germans intervened to limit British constraints on Iraq's resources and sovereignty, the Italians did so to force Britain to share the spoils. One might say that the two states were articulating, if only partially and in embryonic form, two different international visions—the Germans of a world of formally equal sovereign states regulated largely through market competition (which they expected to win); the Italians of a world in which the great powers (among whom Italy liked to count itself) would negotiate their spheres of influence and extract privileges from the more vulnerable. Germany, unsurprisingly, recognized the use to which its arguments were being put and carefully sought to differentiate its position from Italy's. Thus, although Kastl's successor Julius Ruppel joined Theodoli,

Rappard, and Orts in criticizing the IPC's grip on Iraqi oil, he did not support Italy's suggestion that Iraq be required to grant all League states most-favoured-nation status for twenty-five years.[66] Likewise, German Foreign Minister Julius Curtius declined to make common cause with Grandi at that September 1931 Council, stating that Iraq's independence should not be hampered by excessive conditions.[67]

By the PMC's November 1931 session, all cards were on the table. The majority of its members, the Colonial Office knew, remained highly sceptical of Iraq's readiness for independence, and the few that favoured it were far from certain that it was on offer anyway. Even Palacios, who thought it normal and desirable for mandated territories to move towards statehood, worried the Anglo-Iraq Treaty might be a 'step backwards' from the mandate, which at least placed Britain under international oversight.[68] Yet, partly because members could not decide whether Iraq's continued tie to Britain was a scandal or a safeguard, partly because the Foreign Ministers had themselves taken control of the question, and especially (as we shall see) because they were preoccupied with Iraq's minorities, the PMC moved off centre-stage. To the relief of the Colonial Office, the Commission was asked to report merely on whether Iraq had met the conditions outlined in June and not to conduct the negotiations over any special guarantees. This task would fall to the Council, an unsentimental body which British officials could influence. True, they would probably face problems from the Italians but need go no further to meet them.[69] They now had, after all, French support.

Nothing is more revealing of the nature of the independence granted Iraq in 1932 than the role played by France. The Colonial Office had initially expected that France would cause the most trouble. France had, after all, expelled Faysal from Syria and remained very sensitive about Hashemite designs.[70] The Colonial Office was thus quick to attribute the PMC's early obstinacy to malign French influences and feared that Merlin would 'hold out for all sorts of guarantees and undertakings'.[71] But with its pipeline secured, France proved the dog that didn't bark; indeed, as officials at the Quai d'Orsay reflected on the expense, unpopularity, and international censure generated by French behaviour in Syria, they found Britain's Iraq policy—that of creating a cheap client state outside the realm of international scrutiny—increasingly attractive. Journalists and statesmen who had expected to hear the Quai d'Orsay's Robert de Caix condemn Britain's policy thus found him surprisingly mild; indeed, in June 1931 he told the

PMC that France also planned to negotiate a treaty with Syria and then end the mandate.[72] 'This is,' J. E. Hall of the Colonial Office commented, for once speaking the whole truth, 'the most striking compliment yet paid to our Iraq policy.'[73]

## Conditions for independence II: 'minorities protection'

For the Council and the great powers that dominated it, air power and oil mattered most. For the Mandates Commission, however, Iraq's internal situation, and especially the well-being of its minority populations, was just as important. Petitions from Kurdish and Assyrian populations sparked their concern, but so too did the 'Wailing Wall' riots in Jerusalem in 1929, which had claimed both Arab and Jewish lives. The Commission had held a special session investigating Britain's handling of that incident in the summer of 1930, and many of its members—especially Rappard, Orts, Van Rees, and Dannevig—had come to share the Zionist view that Arab leaders had deliberately incited the riots to force a retreat from the Balfour pledge, and that the Labour government, in planning to restrict Jewish immigration, had fallen straight into that trap. Those members drew two lessons from the 'Wailing Wall' controversy: first, that Arabs were excitable, prejudiced, and certainly unready for self-government; and second, that the British government was prone to appease agitators and lacked nerve.[74] Britain's plans for Iraq and the protests arriving from its minority populations lent credence to both those assumptions.

But the Iraq process did not simply reveal minorities' fears; it also helped establish the category of 'minority' within Iraq and indeed within international politics. That category was already much in play during the war and at the Paris Peace Conference, of course, for as polyglot empires dissolved and then were carved into nation states, the problem arose of what to do with those who felt excluded from a now bounded and politicized ethnos. The allied powers in Paris made some initial decisions, requiring new and reborn states across Eastern Europe to grant specific linguistic and cultural rights to minorities now within their borders. The task of managing that 'Minorities Protection Regime', however, fell to the League—as did the tasks of conducting plebiscites in disputed regions, helping to find homes for refugee 'minorities' from Asia Minor, and working out the Greco-

Turkish population exchange in 1923. A laudable concern to protect minorities from harm often underwrote these efforts, but as plebiscites, petitions, and boundary commissions proliferated, and especially as great powers seized on the grievances of particular minorities to pursue territorial or irredentist aims of their own, political effects grew hard to contain. The claim to 'minority' status, like the claim to 'national' status, produced both opportunities and dangers. Religious or ethnic groups claimed 'minority' status to win international support, but emergent states heard those appeals as assaults on their fragile sovereignty.[75]

The emancipation of Iraq brought those questions of nationhood and belonging to the fore. Iraq was imagined as an 'Arab' state, but what exactly might this mean? About half of the population of its three ex-Ottoman provinces of Basra, Baghdad, and Mosul were Shi'i Arabs, sharing the religious traditions of neighbouring Persia. Sunni Arabs and Kurds (mostly in the north) each comprised about a further fifth, with significant groups of Jews, Christians, Turks, and Yezidis making up the rest.[76] Some of these groups had their own 'national' dreams. The Shi'i clerics and tribesmen who had been the backbone of the 1920 rising hoped to bring about an independent and devoutly Islamic Iraq; Kurds strove for the autonomous Kurdistan envisaged in the abortive Treaty of Sèvres, agreed in 1920 by the Ottoman Empire. British guns and the emergence of the Turkish Republic shattered those visions and that treaty, making the marriage of convenience that was the Hashemite Kingdom of Iraq under British mandate possible. But if Faysal's rule rested on British support and the collaboration of much the same Sunni elite that had been the backbone of the Ottoman state, he was aware of the tenuous nature of his legitimacy. His governments thus spoke the language of Arab nation-building, sought to disguise the extent of their dependence on the British, built up an army and bureaucracy capable of uniting (and dominating) this disparate population, and cultivated the loyalty of largely Shi'i rural sheikhs by strengthening their near-feudal hold on their impoverished tenant-cultivators.[77]

Such strategies—along with the summary exile of key Shi'i clerics in the early 1920s—to a degree neutralized Shi'i resistance, and in the cities especially a fragile cosmopolitan culture emerged.[78] The army, too, proved an effective agency for Kurdish assimilation. Yet ethnic antagonisms festered, and the international petition process made them acute. In most territories, as we have seen, petitions were used to articulate collective and often proto-nationalist claims *against* mandatory rule; in Iraq, however, since an Arab government was nominally in control, petitions arrived from those ethnic and religious minorities who feared that government's growing power. Since those petitions did not challenge the mandate, and indeed usually wished to see oversight prolonged, the PMC could take them very seriously. Their impact was further heightened by the fact that the Iraqi government, having no standing in Geneva (yet), could not directly answer petitioners' charges. Only the mandatory power could 'speak' in Geneva. It was Britain's job to persuade the Commission that Iraq's minorities would be safe in the Iraqi state.

British officials faced an uphill battle, for the publication of the new Anglo-Iraq Treaty in 1930 unleashed an avalanche of petitions from Kurds and Assyrians. Both groups had good reason to feel betrayed. Given the recommendations of the Mosul Commission, many Kurds had assumed they would be granted self-government on Iraq's emancipation;[79] when they discovered that there were no such plans, they immediately asked the League to ensure their autonomy.[80] Those claims, British officials insisted, were impossible: the Kurds were 'essentially tribal', 'illiterate and untutored', and 'entirely lacking in those characteristics of political cohesion which are essential to successful self-government'. All that was needed was to protect Kurdish linguistic rights; once the Iraqi government had passed such a law, the Kurds would then have 'no legitimate cause for complaint'.[81] But Rappard was not so sure,[82] and even Humphrys privately admitted that Prime Minister Nuri al-Sa'id was stonewalling. The Iraqi government had already defined Kurdish autonomy as no more than requiring that local administrators know Kurdish; now it proposed to exempt key posts from that obligation. He would prefer not to give further assurances to the League, Humphrys told the Colonial Office, until he was certain that Nuri was acting in good faith.[83]

That day never came. The Iraqi government was trying to create a centralized state, not a federation of ethnic republics, and saw in British solicitude for the Kurds the spectre of the old proposal to create an autonomous Kurdistan. Persia and Turkey also found that prospect unacceptable, and in February 1931 Nuri privately assured Turkey that Iraq would never tolerate Kurdish separatism.[84] Humphrys and the Colonial Office thought this insubordinate and warned Nuri that if news of his action got out, Iraq's Kurdish policy would be regarded as merely 'a facade to impress foreign countries' and its prospects of admission to the League would be 'wholly destroyed'.[85] But while it was certainly true that Iraq's 'Kurdish policy' was a facade, Britain's threat to withdraw its support was (as Nuri surely realized) a bluff. Throughout 1931, although the law the Iraqi government had promised to pass to safeguard Kurdish language rights was whittled down further and risings in the Kurdish areas were suppressed by the Iraqi Army and the RAF, Humphrys and the Colonial Office steadfastly assured the PMC that Kurdish complaints of intimidation were exaggerated or fabricated. Rappard, trying to make sense of this 'jungle of assertions, denials, and explanations' when reporting on the second batch of petitions in mid-1931, became deeply frustrated. 'Never have I felt more keenly the weakness of the Mandates Commission's procedure in the matter of petitions.' Barred from conducting their own investigation, the PMC could only note Kurdish fears and urge the Council to establish meaningful protections at the moment of emancipation.[86]

Moreover, if the Commission was, by 1931, deeply uneasy about the situation of the Kurds, they could hardly contain their worry about the Assyrians. Nor was this anxiety misplaced, for Iraq's tens of thousands of Assyrians were uniquely vulnerable.[87] They were, to begin with, Christian, with a young English-speaking patriarch—the Mar Shimun—who had been educated under the protection of the Archbishop of Canterbury. The Assyrians were, second, Britain's wartime allies, having risen against the Ottomans at Russian instigation and having suffered terribly for their rebellion. Third, many were refugees and thus newcomers to Iraq, unable to return to their historic home in the Hakkiari mountains (now in the Turkish Republic), but reluctant to identify themselves as Iraqis and on poor terms with the Muslim population among which they were dispersed. But the fact that caused particular heart-burning among the Commission was that Assyrians not only were seen to be, but actually were, the shock troops of the British occupation. Excellent soldiers, culturally and ethnically distinct, many served in the 'Assyrian levies', special battalions under exclusively British command that had been used to guard airfields, defend Iraq's borders, and—ominously—put down rebellions among the Kurds.

Like so many imperial collaborators beloved by the commanders they served, the Assyrians found it hard to believe the British would abandon them. When they too discovered that the 1930 treaty did not mention them, however, they too petitioned the League. First through one Arthur Rassam, a former British officer of Assyrian descent who organized a noisy public campaign in their support, and later through their patriarch, they asked to be recognized as a distinct community and to be settled together in northern Iraq.[88] Once again, it was left to the British to assure the PMC that these demands were impossible, and that, if told so firmly, the Assyrians would surely calm down. Pierre Orts, reporting on the petitions, thus gave no support to the demand for political autonomy, although he too underscored the need for minority protections after the end of the mandate.[89] Yet the Assyrians—like the Kurds—manifestly declined to settle down. In October 1931 Assyrians in Mosul concluded that they could no longer live in Iraq and asked that a new home be found for them;[90] the following summer, most Assyrian soldiers resigned from the levies *en masse*. The mandate ended with Assyrian ex-soldiers heading to Syria for support and with a backlog of petitions still awaiting consideration in Geneva.

Nothing so perturbed the PMC as the situation of Iraq's beleaguered minorities. Fissures opened up within the British political elite as well, with the former Conservative Air Minister Samuel Hoare and former High Commissioners Arnold Wilson and Henry Dobbs breaking ranks to remind the government of Britain's historic obligations to the Assyrians and the Kurds.[91] The liberal leadership of the League of Nations Union, although reluctant to criticize publicly a Labour government deeply committed to the League, also began writing jittery private letters to the Foreign Office and Geneva.[92] But what, exactly, was to be done? One obvious solution— that the Assyrians be offered asylum in Britain, the land they had faithfully served—was never proposed, nor was a federal solution to meet Kurdish demands seriously discussed. Iraq was, after all, a state born under the sign of Arab nationalism, and Iraqi ministers worried that decentralization would, as Ja'far al-'Askari put it, 'undermine the foundations on which a settled government have gradually been built'.[93] British officials shared those fears, and although some admitted privately that they were worried about the likely fate of minorities, they exerted considerable pressure in Geneva to ensure that no international guarantees were asked of the Iraqis beyond those previously required of other states.

Humphrys especially proved crucial to this effort. In his discussions with the Commission in June 1931, he dismissed the Mar Shimun as 'an impressionable youth' and Rassam as little more than an adventurer.[94] Claiming that 'he had never found such tolerance of other races and religions as in Iraq', Humphrys stressed that all Iraq's inhabitants should consider themselves equal citizens—and, when all else failed, shouldered the fate of Iraq's minorities himself. 'His Majesty's Government,' he declared, 'fully realized its responsibility in recommending that Iraq should be admitted to the

League... Should Iraq prove herself unworthy of the confidence which had been placed in her, the moral responsibility must rest with His Majesty's Government.'[95] Nothing so impressed and silenced the Mandates Commission as this declaration. Even Rappard and Orts professed themselves 'completely satisfied'; if Britain assumed responsibility, Theodoli added, 'there was very little left for the Mandates Commission to ask'.[96] Although further petitions kept the minorities question to the fore during the PMC's November 1931 session, the British defeated a plan to place a League Commissioner on the ground, agreeing only that Iraq might come under the League's existing minorities' protection regime.[97] Obligations already submitted to by Poland, Albania, and other European states, it was thought, would not humiliate Iraq or derogate from its sovereignty. Britain may not have foreseen, but nor did it forestall, the consequences. In its first year of independence, 1933, the Iraqi Army would sweep through Assyrian villages, massacring as they went.[98]

The final stages of the Iraq drama, as played out in Geneva, were therefore surprisingly anodyne. Asked whether Iraq had met its conditions for independence, at the end of its November 1931 session the PMC gave Iraq what one official termed 'a very grudging "pass degree"'.[99] Paying unconscious tribute to the Colonial Office's success in controlling information, the Commission stated merely that it had 'no information which would justify a contrary opinion' to Britain's assertion of Iraq's preparedness. It specified that Iraq should promise to respect existing contracts, guarantee the rights of foreigners, and offer all League member states most-favoured-nation status for a fixed period. Unsurprisingly, however, it gave pride of place to the question of minorities, requiring Iraq declare its commitment to minority rights and enter the League's minority protection regime. The PMC also underscored Britain's 'moral responsibility', stating that without Humphrys' declaration they could never have contemplated ending a regime 'in the interests of all sections of the population'.[100] The Colonial Office thought the report 'as favourable as could have been hoped'.[101]

The discussion in the Council in January 1932 also went much as expected. No Council member had much direct interest in Iraq's minorities. All were more concerned to protect the privileges of their own citizens and their access to Iraq's lucrative resources and contracts.[102] Nuri al-Sa'id and Sir Francis Humphrys thus had little trouble persuading the Council committee appointed to draft the Iraqi guarantees to whittle down the pledges to the Kurds (the Iraqi Army and the RAF were at that moment

**Figure 9.1** Sir Francis Humphrys congratulating Hamed al-Wadi, the king's chamberlain, on the independence of Iraq, 6 October 1932.

repressing a Kurdish rebellion in northeastern Iraq), but utterly failed to prevent it from requiring that Iraq grant most-favoured-nation status to League members for ten years.[103] In exchange for economic concessions, in other words, Iraq was free to run its internal administration much as it liked. For all the PMC's reservations, this form of 'independence' won international approbation. On 3 October 1932 the thirteenth annual assembly of the League of Nations voted unanimously to admit the Kingdom of Iraq to membership. Three days later, Humphrys was an honoured guest at the celebrations held in Baghdad (Figures 9.1 and 9.2).

★ ★ ★

That assembly was the last attended by a democratic German government. Within months, Hitler would be Chancellor, the Reichstag in flames, Jewish businesses under boycott, and Nazi mobs on the march in Munich and Vienna. We are accustomed to see 1933 as the hinge-year of the twentieth century, and so it was, but that moment was perhaps the pivot of a wider turn, in which one territorial order—that of a world in which much of the globe was under the direct sovereignty of one or other of the European

**Figure 9.2** King Faysal speaking at a celebration in the public garden, Baghdad, on the independence of Iraq, 6 October 1932.

imperial powers—began to give way to a world in which sovereignty would be dispersed and generalized but also redefined.

From his perch at the University of Cologne the conservative law professor and later Nazi apologist Carl Schmitt offered one framework for understanding that transformation. In 'Forms of modern imperialism in international law', written in the year of Iraq's 'emancipation', Schmitt sought to analyse what he took to be the demise of the liberal international order and to perceive what was emerging in its stead. The League was founded on the principle of the equality of all *civilized* states. On the basis of that civilizational claim, 'the civilized assign themselves the right to "educate", that is, to rule, the less civilized'—Article 22 of the League Covenant being 'the most compromised example of the legitimizing function' of that distinction, and thus 'the classic summary expression of an entire epoch'. But that regime, Schmitt insisted, was ending, not only because that 'civilizational' presupposition had become 'very problematic at least' but also because the United States, the coming global power, exercised domination in a different way. Behind the universalism of the League lurked the reality of the Monroe Doctrine, through which the United States claimed hemispheric hegemony over ostensibly independent client states while at the same time shaping, through its rampant economic power, the global order as a whole. Before American power, the power to set 'the forms of speech and even the mode of thought of other peoples', a German could only feel 'like a beggar in rags speaking of the riches and treasures of others', but this was the model of the future.[104] Indeed, some seven years later, we find Schmitt justifying Germany's claim to a *Großraum* of its own.[105]

Schmitt captured something crucial about the reconfiguration of territoriality and power in the 1930s, but he missed much as well. For the League system was not simply a liberal order fated to decline. Instead, as the Iraq case shows, it too was protean and flexible. Indeed, by 'reading' the Iraq episode—an episode Schmitt entirely overlooked—as attentively as scholars now read Schmitt's work, we can see how Britain, that ostensibly declining liberal power, was able to use the League to construct—and win international support for—a form of domination not unlike that crafted by the United States. Schmitt was not the only political thinker to find the model of the Monroe Doctrine seductive, for plenty of English political thinkers had done so as well. Indeed, in 1918, Arnold Toynbee, then at the Political Intelligence Department, had suggested that Britain should embrace self-determination precisely because that ideal would amount to 'a British Monroe Doctrine for Arabia'.[106] The Iraqi bargain, through which the new state's political elites won international recognition and a measure of internal domination by ceding economic and military privileges, was the apotheosis of that British Monroe Doctrine.

What is remarkable about that bargain, however, is that it was negotiated internationally, its ratification contingent upon Britain and Iraq's willingness to promise not only one another, but also other international powers and interests, a share of the pie. Germany needed trade opportunities, Italy a share of Iraqi oil, France a path to clientelist domination in Syria, the Mandates Commission minorities' protection. The Iraqi agreement promised all these things. Once struck, however, those bargains proved unenforceable. Italy's flirtation with the BOD yielded nothing. Within a few years, all concessions for Iraqi oil were back in the IPC's hands.[107] Nor was the Middle East 'internationalized', for France swiftly made it clear that any 'independent' states it built in Syria would remain firmly under its economic and military umbrella.[108] The League had been most genuinely 'international' during the period of German membership, but it could not deliver a form of internationalism that would placate Rome and Berlin. Embittered and unsatisfied, those states now jettisoned 'internationalization' to demand overt territorial revision.

For the Mandates Commission, too, 'Iraq' came to figure as a cautionary tale, a lesson about the willingness of the mandatory powers to lead the PMC down a garden path to perdition. Most members had never been confident of Iraq's fitness for self-government, and when its troops opened fire on the Assyrians in 1933, they could hardly contain their consternation.[109] 'Even though at the time I did everything I could to prevent the premature emancipation of Iraq, I am not yet at peace about the blood spilt as an immediate consequence of the decision I opposed,' Rappard told Robert de Caix in 1936; if he consented to Syria's 'emancipation' and it provoked similar violence, 'I would in my own eyes deserve to be shot.'[110] From 1932 most members of the Commission were openly hostile to Arab nationalism and committed to preventing, not facilitating, any further moves towards independence.

The year 1932 was thus perhaps the last moment when the possibility of crafting a global bargain over empire hung in the balance. Within a year or two, the tide began to flow backwards. The architects of the Anglo-Iraqi agreement thought they were creating a precedent, but in fact the conditions that made that bargain possible—German and Italian willingness to stay at the table, the consent of the Mandates Commission to the terms of the trade—were crumbling. There would be no further 'emancipations' of mandated territories until the revisionist states had been defeated, the European powers crippled, and the League system swept away. Instead, those territories would once again become pawns in the geopolitical game.

# PART
# IV

# Between Empire and Internationalism, 1933–39

# Preface: Multiple Exits

Between 1933 and 1937 three major powers, all permanent members of the Council, left the League. For the Mandates Commission, Germany's exit was most consequential but also the most clear-cut. On 14 October 1933, Hitler took Germany out of the Geneva disarmament conference and, disregarding the requirement of two years' notice, announced its immediate withdrawal from the League. Julius Ruppel absented himself from the Mandates Commission's 24th session which began two weeks later, sending Catastini, his collaborator on many initiatives, a note of thanks and adieu.[1] Although the Nazi regime would wave the flag of colonial revision, and members of the Mandates Commission would watch those manoeuvres with trepidation, Germany was in future more interested in wrecking than joining the mandates system.

The Japanese and Italian exits were more protracted. Japan's withdrawal, although announced first, lasted longest and was punctuated by many backward looks. Japan set great store by its League membership, but it also expected to have its hegemony in East Asia recognized and even—as with European hegemony in Africa and the Middle East—extolled as a work of civilization. That its actions in Manchuria would be interpreted instead as a violation of Chinese sovereign rights struck its nationalist politicians and populace as hypocritical and almost incomprehensible. In December 1932, following an Assembly vote sympathetic to the Chinese case, the Japanese delegation walked out, and six months later, attempts at mediation by Sir Eric Drummond and the Japanese Under-Secretary Yōtarō Sugimura having failed, Japan announced its intention to withdraw from the League.[2]

That decision immediately posed the question of whether Japan should be required to relinquish its South Seas mandate. Many League supporters thought it alien to the spirit of the Covenant to have a non-League state hold a mandate, but others countered that since the mandated territories had been allocated by the allied powers and not by the League, Japan's with-drawal made no difference.[3] Japanese officials made clear that they had no intention of relinquishing the islands anyway.[4] Given that lack of legal clarity, Prentiss Gilbert, the US Consul in Geneva, advised the State Department that the whole question seemed 'a political rather than a jurid-ical problem'.[5]

He was quite right, and political interests strongly inclined all allied pow-ers to leave well enough alone. Neither Whitehall nor the Quai d'Orsay wished to antagonize Japan further, and one British official noted that it was equally 'inconceivable' that the League Council 'would ever bring any pressure on Japan to abandon the islands should she not wish to do so'.[6] Secretariat officials did think the Council should take some steps to 'safe-guard the mandate principle', but were reassured to learn that Japan still intended to participate in such 'technical' and 'non-political' activities as the Health Organization and the Mandates Commission.[7] Nobumichi Sakenobe thus retained the PMC seat he had occupied since 1928, annual reports and accredited representatives were dutifully dispatched, and when Japan's mem-bership formally expired in 1935 the Council simply noted that Japan still considered itself bound by the mandate text.[8] Not until November 1938 did Japan terminate its cooperation and—to Sakenobe's great distress—with-draw its nationals from all League bodies.[9]

By that point, the Commission's colourful, mercurial Italian chairman was gone as well. Of all exits, Theodoli's was the most fraught. Theodoli had led the Commission from its creation, and its character, reputation, and functioning had been sharply marked by his preferences and personality. Moreover, while his colleagues and accredited representatives often com-plained of his 'plaisanteries de mauvais goût',[10] obvious boredom when social questions were discussed, and love of intrigue—he was inclined to make mischief, one British official warned privately in 1935, and was 'never displeased at seeing his colleagues flounder into a mess'[11]—in fact Theodoli had served the Commission well. His jealous defence of its prerogatives, propensity to see most questions through a political (and not administrative or humanitarian) lens, even his obvious manoeuvring in defence of Italian interests, all lent a measure of balance to an institution founded to legitimize allied conquests. Indeed, the very fact that Orts, Rappard, and Lugard all considered themselves 'impartial' and Theodoli 'political', even though Orts colluded with the Belgian Colonial Ministry, Rappard shared confidential information with the Zionist Organization, and Lugard kept open a back-channel to Whitehall, is a sign of how analytically worthless such terms as 'intrigue' or 'bias' are when used in connection with such an intrinsically political institution. (The French members, refreshingly, never bothered pretending to be doing anything but defending French interests.)

But if virtually all members of the PMC 'played politics' in one way or another, not all such games took place in public, sowed discord within the Commission, and endangered the position of the member themselves. Theodoli's behaviour during the Italian conquest of Ethiopia did so. Initially, the Commission studiously ignored the conflict, re-electing Theodoli as chairman at the 28th session that opened on 17 October 1935, two weeks after the Italian invasion. But the Italian bombardment of undefended villages and use of poison gas that winter shocked members. In May of 1936 Valentine Dannevig—always a bellwether for humanitarian sentiments on the Commission—told Lugard that she could not again support the election of someone with fascist sympathies to head an institution charged to protect the welfare of natives.[12] Lugard pointed out that members could not be assumed to support their country's policies,[13] but while Theodoli was again elected, for the first time there was open dissent. Three members, the well-informed German Consul in Geneva reported to Berlin, had voted for Orts.[14]

By this point, Italy's relations with the League were at a nadir. The Italian conquest of Ethiopia was nearly complete. Haile Selassie would flee to Europe a few weeks later. But Mussolini wished to see League sanctions lifted, Ethiopia dismissed from Geneva, and Italian sovereignty internationally recognized. Perhaps Theodoli was under orders to pick a fight; at any rate, at the end of that session he asked the Commission to confirm that the sanctions imposed on Italy ought not to apply in the mandated territories, given that those territories were supposed to be 'international' and kept outside European fights. His colleagues were upset by his intervention, not only because they thought it obvious that League sanctions should apply within territories under League supervision but also because their eroding willingness to support his leadership was conditional on his *not* launching such debates. After a fierce dispute, Orts forced a procedural vote on whether the question should be added to the agenda, in which only the Spaniard Palacios supported Theodoli.[15] Theodoli then walked out, and—since Italy was now boycotting League gatherings—he stayed away from the session in the autumn of 1936 as well.

But Theodoli did not resign and to the distress of his colleagues seemed disinclined to do so. He was desperate to hang on to his post, in early May

1937 even asking Nahum Goldmann of the Zionist Organization to persuade Foreign Minister Count Ciano of the importance of Theodoli's role.
Goldmann had little desire to intercede for a man never friendly to Zionism,
but after promises of future support he did take the matter up with Ciano,
only to be told bluntly that there was no prospect of Italy ending its boycott
of League institutions immediately.[16] Moreover, even had Theodoli been
allowed to return to Geneva, his bid for the chairmanship would have failed.
Opposition had hardened at the October 1936 session. Four of the ten
members were now opposed to Theodoli, and in April 1937 Rappard and
Orts began corresponding privately about how to oust him. Revealingly,
they were troubled less by his unpalatable views on Ethiopia than by his
political manoeuvring and especially—in light of an upcoming special session on Palestine—his anti-Zionism.[17] Orts thus asked Lugard, who had
resigned the previous July, what position his successor would take; Lugard
confirmed that Lord Hailey would also refuse to vote for Theodoli.[18] That
was enough. At the May 1937 session the PMC elected Orts as Chairman
and Rappard as Vice Chairman, positions they would hold for the rest of the
PMC's life.

What was the significance of the revisionist powers' withdrawal from the
mandates regime? One might expect the Commission to have become more
subservient to the mandatory powers. This is not quite what happened. True,
the election of the Belgian Orts was a real retreat. Hitherto both the
Chairman and Vice Chairman had come from the 'non-mandatory' members, and while Orts publicly proclaimed his objectivity, behind the scenes he
advised Belgian and French officials how to 'reinforce tendencies favourable
to the mandatory powers'.[19] Yet a practice and culture established over a
dozen years proved durable, with the piecemeal withdrawal of the German,
Italian, and Japanese members making the Commission if anything more
anxious to appear 'above' international conflict altogether. Appealing to precedent and text, and insisting on their 'technical' and 'apolitical' status, members clung to their Lugardian language and sought to uphold the principles
of anti-annexationism and the open door.

The problem for the members of the PMC was that the foundations for
those norms and for their own authority were crumbling away. In its
'Lugardian' period, the Mandates Commission deployed a language of trusteeship and indirect rule to surmount the challenge posed by wartime
nationalists, rebuild great-power comity, and re-establish the legitimacy of
imperial rule. In its second, 'German', period, it acted as an arena for nego-

tiating grudging agreement over new international norms. As major players left the negotiating table, however, the Commission could no longer fulfil that role. Put simply, once the revisionist powers put all their eggs in the basket of empire-building, they could no longer be appeased by membership in a system that sought to limit the advantages of empire through legal and economic 'de-territorialization'. And once the mandates system ceased to be an arena for conciliation, it not only ceased to matter much to the revisionist powers. It mattered less to the mandatory powers as well.

From the mid-1930s the mandates system thus showed signs of fissure and crisis on every level: ideological, geopolitical, and institutional. To begin with, the successive horrors of Italy's Ethiopia campaign, the Spanish Civil War, and the Nazi regime's brutal anti-Semitism put the claim that Europe acted as the standard-bearer for civilization and progress—a claim on which the rhetoric of trusteeship had been based—under impossible strain. Of course, colonial nationalists, communists, pan-Africanists, and even some European anti-imperialists had long found that claim racist and enraging; now, it began to stick in the craw of European liberal internationalists as well. As consensus frayed, alternative arguments—that indigenous cultures would be better off left entirely alone, say, or that cultural change should be embraced so as to enable subject peoples to move swiftly to independence—found an audience. As we see in Chapter 10, not even the Mandates Commission was immune to such trends, as some members began to question whether European 'tutelage' would ever amount to more than an excuse for labour coercion.

Plagued by internal self-doubts, the regime was also buffeted by external pressures, as the revisionist powers sought to change the rules of the game. The mandates regime had tried to win consent for the Versailles settlement by modestly 'internationalizing' the benefits of those territorial changes, but by the 1930s economic crisis had left that strategy in shreds. Instead, all great powers knit their clients and colonies closer together while at the same time searching, in time-honoured imperial fashion, for some transferable or disposable bits that might lessen antagonisms and make a new settlement possible. Those conversations could not take place through the League, for as Jan Smuts, that wily old operator, wrote to his friend Leo Amery, 'whilst the League was functioning properly, its Council was a Round Table for the Great Powers, but as most of the Great Powers are absent now from that Table, conversations have to take place in a different way'.[20] But once those conversations ceased to work through Geneva, they no longer took the

peace settlement, and especially did not take the mandates system, as their
point of departure. Instead, to the Commission's impotent fury, not only the
avid Germans, but equally the British and French, willingly put the question of some redistribution of the mandated territories back on the table.
Yet, as Chapter 11 shows, although the prospect of a new colonial settlement
was hotly debated in the late 1930s, it was never a realistic option. The
debate discredited and destabilized the League regime but erected nothing
in its place.

Finally, the mandates regime struggled with institutional and leadership
crises, as the League apparatus itself lost prestige and support. The rot started
at the top. Sir Eric Drummond may have reined in Rappard's activism, but
at crucial junctures he defended the independence and authority of the
Commission; by contrast Joseph Avenol, his indolent and pusillanimous successor, paid no attention to the mandates system at all.[21] Poorly led, many
Secretariat sections lost their capacity for independent behind-the-scenes
activism—including the Mandates Section, where Catastini's successor, the
correct Swiss diplomat Edouard de Haller, ran an efficient but entirely
uninspired shop. Initiative rested with the Commission, but that body, hitherto extraordinarily stable, now faced a series of damaging resignations and
retirements. When the German, Italian, and Japanese members left, they
were not replaced, leaving the Commission not only smaller but much less
diverse. Worse, after Martial Merlin retired in 1934 and Lugard in 1936,
France and Britain were represented by a number of short-term members
who were never deeply committed to the work. True, the Dutch former
colonial official and law professor Frederick Van Asbeck, who joined the
Commission in 1935 following the death of Van Rees, was hard-working
and able, but his views were indistinguishable from those of the two dominant members, Rappard and Orts. The great powers were not likely to bow
before 'international opinion' as articulated by a Belgian, a Dutchman, and
a Swiss.

And indeed, such proved the case, with both France and Britain moving
in directions dictated by their geopolitical interests, in defiance of the
Mandates Commission, in the late 1930s. Over time, the Commission's
members had become ever more convinced of the value of international
oversight; all but Palacios were sceptical of self-determination and doubted
that the territories they oversaw would be ready for independence anytime
soon. As Britain and France detected war on the horizon, however, they
became sharply pragmatic, moving to hoard their resources and to get their

clients and allies into line. Since France's commitment to the mandates regime had always been shallow, it had little trouble ignoring the Commission's objections to proposals for Syrian independence and then for the transfer of the Sanjak of Alexandretta from Syria to Turkey, an entirely illegal act. Britain, however, had always been the greatest patron and supporter of the mandates system, and when Britain and the Commission finally came into conflict over Palestine, as Chapter 12 shows, the experience proved more painful and the consequences more severe. With Britain's repudiation of a mandate that British officials had themselves written, we come full circle. 'Internationalization', a strategy devised to reconcile imperial interests to changing political conditions and evolving norms, had run its course. 'Independence' was about to become the only game in town.

# TEN

## Legitimation Crisis

A time will come when the League of Nations will have to deal with racial questions, when it will have to eradicate differences between races which manifest themselves in unfair treatment inflicted on certain races, and constitute a menace to the peace of the world.

Dantès Bellegarde, Delegate for Haiti, Second Assembly,
plenary session, 23 September 1921

The crisis of the mandates system in the 1930s was partly political, for once the revisionist powers exited the League, its institutions and regimes necessarily became more fragile. But it was also ideological, as the presuppositions undergirding the 'sacred trust' came under sustained pressure. Of course, the claim that the European powers were guardians of 'civilization' and would train other peoples in its ways had been contested from the start, not only by the local communities who petitioned or rebelled against their new rulers but also by hawk-eyed humanitarians, anti-colonial intellectuals, and self-appointed guardians of League ideals who suspected the allies would swiftly slip back into their old imperialist ways. Imperial armies had crushed the rebellions, but given those mobilized publics, authority could never be secured through force of arms alone. Instead, faith in the mandate project had to be won through words, over and over and over.

We have seen how the Mandates Commission, influenced heavily by Frederick Lugard but also driven by the need to contain German and Italian criticism, came to articulate a doctrine that both constrained the imperial powers and gave them crucial breathing space in the 1920s. This was not exactly a full-throated defence of the 'civilizing mission', for the Commission was concerned more with protection than with rights, with preserving 'native culture' than with developing native capacity. Shielded from rapacious companies, meretricious consumerism, and 'Western values', subject peoples were to be given a chance to develop—but in their own way, and at a pace that postponed the troubling prospect of them 'standing alone' into the distant future.

In the 1930s, however, that 'Lugardian compromise' came under pressure from all directions. Anti-colonialism had become a global movement, backed by the Soviet Union, sustained by transnational networks, and buoyed by the prestige of an Indian nationalist effort whose leaders' 'civilization' and ethical stature could not be gainsaid.[1] European solidarity and (still more) claims to moral leadership were crumbling as well. Italy's war against Ethiopia in 1935 especially dealt a blow to imperialism's ideological foundations, not only because it was conducted with particular savagery and against a fellow League member, but also because the Italians consciously appropriated the language of trusteeship to justify their campaign. Holding a terrible mirror up to the liberal powers, they claimed to be intervening only to bring law and order to a backwards, warlord-ridden and slave-trading land.[2] Those claims fared badly against the dignified appeals of Haile Selassie and the accounts of Italian perfidy and atrocities filed by the hundreds of foreign correspondents in Addis Ababa at the start of the war.[3] Demonstrations of support and solidarity campaigns sprang up among anti-colonial intellectuals and diasporic populations from Harlem to Jamaica, Cairo to Natal, but in Britain especially support for League sanctions against Italy (although, fatally, not for military involvement) spanned the political spectrum.[4] Some of the early architects of the mandates regime—especially Philip Noel-Baker, now a mainstay of the League of Nations Union, and William Ormsby-Gore, soon to become Colonial Secretary in Stanley Baldwin's government—were among those arguing for strong League action against Italy; any conciliatory response would, they warned prophetically, create 'a sense of rankling injustice and bitter anti-white propaganda throughout Africa'.[5] Selassie's under-supplied armies and the credibility of the 'civilizing' project alike reeled under the onslaught of Italian planes and poison gas, and then the revelation that the British and French were willing to buy a settlement by granting Italy substantial territorial concessions.[6]

Members of the Mandates Commission were well aware of the depth of that ideological challenge. They knew they needed to demonstrate that mandatory rule was *different*—different from the Italians' brutal rule, surely, but different as well from the exploitative and annexationist practices of the imperial past. They had always defined that 'difference' essentially as a kind of disinterestedness. Mandatory powers were to protect native peoples without gaining material advantage from that charge. As the world economy contracted, however, all empires tried to extract more from areas under their own rule. 'Development' became a priority not because it could set such territories on the road to self-government, or even improve living standards and public health, but because it could supply raw materials and markets. The Commission, true to its protective ideals, often took a dim view of unfettered 'development' of this kind. Members criticized labour conditions in the Lupa goldfields in Tanganyika and on plantations in Cameroon. They expressed strong reservations about indentured and contract labour regimes in South West Africa, Rwanda and Burundi, and Mandated New Guinea. From the late 1920s too they woke up to the fact that massive Japanese immigration into the Mariana Islands and the rapid development of the sugar and phosphate industries there threatened to swamp the native Micronesian population entirely. The Japanese, however, retorted that the Sea Islanders were 'absolutely indifferent to the idea of their extinction as a race' and kept up their pell-mell settlement. By 1938 the Japanese outnumbered Micronesians in the mandated territory and comprised 90 per cent of the population of the Marianas.[7] With nationalist movements more clamant, the empires more extractive, and the revisionist powers openly flouting the League, paternalism was consistently forced on the defensive.

We can find some signs of what we might call the legitimation crisis of the mandates regime in virtually every African and Pacific territory by the late 1930s. Yet no territory better reveals those dynamics than Mandated New Guinea. Of all the mandated territories, New Guinea alone possessed a population that was, in most European eyes, unambiguously 'primitive'. In the 1920s the administration had incorporated much of that population into the plantation economy through a highly coercive system of indentured labour, winning the grudging consent of the Mandates Commission by deploying a Lugardian language of cultural preservation. Strict controls on native mobility, pay, and rights, it was held, would prevent urbanization and commercialization and so preserve New Guineans' interesting 'native culture'. In the 1930s, however, violent clashes between New Guineans and whites, combined with the discovery that the hitherto unexplored highlands contained a large population prospering far from 'civilized' control, led some members of the Mandates Commission to wonder whether 'protection'—even in this anthropologically attuned guise—was much more than a justification for exploitation.

These anxieties did not drive the Commission to develop any new rationale or programme for mandatory rule. It was too set in its ways, its members too old and too shaped by humanitarian and 'civilizational' ideas. Yet in the space opened up by the crisis of the Lugardian faith, new ideas and new voices could be heard. If indigenous populations and cultures were actually degraded by Western rule, as anthropologists charged, perhaps they should be quarantined from 'civilization' altogether? Or, alternatively, if the language of 'cultural difference' and 'separate development' really only meant 'permanent repression', as the African American political scientist Ralph Bunche charged, perhaps that paternalistic programme had to give way to robust educational and technical efforts?[8] The mandates system had tried to defer these questions for as long as possible, but by the late 1930s they were squarely on the table. New Guinea, as much as Ethiopia, had put them there.

## New Guinea and the anthropological turn

Mandated New Guinea, comprised of the northeastern quarter of New Guinea and the islands of the Bismarck Archipelago and Bougainville, was one of the larger mandated territories. It was also then (as now) one of the most culturally diverse and polyglot places on earth, home to literally thousands of separate communities speaking hundreds of mutually unintelligible languages. Australia, like Germany before it, claimed to 'rule' that population, but its writ in the 1920s really ran only in the islands and along a thin coastal strip. Population estimates of around 400,000 in the late 1920s were based on the assumption, later proven dramatically wrong, that the interior was only sparsely inhabited.

How could the mandate administration headquartered in Rabaul bring 'civilization' to this rugged and unimaginably different world? The obvious course would have been to follow the lead of Sir Herbert Murray, from 1908 the Lieutenant Governor of Papua, the similarly sized southeastern quarter of New Guinea also under Australian rule. The two regimes did resemble one another in some ways. Both relied on patrol officers to expand the reach and enforce the rule of government; both then appointed village headmen (*luluais*) and assistants (*tultuls*) to carry out basic tasks; both depended for revenue on a plantation sector producing copra, the main export crop; in both, virtually all New Guinean wage labour was indentured. Yet, already in the 1920s sharp differences had emerged. For Murray thought of Papuans more as peasants than as primitives and deliberately kept the plantation sector small; he also worked hard to limit the level of violence that officers could use to bring new or unruly areas under control. As a result, when outsiders looked at the two territories in the 1920s, it was Papua that seemed to be following 'mandate' principles. Murray looked very much like Lord Lugard under the Southern Cross.[9]

In the mandated territory, by contrast, Australia had inherited German New Guinea's much larger plantation sector and was determined to make it pay. This proved difficult, for copra prices were low for much of the inter-war period and the plantations' new owners, often ex-servicemen given mortgages on preferential terms, lacked experience and were soon mired in debt. Isolated, embittered, and (if import figures for spirits are any guide) heavy drinkers to a man, they had no plan for economic revival beyond the demand—repeated with mind-numbing frequency in every planters' meeting and letter to the *Pacific Islands Monthly*—that the administration grant them the right to flog their workers. Brigadier General Evan Wisdom, the territory's administrator from 1921 until 1932, would not go that far. 'Paternal chastisement', although widespread, remained against the law. But Wisdom and all subsequent administrators thought it their job to ensure planters, traders, and (once gold mining commenced in earnest in the mid-1920s) mining companies a copious labour supply.[10]

In a sense, indeed, the Mandated Territory's main 'industry' was the production of indentured labour, a most profitable 'trade' that kept hundreds of licensed private recruiters in work and the whole territory running. Recruiters moved ever further inland as coastal populations were depleted, offering payments to village headmen to produce a complement of 'boys'— males aged over twelve who were liable for recruiting. (Whites called all native men 'boys', all native women 'marys', all native boys, astonishingly, 'monkeys', and native girls nothing at all.) Workers were delivered first to a District Officer to confirm their three-year contract and then to private employers for a price of about £10 per head, although when the first big gold strike at Edie Creek in the Morobe district drew a motley assortment of prospectors and adventurers to New Guinea, that price rose as high as £20. Wages, by contrast, averaged around 6 shillings per month or just over £10 for the entire term (compared to 10s per month in Murray's Papua), with two-thirds paid on release. In the mid-1920s approximately 25,000 men were under indenture in the Mandated Territory, rising to around 30,000 in 1930 (compared to 9,000 in Papua)—a figure amounting to perhaps a quarter or a third of the adult men living on the islands and in the coastal areas under government control.[11]

Unsurprisingly, the Mandates Commission (with the exception of the Portuguese Freire d'Andrade, always eager to put in a good word for forced labour) had trouble seeing how that labour regime fulfilled Australia's obligation 'to promote to the utmost the material and moral well-being and the social progress of the inhabitants of the territory'. Members voiced alarm about specific abuses—planters flogging workers, recruiters taking hostages in order to force villagers to produce 'boys', dysentery and high death rates in the goldfields, officials launching punitive raids to crush any resistance— but they also disapproved of indenture per se and thought the proportion of the population under it far too high. Lugard, Rappard, and Grimshaw (the ILO representative) proved particularly tenacious interrogators, asking the Australian representative year after year whether such wholesale recruitment would foster disease, population decline, and social dislocation. Kept abreast of local scandals by the League's excellent newspaper clipping service and regular mailings from the Mandates Section, they easily outwitted the officials sent to answer their questions—most of whom, according to the *Rabaul Times*, were distinguished by their 'blissful ignorance' of the territory.[12] To the Australian government's great irritation, Lugard also had access to the best of all possible 'back-channels', for Papua's Murray, who was highly critical of the mandated territory next door, felt quite free to pass along damaging information to his brother Gilbert Murray, the Oxford University Professor of Greek and League of Nations Union stalwart, who forwarded it privately to Lugard. There was 'a certain amount of discrepancy between the information obtained from official sources and that coming from unofficial sources,' Rappard said bluntly in 1928. Everything the Commission heard about the Mandated Territory suggested that Australia was sacrificing native well-being to satisfy the greed of the white population.[13]

Nonplussed, wrong-footed, and very much on the defensive, Australian officials fell back on an old but dated argument about the civilizing virtues of work. Plantation work was 'the most hopeful means of introducing the native to civilization', giving him 'something to replace the occupations and excitements of his former savage life', the administration had written in the 1922 report.[14] Beginning in the mid-1920s, however, the mandate administration also deployed a rather different language and set of policies that pleased the Commission better and blunted its criticism. Perhaps more than any other

Figure 10.1  E. W. P. Chinnery by a monoplane, 1933.

colonial power, Australia turned to anthropology, professing its commitment
to 'think black' (as one official put it) in order to better adapt its administration
to native life.[15] In 1924 Evan Wisdom followed Hubert Murray's lead in Papua
and appointed E. W. P. Chinnery, a former patrol officer who had studied for
a time with the Cambridge ethnologist A. C. Haddon, as 'government anthropologist' (Figure 10.1). Concerned about the low quality of his officers,
Wisdom also joined Murray in creating a 'cadet' scheme under which recruits
would serve two years in the field and then be sent to Sydney for an anthropology course conducted by the charismatic A. R. Radcliffe-Brown, who had
been appointed Professor of Anthropology in 1926. The first cadets arrived for
their special course in 1928, and the scheme continued—although with set-
backs and occasional lapses—through the 1930s.[16]

Historians examining that early alliance of anthropology and colonial administration have disagreed about its significance and particularly about Chinnery's role.[17] Kept busy handling 'all sorts of routine and emergency jobs, such as investigating uprisings or a falling birth rate', Chinnery never did much sustained fieldwork, and unlike F. E. Williams, Murray's appointee in Papua, never gained a serious scholarly reputation. His role was more that of 'gatekeeper', and since he controlled access to some of the most untouched and sought-after fieldwork sites in the world, even those (like Margaret Mead) who thought nothing of his scholarly credentials went to some trouble to please him.[18] The cadet scheme also had a rocky existence, for Wisdom restricted participation when funds or manpower were tight, while Murray (who came to feel anthropologists were too quick to defend native practices that genuinely required suppression) ceased to send cadets in the 1930s.[19] Yet, for the Mandated Territory in particular, the 'anthropological turn' *was* important, not only because it helped officers distance themselves from a pervasive planter culture that saw 'the native' as (in the words of one all too representative employer) 'a child, but...also a born thief, liar and black-mailer',[20] but also because it provided that administration with a language, policies, and a person—Chinnery—able to reconcile their labour policy to the norms of the 'sacred trust'.

How, precisely, could what Chinnery termed 'applied anthropology' do that work? It is important to note, first, that it did not and could not limit the exactions of the indenture regime. Indeed, Chinnery, who had managed native labour for Papua's copper mines for three years before his appointment in the Mandated Territory, accepted from the outset both that the government had an obligation to maintain the labour supply and that European 'civilization' would transform native culture beyond recognition. What anthropologically informed administration could do, however, was to slow the *pace* of change and lessen the social dislocation that accompanied it. Listening to Chinnery's statements, it becomes clear that his aim was less to understand native culture ('it was never possible to know how a native would react,' he told the Mandates Commission in 1930)[21] than to strike a balance between the claims of 'trusteeship' and those of 'development', between placating the PMC and giving New Guinea's plantation owners and miners what they needed. And viewed from this angle, the indenture system could prove a blessing, for by limiting workers' independence, it preserved the village as the appropriate heart of native life.[22]

There was a degree of make-believe in all this, of course, for indentured labour radically transformed native culture, and the missions—which had exclusive control of primary education—worked hard to undermine it further. Inevitably, indentured labourers learned skills, grew accustomed to machinery and money, and developed a taste for modest consumer goods. Shipped far from home, surrounded by speech they could not understand, they learned pidgin (Tok Pisin), conversing for the first time with others beyond their community and region. Those experiences could not but be transformative: indeed, just how transformative became clear on 3 January 1929 when the white population of Rabaul awoke to find that virtually the whole three-thousand-plus native workforce of the town, from Sergeant Major Rami who helped plan the action to the lowliest sweeper, had struck for higher wages.[23] Under pressure from the whites, the administration responded harshly, sentencing the ringleaders to three years' hard labour, curtailing New Guineans' rights to move about Rabaul freely, and posting Chinnery off to Geneva to assure the Mandates Commission that labourers paid 6s a month had 'no reason at all for striking'.[24] But the strike also strengthened the administration's determination to limit cultural change by repatriating workers to their home villages at the end of their contract and, especially, by excluding women from indenture almost entirely—a decision no doubt intended to protect women from sexual predation but that also left them barricaded in the villages, with little access to new skills and goods, as men became modern. Revealingly, only Margaret Mead, doing fieldwork on Manus in the Admiralty Islands in the late 1920s, had the wit and human sympathy to notice the way this 'new social system' of male migration and female rootedness inscribed gender hierarchy into native life, and to wonder what would become of women 'when all the men speak a common tongue and the women still speak a dozen mutually incomprehensible ones'.[25]

This was not a question Chinnery asked himself. His was very much a 'Lugardian' approach, and the Commission unsurprisingly endorsed it wholeheartedly. Members welcomed Chinnery's appointment, expressed great interest in his reports, were delighted when he was sent (at great expense and waste of time) to Geneva for sessions in 1930 and 1934, and warmly congratulated him on his promotion in 1932 to Director of District Services and Native Affairs—a position that put him in charge of a labour regime that the Commission assumed would now be run along 'anthropological lines'.[26] Lugard had always thought native 'well-being' should take precedence over 'development', and 'tradition' over change; he was, then,

greatly reassured to learn that plantation labour was treated only as an episode and not as a career. True, he urged that wives accompany their hus-
bands, but this was only because he thought they could act as a prophylactic
against prostitution, venereal disease, homosexuality, and rape, not because
he thought women too needed access to money or the common tongue.[27]
The labour conditions Chinnery described were 'excellent', Lugard said in
1930. Indenture prevented the emergence of a casual labouring class.[28]

'Applied anthropology' thus did some ideological work, winning the
Commission's grudging consent to the only mandatory labour regime in
which virtually all native labourers were deployed under long-term state
contracts enforced through the criminal law. But the Commission's tolera-
tion was always conditional on the administration indeed being in control,
able to act as the lawmaker and go-between, bending both settlers and
natives to its will. Even in the 1920s the PMC had doubts on that score, and
in the early 1930s—when the lust for gold drove prospectors ever further
into the 'uncontrolled' interior—its faith eroded further. Tales of clashes
between whites and natives were reaching the Commission—of prospectors
shooting natives, of missionaries and prospectors killed in turn, of officials
ambushed or carrying out punitive expeditions to reassert control. And hard
on the heels of those worrying reports came the astonishing news that prospectors pressing into the New Guinea highlands had stumbled across hundreds of thousands of people, living in neat villages and tending lush gardens,
far beyond administration control. Those revelations not only exposed the
real limits to the administration's rule but also called into question the desir-
ability and status of 'Western civilization' itself, for the societies discovered
appeared to be healthy, productive, and well ordered, whereas gun-toting
prospectors, as Rappard put it drily, were hardly 'civilizing agents'.[29] One set
of expeditions touched the Commission particularly closely, those led and
then chronicled by the Australian prospector and explorer Michael Leahy.
In the Leahy expeditions and the Commission's awkward response, we
begin to see that Lugardian consensus—and with it the authority of
'civilization'—come apart.

## Michael Leahy's excellent adventure

Michael Leahy (always 'Masta Mick' to his 'boys') was born in 1901 to Irish
immigrant parents and grew up in rural Queensland, hunting rifle and

**Figure 10.2** Michael Leahy in the Wahgi valley, 1933.

fishing tackle ever to hand. He had worked, none too happily, as a railway
clerk and then a labourer when news of the Edie Creek gold strike broke
in 1926. Leahy caught the next boat out; over the next few years his brothers
Daniel, Patrick, and James would join him. Driven and well organized,
Leahy made some money at Edie Creek, but he was too adventurous a man
to remain there, especially as operations routinized and mining companies
bought out individual claims. First with his friend Mick Dwyer, and then
with various brothers and the backing of the mining companies, between
1930 and 1934 Leahy made many trips into the 'uncontrolled' interior in
search of a new El Dorado (Figure 10.2).[30]

On the first trip in 1930, Leahy, Dwyer, and a strong group of carriers
trekked from Lae up the Markham River and into the Upper Ramu valley,
panning for gold as they went. They then crossed the Bismarck range and,
realizing themselves lost but unwilling to turn back, followed the rivers that
flowed into the Purari and eventually debouched the party into the Gulf of
Papua on the other side of New Guinea—an astonishing and inadvertent
cross-island feat reminiscent of C. H. Karius and Ivan Champion's crossing
from the Fly to the Sepik three years earlier. The next year Leahy, Dwyer,
and Pat Leahy contracted with New Guinea Goldfields Limited to explore

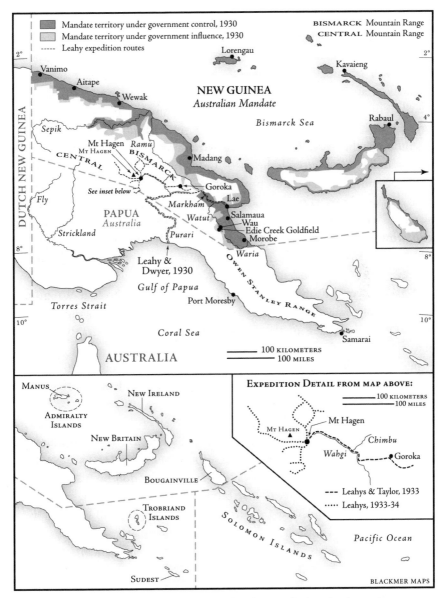

**Map 5.** Exploration and Control in Mandated New Guinea in the early 1930s.

the tributaries of the Watut and Ramu. Spring and summer 1933 found Michael and Daniel Leahy teaming up with Assistant District Officer James L. (Jim) Taylor to take a large and well-armed joint expedition up into the Wahgi River valley and to Mount Hagen, building a landing field to supply

a base camp from which they made further forays into surrounding territory. They also established the first mining operation in the Hagen area at
Ewunga Creek (named for Mick's indispensable 'boss boy', Ewunga Goiba),
using local labour. On the strength of that discovery, Mick returned to
Australia that winter and amassed a group of financial backers (including
newly retired Evan Wisdom) for further explorations. In 1934 he and Dan
pressed further into the grassy highlands beyond Mount Hagen (Map 5).[31]

Although the operation at Ewunga Creek proved viable, and Mick and
Dan would work it through the 1930s, the rich strike the brothers hoped for
eluded them. They had been promised £10,000 per dredge for any claim
that warranted mechanical dredging, but no area they investigated met that
standard. Mick claimed he didn't care: 'it was the search and the thrill of
exploring new country...that had so fascinated me'.[32] Leahy was not the
only white man tramping into the highlands in these years, for patrol
officers, prospectors, and missionaries were all making incursions, but he
and Taylor were the first to 'discover' the densely cultivated Wahgi and
Chimbu valleys near Mount Hagen that Taylor estimated contained at least
150,000 people (Figure 10.3).[33] Leahy was the first to photograph and then
film their lovely fenced villages, thatched houses, ornamented ceremonial
grounds, ingenious irrigation ditches, and neat gardens, and the first white
man to communicate—if only by hand gestures—with them. It was the
defining experience of his life.

In 1935 the brothers sold their Watut stake for £10,000, and Mick and
his brother Jim headed to Europe for a grand holiday. Mick also wanted to
defend his claim, contested by Papuan officer Jack Hides, to have been the
first white man into the Mount Hagen area. In London he persuaded the
Royal Geographical Society to give him a hearing and that November gave
a public lecture complete with map and slides.[34] As we shall see, that event
placed him on a collision course with the Anti-Slavery Society and the
Mandates Commission, but before we anatomize that scandal, it is worth
asking just what happened in those highland villages when 'Masta Mick'
and his line of carriers and 'shoot-boys' walked in. Some of our information comes from Leahy himself, for he told his story several times—in his
lecture, which was published in the *Geographical Journal*, in a popular book
co-authored with Maurice Crain in 1937, and once more in a comprehensive account based on his diaries and notes, written in the 1960s and published after his death.[35] Yet, because Leahy was such a very modern explorer
indeed, carrying a typewriter and a film camera, he also left an astonishing

**Figure 10.3** Jim Taylor making first contact, 1934.

and now famous visual record—a record that, many years later, inspired two other filmmakers to retrace his steps and recover the 'encountered' peoples' stories.[36] Not all of those sources say the same thing, and if we are also attentive to what Leahy sought to conceal as well as what he confessed, we can begin to glimpse an episode of 'culture contact' that looks neither like the untrammelled exploitation of the Anti-Slavery Society's fears nor the protective paternalism of Chinnery's 'applied anthropology' but something much more complex, human, and, in a peculiar way, *reciprocal* (Figure 10.4).

Leahy went into the uncontrolled areas with the administration's permission and under regulations established in 1925, when the lust for gold began driving prospectors inland. Since many New Guinea tribes were known to be warlike, parties were required to be adequately armed. Yet they were also to stay out of the way of native inhabitants. They were not to recruit locals for portage, not to ask them for food, not to camp within a quarter-mile of their villages.[37] These rules were sensible enough, for the administration could not guarantee the safety of prospectors and did not want to endanger its own officers' lives rescuing them, but the rules were often violated. The expeditions Leahy undertook flouted each one. For Leahy did not intend to observe the local population and leave. Instead, he saw himself as the advance guard of a permanent presence, one that would alter the local landscape and

**Figure 10.4** Local people with one of Leahy's men, 1934.

culture in irreversible ways. His goal was to find workable deposits of gold.
If he did so, machines, miners, health officials, and an army of 'boys' and
camp followers would follow. Prefaced by aerial surveillance, sustained by
base camps and airstrips, and provisioned through trade with the locals and
by air, these were no fleeting forays but an attempt to establish permanent
enterprises and solid relations with the native population. Leahy was
involved in four such relations or 'trades'—war, the trade in goods, the
labour market, and the sex trade.

After Leahy returned, it was the first set of relations—the relations of
force—that attracted the PMC's attention. Leahy, certainly, paid close attention to what one might call the military side of things. He chose his 'boys'
for their strength and their fighting skill, brought along several good guns
and fierce dogs, and always—particularly after his second expedition, on
which he was clubbed and his brother Pat wounded by an arrow—made
sure that they could swiftly respond to an attack. Even when villagers were
friendly, the expedition required their hosts to disarm by releasing their
bow-strings. Sometimes, they would shoot a pig to make sure the locals
understood the power of their guns, and they also followed the common
practice of stringing a line of fish wire around their camp and allowing no

native to pass. (Leahy photographed crowds of hundreds watching curiously from the wire.) On the march, he kept his 'shoot-boys' nearby and always slept with a revolver and a flashlight by his pillow. When the party was attacked (or, perhaps, seemed about to be attacked), he shot to kill. Leahy's field notes mention forty-one locals killed, but the total was unquestionably higher.[38]

In his books, Leahy presented these measures as no more than essential common sense, dictated by New Guineans' fierce traditions of inter-tribal warfare, their skill with the spear and the bow, and their understandable desire for plunder. Lack of preparedness was, for him, a crime. Indeed, he attributed the recent murders of his friends and fellow prospectors Hermann Baum and Bernie McGrath (whose body he had helped to recover) to the two men's naiveté about 'primitive man' and to the ludicrous theories of 'do-gooders' and 'armchair administrators' who had never faced 'club-wielding savages'.[39] 'There is no law among these savages but the law of might,' he insisted; 'clashes could be avoided only if white men stayed out of the country altogether.'[40] Leahy thought that impossible, but he was not hypo-critical enough to pretend that 'pacification' would come without a price. In *The Land that Time Forgot*, the account of his travels Leahy co-authored with Crain, that ambivalence is expressed in the form of an ongoing argu-ment between the realist Mick and the idealist brother Dan. Dan, for example, will admire the lovely floral borders of a ceremonial ground; Mick will point out that the aesthetically gifted gardeners just burnt a neighbouring village to the ground; Dan will retort that 'at least these benighted heathen haven't descended to using poison gas'.[41] We are a long way here from the confi-dence of the *Dual Mandate*. The march of 'civilization' is inexorable, but just what natives have to gain from it is not altogether clear.

Yet Leahy did feel that *trade* could have tangible benefits. Trade was an equal exchange, from which all parties could profit. Leahy's expeditions traded mightily for food and for labour, exchanges that brought some satis-faction—emotional as well as material—to all sides. The explorers traded shell and steel knives for pigs, sweet potatoes, beans, and other garden pro-duce. They persuaded local people to help clear a landing field and filmed the dances that flattened the surface down. As locals and explorers grew more familiar with one another, locals provided other services—introduc-tions to the people of the next valley or village, for example—or attached themselves semi-permanently to one expedition or another for a time. Young men were recruited as carriers, returning to their villages, full of stories, months later. When the mining operation started up, locals were paid in shells for the hard work of breaking rock and washing it for gold. Far from the reach of government and with land and gardens to sustain them, those 'workers' could not be coerced. They came and went as they wished. When the first lorry was flown in and assembled, local men were taken for rides. One or two were even brought along on a supply flight to the coast. Leahy didn't just record these stories. He named the men and sketched their personalities.

He was more reticent, however, about one final trade in which he was involved, which we can only call the sex trade. In his talk to the Royal Geographical Society, Leahy mentioned the sex trade only in passing and only to attribute it to the loose behaviour of the local villagers. The people of the Mount Hagen area, he stated, were 'very immoral', and 'the younger and apparently unmarried girls spent most of their time around our roped-off camping area offering themselves to our boys for a few shells', aided and abetted by their men. In a description of a later expedition, he likewise mentioned the girls offering themselves and the 'boys' 'picking out their sleeping partners for the night and obtaining from us the necessary shells with which to foot the bill in the morning'.[42] The trade, in other words, was driven by ready supply and by the moral depravity of the native population.

Leahy's later accounts, however, give a somewhat different story. Shells were currency in highland New Guinea and prized beyond measure: this is why the company carried quantities of them. But the highlanders had nothing to trade for these riches but labour, food (of which the expedition quickly had a surfeit), and women. Given those untrammelled desires (for bodies, for shell), Leahy concluded he had no hope of stopping the sex trade, but since he needed to restrict spending, 'we had to control the traffic'. He thus insisted that all liaisons be cleared with him. Concerned not to antagonize the locals, he also set a penalty—twenty strokes of the cane—for rape. Although it was 'strictly illegal to strike a work boy', he thought it crucial to convince 'the kanakas that white men would not tolerate injustice'.[43]

This system, he found, worked well. His 'boys', well-fed, well-companioned, and often with the odd volunteer to carry their load, were having the time of their lives, and the incorporation of 'wives' into the line of carriers reassured other villages that they came in peace. Of course, sometimes discipline was required. When the father of one Mount Hagen girl protested that his daughter had been raped by three of Leahy's 'boys', Leahy not only thrashed all three until even the complainants begged him to stop but also gave the father a valuable gold-lip shell and the girl some small shells. This was the context of one of the principal demonstrations of 'immorality', for the next morning, Leahy wrote, 'the old men brought along all the female youth and beauty of the village and said that if we had any more gold lip shells we could rape the lot'. But was this not, in fact, the analogue of Leahy's own attempt to 'control the traffic'? The local fathers clearly agreed that the couplings of Leahy's 'boys' and the village girls should occur under terms set by older men.[44]

But even those 'thicker' accounts of the sex trade left one crucial fact out. This was that Leahy was a customer and not only a regulator of the trade. If we had nothing but his writings to go on we would never know this, for he censored himself—in this respect (as in his 'use' of local women) conforming to white norms. Sexual relations (voluntary and forced) between white men and New Guinean women were widespread, although the Territory's administrators tried hard to stamp them out. They were hamstrung, however, not only by the fact that (as Evan Wisdom complained in one case) an officer who procured or raped native women did not always think 'that he had done anything very wrong', but also by their desire to avoid publicity, protect white prestige, and shield officers' families from the truth. So they doctored the record, trying officers who raped local women on other charges or offering them a chance to resign.[45]

Australian archives reveal a fuller story, and in the case of Leahy's expeditions, his astonishing film footage induced later scholars to take a closer look. Some fifty years after those riveting scenes were shot and after Leahy himself was dead, the documentary filmmakers Bob Connelly and Robin Anderson returned to those valleys to find the villagers whose lives were transformed through 'first contact'. There were plenty who remembered that moment. In village after village, locals recalled their fear of the guns, their grief when conflicts left family members dead, their amazement when an airplane landed with a belly full of cargo. As for the 'whiteman' himself: some peoples had thought he was a spirit and his carriers were their own dead kin, brought back from the dead. But they soon discovered that these men had needs and desires like theirs and the goods to pay for them—steel axes, knives, and amazing quantities of shells.

Some of the women who were 'traded' were at those gatherings, and they remembered those transactions perfectly well. 'We were given to the white man's carriers in return for shells,' one said. 'As the white men were giving out good things for women my husband asked me to go to them,' said another. One can imagine what Lugard and Valentine Dannevig would have thought of all this. For Lugard, such sexual contact represented an unforgivable lapse in white civilizational codes, to be punished but never publicly acknowledged. For Dannevig, it was simply trafficking, an abuse of male power. But those responses were forged in a culture suffused with humanitarianism, racism, and romanticism alike, and the women themselves were more philosophical. Yes, they had been terrified and had begged their parents to be spared, but they understood the bargain. 'To get these gifts,' one recalled, 'I overcame my fear.' They had been kindly treated, photographed, and fed, and there were some lasting compensations. 'Out of this I bore a mixed-race son,' one stated, 'which is good.'

And they bought precious knowledge with their bravery, knowledge useful to themselves and their disoriented community. For nothing so punctuated myths of supernatural origin or racial supremacy as those commonplace transactions of sex, surely one reason why Lugard found them so reprehensible. Since our colonizing men and the imperial archive alike worked so hard to erase these women from our story, as we leave the New Guinea highlands and turn to the Genevan response we should let their hard-won knowledge stand as the last word.

'We had sex together then we knew they were men.'

'That's right.'

'That's right—not spirits—just men.'[46]

## The Lugardian model in crisis

Michael Leahy had used airplanes, guns, film cameras, and trade goods to bring the natives where he built his base camps into relations of collaboration if not quite control. His transactions left lasting traces—airfields, a mining operation, new trades and wants, three never acknowledged mixed-race sons. Two of those sons, Clem and Joe, would become important coffee-growers in the highlands, and Mick's brother Dan Leahy would remain there, raising crops and children with two strong-minded common-law New Guinean wives.[47]

When Leahy first described his explorations to the Royal Geographical Society, however, he downplayed those ambiguous and complex relationships to present himself as a modern embodiment of the hero/explorer, bringing savage nature *and savage people* under his control. It was the latter aspect that caught the public eye and that shifted attention away from the drama of exploration to the problems of 'contact' and governance. By November 1935, with the spectacle of Italy's brutal war in Ethiopia unfolding, even the members of the Geographical Society knew they could not avoid those questions. The Vice President, Sir William Goodenough, commended Leahy's achievement but noted that human life had appeared 'pretty cheap' and urged that 'these people and their country' not be 'in any way exploited'—an intervention one scholar sees as marking a decisive shift in attitude.[48] And if Goodenough expressed reservations, when J. H. Harris of the Anti-Slavery Society read Leahy's account he felt only anger and scorn. Leahy had mentioned shooting one or more natives on at least eight separate occasions, Harris wrote in a bristling letter to the Australian High Commissioner the following June. The Anti-Slavery Society would thus like to know whether Leahy had had a permit to enter uncontrolled areas, whether he had reported those clashes, whether they were being investigated, and whether the government was likely to prosecute. Four months later, Harris asked the PMC to investigate as well.[49]

The Commission was happy to have Harris's petition, one of the very few ever received about New Guinea, for it had been worrying about prospectors' untamed behaviour for a long time. As early as 1928, Lugard had urged the administration to bring new areas under control before allowing prospectors entry,[50] and in the 1930s, as the Commission came to grasp how much of New Guinea lay ungoverned and how populous those areas might be, members grew still more anxious.[51] From the Pacific Islands' press, they knew that prospectors were still entering those regions with impunity and had heard about the clashes that had led to the deaths of Baum and McGrath. Lugard also knew through Gilbert Murray of the brutality of the punitive expeditions sent out against tribes thought responsible for murder.[52] Indeed, at the June 1935 session, well before Harris's petition but after it was aware of the clashes in the Mount Hagen area, the Commission subjected the Australian representative to a thorough drubbing for the obvious ineffectiveness of the administration's regulations and permits, the way prospectors were endangering the lives of both the locals and their own carriers, and its delinquency in not keeping them under control.[53] The highlands should be closed to all but government officials until order had been clearly established.

The administration, rattled by the number of fatal collisions between whites and natives in the uncontrolled areas, had already moved in this direction. In 1935 the Uncontrolled Areas Ordinance was amended to allow the administration to impose different gradations of control, and the Upper Ramu and Mount Hagen areas were closed to new expeditions. The following year the administration also took the unprecedented step of executing Ludwig Schmidt, a (fortuitously German) prospector who had inaugurated a 'reign of terror' along the Upper Sepik.[54] Some entry was still allowed. Miners (including the Leahy brothers) who were already working claims in the Hagen area and missionaries in the Upper Ramu were tolerated, provided they did not extend their reach.[55] But the government went to some trouble to contain criticism. It conducted an investigation into charges by the Anti-Slavery Society; that investigation, entrusted to the very Jim Taylor who had led the joint 1933 expedition, unsurprisingly found that the party had always acted in self-defence.[56] The government also dispatched Colonel Walstab, Superintendent of Police, to Geneva to assure the Commission that the administration had closed some areas entirely and would issue permits for others only if it was certain that it could do so safely.[57]

Since Australia had already taken these steps, the Commission's report on the Leahy petition, written by Malcolm Hailey (who had just replaced Lugard as British member), thus covered familiar ground. The mandatory power was obliged to secure the rule of law. *All* permits should be withheld until the administration was firmly in control.[58] Yet in the Geneva discussions over Leahy's explorations we also hear a new theme—the suggestion that perhaps 'primitive peoples' might be better off without intrusion from 'civilization' altogether. That note was sounded mostly by the woman member, Valentine Dannevig, who had by this point served on the Commission for about half a dozen years. Dannevig, a progressive and a feminist, had hitherto urged the mandatory powers to make ever greater efforts to 'uplift' and 'civilize' native populations; a school director, she was hardly someone to favour benign neglect. In this instance, however, Dannevig questioned whether 'contact' had much to offer the New Guinea highlanders at all, instead asking what the government might do to preserve 'the ethnological characteristics of the people, who evidently exhibited a comparatively high degree of culture'. She could see little reason to allow anyone save officials and anthropologists access to the highlands, and hoped that its peoples 'would be left alone for as long a time as possible'.[59]

Dannevig's response to the Leahy petition bears watching, for it signals that what we might call the cultural-relativist position was spreading beyond academics and travellers to influence liberals and 'Lugardians' as well. Indeed, just as anthropologists and ethnologists made so-called 'primitive' cultures appear coherent and sophisticated, European intellectuals were also deploring the meretricious and commercialized values suffusing mass culture in the West. (The Mandates Commission, when asked, unsurprisingly thought natives should be protected from the debasing excitements of Hollywood Westerns and romantic comedies.)[60] In Dannevig's case, however, that 'anthropological turn' produced discomfort with civilizational and moral rankings. Thus in 1937 we find her still fulminating against the statements (made three years earlier) of Eric Louw, the South African High Commissioner, that the Bushmen were 'a low type, a deteriorating race and rapidly dying out', and that they 'lived like animals in caves in the ground and…were not susceptible either to education or to civilization'.[61] To the contrary, she said (and the new Dutch member, Baron Van Asbeck, strongly agreed), ethnologists had found the Bushmen 'an interesting people with peculiar qualities fitting them for life in the desert and no small culture'. Indeed, they might be considered the Southwest African analogue to the Laplanders in Norway—and no one, Dannevig pointed out tartly, had suggested that the Laplanders be exterminated.[62]

Yet Dannevig's new scepticism about 'contact' was a sign of something more—a growing disillusionment with the mandate project altogether. That project's legitimacy depended, after all, on the claim that the mandatory powers were developing native *capacities*, and not simply native productivity, so that that population might gradually take control of its own destiny. For Dannevig that meant vastly expanding education, the area she had made her own life's work and that was her particular brief on the PMC. Yet especially in New Guinea and South West Africa, the territories in which need might be greatest and natives' desire for schooling well-documented, administrations thought native education of no importance at all.[63] New Guinea in the mid-1930s left virtually all education to the missions and declined to subsidize their work; South West Africa spent 90 per cent of its education budget on that 10 per cent of children who happened to be white. (Indeed, in 1937 the entire education budget for Ovamboland, with its 100,000 people, was £200.) Dannevig was far from radical in her advocacy. Like Lugard, she favoured vernacular instruction, technical and practical education, and village schools. But by the mid-1930s she was tired of hearing that natives

didn't want education, that they shouldn't be taught anything that might
enable them to compete with whites anyway, and that whites—however
much they profited from African labour—couldn't be taxed to provide services to natives.

Hence her remarkable report, written in 1938, in which she expressed
most clearly her doubts about the mandatory powers' good faith. She had
been tracking educational provision for ten years now, she wrote, and had
seen little progress. Those powers professed themselves unable to raise
taxes—but then, she pointed out, those governments themselves forced
natives 'to work in mines and on farms for the benefit of the white companies and settlers for wages which are so low as barely to enable them to pay
their taxes'. 'I have often wondered,' she continued:

> what must be the thoughts and the feelings of thinking natives towards the
> European Governments who come and make themselves masters of their land
> and its natural riches for their own benefit, and who have not yet found it
> possible to give the original owners of the land a fair share of the considerable
> profits, for instance, by erecting schools to help them to improve their standard
> of life and further their intellectual development so as to enable them, in a
> future not too far removed, to take an effective part in the management of
> their own affairs and the development of their country, as is, in fact, implied
> by the mandates.[64]

Thus Dannevig, in her most honest moment. Mandate administrations had
exploited their position to their own economic benefit; the pledge to put
native interests first had been broken. Lugard's vision of colonial administration as a *reciprocally* beneficial practice, one that raised European living
standards and native 'civilization' alike, had not been realized—or, at least,
Dannevig had crossed over into the swelling ranks of those who found it
hollow. Indeed, just how much that earlier Lugardian consensus had eroded,
and what was crystallizing in its wake, becomes clear when we look at two
further expeditions to mandated territories in the 1930s.

## Coda: Theodoli in Ovamboland,
## Ralph Bunche in Lomé

Nothing exposes more sharply the debased uses to which Lugardian ideals
could be put than the trip the Marquis Theodoli made at the invitation of
Prime Minister Hertzog to South Africa and the mandated territory in the

summer of 1935.[65] For a dozen years Theodoli had been one of South Africa's harshest critics, but as High Commissioner Te Water wrote to Hertzog that June, he had 'metamorphosed his opinions on the native aspect of the mandatory system since his own country has become involved in the Abyssinian affair'. At the most recent Commission session, Theodoli had shocked Dannevig with his dismissive comments about Africans' primitivism, and his colleagues were greatly relieved when he made it clear that he would travel wearing his 'Italian' and not his 'League' hat. As Te Water noted shrewdly, however, in the eyes of the public unquestionably 'the Marquis Theodoli comes to South Africa as Chairman of the Mandates Commission', his trip transparently an attempt to bring Italy and South Africa—two states whose aggressive regional expansionism had left them in bad odour with the League—closer together.[66]

Eager to further that cause, South West African officials corresponded intensely about the visit. As Theodoli was known to have interests in mines and farms in Italian Somaliland and also to be a keen sportsman, a three-week itinerary took shape that, by using air travel to ferry him across long distances, could show him much of the territory. He was to visit Windhoek, Grootfontein, Lüderitz, and Walvis Bay; to see farms, mines, and native reserves; to meet Hosea, chief of South West Africa's Herero people, and other notables; and to stop whenever possible to 'shoot something'. But the highlight of the trip was a four-day excursion to Ovamboland, the 'native reserve' north of the Police Zone that was home to about half of South West Africa's African population and the territory's showcase for 'indirect rule'. There, the Marquis would 'sleep in the veldt', visit the missions and the Oruahakana falls, go shooting, and—the *pièce de résistance*—attend 'tribal' ceremonies in the company of the area's Native Commissioner, Major C. H. L. Hahn.[67]

'Cocky' Hahn, as he was known to his friends (the Ovambo called him *Shongola*—'the whip'), presided over Ovamboland for the whole of the mandate period. Raised in Cape Province, Hahn had taken part in the South African invasion in 1915 and in the campaign to subdue Ovamboland's last Kwanyama king, Mandume ya Ndemufayo, before being appointed Native Commissioner in 1920. In that role his task—rather like Chinnery's in New Guinea—was first and foremost to keep the supply of male contract labour flowing to the territory's mines and farms.[68] Like Chinnery too, Hahn tried to contain the social dislocation that resulted by restricting the mobility of women, bolstering the authority of older men, and adopting a Lugardian language of ethnography and indirect rule. In personality and temperament, however, Hahn resembled Mick Leahy much more than Chinnery. Physically tough, authoritarian, attached to his dogs and guns, and a gifted amateur photographer, Hahn used the camera and the pen as well as taxes and the whip to bring Ovamboland's population under control.[69] In the early years that control was more desired than real, but at the time of Theodoli's visit in 1935, following a period of famine and economic crisis, Hahn was at the height of his power. And what he produced for his aristocratic visitor was a dramatization of African 'difference' that at once effaced and legitimated white rule.

We have Hahn's carefully composed photographs of that event. There are rows of bare-breasted young women carrying vessels filled with beer on their heads, to be offered as tribute to the Native Commissioner. There are the excited participants in the *efundula* ceremony, the ritual marking female initiation. There are group portraits: impeccably dressed Europeans individualized, front and centre, and the black Africans massed in the background. Hahn's photographs are visually arresting and do important ideological work. As Patricia Hayes astutely notes, they 'construct the space of Ovamboland as intensely African', effacing signs—Western clothing, Christian symbols—of the massive social change the territory was undergoing.[70] Outside the frame, of course, activities have taken place to produce that performance of European civilization. Hahn has mobilized African labour to build two landing strips for the white dignitaries' planes. He has flown in brandy and cigars, tinned asparagus and good cheeses, so the Marquis can eat as a Marquis should.[71] Through these technologies, the impresario renders civilizational difference and hierarchy—those fine wines in the veldt, recognizable precursors of the luxurious and artfully rustic accoutrements of today's 'wilderness' tourism, saying everything that needed saying about the location of power and 'civilization'.

We cannot know what Theodoli thought of all this but it certainly served Hahn well, for two years later whom do we find in Geneva but 'Shongola', now sporting an MBE, accompanying the new High Commissioner Courtney Clarke in his first appearance before the PMC. The two were there to explain why it would be unwise to try to 'civilise too rapidly' South West Africa's interesting native peoples.[72] Probably to Hahn's surprise, however, the PMC seem not to have found that joint performance very persuasive. For while Hahn may have spoken impeccable 'Lugardian', Lugard was now retired from the Commission and Theodoli absent as well, the expense of his South African adventure wasted. Courtney Clarke and Hahn faced, instead, a gathering well informed about those things—the coercive contract labour regime, the utterly inadequate social and educational provision— that the Ovamboland performances had been designed to occlude. The Commission did not speak with a single voice. Its members wanted *both* stronger efforts to safeguard native 'well-being' *and* a less economistic and exploitative definition of 'development'; Dannevig wanted the administration both to try to preserve the distinctive culture and lifestyle of the Bushmen *and* to meet the Hereros' demands for more extensive education. In that sense the Commission was still 'Lugardian', still trying to imagine a form of government that would both 'preserve' cultural difference and help those 'different' peoples survive in an ineluctably Western-dominated world. Yet its members had become more sceptical of that project, with a few— Dannevig, Van Asbeck, Palacios—now conscious of the ways in which the trope of cultural difference had been deployed to justify repression. The Mandates Commission could not really generate that critique. It was too European, too white, and much too wedded to the very tropes and language some members were beginning to question. But as the Commission grew uncertain, other voices and positions became audible and credible.

What makes it possible to see a system whole—to see, that is, the play and flow of power, but also to recognize one's own position in its deployment? W. E. B. Du Bois, the brilliant African American philosopher and an early radical critic of the mandates system, called this capacity 'double consciousness', attributing it to those who live at once within and aslant a dominant culture, who have the training and capacity to speak in universal terms but bear some mark, some sign of particularity or difference, that also enables them to discern how other particularisms—whiteness, for example—flourish in a 'universalist' disguise.[73] Our second traveller, Ralph Bunche, was one such man. As the architect of the United Nations' Trusteeship regime, Bunche would become in a sense Theodoli's successor. In the early 1930s, however, he was simply a young albeit supremely talented academic, completing a PhD at Harvard University while teaching political science at Howard University in Washington, DC, the pre-eminent institution of African American higher education (Figure 10.5). Having decided to compare French administration in mandated Togo with French administration in the colony of Dahomey, in the summer of 1932 Bunche set off for Paris, Geneva, and West Africa. He spent some two months in Senegal, Togo, and Dahomey, travelling there on a ship along with French civil servants returning after a spell of home leave.[74]

Figure 10.5  Ralph Bunche at Howard University, 1932.

Bunche had had some trouble settling on a dissertation topic, and it still is not clear just why he chose the one he did. He may have been influenced by the philosopher Alain Locke and the historian Rayford Logan, two other members of the brilliant coterie of internationally inclined African American intellectuals then on the faculty at Howard, both of whom had written general studies of the mandates regime in the late 1920s.[75] That most influential American scholar of contemporary Africa, Raymond Leslie Buell, whom we have met in Chapter 8, also pushed Bunche in this direction, for Buell, who had left Harvard in 1927 to become research director of the Foreign Policy Association, was eager to interest 'American negroes' in the mandates regime. (He had, for example, arranged funding for Locke's research trip to Geneva.)[76] Buell lent Bunche materials, helped him to clarify his research design, and especially impressed upon him the importance of fieldwork in Africa. And while Bunche could not travel, as Theodoli had,

as a distinguished guest (indeed, as a mixed-race scholar, he took the precaution of gathering testimonials about his *bona fides* from French academics
before setting off), the trip was decisive, providing him with a gut-level
understanding, a kind of moral optic, through which to read the mandates
regime.[77]

Bunche's dissertation, 'French Administration in Togoland and Dahomey',
which was submitted in 1934 and won the Toppan Prize for the best dissertation on comparative politics in the Harvard Government Department
that year, was a meticulous survey of French administrative practices in two
differently governed territories. On another level, however, it was an
extended engagement with the 'civilizational' justification for empire and
with arguments about African 'difference' articulated—in very different
ways—by Smuts, Lugard, and even Buell. Indeed, as Pearl T. Robinson points
out, Bunche clearly wrote his dissertation with Buell's *The Native Problem in
Africa* at his elbow, and while he remained indebted to that work for his
questions and method, he came to very different conclusions. Both Buell
and Bunche attempted to specify what difference League oversight made,
and both concluded that it had established progressive norms and even, to a
degree, induced mandate administrations to follow them. Yet Bunche was
far more outspoken about the regime's limitations. It wasn't just that he
found economic policies in colonies and mandated territories alike far too
exploitative (Buell had too), nor that he caught official reports misrepre-
senting facts (Buell had too), nor even that he thought the Mandates
Commission sorely in need of powers of on-the-spot investigation, for
Buell had proposed that as well. It was, rather, that he found the regime's
very ideals, which Buell considered progressive and commendable,
mean-spirited, outdated, and, in a word, racist.[78]

Those differences came out especially sharply in Bunche's treatment of
the relative merits of British and French colonial practices. Buell, recall, had
been critical of France's cavalier attitude towards 'native culture' and had
thought the British practice of strengthening the 'traditional' authority of
'native chiefs' through 'indirect rule' far more progressive. To Bunche, however, that British solicitude for African difference was at best patronizing
and at worst a cloak for white supremacy. Smuts' claim that 'the African'
would always remain something different, 'a child-type', 'mysterious and
wild', was retrograde and simply empirically wrong. Only a fool would
think the Togolese of Lomé, who 'speak fluently German, English and
French, as well as their native languages', less 'civilized' than their monolin-

gual rulers.[79] Africa was changing, and that change had to be managed and embraced, not—as Lugard proposed—contained within outdated 'chiefly' structures that educated Africans found profoundly irksome. Bunche was, by contrast, genuinely impressed by (and may have exaggerated) the lack of open racial prejudice and easy social mixing he found in the French colonies—the French women serving Africans in restaurants, the African and European children and soldiers trained side by side—and by France's willingness to embrace (if in their own interest) an ethos of progress. True, France's more confident 'civilizational' approach could make educated Africans too francophile, but by breaking down regional and ethnic loyalties at least it made national consciousness possible. 'Detribalization', anathema for Lugard and Buell alike, was for Bunche the precondition of African self-determination.

What you see depends on which way you are headed. Theodoli, struggling to justify Italy's claim to Ethiopia, 'saw' in Ovamboland confirmation of African primitivism. Buell, academic entrepreneur and liberal internationalist, saw in Tanganyika and South Africa's 'native reserves' a model of government that would allow Africans to 'progress' in their own way without unleashing the spectre of racial antagonism. Bunche, however, went to Africa persuaded that 'knowledge is of a universal character and knows neither race nor national boundaries', and found nothing in Africa to shake that faith. Africa was weak—politically, economically—but the 'natural differences' among its peoples were 'identical in terms of class, wealth and aspirations with those of Western peoples'. With time and technical aid, Africans were no less capable than other peoples of exercising the rights of free men.[80]

Bunche did not think that would happen anytime soon. He too thought independence was probably 'many generations removed from the present day'.[81] The 1930s were the devil's decade: the European empires were strong; the revisionist powers determined to expand as well. Bunche could not know that ten years hence, those empires having almost self-destructed, he would be drafting the chapters of the United Nations Charter dealing with non-self-governing territories, or that, at the Trusteeship Council a few years after that, he would begin planning the steps towards statehood. Already in 1934, however, Bunche had broken with the cultural and racial reasoning that was a hallmark of the interwar years to cast political development more as a matter of technical capacity and education. He was waiting in the wings and would not change his mind. The authority of 'civilization' was ending.

# ELEVEN

## When Empire Stopped Working

As far as I know, no one has ever asked or suggested that the British Empire should give up any of its Colonies, and I need hardly say that, if any such demand were made, it could not possibly be entertained for a moment. Mandated territories are not Colonies; they are in a somewhat different category, and are only part of the British Empire in what I may call a colloquial sense.

Neville Chamberlain, Chancellor of the Exchequer, House of Commons, 6 April 1936[1]

I have never known negotiations helped by encouraging hopes that cannot be realised, and for my part, not only do I think that we have not the right to part with our Mandated Territories to anyone except the people themselves when they become fit to rule and defend them, but I say that I cannot take upon my shoulders the guilt of putting another human being under a Government which refuses in its own country to its own people the rights of citizenship and makes them serfs.

Austen Chamberlain, former Foreign Secretary, House of Commons, 27 July 1936[2]

The mandates regime may have been in the midst of a full-blown crisis of confidence and legitimacy by the mid-1930s, but the British liberal internationalists who had always been its strongest backers did not respond quite as one might have expected. To the horror of the Mandates Commission and the embitterment of colonial nationalists everywhere, the late 1930s in Britain saw the emergence of a major public movement aimed not at 'emancipating' further mandated territories along the lines pursued in Iraq, but rather at bringing about a new colonial repartition. Now made aware by the Italo-Ethiopian war of the determination of the revisionist powers to force their claims, a growing number of British internationalists and politicians—a group that came to include Neville Chamberlain himself—concluded that they could only calm international tensions and bring Germany back into the League club by offering it territories in Africa.

This movement for 'colonial appeasement' generated an extraordinary level of public debate and attention between 1936 and 1938 and generated numerous practical proposals, culminating in Neville Chamberlain's 'colonial offer' to Hitler in March 1938, which was rejected.[3] The diplomacy that underlay those proposals has received close scholarly attention, and we now know how little interest Hitler took in those overseas territories, how instrumentally he deployed these claims, and, in consequence, just how futile and misguided those British efforts really were.[4] Yet the debate over 'colonial appeasement' mattered, not only because it decoyed so many internationalists into a profound misreading of German aims but also because it further discredited the project of 'internationalizing' empire itself. Not only desperate allied statesmen but equally British liberals and humanitarians, it became clear, could imagine handing Africans over to Nazis in order to preserve peace in Europe. The racial and cultural hierarchies and interests underpinning the League order could hardly have been more sharply revealed.

To track the genealogy of this particularly quixotic effort, we might turn to Arnold Toynbee, doyen of British liberal internationalists, ensconced at Chatham House in the early 1930s writing the annual *Survey of International Affairs*. When working for the Political Intelligence Department of the Foreign Office in 1919, Toynbee like so many others had been afire for the ideal of national self-determination. As time passed, however, and as he observed ethnic nationalisms in conflict in one area after another—Vilna, Corfu, Bulgaria, Palestine—that enthusiasm had palled. But Toynbee didn't only fear that Wilsonianism had promoted cultural chauvinism and intolerance; he also thought the doctrine had been unfairly applied. Toynbee had no sympathy for Italian claims: he would argue strenuously for a strong, even military, response to its attack on Ethiopia. But he thought the Versailles settlement unjust to Germany in particular, for it left too many ethnic Germans outside the Weimar borders. This was, of course, precisely what the Germans had been saying ever since 1919, and Toynbee was far from the only liberal intellectual to have come to regret the part he played in constructing that settlement. What is significant about Toynbee's role, however, is how hard he worked to promote territorial revision *after* the Nazi seizure of power in January 1933.

Toynbee undertook this work partly through the International Studies Conference—an organization initially founded under the auspices of the

League of Nations Institute for Intellectual Cooperation that brought together scholars of international politics and law. Initially, these biannual conferences had tried to establish common disciplinary practices in this new field of international relations. As tensions worsened in the 1930s, however, the conference became a forum through which well-connected liberal intellectuals in Britain, France, and the United States sought to shape diplomacy and policy. Each conference took two years to plan, with national think tanks like the Council on Foreign Relations in the United States or the Royal Institute for International Affairs in Britain choosing national delegations and commissioning preparatory studies on the designated topic. The 1933 conference addressed international trade (a topic chosen at the depths of the Depression in 1931); the 1935 conference dealt with collective security.

German political scientists had been avid participants in the International Studies Conference, but Germany's withdrawal from the League followed by the Nazification of all academic institutions threatened that participation. Toynbee tried to keep up contacts, and on a visit to Berlin in 1934 entered into conversations with Fritz Berber, an international lawyer now at its Institute for International Law. In the post-war period, Toynbee would downplay the extent of his contacts with Berber (quite possibly because, writing hundreds of letters monthly, he had simply forgotten them), but he took considerable trouble to secure Berber's welcome as an 'observer' at the 1935 conference.[5] That conference also agreed that their next topic would be 'peaceful change'—or, in other words, the process by which changes might be made in the international order without resort to war.

Everyone understood just *why* that question was urgent. Those states which were coming to be known as the 'have-not' powers—Japan, Italy, Germany—had made clear that they *would* resort to war if the balance of resources and territories were not shifted in their favour: Japan had already done so in Manchuria; Italy was massing troops on Ethiopia's borders. That autumn Toynbee thus sat down to think through just how the global order could be changed without war. By the time he presented his conclusions at Chatham House in December, it was too late: Italy had struck deep into Ethiopia, and Foreign Secretary Sir Samuel Hoare, scapegoat for a reviled proposal to secure a settlement by granting Mussolini significant territorial gains, would resign the next morning. But to the clutch of internationalists who gathered to hear Toynbee, that failure just made their task more urgent. If war was not to engulf the European continent, some mechanism had to be devised to adjust resources and boundaries to a shifting global balance of power.

How could that be done? As Toynbee saw it, internationalists needed first to recognize that they had left Versailles with their work unfinished. Yes, the Covenant had established a system of 'collective security' to safeguard that settlement against attempts to change it by force—but that was only half the battle. For, as the world changed, the international order had to change with it. Thus, argued Toynbee, 'we have also...to work out some method of "peaceful change" as an alternative to the violent method of change' through war. 'Dissatisfied' powers were making open territorial claims, and although some of those were specious and exaggerated, others, like Germany's claim for wider economic opportunities, were more justified. How could those grievances be met, and the world rendered less dangerous?

What is illuminating about Toynbee's response to that question is that he first sought to shift the terms of debate altogether. International tensions and revisionist resentments would not be eased by nationalist moves—that is, by giving in either to 'essentially irrational' colonial claims or to the 'caveman psychology' of those British imperialists who refused to contemplate any territorial concessions. Rather, the best approach would be to make sovereignty and territory matter less *tout court*. Between the opposing but similar programmes of colonial transfer and imperial annexation, Toynbee located a third alternative: that of 'internationalizing' all benefits of territorial control so that they could be enjoyed by the 'haves' and the 'have-nots' alike. Such had been the initial aim of the mandates system, and Toynbee, revealingly, looked back to that original impulse. Rather than returning territories to their former sovereigns, why not bring all non-self-governing territories under the mandates regime? If colonial control were truly internationalized, all grounds for resentment would vanish.[6]

Toynbee did not see this proposal as a veiled apology for Italian or German aggression. His aim was to prevent such resorts to force, not to condone them. It is also true, however, that Toynbee was far more sympathetic to Germany than to Italy, and while he may not have sought to stoke German territorial demands, his interventions had that effect. Toynbee's ideas were welcomed by German colonial lobbyists who registered his sympathy for their claims while ignoring his internationalism, and he became one conduit by which what has come to be known as the project of 'colonial appeasement' gained international traction and then British Cabinet

**Figure 11.1** Arnold Toynbee in Germany, 1936.

support (Figure 11.1). But he was only one such conduit. So, let us now examine how, over the next three years, that unthinkable proposal—giving colonies to Germany—became a popular cause.

## German revisionism and British internationalism: a dialogue of the deaf

German colonial revisionists lived through the period of League member-ship in a state of irritation and sometimes rage. They were pleased that the ex-colonies had opened to German trade and tourism and knew member-ship on the Mandates Commission brought opportunities for colonial propaganda and a kind of prestige. Yet League membership had also forced them to play a particular 'mandate' game: to pose as defenders of interna-tional law, to insist on strict enforcement of the principles of trusteeship and the 'open door', and to advocate colonial independence. In the Stresemann era, the Wilhelmstrasse slipped easily into that role, winning Germany an enviable reputation among anti-colonial nationalists. For the colonial movement, however, there was a sting in the tail. Embittered ex-governors and nostalgic old soldiers were not much interested in trade balances or (still less) anti-colonialist kudos; they just wanted those territories back. And there was no real sign, in 1933, that League membership had brought that goal any nearer.

Throughout the Weimar period the colonial movement thus concentrated not on building international ties but rather on converting the German people to their cause. Exhibits, lectures, and articles strategically placed in the daily press hammered familiar arguments home—that Germany had been 'illegally' deprived of its property in violation of Wilsonian pledges by the 'Diktat' of Versailles; that charges of colonial brutality were lies hypocritically levelled by those responsible for the Amritsar massacre or the Congo regime; that, to the contrary, the German colonies had been near-utopias of flourishing plantations and happy, productive natives; and that those territories and peoples were now going to rack and ruin under brutal or incompetent French or Australian rule.[7] 'It is no use saying that the old German colonies were only a source of expense and weakness, or that no German ever went to them, or that they served no really useful purpose in any way,' Britain's ambassador in Berlin, Sir Ronald Lindsay, advised the Foreign Office as early as 1928. 'The fact remains that their loss is resented and their recovery is desired, and in the course of time the resentment is likely to become bitter and the desire more ardent.'[8] He was exactly right, and the fact that all great powers responded to the deep economic crisis of the early 1930s by introducing tariffs or imperial preferences made German complaints of being unfairly deprived of raw materials and markets more strident and believable. In 1932 Heinrich Schnee resigned from the Deutsche Volkspartei and cast his lot with the Nazis (Figure 11.2).

His followers, too, greeted the Nazi takeover enthusiastically. The Nazis might be lukewarm about the colonialists' cause—*Mein Kampf* contained unflattering references to it—but common loathing for the Versailles framework made the two natural allies. Finally, colonialists could cast off their uncomfortable internationalist disguise and openly demand not a 'mandate' but rather the return in full sovereignty of *all* the former German colonial possessions.[9] The Nazis' flair for propaganda rubbed off. Brightly coloured posters in train stations reminded passers-by that 'their' colonies could provide raw materials and *Lebensraum* (Figure 11.3); striking charts compared the huge expanse of territory supporting each British or Belgian

**Figure 11.2** Heinrich Schnee at the opening of the film, *Der Reiter von Ost-Afrika*, 1934.

man (their native inhabitants conveniently forgotten) with their German counterpart's sorry state; postage stamps bedecked with colonial 'heroes' dropped into letter boxes. Public statues of colonial conquerors were rededicated, colonial exhibitions mounted, 'talkies' and documentary films about German colonies produced, and in 1934 the fiftieth anniversary of the founding of German South West Africa observed in the schools. All this did not win a mass following. French intelligence estimated total membership in the raft of German colonialist organizations at no more than 75,000 in 1935.[10] But it nourished resentful fantasies about the joys of African life and turned the 'unfairness' of Germany's lack of colonies into unexamined 'common sense'.[11]

The year 1936 was revisionism's *annus mirabilis*. Hitler repeatedly stressed German colonial demands and the Reichsbank President and his Minister of Economics, Hjalmar Schacht, brought them up with British and French counterparts. Sympathetic articles sprouted in the British press, and the British government began privately—and then not so privately—considering ways to meet those demands. Yet, like so many other right-wing movements

Einladung

zur feierlichen Eröffnung der

## großen Kolonial=Ausstellung

am Sonntag, den 16. Juni 1935, vormittags 11 Uhr

### in der Städtischen Festhalle

Horst=Wessel-Straße

Figure 11.3 'Here too is Living Space': poster for a colonial exhibition, 1935.

initially euphoric about Hitler's rise, the colonial movement found the Nazi embrace suffocating. This was also the year when the old established colonial associations were disbanded and Schnee, protesting, was pushed aside.[12] Henceforth Ritter von Epp, the head of the Nazi Party's Colonial Bureau, former Freikorps leader, and veteran of the genocidal war against the Herero, would be the public face of German colonialism—although policy was usually set by the hardline ambassador to Britain and later Foreign Minister, Joachim von Ribbentrop. It also shifted to serve Hitler's vision, which was never about restitution of some particular African land but rather about Germany's apotheosis as a racially purified self-actualizing global power. There was 'no such thing as "colonial policy in itself"', the Nazi Party's Office of Colonial Policy instructed its propagandists. 'Colonial issues should be judged exclusively from the standpoint of *Germany's national needs*.'[13] And in 1936 those 'needs' were to forge an Anglo-German alliance, disrupt the Anglo-French entente, and win Britain's implicit consent to Germany's expansion eastwards. If colonial propaganda sought to make Germans 'colonial-minded', then it was also, French intelligence reported, 'always directed at London'.[14]

There was good reason for that, for Britain was revisionism's most fertile ground. It wasn't only that Lloyd George and so many of the bright young men behind the scenes at Versailles came to feel that settlement too punitive, nor only that virtually all British statesmen were eager to avoid commitments in eastern Europe, nor even that strong cultural prejudices against slippery Latins and primitive Slavs made many resist the close French alliance or prefer Germans to Poles and Russians.[15] Of course those factors mattered, and a small group of Germanophiles or Nazi sympathizers (most notably the historian W. H. Dawson and, from 1934, the *Daily Mail* proprietor Lord Rothermere) gave vocal and early support to German claims.[16] Perhaps more important, however, was the fact that Britain had a democratic political culture in which *foreign* as well as domestic policy was scrutinized and debated by a vigilant and informed Parliament and press. As a result, unlike in France, where the Foreign Ministry worked hard to keep policy out of parliamentary sight and in expert hands,[17] in Britain a great number of ordinary people fell into the habit of thinking of themselves as policymakers, unselfconsciously using the word 'we'—just as Toynbee did—when they discussed Britain's world role. And those volunteer 'world-orderers', while anything but pro-fascist, nonetheless provided the grounds on which revisionism could flourish for the simple reason that they instinctively favoured conciliation and sought internationalist responses to conflicts between states. The British were more sympathetic to colonial revision than other imperial powers, in other words, not because they were particularly defeatist but because they were particularly *internationalist*—without, however, interrogating too closely their reflexive identification of internationalism with British ideals.

Take, for example, the treatment of German colonial claims in *Headway*, the house organ of Britain's 400,000-strong League of Nations Union. *Headway* printed a letter from one Colonel Kelsall in March 1935 supporting the return of Germany's ex-colonies, and for more than a year every issue contained correspondence on this question. First came the retorts, by the Fabian colonial expert Lord Olivier among others, that territories could no longer be handed about without regard to the interests of the inhabitants. Those then produced several interventions (including one from Heinrich Schnee) warning that German expansion was inevitable and pointing out that African views had hardly been considered when the mandates had first been allocated.[18] What is striking, however, is how quickly correspondents tried to move the issue away from rival national claims. 'A lasting solution of the whole problem will not be achieved until the Great Powers of Europe admit that two standards of behaviour towards subject peoples are incompatible—the "Colonial Possession" standard and the "Mandate" standard,' the former Iraqi intelligence officer Philip Mumford argued; 'the Mandates system must become universal'.[19] Although some correspondents contended that the Nazis' 'marauding instinct' and loathsome racial policies disqualified Germany from ruling Africans at all,[20] others held out the hope that a universal system would induce the regime to adopt international humanitarian norms.[21]

In Parliament and the press, League supporters thus looked to international agreements to ease nationalist grievances. Indeed, the level of popular enthusiasm for various 'world-ordering' proposals greatly worried a moderate League supporter like Lugard, who in September 1935 and January 1936 laid out his own views in four closely argued letters to *The Times*. Lugard defended Britain's colonial record and challenged the German case, but his main aim was to expose how impractical the proposals for international control really were. Whether Britain held its own territories under sovereignty or under mandate was a matter of supreme indifference to Germany or Italy, who were concerned only to have territories of their own. The idea that inexperienced powers or, still less, committees of international bureaucrats could do a better job administering dependent territories than experienced colonial officials was downright absurd. Lugard, an old free-trader, did think the 'open door' should apply to all African colonies, but he viewed proposals to 'internationalize' all dependent territories as so much moonshine, and said so.[22]

As the debate heated up, diehard imperialists mobilized as well. A Labour motion of 5 February 1936 calling on the government to instigate that international inquiry raised the stakes, for Lloyd George blurted out that he 'did not believe they would make peace in the world until they met all the nations in a friendly spirit and said that the British Empire was willing to reconsider the question of mandates'. He was sharply rebuked by Leo Amery, who retorted that Germany had lost its territories in a war it had itself provoked and should look to the 'great markets of Central Europe' and not to Africa for an economic zone.[23] Amery didn't think Britain should object to German dominance in Central Europe (in August 1935 he had told Hitler as much),[24] but he insisted that Britain's security rested on tightening imperial ties. Five days later Amery, Churchill's son-in-law Duncan Sandys, and a dozen other MPs gave notice of a motion opposing the transfer of any British colonies or mandated territories.[25] As an issue, 'colonial revisionism' had well and truly arrived. *The Times* would publish 160 articles on the subject in 1936 alone.[26]

What was new about this public discussion? First, it *preceded* any serious Cabinet-level consideration; 'public opinion' raced ahead of official plans. Second, virtually all policy options were on the table from the start. There were, after all, only three possible responses to German colonial demands: to surrender the ex-German territories, to incorporate them more fully into the empires of the mandatory powers, or to try to find a 'third way' by tying the issue to other internationalist goals—economic liberalization, say, or the universalization of mandate principles, or the crafting of a 'general settlement'. Of these three, however, in Britain 'internationalist' arguments predominated. They were clever, interesting, and appealed equally to well-connected liberal intellectuals quick to take up their pens and a public desperate to avoid war. Over the course of 1936 and 1937, a network of liberal intellectuals, loosely coordinated by Toynbee and the Labour peer Noel-Buxton (both of whom travelled to Germany), promoted the plan to conciliate Germany by redistributing colonies under an expanded system of international control. Those revisionist plans were always hedged about, of course, with various high-minded conditions. All powers administering dependent peoples were to enforce principles of trusteeship and the 'open door'; no transfers were to be made without the inhabitants' consent. But the crucial point is that, for more than a year, the 'world-orderers' dominated the airwaves.[27]

These proposals were hardly what German colonialists had in mind, and they quickly grew frustrated with their self-referential British counterparts. Theodor Gunzert, former head of the Foreign Ministry's Colonial Bureau, told a French informant in late 1936, and again in January 1937, that he had lost all confidence in Toynbee and his proposals for 'peaceful change'. British revisionists seemed unable to grasp what to the French was crystal clear: since the Germans were interested in *less* international constraint rather than more, expanding the mandates system was no longer a basis for discussion. The Germans were happy to let the debate continue, French intelligence experts thought, mostly because it drew attention away from 'the specific and central question of Cameroon's strategic position and the political impact on French West Africa of its return to Germany'.[28] But if British liberal intellectuals were deluded to think the Nazis might be interested in their internationalist fixes, the Nazis were equally deluded to think the British might accept transfers outside an internationalist framework. For not only were powerful if less vocal interests uninterested in territorial revision (the Conservative Party conference, for example, proclaimed it in 1936 and 1937 'not a discussable question'),[29] but even those that *were* interested had no intention of unconditionally restoring German sovereignty. Once the negotiations started, that incompatibility would become apparent.

## Making offers he could only refuse

The British government's consideration of German claims can be divided into three episodes: the secret review conducted by a subcommittee of the Committee of Imperial Defence between March and June 1936; the intermittent Anglo-French consideration of the economic case made by Hjalmar Schacht, Reichsbank President and German Minister of Economics, through the winter and spring of 1936–37; and finally the crafting by Neville Chamberlain and a few trusted associates of a 'colonial offer' in late 1937 and early 1938. Prior to those investigations, when asked about German claims in the Commons, ministers stated bluntly that the government had not considered transferring any of its mandated territories and were not considering such transfers in the future. When Hitler raised Germany's 'moral and legal' claim to colonies with Sir John Simon in March 1935, Simon said flatly that he could not hold out hope of concessions.[30]

But there was cautious movement behind the scenes. In early 1935 the Foreign Office conducted a long review of the question.[31] Some ministers and officials thought that, if peace could be bought by handing over one of the ex-German colonies, it would be cheap at the price. Sir Robert Vansittart, the powerful Permanent Under-Secretary at the Foreign Office, for example, thought Britain would have to allow German expansion either in Eastern Europe or Africa and much preferred the latter. That would come 'at our own expense', whereas 'any attempt at giving Germany a free hand to annex other people's property in central or eastern Europe is both absolutely immoral and completely contrary to all the principles of the League which form the backbone of the policy of this country'.[32] Neville Chamberlain and J. H. Thomas (then Chancellor and Colonial Secretary respectively) also told a Cabinet subcommittee in February 1936 that they'd be happy to trade Tanganyika for a lasting settlement.[33] African concessions could buy European peace.

This should not surprise us: this is how empires think. They often buy goodwill by handing dependent bits of territory and their inhabitants around. But could they do so in this case? Vansittart recognized that 'League principles' might make it hard to hand Hitler the Ukraine, for example; he failed, however, to realize that they might make other territorial transfers tricky as well. For if Britain was not 'sovereign' in (say) Tanganyika, and if it took the obligations of trusteeship seriously, how could transferring African populations to Germany be a private, even a generous, act? British consideration would founder, over and over, on this question.

## The Plymouth Committee

The British government's first serious consideration of the German claim was sparked by Hitler's so-called 'peace offer' of 7 March 1936, the day German troops reoccupied the Rhineland. That document laid out the conditions under which Germany might return to the League and referred to the hope that 'the question of colonial equality of right' could be settled 'through friendly negotiation'. If Hitler's aim was to throw sand in the eyes of the Locarno powers, he achieved it, for the next day Anthony Eden, the Foreign Secretary, told Prime Minister Stanley Baldwin that the time had come to consider the question of transferring a mandate or mandates to Germany. One day later Baldwin turned over that task to a secret subcommittee of the Committee of Imperial Defence under the chairmanship of the Colonial Under-Secretary, Lord Plymouth, and with representatives from the service ministries, the Colonial, Dominions, and Foreign Offices, and the Board of Trade. The Plymouth Committee began work immediately.[34]

The Foreign Office representatives were the most favourable, thinking restitution worth doing if it contributed to a general settlement and if humanitarian safeguards similar to those applied to the mandated territories were imposed. The service ministries, although pessimistic, were not obstructive, with the Admiralty stating that since 'we cannot claim a monopoly for ports and naval bases overseas', German overseas possessions would not pose any problems Britain hadn't faced before.[35] The Colonial Office representatives, however, thought the very notion that one could transfer people 'obsolete' and succeeded in making other members take its arguments seriously. 'I think the striking thing about our lengthy deliberations,' one official noted when it was all over, 'was the way in which even those... who were most anxious to find in the colonial field some opportunity for generosity to Germany, became, as they considered the matter, more and more convinced that the return of territory to Germany would create more problems than it would solve.'[36]

The Committee's June 1936 report laid all those problems out. Terminating a mandate would require consent of the League, and since Germany was not even a League member, raising this in Geneva might destroy the mandates system altogether. It would be a retrograde step, amounting to 'a reversion to the doctrine of exploitation and to a retreat from the enlightened principles enshrined in the mandates which the United Kingdom Government have always claimed are applied already throughout the Colonial Empire'. Inevitably, such a move would be interpreted as a sign of weakness, not only by Britain's imperial allies and by the British Dominions, all of whom were deeply opposed, but equally by colonial peoples themselves.

That was an accurate view of how little colonial concessions would do to ease global tensions. Revealingly, however, the Plymouth Committee didn't feel able to stop there. Instead, thinking that 'wider considerations' might necessitate concessions anyway, they took it upon themselves to lay out the minimum requirements such a transfer must meet. These were, first, that it should not endanger the principles of trusteeship; second, that it should not be achieved through a German *fait accompli*; third, that it should be condi-tional upon Germany's continued good behaviour; and finally, that it should be part of a wider global settlement. Letting loose some speculative hares that would never be run down, they also suggested that if some concession had to be made, Togo and Cameroon would be much more easily relinquished than Tanganyika—unsurprisingly, since those territories were largely in French hands.[37] While insisting that territorial transfer was a terrible idea, the committee thus went quite far towards making it imaginable.

That conceptual leap mattered more than the well-grounded reservations. Information about the Plymouth Committee's deliberations leaked out, and on 6 April 1936, Churchill, Sandys, and others asked for reassurances in the House of Commons that no territorial transfers were contemplated. Neville Chamberlain, when replying for the government, prevaricated. Although the surrender of British colonies was unthinkable, 'mandated territories were not colonies' and their disposition—while subject of course to consid-erations of native welfare—was, in part, a matter for the League.[38] The sound barrier had been broken. Eden would inform the Commons at the end of July that the government had concluded that 'any transfer of Mandated Territories would inevitably raise grave difficulties, moral, political and legal, of which His Majesty's Government must frankly say that they have been unable to find any solution', but his regretful tone revealed how much the Foreign Office at least wished otherwise. The government could see no way forward but refused to shut the door.[39]

## Hjalmar Schacht and the economic case for transfer

For the next year, amid intense public interest, proposals for colonial res-titution proffered by an assortment of real and would-be diplomats landed on Whitehall desks. Some reached for the panacea of a 'general settlement', but others sought mostly to reknit frayed European economic ties. Liberal economists within the League's Economic and Financial Organization and advising the British government were by the early 1930s very worried about how protectionist policies had deepened global antagonisms and guiltily aware that the United States and the United Kingdom had—with the Smoot-Hawley tariff of 1930 and the Ottawa agreements on imperial protection in 1932—been among the worst offenders. Those economists knew that Germany, a trading power with-out a dependent empire, had fewer options. Sailing athwart the trends of the times, they now tried to use international organizations to promote trade liberalization.[40] In September 1935, Foreign Secretary Sir Samuel Hoare had promised the League Assembly that Britain stood ready to equalize access to raw materials.[41]

The man who did the most to insert German colonial claims into these economic discussions was the Reichsbank President and the Nazi regime's Minister of Economics in the mid-1930s, Hjalmar Schacht. Schacht was one of Germany's most powerful men, having not only helped orchestrate its economic recovery from the nadir of 1934 but done so in such a way as to lessen its dependence on American loans, hold down domestic consumer spending, and make possible the hothouse arms build-up to which Hitler was absolutely committed. Schacht refused to allow Germany's choices to be constrained by its serious foreign-exchange problems, taking a hard line with its creditors and negotiating clearing arrangements that drew its continental trading partners (especially in southeastern Europe) ever closer into its economic orbit.[42] Always on the lookout for markets and materials that could aid Germany's growth, Schacht updated the colonial case to fit a protectionist, bloc-oriented world. The pre-war world had enjoyed free trade, ready credit, open emigration, long-term commercial treaties, and a universal gold standard, he pointed out in a much-cited article in *Foreign Affairs*. But that economic liberalism had vanished, and with global trade down by as much as two-thirds, the great trading powers now looked to their empires or to their vast internal markets. Germany thus needed colonies not to recover the products those territories had once supplied, but rather to build a comparable market within its own currency area.[43]

That move towards global trading blocs that Schacht emphasized was quite real. The proportion of French exports going to its colonies rose from just over a fifth in 1931 to almost a third in 1935, by which point just under half of British exports went to imperial destinations.[44] But it was less that economic shift than the June 1936 advent of the Popular Front government in France that won Schacht a hearing. The new Socialist Prime Minister Léon Blum was too beset by domestic and European strife to set a high price on France's African mandates and told Schacht he was willing to contemplate concessions if Britain would as well. For the first time the French appeared to be running ahead of the British, driving Eden to remind Blum and his Foreign Minister, Yvon Delbos, that Britain opposed negotiating on the colonial question alone. Blum thus told Schacht in December that any colonial agreement had to be part of a general settlement.

Revealingly, Hitler made no mention of those offers in his speeches, but they were followed up, with the British government's chief economic advisor, Frederick Leith-Ross, meeting with Schacht in early 1937. That March and April the British Cabinet reviewed Schacht's proposal to Blum, in which he offered arms limitations and Germany's re-entry into the League in exchange for Togo and Cameroon, a reduction of interest on debt, and other economic concessions. It ultimately decided that if France wished to enter into negotiations, Britain would go along. Yet Schacht's proposal went no further, for there were numerous practical impediments. Timing was a major problem. By the time the British government considered Schacht's case, the Blum government was in crisis (it would fall in July 1937), and Schacht's star was in decline as well. Divisions within the French and British governments also mattered, for if Delbos and to a lesser extent Eden wanted to make a deal, French Colonial Minister Marius Moutet was horrified and had no qualms about telling the papers so, and his British counterpart William Ormsby-Gore felt much the same way. And had negotiations proceeded, they would likely have quickly foundered. Yes, Schacht and his Anglo-French interlocutors had similar understandings of the ways in which the global economy had changed, but they had diametrically opposite ideas about what to do about it. Blum, Eden, and Leith-Ross wanted all powers to retreat from 'bloc' construction and restore freer trade and better relations across international lines. Schacht just wanted Germany to have a bloc of its own.[45]

Thus while the period from Hoare's speech up until the Second World War saw many investigations into trade relations, access to raw materials, and the relationship of those matters to colonial control, these never produced proposals that Schacht, much less Hitler, wanted. Instead, both the British government's internal study of access to raw materials and the League inquiry authorized by the 1936 Assembly concluded that since the vast majority of raw materials came from sovereign and not colonial territories and were traded openly on international markets, trade restrictions and not colonial control was the main problem. The League report pointedly added that if certain countries had difficulty purchasing all they needed, that might be due to an unwillingness to devalue or to excessive spending on arms.[46] The many scholarly studies of 'peaceful change' undertaken in Western Europe and the United States between 1936 and 1940 came to the same conclusion.[47] As the economist J. B. Condliffe explained:

The real alternative to a restoration of international co-operation on a regulated but expanding basis is the grouping of nations into great trading blocs or empires. Apart from the tremendous losses of investments, trading connections and specialized capacities which such a development would involve, it seems clear that the risk of war between such great units would be enhanced, while the situation of the independent small nations would be gravely prejudiced. The most promising road to lasting peace and fruitful co-operation among the nations is not the further aggrandizement of great states, but the limitation of state rights in a world community. Not the re-building but the transformation of empires is needed by the granting of self-government where circumstances justify it and the vitalizing and extension of a true mandatory system where self-government is unwise in the best interests of the native populations. A first step in that direction might well be a reversal of the recent tendency to close colonial markets for the benefit of the governing power. It is difficult to justify this tendency as being in the interest of the colonial peoples or of world peace.[48]

This was just the liberalizing programme in which Schacht had no interest—and, it is worth adding, that the British government (as opposed to British liberal internationalists), now committed to imperial preference, proved unwilling to pursue either.

But the final reason why Schacht's proposals could not succeed is simply because they were not what Hitler wanted. Yes, Germany needed *Lebensraum* and subject territories to provide raw materials and agricultural supplies, but those territories should directly adjoin the Reich. In a now-famous meeting on 5 November 1937, Hitler made clear that Eastern Europe and the Balkans were to be those 'colonies'. Those states, thanks to Schacht's hard-driven bargains, were already bound to the Nazi economy, and Hitler instructed his military chiefs to prepare for the *Drang nach Osten* that would follow.[49] But if Schacht had helped secure that economic hinterland, by doing so he had worked himself out of a job. One month after that meeting, he was dismissed as Minister of Economics. He and Blum would meet again near the end of the war—both political prisoners in Dachau.

If Hitler's eastern plans were set, however, he managed to keep the British and French in the dark. In public he still harped on colonies, and British internationalists fell lemming-like into line. On 7 October, only days after Hitler's bitter attack on those powers who insisted that colonies were only a burden but nevertheless refused to share them, Toynbee, Gilbert Murray, Noel-Buxton, and Vernon Bartlett (liberal internationalists all) published a collective letter urging some effort to satisfy German colonial claims.[50]

Three weeks later *The Times* called for 'a genuine attempt to find for Germany some acceptable field for development', and two weeks after that *The Manchester Guardian*, usually a fierce critic of the Nazi state, published a self-flagellating argument for concessions as well—one reprinted, the French ambassador reported, in every Berlin newspaper.[51] In the House of Lords an odd alliance of progressive peers and isolationist or francophobe backwoodsmen joined together to urge the government to consider German claims in the context of a 'general settlement',[52] while the Council of the League of Nations Union called for the transfer of all non-self-governing territories to the mandates regime.[53] This was the high-water mark of British colonial revisionism, the enabling context for Chamberlain's final and misguided attempt at colonial appeasement.

## Chamberlain's colonial offer

On 19 November 1937, Viscount Halifax, Lord President of Council and Neville Chamberlain's closest ally, met with Hitler at Berchtesgaden to test the ground. Hitler was alternately aggrieved and self-justifying, complaining of the attacks upon him in the British press, and showing very little interest in Halifax's suggestion of a four-power conference. Yet perhaps because Hitler said that 'there was only one difference, namely the colonial question' marring Anglo-German relations,[54] and perhaps because Halifax met the colonies-obsessed Schacht the next day, he left Germany persuaded that 'a colonial settlement *on broad* lines' might be used 'as a lever upon which to pursue a policy of real reassurance in Europe'. In other words, he clarified, 'instead of trying to do a bargain on the line of getting [Hitler] to drop colonies as a return for a free hand in Europe, to try for the more difficult but possibly sounder bargain of a colonial settlement at the price of being a good European'.[55] (Figure 11.4)

This was what Neville Chamberlain wanted to hear. Ignoring Eden's warning to the Cabinet that 'Germany clearly did not now wish to connect Central Europe with the colonial question', Chamberlain speculated that the '*quid pro quo* for colonies' might include 'not only Central Europe but also some agreement on the League of Nations and on armaments'.[56] He met immediately with the new French Prime Minister, Camille Chautemps, and Foreign Minister Yvon Delbos in London and, buoyed by a surprisingly restrained reception in the Commons, began to sketch out a plan. He likely drew on Schacht's last conversation with Halifax, which had proposed the

**Figure 11.4** Mass meeting of the Reichskolonialbund at the Berliner Sportpalast, December 1937. Note the banner: 'Germany needs colonies!'

straight return of Togo and Cameroon and the transfer under mandate of a Central African territory carved out of Belgian Congo and Portuguese Angola; on private conversations with the French Secretary General of the League, Joseph Avenol; and on Colonial Office thinking about possible extensions of the mandates regime. Chamberlain's plan was 'imperial' in that horse-trading over Africa was, again, to do the work of European reconciliation. The whole of Central Africa—essentially everything below the fifth parallel (including Cameroon but excluding the Sahara and most of West Africa) and above the Zambezi River—would be put in a common pot and then distributed among all interested European powers. Yet it was also 'international' in that all powers would be obliged to administer their territories under common economic and humanitarian norms. In other words, Chamberlain was planning to reform the mandates system to reflect the realities—and, he hoped, abate the dangers—of the shifting European balance of power.[57]

Chamberlain's colleagues reacted cautiously at the Cabinet Committee on Foreign Policy on 24 January 1938. Eden doubted 'that we could get away with this question on the backs of other powers', and indeed, British machinations (about which they had some knowledge) worried and angered the Portuguese and Belgians in particular. The Colonial Secretary, Ormsby-Gore, also warned that 'the whole of the coloured world . . . would be greatly disturbed and would intensely resent the idea of our handing over native populations to another Power'.[58] But if Chamberlain was playing fast and loose with the interests and loyalties of Britain's European allies and the inhabitants of the African territories alike, he was also wilfully ignoring what the Nazis were saying. Von Ribbentrop, convinced (like Hitler) that the eastern settlement could only be undone by force and determined to do nothing to restrain Germany's freedom of action, had told Halifax and Chamberlain point-blank in mid-December 1937 that the German colonial claim was not a bargaining point[59]—a message that Neurath repeated to British ambassador Sir Nevile Henderson in the most explicit way in late January 1938.[60] Yet Chamberlain proceeded anyway, recalling Henderson to London in early February to discuss the proposal (the substance of which was soon known to the German Embassy)[61] and then instructing him to request an early audience with Hitler to present it. On 1 March, when Henderson asked for that meeting, he was again told that Germany's colonial demands were 'a legal claim' and non-negotiable.[62]

Henderson dutifully met with Hitler on 3 March 1938 anyway. 'There was no question of a bargain,' he (implausibly) insisted, 'but rather of an attempt to create the basis for a real and sincere friendship with Germany.' German cooperation on arms agreements and on Czech and Austrian politics was essential to European peace, but the British government was also ready to make progress on the colonial question; indeed the Prime Minister 'had devoted his personal attention to this matter'. With the aid of a globe, Henderson explained Chamberlain's proposal, assuring Hitler that while all powers would be asked to subscribe to common principles about demilitarization, free trade, and native welfare, Germany would hold some territory in sovereignty. Would Germany be ready to take part in such a regime? And, if so, what contribution would Germany make 'for general order and security in Europe'?

Hitler responded truculently. The main contribution Britain could make towards peace would be to prohibit the incessant attacks made upon him in the British press. Central Europe was no concern of Britain at all. Just as Germany 'would never think of interfering in the settlement of relations between England and Ireland', so too 'Germany would not tolerate any interference by third powers in the settlement of her relations with kindred countries or with countries having large German elements in their populations.' As for Chamberlain's cherished colonial plan, Hitler failed to see the point of it. 'Instead of establishing a new and complicated system,' he asked Henderson, 'why not solve the colonial problem in the simplest and most natural way, namely, by returning the former German colonies?' That was all Germany wanted, and if France and Britain were not interested in that proposal, Germany would prefer to wait quietly 'for 4, 6, 8, or 10 years' until they might change their minds; nor did he wish to burden countries that had nothing to do with German claims. Henderson patiently ran through the whole thing again, adding that if Germany were interested, he believed Belgium, Portugal, France, and Italy would eventually all come round. Hitler made no reply, but promised to send a written response.[63]

That missive never arrived. Instead, on 12 March, nine days after Henderson's meeting with Hitler, German troops marched into Vienna. The Führer, Chamberlain learned the hard way, would not be deflected from his eastern plans; indeed, the Munich accords were built on that realization. Yet Hitler's response signalled not only a refusal to trade eastern for African 'colonies'. It was also an absolute rejection of the international order the British had been trying desperately to reconstruct. From 1936 until 1938 British politicians and the British public had tried to use the colonial issue to lure Germany into a programme of trade liberalization, 'de-territorialization', and 'peaceful change'. That effort failed in part because Britain was now protectionist as well, but also because Germany was never interested. The whole purpose of colonies, for Schacht as well as Hitler, was to *limit* Germany's dependence on an Anglo-American international economic and political order.

After this debacle, the British government gave up on colonial conciliation. Instead, in October 1938, Chamberlain forced the Czechs to play the Africans' role. Since Hitler kept harping, public interest lasted a little longer. Indeed, distressingly, on the night of 9 November, as mobs rampaged through German cities attacking Jews and sacking their properties, the Mandates Committee of the British League of Nations Union was putting the finishing touches to their proposal for extending international control as part of a 'general settlement'.[64] Those pogroms shattered these illusions. As the French ambassador to London reported with some relief the next month, left and Liberal opinion was now strongly opposed to turning native peoples over to a totalitarian state.[65] 'Don't let Neville underestimate the profound change...caused by the revelation of the Nazi character,' Amery wrote to Halifax on 15 November; ' "appeasement" had better lie low for some time to come.'[66] The French had always been less optimistic about colonial *Danegeld* anyway, and on 16 November Prime Minister Edouard Daladier stated, decisively if not entirely truthfully, that 'no cession has ever been considered, nor can it be'.[67] But by that point, the mandates system was coming apart at the seams.

## Seeking shelter from the storm: 'internationalized' territories in a territorializing world

The geopolitical quakes of the mid-1930s shook every mandated territory. But their governors had no common response. Each ran for cover or, worse, volunteered neighbouring territory as booty. Those responses show how reliant on imperial comity the mandates system was, and, still more, how utterly that comity had come apart.

New Zealand was the least affected, being remote from the centres of power and too weak to take an independent line. Australia, however, had already refused Germany's request to be allowed to purchase property in New Guinea, and at the imperial conference in 1937, made clear that it would not change course. Yet opinion among those merchants, businessmen, and settlers active in New Guinea itself was less clear-cut, with some feeling that Australia had done too little to develop the territory and needed all the help it could get against the growing Japanese threat.[68] From the mid-1930s white opinion in the mandated territory grew more critical of the non-fortification clauses of the mandate text and more favourable towards amalgamation with Papua. After 1945, Australia would insist on its right to fortify the new Trust Territory and would unite it to Papua.

Japan, to the north, was also moving towards re-imperialization. Suspicions abounded that Japan was illegally fortifying its mandated territory, and although Japanese representatives firmly denied those charges at the 1932 and 1934 PMC sessions, its unwillingness to allow foreign visitors and vessels access meant the suspicions never died down.[69] Throughout the 1930s the odd missionary, scientist, or stranded seaman passed along accounts of inexplicably large cargos and furious activity, as evidence mounted of major communications, airfield, oil storage, and harbour works underway on Saipan, Ponape, Truk, and the Palaus.[70] Japan insisted that its improvements were purely economic in aim, and historians have found little evidence of open militarization (that is, of fortification) before 1939, but those works, not to mention ever-increasing settlement and investment, certainly bound the islands tightly into the Japanese 'sphere'.[71]

Germany understood what this meant. As its ambassador in Tokyo told the Wilhelmstrasse early in 1938, 'Japan will under no circumstances, even at the risk of losing Germany's friendship, relinquish the South Sea Islands.'[72] But Tokyo, estranged from its former allies and now tied to Germany through the 1936 anti-Comintern pact, would not accept League authority either. Hence Japan's sporadic and surreptitious offers from 1938 to buy the islands from Germany—a solution that would have repudiated 'international' sovereignty and acknowledged Germany's claim while also permanently establishing Japanese ownership. In 1938 Germany rejected these initiatives,[73] but in 1940 its representatives at the tripartite negotiations in Tokyo agreed to transfer residual sovereignty into Japanese hands.[74]

Japan was the only mandatory power openly to repudiate League control in this way, but South Africa certainly flirted with defiance. South Africa had always said that South West Africa would ultimately become a fifth province, and the world economic crisis and the emergence of an irredentist Nazi movement among German settlers forced the question (Figure 11.5). In 1934 the embittered and jittery non-German majority of the whites-only Legislative Assembly appealed openly for annexation, and in Geneva, South Africa refused to disavow that prospect. Indeed, in September 1936 a South African commission found 'no legal obstacle to the government of the Mandated Territory as a province of the Union, subject to the Mandate'—which had always been interpreted by South Africa to mean only that one had to restrict the African population's access to firearms, alcohol, land, votes, and other things reserved for adults.[75]

Yet the Union government did not annex the territory. No doubt it didn't relish further conflict with Geneva, but like Japan it also did not wish to antagonize Germany. South Africa and Germany had long had close trading ties, and from 1934, Schacht's ingenious barter arrangements bound them still more tightly together. Through the 1930s the Reich was the single most important market for South African wool.[76] In 1935 and 1936 Smuts and the South African Prime Minister, J. B. M. Hertzog, let British friends and officials know that they favoured concessions to Germany (provided South African hegemony below the Zambezi was acknowledged), and in September 1937, when debate was hottest, High Commissioner Charles Te

**Figure 11.5** Two thousand whites attend a Hitler Youth rally in Windhoek, 1936.

Water made that view public.[77] South Africa's Germanophile Defence Minister, Oswald Pirow, was still more enthusiastic, telling the crew of a German ship in 1935 that 'at a time like the present, when the coloured tide rises higher and higher', South Africa could only welcome the return of such a staunchly white supremacist power. Pirow met with well-placed Britons (including Lugard) and tried fruitlessly to persuade the government that his excellent Nazi contacts made him a perfect intermediary.[78]

Tanganyika was buffeted by many of the same forces. It too had a significant German presence, for German nationals had been allowed to enter the territory after 1924 and with German government loans swiftly re-established themselves on the sisal estates. By 1939, Germans outnumbered Britons in the non-official 'European' population.[79] As in South West Africa, that German population proved a receptive target for Nazi sentiment; as in South West Africa, too, German revanchism revived appeals from other whites for 'closer union' with neighbouring British possessions. Yet, with the white-settler population numbering only 10,000 of a total of five million, Anglo-German antagonisms never became as fierce as in South West Africa. Indeed, visiting the territory in 1938, the American consul in Nairobi found German plantation owners 'rather lukewarm' about the prospect of Germany's return.[80] British officials in Tanganyika, the territory's mobilized Indian population, and powerful voices on all sides of the political spectrum—among them Lugard, Amery, and Ormsby-Gore—also loathed the idea of retrocession, and said so. Tanganyika had always been the flagship for mandatory trusteeship, and for anyone who took that language seriously (as Lugard did), to turn five million Africans over 'like cattle' to a country that 'has shewn such ruthless cruelty to those whom it considers an inferior race' was 'simply unthinkable'.[81]

But this left the West African mandates, which many British statesmen appeared to think dispensable. Smuts, Pirow, Chamberlain, Leith-Ross, the Plymouth Committee: all cheerfully identified Cameroon as the territory Britain could most easily do without. Of course it could, for five-sixths of mandated Cameroon was in *French* hands, and as French officials bitterly remarked, the British had already surrendered their portion to German firms anyway.[82] Britain had extended the Nigerian system of 'indirect rule' in their northern Cameroon holdings (at independence, those areas would join Nigeria), but in southern Cameroon German companies and shipping lines operated almost unchecked. Repurchased German plantations in the British sector were operating at pre-war capacity within a year of the owners' return in 1925, and by 1936, 293,678 acres were in German hands (compared to 19,053 acres in British hands). German firms expanded the port facilities at Tiko and Victoria and shipped the entire banana crop and most of the cocoa crop directly to Bremen and Hamburg where— avoiding the need for currency conversion—they were traded against German products which were sold to those plantations' workforces in company stores. (In the late 1930s the Mandates Commission woke up to the fact that those African workers were forced to accept a portion of their wages in credit redeemable only at those stores, driving Colonial Secretary Ormsby-Gore to ask the Governor to look into that practice.)[83] By 1938, European plantations employed more than 25,000 Africans (up from about 13,000 a decade earlier), about 25 per cent drawn from French Cameroon and another 10 per cent from Nigeria, and 285 of the 448 non-Africans in the territory were Germans sometimes openly sympathetic to the Nazi regime (Figure 11.6). 'British administration' was a thin veneer on this German world.[84]

French mandate authorities found British choices baffling and dangerous. Even in the 1920s they had kept Germans in Douala and Lomé under close surveillance and after 1933 moved quickly to integrate their territories more tightly into neighbouring imperial holdings. By December, Paul Bonnecarrère (now Governor in Cameroon) was planning better roads to

**Figure 11.6** Celebrating the annexation of Austria, in Cameroon, 1938: 'Germans in Cameroon thank the Führer!'

Gabon and a railroad to Chad,[85] and the following year the Colonial Ministry assigned key services and positions in Togo to officials in neighbouring Dahomey—although sharp criticism by the Mandates Commission and by the main French official who was to run the residual operation in Lomé curtailed the scope of that reform.[86] (Britain, having administratively integrated their portion of Togo into Gold Coast more than a decade earlier, escaped such criticism, paving the way for its permanent incorporation into Ghana at independence.) Those French moves were prescient, for from 1935 the German colonial movement worked hard to destabilize France's West African mandate administrations, including by sending one high-profile ex-Governor, scientist, film-maker, or celebrity after another on tour there. French consuls in Germany and local officials in Yaoundé rejected many of those visa applications and found the lackadaisical attitude of the British over the border exasperating.[87] In 1936, for example, when the former Governor of German Cameroon, Theodor Seitz, landed in Douala and toured the town even though he had been refused a visa, local authorities were annoyed to learn that Seitz had lunched with the British Resident and visited German plantations over the border.[88] By the late 1930s, French

Cameroon was finally booming, its plantation sector growing, and its lack of public debt allowing the administration to devote substantial tax revenues to public works. However menacing the Germans and pusillanimous the British, French colonial authorities would not let this prize slip from their hands.

Yet that shifting geopolitical balance did produce one transfer of French-mandated territory in the late 1930s. Between 1936 and 1939 France helped to orchestrate the cession of the ethnically polyglot Sanjak of Alexandretta, hitherto administered under the Syrian mandate, to Turkey.[89] The Sanjak, along with Mosul, had been one of the sticking points in the Near Eastern settlement, for a significant minority of its population was identified as Turkish, and Turkey claimed a strong interest in its fate. In 1921, France and Turkey had concluded an agreement providing a measure of administrative autonomy for the Sanjak and guaranteeing its Turkish minority linguistic and cultural rights. In 1936, as plans for Syrian independence proceeded, Ankara made it clear that Turkey (which had joined the League in 1932) would resist the Sanjak's inclusion in Syria. The matter was thus referred to the League Council, which—over the objections of Pierre Orts, now Vice Chairman of the Mandates Commission[90]—allowed France and Turkey to negotiate bilaterally. In 1937 those negotiations produced plans for an autonomous Sanjak federated to Syria but under continued League supervision and joint Franco-Turkish guarantee (a proposal already seen as a defeat in Syria), but the worsening international situation, Allied desperation to secure Turkish neutrality in any coming war, and open meddling within the Sanjak itself pushed matters still further. In 1939, with French consent, the Sanjak was incorporated into Turkey.

This violated the mandate's charge to safeguard territorial integrity, and much subterfuge was necessary for France and Turkey to pull it off. The Council had to tell the Mandates Commission that Alexandretta was now a matter for international negotiation and none of its business. Next, Britain's tacit consent was secured, a statute establishing the region's autonomy was approved by the League Council, the dependent Syrian government was forced to accept that new dispensation, and a League Commission was dispatched to register the region's inhabitants by ethnicity and religion. Then, when it became clear that registration would not produce a Turkish majority, a secret Franco-Turkish agreement had to be reached to do whatever was necessary to produce one; intimidation and pressure were organized; a helping hand was lent to the communal violence and entry by the Turkish army that followed; elections were held and their pre-agreed results proclaimed; the region's independence as the 'Republic of Hatay' was declared—and, when that Republic rapidly fell into chaos, a referendum was organized to approve its incorporation into Turkey. By the last stages of this sordid process the Mandates Commission was raging impotently on the sidelines. 'The guardian,' Rappard hectored Robert de Caix in June 1939, 'in an interest which was essentially his own, had abandoned to a third party a portion of the ward's inheritance, after having been entrusted with its defence.'[91] De Caix would not discuss the agreement, no doubt because its provisions were, as the Quai d'Orsay admitted privately, 'almost all in conflict with the mandate'.[92] Between 1938 and 1940 some 50,000 Armenians and Arabs fled the Sanjak for Syria.

Border revision in the Sudetenland and Syria, rather than African repartition, thus showed the world how the great powers were likely to conduct 'peaceful change'. But if the Czech 'settlement' received the most attention, only the Syrian carve-up achieved what was intended. Just before the war with Germany broke out, Britain and France signed mutual assistance and non-aggression treaties with Turkey, which remained neutral through the whole conflict. But the opprobrium this transaction evoked, not to mention the inability of revisionists to pull off something similar in Africa, reveals how the principles and practices of liberal internationalism had taken hold. Everyone wanted 'peaceful change', but imperial handovers were getting harder to achieve.

★ ★ ★

On 28 June 1937, almost two years to the day before that Franco-Turkish Treaty was signed, the International Studies Conference on 'Peaceful Change' opened in Paris. Sponsored by the League's International Institute for Intellectual Cooperation, the conference was the culmination of two years of research and planning. Preparatory studies of population pressures, access to raw materials, and the colonial question had been written; memoranda from the various national coordinating committees submitted; delegations of economists, political scientists, lawyers and politicians chosen. An astonishingly distinguished phalanx of liberal academics—Henri Labouret, Hersch Lauterpacht, James Shotwell, Quincy Wright—attended; statesmen who had led some of the League's most high-profile efforts at 'peaceful change'— Count Paul Teleki of the Mosul Commission, Lord Lytton of the Manchuria Commission—showed up as well. Even Germany and Italy sent observers.

Territorial transfer, at that point the hottest of hot topics, was discussed by the round-table on colonial questions. Revealingly, however, when the debate opened, another option—'gradual disappearance of colonial status as the result of the emancipation of the native population'—had been added to the agenda. As the chairman explained, while at the outset only two models for colonial 'peaceful change' had really been envisaged, 'the transfer of the territory of a colonial Power to some other national sovereignty, and of a colonial Power to an international sovereignty', it had later been thought worthwhile to consider 'this third solution, which consists in the progressive disappearance of the colonial status as the result of the emancipation of the tributary populations'. Rather than transferring sovereignty, sovereignty—or, we might say, a form of sovereignty—would be conferred on the native population itself.[93] 'Self-determination' was back on the table.

With an almost audible sigh of relief, the conference's Anglo-American scholars and statesmen swung behind this 'third way'. Perhaps they were influenced by devolution in India or the 'emancipation' of Iraq, but they also needed an exit from the sterile opposition between a German claim now stated in terms of property and legal rights and the Franco-Belgian insistence that their 'sacrifices' justified their imperial role.[94] There was no reason save 'historical accident' and rapid Western technological advance for the current distribution of colonies anyway, Quincy Wright argued, and the fifty or sixty countries who lacked them found the empires' rhetoric about their 'burden' unpersuasive at best. 'There is something inherently unnatural in the government of a people of very different culture by a metropolitan center.'[95] Professor Richardson from the University of Leeds eagerly agreed, but worried that the process might take a long time. Labour's former Colonial Under-Secretary, Drummond Shiels, demurred: if a real effort at education were made, 'the period need not be so long as is sometimes thought'.[96]

No one invited W. E. B. Du Bois or Dantès Bellegarde to the conference. It was a very white event indeed. In 1919 those men had been where Shiels wound up in 1937, seeing the mandates system as a mechanism for moving subject peoples *swiftly* to independence, but two decades of repression and re-imperialization had cured them of that naiveté. The colonized populations whose interests were so freely cited were not represented either; in the eyes of the conference-goers, they were clearly peoples still unable to stand—or indeed speak—on their own. But Ralph Bunche was at Howard University awaiting his call, and buried in League of Nations and Colonial Ministry archives in Geneva, Paris, and London we find plenty of evidence of 'voice'. Just before the conference gathered, members of the Negro Welfare Association in Port of Spain wrote to denounce 'the plotting of British, Italian and French imperialism for the handing over of African colonies to the Fascist Nazi gangs of Germany', while making clear they were not so thrilled with the current regimes either. 'The Negro people of the former German Colonies who are struggling against their present British and French exploiters must be given the right to determine their own form of Government.'[97] For those nationalists-in-formation, the haggling over colonial transfer was a shock, but also an illumination.

# TWELVE
## When Internationalism
## Stopped Working

The open question, as I see it, is not whether, at the end of those dozen years, we [the British] shall go or stay [in Palestine]. I do not think that that is an open question. I think that, within that number of years, we shall find ourselves going out of Palestine anyway. The real question, I think, is whether we shall go out of Palestine, as we are going out of 'Iraq, with our mandate fulfilled, leaving a peaceful country and a stable government behind us as the fruits of our labours; or whether we shall go out of Palestine, some time in 'the nineteen-forties', as the French went out of Cilicia in 1920, and as the Greeks went out of Smyrna in 1922.

Arnold Toynbee, Address to the Royal Institute<br>of International Affairs, 9 December 1930[1]

Clearly the Palestine problem has become an 'international' problem, and Geneva will treat it as such. Meanwhile we shall be expected to hold the situation in Palestine and deal firmly with any disorder... In fact our 'mandate' while the whole future of Palestine is under debate is primarily to maintain law and order and the status quo—including the continuance of Jewish immigration.

Colonial Secretary William Ormsby-Gore to High Commissioner<br>Arthur Wauchope, 24 August 1937[2]

By the late 1930s the League of Nations was in decline. The impressive so-called 'technical' organizations continued their work—tracking epidemics, analysing economic data, managing cross-border traffics and exchanges, negotiating labour standards, and promoting humanitarian norms. But the security apparatus deteriorated after the Abyssinian debacle. The Spanish Civil War, the Austrian *Anschluss*, and the Czech crisis were all handled outside the League. At Munich in 1938, indeed, we see a great-power

Concert of Europe back in operation, although Hitler's determined expansionism quickly rendered any agreements worthless.

The mandates regime reeled under those political shocks. The apparatus of review, now highly institutionalized, carried on. Petitions flowed in in ever larger numbers, those relating to Syria, Lebanon, and Palestine often produced by highly organized diaspora networks around the globe. Yet with Germany and Italy irreconcilable, the political foundations for the regime had crumbled. Now with little to gain from League approbation, the mandatory powers drew their territories more tightly into the imperial net.

Britain had always been the mainstay of the League system. British officials had drafted its rules; British pressure had brought the other allied powers on board. Britain, in other words, had fostered the process of internationalization, driven equally by a desire to exercise moral leadership in the world and to legitimate its own imperial practices. In Britain, far more than in any other country, the mandates system was regularly cited as a signal achievement of the League and of British leadership alike; for years, the system relied on British official and public support. In the late 1930s, however, that alliance suddenly and dramatically ruptured. The reason for this was Palestine.

'Internationalization'—that is, the process of gaining international sanction for particular foreign-policy aims—had been crucial to British policy in Palestine from the start. The conviction that Jews were a powerful international interest, one whose support would count in the First World War, had been one motive behind the Balfour Declaration, and at San Remo in 1920 and in London in 1922 Britain had deployed considerable pressure to persuade its sceptical French and Italian allies to write that promise into the Palestine mandate. We have seen, too, how British politicians and their Zionist collaborators were able to use the Council to reprimand the Mandates Commission for its early criticism of the Zionist effort.[3] Britain, in other words, had worked hard to make sure that its policy of facilitating the Jewish National Home received international approbation.

That very strategy of 'internationalization' proved Britain's undoing. For Jews were not the only people outside Palestine to claim an interest in its fate. Pan-Arab nationalists, the emerging Arab states, and (especially after 1933) a host of European regimes and organizations did so too. Yet when the British administration in Palestine and then British governments in London woke up to the fact that Arab opposition to Jewish immigration could not be abated—and, indeed, that anti-Zionism had become the touchstone of

Arab nationalism throughout the Middle East—it was too late to win international support for a change of course. Not only was the majority of the Mandates Commission by 1930 staunchly Zionist, but from the mid-1930s both Western humanitarians eager to save Jews and Central European anti-Semitic regimes eager to rid themselves of Jews were determined to keep the gates of Palestine open. That altered international reality—one in which Palestine was viewed in the Middle East as an imperialist affront but within Europe almost entirely as a means of resolving Europe's 'Jewish Question'—placed Britain on a collision course with the Mandates Commission, with serious consequences for Britain, for Jews in Palestine and Europe, for Arab populations in Palestine and neighbouring Arab states, and indeed for the mandates regime.

That conflict could not be resolved. As the British finally were forced to admit, Arab and Jewish interests in Palestine genuinely were incompatible, and the regional and international interests elbowing their way into the room were irreconcilable as well. Britain ultimately withdrew from Palestine in disgrace, unable to hand over power to any waiting government at all: asked to whom he would turn over the keys to office in 1948, the Chief Secretary of the Palestine administration famously replied, 'I shall put them under the mat.'[4] But the fact that the Yishuv (the Jewish community in Palestine) was, by 1948, able to survive and emerge as a state was due not only to international sympathy for the Zionist cause in the wake of the Holocaust, nor even to division and disarray among Zionism's Arab opponents, but also to the fact that the deadlock created by 'internationalization' had offered a window of opportunity for state-building.

To a considerable extent, of course, Israel 'made' itself—but it was also, like Iraq, 'made' by the mandates system.[5] Unlike in Iraq, however, in Palestine the Mandates Commission as much as the mandatory power acted as midwife. By elevating the obligation to support Jewish immigration above the obligation to foster representative institutions in the 1930s, and by opposing concessions to the Arabs during and after the Arab Revolt of 1936–39, the Mandates Commission helped to preserve Palestine as a target of Jewish immigration and made its emergence as a Jewish state possible. The Commission's deepening fidelity to a largely Zionist interpretation of the mandate precisely as British policy was moving the other way drove a wedge between Britain and the Commission and, in time, between Britain and the system it had largely created. Let us trace that history step by step.

# The Western Wall riots, and the Mandates Commission's Zionist turn, 1929–31

Neither the Balfour Declaration nor the Mandate for Palestine promised a Jewish state. Nor did those founding texts promise a Jewish 'national home'. What they promised, rather, was that the British government would 'look with favour' (as the Balfour Declaration put it) on the Jewish effort to create that home themselves. The mandate was explicit on this point. Britain, as the mandatory power, was 'responsible for placing the country under such political, administrative and economic conditions as will secure the establishment of the Jewish national home' (Article 2). It was, therefore, both to 'facilitate Jewish immigration' and to encourage 'close settlement by Jews on the land' (Article 6). No mention was made, however, of a Jewish state. Indeed, the mandate instructed Britain to establish a common Palestinian citizenship and to foster self-governing institutions for the population as a whole.

It was Chaim Weizmann's particular genius to understand that this pledge was enough. It was, in fact, more than enough, for if the British had said frankly (as the revisionist Zionist Vladimir Jabotinsky put it in 1923) that Zionism, like all forms of colonization, had to override the interests of the native population and that the job of the British was simply to provide an 'Iron Wall' behind which settlement could proceed, not only the British but many Zionists would have recoiled in horror.[6] For Zionism was, in the interwar years, a liberal and progressive cause, and the assertion that it meant no harm to the Arab population—and, indeed, would do more to improve the lot of ignorant peasants than the wily 'effendis' opposing Jewish settlement—was crucial to its appeal. Zionists thus did not need to be promised a Jewish state. What they needed was simply for Britain to hold to policies—Jewish immigration up to the 'economic absorptive capacity' of the territory (as the 1922 White Paper put it), a relatively free market in land, and a moratorium on the introduction of responsible government in Palestine until either the Arab population had become reconciled to Jewish immigration or the demographic balance had turned in their favour—that kept that possibility open. But they needed one more amorphous thing as well—a willingness, on the part of the British, to let textual interpretation trump political negotiation and European interests trump local concerns, when deciding policy in Palestine. This is where the Mandates Commission came in.

For, from 1930, the Mandates Commission acted essentially as a conduit for Zionist claims within the international arena. Several factors contributed to the Commission's 'Zionist turn'. Personal affinity was part of it, for all members of the Commission admired Weizmann, and Victor Jacobson, a convivial and likeable man who managed the Zionist Organization's Geneva office, developed amicable relations with Rappard, Orts, Lugard, and other Commission members in the 1920s. Adept political activity mattered too, for through private connections in the Secretariat, Jacobson gained access to the uncorrected minutes of Commission sessions and other secret documents, enabling the Executive in London to carefully calibrate its reports to speak to the Commission's concerns. More important, however, was the fact that the Zionist Organization and the Commission shared a common culture and orientation—a common *habitus*, one might say—that made collaboration easy and natural. These were men comfortable with legal and textual argument, and since the mandate was, as J. C. Hurewitz noted, 'framed unmistakably in the Zionist interest', with precise clauses stipulating Britain's obligations towards the Jews, that common 'textualism' inevitably favoured the Zionist side.[7] Zionists could claim with some justice that their project had received the approbation of the 'international community' (a term nearly synonymous with the West in this period), and that the Commission need only be 'impartial' to uphold it. Finding this cooperative stance a relief from the angry protests of Arab nationalists, the Commission fell into the habit of treating Zionist officials as confidential interlocutors and Zionist memoranda as impartial guides to Palestinian affairs.

Yet the mandate did contain textual ambiguities, on which basis Palestine's Arabs too appealed for the Commission's support. For those same articles of the mandate that instructed the mandatory power to promote Jewish immigration and settlement also required it to foster 'the development of self-governing institutions' (Article 2) and to ensure 'that the rights and position of other sections of the population are not prejudiced' (Article 6). True, by 1928, Rappard had already decided that those obligations were secondary, arguing in a report on an Arab petition that democratic institutions were specifically excluded in a mandate regime. ('One sees how his report has been largely shaped by our memorandum,' Jacobson—who got hold of the confidential report in draft—reported to the Zionist Executive in London.)[8] At this stage, however, most of his fellows disagreed, accepting that Arab desires for self-government were in line with pledges implicit in Article 22.[9] The Commission thus endorsed *both* Zionist appeals to uphold

**Figure 12.1** Palestine police searching suspects by the Jaffa gate during the 1929 disturbances.

Jewish immigration and land rights *and* Arab appeals for progress towards representative government—that is, until 1929, when riots in Palestine forced the Commission to decide whose claims must be given precedence.

Tensions had been building over rival Jewish and Muslim claims to Jerusalem's sacred sites for some time, and especially over Jewish attempts to bring chairs and screens to aid their worship at the Western Wall, but the communal mobilization and subsequent Arab attacks on Jews that summer took the administration by surprise. The police were reinforced and order was eventually restored (Figure 12.1), and the British government appointed an all-party commission (the Shaw Commission) to travel to the country, ascertain the causes of the violence, and make recommendations. But Sir John Chancellor, the new High Commissioner for Palestine, was already persuaded that Jewish immigration had undermined the status of Palestine's rural Arab cultivators, and that more had to be done to safeguard their rights. In January 1930, Chancellor informed the Cabinet of his plans to limit immigration, prevent further sales of Arab land, and move towards representative government. Since the Jewish Agency had access to Chancellor's secret correspondence through sympathizers within his office, the Zionist Organization learned of his plans as he made them.[10]

That the League would have something to say about this was clear from the outset. At the League Council in September 1929 several states—including, ominously, Poland and Romania, new or reborn states in the grip of ethnic nationalism and eager to reduce their 'minority' populations—urged Britain swiftly to restore order. The Foreign Secretary, Arthur Henderson, and Prime Minister Ramsay MacDonald assured the Council and (at Weizmann's urging) the League Assembly that Britain had no intention of deviating from the Balfour Declaration and the mandate, but the Council nevertheless asked the Mandates Commission to 'thoroughly examine' whatever recommendations the Shaw Commission advanced.[11] Invited to put in its oar, the PMC agreed to hold a special session on Palestine alone.[12]

A period of intense negotiation and lobbying followed, with both Zionist and Arab representatives working hard through the spring of 1930 to influence the Shaw Commission's report and shape future British policy. In Palestine and in a delegation to London that included both Hajj Amin al-Husayni, the Mufti of Jerusalem, and his rival, Jerusalem's Mayor Ragheb bey Nashashibi, Arab leaders put forward familiar arguments for an end to Jewish immigration and land sales, and for the establishment of an independent national government.[13] Weizmann opposed those claims by insisting, in meetings and in countless private letters to his formidable network of friends, politicians, and officials, on the prior and inviolable nature of the Balfour pledge. Yet Weizmann, aware that a Labour government pledged to grant devolution to India and independence to Iraq found the autocratic Palestine administration anomalous and embarrassing, also sought to appropriate the language of self-determination to Zionist ends. Self-determination was a right to be exercised by peoples, he pointed out, and not by individuals, and since Arabs had been granted self-governing states elsewhere, they could not justly stand in the way of Jewish aspirations in Palestine.[14] Further, since the Balfour pledge had been made to the Jews of the world, Palestine's existing inhabitants could not 'be considered as owning the country in the sense in which the inhabitants of Iraq or of Egypt possess their respective countries'. To set up self-government now 'would be to assign the country to its present inhabitants' and to cancel 'in an underhand manner' the policy of the National Home.[15]

As Weizmann feared, the Shaw Commission's majority report published on 31 March 1930 mirrored Chancellor's views. Against the Zionist claims, it held that the riots had not been fomented by a cabal of nationalist leaders but rather reflected the Arab population's genuine anxieties about the Zionist project, and it endorsed immigration restrictions and a moratorium on land sales pending a survey of the economic capacity of the territory. Attention then swung to Geneva, where the Commission would soon convene for its extraordinary session. On 20 May the British government wrote to the League accepting the Commission's findings and outlining plans to conduct a land survey and to introduce a measure of local self-government.[16] Weizmann arrived to meet with Rappard, Orts, the French member Martial Merlin, and Lugard (who helpfully leaked the not-yet-published British statement to him); he also mobilized other sympathizers to approach the German member and Theodoli.[17] The Zionist Organization also prepared a detailed response to the Shaw Commission report, which the British government honourably (if stupidly) forwarded to the PMC even though the Colonial Office had not had time to prepare accompanying comments. The Arab delegation also visited Geneva, and the Commission received over a hundred separate petitions or protests from Arab and Jewish organizations around the world.

The PMC's session opened on 3 June 1930 with Labour's Colonial Under-Secretary, Drummond Shiels, present to answer questions. It's fair to say he was unprepared for the hostility with which he was confronted. On the basis of the Zionists' report, Orts, Rappard, and the voluble Dutch member, Van Rees, challenged Shiels over the validity of the Shaw Commission's findings. Monopolizing most of the third day, Van Rees argued that the Arab attacks were the premeditated work of a revolutionary movement led by al-Husayni, that the British response had been culpably weak, that the British had failed adequately to support the Zionist effort, and that Arab claims to rights in Palestine were without foundation anyway since the British had conquered the country and could thus dispose of it as they wished—an argument hardly in keeping with Van Rees's normally anti-annexationist stance. Shiels, taken aback, objected to the way Van Rees's arguments echoed the Zionists' memorandum; had the Arabs written a similar memorandum, they too 'might have made out a case that seemed convincing, taken by itself'.[18] In its report to the Council, however, the PMC both defended its 'special attention to the memorandum from the Jewish Agency' and dissented from the Shaw Commission's 'kindly judgement' about the behaviour of the Arab leaders.[19] Only very rarely did the PMC accept third-party claims over the statements of the mandatory power. The fact that it did so in this case helped to discredit the Shaw Commission—already under attack in the House of Commons—further.[20]

To the government's distress, the PMC also followed the Zionists' lead in ascribing some responsibility for the riots to the 'hesitant' policy of Britain's Palestine administration.[21] This criticism too caught the British off-guard. At the League Council, Arthur Henderson thought it a matter for congratulation that the British administration had not imposed martial law and tried rioters in ordinary civil courts.[22] At the PMC session, however, Rappard, Merlin, Van Rees, and Orts (not coincidentally the four who drafted the Commission's report) all charged the administration with weakness, suggesting that it should have censored the press more strictly, relied less on Arab police, responded much more forcefully to the riots, and, especially, not have suspended Jewish immigration, which signalled a willingness to shift policy in the face of violence.[23] Surely, Shiels protested, the Commission was not suggesting that Britain should hold Palestine 'by force of arms'? That would 'scarcely be a tribute to the success of its regime'.[24] The Commission, again echoing the Zionist Organization's arguments, countered that with strong government, violence might never have occurred. If the British now pursued an active economic policy, one that 'would develop the country's capacity to receive and absorb immigrants in larger numbers with no ill results', the hostility of the Arab population would likely abate.[25] More Jewish immigration and stronger government, in other words, were to *lessen* Arab discontent—a prediction that reveals how little the Commission understood the situation on the ground.

Most importantly, in the face of what it saw as British prevarication, the PMC offered a definitive interpretation of the mandate itself. The Shaw Commission had advised the British government to do this, but the Commission pre-empted that role. Thus far, the Commission had simply accepted the British claim that its obligations to the Jews and the Arabs were *equal but reconcilable*. Now, it clarified just *how* those obligations could be harmonized. Rappard thought it was obvious that Jewish claims were paramount. 'It was the duty of the mandatory Power to establish the National Jewish Home and to develop self-governing institutions so far as was compatible with such establishment,' he stated. If the Arabs rejected that first provision of the mandate, then 'the Mandatory could not be censured for failing to apply the second part'. Theodoli, however, disagreed. All mandates were subject to Article 22, which placed the welfare of the inhabitants first.

The establishment of the National Home for the Jews must thus 'be made compatible with the introduction of autonomous institutions' or this fundamental purpose of the mandate was compromised.[26] In Rappard's view, self-government must give way to Jewish immigration, while Theodoli, relying on the Covenant, argued the opposite. Who was right? How could the mandate's two obligations really be reconciled?

In its report to the Council the PMC finally settled on a formulation. Yes, the obligations to facilitate the national home and to encourage self-government were of equal weight and reconcilable, but it was necessary to distinguish the *objects* of the mandate from its *immediate obligations*. Building the Jewish National Home and establishing self-government were *objects* of the mandate but their achievement understandably would take time. The mandate had thus laid on the mandatory power two more limited *immediate obligations*, which were 'to place the country under such conditions as would secure' those ultimate objects. The mandatory power could thus not be blamed for the fact that the National Home and self-government had not yet been achieved. It would be culpable only if 'it aimed at crystallizing the Jewish National Home at its present stage of development, or rigidly stabilizing the public institutions of Palestine in their present form'.[27] Formally, this interpretation looked even-handed. Practically, however, since it turned continued Jewish immigration into an 'immediate obligation' while leaving self-government a more remote 'object', it implicitly accepted that self-government could be introduced only if the Arabs dropped their opposition to the policy of the 'National Home' (a development Zionist leaders and politicians in Britain—but not in Palestine—always assured the Commission was just around the corner) or the demographic balance turned in the Jewish favour. The PMC's 'interpretation' did not stipulate that a Jewish state would arise in Palestine—indeed, since the 1922 White Paper pledged neither to displace the existing population nor to make Palestine 'Jewish', it could hardly do so—but it did make clear that no move towards representative government could be made that might in any way hamper the Zionist project.

The British government greeted the PMC's report with consternation. G. L. M. Clauson at the Colonial Office called it 'a damaging and rather vicious attack on the British Government' and Ramsay MacDonald 'a dreadful document which every enemy of England had had a hand in drafting'. Its inspiration was 'clearly Jewish', Clauson minuted, and he wondered whether the government shouldn't perhaps try to get the Council to crack down on the Zionists' 'very objectionable' practice of maintaining lobbyists in Geneva.[28] He was (no doubt wisely) overruled, and the government contented itself with a sharp protest against the PMC's reliance on 'ex parte statements',[29] but the Council session at which the PMC's report was reviewed was a bit rocky anyway. The Commission's 'close and serious examination, conducted with frankness, conscientiousness and calmness,' Van Rees complained, had not been given quite the welcome it 'might in all justice have expected'.[30]

As we know, in the Passfield White Paper issued shortly after this Council meeting, the government proposed to restrict Jewish immigration and land sales in line with the Shaw Commission's recommendations and reiterated its commitment to develop self-governing institutions. Yet, as we also know, those provisions on immigration and land sales were virtually nullified by Ramsay MacDonald's letter to Chaim Weizmann some three months later. Historians usually credit Weizmann's effective lobbying for that volte-face, but it is clear that the machinations in Geneva mattered as well.[31] For, at that Council meeting, Britain let the Commission's interpretation of the mandate stand (only the Persian delegate objected)[32] and when debate moved to the House of Commons, MPs repeatedly cited the Commission's criticisms.[33] Had MacDonald decided to stay the course, then, he may well have faced censure both in Parliament and at the Commission's next session in Geneva.[34] Instead, the government backed down. In 1931 Sir John Chancellor, who had learned the hard way that he was not really master in his house, left Jerusalem in humiliation. The battle to safeguard the Balfour pledge, Weizmann had warned in January of 1930, would be won not in Palestine or through negotiations with the Arabs, but 'in London, in Westminster, and after the voice of Westminster has been heard, in Geneva'.[35] The fate of the Passfield White Paper showed how right he was.

## Tipping point: competitive internationalization and the fate of the Legislative Council proposal

After the Labour government's retreat, the work of building up the National Home accelerated. Between 1931 and 1936, according to official figures, the Jewish presence in Palestine more than doubled, from 175,000 to 370,000 or from 17 per cent to 27 per cent of the population. The number of registered Jewish immigrants jumped from 11,289 in 1932 to 31,977 in 1933, to 42,349 in 1934, and to a peak of 64,147 in 1935—and these figures did not include illegal immigrants, also entering in considerable numbers. Sale of land to Jews continued, and the Jewish share of GDP also expanded rapidly, reaching 57 per cent by 1933. Tel Aviv sprung up, an entirely Jewish city of tree-lined boulevards and Bauhaus villas, its population passing the 100,000 mark by the mid-1930s. Jewish enterprises, cultural institutions, and newspapers flourished. And, as the Jewish state took shape before their eyes, Zionist leaders grew more confident. In 1931, under criticism for his close ties to the English establishment, Weizmann gave up the Presidency of the Zionist Organization, although he remained important in its counsels and would return in 1935. Increasingly, however, policy was set by the Zionist Executive in Palestine, especially by that gifted and uncompromising state-builder and Labour Zionist, David Ben-Gurion.[36]

A menacing international context lay behind that rapid transformation. The Nazi seizure of power in 1933 utterly transformed the situation of European Jews and with it the politics of Palestine. Once a magnet for convinced Zionists alone, the territory now became a potential refuge for hitherto unanticipated numbers of Jews. For the Nazi takeover not only imperilled Germany's own relatively assimilated Jewish population but also unleashed a wave of copycat and competitive anti-Semitism, as other East European states scrambled to show how eager they too were to rid themselves of their (much larger) Jewish populations. Throughout Central and Eastern Europe, Jews found their civic status eroding, discriminatory measures and practices proliferating, and demagogues blaming them for everything from the economic depression to the deteriorating international situation. In Poland, where the government became explicitly anti-Semitic following the death of Marshal Pilsudski in May 1935, the Socialist Party and the Jewish Bund put up a brave fight against the ethnic nationalist tide, but the Zionist argument that Jews could never achieve full freedom except in a state of their own began to seem incontrovertible.[37] In 1935 Jabotinsky's revisionists formed the New Zionist Organization, which was committed to bringing one million Jews to Palestine within ten years (in 1939, the timeframe was cut to two years in view of the worsening situation of Europe's Jews) and to a Jewish state on both banks of the Jordan.[38] The majority of the Zionist movement continued to stress the need for gradual immigration within the framework of the mandate and equally to defend the rights of Jews within the diaspora, but as those rights eroded, even European and American liberals and assimilationist Jews moved into sympathy with Zionism.[39] It seemed the one thing Zionists, European liberals, and anti-Semitic regimes could agree on in the 1930s was that (as the old cynic and anti-Zionist Robert de Caix sardonically put it) 'the Palestinian hen' should be forced 'to swallow Zionist colonists whether she wants them or not, securely pinned between the knees of the English tutor'.[40]

The Arab population and its divided leadership had difficulty responding to that rapidly changing situation. The demographic balance was now shifting, but the determination of European liberals and anti-Semites alike to see Palestine primarily as an emigration destination for Europe's unwanted Jews meant that no European state would oppose that transformation. Nazi ideology, of course, entirely deplored the possible construction of a Jewish state, but while the Nazi regime gave lip service and a bit of modest aid to Arab intellectuals (notably the Arslans and later the Mufti), it was too eager to rid itself of its own Jews and until 1938 too reluctant to antagonize Britain to commit itself deeply to what it considered a marginal cause.[41] Palestine's Arab nationalist leadership also found its inability to staunch the flow of land sales particularly demoralizing, especially as local rather than absentee landlords constituted an ever larger proportion—from 1933, the majority—of sellers. Jewish purchases were, in absolute terms, small—by 1937 Jews had acquired only about 1.2 million of Palestine's 26 million *dunams* of land—but those acquisitions were concentrated in the most cultivable valleys and coastal plains. Much Arab land was heavily indebted, and with prices high, landowners sought relief through piecemeal sales, their actions made easier by the fact that the Jewish National Fund could be counted on to keep their identities secret. The Fund did, however, want to receive the land unencumbered, a stipulation that tarred Arab landowners with the opprobrium of forcing *fellaheen* off the land, deepened social antagonisms, and sowed fear and mistrust within the rural population.[42]

Yet Palestine's Arabs were not without international support. Arab papers and populations everywhere had followed the Western Wall conflicts, with sympathy strikes and riots breaking out in Egypt, Iraq, and Syria. Now, as disillusionment with the British grew, activists within Palestine looked abroad for sustenance. 'Let us leave this Government to flatter the Jews as much as they desire,' declared the Arab Executive following MacDonald's 'Black Letter', 'and let us seek help from ourselves and the Arab and Islamic World'.[43] In the Middle East as in Europe, the struggle for Palestine 'internationalized'. Hajj Amin al-Husayni, the Mufti of Jerusalem, reached out to Muslim leaders in India and elsewhere, convening an international Islamic

Congress in Jerusalem in December 1931, while a younger generation already impatient with the Arab Executive turned to exiled Syrian nationalists in Transjordan and Europe (including Shakib Arslan) for support and inspiration. There were also independent Arab states eager to lend a hand. By 1932, Yemen, Iraq, and Saudi Arabia were all formally independent, and in 1937 Egypt—which Britain had unilaterally declared independent in 1922—would join the League. Transjordan too, while still under the Palestine mandate, gained autonomy through a treaty negotiated in 1928. Even the French were searching for a way to come to terms with nationalists in Syria. True, there were tensions within this supposed Arab community. Faysal in Iraq and Abdullah in Transjordan were rivals as well as brothers; the Hashemites speculated anxiously about the intentions of Ibn Saud; Syria's republican nationalists were wary of monarchies altogether. Yet pan-Arabism enabled rather than hampered Palestinian nationalism. Hopes of Arab federation and of representative government in Palestine went hand in hand.[44]

Most of those Arab states were British allies or British clients, and as inter-communal relations in Palestine worsened, the Foreign Office grew concerned about the damage the Zionist project was doing to those ties. Throughout the 1930s British officials tentatively explored the possibility of Arab federation, likely under Hashemite leadership, within which a Jewish population might possibly be seen as an asset rather than a threat—a prospect that Ben-Gurion, too, considered.[45] Yet the government also remained formally committed to the one policy proposal within the Passfield White Paper not effectively nullified by the MacDonald Letter: the plan to establish a Legislative Council. Indeed, the Baldwin government confirmed in April 1932 that it still favoured such a Council, while also deciding that there should be no public discussion until the new High Commissioner, Arthur Wauchope, had a chance to meet with the Mandates Commission that autumn.[46]

Wauchope was well aware of just how impossible it might be to find any constitutional formula on which both Jews and Arabs could agree. For as Arnold Toynbee had pointed out in a brilliant talk given at Chatham House in December 1930, such an agreement could only be crafted if all parties accepted three basic realities: that the British would certainly find it impossible to remain in Palestine for more than another decade or so; that the pledges Britain had made to Arabs and Jews under pressure of war were frankly incompatible; and that, as a result, no party could enjoy exclusive 'national self-determination' in Palestine. The only honourable course, Toynbee concluded, was thus 'to build up in Palestine a non-national fully self-governing State in which there will be national homes for Jews and for Arabs side by side'—a state, in other words, founded not on 'the odious doctrine of Western Nationalism...that a country is the national home of one nationality only', but rather on the principle 'that this doctrine of intolerance and fanaticism is not to prevail'.[47] The Passfield White Paper and Wauchope's Legislative Council scheme were attempts to move in that direction.

The problem was that that vision ran athwart both Palestinian Arab desires for a national status comparable to that achieved by their Arab neighbours and most Zionists' hopes of a specifically Jewish state. From the outset, Weizmann had been well aware of the danger ostensibly democratic measures posed to Zionist goals. Indeed, when his proposal in 1920 that the mandate endorse the aim of a self-governing *Jewish* Commonwealth in Palestine was changed to a pledge to develop 'self-governing institutions', he had presciently (if unsuccessfully) tried to have the clause deleted altogether.[48] In the 1920s, fortunately for the Zionists, the Palestinian Arab Congress had rejected all attempts to build representative institutions that were not based on majoritarian principles or excluded the key subjects of immigration and land from their remit, but by the early 1930s most Arab leaders had concluded that that uncompromising stance had backfired. When the High Commissioner began to take soundings about a Legislative Council, he found even al-Husayni willing to consider the question. True, with the exception of a few leaders and groups committed to 'bi-national' political development, the Jewish organizations in Palestine and abroad were opposed, and as the size of the Jewish community grew, that opposition hardened.[49] The Cabinet agreed, however, that the British government could not allow one party alone to prevent progress. At the November 1932 session Wauchope thus informed the Mandates Commission that the government intended to establish the Legislative Council.

The Zionist Organization had learned of Wauchope's intentions only that October, and the news caused consternation. Viktor Jacobson in Geneva was told to do his best to persuade the Commission to oppose or at least delay the plan, but felt himself, as he told Selig Brodetsky, head of the political department of the Zionist Organization in London, 'very badly prepared' for the job.[50] Yet Jacobson immediately got to work, meeting privately with PMC members Rappard, Van Rees, Merlin, Ruppel, Sakenobe, Palacios,

Theodoli, and Weaver, sending a memorandum on the subject to Rappard, Van Rees, Ruppel, Merlin, and Palacios, and persuading Rappard's great friend William Martin to write an article against the plan in the *Journal de Genève*. In those meetings, Jacobson played on divisions within the Commission, alerting Rappard, Orts, and Van Rees to the propensity of Theodoli and Catastini to slip their own anti-Zionist views into the Commission's resolutions, and argued that it would be 'intolerable' for such a plan simply to be announced without 'an authorized voice, such as that of the Permanent Mandates Commission' calling attention to possible dangers or at least indicating possible reservations by a 'silence significatif'.[51]

The battle was hard-fought nonetheless. The Commission had endorsed movement towards a Legislative Council only last year, and at the outset a majority still favoured the plan. Moreover, although the Arabs had no one with Jacobson's access and skill, the Commission did have a long petition from the Palestine Arab Women's Congress condemning Palestine's auto-cratic form of government, calling for a series of educational and social reforms, and demanding the introduction of responsible government. Rappard insisted that the Commission must rule the latter demand inadmis-sible since it called 'for the abrogation of the regime, the application of which it is its duty to supervise'—and anyway, the petitioners only 'wished to have autonomous government so as to rid themselves, among other things, of the Balfour Declaration'. Palacios and Theodoli countered that representative government was 'a natural aspiration which, moreover, was expressly authorized by the Covenant and the mandate'.[52] Yet, with Merlin and Orts opposed to Arab self-government and the Commission's 'inde-pendents'—Ruppel, Van Rees, Dannevig—wavering, Jacobson's careful work and Rappard's selective textualism narrowly won out. Having once again managed to get hold of the confidential minutes in draft, which showed a six-to-five split, Jacobson wrote to Brodetsky in relief that:

> It is now clear to me that I've managed to bring even a difficult man like Rappard on board, to persuade stubborn Palacios for once not to insist on his usual endorsement of 'autonomous institutions', to erode Ruppel's indif-ference, to put all of them on their guard against any intrigue between Catastini and Theodoli, to frustrate that intrigue itself, and thus to avert a real danger![53]

In its report to the Council that year, the Commission thus merely 'noted'— and not, as in 1931, 'welcomed'—the statement that Britain would move forward on the Legislative Council plan.[54] If the British government wished to introduce representative institutions, it would do so without the blessing of the PMC. Zionist legal scholars astutely recognized the significance of this tiny textual shift.[55]

The Commission never showed much sympathy for representative government again. Indeed, the events of 1933—the coming to power of an overtly anti-Semitic and eliminationist regime in Germany, and the massacre of Assyrian villagers by the army of a newly independent Iraq—left Rappard, Lugard, and Orts guilt-ridden about their acquiescence in Iraqi independence and determined to protect Syria's minorities and Palestine's Jews. The British government could not let the constitutional issue die, however, and throughout 1933 and 1934 Wauchope attempted at once to increase Palestinian participation on various advisory boards, to reorganize local authorities, and to win support for a Legislative Council. The proposal that crystallized in 1934 and 1935—for a Council without an official majority, with members elected based on their proportion in the population but supplemented by additional nominated members and officials to lessen Muslim preponderance, with questions of immigration excluded from the Council's remit, and with the High Commissioner holding the power of veto—was accepted at least as a basis for discussion by several Arab parties but was entirely opposed by the Zionists, who vowed to boycott it.[56]

Yet, as with the Passfield White Paper, opinion in London and Geneva outweighed opinion in Jerusalem, Baghdad, or Amman. The growing anxiety of European liberals about the worsening situation of Europe's Jews helped to tip the scales. The main problem confronting civilization, Josiah Wedgwood pointed out in a key debate in the Commons, was the shameful persecution of Jews, not only in Germany but in Poland and Eastern Europe as well, and if 'we cannot do much here now' for those persecuted people, 'at least we rule Palestine ... almost the only hope for the Jewish people'. In both chambers, speaker after speaker—among them Churchill, Leo Amery, and the Liberal leader Archibald Sinclair—insisted that Jewish immigration had improved the living standards and well-being of Palestine's peasants, that opening Transjordan to Jewish immigration could only spread those benefits, that Britain had done ample justice to Arabs already by creating states in Iraq and Transjordan, and that any Legislative Council proposal was premature, given the ignorant state of the Arab peasantry and the unscrupulous and extremist nature of the Arab leadership.[57] The Arab parties in Palestine were shocked, and as it became clear that the British government would not move forward in the face of such strong parliamentary and Zionist criticism, those (such as the Nashashibis) who had strongly urged cooperation with Wauchope's plan found themselves discredited.[58]

By the time the Mandates Commission met in June 1936 an Arab general strike had already begun. The Commission was 'most bitter' about the British government's unwillingness to provide full information about the current disorders, Jacobson's successor Nahum Goldmann in Geneva wrote to Ben-Gurion, and was likely to insist on a special session on Palestine alone.[59] Goldmann also sent along the 'quite secret' provisional minutes he had somehow acquired, which made clear that the Commission's majority was 'very friendly to us'. Members had been concerned mostly to fend off any move that would restrict Jewish immigration (the Arabs, Goldmann warned, were now arguing that as the mandate had promised a 'national home' and not a Jewish state, its purpose had been accomplished),[60] but they made clear their hostility to the Legislative Council as well.[61] Representative institutions, Lugard opined, were 'quite unsuited to Oriental peoples', and the Jews would rightly resent any system that might give a majority to a party opposed to 'the mandate' itself. This argument echoed Weizmann's interpretation, made in letters to Lugard and Rappard that winter, that that text's main aim had been to ensure that 'in this one corner of the earth', Jews were to have 'full freedom of national development' and not the status of a 'minority'.[62] Palacios retorted that the denial of representative government would push Arab dissent out of the League and into the streets, but his colleagues were willing to run that risk. For the Mandates Commission, the Palestine mandate now amounted to little more than the steady maintenance of Jewish immigration, whatever the impact on the Arab population.

## Revolt and the Peel Partition Plan, 1936–38

The Arab revolt, which began with a general strike in April 1936 and lasted until British troops mopped up the last pockets of rural resistance in 1939, did not 'internationalize' (Figure 12.2). It was international from the start. Born of the failure of Arab political efforts, and drawing heart from the successful example of the general strike in Syria next door (which had brought France swiftly to the bargaining table), the revolt was seen across the Muslim world as an anti-imperialist cause. Volunteers arrived from Iraq,

Figure 12.2 Arabs in Abu Ghosh pledge support for the rising, Spring 1936.

Transjordan, and Syria—including the redoubtable Fawzi al-Qawuqji, the exiled leader of the 1925 Syrian rising in Hama, who had spent much of the preceding decade helping Ibn Saud build up his army. Neighbouring Arab governments took an interest in the conflict, their claims to *locus standi* strengthened by the role of the 'Arab kings' in ending the general strike in October 1936.[63]

East European states quickly claimed an interest as well. On the League Council both Poland and Hungary stressed that Palestine must have (as Poland's Colonel Beck put it in the League Council in 1937) 'a maximum capacity of absorption'.[64] Immigration to Palestine, Romania's Nicolas Comnene added the following year, would 'assist appreciably in relieving the congestion in the Central and Eastern European countries, and would thus make it possible to look forward to a final solution' to Europe's Jewish Question.[65] Now shamelessly aping both Germany's demand for colonies and its drive to purge itself of Jews, Poland also put in a bid for membership on the Mandates Commission and advertised its willingness to take over the Palestine mandate.[66] In Geneva those concerned to save Jews and states eager to rid themselves of Jews both

Figure 12.3 British engineers dynamite Jaffa old town, June 1936.

pressed Britain to get Palestine under control so that it could take in as many Jews as possible.

Britain tried to restore order. In June, Ormsby-Gore, who had just replaced J. H. Thomas as Colonial Secretary, announced measures—including censorship, curfews, collective punishments, the destruction of houses found harbouring weapons, and the introduction of the death penalty for bombing—to deal with Arab violence.[67] Although the rebels for a time controlled much of rural Palestine and even briefly held Jerusalem's Old City, harsh counter-insurgency techniques—including the dynamiting of many houses in Jaffa's old city in June 1936, the use of armed convoys and construction of fortified police posts, and massive infusions of British troops—finally drove the rebels to the wall (Figure 12.3).[68] By the summer of 1938, there were 20,000 British troops in Palestine, a figure equal to one soldier for every fifty Arabs of all ages and sexes, and the hard-pressed rural population was suffering under the exactions and bloodletting of increasingly out-of-control bands as well. Indeed, in the end the main victim of the revolt was the Arab population itself, which not only suffered significant casualties but also lost ground to the Jewish population. The general strike and the policy of non-cooperation proved ineffective, for Jewish settlements and importers were able to provision the cities, while the withdrawal of Arab workers simply shifted more of the economy into Jewish hands. The administration also attempted to disarm Arabs, while eventually arming Jewish settlements and disproportionately incorporating Jews into the supernumerary police force and Orde Wingate's paramilitary 'Night Squads'. The Yishuv thus emerged from the maelstrom of the revolt more productive, better armed, and more 'state-like' than ever.

If the Arab Revolt accomplished little else, however, it finally convinced the British that the Arab population would never be reconciled to Zionism and that all hope of a unitary bi-national state in Palestine was dead. In August 1936 the British government appointed a Royal Commission under Lord Peel to inquire into the causes of the disturbances and to suggest remedies, but the unrest was so serious that the Commission did not arrive in Palestine to begin to interview witnesses—among them Weizmann and Hajj Amin al-Husayni—until November (Figures 12.4—12.6). The Commission's 400-page report, issued in July 1937, surveyed virtually every aspect of the territory's life, but only two conclusions truly mattered. The first was that the mandate was unworkable and would have to be abandoned. The report was entirely unambiguous on that score. 'The obligations Britain undertook towards the Arabs and the Jews some twenty years ago' may have lost none of their 'moral or legal weight', but 'they have proved irreconcilable'. 'To put it in one sentence, we cannot—in Palestine as it now is—both concede the Arab claim to self-government and secure the establishment of the Jewish National Home.' The argument that the Arabs would grow reconciled to Jewish immigration as it brought prosperity to the country had been proven false; to the contrary, economic improvement and efforts at conciliation had merely deepened communal antagonism. Both communities had become irredeemably 'national', and 'to maintain that Palestinian citizenship has any moral meaning is a mischievous pretense'. The separate educational systems had become 'schools of nationalism'; violent outbreaks had become common; efforts 'to enforce respect for law and order have proved ineffectual'. Moreover, 'it seems probable that the situation, bad as it now is, will grow worse', for Palestinian Arab claims to sovereignty and pressures to grant refuge to Europe's hard-pressed Jews could only grow stronger. No constitutional settlement could possibly reconcile the two sides; instead, 'peace, order and good government can only be maintained . . . by a rigorous system

of repression'. 'The moral objections to maintaining a system of government by constant repression are self-evident', and practically too the policy
would lead nowhere. It would further exacerbate relations between Arabs
and Jews; it would damage British interests and British prestige in the world;
it would 'mean the gradual alienation of two peoples who are traditionally
our friends'. No more devastating indictment of the mandate could have
been imagined.[69]

Indeed, so desperate was the situation, so deep the wound, that a more
drastic remedy—a 'surgical cut'—might be necessary. The frank avowal of
failure set the stage for the Commission's explosive second finding. As there
was no hope of lasting peace in Palestine under the mandate, 'the Government
should take the appropriate steps for the termination of the present Mandate
on the basis of Partition'. Such a plan, obviously, would be replete with difficulties, yet it alone offered some chance of meeting the national aspirations of both communities. A further inquiry on the ground would work

**Figure 12.4** Members of the Palestine Royal Commission at the King David
Hotel, Jerusalem. From left: Sir Harold Morris, Professor Reginald Coupland,
Lord Peel (Chairman), Sir Horace Rumbold (Vice Chairman), Sir Laurie
Hammond, Sir Morris Carter, J. M. Martin (Secretary to the Commission), and
Mr Heathcote-Amory (Secretary to Peel).

Figure 12.5   Chaim Weizmann arriving to give evidence to the Royal Commission.

the details out; provisionally, however, the Commission suggested that the northern coastal areas and Galilee become a Jewish state, the interior and the Negev be joined to Abdullah's Transjordan as an Arab state, and a final region around Jerusalem with a corridor to the sea remain under mandate. Adjustments and inducements would be necessary. Since the Jewish population was better off and the Jewish state would contain the better land, it should provide a subvention to the Arab state. Some economic benefits would need to be shared and trade relations regularized. Most critically, since the Commission carved out a Jewish state of a certain size by including districts inhabited by some 225,000 Arabs (compared with only 1,250 Jews in the proposed Arab state), those lands and populations would need to be transferred, with the understanding that often 'in the last resort the exchange would be compulsory'.[70]

Partition had been in the air for some time and was after all a tried and true imperial method of abating communal strife through 'territorialization'.[71] In Ireland, however, partition had been used to give territorial expression to a communal division that was three hundred years old, while in Palestine it was proposed to create a state for a community that, while possessing an indisputable historical connection to, and an unbroken presence

**Figure 12.6** Hajj Amin al-Husayni after giving evidence to the Royal Commission.

in, Palestine, had recently made up no more than 10 per cent of the population. True, that population was now rapidly expanding, but because Jews
needed refuge from European—not Arab—violence and hatred. The Peel
Commission admitted this, but pointed out that while the sacrifice demanded
of Palestine's Arabs might be great, 'it is not only the people of that country
that have to be considered'. For:

> The Jewish Problem is not the least of the many problems which are disturb-
> ing international relations at this critical time and obstructing the path to
> peace and prosperity. If the Arabs at some sacrifice could help to solve that
> problem, they would earn the gratitude not of the Jews alone but of all the
> Western World.[72]

That the Royal Commission would in the end conclude that Arabs should
'sacrifice' to solve a 'problem' of European invention should not surprise;
nor should the fact that the Arab national movement rejected this call to
sacrifice. More revealing is the response of the Mandates Commission to
the Peel plan.

The Commission was very discontented with the British government
by the summer of 1937. As the Colonial Office warned the Palestine

administration, its members were itching to interrogate them about the causes and handling of the rising and had only reluctantly agreed to wait until the Royal Commission reported.[73] When that inquiry dragged on and the Commission's proposed special session had to be repeatedly postponed, Foreign Minister Anthony Eden had 'considerable difficulty... avoiding an open dispute' with Orts at the League Council.[74] Under the leadership of Orts and Rappard, and with Theodoli kept in Rome by Mussolini's anti-League policy, the Commission had also become more strongly Zionist, the Spaniard Palacios being now the only Arab sympathizer. And all members—including Orts, Rappard, Dannevig, the new Dutch member Van Asbeck, and indeed Palacios himself—were anxious about the violence in Palestine and profoundly worried about the deteriorating situation of Europe's Jews. In early July 1937, when the Royal Commission's report was finally ready, it was sent directly to the PMC members.[75] With the grudging consent of the House of Commons, Ormsby-Gore gathered his officials and headed for Geneva.[76]

He found the PMC 'deluged with propaganda', with Weizmann (cautiously pro-partition), Rabbi Stephen Wise (anti-partition), and an Arab delegation including the Mufti's kinsman Jamal al-Husayni (adamantly opposed) all in town, and the British papers and the Geneva press corps poised for action.[77] Behind the scenes, too, a great deal of negotiation was going on. Orts had met twice with Nahum Goldmann in June, and in another two-hour meeting with him in late July, right before the PMC session opened, he made clear his commitment to the Zionist cause. As Goldmann reported, Orts had agreed wholeheartedly that the Zionists 'could not possibly agree to anything which would make us a permanent minority in the country', and had asked what policy the Zionists would prefer. When told that the desiderata was either for the mandate to be applied 'in the manner it was intended' or for a Jewish state to be set up in all areas west of the Jordan (a policy that 'would represent no injustice to the Arabs' as they had been given Transjordan already), Orts replied that those two options were not presently possible, but that the Jewish state suggested by the Royal Commission was 'ridiculously small in relation to the problem with which we had to deal' and should certainly be enlarged to include the whole coastal area from Lebanon to Egypt and the Negev. He also expressed great interest in a possible population transfer and was very impressed to hear that a million Jews might be settled if those 225,000 Arabs could be removed. He had asked for a memorandum on this point, 'as he thought this would be of considerable importance for the Mandates Commission'.[78]

Weizmann, heartened, sent Orts a copy of his *in camera* evidence to the Royal Commission and several letters making the case for additional land, including the Negev.[79]

The PMC's session opened on 30 July and lasted until 18 August, with Ormsby-Gore present for eleven of twenty-four of its meetings and Hathorn Hall, former Chief Secretary of the Palestine administration, for fully eighteen. In this tense atmosphere—'the Mandates Commission very critical & difficult, the Jews bad and the Arabs impossible'—Ormsby-Gore tried to muster support for partition.[80] For seventeen years, he told them, the British had sought, without success, to reconcile Arab and Jewish aspirations, and current conditions—the urgent search for Jewish refuge in the face of European anti-Semitism, the growing force of Arab nationalism—made any prospect of success recede further. Partition was 'the best and most hopeful solution' to this deadlock, and he asked the Commission simply to authorize Britain to investigate options and return with a scheme. A summary of Ormsby-Gore's opening statement was released to the press, and he then settled down to face almost two weeks of interrogation (Figure 12.7).[81]

**Figure 12.7** William Ormsby-Gore (seated in the middle of the front table) before the Mandates Commission's special session on Palestine, 1937.

After it was all over, Ormsby-Gore wrote a long, perceptive summary for High Commissioner Wauchope. Orts, Rappard, Van Asbeck, Dannevig, and Lugard's successor, Malcolm Hailey, dominated the proceedings, and there was no disguising that all but Hailey were 'strongly prejudiced in favour of the Jews and against the Arabs'. They were 'particularly resentful' of the involvement of the Arab states (as, indeed, was Weizmann),[82] and Iraqi claims to represent the Palestinians made them 'all the crosser'. Ormsby-Gore had great difficulty leading them to view Palestine as part of a regional system at all, for they saw it almost entirely as a 'refuge for persecuted Jews of Central Europe'. They were thus 'vividly conscious' that Poland, an important member of the Council, wanted to get 'as many Jews out of Poland and into Palestine as possible'. (Indeed, the Polish Foreign Ministry was busy calculating the number of Jews that could be shoehorned into the Jewish area and lobbying for it to include the Negev as well.)[83] The Commission's main interest in partition was the opportunity it offered of transferring Arabs out of any Jewish territory and into Transjordan. 'I was asked endless questions on this subject,' Ormsby-Gore wrote to Wauchope.[84]

Once the PMC had started their private discussions, Hailey wrote to Ormsby-Gore to say that he thought he could persuade the Commission to authorize Britain to explore all options, including partition.[85] Yet, it was quite clear to Ormsby-Gore that no member—not even Hailey—had much faith in the ability of either the Arabs or the Jews to govern themselves, still less to treat the other group fairly.[86] And indeed, while the Commission did grudgingly permit Britain to explore various options, its report forthrightly opposed the immediate creation of two independent states, pointing out that neither could possibly meet the minimal requirements of administrative and defensive capacity that the PMC had laid down for Iraq. There would have to be 'a prolongation of the period of political apprenticeship', whether this took the form of cantonization or of Britain holding two separate mandates for the prospective Arab and Jewish states.[87]

Indeed, what had absorbed the Commission was less the prospects for the future than the errors of the past. Although Ormsby-Gore insisted that repression had if anything worsened communal antagonisms, the bulk of the Commission refused to believe him. With the Zionists, they argued that what had failed was Britain's policy of 'extreme conciliation'; had the mandatory power been firmer in support of 'the mandate'—by which they meant in support of Jewish immigration—violence might never have broken out. What had caused all the trouble, Baron van Asbeck insisted, was the view that the mandate contained a 'dual obligation' when its original purpose had clearly been to create a Jewish state in which non-Jews would be protected as minorities—a declaration of 'original intent' in keeping with the humanitarian needs of the 1930s but at odds with virtually every official statement Britain had made. If one were to see it as a blueprint for a Jewish state, van Asbeck argued, the mandate was perfectly workable, 'provided, however, that a strong government was imposed on the country'.[88] That the British had not imposed such a government was taken as given; indeed, the Commission's wholesale endorsement of repressive measures shocked some readers when the minutes of the session were published and makes for strange reading today.[89] According to Rappard, Orts, Van Asbeck, and Dannevig (and, in retirement, Lord Lugard),[90] the administration should have imposed martial law immediately; it should have replaced Arab policemen, imported more troops, and armed Jews; it should have exercised stricter censorship and shut down opposition newspapers; it should have arrested and tried the Arab officials who sent a petition critical of government policy; it should have imposed the death penalty more readily; it should have threatened to bomb villages that harboured rebels.

Dragged back to Geneva towards the close of the session to give his opinion about whether such a policy might have successfully deterred Arab violence, Ormsby-Gore emphatically said it would not. To the contrary, ruthless treatment would likely spread Muslim-Jewish antagonism beyond Palestine and was in any case unjust. There genuinely were two communities in Palestine, and no amount of legalistic interpretation of an inherently ambiguous founding text could make one disappear or reconcile their conflicting, but both legitimate, claims. Nor could that be done by force—at least, not by a democratic government. 'For better or worse, the people of Great Britain were a liberal and democratic people,' Ormsby-Gore insisted, and would not 'for long be persuaded to use military force to settle a conflict between right and right.'[91] An entirely new, robustly political, approach was necessary.

And yet, throughout the process, Ormsby-Gore—and, in the Council, Anthony Eden—never ceased to acknowledge the League's authority or appeal for its aid. The British government could not work out a partition plan without the League's approval, they stated; only with strong League support had Britain some hope of securing Arab and Jewish collaboration.[92] That attempt to win international backing made sense, for with strong international and domestic support Britain could perhaps have forced through the Peel plan, but it was not successful. For the dominant view in Geneva, as in the House of Commons, was that partition was unacceptably unfair to the Jews—this despite the fact that it was the Arabs who unambiguously rejected it and that many Zionists (persuaded, unlike the British, that the Yishuv could survive, and eager to have Britain handle the tricky task of forcible population transfer) had themselves cautiously turned favourable.[93] Nahum Goldmann was strenuously supportive from the start, believing the plan offered the only real prospect of providing refuge to a considerable number of Jews. Weizmann too came to realize that if partition failed something better was unlikely to follow. Yet his carping response, not to mention his very success in persuading his Gentile supporters in London and Geneva that the main problem was not the mandate itself but British weakness in enforcing it, lessened the interest of those fellow-travellers in a proposal that, at least in some measure, recognized and sought to reconcile *both* Jewish and Arab claims.[94]

Internationalization alone did not doom the partition plan—the hostile parliamentary response was important too[95]—but the PMC's obvious scepticism certainly contributed to its demise. Unsurprisingly, at its session the following year the PMC spent much of its time reviewing the administration's anti-terrorism measures and criticizing its immigration restrictions.[96] Weizmann had protested to Ormsby-Gore that any departure from the old principle of basing immigration on 'economic absorptive capacity' was a violation of the mandate.[97] When Ormsby-Gore refused to budge, Weizmann appealed to Rappard '*in extremis*... to defend the principles of elementary justice and political decency'.[98] The PMC did not disappoint, reporting to the Council that it considered the mandate had been 'partially suspended', since 'some of its essential objects' were not being pursued.[99] Of course, one might say that many of the mandate's ostensible objects were not being pursued, among them the development of self-governing institutions and (since the territory was under virtual lockdown) the protection of the local population's civil rights, but this was not what the Commission had in mind. The British government replied that it could not agree that its immigration controls amounted to 'a partial suspension of the mandate', but the meaning of that text had long passed out of its hands.[100]

# Britain against the League: the 1939 White Paper

The slow death of the partition plan, still under fruitless consideration through the autumn of 1938, left the British with the unenviable task of administering a mandate they had publicly declared unworkable under the full glare of the hostile publicity of the League, the House of Commons, the Zionists, and Arab nationalists alike. Publicly, the government put a brave face on the disaster. In May 1938 Ormsby-Gore—'a broken reed' in Blanche Dugdale's words[101]—went off to the House of Lords as Lord Harlech, leaving his successor Malcolm MacDonald (Ramsay MacDonald's able son) to bury the partition plan, supervise the final crushing of the Arab Revolt with policies quite as draconian as the most avid anti-terrorist could wish, and then bring together the new High Commissioner, Harold MacMichael, and the Foreign and Colonial Office staffs to devise a new policy.

Jabotinsky's New Zionist Organization, now in a 'marriage of convenience' with the Polish government, thought that Poland, surely a more important ally than a coterie of dependent Arab states, could put pressure on the British to keep the gates of Palestine open. Ben-Gurion understood, however, that such lobbying would likely be viewed as 'a case of pogromists preaching morality' and would only be counter-productive.[102] For by 1938 it was obvious to all that anti-Semitism, and not a concern for the aspirations of its Jewish citizens, was driving Polish, like German, policy. Meeting with Nahum Goldmann's colleague Meir Kahany in Geneva in November 1938, just after the Kristallnacht pogroms in Germany, Poland's representative to the League, Titus Komarnicki, revealed that his government admired Germany's success in expelling Jews and hoped to follow suit. Kahany tried to persuade him that such extremism was a tactical error. Poland, by speaking in the name of three and a half million Jewish citizens, had a strong claim to influence international policy towards Palestine, but if it said that other lands had to be opened up as well, all hope of Western cooperation would vanish. Komarnicki retorted that his government was convinced that with Germany, Italy, Poland, and all other East European regimes of one mind both on colonial revision and on the Jewish question, England would be forced to give way. Jews would have to suffer a good deal if the Western powers failed to arrange their emigration, he warned, for Poland would then be 'forced to take legal measures to make the situation of the Jewish diaspora [*Zuflucht*] in Poland as difficult as possible'. The fact that only a shocking (*unerhört*) pogrom had produced action on the problem of Germany's Jews was the sorry proof 'that the Western powers would only grant concessions when forced by acts of violence'.[103]

If this was true, however, Britain's concerns about Arab violence in Palestine ultimately trumped their worries about European violence against Jews. As the Foreign Office understood, Britain had nothing to gain by conciliating East European anti-Semites, especially since—should the Germans actually turn on the Poles—Poland would have no alternative but to be on Britain's side. If war was coming, however, and it now looked likely it was, Britain would need to be able to rely on its Arab client states and to reduce its troop commitments in Palestine. In the spring of 1939 Britain thus invited not only Palestine's warring parties but the neighbouring Arab states as well to a Round Table conference aimed at forcing a new settlement. Out of that consultation arose, as we know, the White Paper of May 1939—a document that, while allowing entry to a further 75,000 Jews (a figure close to that of the entire Jewish population of Palestine in 1919), proposed to make all subsequent entry subject to Arab consent and envisaged the creation of a unitary state in Palestine within ten years.[104] Although the Jewish minority was to be protected, this would be an Arab and not a 'bi-national' state. There would be no Jewish state in Palestine.

The White Paper was rejected by the Arabs as inadequate (despite some arguments in favour of acceptance), and since it would have entailed a permanent minority status for Jews in an independent Palestine, was anathema to the Zionists as well (Figure 12.8). Malcolm MacDonald, once Weizmann's conduit to his father, was reviled as a traitor—his name linked, in Weizmann's correspondence, with 'Jewish detractors, from Pharaoh to Hitler'.[105] This was not quite fair: records of the Interdepartmental Committee that hammered out the Round Table policy reveal MacDonald striving to keep open the possibility of continued Jewish immigration and an eventual Jewish state against the advice of his officials, most of whom wanted Britain to declare forthrightly that it would no longer be bound by what his Under-Secretary the Marquis of Dufferin called 'Lord Balfour's error of judgement'. Britain, they insisted, should now come to terms with the Arabs—including, if necessary, with the Mufti himself. ('But His Majesty's Government cannot treat with instigators of murder!' the High Commissioner exclaimed. 'On the contrary,' retorted the Colonial Office's Sir Grattan Bushe, 'peace in Ireland was made by a treaty between Cabinet Ministers and "murderers."')

**Figure 12.8** 'Tear up the evil decree'. The demonstration against the White Paper, Jerusalem, 18 May 1939.

MacDonald would not go this far. The government was hoping to buy just a few years of peace, he told his officials, not to craft a lasting settlement.[106] He did, however, think it both wrong and politically imprudent to coerce Palestine's Arab population forever, and understood that, with war threatening, the friendship of the Arab states might be a more valuable asset than the crippled League's approbation. For the first time, British ministers thus made it clear that they would not defer to the League. The government was certain that their new policy was reconcilable with the mandate, Lord Dufferin stated in the Lords, but if the League Council were to take a different view the government 'would immediately ask the Council to alter the Mandate so as to bring it into accordance with the policy laid down in the White Paper'. No one, he concluded pointedly, should have 'a shadow of hope that this policy will not go through'.[107] Legalism would have to bow to politics in the end.

Opponents of the White Paper looked to the League for salvation nonetheless. Hostile amendments were introduced in both Houses urging Parliament to defer its vote on the White Paper until the Mandates Commission had had a chance to express its view, and while the government forced approval through the Commons in late May anyway, Churchill,

Amery, and nearly one hundred other prominent Conservatives withheld their support—a larger dissenting bloc than had broken with Chamberlain over Munich.[108] In Geneva, Rappard girded himself for a fight. The Mandates Commission had been 'trailing along' behind government policy for years, he told R. A. Butler, the Foreign Office Under-Secretary, and 'many of its members' wished to 'save their self-respect by stating their position a little more clearly this time'.[109] Weizmann, who had already met with Rappard and Orts and had a Dutch friend lobby Van Asbeck,[110] now sent Rappard a final appeal. The government was 'flouting both the League and public opinion'; the PMC was now 'the only body still left in this distracted world which has courage and [is] capable of an independent judgment'.[111]

The PMC's three-week session opened in Geneva on 8 June 1939. One week later Malcolm MacDonald arrived to defend his policy. Britain had kept its pledge to the Jews, he insisted, for a community numbering some 80,000 at the beginning of the mandate had grown to 450,000. The 'National Home' was established, and while the mandate did not *preclude* its further development into a Jewish state, it did not require such a development either, nor was it a violation of the mandate for Britain to refuse to impose such a state on Palestine against the will of its Arab inhabitants. Britain had tried hard to secure Arab consent to the Zionist project but it had failed. To the contrary, Arab opposition had swelled into a 'wide, patriotic national protest'. 'Sooner or later,' MacDonald told the PMC, 'the time must come when the mandatory Power, which is charged to safeguard "the rights and position" of the Arabs, is duty bound to take serious note of this passionate protest.'[112] It could not just 'slay large numbers of Arabs' indefinitely, especially when the Covenant had clearly envisaged that the mandate was to be temporary. 'It was impossible to set one's face against the whole spirit of the twentieth century, which in many countries was a steady movement towards self-government.'[113]

Most of the PMC, however, flatly disagreed. Palacios had been unable to attend this crucial meeting, and in his absence Rappard, Orts, Van Asbeck, and Dannevig dominated the questioning. All were not only hostile to MacDonald's policy but frankly dismissive of his claim that the right to self-government envisaged under Article 22 of the Covenant applied to Palestine's Arabs anyway. It was not possible for two peoples to be granted the 'rights of a free people' in a single territory, Rappard stated, so the 'civil and religious rights' guaranteed to Arabs under the mandate must not include the right to political development. By contrast, Dannevig stated, the pledge to the Jews was part of the peace agreement; thus, even if that pledge 'was clearly against the will of the Arabs, they had to submit to it'.[114] The fact that the Arabs were self-evidently *not* submitting was no reason to change course. She was sorry she had ever supported British plans to introduce self-governing institutions in Palestine, Dannevig told MacDonald. She now thought self-government a very long way off indeed—perhaps fifty or one hundred years, not five or ten.[115]

The PMC was clearly hostile, but would it publicly condemn British policy? When the official representatives withdrew, four of the seven members—Rappard, Dannevig, Van Asbeck, and Orts—were eager that it do so. The fact that it did not (quite) was owing to the intervention of one man, Sir Maurice Hankey, who had just retired as Cabinet Secretary and had been hastily (and, for some Labour MPs, entirely inappropriately) appointed as British member following Lord Hailey's sudden resignation only a few weeks earlier.[116] This was Hankey's first—and, as it would turn out, only— PMC session; he was by his own admission ill-prepared; and Weizmann expected him, as a neophyte, to cut no ice.[117] But Hankey was a skilled political operator with a rooted mistrust of the League. In 1919, after all, he had concluded that 'the British Empire is worth a thousand Leagues of Nations' and had turned down Lloyd George's offer to become the organization's first Secretary General.[118] Now, he had no intention of letting Rappard, Dannevig ('the old "School Marm"'), or Orts ('the most bigoted and intransigent of the whole narrow-minded, legalistic crew') slap his empire's wrist.[119] When the Commission tried to exclude Hankey from the committee appointed to draft a report, he declined to leave; when it voted four-to-three to issue majority and minority reports and have done with it, he flatly refused to accept the vote.

Over four days of argument, Hankey wore his colleagues down. It was hard going. Rappard was 'desperately keen on publishing his Report denouncing the White Paper', Hankey reported to MacDonald, and Orts, Dannevig, and Van Asbeck were lined up behind him. Only the French and Portuguese members thought the White Paper policy right, and not even they felt comfortable simply asserting that it was in conformity with the mandate. For a time it looked as if the Commission would issue three separate reports, an outcome Hankey said would make them all look ridiculous. By tea-time on the third day, the majority began to crack.[120] In place of the fierce denunciation Rappard intended, the report simply stated that while the White Paper was not in accord with the interpretation the PMC had *hitherto* placed on the mandate, the Commission could not decide whether it was contrary to the mandate itself. Four members felt that it was while three did not—and with that the Commission referred the Council to the minutes for the members' different views.[121]

In this battle with his fellows, and especially in a long speech *not* published in the minutes, Hankey argued, in essence, that politics mattered. When Rappard and Orts insisted that the PMC was a technical body, charged only to interpret text, and therefore need not consider the worsening situation in Palestine itself, Hankey retorted that this position was naive and even immoral. As a political creation intervening in a charged field, the Commission was obliged to consider the context within which it acted; should it fail to do so, it would bear a share of responsibility if bloodshed ensued. Moreover, even on the narrow issue of the proper interpretation of the mandate, he charged, the PMC had been far too legalistic and rigid. The Commission behaved as if the mandate could be made workable if it was given an authoritative interpretation but if anything the opposite was true, for the simple reason that only the text's ambiguity, intentional from the outset, could allow for adjustments of policy as conditions changed. The essence of good government, after all, was adaptability; governments were *right*, not weak, to tack when the winds changed.[122] The British government's written response to the PMC's report reiterated just these points. It was the government's 'clear duty' to attend to political conditions and to adjust its policy accordingly. The mandate, 'drawn up at a time when future developments could not be foreseen', had been 'naturally worded in the most general terms' precisely so that it could be flexibly applied 'in accordance with the fundamental principles of good government'. And one such principle, surely, was that 'government should be not by force but by consent'.[123]

Few of the League's dwindling band of supporters in the summer of 1939 accepted this justification. They wanted to resist Hitler, not pacify Palestine, and hoped the League would take a strong stance in defence of the Jews. The PMC majority's condemnation of the White Paper heartened them. Nahum Goldmann, speaking to the Zionist Congress in Geneva on 18 August, called it 'a ray of light'.[124] Now desperate to strengthen its Middle East alliances and willing to ignore the crippled League, the British government imposed the White Paper anyway. As a tool of reconciliation, however, it was a failure, for it infuriated Zionists in Palestine and abroad without in any measure 'appeasing' Palestine's Arabs. Indeed, what was most significant about the 1939 White Paper was simply its belatedness, for it imposed a policy that all Palestine High Commissioners, the Foreign Office, and even one or two Colonial Secretaries, had favoured at least since 1929. That the British found it impossible to change course earlier, and thus that the Yishuv went into the crucible of the Second World War with the demographic capacity to surmount later challenges, was due not only to the Zionist movement's superior political skills and the sentiments of the House of Commons. It was due also, in some measure, to the political inflexibility and stasis created by the dynamic of competitive internationalization, and to the Permanent Mandates Commission of the League of Nations.

★ ★ ★

On 8 December 1938, when the partition proposal was in its death throes, the House of Lords debated the government's new plan for a Round Table conference. Since so many colonial administrators wound up their careers in the Lords, several prominent architects of Britain's Palestine policy were in the chamber. There were moments of recrimination and self-justification. Lord Snell read passages from his decade-old Minority Report on the Shaw Commission to show he had been right all along. Herbert Samuel defended his even older decision to appoint Hajj Amin al-Husayni as Mufti of Jerusalem. Yet, by the ferocious standard of parliamentary debates on Palestine, the tone was melancholy and rather mild, imbued as it was with the realization that many in the room had acted with sincerity and what they thought was impartiality, but had nevertheless failed. Ormsby-Gore, who was quite possibly the most capable interwar Colonial Secretary but who nevertheless ended his term of office humiliated and diminished, tried to shift a portion of the blame in the direction of Geneva. The mandate text 'has been the bane of all administration by successive governments in Palestine'. It had forced Britain to continue policies it had already learned were unworkable; worse, it was accompanied by a legalistic oversight apparatus that made flexible decision-making impossible. He knew the Cabinet had been precipitate in their adoption of partition, he said, but 'the parties at Geneva had adjourned and demanded from the Mandatory Power an immediate explanation of their policy and an immediate statement. I had to go hot foot to Geneva, which was waiting... in order to produce something.'[125] The need to placate 'Geneva', in other words, had started to drive Palestine policy itself.

One can understand the noble Lords' frustration, but their shackles were of their own making. Ormsby-Gore had helped draft the Balfour Declaration, and he and Herbert Samuel had helped secure its incorporation into the mandate text. All British governments had worked hard to enhance the prestige of that document and of the consultative and oversight bodies in Geneva. That attempt to construct, and then defer to, international author- ity was part of a wider effort to reconcile imperial interests and Wilsonian values, and in Tanganyika, Togo, and even Iraq, that effort paid off. When it came to Palestine, however, that strategy of internationalization backfired, for the simple reason that it made any shift in policy almost impossible. In the early 1920s Britain had forced the PMC (initially against its own better judgement) to treat the implausible claim that the Balfour pledge did not damage Arab interests as a 'fact'—but, once the PMC had done so, and had issued fifteen years of assessments and judgements on that basis, that claim took on the status of 'law'. Britain's persistent efforts after 1929 to change course thus only exposed it to the PMC's reprimands—chastisements it could not easily flout without undermining its status as the mainstay of the League and a guardian of international law.

Until 1939, Britain thus put the League first, deferring less to the Zionists per se than to an ostensibly global institution that nonetheless saw the world through indelibly European eyes. The Zionist project, although initially divisive, came to speak to many European interests—to anti-Semitic regimes eager to reduce their Jewish populations, to liberals horrified by Nazi doc- trines and seeking refuge for Jews, to a Mandates Commission eager to do what it could to aid in that refugee crisis, and to Eastern European Jews inspired by the nation-building project. Indeed, precisely because of its mul- tivalent Western appeal, the Zionist project in Palestine came to be seen as the quintessential League effort, a test of the capacity of 'the international' to reshape the global order in line with ostensibly textually defined but often politically determined collective norms. How one evaluates that pro- ject depends entirely on where one stands in relation to what Ormsby-Gore so presciently called the 'battle between right and right'. British patronage, maintained through international pressure long past the sell-by date of British interest, enabled some members of the European Jewish diaspora to find refuge in Palestine from the hatred of non-Jewish fellow Europeans, but at the cost of subjecting an existing population initially quite uninter- ested in that quarrel and afire with those same ideals of self-determination. It is hard to imagine that, absent the League, the British would have sup- ported the Zionist project for so long, especially once Britain's global and regional interests favoured another direction.

By the time Britain repudiated the Palestine mandate, the mandates system was already in crisis. France had given Alexandretta to Turkey, in direct violation of the Syrian mandate, refusing to allow the Commission even to discuss the question. Japan had formally incorporated the South Sea mandated islands. All mandatory powers were 'imperializing' their African holdings, drawing mandates and colonies into closer strategic and economic cooperation as global antagonisms worsened. Britain, as the system's main author and beneficiary, was the last to break faith, but when the logic of interest became irresistible, Britain too made clear that imperial imperatives, and not League doctrine, would drive policy.

In Geneva the shaken smaller powers realized what was happening, and stopped clamouring for League positions and perks. In 1938, the German, Italian, and Japanese members having withdrawn, the Council had been pestered by states—notably Poland—eager to take over their seats on the Mandates Commission. By the spring of 1939, however, those requests had dried up. The director of the Mandates Section, Edouard de Haller, wrote to the Secretary General, Joseph Avenol, that in April the Council had asked him to look into the problem of PMC membership, but while 'in normal times this announcement would have led to demands from various quarters', they had heard 'no comment at all'. 'This silence is a bit embarrassing.'[126] The mandates system was ending.

# Conclusion
## Mandatory Statehood in the Making

So here I am, in the middle way, having had twenty years—
Twenty years largely wasted, the years of *l'entre deux guerres*—
Trying to learn to use words, and every attempt
Is a wholly new start, and a different kind of failure...

                    T. S. Eliot, 'East Coker', *Four Quartets*

The European War that broke out in September 1939 would sweep away the League of Nations, transplanting internationalism's beating heart from Geneva to New York. But no one knew that at the time. For if Britain and France were at war in the autumn of 1939, the League was not; indeed, the vast majority of the institution's remaining member states (including most European states) were neutral. Not that they condoned 'aggression'. In December a brief Assembly was convened to expel the Soviet Union for its unprovoked attack on Finland—a quixotic and principled gesture the Soviets never forgave. Yet for most states, and indeed for the Secretariat, the war posed starkly the question of whether the League was something more than the handmaiden of the Allied powers. Could the institution act as the guardian of international values, keeping its 'non-political' sections and its capacities alive until the present conflict was over?

The Mandates Commission faced that question as well. Since the Secretariat had agreed to carry on with 'non-political' work, members were summoned in December 1939 for the 37th session.[1] All but Leopoldo Palacios attended, and after some initial grumbling and infighting the mandatory powers sent reports and representatives as well. In Britain officials at the Colonial Office were so incensed by the 'severe handling and deplorable lack of comprehension' which they felt they had received over Palestine that they would gladly have seen the system collapse entirely; only the Foreign Office's concern not to antagonize American and neutral opinion drove the Colonial Office to dispatch representatives to answer the Commission's questions at the session in Geneva.[2] There those officials expected, and received, yet more criticism from an institution trying to protect its precarious claim to neutrality. PMC members were well aware that Britain and France had introduced wartime measures in West Africa and Tanganyika incompatible with the rules on economic equality and non-militarization; they knew too that Germany, calling the kettle black, had protested this violation of international law. The war thus hung over the gathering, and towards the end of the session, William Rappard forthrightly raised the question of whether territories administered by powers at war with Germany must be considered to be at war as well. The British member Malcolm Hailey, surprised, interjected that he thought they obviously were, but Rappard retorted that the situation was not so clear. After all, Britain and France administered those areas on behalf of the League, and the League was not at war. 'Everywhere,' he stated, 'great curiosity exists as to whether the League is exclusively at the services of those powers now at war with Germany, or whether, to the contrary, she exercises oversight, in the name of the international community, which is independent of such purely national influences.' If the mandatory powers used their territories to support the war effort, and the Commission disbanded without questioning that use, 'they risk weakening their authority not only in the eyes of the Council but still more in relation to public opinion outside the League'. Three other members from neutral states—Orts (Belgium), Van Asbeck (Netherlands), and Dannevig (Norway)—agreed and in the most circuitous way possible made clear that they expected the mandatory powers to confirm the 'international' character of the mandated territories at the June 1940 session.[3]

That session was never held. In April 1940 Hitler's armies attacked neutral Denmark and Norway, and that May swept through neutral Luxembourg, Belgium, and the Netherlands en route to France. In Brussels, Pierre Orts bundled his daughters-in-law and grandchildren into a car and drove south before the advancing armies, alerting Rappard some weeks later that they had arrived safely at Arcachon on the French coast.[4] Those lightning campaigns caused turmoil in the Secretariat too. Through the winter of 1939–40, with Swiss anxiety about harbouring an 'Allied' organization growing, the

French Secretary General Joseph Avenol had radically reduced the League staff and considered moving the organization to France, but the precipitous French surrender in June left those plans in shambles. A period of intrigue followed, during which Avenol dismissed many long-serving officials and fantasized about whether the organization might serve a 'new order' led by the victorious Germans. But by August he had finally resigned, the archives and staff of the Economics Section were on their way to their wartime home at the Institute for Advanced Study in Princeton, New Jersey, and Avenol's deputy Sean Lester, a laconic but principled diplomat from neutral Ireland, had been sworn in as Secretary General. For the next five years Lester and a skeleton staff would keep a lonely vigil in the ghostly Palais des Nations in Geneva, waiting for a time when the League would again be needed.[5] Peter Anker, a young Norwegian official (and protégé of Rappard's), dealt with the small amount of wartime correspondence about the mandated territories.

By 1944 those men knew they had been superseded. The war might have begun as a battle between the League's main imperial backers and the revisionist states, but after the fall of France it quickly changed character. Once the German offensive of June 1941 and the Japanese attack on Pearl Harbor that December brought the Soviet Union and the United States into the war, the British Empire became only one of three major Allied belligerents—and, as British officials grew ever more aware, by no means the most powerful one. Those new entrants made the final Allied victory possible, but the shifting balance of forces brought new ideological commitments and political possibilities in its train. A war against German and Japanese imperial ambitions, one fought by soldiers of all colours and nationalities, could not have as its purpose the preservation of European colonialism or white supremacy; in India and elsewhere, independence quickly became the condition of colonial nationalists' support. Through the Atlantic Charter in 1941, as in the aftermath of Wilson's Fourteen Points more than two decades earlier, Britain and the United States disavowed any interest in territorial gains, agreed that all adjustments would be made with the consent of the people concerned, and endorsed the right of all peoples to self-determination—principles approved in 1942 by the Soviets and other members of what was coming to be known as the 'United Nations'. That a new international organization would be needed to oversee any post-war settlement virtually went without saying; that neither the Soviets nor the Americans wished it to be the League was soon apparent as well. Following

a first planning conference held at Dumbarton Oaks in the autumn of
1944, the United Nations met in San Francisco the following summer
to agree on a founding Charter, which included a declaration endorsing
political advancement towards 'self-government' for all non-self-governing
territories, and two chapters laying out a trusteeship system to succeed
the mandates system of the League of Nations. There was much evocation
of new orders and new worlds, and as little mention as possible of the
organization that had gone before. Indeed, although the United States
belatedly invited Lester and two other League officials to attend the San
Francisco conference, they were given no role and only seats in the last
row of the gallery—a clear sign of how little the two main powers wanted
them there at all.[6]

The mandated territories whose futures were under the conference's eye
had—like the rest of the colonial world—emerged from the maelstrom of
the war much changed. The Middle East territories were exiting 'oversight'
entirely, for British forces had ousted the Vichy regime from Syria and
Lebanon and then (over De Gaulle's objections) collaborated with nationalist leaders to support their independence in 1946—the year Transjordan
also gained nominal independence and that Britain finally grasped that it
could not work out any viable transition in Palestine.[7] The Pacific mandated
territories had also been caught up directly in the war. Island populations
suffered labour conscription, forced evacuation, epidemics, privations of all
kinds, bombardment, and sometimes outright massacres as the Japanese
advanced and then were beaten back; New Guineans were impressed as
labourers and carriers as the Japanese army fought a terrible campaign
against a rag-tag Australian army in their highlands; Nauru was occupied
and much of its population forcibly relocated. The Samoan islands were
spared this fate, their use by the United States Army as supply bases and sites
for soldiers' 'rest and recuperation' instead bringing both wealth and cultural
dislocation.[8] Sub-Saharan Africa, too, was this time not a field of battle, but
the British, the Vichy regime, and the Free French (who used Cameroon as
a base of operations) placed heavy demands on Africans as soldiers and
labourers. Those demands elicited claims in their turn for a new status for
Africans and African nations, whether they remained within the imperial
framework or out of it.[9]

Yet however strenuously nationalist critics and wartime planners alike
disavowed the institutions that had gone before, the new trusteeship system drew on League personnel and precedents. True, when the American

Under-Secretary of State, Sumner Welles, first pulled together a committee to plan the post-war order in 1942, he envisaged bringing *all* colonized territories under international supervision.[10] But when Leo Pasvolsky, the Russian political scientist brought in to run the State Department's Division of Social and Economic Studies, hunted for staff to think through how to operate such supervision, he turned the question over to Benjamin Gerig, an American who had written a dissertation on the mandates system with Rappard's support at the University of Geneva in the late 1920s and had then worked for the League's Information Section for ten years.[11] Gerig lured Ralph Bunche, the brilliant African American political scientist, whom we last met in West Africa gathering data for his Harvard dissertation, from another State Department section to help him. In San Francisco both men were part of the US delegation's team working on the trusteeship issue, which fell under the conference's Second Commission, whose Executive Officer was none other than our old friend from the Mandates Section, Huntington Gilchrist. Gerig and Bunche were also part of the American delegation to the Preparatory Commission of the United Nations that met in London three months later, where the 'Fourth Committee' dealing with Trusteeship included those former PMC members Van Asbeck and Orts, now straightforwardly representing Dutch and Belgian imperial interests.[12] Peter Anker, who had at Lester's request written a summary of the mandates system for the use of these planners, supplied tranches of documents about the system to Bunche's assistant Lawrence Finkelstein in New York.[13]

   It should not surprise us, then, that the trusteeship system which emerged out of those considerations and negotiations drew on League precedents. It too was a regime of international oversight, not international government, with a specific state administering a specific territory, according to stipulations laid out in a text agreed between the administering power and the United Nations, under the supervision of a specific United Nations body (now the Trusteeship Council), supported by a Secretariat section (now the Trusteeship Division). The core procedures of the mandates regime—annual reports, regular meetings, and a petition process—were retained. Yet there were changes too. Perhaps inevitably in the wake of a devastating war, the need to 'further international peace and security' became the system's first objective, and trust territories were to contribute to, and not be held apart from, security arrangements. The rhetoric of 'civilization' was swept away, as was all reference to the incapacity or immaturity of the populations governed 'in trust'. Instead, the goal of explicitly *political* advancement—of 'progressive development towards self-government or independence as may be appropriate to the particular circumstances of each territory' and in line with its people's 'freely expressed wishes'—was avowed for all. The obligation 'to encourage respect for human rights and for fundamental freedoms for all without distinction to race, sex, language or religion' was also new, the explicit endorsement of racial equality in sharp contrast with the racial underpinnings of the League system.[14]

Perhaps the most significant changes were found, however, in the details. For Bunche, together with representatives of former colonized states and of the Soviet republics, cannily wrote new capacities and rights for the Trusteeship Council and populations under mandate into the rules agreed in San Francisco and London. Inhabitants were allowed to petition the Council directly, rather than through the medium of the administering power, and Orts' attempt in London to exclude all petitions that could be pursued in local courts failed. Unlike the Mandates Commission, the Trusteeship Council could conduct official visits and inquiries in the trust territories, a stipulation the Syrian representative at the London meeting considered especially important 'on account of the unfortunate experience of the Permanent Mandates Commission in the past'. A Ukrainian resolution on which the imperial powers abstained empowered such inquiries 'to use various methods to ensure the fullest possible expression of the wishes of the local population', including by holding elections for spokesmen or conducting a popular referendum.[15] Most importantly, the Council reported not to the Security Council but rather to the General Assembly—a stipulation that, as Bunche surely realized, meant that pressures for decolonization would grow as the Assembly became less European and less white. Indeed, as Meredith Terretta and Ullrich Lohrmann have shown, by the 1950s local activists within the trust territories were able to exploit those provisions to inundate the Trusteeship Council with tens of thousands of petitions, lobby visiting missions, form alliances with such international human-rights and anti-colonial organizations as the International League of the Rights of Man and the Movement for Colonial Freedom, and take advantage of growing sympathy among non-aligned and newly independent states to state their case on the floor of the United Nations General Assembly itself.[16] The practice of using international mechanisms and the international arena as a sphere of colonial contestation, already visible during the mandate period, here reached its apotheosis.

But if the trusteeship system was more self-consciously 'progressive' than the mandates regime, it is important to note that it was smaller as well. This was partly because the war brought the Middle East mandates to an end, but it was also because, when it came down to it, the United States proved much less 'anti-imperialist' than its rhetoric might suggest. True, the war had again spurred claims for national self-determination across the globe. Within Gerig's team in the State Department, not to mention within the African American movement, there had been much enthusiastic talk of bringing all colonial territories under the new trusteeship regime and then swiftly to statehood.[17] Yet, as Roger Louis has shown, Churchill's intransigence on imperial questions, adept British diplomacy, Welles' expulsion from the State Department in 1943, and the Americans' steady defence of their own (publicly disavowed) imperial interests defeated those plans. By the time of the San Francisco conference, the United States and the United Kingdom were working in tandem, collaborating to defeat attempts by the delegates from Egypt and the Philippines to have the United Nations endorse independence (and not simply, as the British were willing to allow, self-government) as the goal for *all* non-self-governing territories. Instead, that aim appeared in the chapter on trusteeship alone, and the placement of any territory under that system was left up to the controlling power. 'We have no such intention, and I'm sure no other power has,' one member of the British delegation noted drily in his diary.[18] He was quite right. The only non-mandate territory placed under the trusteeship system was Somaliland, which had been seized from Italy but was then—in sharp contrast to the treatment of Germany in 1919—restored in 'trust'.[19]

The Americans, revealingly, also placed their own conquests in a special class. While Gerig and Bunche's team at the State Department were crafting their trusteeship proposals, American troops were taking one devastated island after another in the bloody Pacific theatre, and the military men orchestrating that advance had very different plans for their conquests. According to the service chiefs, the former Japanese islands were of strategic importance to the United States, had been paid for with American lives, and should be annexed—a plan utterly in conflict with the principles of the Atlantic Charter and that echoed nothing so much as Smuts' schemes for South West Africa and Billy Hughes' table-thumping perorations about New Guinea two decades earlier. And since the United States was the sovereign who could decide the exception, the Americans (unlike the Australians in 1919) got their way. Thus, Britain, France, Belgium, Australia, and New Zealand (but not South Africa)[20] all concluded trusteeship agreements for their African or Pacific mandated territories (in the case of Western Samoa and Nauru over the strong reservations of local populations, who speculated that the dollar-laden Americans might be better guardians).[21] But the United States forced the creation of a special category—the 'strategic trust'—for the former Japanese mandated islands, under which the United States answered for their administration not to the General Assembly but rather to the Security Council, on which it had a veto. The islands were used as military bases and, in the case of the Marshall Islands, for atmospheric nuclear tests that rendered some toxic and uninhabitable.[22]

If the trusteeship regime deferred more to the ideal of 'self-government or independence' than the mandates system had done, then, it was also much more 'statist' and conceded more to the realities of power.[23] The exception accorded the Americans was one such concession; that security was allowed to trump indigenous interests was another; that administrative integration into neighbouring colonies—so strenuously resisted by the Mandates Commission—was now allowed was a third; that the Trusteeship Council was to be composed not of long-serving 'independent experts' but rather of representatives of member states (and that fully half would come from the five permanent members and the administering powers and serve without fixed term, while the other half would serve fixed three-year terms) was a fourth. Bunche's observant former colleague from Howard University, the African American historian Rayford Logan, found that deference to the administering powers and their 'security' interests particularly worrying, and Rappard, watching from Geneva, did so as well. The 'one redeeming feature' of the mandates system had been the independence of its Commission, Rappard wrote to Arthur Sweetser, his old American friend from the Secretariat, now in the thick of the UN plans. Had the members been government delegates, as those named to the Trusteeship Council would be, 'we would have become mute or at least so discreet as to have been quite ineffective'.[24] Rappard's self-serving history was not, of course, quite correct. This book has detailed countless instances of Commission members defending the interests of their states, and many others in which they upheld what one might call the 'interest' of the European empires as a whole. Yet it is true that the trusteeship system, by accepting that Council members would inevitably represent the interests of states and that 'the international' was little more than the arena in which their battles would be fought out, threw out the internationalist baby with the imperialist bathwater. Scholars who followed the trusteeship system in its early years were astounded at how quickly and thoroughly it became permeated by Cold War antagonisms; indeed, those tensions were palpably present at those Preparatory Commission meetings in London in the autumn of 1945.[25] The trust territories would make their way to statehood, but the kind of states (or 'quasi-states') that emerged would be hobbled by economic concessions and by the clientelist entanglements of the Cold War world.[26]

In April 1946, shortly after the meeting in London of the UN Preparatory Commission, delegates of some thirty mostly European member states of the League of Nations met in Geneva to wind up their organization and exit the stage. The wind of self-determination was at gale force, and they bent before it. In the way of politicians everywhere, they rewrote the past to accommodate the present, suggesting that state-building had been the purpose of the mandates system all along. The Assembly thus warmly welcomed the termination of the Syria, Lebanon, and Transjordan mandates, and thanked the Mandates Commission for its years of devoted work, noting especially how the League had helped Iraq 'to progress...to a condition of complete independence'.[27] Thus was the League subsumed into a genealogy that would credit enlightened European internationalism with the extension to all men of that Hegelian destiny: the construction of the state as the achievement of national freedom.

If this book has convinced you of nothing else, I hope it has shown how profoundly this causal narrative misreads history. The 'emancipation' of Iraq, for example—or, let us say, the creation of a client state in Iraq—was a joint project of Iraqi nationalists and British officials seeking to reach a mutually beneficial agreement, one that would also limit international oversight, economic access, and diplomatic meddling. It was disliked by the Mandates Commission, which was profoundly and justifiably sceptical of British motives but equally doubtful of non-Western peoples' readiness for self-government. Indeed, at no point did the Mandates Commission unambiguously endorse plans to create independent states; British and later French efforts to move in this direction in Iraq, Transjordan, Syria, and finally Palestine were met with carping and criticism. With a few rare exceptions—the Spaniard Leopoldo Palacios was one—members simply could not think in such terms. For them, the mandates system was a mechanism for producing what Winifred Holtby, that brilliant and astringent critic of the 'benevolent imperialism' of the 1930s, once called 'better and brighter natives', not a crucible for independent states.[28] That the system lurched towards normative statehood anyway was unintended and inadvertent—the result not of any conscious plan but rather of the uncontainable dynamic of the system itself.

The mandates system, as it was cobbled together in Paris and then reinvented in Geneva, began as a project of imperial reconciliation and legitimation. Galvanized by Woodrow Wilson's insistence on an 'anti-annexationist' peace and by an explosion of demands for self-determination across the globe, British statesmen in particular shaped this new international regime, one in which territorial control was redefined as a means for the 'civilized' world to promote the 'well-being and development' of backwards areas and peoples alike. That system was only grudgingly accepted by the other mandatory powers and was sharply contested by local populations and indeed by such self-appointed guardians as the Anti-Slavery Society from the start. It could be imposed on Syria and Iraq in 1920 only at the point of a gun, and groups in South West Africa, Syria, and Western Samoa all rose against their 'tutors' in the regime's early years. That level of discontent forced the creation of a petition process—a practice that became a persistent thorn in the side of the mandatory powers and that did much to train local elites in the skills of international organizing, claim-making, and representation. When faced with open resistance or such political claims, the League almost invariably supported the imperial powers, reiterating the system's paternalistic and not emancipatory intent. There is little evidence that populations under mandate found the subject position offered them attractive; indeed, the mandates system served in these early years less as a means of reconciling mandated populations to their rulers than of reconciling the quarrelsome imperial powers among themselves.

The system could play that conciliating role because the 'League of Nations' was, in the early 1920s, also a 'League of Empires': with the United States and the Soviet Union absent, and Germany a pariah, the imperial powers—not only Britain and France, but Italy, Japan, Belgium, the Netherlands, and Portugal as well—set the tone. That situation changed dramatically when Germany entered the League in 1926, for Germany was not only the sole European great power without an empire but also the former sovereign of most of the territories under mandatory rule. German entry thus ushered in the mandate system's most creative period, as the Mandates Commission struggled to articulate norms that might reconcile the revisionist powers to the League regime. It was during this period that the Commission forced the Council to agree that the mandatory powers were *not sovereign* in mandated territories, and during this period that Germany sought to take full advantage of the provisions of the 'open door'. It was in this period too that Germany self-interestedly promoted Arab and African claims for independence and that British officials worked overtime to craft a version of 'independence' in Iraq that would preserve their military and economic advantage once formal empire had gone. 'Statehood' thus began to appear in these years as a possible destiny for all dependent territories, and the mandates system as an engine for such a transformation, not because the members of the Mandates Commission saw it that way, but rather because this was a project that just might win the support of the imperial powers, revisionist states, and clamant local nationalists alike.

Within the mandates system 'statehood' thus came into play not as the result of international oversight but rather as an alternative to that oversight, a means of securing alliances and advantages in a formally decolonizing world. The cataclysms of the 1930s—economic collapse, the Nazi seizure of power, and then the move towards territorialization and bloc-creation that followed—put an end to such experimentation. Instead, all powers sought to draw clients and colonies closer into their nets. 'Internationalization', as a strategy for reconciling great-power interests, had failed; by this point, however, it had lost its ideological force as well. For with the great empires and the revisionist states at loggerheads, and Japan and Italy describing their rule in Manchuria and Ethiopia as a version of the 'sacred trust', even the stalwarts of the Mandates Commission found claims of Western civilizational superiority, and likewise of alien rule as a form of tutelage, hard to defend. For them, the mandates system had always been something more than a means of reconciling warring states or containing unruly populations: it was a mechanism for defining norms of good governance and promoting imperial 'best practice' across the globe. That project had always been more rhetorical than real, always more a matter of talk in Geneva and London than practice in Jerusalem or Lomé. And when geopolitical imperatives made that disjuncture between rhetoric and imperial policy apparent, the system lost its moorings.

What conclusions might we then draw from this far from linear story? Where do we locate the significance of the mandates system? What difference did it all make? I would make three final points.

First, the mandates system mattered because it was always a strategic part of the geopolitical order of the interwar era. It cannot be understood except within this context. The need to use the system to stabilize that order—initially by containing challenges to imperial rule and reconciling British and French aims, later by placating the revisionist powers—was always paramount. The mandates system was significant not because the territories to which it was applied were particularly valuable (although some, notably Iraq, were), but rather because they were part of what H. Duncan Hall, the former League official and author of the first comparative study of the mandates and trusteeship regimes, perceptively called the 'international frontier' of the interwar era—the conflict zone where empires clashed and territory changed hands.[29] We have forgotten this, and forgotten too that in this respect the mandates system and the trusteeship system were not alike at all. For the mandated territories were in analytical terms the interwar equivalents not of the post-war trust territories (which were, in the Cold War era, relative backwaters) but rather of Korea, Vietnam, Malaya, Congo, or any number of those states where the great powers fought for dominance.[30] Not until the revisionist powers were well and truly defeated did the mandated territories lose their significance, and in the Middle East not even then. The mandates system is part of the history of the tense geopolitics of the interwar period—an era in which the effort to rehabilitate and 'tame' Germany, but also to reconcile British and French strategies and to secure American participation in maintaining the global settlement, were all important. The mandates system was a stake, and Geneva a site, in that effort at global stabilization.

But if the geopolitical conflicts of those years shaped the character of the mandates system, pressures generated by what we might call a dynamic of internationalization mattered too. Bringing to light the significance of that dynamic has been the second main contribution of this study. For the great powers in 1919, partly inadvertently and partly deliberately, decided to manage the geopolitical order not through the balance of power or an armed stand-off but rather by creating an international institution, the League of Nations, so that conflicts could be dealt with through deliberations conducted among member states but visible to informed publics around the world. By doing so, however, they unleashed a force that could not be contained, as the League swiftly became an engine for the mobilization of new constituencies, the generation of new claims, the elaboration of new practices, and the articulation of new norms. The colonial repartition of 1919, like the territorial settlement in Eastern Europe, was to be rendered acceptable through international oversight; in both cases, however, those oversight regimes made those settlements more contestable and vulnerable. For by subjecting the mandatory powers to regular questioning, by providing a

mechanism for petitions and protests, and especially by publishing and distributing their records and reports, the mandates system opened up imperial
rule to an uncontainable wave of scrutiny and 'talk'. Not only W. H. Harris
of the Anti-Slavery Society and Quincy Wright of the University of Chicago
but also Shakib Arslan of the Syro-Palestinian Congress and Olaf Nelson of
the Samoan Mau made use of the opportunities offered. If the Mandates
Commission did its best to discredit and silence many of these voices—to
bar them from their meetings, to reject their petitions, to impugn their
motives—they could never quite shut them up. Their words were out in the
world, a world now remade by literacy, print, air travel, and radio waves, and
could not be recalled.

If we would seek for an explanation of the course and consequences of
the mandates system, it is to be found in the interaction between these two
dynamics—the play of geopolitical interest and the force of international
scrutiny and 'talk'. The explanation for how imperialism and internationalism interacted in these years—that is, for how the League, against its own
desires and intentions, helped to bring the European empires down—is to
be found here. This is my third claim, and it is a methodological one as well.
This book has anatomized a system, a system in motion. It has sought to
explain not what the League *said* it did, but rather to show how its practices
and proclivities—scrutiny, publicity, verbosity, legalism—bumped up against
the aims, claims, and interests of the powers and peoples with which it was
involved, and by doing so produced meanings and outcomes no one had
intended. The League helped make the end of empire imaginable, and normative statehood possible, not because the empires willed it so, or the
Covenant prescribed it, but because that dynamic of internationalization
changed everything—including how 'dependent peoples' would bid for
statehood, what that 'statehood' would henceforth mean, and whether
empires would think territorial control essential to the maintenance of
global power.

The men and one woman who had been the heart and soul of the
mandates system, the surviving members of the Permanent Mandates
Commission, watched the death of the League and the emergence of the
trusteeship system with mixed emotions. Long-serving and for the most
part like-minded, by 1940 they had become friends as well as co-workers.
William Rappard, living in his house in the Geneva hills, still hard at work
in the university, tried through the war to keep track of the fate of his colleagues. He managed to get to London in the summer of 1942, where he

saw Lord Lugard before his death in 1945, and to swing through Madrid to visit Leopoldo Palacios on the way home—although he found the latter (he reported to Lugard) 'neither as fat nor as happy as he used to be when I tormented him on the Mandates Commission'.[31] Rappard met up with Malcolm Hailey, Orts, and Frederick van Asbeck—the latter having survived wartime internment—in London in 1945.[32] Once the war was over, Vito Catastini—hard up, looking for work, and very much repenting his fascist past—also got in touch, and passed on the news that Alberto Theodoli, to no one's surprise, had survived the war unscathed.[33] Rappard appears to have lost touch with Ludwig Kastl, who was expelled from the legal profession for Jewish ancestry in the Nazi period but who—much more remarkably—also survived the war, going on to advise many German companies during the post-war recovery and to receive the prestigious *Bundesverdienstkreuz* from the Federal Republic in 1953. But Rappard saw Valentine Dannevig, now very deaf, in Oslo in 1952, as well as the former Mandates Section director Edouard de Haller, who was now Swiss ambassador to Norway.[34] (Rappard's young protégé Peter Anker, in a nice parallel, became Norway's ambassador to Switzerland.) And through it all, Rappard kept in touch with Orts, his closest collaborator. Theodoli died in 1955, and Rappard passed along his widow's inimitable reply to Catastini's letter of condolence: 'For a long time, you and I, Monsieur, were no doubt the deceased's most pitiable victims.'[35]

But Rappard and Orts were now old men, out of sympathy with their age. Rappard was still a Wilsonian, entirely persuaded that civilized men exercising impartial judgement could solve the problems of the world, and he found the 'realistic militancy' of the post-war trusteeship system—and the post-war order more generally—regressive.[36] Orts had always been more conservative, and at the end of his life still thought even mandatory rule (as opposed to direct imperial administration) uncalled for in 'territories peopled by primitives'.[37] They were pleased to have played a part in the emergence of the state of Israel—in November 1949 Rappard spent a week there, staying with the Weizmanns and feeling 'quite exceptionally, indeed almost abnormally, happy'[38]—but beyond that, they were no longer quite sure just what they had achieved. The more the United Nations grows in size and powerlessness, Orts told Rappard in 1952, the better the League looks—and Rappard entirely agreed.[39] Both men died in the spring of 1958, inadvertent architects of a world they had not imagined.

# *Appendix I*
## Article 22 of the Covenant of the League of Nations

To those colonies and territories which as a consequence of the late war have ceased to be under the sovereignty of the States which formerly governed them and which are inhabited by peoples not yet able to stand by themselves under the strenuous conditions of the modern world, there should be applied the principle that the well-being and development of such peoples form a sacred trust of civilisation and that securities for the performance of this trust should be embodied in this Covenant.

The best method of giving practical effect to this principle is that the tutelage of such peoples should be entrusted to advanced nations who by reason of their resources, their experience or their geographical position can best undertake this responsibility, and who are willing to accept it, and that this tutelage should be exercised by them as Mandatories on behalf of the League.

The character of the mandate must differ according to the stage of the development of the people, the geographical situation of the territory, its economic conditions and other similar circumstances.

Certain communities formerly belonging to the Turkish Empire have reached a stage of development where their existence as independent nations can be provisionally recognized subject to the rendering of administrative advice and assistance by a Mandatory until such time as they are able to stand alone. The wishes of these communities must be a principal consideration in the selection of the Mandatory.

Other peoples, especially those of Central Africa, are at such a stage that the Mandatory must be responsible for the administration of the territory under conditions which will guarantee freedom of conscience and religion, subject only to the maintenance of public order and morals, the prohibition of abuses such as the slave trade, the arms traffic and the liquor traffic, and the prevention of the establishment of fortifications or military and naval bases and of military training of the natives for other than police purposes and the defence of territory, and will also secure equal opportunities for the trade and commerce of other Members of the League.

There are territories, such as South-West Africa and certain of the South Pacific Islands, which, owing to the sparseness of their population, or their small size, or their remoteness from the centres of civilisation, or their geographical contiguity to the territory of the Mandatory, and other circumstances, can be best administered under the laws of the Mandatory as integral portions of its territory, subject to the safeguards above mentioned in the interests of the indigenous population.

In every case of mandate, the Mandatory shall render to the Council an annual report in reference to the territory committed to its charge.

The degree of authority, control, or administration to be exercised by the Mandatory shall, if not previously agreed upon by the Members of the League, be explicitly defined in each case by the Council.

A permanent Commission shall be constituted to receive and examine the annual reports of the Mandatories and to advise the Council on all matters relating to the observance of the mandates.

# *Appendix II*

## Principal Administrators of the Mandated Territories and Appearances before the PMC

This list excludes most administrators who served during the Second World War or for less than a year. Those marked with an asterisk (*) appeared as 'accredited representative' before the Permanent Mandates Commission at the session noted.

### 'A' MANDATES (BROUGHT INTO EFFECT ON 29 SEPTEMBER 1923 IN SYRIA AND PALESTINE, AND ON 27 SEPTEMBER 1924 IN IRAQ)

**French High Commissioners in Syria and Lebanon**

Henri Gouraud, 1919–23

Maxime Weygand, 1923–24

Maurice Sarrail, 1924–25

*Henry de Jouvenel, 1925–26 (9th session, June 1926)

*Henri Ponsot, 1926–33 (18th session, June–July 1930; 22nd session, November–December 1932)

Damien de Martel, 1933–39

Gabriel Puaux, 1939–40

**British High Commissioners in Palestine**

*Sir Herbert Samuel, 1920–25 (5th session, October–November 1924)

Herbert Plumer, 1st Viscount Plumer, 1925–28

*Sir John Chancellor, 1928–31 (15th session, July 1929)

*Sir Arthur Wauchope, 1931–38 (22nd session, November–December 1932)

Sir Harold MacMichael, 1938–44

### BRITISH HIGH COMMISSIONERS IN IRAQ

Sir Percy Cox, 1920–23

*Sir Henry Dobbs, 1923–28 (10th session, November 1926)

Sir Gilbert Clayton, 1928–29

*Sir Francis Humphrys, 1929–32 (20th session, June 1931; 21st session, October–November 1931)

## 'B' MANDATES (BROUGHT INTO EFFECT ON 20 JULY 1922)

### Commissioners of the French Republic for Cameroon
Lucien Fourneau, 1916–19 (military occupation)
Jules Carde, 1919–23 (military occupation, then mandate)
★Théodore Marchand, 1923–32 (15th session, July 1929; 21st session, October–November 1931; 22nd session, November–December 1932)
Paul Bonnecarrère, 1932–34
★Jules Repiquet, 1934–36 (30th session, October–November 1936; 37th session, December 1939)
Pierre Boisson, 1937–38
Richard Brunot, 1938–40

### Commissioners of the French Republic for Togoland
Gaston Fourn, 1916–17 (military occupation)
Alfred Louis Woelfel, 1917–22 (military occupation)
★Paul Bonnecarrère, 1922–31 (6th session, June–July 1925, 18th session, June–July 1930)
Robert Paul Marie de Guise, 1931–33
Maurice Léon Bourgine, 1934
Léon Guismar, 1935–36
Michel Lucien Montagné, 1936–41

### Cameroon under British Mandate
The British-mandated territory of Cameroons was divided into two provinces, Cameroons Province and Northern Cameroons, each of which was further subdivided and, in the case of Northern Cameroons, administratively integrated into adjoining Nigerian provinces. No official held responsibility for administration of the mandated territory alone.

### Togo under British Mandate
The British-mandated territory of Togo was divided into two territories, each of which was administratively integrated into the adjoining territories of the Gold Coast. No administrator held responsibility for the mandated territory alone.

### British Governors, Tanganyika Territory
Sir H. A. Byatt, 1916–25 (military administrator, then governor)
★Sir Donald Cameron, 1925–31 (11th session, June–July 1927)
★Lieut. Col. G. Stewart Symes, 1931–34 (23rd session, June–July 1933)
★Harold MacMichael, 1934–38 (27th session, June 1935)
Sir M. A. Young, 1938–41

### Belgian Royal Commissioners in Ruanda-Urundi; from 1926 Governors of Ruanda-Urundi and Deputy Governor Generals, Belgian Congo
Charles Tombeur, 1916 (military governor, Belgian occupation)
J. P. F. M. Malfeyt, 1916–19 (Royal Commissioner, Belgian occupation)

*Alfred Marzorati, 1919–29 (occupation, then mandate) (9th session, June 1926; 16th session, November 1929)
Louis Joseph Postiaux, 1929–30
Charles Henri Joseph Voisin, 1930–32
Eugène Jungers, 1932–46

## 'C' MANDATES (BROUGHT INTO EFFECT ON 17 DECEMBER 1920)

### South African Administrators, South West Africa
Sir E. H. L. Gorges, 1915–20 (military administrator)
*Gysbert R. Hofmeyr, 1920–26 (4th session, June–July, 1924)
*A. J. Werth, 1926–33 (14th session, October–November 1928)
*D. G. Conradie, 1933–43 (27th session, June 1935)

### Australian Administrators, Mandated New Guinea
Col. William Holmes, 1914–15 (military administrator)
Sir Samuel Augustus Pethebridge, 1915–17 (military administrator)
Brig. Gen. George Jameson Johnston, 1918–20 (military administrator)
Brig. Gen. Thomas Griffiths, 1920–21 (military administrator)
Brig. Gen. E. A. Wisdom, 1921–32
Brig. Gen. Thomas Griffiths, 1932–34
Sir Walter Ramsay McNicoll, 1934–42

### New Zealand Administrators in Western Samoa
Lieut. Col. Robert Logan, 1914–19 (military administrator)
Col. Robert Ward Tate, 1919–23 (military then mandate administrator)
*Brig. Gen. Sir George Richardson, 1923–28 (13th and 14th session, June and October–November 1928)
Col. Stephen S. Allen, 1928–31
Brig. Gen. Herbert E. Hart, 1931–35
Alfred Turnbull, 1935–43 (acting), 1943–46

### Australian Administrators, Nauru
Mr. G. B. Smith-Rewse, 1914–20 (administrator during occupation)
Brig. Gen. Thomas Griffiths, 1921–27
William Newman, 1927–32
Commander Rupert Garsia, 1932–38
Frederick Royden Chalmers, 1938–42 (Nauru occupied by Japanese, August 1943)

### Governors, Nan'yō-chō (Japanese South Seas mandated territory)
Tezuko Toshira, 1922–23
Yokota Gōsuke, 1923–31
*Horiguchi Mitsuda, 1931 (22nd session, November–December 1932)
Tawara Kazuo, 1931–32
Matsuda Masayuki, 1932–33

Hayashi Hisao, 1933–36
Kitajima Kenjiro, 1936–40

## OTHER HIGH OFFICIALS APPEARING BEFORE
## THE MANDATES COMMISSION

### Colonial Governors of adjacent colonies administratively tied to mandated territories

Sir A. Ranford Slater, Governor of Gold Coast, 14th session, October–November 1928 (for British-mandated Togo)

Sir Donald Cameron, Governor of Nigeria, 22nd session, November–December 1932 (for British-mandated Cameroon)

Pierre Ryckmans, Governor General of Belgian Congo, 30th session, October–November 1936 (for Ruanda-Urundi)

### Government ministers

The Hon. William Ormsby-Gore, 3rd session, July–August 1923; 4th session, June–July 1924; 6th session, June–July 1925; 7th session, October 1925; 10th session, November 1926; 12th session, October–November 1927 (as Colonial Under-Secretary); 32nd session, July–August 1937 (as Colonial Secretary)

Thomas Drummond Shiels, Under-Secretary of State, Colonial Office, 17th session, June 1930, and 20th session, June 1931

Earl of Plymouth, Under-Secretary of State, Colonial Office, 22nd session, November–December 1932

Lord De la Warr, Under-Secretary of State, Colonial Office, 31st session, May–June 1937

Malcolm MacDonald, Colonial Secretary, 36th session, June 1939

### Officials from national colonial ministries

Albert Duchêne, Conseilleur d'Etat, Director of Political Affairs, French Colonial Office, present at all discussions of French Togo and Cameroon, 1923–29; later Maurice Besson took over that role 1931–39

Halewyck de Heusch, Director General of Political and Administrative Affairs, Belgian Ministry for the Colonies, present at all discussions of Ruanda and Urundi save first, 1924–39

Robert de Caix, present at every session dealing with Syria, 1924–39

# Acknowledgements

When the pioneering political scientist Raymond Leslie Buell headed to Africa in 1925 to study European colonial administrations, American dollars, power, and privilege eased his way. In October the Governor of Tanganyika, Sir Donald Cameron, fulminated to his old mentor Sir Frederick Lugard that 'a dreadful young American pup ... by name of Buell' had shown up in Dar es Salaam assuming he'd be put up at Government House. Cameron sent Buell off to a hotel instead, but the Governor and his Portuguese, French, and Belgian counterparts across Africa did let the well-connected young American travel freely through their territories, gathering impressions and testimony as he went. Introductions from London and Geneva, funding from the Laura Spelman Rockefeller Foundation, backing from Harvard University and the Foreign Policy Association, and, bluntly, whiteness, made Buell impossible to expel. Three years later, Buell's revelations about forced labour and administrative corruption in his two-volume, 1,000-page compilation, *The Native Problem in Africa*—explored in Chapter 8—fuelled petitions to the Mandates Commission and fury within the corridors of the foreign ministries of the imperial powers.

I began this book at the close of the American century and not at its optimistic beginnings; I certainly never thought I'd put up at Government House. Yet, there are parallels here that are close enough to give pause. The foundations and institutions that made Buell's extraordinary travels possible sustained this project too. Wealth amassed more than a century ago by Rockefeller, Mellon, Carnegie, and others still provide some American academics with the resources—time, leaves, funding, intellectual communities—required for projects of this scope. Access to those resources has left me with many debts to acknowledge, but it brought its own hazards as well. Travelling across continents, a bird of passage in archives where specialists spend their lives, I grew intensely aware of the way international history can shift the focus back to the metropole, re-enacting in scholarly terms just that drive to control disparate local cultures and places that I was documenting. I have tried instead to write a genuinely multilocal history, one as attentive to actors in Damascus or Windhoek as in London or Berlin. But to do that I had to read deeply—or as deeply as I was able—in a host of different fields, an immersion that has left me beholden in many ways. My first thanks must thus go to the hundreds of historians of Africa, the Middle East, and the Pacific islands on whose brilliant and painstaking work I have promiscuously drawn. The copious notes in this book aren't only a sign of my obsessive character; they are also a tribute. *Je vous salue, mes collègues.*

I am equally indebted to the record-keepers, especially those who built up and safeguard collections that cut against the grain. The gratitude I feel to the guardians of the League archives stretches across generations. Were it not for the Secretariat's long-forgotten interwar clerical staff—an idealistic, greatly overqualified, disproportionately English, and largely female band—those meticulous records would not exist at all. Equally, for their generous assistance across many years, I thank Bernhardine Pejovic, Jacques Oberson, Lee Robertson, and the Chief of the Archives Department, Mme Blandine Blukacz-Louisfert. Werner Hillebrecht of the Namibian National Archives helped me navigate archives off my usual track; Anat Stern sat with me translating indexes from Hebrew at the Central Zionist Archives in Jerusalem. I was not able to visit the New Zealand archives in Wellington, but Peter Carter surveyed and retrieved dossiers for me, while Jemina Mowbray finished up my periodicals research at the University of Sydney. A host of students, some now professors, provided research assistance over the past dozen years: I thank Anna Danziger-Halperin, Aimee Genell, Toby Harper, Michelle Iden, Miguel Lopez, Kevin O'Brien, Erik Saari, and Ken Weisbrode.

Two years of intensive research in 2005–6 and 2008–9 were supported by fellowships from the Guggenheim Foundation, the Wissenschaftskolleg zu Berlin, and the American Academy in Berlin, and by visiting fellowships at the Ecole des Hautes Etudes en Sciences Sociales, Paris, and the University of Sydney. I thank Laura Lee Downs for the invitation to Paris, Glenda Sluga and Chris Hilliard for hospitality in Sydney, Gary Smith for welcoming me to Wannsee, and Dieter Grimm and the amazing Wiko staff for creating the closest thing to a scholarly utopia I've known. The Faculty of Arts and Sciences at Columbia University supported this project in many ways, not least by allowing me eighteen months' leave to write in 2011–12. During this time I held a fellowship funded by the Society of Institute Fellows at the Institute for Advanced Study, Princeton, and then was John Birkelund Fellow at the Cullman Center for Writers and Scholars at New York Public Library, a garden of humanistic values beautifully tended by Jean Strouse. I was able to test my ideas and undertake final revisions while Ford's Lecturer and Fellow of All Souls College at Oxford University in Hilary Term 2014; I thank especially Roy Foster and the Warden of All Souls, Sir John Vickers, for making my stay there so strange and wonderful. I could not possibly have kept on top of my administrative responsibilities at Columbia while completing this book but for Rose Razaghian.

My agent Clare Alexander and Christopher Wheeler of Oxford University Press supported this project while it was still a gleam in my eye; Robert Faber and Tim Bent of OUP's Oxford and New York offices have seen it through. I am grateful, too, to the impeccable production team that OUP assembled, especially my copy-editor Richard Mason and Liz Fawcett who compiled the index. Manuel Bautista González first compiled the charts; Kate Blackmer, brilliant cartographer, then drew the revelatory maps and tables you see here. Every effort has been made to identify the original copyright holders of the photographs reproduced in the book; full credits are listed separately below.

This history of international connections was nourished by intersecting scholarly communities. I thank especially my matchless colleagues of the Columbia history department (especially my fellow Europeanists Mark Mazower, Sam Moyn, Emmanuelle Saada, and Victoria de Grazia); the many brilliant Columbia graduate students who took part in my courses on colonial governance, the League, and interwar internationalism (especially Sayaka Chatani, Aimee Genell, Tom Meaney, and Natasha Wheatley); my fellow participants in the vibrant transnational Oslo Contemporary History Network, which met each summer from 2010 to 2012; and the 'Geneva team'—a sprawling, transnational caravansarai of scholars, many of whom came together at the conference on new work on the League that Patricia Clavin, Davide Rodogno, Corinne Pernet, and I organized in Geneva in the summer of 2011. To our amazement, fifty graduate students working on League-related projects showed up. I have been privileged to watch, and in a small measure to facilitate, the emergence of a new scholarly field.

Interventions at key moments proved critical. Daniela Caglioti, Laurie Green, Stephen Pierce, and especially Judith Surkis lent their sharp minds over a crucial lunch that finally settled the book's structure. Ananda Burra, Caroline Elkins, Aimee Genell, Rashid Khalidi, Peter Mandler, Greg Mann, Penny Sinanoglou, Stephen Wertheim, Natasha Wheatley, and Ben White offered smart criticism on one or more chapters. It is evident that Peter Sluglett was one of the reviewers for my *American Historical Review* article on British policy towards Iraq; I am grateful for his wise advice. Ann Summers reminded me of women's importance in the history of internationalism and insisted I write an essay on the subject for *History Workshop Journal*: she was right to do this, and I thank her. Carol Fink, Roger Louis, Zara Steiner, and Bernard Wasserstein shared their deep expertise; Robert Vitalis challenged my thinking at a key moment. Patricia Clavin and Glenda Sluga, closest of co-conspirators, share not only my interests but also my commitments: I cannot imagine pursuing this work without them. Years of conversation with Catherine Evtuhov and Peter Mandler have made me, and this book, wiser. Deborah Cohen, best of readers and most generous of friends, subjected the entire manuscript to her searching eye.

The family usually features last in acknowledgements and usually for their forbearance. But I am not certain my children Saskia and Carl have suffered from their academic childhoods. Yes, they probably know more about the mandates system than any other two teenagers in America, but they have emerged a firm-minded pair—hard bargainers, and, unlike so many people held in trust, well able to defend their rights. The price of Carl's presence at a Florence conference was tickets to see Fiorentina play; Saskia put up with the League historians to spend a week exploring Geneva's museums and food. Their adventurous spirits made my ambitious research agenda imaginable, but still more consequential were choices made by my husband, Tom Ertman. Were it not for Tom's decision to raise our children bilingually and to build a NYU programme in Berlin, I would never have slowly mastered German, sought out research berths in Berlin, or biked off to the German Foreign Ministry archives to discover the record of German colonial revanchism which is one of the anchors of this book. My German is still a source of family merriment, but for forcing our family to live in two worlds and for entirely failing to sympathize with my linguistic limitations: my love, thank you.

# A Note on Sources

This study of the mandates system is based upon the records of the empires and local governments administering mandates; of the League of Nations overseeing that administration; and of a host of individuals and organizations involved in running, contesting or evaluating that effort. Much of that record is unpublished and available only in archives, but the League's stated commitment to publicity means that some key sources—notably the Reports and Minutes of the Permanent Mandates Commission and the Annual Reports sent by each mandatory power on their administration—were published and are readily available in many libraries, as are runs of some key government documents. Digitization is steadily making available more such materials, as well as many contemporary newspaper sources. The archives, League records, printed government documents, and newspapers consulted are listed here. Abbreviations and an explanation for the citation method for printed League documents are given at the beginning of the Notes. A bibliography of contemporary and post-1945 printed books and articles follows the Notes.

### GOVERNMENT ARCHIVES

*Australia*
National Archives, Canberra

*Belgium*
Archives Africaines, Brussels
Archives Générales du Royaume, Brussels

*France*
Archives de la Ministère des Affaires Etrangères, Paris
Archives Nationales d'Outre-Mer, Aix-en-Provence

*Germany*
German Foreign Ministry Archives, Berlin

*Israel*
Central Zionist Archives, Jerusalem

*Namibia*
Namibian National Archives, Windhoek

*New Zealand*
National Archives, Wellington

*United Kingdom*
The National Archives, London

*United States*
The National Archives, College Park, Maryland

### LEAGUE OF NATIONS RECORDS

League of Nations Archives, Geneva
League of Nations Documents, 1919–46 (microform collection), New Haven: Research Publications, 1973–75
League of Nations Permanent Mandates Commission, Minutes and Reports
Annual Reports to the League of Nations on the administration of the different mandated territories (these are cited by territory and date alone)

### ARCHIVES OF INDIVIDUALS AND ORGANIZATIONS

Leo Amery Papers, Churchill Archives Centre, Cambridge
Anti-Slavery and Aborigines' Protection Society Archives, Rhodes House, Oxford
George Louis Beer diary, Library of Congress, Washington DC
Brogyntyn Estate Records (William Ormsby-Gore Papers), National Library of Wales
Raymond Leslie Buell Papers, Library of Congress, Washington DC
Robert Cecil Papers, British Library
Huntington Gilchrist Papers, Library of Congress, Washington DC
Nahum Goldmann Papers, Central Zionist Archive, Jerusalem
Maurice Hankey Papers, Churchill Archives Centre, Cambridge
League of Nations Union Archives, British Library of Political and Economic Science
Frederick Lugard Papers, Rhodes House, Oxford
Alfred Milner Papers, Bodleian Library, Oxford
Gilbert Murray Papers, Bodleian Library, Oxford
Philip Noel-Baker Papers, Churchill Archives Centre, Cambridge
Pierre Orts Papers, Archives Générales du Royaume, Brussels
Margery Perham Papers, Rhodes House, Oxford
William Rappard Papers, Swiss Federal Archives, Bern
Heinrich Schnee Papers, Geheimes Staatsarchiv Preussischer Kulturbesitz, Berlin
Arnold Toynbee Papers, Bodleian Library, Oxford
World Zionist Organization/Jewish Agency for Palestine Archives, Central Zionist Archives, Jerusalem
Quincy Wright Papers, University of Chicago Library

### PRINTED GOVERNMENT DOCUMENTS

British Documents on Foreign Affairs
Débats et Documents Parlementaires (France)

Documents Diplomatiques Françaises
Documents on British Foreign Policy
Documents on German Foreign Policy
Foreign Relations of the United States
House of Commons Debates (UK)
House of Lords Debates (UK)
Parliamentary Papers (UK)
Verhandlungen des Reichstages (Germany)

## SELECTED PERIODICALS

*L'Afrique Française*
*Allgemeine Zeitung* (Windhoek)
*American Journal of International Law*
*Anti-Slavery Reporter and Aborigines' Friend*
*L'Asie Française*
*Foreign Affairs* (UK)
*Headway*
*The International* (Johannesburg)
*Journal de Genève*
*Journal Officiel*
*Koloniale Rundschau*
*League of Nations Official Journal*
*Manchester Guardian*
*Pacific Islands Monthly*
*Pacific Magazine*
*Political Science Quarterly*
*Rabaul Times*
*Round Table*
*Samoa Guardian*
*The Scotsman*
*Today and Tomorrow*
*Le Temps*
*The Times* (London)
*Windhoek Advertiser*

# Notes

ABBREVIATIONS

| | |
|---|---|
| AA | Archives Africaines (Brussels) |
| ANA | Australian National Archives (Canberra) |
| ANOM | Archives Nationales d'Outre-Mer (Aix-en-Provence) |
| ANZ | Archives New Zealand (Wellington) |
| ASAPS | Anti-Slavery and Aborigines' Protection Society Archives (Rhodes House, Oxford) |
| *ASRAF* | *Anti-Slavery Reporter and Aborigines' Friend* |
| *BDFA* | *British Documents on Foreign Affairs* |
| BL | British Library |
| BLPES | British Library of Political and Economic Science (London) |
| CAC | Churchill Archives Centre (Cambridge) |
| CZA | Central Zionist Archive (Jerusalem) |
| *DBFP* | *Documents on British Foreign Policy* |
| *DGFP* | *Documents on German Foreign Policy* |
| *FRUS* | *Foreign Relations of the United States* |
| GStA PK | Geheimes Staatsarchiv Preußischer Kulturbesitz |
| *H.C. Deb.* | *House of Commons Debates* (UK) |
| *H.L. Deb.* | *House of Lords Debates* (UK) |
| *J.O.* | *Journal Officiel* (France) |
| LC | Library of Congress (Washington) |
| LNA | League of Nations Archives (Geneva) |
| LNDM | League of Nations Documents, 1919–46: microform collection |
| *LNOJ* | *League of Nations Official Journal* |
| LNU | League of Nations Union |
| *LPCW* | *Letters and Papers of Chaim Weizmann* |
| MAE | Archives of the Ministère des Affaires Etrangères (Paris) |
| NA | National Archives (London) |

NAN        Namibian National Archives (Windhoek)
PA         Politisches Archiv des Auswärtigen Amts (German Foreign Ministry
           Archives) (Berlin)
PMC        Permanent Mandates Commission/Commission permanente des
           mandats
*PMCM*       *Minutes of the Permanent Mandates Commission*★
QW         Quincy Wright Papers, Department of Special Collections,
           Regenstein Library, University of Chicago
RH         Bodleian Library of Commonwealth and African Studies at Rhodes
           House (Oxford)
SFA        Swiss Federal Archives (Bern)
USNA       United States National Archives (College Park)

★ The PMC's published *Minutes* are the major source for the Commission's work
and include somewhat sanitized minutes of the discussions, some petitions and
reports on petitions, special reports by the Commission on subjects of interest, the
Commission's official observations on the various territories, and its Report to the
Council. The Minutes are cited in the notes by session number and page number
only (e.g. 4 *PMCM*, 43–4). The complete list of sessions and their dates is as
follows:

1st: 4–9 October 1921
2nd: 1–11 August 1922
3rd: 20 July–10 August 1923
4th: 24 June–8 July 1924
5th: 23 October–6 November 1924
6th: 26 June–10 July 1925
7th: 19–30 October 1925
8th: 16 February–6 March 1926 (extraordinary, Rome)
9th: 8–25 June 1926
10th: 4–19 November 1926
11th: 20 June–6 July 1927
12th: 24 October–11 November 1927
13th: 12–29 June 1928
14th: 26 October–13 November 1928
15th: 1–19 July 1929
16th: 6–26 November 1929
17th: 3–21 June 1930 (extraordinary)
18th: 18 June–1 July 1930
19th: 4–19 November 1930
20th: 2–27 June 1931

21st: 26 October–13 November 1931
22nd: 3 November–6 December 1932
23rd: 19 June–1 July 1933
24th: 23 October–4 November 1933
25th: 30 May–12 June 1934
26th: 29 October–12 November 1934
27th: 3–18 June 1935
28th: 17 October–2 November 1935
29th: 27 May–12 June 1936
30th: 27 October–11 November 1936
31st: 31 May–15 June 1937
32nd: 30 July–18 August 1937 (extraordinary)
33rd: 8–19 November 1937
34th: 8–23 June 1938
35th: 24 October–8 November 1938
36th: 8–29 June 1939
37th: 12–21 December 1939

## NOTES FOR THE INTRODUCTION

1. 1 *PMCM*, 2–6.
2. Du Bois was delivering the resolutions of the second Pan-African Congress. For those resolutions, which Secretary General Sir Eric Drummond circulated to the Council, and Rappard's meeting, see LNA, R39, 1/15865/13940 and 15866/13940; for the Congress, see David Levering Lewis, *W. E. B. Du Bois: The Fight for Equality and the American Century, 1919–1963* (New York: Henry Holt, 2000), 37–50.
3. LNA, R21, 1/14993/4284, Rappard memo, 24 Aug. 1921.
4. 1 *PMCM*, 2–6.
5. Some of the earliest and most insightful scholars of the mandates regime concluded that, on balance, the system operated to spread colonial 'best practices'; see, e.g., Quincy Wright, *Mandates under the League of Nations* (1930; New York: Greenwood Press, 1968); Raymond Leslie Buell, *The Native Problem in Africa*, 2 vols. (New York: Macmillan, 1928); Ralph J. Bunche, 'French Administration in Togoland and Dahomey', Dissertation, Harvard University, 1934; Rayford Logan, 'The Operation of the Mandates System in Africa', *The Journal of Negro History*, 13:4 (Oct. 1928), 423–77. Works by recent scholars coming to a similar conclusion include Neta Crawford, *Argument and Change in World Politics: Ethics, Decolonization and Humanitarian Intervention* (Cambridge: Cambridge University Press, 2002); Michael D. Callahan, *Mandates and Empire: The League of Nations and Africa, 1914–1931* (Brighton: Sussex Academic Press, 1999), and *A Sacred Trust: The League of Nations and Africa, 1929–1946* (Brighton: Sussex Academic Press, 2004).

Yet, when mandate administration is compared systematically to colonial admin-istration, such claims become harder to sustain. The former League official H. Duncan Hall, in a study written for the founding conference of the United Nations, pointed out that only in two cases—those of New Zealand's mandate in Western Samoa (which could be compared to American Samoa) and of Australia's mandate in German New Guinea (which could be compared to Australia's neighbouring colony of Papua)—was comparison really suitable, and in neither of these two cases was the mandatory administration more pro-gressive. See H. Duncan Hall, *Mandates, Dependencies and Trusteeship* (Washington: Carnegie Endowment for International Peace, 1948), 59–62. The anachronistic argument that the mandates system safeguarded 'human rights' (a term not used at the time) is found in Paul Gordon Lauren, *The Evolution of International Human Rights: Visions Seen* (Philadelphia: University of Pennsylvania Press, 1998), 117–18; it is not persuasive.

6. CAC, NBKR 4/444, Baker to Drummond, 6 June 1921.
7. We are in the midst of a great revival of scholarly interest in the League. The proliferation of new work is too large to cite here, but for a recent (yet already outdated) summary, see my 'Back to the League of Nations', *American Historical Review*, 112:4 (Oct. 2007), 1091–117. Notable contributions since that date include Mark Mazower, *Governing the World: The History of an Idea* (New York: Penguin, 2012); Mark Mazower, *No Enchanted Palace: The End of Empire and the Ideological Origins of the United Nations* (Princeton: Princeton University Press, 2009); Glenda Sluga, *Internationalism in the Age of Nationalism* (Philadelphia: University of Pennsylvania Press, 2013); Patricia Clavin, *Securing the World Economy: The Reinvention of the League of Nations, 1920–1946* (Oxford: Oxford University Press, 2013); Isabella Löhr and Roland Wenzlhuemer, *The Nation State and Beyond: Governing Globalization Processes in the Nineteenth and Early Twentieth Centuries* (Heidelberg: Springer, 2013).
8. There is a considerable literature on the relationship of various states to the League; among these, Joachim Wintzer's recent study of the German Foreign Ministry's policies towards Geneva in the early 1920s, Christoph Kimmich's account of Germany's League relations, and Thomas Burkman's recent study of Japan's place in the League, are especially useful; see Joachim Wintzer, *Deutschland und der Völkerbund, 1918–1926* (Paderborn: Ferdinand Schöningh Verlag, 2006); Christoph Kimmich, *Germany and the League of Nations* (Chicago: University of Chicago Press, 1976); and Thomas W. Burkman, *Japan and the League of Nations: Empire and World Order, 1914–1938* (Honolulu: University of Hawaii Press, 2008). Scholars have also begun to grasp the crucial role the Americans played within the League, not only through official participation on some 'technical' bodies and at moments of crisis, but also through extensive contacts between American and European internationalists and voluntary organizations, through the pres-ence of Americans in the Secretariat, and through American foundations like

Carnegie and Rockefeller which allocated considerable resources to various League bodies and projects. Amid a growing literature, see especially Warren F. Kuehl and Lynne K. Dunn, *Keeping the Covenant: American Internationalists and the League of Nations, 1920–1939* (Kent, OH: Kent State University Press, 1997); Patrick Cohrs, *The Unfinished Peace after World War I: America, Britain, and the Stabilisation of Europe, 1919–1932* (Cambridge: Cambridge University Press, 2006); Katharina Rietzler, 'Experts for Peace: Structures and Motivations of Philanthropic Internationalism in the Interwar Years', in *Internationalism Reconfigured: Transnational Ideas and Movements between the Wars*, ed. Daniel Laqua (London: I. B. Tauris, 2011), 45–65.

9. Alois Derso and Emery Kelen, *Le Testament de Genève: 10 années de coopération internationale* (Paris: Georges Lang, 1931), vividly depicts the League's leading personalities and culture, and for a brilliant record of the entire Geneva world (the speeches at the Assembly, the journalists outside the door, Stresemann drinking with friends), see Janos Frecot, ed., *Erich Salomon 'Mit Frack und Linse durch Politik und Gesellschaft': Photographien 1928–1938* (Halle, Leipzig, and Passau: Schirmer/Mosel, 2004). Haile Selassie's speech to the League in 1936 is now readily available online.

10. Leo Amery, *My Political Life*, vol. 2, *War and Peace, 1914–29* (London: Hutchinson, 1953), 332.

11. For the Assembly and its powers, see Margaret E. Burton, *The Assembly of the League of Nations* (University of Chicago Press, 1941; rpt. NY: Howard Fertig, 1974).

12. See BL, Add MS 51110 and 51112, for Drummond's correspondence with Cecil about the requests of various states for seats and Secretariat positions. Observers at the time were also alert to the way the expansion of the Council lent its deliberations—as Rappard put it—'a character of unreality and insincerity'. See William E. Rappard, *The Geneva Experiment* (London: Oxford University Press, 1931), here quoted 48–9; also C. Howard-Ellis [Konni Zilliacus], *The Origin, Structure and Working of the League of Nations* (Boston: Houghton Mifflin, 1929), 139–59.

13. A new history of the League Secretariat is much needed, especially now that the personnel files are all open. Still authoritative for the present is Egon F. Ranshofen-Wertheimer, *The International Secretariat: A Great Experiment in International Administration* (Washington: Carnegie Endowment for International Peace, 1945); this is particularly good on the problem of spying. The ethos of the Secretariat is, however, probably best captured by the novels of Frank Moorhouse, who researched them in the League archives and incorporated many historical figures into the texts, and by Salvador de Madariaga's wonderful memoirs *Morning without Noon* (Farnsworth, England: Saxon House, 1974). See Frank Moorhouse, *Grand Days* (Sydney: Pan Macmillan, 1993), and *Dark Palace* (New York: Knopf, 2000), and Mary Kinnear's recent biography of Mary McGeachy, on whom Moorhouse modelled his main character, *Woman of the*

*World: Mary McGeachy and International Cooperation* (Toronto: University of Toronto Press, 2004). For the French staff at the League, see Christine Manigand, *Les Français au service de la Société des Nations* (Bern: Peter Lang, 2003). Elisabetta Tollardo is completing a dissertation at Oxford on Italians in the League Secretariat.

14. For that 'League around the League' see esp. Emery Kelen, *Peace in their Time: Men Who Led Us In and Out of War, 1914–1945* (New York: Alfred A. Knopf, 1963), 178–201, and Andrew Arsan, Su Lin Lewis, and Anne-Isabelle Richard, 'The Roots of Global Civil Society and the Interwar Moment', *Journal of Global History*, 7:2 (2012), 157–65.

15. CAC, HNKY 1/5, diary entry 29 Dec. 1920.

16. CAC, HNKY, 1/5, diary entry 21 Oct. 1922.

17. The management of the conference is thoroughly canvassed in Carole Fink, *The Genoa Conference: European Diplomacy, 1921–1922* (Chapel Hill: University of North Carolina Press, 1984).

18. A comprehensive history of the Federation of League of Nations Societies, which met annually and provided a vehicle for much civil society lobbying, remains to be written; the best beginning is Anne-Isabelle Richard, 'Competition and Complementarity: Civil Society Networks and the Question of Decentralizing the League of Nations', *Journal of Global History*, 7:2 (2012), 233–56, and for the influential and enormous British League of Nations Unions, Helen McCarthy, *The British People and the League of Nations: Democracy, Citizenship and Internationalism, c. 1918–45* (Manchester: Manchester University Press, 2011).

19. William E. Rappard, *International Relations as Viewed from Geneva* (1925; rpt. New Haven: Yale University Press, 1975).

20. Understandably, most early accounts concentrated largely on the 'collective security' narrative, the classic critical account being of course E. H. Carr, *The Twenty-Year Crisis, 1919–1939: An Introduction to the Study of International Relations* (London: Macmillan, 1940). The former Deputy Secretary General Francis P. Walters authored the classic defence, *A History of the League of Nations* (Oxford: Oxford University Press, 1952); for a balanced and reliable assessment, see F. S. Northedge, *The League of Nations: Its Life and Times* (Leicester: Leicester University Press, 1986). James Barros also published over several decades fine studies of the secretary-generalships of Drummond and his successor Joseph Avenol as well as of the various international crises handled by the League in the 1920s. Among an extensive recent literature on the effort to strengthen legal sanctions against war and to reduce armaments, see Lorna Lloyd, *Peace through Law: Britain and the International Court in the 1920s* (London: Royal Historical Society, 1997), and Andrew Webster, 'The Transnational Dream: Politicians, Diplomats and Soldiers in the League of Nations' Pursuit of International Disarmament, 1920–1938', *Central European History*, 14:4 (Nov. 2005), 493–518.

21. See David Mitrany, *A Working Peace System: An Argument for the Functional Development of International Organization* (New York: Oxford University Press, 1944).

22. For two important early articles on the steady expansion of this side of the League, see Martin David Dubin, 'Transgovernmental Processes in the League of Nations', *International Organization*, 37:3 (1983), 469–93, and 'Towards the Bruce Report: The Economic and Social Programmes of the League of Nations in the Avenol Era', in *The League of Nations in Retrospect* (Berlin: W. de Gruyter, 1983), 42–72. Amid recent work, Patricia Clavin's pathbreaking account of the Economic and Financial Section, *Securing the World Economy*, stands out. For the tip of a deepening iceberg, see also Iris Borowy, *Coming to Terms with World Health: The League of Nations Health Organisation, 1921–1946* (Frankfurt: Peter Lang, 2006); Barbara H. M. Metzger, 'Towards an International Human Rights Regime during the Inter-War Years: The League of Nations' Combat of Traffic in Women and Children', and Kevin Grant, 'Human Rights and Sovereign Abolitions of Slavery, c. 1885–1950', both in *Beyond Sovereignty: Britain, Empire and Transnationalism, c. 1880–1950*, ed. Kevin Grant, Philippa Levine, and Frank Trentmann (London: Palgrave Macmillan, 2007), 54–79 and 80–102; Claudena M. Skran, *Refugees in Inter-War Europe: The Emergence of a Regime* (Oxford: Clarendon Press, 1995); and Carol Miller, 'The Social Section and Advisory Committee on Social Questions of the League of Nations', in *International Health Organizations and Movements*, ed. Paul Weindling (Cambridge: Cambridge University Press, 1995), 154–76.

23. There is a very substantial literature on the minorities protection regime, as well as on its impact on particular states and ethnic groups, but for a good recent account see Carole Fink, *Defending the Rights of Others: The Great Powers, the Jews, and International Minority Protection, 1878–1938* (Cambridge: Cambridge University Press, 2004).

24. The only comprehensive accounts of the mandates system in English, both very dated but still impressive and useful, are the previously cited accounts by the Chicago law professor Quincy Wright, *Mandates Under the League of Nations*, and by H. Duncan Hall, *Mandates, Dependencies and Trusteeship*. Relatively few works were published on the mandates system in the period of decolonization, especially important exceptions being Wm. Roger Louis's crucial articles, now collected in his *Ends of British Imperialism: The Scramble for Empire, Suez and Decolonization* (London: I. B. Tauris, 2006), and Ralph A. Austen, 'Varieties of Trusteeship: African Territories under British and French Mandate, 1919–1939', in Prosser Gifford and Wm. Roger Louis, eds., *France and Britain in Africa* (New Haven: Yale University Press, 1971), 515–42. A landmark publication for the Middle East mandates was the conference volume edited by Nadine Méouchy and Peter Sluglett, *British and French Mandates in Comparative Perspective* (Leiden: Brill, 2004), and for the British and French 'B' mandates, the two-volume study by Michael D. Callahan,

*Mandates and Empire: The League of Nations and Africa, 1914–1931* (Brighton: Sussex Academic Press, 1999), and *A Sacred Trust: The League of Nations And Africa, 1929–1946* (Brighton: Sussex Academic Press, 2004). An important recent study placing the mandates system within the context of imperialism and international law is Antony Anghie, *Imperialism, Sovereignty and the Making of International Law* (Cambridge: Cambridge University Press, 2004). Many studies of the system's operation in individual territories are cited throughout this work.

### NOTES FOR CHAPTER 1

1. Bodleian, MSS Milner 46, 'Extract from a letter written by Lord Milner of August 14th, 1919'.
2. LC, MSS 4954, Diary of George Louis Beer, entry for 10 Aug. 1919, 131.
3. Quoted in H. A. Byatt, Administrator, to the Secretary of State for the Colonies, 22 March 1918, in *Correspondence Relating to the Wishes of the Natives of the German Colonies and to their Future Government*, PP 1918, Cd. 9210, 25.
4. Beer diary, 9 and 10 Dec. 1919. For Beer's role at the peace conference, see Wm. Roger Louis, 'The United States and the African Peace Settlement of 1919: The Pilgrimage of George Louis Beer', *The Journal of African History*, 4:3 (1963), 413–33.
5. Beer diary, 3 June 1919.
6. George Louis Beer, *African Questions at the Paris Peace Conference* (London: Dawsons of Pall Mall, 1968), 179.
7. Beer diary, 16 March 1919, 41.
8. Beer, *African Questions*, 182.
9. On the Japanese Navy's central and independent role in the islands' conquest, see J. Charles Schencking, 'Bureaucratic Politics, Military Budgets and Japan's Southern Advance: The Imperial Navy's Seizure of German Micronesia in the First World War', *War in History*, 5:3 (1998), 308–26. For Western Samoa, Mary Boyd, 'The Military Administration of Western Samoa, 1914–1919', *The New Zealand Journal of History*, 2:2 (Oct. 1968), 148–64.
10. NA, Cab. 16/36, Committee of Imperial Defence, Committee on Territorial Changes, 'Brief Summary of Colonial Campaigns in the Present War', March 1917; and for the full story, Hew Strachan, *The First World War in Africa* (Oxford: Oxford University Press, 2004). Accounts of wholesale rape by soldiers under Belgian command made their way to London, for which see Bodleian, Milner 46, 'Belgian Administration of East Africa', Secret [1916].
11. NA, Cab. 16/36, Committee of Imperial Defence, Sub-Committee on Territorial Changes, esp. Memorandum 4, 'Note by the General Staff as to the Policy to be Pursued in Regard to the German Colonies' (8 Sept. 1916), and for a discussion of the Committee's work, Wm. Roger Louis, *Great Britain and Germany's Lost Colonies, 1914–1919* (Oxford: Clarendon Press, 1967), 70–4; NA,

Cab. 21/77, Minutes of the Imperial War Cabinet Committee on Terms of Peace (Territorial Desiderata), and 'Report' (28 April 1917).

12. Records of those unofficial discussions can be found in the Archives Générales du Royaume, Brussels, Orts Family Papers, file 433, and for the ever more ambitious and unrealistic war aims in Africa of the French colonial lobby see C. M. Andrew and A. S. Kanya-Forstner, 'France, Africa, and the First World War', *The Journal of African History*, 19:1 (1978), 11–23.

13. For Italian claims, see René Albrecht-Carrié, 'Italian Colonial Policy, 1914–1918', *The Journal of Modern History*, 18:2 (June 1946), 123–47.

14. For the disastrous Mesopotamia campaign, see Charles Townshend, *Desert Hell: The British Invasion of Mesopotamia* (Cambridge, MA: Harvard University Press, 2011).

15. There is an enormous historiography detailing the wartime Anglo-Arab relations and negotiations. Three relatively good recent synthetic accounts are Jonathan Schneer, *The Balfour Declaration: The Origins of the Arab-Israeli Conflict* (New York: Random House, 2010), David Fromkin, *Peace to End All Peace: The Fall of the Ottoman Empire and the Creation of the Modern Middle East* (New York: Henry Holt, 2001), and D. K. Fieldhouse, *Western Imperialism in the Middle East, 1914–1958* (Oxford: Oxford University Press, 2006). But older accounts by participant observers are still valuable, notably George Antonius, *The Arab Awakening: The Story of the Arab National Movement* (London: Hamish Hamilton, 1938), and Stephen H. Longrigg, *Syria and Lebanon under French Mandate* (Oxford: Oxford University Press, 1958). Most useful of all are perhaps the close studies of individual mandates, cited below.

16. Meir Zamir, *The Formation of Modern Lebanon* (Ithaca and New York: Cornell University Press, 1985), esp. 38–45.

17. 'Arrangement of May 1916, commonly known as the Sykes-Picot agreement', in *BDFA*, pt. II, ser. I, vol. 11, 26–7; and for a detailed account of Anglo-French negotiations, Christopher M. Andrew and A. S. Kanya-Forstner, *France Overseas: The Great War and the Climax of French Imperial Expansion* (London: Thames and Hudson, 1981), 87–102.

18. Few agreements have been more exhaustively written about than the Balfour declaration, and this study cannot revisit that debate. For a good and responsible account based on the latest research, see Schneer, *The Balfour Declaration*.

19. Erez Manela has written an influential account of the 'Wilsonian moment' in the non-Western world—*The Wilsonian Moment: Self-Determination and the International Origins of Anticolonial Nationalism* (Oxford: Oxford University Press, 2007)—but it is clear that that 'moment' was echoed not only in the Asian and Middle Eastern countries he investigates but in the occupied African and Pacific territories as well.

20. Whole library shelves groan under the weight of books written on the founding of the League of Nations. Two reliable standard accounts of Wilson's role are

Thomas J. Knock, *To End All Wars: Woodrow Wilson and the Quest for a New World Order* (Princeton, NJ: Princeton University Press, 1992), and John Milton Cooper, *Breaking the Heart of the World: Woodrow Wilson and the Fight for the League of Nations* (Cambridge: Cambridge University Press, 2001). The process has been traced from the British side in George W. Egerton, *Great Britain and the Creation of the League of Nations* (Chapel Hill: University of North Carolina Press, 1978), and most thoroughly and with particular attention to the key role of Lord Robert Cecil, in Peter Yearwood, *Guarantee of Peace: The League of Nations in British Policy, 1914–1925* (Oxford: Oxford University Press, 2009). Mark Mazower has recently delineated the specific American and British contributions to the League projects in *Governing the World: The History of an Idea* (New York: Penguin, 2012), esp. 116–41, and with particular attention to the role of Jan Christiaan Smuts, in *No Enchanted Palace: The End of Empire and the Ideological Origins of the United Nations* (Princeton: Princeton University Press, 2009). This is merely the tip of a mountain of scholarship, including much from the 1920s and 1930s that is still well worth reading by such scholars as Thomas Parker Moon, Pitman Potter, James Shotwell, Quincy Wright, and others.

21. 'Native Races and Peace Terms', *ASRAF*, V, 6:2 (July 1916), 34–5.
22. 'Conference on the Future of German Colonies', *ASRAF*, V, 7:3 (Oct. 1917), 50–9, and 7:4 (Jan. 1918), 89–95; and 'The German Colonies and International Control', *ASRAF*, V, 8:1 (April 1918), 1–4. For the influence of the anti-slavery lobby on the formation of the mandates regime, see esp. Kevin Grant, *A Civilized Savagery: Britain and the New Slaveries in Africa, 1884–1926* (New York: Routledge, 2005), ch. 5.
23. For that genealogy, see esp. William Bain, *Between Anarchy and Society: Trusteeship and the Obligations of Power* (Oxford: Oxford University Press, 2003), and Kevin Grant, 'Trust and Self-Determination: Anglo-American Ethics of Empire and International Government', in *Critiques of Capital in Modern Britain and America: Transatlantic Exchanges*, ed. Mark Bevir and Frank Trentmann (London: Palgrave, 2002), 151–73.
24. 'Mr Lloyd George and the Peace Terms', *The Manchester Guardian*, 30 June 1917, 5.
25. 'The Premier and War Aims', *The Observer*, 6 Jan. 1918, 7.
26. NA, FO 608/215/955, Comment by Spicer, 29 Jan. 1919. For those testimonials, see *Correspondence Relating to the Wishes of the Natives of the German Colonies as to their Future Government*, PP 1918, Cd. 9210.
27. Bodleian, Milner 46, Milner to Lloyd George, 16 May 1919.
28. National Library of Wales, Brogyntyn manuscripts, PEC 10/1/10, Ormsby-Gore to his mother, 12 June 1916.
29. National Library of Wales, Brogyntyn manuscripts, PEC 11/1, Ormsby-Gore, note, n.d.
30. National Library of Wales, Brogyntyn manuscripts, PEC 10/1/11, Ormsby-Gore to his mother, 2 Feb. 1918.

31. Curzon, in Eastern Committee Minutes, 5 Dec. 1918, Secret, Milner Papers, quoted in Wm. Roger Louis, 'The Repartition of Africa during the First World War', in *Ends of British Imperialism: The Scramble for Empire, Suez and Decolonization* (London: I. B. Tauris, 2006), 205.

32. A great deal has been written on the emergence of the mandates plan. Among the most authoritative treatments are: Wm. Roger Louis, 'The United Kingdom and the Beginning of the Mandates System, 1919–1922', *International Organization*, 23:1 (1969), 73–96 (this essay, and Louis's other pathbreaking works on the regime's founding, have been collected in *Ends of British Imperialism*, chs. 6–10); Michael D. Callahan, *Mandates and Empire: The League of Nations and Africa, 1914–1931* (Brighton: Sussex Academic Press, 1999); Andrew J. Crozier, 'The Establishment of the Mandates System, 1919–25: Some Problems Created by the Paris Peace Conference', *Journal of Contemporary History*, 14:3 (July 1979), 483–513.

33. J. C. Smuts, *The League of Nations: A Practical Suggestion* (New York: The Nation Press, 1919), 12.

34. LNA, R13, 1/2372/2372, G. S. Spicer (Foreign Office), 'Some of the principal points concerning Africa to be dealt with at the Peace Conference', 17 Jan. 1919; and NA, FO 608/240/1408, 'Minutes of a Meeting held in Lord Robert Cecil's Room on Jan. 20, 1919'.

35. Andrew and Kanya-Forstner, *France Overseas*, 170–2.

36. Beer diary, 15 Jan. 1919.

37. Andrew and Kanya-Forstner, *France Overseas*, 180–2.

38. Beer diary, 18 March 1919.

39. *BDFA*, pt. II, ser. I, vol. 2, Supreme Council Minutes, 24 Jan. 1919, 9–15; 27 Jan. 1919, 19–29; 28 Jan. 1919, 29–42, Simon at 36–7, Wilson at 38.

40. *BDFA*, pt. II, ser. I, vol. 3, British Empire Delegation, Minutes, 27 Jan. 1919, 338–41, and 28 Jan. 1919, 342–4.

41. *BDFA*, pt. II, ser. I, vol. 2, Supreme Council Minutes, 30 Jan. 1919, 51–68, draft resolutions at 56, Lloyd George's statement at 61.

42. NA, FO 608/219/919, note by Sir Charles Strachey, 29 Jan. 1919; and Travers Buxton, Honorary Secretary, Anti-Slavery Society, to Balfour, 14 Feb. 1919, enclosing ASS to delegations of France, Italy, United States, Belgium, and Portugal.

43. David Levering Lewis, *W. E. B. Du Bois: Biography of a Race, 1869–1919* (New York: Henry Holt, 1993), 574–8.

44. Duala appeals are mentioned in Richard Joseph, 'The Royal Pretender: Prince Douala Manga Bell in Paris, 1919–1922', *Cahiers d'Etudes Africaines*, 14:54 (1974), 339–58. A Samoan petition in January 1919 to have the mandate granted to the United States rather than New Zealand is discussed in Mary Boyd, 'The Military Administration of Western Samoa, 1914–1919', *New Zealand Journal of History*, 2: 2 (Oct. 1968), pp. 148–64. Rehoboth appeals for autonomy within South West Africa were sent to Milner by Theo Schreiner, 14 Feb. 1919, and

ignored (see Bodleian, MSS Eng. Hist. C. 702), and for petitions to the Peace
Conference about Togo, see esp. Octaviano Olympio to Colonial Secretary
telegram, FO 608/216/6643. Arab, Kurdish, and Armenian petitions were
flooding the conference too.

45. Bodleian, MSS Eng. Hist. C. 700, Milner to Massey, 30 Jan. 1919. Lloyd George,
concerned about the impact the Dominions' discontent might have on Milner,
had Philip Kerr write to him in confidence to point out that Wilson had
wanted all territories placed under direct League control with no naming of
mandatories at all, and that the decision to accept mandates for the Dominions
secured those territories and also enabled Britain to prevent the Japanese from
annexing the northern islands. See Bodleian, MSS Eng. Hist. C. 700, Philip
Kerr to Milner, 31 Jan. 1919.

46. Bodleian, MSS Milner 389, W.C.P. 211, 'Mandates. Memorandum by Lord
Milner' (8 March 1919). Leo Amery, who was Milner's under-secretary at the
Colonial Office, reiterated the point about sovereignty resting with the manda-
tory power (in view of the local population's incapacity) subject only to 'certain
servitudes', in Bodleian MSS Milner 46, Amery to Philip Kerr, 14 March 1919.
Note, by contrast, that the Anti-Slavery Society's draft mandate allowed for the
territory to be reassigned if the mandatory power abused its position. See
Bodleian, Milner 390, Anti-Slavery Society, 'Memorandum on the Colonial
Mandates for the Late German Colonies', n.d.

47. NA, FO 608/215, Memo by Strachey, 7 March 1919.

48. Bodleian, Milner 46, WCP 745, Hankey, 'Mandates. Note for the British Empire
Delegation' (7 May 1919).

49. For these meetings, Bodleian, Milner 46, Colonial Committee meetings of 15,
19, and 28 May 1919, and Milner 389, Milner, '"Equitable Compensation" for
Italy in Africa', 30 May 1919.

50. For the strong opposition from many quarters to ceding Rwanda and Burundi
to Belgium, see NA FO 608/216; also Bodleian, Milner 389, Amery to Milner,
27 Feb. 1919. The very complex negotiations between Milner and Orts, through
which Belgium initially tried to barter its position in East Africa for Portuguese
territory at the mouth of the Congo, are thoroughly explained in Wm. Roger
Louis, *Ruanda-Urundi, 1884–1919* (Oxford: Clarendon Press, 1963). Orts' records
of those transactions are in Archives Générales du Royaume, Brussels, Orts
Family Papers, File. 434; and for Milner's summary of those negotiations, see
Bodleian, Milner 389, Milner, 'Memorandum. Negotiations with Belgium
about German East Africa'.

51. Bodleian, Milner 389, Milner, 'Memorandum. Cameroons and Togoland' (29
May 1919).

52. Bodleian, Milner 46, Milner to Simon, 29 May 1919.

53. Christoph Kimmich, *Germany and the League of Nations* (Chicago: University of
Chicago Press, 1976), 20–1.

54. 'Observation of the German Delegation on the Conditions of Peace', 29 March 1919, *BDFA*, pt. II, ser. I, vol. 7, 298–349, here at 324.
55. 'Reply of the Allied and Associated Powers to the Observations of the German Delegation on the Conditions of Peace', 16 June 1919, *BDFA*, pt. II, ser. I, vol. 7, 374–80, here at 378.
56. The complete minutes of the Commission can be found in LNA, R1, 1/2366/52; another copy is in NA, FO 608/152/15892.
57. LNA, R1, 1/2366/52, Commission on Mandates, Minutes, 8 July 1919.
58. LNA R1/771/161, Sir Cecil Hurst, legal advisor to the Foreign Office, to Balfour, 20 July 1919.
59. LNA, R1/563/52, Simon to Milner, 1 Aug. 1919.
60. LNA, R1/1223/161, Milner to Dutasta, 6 Aug. 1919.
61. NA, FO 608/152/17580, Milner to Balfour, 8 Aug. 1919.
62. Milner to Lloyd George, 8 March 1919, quoted in John Fisher, 'Syria and Mesopotamia in British Middle Eastern Policy in 1919', *Middle Eastern Studies*, 34:2 (April 1998), 129–70, here at 144.
63. Bodleian, Milner 390, Cecil to Milner, 11 July 1919; and see NA, FO 608/152/17578, Drummond to Balfour, 7 Aug. 1919; LNA, R1, 1266/161, Drummond to Milner, 23 Sept. 1919, and Milner to Drummond, 25 Sept. 1919.
64. LNA, R13, 1/1970/1970, Milner to Cecil, 2 Nov. 1919 (copy).
65. The many American supporters of the League were embarrassed by, and sharply critical of, that American obstructionism. For one such critique, see Quincy Wright, 'The United States and the Mandates', *Michigan Law Review*, 23:7 (May 1925), 717–47. The fierce and protracted conflict between the Japanese and the USA over possession of Yap (which the Japanese insisted had been granted them as part of their mandate and for which Wilson insisted he had secured an exception) cannot be detailed here, but see Sumitra Rattan, 'The Yap Controversy and its Significance', *The Journal of Pacific History*, 7 (1972), 124–36.
66. *DBFP 1919–1939*, ser. 1, vol. 8, 169.
67. Sokolow and Weizmann to Zionist Bureau London, 27 April 1920, in *The Letters and Papers of Chaim Weizmann* (henceforth *LPCW*), vol. 9, ed. Jehuda Reinharz (New Brunswick, NJ, 1977), p. 342. For the San Remo discussions more generally, see Tom Segev, *One Palestine, Complete: Jews and Arabs under the British Mandate* (New York: Metropolitan Books, 2000), pp. 142–4, and for Curzon's reluctant acquiescence, David Gilmour, 'The Unregarded Prophet: Lord Curzon and the Palestine Question', *Journal of Palestine Studies*, 25:3 (Spring 1996), 60–8.
68. MAE, SDN 564, Gouraud to MAE, 26 Jan. 1920.
69. For this history, see Zamir, *Formation*, and Zamir, 'Faisal and the Lebanese Question, 1918–20', *Middle Eastern Studies*, 27:3 (July 1991), 404–26; and Kais M. Firro, *Inventing Lebanon: Nationalism and the State under the Mandate* (London: I. B. Tauris, 2003).

70. The King-Crane report was finally published (and made its way to the League) in 1922:'King-Crane Report on the Near East', *Editor & Publisher*, 55:27 (2 Dec. 1922). But while it was suppressed and did not affect the peace settlement, the Commission—like so many League of Nations activities—helped foster and channel rival Syrian nationalisms, for which see James L. Gelvin, *Divided Loyalties: Nationalism and Mass Politics in Syria at the Close of Empire* (Berkeley: University of California Press, 1998).

71. Zamir, *Formation*, 55–7.

72. Andrew and Kanya-Forstner, *France Overseas*, 203–4.

73. Andrew and Kanya-Forstner, *France Overseas*, 204.

74. Andrew and Kanya-Forstner, *France Overseas*, 216.

75. Allenby to Curzon, 13 May 1920, *DBFP*, ser. 1, vol. 13, 257.

76. MAE, SDN 564, Gouraud to MAE, 17 March 1920. For a detailed but analytically unsophisticated account of the conflict between Faysal and the French, see Dan Eldar,'France in Syria: The Abolition of the Sharifian Government, April–July 1920', *Middle Eastern Studies*, 29:3 (July 1993), 487–503.

77. Faysal to Curzon, 5 June 1920, contained in Allenby to Curzon, 19 June 1920, in *DBFP*, ser. 1, vol. 13, 289.

78. De Caix's absolutely critical memoranda for the 1919–23 period have been brilliantly analysed and edited by Gérard D. Khoury, *Une Tutelle coloniale: Le Mandat français en Syrie et au Liban: Ecrits politiques de Robert de Caix* (Paris: Belin, 2006); see De Caix, 'Esquisse de l'organisation de la Syrie sous le mandat français', 248–70, quoted 249.

79. Hardinge to Allenby, 16 July 1920, *DBFP*, ser. 1, vol. 8, 313.

80. MAE, SDN 565, Gouraud to MAE, 24 and 27 July 1920.

81. 'House of Commons', *The Times*, 20 July 1920, 16; and MAE, SDN 565, Gouraud to MAE, 20 July 1920.

82. Curzon to Grahame, 28 July 1920, in *DBFP*, ser. 1, vol. 13, 321.

83. For the revolt, Townshend, *Desert Hell*, 463–78, and Amal Vinogradov,'The 1920 Revolt in Iraq Reconsidered: The Role of Tribes in National Politics', *International Journal of Middle Eastern Studies*, 3:2 (April 1972), 123–39.

84. H. W. Young, 'Memorandum on the Future Control of the Middle East', 17 May 1920, *DBFP*, ser. 1, vol. 13, here at 264.

85. Much the best account of the formation of Iraq is Peter Sluglett, *Britain in Iraq: Contriving King and Country, 1914–1932* (New York: Columbia University Press, 2007).

86. Wilson to Edwin Montagu, Secretary of State for India, 31 July 1920, in *DBFP*, ser. 1, vol. 13, 323–4.

87. 'British Secretary's Notes of an Anglo-French Conference, held at Lympne on Sunday August 8, 1920', *DBFP*, ser. 1, vol. 8, 718–19.

88. MAE, SDN 565, Gouraud to MAE, 15 Aug. 1920.

89. D. K. Fieldhouse, ed., *Kurds, Arabs and Britons: The Memoir of Wallace Lyon in Iraq, 1918–1944* (London: I. B. Tauris, 2002), 94–5.

90. For the Nebi Musa riots, see esp. Segev, *One Palestine*, ch. 6.
91. Allenby to Curzon, 6 May 1920, *DBFP*, ser. 1, vol. 13, 255, and see Faysal's protest in Allenby to Curzon, 9 July 1920, in *DBFP*, ser. 1, vol. 13, 284–5.
92. Yoav Alon, *The Making of Jordan: Tribes, Colonialism and the Modern State* (London: I. B. Tauris, 2007), 14–20.
93. Samuel to Curzon, 22 Aug. 1920, in *DBFP*, ser. 1, vol. 13, 342–3.
94. For the founding of Transjordan, and Abdullah's role in particular, see esp. Mary C. Wilson, *King Abdullah, Britain and the Making of Jordan* (Cambridge: Cambridge University Press, 1987), ch. 4.
95. NA, Cab/24/126, 'Report on the Middle East Conference held in Cairo and Jerusalem' (June 1921).
96. MAE, SDN 565, De Caix to MAE, 3 April 1921.
97. Cecil's statement is referenced in 'Memorandum by Major Young', 6 Nov. 1920, *DBFP*, ser. 1, vol. 13, 379.

## NOTES FOR CHAPTER 2

1. LNDM, 'Minutes of the Directors' Meetings', Reel 1 of 4, appended to the collection.
2. *Procès-Verbal of the Eighth Session of the Council of the League of Nations* (Geneva: League of Nations, 1920), 41.
3. On Drummond, see James C. Barros, *Office without Power: Secretary-General Sir Eric Drummond, 1919–1933* (Oxford: Clarendon Press, 1979).
4. CAC, Maurice Hankey Papers, HNKY 8/13, [Sir Maurice Hankey], 'The League of Nations: Sketch Plan of Organisation', printed, 31 March 1919.
5. The best study of the League Secretariat, on which I have selectively drawn in this section, remains Egon F. Ranshofen-Wertheimer, *The International Secretariat: A Great Experiment in International Administration* (Washington: Carnegie Endowment for International Peace, 1945).
6. LNA, R1, 1/1365/52, Drummond to Beer, 3 Oct. 1919, and Beer to Drummond, 15 and 28 Oct. 1919; also LNA, R13, 1/1742/1742, Beer to Drummond, 11 Nov. 1919.
7. LNA, R1, 1/2173/52, Minute by Drummond, 8 Dec. 1919.
8. These records are in LNA, R1, see 1/771/161, and Baker to Drummond, 12 Sept. 1919.
9. LNA, R1, 1/661/161, Van Hamel to Drummond, 8 Aug. 1919. For Baker's early espousal of this approach and Drummond's agreement, see LNA, R1, 1/2054/161, Baker to Drummond, 14 Oct. 1919; 1/2760/161, Minute by Baker, 17 Jan. 1920; 1/2458/161, Drummond to Nicolson, 13 and 21 Dec. 1919.
10. LNA, R1, 1/4862/161, *The Responsibility of the League of Nations arising out of Article XXII of the Covenant: Memorandum by the Secretary-General*, Council Doc. 48; the jacket indicates the author as Baker, date as 8 June 1920; distribution to the Council on 13 July 1920.

11. The latter was agreed in discussion and not in the text itself. The draft as adopted by the Council on 5 August 1920 is in LNA, R1, 1/5958/161; it was printed as 'Obligations falling upon the League of Nations under the terms of Article 22 of the Covenant (Mandates)', *LNOJ*, Sept. 1920, 334–41.

12. For the character of the League Assembly, see Margaret E. Burton, *The Assembly of the League of Nations* (University of Chicago Press, 1941; rpt. NY: Howard Fertig, 1974). Burton stresses the key role of the Assembly in providing a platform for statesmen from smaller states and for public opinion.

13. LNA, R2, 1/8132/161, Minute, Baker to Rappard and Drummond, 10 Nov. 1920.

14. The German protest of November 1920 was printed in French and English and distributed to all member states at the First Assembly. For copies, see PA, R70002, and in LNA, R2, 1/8451/161.

15. The original correspondence is in LNA, R2, 1/9550/161; it is summarized in *Journal of the First Assembly of the League of Nations*, no. 36 (19 Dec. 1920), 296. For the Committee's proceedings, see *Procès-Verbaux of the Committees of the First Assembly of the League of Nations*, no. 2 (25 Nov. 1920), and for an intelligent insider's summary (written by Cecil), *The First Assembly: A Study of the Proceedings of the First Assembly of the League of Nations* (London: Macmillan, 1921), 227–30.

16. *Journal of the First Assembly of the League of Nations*, no. 36 (19 Dec. 1920), 291–5.

17. Fourth Assembly, Plenary Meeting, 26 Sept. 1923, *LNOJ*, Special Suppl. no. 13 (Oct. 1923), 92.

18. For a comprehensive reassessment of Cecil's role within the League, see Peter Yearwood, *Guarantee of Peace: The League of Nations in British Policy, 1914–1925* (Oxford: Oxford University Press, 2009).

19. CAC, NBKR4/463, Baker to Cecil, 3 May 1921.

20. SFA, Rappard Papers, Box 1977/135 74, Drummond to Rappard, 9 Oct. 1920.

21. For Rappard, see Victor Monnier, *William E. Rappard: Défenseur des libertés, serviteur de son pays et de la communauté internationale* (Geneva: Slatkine, 1995), and for his work at the League, Ania Peter, *William E. Rappard und der Völkerbund: Ein Schweizer Pionier der internationalen Verständigung* (Bern: Lang, 1973). I have drawn on Peter in particular.

22. Drummond had asked Rappard to take over the role of Director of Internal Administration, which Rappard interpreted as an offer to take on the tasks hitherto reserved for Raymond Fosdick, the American who was to have been appointed at the rank of Under-Secretary General. Drummond, however, could not possibly have appointed a Swiss to one of the League's precious under-secretaryships (all of which were reserved for nationals of the great powers), and once Rappard concluded that he would be a sort of glorified office manager, he refused, then grudgingly accepted in Switzerland's interest, and then was gently let down by Drummond. This episode, the correspondence for

which is in SFA, Rappard Papers, Box 1977/135 74, captures well the differences between the two men and their respective limitations. Rappard wanted to be in a post with an important policy role; Drummond knew that much power would be held by the Secretariat, but only if they pretended never to exercise it. See also Monnet to Rappard, telegram, 15 Oct. 1920, in SFA, Rappard Papers, Box 1977/135 74.

23. See LNA, R3, 1/12756/161, Rappard, Minute, 5 May 1921; LNA, R3, 1/13446/161, Rappard to Drummond, 21 June 1921, Drummond to Fisher, 23 June 1921, and Rappard to Drummond, 24 June 1921; also LNA, R3, 1/19376/161, Rappard to Drummond, 6 March 1922, and Drummond to Poincaré and Lloyd George, 13 March 1922.

24. AA, AE/II (3288), 1848, Hymans to Drummond, 17 Dec. 1920.

25. LNA, R2, 1/9769/161, Baker to Drummond, Van Hamel, and Rappard, n.d. [Dec. 1920?].

26. The parliamentary questions and press interventions are too numerous to cite, but for discussions about pressure and strategy, it is useful especially to look at the records of the LNU, and notably of its Mandates Subcommittee, chaired by Ormsby-Gore, which can be found in the BLPES, LNU Archives, Microfilm Reel 430, and articles in the LNU journals *Today and Tomorrow* and *Headway*; also at Harris's correspondence in RH, ASAPS Archives, and articles in the *ASRAF*. The Anti-Slavery Society's draft mandate was published in *ASRAF*, 9:3 (Oct. 1919), 63–71; the LNU's can be found in *Today and Tomorrow*, Nov. 1920, 323–5. For Harris's early role shaping the mandates system, see also Amalia Ribi, ' "The Breath of a New Life"? British Anti-Slavery and the League of Nations', *Internationalism Reconfigured: Transnational Ideas and Movements Between the World Wars*, ed. Daniel Laqua (London: I. B. Tauris, 2011), 93–113.

27. RH, ASAPS, G401, Harris to Rappard, 6 Jan. 1921.

28. LNA, S284 1 (9), Ormsby-Gore to Rappard, 17 Jan. 1921.

29. LNA, S284 1 (9), Rappard to Ormsby-Gore, 19 Jan. 1921.

30. LNA, S1608 no. 1 (1920–1939), Rappard, 'Relations between the Secretariat of the League of Nations and the Permanent Mandates Commission', 3 March 1921, and LNA, R7, 1/11502/248, Ormsby-Gore to Rappard, 8 March 1921, and Drummond to Rappard, 14 March 1921.

31. LNA, S284 1 (9), Rappard to Ormsby-Gore, 29 March 1921.

32. LNA, R3, 1/14861/161, Rappard to Drummond, 20 Aug. 1921, and note by Drummond, 20 Aug. 1921.

33. *Records of the Second Assembley: Plenary Meetings* (Geneva, 1921), 342–57; see also, H. W. V. Temperley, *The Second Year of the League: A Study of the Second Assembly of the League of Nations* (London: Hutchinson, 1922), 81–91.

34. Minutes of the 19th session of the Council, 18 July 1922, *LNOJ*, Aug. 1922, 791–3.

35. For Catastini colluding with the German PMC member and leaking information, see e.g. PA, R96535, Grobba, 'Zu Punkt 2 der Tagesordnung der 54. Tagung

des Völkerbundsrates. Mandate. Irak' (28 Feb. 1929), and R96517, Trendelenburg to Kamphövener, 6 Sept. 1933. The German Foreign Ministry, unsurprisingly, wanted to see Catastini's contract renewed in 1933: see R96549, Note by Brückner, 8 Sept. 1933.

36. LNA, S263, File on 1st and 2nd meetings, 1922, John Palmer to Rappard, 12 Aug. 1922.

37. Some of these 'monthly distributions' for the early 1920s, which are quite substantial, can be found in LNA, S241.

38. The fascinating correspondence about this question can be found in LNA, R74, Files 1/58136/41289 and 1/41289/41289. The monthly *Analyses de presses Arabes* from 1928 to 1930 are in S258.

39. See, e.g., *List of Works Relating to the Mandates System and the Territories under Mandate Catalogued in the Library of the League of Nations* (Geneva: League of Nations, 1934), copy in LNA R4137.

40. 1 *PMCM*, 40.

41. 1 *PMCM*, 40.

42. LNA, Rappard personnel file, Rappard to Drummond, 20 May 1924.

43. LNA, Rappard personnel file, Note by Drummond, 22 May 1924.

44. 5 *PMCM*, 149, and LNA, R8, 1/40493/248, Minute by the Secretary General, 3 Nov. 1924.

45. 5 *PMCM*, 149, and LNA, R8, 1/40493/248, Drummond to Rappard, 20 Dec. 1924.

46. Baker, assuming that the Commission would be appointed before the Peace Conference concluded, drafted a first proposal in February 1919: see NA, FO 608/240, file 2885, Baker, 'The Permanent Mandates Commission of the League of Nations', 22 Feb. 1919, and comment by Ormsby-Gore, 27 Feb. 1919. Beer mentions working on a memorandum about the organization of the mandates section and mandates commission in his entry on 2 July 1919; see LC, MSS 4954, Diary of George Louis Beer. A later version of this memorandum is in LC, Gilchrist Papers, Box 20, Beer, 'The Mandatory Commission and the Mandatory Section of the Secretariat' [n.d.]; another copy can be found in Milner 390, and various plans by Beer, Drummond, and Baker in LNA, R6.

47. LNA, S1608, no. 1 (1920–39), Anon. [Baker], 'Mandates Commission: Memo for the Secretary General', 17 Sept. 1920, and P. J. Baker, 'Mandates Commission: Basis of Discussion', 23 Oct. 1920.

48. 'Constitution of the Permanent Mandates Commission', *LNOJ*, Nov.–Dec. 1920, 87–8.

49. Albert Thomas, Director of the ILO, insisted on ILO representation. See LNA, R2, 1/8627/161.

50. MAE, SDN 620, Sarraut to George Leygues, 13 Dec. 1920.

51. LNA, R6, 1/11046/248, Arthur Henderson to Drummond, 18 Feb. 1921; 1/10518/248, correspondence on the candidacy of Claparède.

NOTES TO PAGES 61-65

52. LNA, R39, 1/15865/13940, W. E. Burghardt Du Bois, Secretary, Second Pan-African Congress, to the President of the Council of the League of Nations, 15 Sept. 1921 (printed as Assembly Document A.148); *Minutes of the First Assembly*, 355–7; CAC, NBKR 4/440, Noel-Baker to Ormsby-Gore, 24 Sept. 1921.

53. Correspondence about Orts' appointment is to be found in Archives Générales du Royaume, Brussels, Orts Family Papers, File 172.

54. Information on the various members of the PMC is gathered from standard biographical dictionaries as well as from the files on the various members in the LNA: see, especially, the Section files containing correspondence with and about each member in S284 and S1626–1628, as well as in R2327. Theodoli published an autobiography, *A Cavallo di Due Secoli* (Rome: La Navicella, 1950), but it does not discuss his work on the Commission at length.

55. LNA, S284 1 (6), File on Count de Ballobar, Rappard to Drummond, 14 June 1924.

56. For Japan's representatives on the PMC, see esp. Thomas W. Burkman, *Japan and the League of Nations: Empire and World Order, 1914–1938* (Honolulu: University of Hawaii Press, 2008), 126–33.

57. LNA, S284 1 (1) File on Bugge-Wicksell, Bugge-Wicksell to Drummond, 22 March 1921. There is a biography by Liv Wicksell Nordqvist, *Anna Bugge Wicksell: En Kvinna före sin tid* (Malmö: Liber Förlag, 1985), but it contains very little on her work on the PMC. For the work of Bugge-Wicksell and Dannevig, see Pedersen, 'Metaphors of the Schoolroom: Women Working the Mandates System of the League of Nations', *History Workshop Journal*, 66 (2008), 188–207.

58. For the argument over the appointment of Ormsby-Gore, see Callahan, *Mandates and Empire: The League of Nations and Africa, 1914–1931* (Brighton: Sussex Academic Press, 1999), 71–3. Callahan states that Ormsby-Gore had 'no colonial experience', overlooking his wartime experiences in the Middle East.

59. RH, ASAPS, G401, Harris to C. P. Scott, 22 Feb. 1921; Harris to Rappard, 28 Feb. 1921; and Letter, *The Times*, 22 March 1921.

60. Van Rees, D. F. W., *Les Mandats internationaux: Le contrôle de l'administration mandataire* (Paris: Librairie Arthur Rousseau, 1927); Van Rees, D. F. W., *Les Mandats internationaux: Les principes généraux du régime des mandats* (Paris: Librairie Arthur Rousseau, 1928); Leopoldo Palacios, *Los Mandatos internacionales de la Sociedad de Naciones* (Madrid: Librería General de Victoriano Suarez), 1928; and among many talks and articles, especially, William Rappard, 'The Practical Working of the Mandates System', *Journal of the British Institute of International Affairs*, 4:5 (Sept. 1925), 205–26.

61. LNA, S 284 1 (1), Bugge-Wicksell to Rappard, 7 June 1922.

62. 1 *PMCM*, 40.

63. After Germany joined, the Commission discussed the question of holding meetings in public again, and concurred that it was unwise; see 12 *PMCM*, 59–61.

64. LNA, R78, 1/52914/52914, Minute by Gilchrist, 22 July 1926, and list of recipients of mandates documents.
65. Rappard went to Palestine with Balfour in 1925 for the founding of Hebrew University, and Grimshaw and Bugge-Wicksell both travelled there as well; Orts went to Tanganyika and Belgian Congo in 1928; Ruppel went to Palestine and Syria in 1933 (his movements monitored closely by the Colonial Office and the Quai d'Orsay); Theodoli and Da Penha Garcia both visited South West Africa in the mid-1930s. After resigning from the Commission, Ruppel visited the African mandated territories and made no secret of his hope that they would soon again be German.
66. 3 *PMCM*, 8.
67. 1 *PMCM*, 9, 14. Theodoli announced the textual revision in the next session; 2 *PMCM*, 3.
68. Theodoli's oral summary to the Council on 10 Oct. of their work and the issues they wished clarified, as well as a copy of the questionnaire, is in *LNOJ*, Dec. 1921, 1124–33.
69. CAC, NBKR 4/440, Baker to H. Wilson Harris, 11 Oct. 1921.
70. The content of the speech, and Smuts' reply to Rappard, were reprinted in 2 *PMCM*, 91–2. For the very conciliatory German text, see NAN, Accession 312, File 9/24.
71. 1 *PMCM*, 33–5.
72. 'Resolution adopted by the Council on October 10, 1921', *LNOJ*, Dec. 1921, 1126, 1133.
73. NA, CO, 323/884/61, 'Minutes of a meeting held at the Colonial Office on Oct. 28th to discuss various questions concerning mandates'; and NA, CO 323/882, 'Minutes of a meeting held at the Colonial Office at 12 noon 23rd Nov. 1921'.
74. 2 *PMCM*, 16–19. The subcommittee's report can be found in LNA, R57, 1/17831/16844, 'Preliminary Report for the Secretary General on the Mission of the Sub-Committee of the Permanent Mandates Commission charged with the duty of ascertaining the views of the Mandatory Powers on the question of the national status of the inhabitants of mandated territories', 2 Dec. 1921. For the Belgian meeting, see the next note; French deliberations are covered in Callahan, *Mandates and Empire*, 112–14.
75. AA, AE II/(2977) 935, 'Compte-rendu des délibérations de la Sous Commission des Mandats, chargée d'examiner la question de la nationalité des sujets des territoires à mandat, Brussels, 26 Nov. 1921'.
76. LNA, R57, 1/17831/16844, 'Preliminary Report for the Secretary-General on the Mission of the Sub-Committee of the Permanent Mandates Commission charged with the duty of ascertaining the views of the Mandatory Powers on the question of the national status of the inhabitants of mandated territories', 2 Dec. 1921.
77. Minutes of the 24th session of the Council, 6th and 14th meetings, 20 and 23 April 1923, *LNOJ*, June 1923, 567–72, 603–4.

78. LNA, S1652 (1), 'The "London Agreement", 1923' typescript. Some 90% of the adult Germans in SWA accepted that offer, becoming British citizens on 15 March 1925; in 1926 children of naturalized Britons became British as well. For the German community's response, and especially for its attempt to preserve its 'Deutschtum' despite naturalization, see Daniel Joseph Walther, *Creating Germans Abroad: Cultural Policies and National Identity in Namibia* (Athens, OH: Ohio University Press, 2002), 153–65.

79. For Musinga's protest to King Albert, see AA, AE II/(3296), 1885, File: 'Musinga 1920–1930', Juyi Musinga to Albert, 16 June 1920, and for local concerns about his disaffection and their inability to rule unless he were satisfied, see AA, RWA (1) 12, Marzorati, Auditeur Militaire, to Minister of the Colonies, 8 July 1921. The British-Belgian conflict over Gisaka, which seriously compromised relations between the Belgians and Musinga, is discussed in some detail in Jean Rumiya, *Le Rwanda sous le régime du mandat belge (1916–1931)* (Paris: L'Harmattan, 1992), 79–129.

80. 1 *PMCM*, 24.

81. The original memoranda by Pastor H. Anet and Monseigneur Classe, and protests by Musinga, are in LNA, R9, 1/22262/1025 and 1/220403/1025; see also 2 *PMCM*, 69–72, and Annexes 8 and 9, and *Rapport sur l'administration belge du Ruanda et de l'Urundi pendant l'année 1921*, 12–13.

82. The involvement of the League in this dispute is summarized in LNA, R70, 1/29958/29952, 'Territory of the Former Colony of German East Africa under Belgian and British Mandates. Proposals of the Belgian and British Governments. Memorandum by the Secretary General' (16 Aug. 1923). The British and Belgian correspondence was published in *Correspondence Regarding the Modification of the Boundary between British Mandated Territory and Belgian Mandated Territory in East Africa*, PP 1923, Cmd. 1974.

83. For Classe's initial involvement in the controversy, and then his offer to the Belgian government, see AA, AE II/(3296), 1885, File: 'Musinga 1920–1930', Classe to Resident, 25 Feb. 1920, and Auditor-General of Ruanda, to the Colonial Minister, 19 April 1921.

84. Orts' account of his approach to Ormsby-Gore is in Archives Générales du Royaume, Brussels, Orts Family Papers, File 434, 'Note pour messieurs les Ministres des Affaires étrangères et des colonies', 15 Oct. 1921; Ormsby-Gore's first mention of the matter to Churchill is in NA, CO 323/884/61, Ormsby-Gore to Churchill, 17 Oct. 1921; also, for the failure of that first démarche, NA, CO 323/884/61, Louwers to Orts, 12 April 1922.

85. For Orts' account of his work at the second session, see AA, AE/II (3288) 1848, Orts to Colonial Minister, 15 Aug. 1922. Halewyck de Heusch wrote to thank him: Archives Générales du Royaume, Orts Family Papers, File 434, Halewyck to Orts, 19 Aug. 1922.

86. Rappard in 1 *PMCM*, 24.

87. 2 *PMCM*, 70; AA, AE/II (3288) 1848, Orts to Colonial Minister, 15 Aug. 1922.

88. 3 *PMCM*, 92.
89. Bodleian, Milner C 700, Lloyd George to Milner, 22 April 1919.
90. Records about these negotiations are in Bodleian, Milner C 700, but for a cogent summary of their final provisions, see A. H. Charteris, 'The Mandate over Nauru Island', *British Year Book of International Law*, 137 (1923–24), 137–52.
91. *H.C. Deb.*, ser. 5, vol. 130, 16 June 1920, here at cols. 1308–13 (for Ormsby-Gore), 1317–21 (for Cecil), and 1321–23 (for Asquith). The 77 to 217 vote rejecting Ormsby-Gore's amendment is at col. 1349.
92. 'Phosphates and Principles: Debate on Nauru Agreement, Mandate and League', *The Times*, 17 June 1920, 12. Some three weeks later, Cecil managed to force through an amendment making the bill subject to Article 22 of the Covenant, but when it got to the Lords. Milner insisted that there was no conflict with the Covenant anyway, since the 'open door' policy did not apply to 'C' mandates. 'Phosphates of Nauru: Government Defeat in Committee', *The Manchester Guardian*, 7 July 1920, 6; *H.L. Deb.*, ser. 5, vol. 41, 29 July 1920, cols. 627–31.
93. 2 *PMCM*, 38–57; National Library of Wales, Brogyntyn manuscripts, PEC 10/1/12, Ormsby-Gore to his mother, 10 Aug. 1922.
94. 'The Nauru Mandate: League Commission's Misgivings', *The Times*, 12 Aug. 1922, 7.
95. Roger C. Thompson, 'Edge of Empire: Australian Colonization in Nauru, 1919–1939'. in Donald H. Rubinstein, ed., *Pacific History: Papers from the 8th Pacific History Association Conference* (Mangilao: University of Guam Press, 1992), 273–80.
96. Christopher Weeramantry, Chairman of the three-person Commission of Inquiry established by the Government of Nauru into legal responsibility for environmental damage to Nauru during the mandate and trusteeship period, provides an exhaustive summary of the Commission's findings in *Nauru: Environmental Damage under International Trusteeship* (Melbourne: Oxford University Press, 1992). For the later history of Nauru's claim, see esp. the account by Antony Anghie, who acted as research assistant to the Commission and went on to write influential works on international oversight regimes, '"The Heart of my Home": Colonialism, Environmental Damage, and the Nauru Case', *Harvard International Law Journal*, 34:2 (Spring 1993), 445–506. For the full story of the exploitation of the guano-producing Pacific islands, see Gregory T. Cushman, *Guano and the Opening of the Pacific World: A Global Ecological History* (Cambridge: Cambridge University Press, 2013).

### NOTES FOR CHAPTER 3

1. RH, ASAPS, G401, Joseph Bell to Anti-Slavery Society, 30 Aug. 1919.
2. A few scholars have considered the PMC's petition process. The most thorough treatment, which includes comprehensive statistics on petitions received by the

PMC, is A. H. M. Van Ginneken, 'Volkenbondsvoogdij: Het Toezicht van de Volkenbond op het Bestuur in Mandaatgebieden, 1919–1940,' Dissertation, University of Utrecht, 1992. Aleksandar Momirov relies on Van Ginneken's research in his discussion of the differences between the Mandate and Trusteeship systems of petitioning; see 'The Individual Right to Petition in Internationalized Territories: From Progressive Thought to an Abandoned Practice', *Journal of the History of International Law*, 9 (2007), 203–31. Balakrishnan Rajagopal places the PMC's regime within an account of the way pressures from below shaped international law: see *International Law from Below: Development, Social Movements, and Third World Resistance* (Cambridge: Cambridge University Press, 2003), 67–71. Israel de Jesús Butler mentions the PMC regime in a genealogy of the practice; see 'A Comparative Analysis of Individual Petition in Regional and Global Human Rights Protection Mechanisms', *University of Queensland Law Journal*, 23:1 (2004), 22–53.

3. LNA, R1, Minutes of the Commission on Mandates (Milner Commission), 4th meeting, 9 July 1919.

4. For Ottoman precedents, see Andrew Arsan, ' "This is the Age of Associations": Committees, Petitions, and the Roots of Interwar Middle Eastern Internationalism', *Journal of Global History*, 7 (2012), 166–88; for Samoan and Dualan petitions to the Reichstag, see J. W. Davidson, *Samoa mo Samoa: The Emergence of the Independent State of Western Samoa* (Melbourne: Oxford University Press, 1967), 90; Ralph A. Austen and Jonathan Derrick, *Middlemen of the Cameroons Rivers: The Duala and their Hinterland c. 1600–c. 1960* (Cambridge: Cambridge University Press, 1999), 128–9.

5. For the merchant protests, see NA, FO 608/215/955, Jonathan C. Holt, John Holt & Co. (Liverpool), to Balfour, 25 Jan. 1919, and FO/608/215/2910, Association of West African Merchants to FO, 13 Feb. 1919. For the partition of Cameroon, see Peter J. Yearwood, ' "In a Casual Way with a Blue Pencil": British Policy and the Partition of Kamerun, 1914–1919', *Canadian Journal of African Studies*, 27:2 (1993), 218–44, and for Duala protests against that partition and against French occupation in 1919, see Michael D. Callahan, *Mandates and Empire: The League of Nations and Africa, 1914–1931* (Brighton: Sussex Academic Press, 1999), 43–4, and Ralph A. Austen and Jonathan Derrick, *Middlemen of the Cameroons Rivers*, 144–8. Ewe protests against the Togo partition are dealt with in some detail in D. E. K. Amenumey, *The Ewe Unification Movement: A Political History* (Accra: Ghana Universities Press, 1989), 9–26; see also Benjamin Lawrance, 'Petitioners, "Bush Lawyers", and Letter Writers: Court Access in British-Occupied Lomé, 1914–1920', in Benjamin N. Lawrance, Emily L. Osborn, and Richard L. Roberts, eds., *Intermediaries, Interpreters and Clerks: African Employees and the Making of Colonial Africa* (Madison: University of Wisconsin Press, 2006), 94–114.

6. NA, FO 608/216/2239, Hugh Clifford, Governor, Gold Coast, to Walter Long, Colonial Office, 17 Dec. 1918; NA, FO 608/215/2050, Edward Holder to FO, 27 Dec. 1918.

7. NA, FO 608/215/2050, Comment by Strachey, 15 Feb. 1919.

8. Harris's many letters and articles about the delay approving mandates and possible violations of League principles in French-mandated Togo and Cameroon are in ASAPS, G401.

9. Michael Callahan has unearthed Mensah's 1920 petitions to Milner and Lloyd George, and the fate of his 1921 petition sent to the Liverpool Chamber of Commerce, for which see *Mandates and Empire*, 52, 117–19; see also ASS G402, Mensah to Charles Roberts, LNU, 7 May 1921, and Harris to Mensah, 7 July 1921, and G401, Rappard to Harris, 3 June 1921.

10. BLPES, LNU Archives, Microfilm Reel 430, Mandates Committee minutes, 12 Jan. 1921.

11. 'British Mandate for Palestine', *The Times*, 5 Feb. 1921, 7.

12. LNA, R21, 1/11100/4284, Faysal to Drummond, 16 Feb. 1921. King Husayn's protests, which were ruled 'not receivable' by the Council on the dubious grounds that a peace treaty had not yet been concluded with Turkey, can be found in LNA R21, and are discussed in Hussein D. Alkhazragi, 'Un Petit Prince à la SDN: La lutte du roi Hussein du Hedjaz pour l'indépendance des provinces arabes de l'empire ottoman', *Relations Internationales*, 146 (2011–12), 7–23.

13. The first Syro-Palestinian Congress is discussed by several experts but often misdated, Khoury stating that it took place in June and Patrick Seale in July; see Philip S. Khoury, *Syria and the French Mandate: The Politics of Arab Nationalism, 1920–1945* (Princeton: Princeton University Press, 1987), 221, and Patrick Seale, *The Struggle for Arab Independence: Riad el-Solh and the Makers of the Modern Middle East* (Cambridge: Cambridge University Press, 2010), 180. Both cite Marie-Renée Mouton's article, 'Le Congrès syro-palestinien de Genève', *Relations Internationales*, 19 (Autumn 1979), 313–28, who rightly gives the Congress's opening as 25 Aug. For a fuller account of the participants, see Friedhelm Hoffmann, *Die Syro-Palästinensische Delegation am Völkerbund und Šakīb Arslān in Genf, 1921–1936/46* (Berlin: Lit, 2007).

14. LNA, R21, 1/5947/4284, Note by Philip Baker for Captain Walters, 11 Sept. 1920.

15. LNA, R15, 1/15299/2413, Drummond to Shibly Jamal, 3 Sept. 1921; 1/12676/2413, Walters to Rappard, 16 Sept. 1921, and Wellington Koo to Hammad, 30 Sept. 1921.

16. LNA, R21, 1/14993/4284, Memo by Rappard, 24 Aug. 1921; R15, 1/15299/2413, Rappard to Drummond, 31 Aug. 1921.

17. This rather tense correspondence is in LNA, R15, 1/15299/2413; see esp. Rappard to Drummond, 1, 22, and 23 (misdated 22) Sept. 1921, Drummond to Rappard, 23 Sept. 1921.

18. LNA, 1/16448/2413, Rappard to Drummond, 11 Oct. 1921, quoted in Ania Peter, *William E. Rappard und der Völkerbund: Ein Schweizer Pionier der internationalen Verständigung* (Bern: Lang, 1973), 123.

19. 1 *PMCM*, 22–3. Under the treaties agreed at the end of the war, most new or reconstituted Eastern European states granted specific rights to ethnic minorities now within their borders, and a mechanism had been established for the Council to hear petitions about alleged violations. If Rappard and Ormsby-Gore were aware of the petition process established under the minorities regime, which allowed *governments* to transmit allegations about possible violations of those treaties to the Council (a process that meant petitions were considered mostly if they received backing from a sympathetic 'kin-state'), they clearly did not find it attractive, for the mandates procedure allowed individuals to petition and was quite different. For the minorities' regime, see esp. Carole Fink, *Defending the Rights of Others: The Great Powers, the Jews, and International Minority Protection, 1878–1938* (Cambridge: Cambridge University Press, 2006).

20. For a close analysis of the impact of the delegation and efforts to overturn the mandate in 1921–23, see Sahar Huneidi, *A Broken Trust: Herbert Samuel, Zionism, and the Palestinians* (London: I. B. Tauris, 2001), chs. 3, 7. The delegation managed to get its views into the mainstream press: see, e.g., Moussa Pasha Kazim El Husseini and Shibly Jamal, 'The Future of Palestine', *The Times*, 19 Dec. 1921, 6, and subsequent articles on Arab disaffection on 4 April, 11 May, and 3 June. For the Lords debate, *H.L. Deb.*, ser. 5, vol. 50, 21 June 1922, cols. 994–1033; 'The Palestine Mandate', *The Times*, 23 June 1922, 17.

21. The Zionist Organization accepted the White Paper (Weizmann having been consulted about its contents), while the Palestinian delegation, prophesying that it presaged the 'extinction' of the Arab population, rejected it. For those responses, *Palestine: Correspondence with the Palestine Arab Delegation and the Zionist Organisation*, PP 1922, Cmd. 1700, 17–21. For discussions of the White Paper, see esp. Huneidi, *A Broken Trust*, 156–61, and Bernard Wasserstein, *The British in Palestine: The Mandatory Government and the Arab-Jewish Conflict, 1917–1929* (1978; 2nd ed. Oxford: Basil Blackwell, 1991), 118–21.

22. Minutes of the 19th session of the Council, *LNOJ*, 3:8 (Aug. 1922), 824.

23. Weizmann to Simon, 16 July 1922, in *LPCW*, vol. 11, ed. Bernard Wasserstein (New Brunswick, NJ: Transaction Books, 1977), 143–7.

24. 2 *PMCM*, 8.

25. LNA, Box R60, 1/22099/22099, 'Submission to the League of Nations of Petitions from Inhabitants of Mandated Territories. Memorandum by the British Representative on Procedures to be Adopted' (24 July 1922).

26. 2 *PMCM*, 15, and LNA, R50, 1/23071/22099, 'Procedure to be followed in communicating...petitions' (1 Sept. 1922).

27. Minutes of the 23rd session of the Council, 29 and 31 Jan. 1923, *LNOJ*, March 1923, 200–1, 211.

28. *Records of the 3rd Assembly*, vol. 1, *Minutes*, Plenary session, 20 Sept. 1922, 156.

29. ASAPS, G403, Henry Kau Gaba to Harris, 14 June 1924.

30. 15 *PMCM*, 140.

31. 8 *PMCM*, 165–6.
32. 9 *PMCM*, 48.
33. LNA, Box 2321, File A/15731/708, CPM 967, 'Petitions. Note by M. Merlin' (18 Nov. 1929).
34. LNA, R60, 1/24276/22099, 'Pétitions d'habitants des Territoires sous Mandat. Projet de rapport soumis aux Membres de la Commission permanente des Mandats par le Marquis Alberto Théodoli, Président' (Oct. 1922).
35. The decision not to accept petitions on matters justiciable in local courts was taken at Lugard's urging; see 'General Procedure regarding Petitions: Note by Sir F. Lugard', in 4 *PMCM*, Annex 6, 178–9.
36. Theodoli was already making decisions about 'receivability' in 1924; see, for example, his report to the Commission in 4 *PMCM*, 146. Those procedures—including the decision not to exclude petitions couched in 'violent language'—were clarified during the Commission's discussion of petitions in 1925 (7 *PMCM*, 133); see also the 1925 memoranda by Huntington Gilchrist in LNA R77, and C.P.M. 558 (1), 'Summary of the Procedure to be Followed in the Matter of Petitions Concerning Mandated Territories', Annex 4 in 12 *PMCM*, 176–8. Theodoli also wrote a brief report for each session listing petitions he had rejected and explaining his reason for doing so. On the minorities' regime's rules about 'violent language', see Jane Cowan, 'Who's Afraid of Violent Language? Honour, Sovereignty and Claims-Making in the League of Nations', *Anthropological Theory*, 33:3 (2003), 271–91.
37. Van Ginneken, 'Volkenbondsvoogdij,' 217.
38. Theodoli especially did this: see 11 *PMCM*, 18, 163; for the Dutch member Van Rees asking for similar information, see 12 *PMCM*, 62–3.
39. The Section Register can be found in LNA, S1681.
40. Van Ginneken presents comprehensive statistics about the source, subject, treatment, and publication of all petitions in her dissertation, 'Volkenbondsvoogdij', 211–18.
41. For which see Simon Jackson, 'Diaspora Politics and Developmental Empire: The Syro-Lebanese at the League of Nations', *Arab Studies Journal*, 21:1 (Spring 2013), 166–90.
42. For petitioning under the Palestine mandate, see esp. Natasha Wheatley, 'Mandatory Interpretation: Legal Hermeneutics and the New International Order in Arab and Jewish Petitions to the League of Nations', *Past and Present*, no. 227 (May 2015).
43. The suppressed history of Nauruan protests has been recovered in Roger C. Thompson, 'Edge of Empire: Australian Colonization in Nauru, 1919–1939', in Donald H. Rubinstein, ed., *Pacific History: Papers from the 8th Pacific History Association Conference* (Mangilao: University of Guam Press, 1992), 273–80.
44. Benjamin N. Lawrance, 'Bankoe v. Dome: Traditions and Petitions in the Ho-Asogli Amalgamation, British Mandated Togoland, 1919–1939', *Journal of African History*, 46 (2005), 243–67.

45. For which see Tilman Dedering, 'Petitioning Geneva: Transnational Aspects of Protest and Resistance in South West Africa/Namibia after the First World War', *Journal of Southern African Studies*, 35:4 (Dec. 2009), 785–801, and Rudolf G. Britz, Hartmut Lang, and Cornelia Limpricht, *A Concise History of the Rehoboth Basters until 1990* (Windhoek: Klaus Hess, 1999), 28–39.

46. For a sophisticated account of the emergence and transformation of the Bund over two decades, see Benjamin N. Lawrance, *Locality, Mobility, and 'Nation': Periurban Colonialism in Togo's Eweland, 1900–1960* (Rochester, NY: University of Rochester Press, 2007), ch. 5. The fate of the Bund and Duala petitions are exhaustively traced in Callahan, *Mandates and Empire*, 149–54, and *Sacred Trust*, 48–52. Andreas Eckert also discusses the Duala petitions in *Die Duala und die Kolonialmächte: Eine Untersuchung zu Widerstand, Protest und Protonationalismus in Kamerun vor dem Zweiten Weltkreig* (Münster and Hamburg: Lit, 1991), as do Austen and Derrick in *Middlemen*, 144–52.

47. For the Adjigo dispute, see Lawrance, *Locality, Mobility, and 'Nation'*, ch. 2, and Callahan, *Mandates*, 118–20. One member of the clan wrote to Harris repeatedly between 1922 and 1924, and Harris did write to Drummond and attempt to get the deportation reversed; this correspondence is in ASAPS, G402 and G403. For Casely Hayford, as well as for information on many other significant but often overlooked anti-colonial activists, see esp. Jonathan Derrick, *Africa's 'Agitators': Militant Anti-Colonialism in Africa and the West, 1918–1939* (New York: Columbia University Press, 2008).

48. These incidents troubled the Commission and gave M. Besson, the French accredited representative, some bad hours. For the 'Lomé incidents', see 24 *PMCM*, 52–5, 122–6, and Lawrance, *Locality, Mobility, and 'Nation'*, 69–89 and 139–40 (including footnotes 110 and 111). For the Cameroonian women's protest, Austen and Derrick, *Middlemen*, 151–2.

49. This summary of the sources and subjects of petitions is derived from my study of the PMC's reports and the League archives. The fascinating appeals from the Pan-African Congress and the Garveyites, most of which were simply rejected without report, can be found in LNA, Boxes R39, R41, R60, R2344, R4123.

50. Van Ginneken, 'Volkenbondsvoogdij', 218.

51. 24 *PMCM*, 54.

52. Balakrishnan Rajagopal, *International Law From Below: Development, Social Movements, and Third World Resistance* (Cambridge: Cambridge University Press, 2003), 69.

53. 24 *PMCM*, 54. The 'Bund' aroused the anger of the Belgian and French PMC members in particular, who assumed that it was being manipulated by Germans eager to reclaim their colonies. In 1927, for example, Merlin and Orts joined the representative of the French government in roundly abusing the petitioners as cranks with fraudulent claims; see 11 *PMCM*, 36–42.

54. 'Procedure in Respect of Petitions Regarding Inhabitants of Mandated Territories: Report by M. Salandra', *LNOJ*, 4:3 (March 1923), 299.

55. *LNOJ, Special Supplement No. 11, Records of the Third Assembly: Plenary Meetings*, vol. 1 (1922), 165.

56. For these developments in the 1920s, see esp. Barbara J. Smith, *The Roots of Separatism in Palestine: British Economic Policy, 1920–1929* (Syracuse, NY: Syracuse University Press, 1993).

57. Bernard Wasserstein attends to the ways in which Samuel's travels in Palestine in 1919 and then his time as High Commissioner persuaded him of the depth of Arab opposition to Zionism and led to repeated efforts at conciliation. See Bernard Wasserstein, *Herbert Samuel: A Political Life* (Oxford: Oxford University Press, 1992), ch. 9.

58. For the challenge to the Balfour policy in 1922–23, and its reaffirmation, see esp. Sahar Huneidi, 'Was Balfour Policy Reversible? The Colonial Office and Palestine, 1921–23', *Journal of Palestine Studies*, 27:2 (Winter 1998), 23–41.

59. See 'Report on the State of Palestine During the Four Years of Civil Administration', Annex 2, and 'Letter from the President of the Executive Committee of the Palestine Arab Congress', Annex 3, both in 5 *PMCM*, 166–74. Abdelaziz A. Ayyad's *Arab Nationalism and the Palestinians, 1850–1939* (Jerusalem: PASSIA, 1999), surveys the history of the Executive Committee of the Palestine Arab Congress, including its appeals to the League.

60. Weizmann to Morris Rothenberg and Emanuel Neumann, 9 Nov. 1924, in *LPCW*, vol. 12, ed. Joshua Freundlich (New Brunswick, NJ, 1976), 249.

61. LNA, S298 (2), 'Record of a Conversation with Sir Herbert Samuel…June 17, 1922'.

62. 5 *PMCM*, 65; Ormsby-Gore had said much the same thing at the 4th session, 24 June–8 July 1924, 88.

63. 4 *PMCM*, 89.

64. PMC, 'Report', in 5 *PMCM*, 188–9.

65. Weizmann to Rothenberg and Neumann, 9 Nov. 1924, in *LPCW*, vol. 12, 249.

66. Weizmann to Samuel, 13 Nov. 1924, in *LPCW*, vol. 12, 255.

67. Weizmann to Shuckburgh, 13 Nov. 1924, to Samuel, 13 Nov. 1924, to Rappard, 15 Nov. 1924, to Drummond, 17 Nov. 1924, in *LPCW*, vol. 12, 252–70, and LNA, S298 (2), Weizmann to Rappard, 14 Nov. 1924 (for the 'official' letter).

68. LNA, S298 (2), Rappard to Drummond, 24 Nov. 1924.

69. LNA, S298 (2), Rappard to Drummond, 18 Nov. 1924, and Note by Rappard, 5 Dec. 1924.

70. Evidence of the Zionist organization's successful infiltration of the Secretariat, documented in the Central Zionist Archives, is presented in Chapter 12 below.

71. Weizmann to Ludvik Singer, 21 Nov. 1924, Alexander Cadogan, 25 Nov. 1924, and Jean Fischer, 27 Nov. 1924, in *LPCW*, vol. 12, 272–3, 275, 277–8.

72. Minutes of the 32rd session of the Council, 10 December 1924, in *LNOJ*, 6:2 (Feb. 1925), 134.

73. Records of various Secretariat kerfuffles about how to treat Jacobson and the Zionists' claim for 'official' status are in LNA, S263. The Foreign Office in 1936 also objected that Zionist representatives were being admitted to areas during Assembly sessions reserved for delegates of member states; for this, see S1609, De Haller to Makins, 3 Dec. 1936.

74. Correspondence between Weizmann and many members of the PMC can be found in LPCW, as well as in the Lugard and Rappard Papers; see also Chaim Weizmann, *Trial and Error: The Autobiography of Chaim Weizmann* (New York: Harper and Brothers, 1949), 375–8. For Goldmann's arduous travels, see the records of the Geneva Office, now held at the CZA, Israel, esp. Goldmann's diaries for 1934–41 in CZA, Z6/1932; and Nahum Goldmann, *The Autobiography of Nahum Goldmann: Sixty Years of Jewish Life* (New York: Holt, Rinehart, and Winston, 1969), 137–44.

75. For Rappard's trip to Palestine, see esp. Victor Monnier, *William E. Rappard: Défenseur des libertés, serviteur de son pays et de la communauté internationale* (Geneva: Slatkine, 1995), 332–46, and Peter, *William E. Rappard*, 126–7.

76. 7 *PMCM*, 127.

77. For which see Weldon C. Matthews, *Confronting an Empire, Constructing a Nation: Arab Nationalists and Popular Politics in Mandate Palestine* (London: I. B. Tauris, 2006), 34–42, and Philip Mattar, *The Mufti of Jerusalem: Al-Hajj Amin al-Husayni and the Palestinian National Movement* (New York: Columbia University Press, 1988), ch. 2.

78. J. C. Hurewitz notes, rightly, that 'the mandate for Palestine was framed unmistakably in the Zionist interest'; see J. C. Hurewitz, *The Struggle for Palestine* (1950; new ed. New York: Schocken Books, 1976), 18.

79. Wheatley, 'Mandatory Interpretation.'

80. See the two petitions from the Palestine Arab Congress, Palacios' report on those petitions, and the PMC's observations thereon, in 7 *PMCM*, 160–73, 180–1, 219.

81. Wheatley, 'Mandatory Interpretation'.

82. 'Petition, dated April 25, 1927, from the "Executive Committee of the Palestine Arab Congress": Report by M. Palacios', in 11 *PMCM*, 208.

## NOTES FOR PART II

1. RH, Lugard 119/4, Lady Lugard to Major E. J. Lugard, 22 July 1923.
2. RH, Lady Lugard to Major E. J. Lugard, 29 July 1923.
3. RH, Lugard 119/2, Ormsby-Gore to Lugard, 16 Feb. 1923.
4. RH, Lugard, 151/1/16, Ruppel to Lugard, 24 Feb. 1933.
5. Lord Lugard, *The Dual Mandate in British Tropical Africa* (1922; rpt. Hamden, CT: Archon Books, 1965).
6. See Véronique Dimier's perspicacious comments on *The Dual Mandate* in *Le Gouvernement des colonies, regards croisés franco-britanniques* (Brussels: Editions de l'Université de Bruxelles, 2004), 206–10.

7. *Dual Mandate*, 48–58.

8. *Dual Mandate*, esp. 197–229, and quoted 217.

9. A great deal has been written on British colonial administration, but for an especially astute summary of 'indirect rule' see Karen E. Fields, *Revival and Rebellion in Colonial Central Africa* (Princeton: Princeton University Press, 1985), pp. 30–60, and for the articulation of the Kenyan model, Bruce Berman and John Lonsdale, *Unhappy Valley: Conflict in Kenya and Africa* (London: John Currey, 1992).

10. LNA, R6, 1/10005/248, jacket 1, Rappard to Lugard, 12 Feb. 1923.

11. *Dual Mandate*, 197–8.

12. LNA, S284 1 (9), Ormsby-Gore to Rappard, 17 Jan. 1921.

13. *Dual Mandate*, 198.

14. For which see Benoît de L'Estoile, 'Internationalization and "Scientific Nationalism": The International Institute of African Languages and Cultures between the Wars', in Helen Tilley with Robert J. Gordon, ed., *Ordering Africa: Anthropology, European Imperialism and the Politics of Knowledge* (Manchester: Manchester University Press, 2007), 95–116.

15. Lugard's ideas about race come out more explicitly in a discussion at the British Institute of Philosophical Studies in which he participated, 'The Problem of Colour in Relation to the Idea of Equality', *Journal of Philosophical Studies*, 1:2 (April 1926), 211–33, and in Lugard, 'The White Man's Task in Tropical Africa', *Foreign Affairs*, 5:1 (Oct. 1926), 57–68. George W. Stocking Jr. notes their dated character in *After Tylor: British Social Anthropology, 1888–1951* (Madison: University of Wisconsin Press, 1995), 383–4.

16. LNA, S284 1 (9), Ormsby-Gore to Rappard, 17 Jan. 1921.

17. Albert Sarraut, *La Mise en Valeur des colonies françaises* (Paris: Payot, 1923), and for the shift to 'association', Alice L. Conklin, *A Mission to Civilize: The Republican Idea of Empire in France and West Africa, 1895–1930* (Stanford: Stanford University Press, 1997), ch. 6. On Sarraut, see Martin Thomas, 'Albert Sarraut, French Colonial Development and the Communist Threat', *Journal of Modern History*, 77:4 (Dec. 2005), 917–55.

18. He was acquitted, but some harsh words were said about him. See the correspondence in MAE, SDN 556.

19. NA, CO 323/956/32, Note by J. E. W. Flood, 15 Sept. 1926.

20. Margery Perham, *Lugard: The Years of Authority, 1898–1945* (London: Collins, 1960), 645.

### NOTES FOR CHAPTER 4

1. 3 *PMCM*, 117–18.

2. *Records of the Third Assembly*, vol. 1, *Minutes*, session of 8 Sept. 1922, 76, 81; for Walton's deposition of the report, see session of 5 Sept., 38–9. For Bellegarde, see Patrick D. Bellegarde-Smith, 'Dantès Bellegarde and Pan-Africanism', *Phylon (1960–)*, 42:3 (1981), 233–44.

3. *Records of the Third Assembly*, vol. 1, *Minutes*, session of 19 Sept. 1922, 142–3, and 20 Sept. 1922, 152–66.

4. Helmut Bley provides a chilling account of the German system in his *Namibia under German Rule* (new ed., Hamburg: Lit, 1996), 249–79; see also Tony Emmett, *Popular Resistance and the Roots of Nationalism in Namibia, 1915–1966* (Basel: P. Schlettwein, 1999), 73–5.

5. For the 1917 petition, and discussions with Milner about the implications for allocating the territory to South Africa, see Bodleian, Milner C. 702, Schreiner to Milner, 20 Jan. and 14 Feb. 1919.

6. Union of South Africa, *Report on the natives of South West Africa and their treatment by Germany*, PP 1918, XVII, Cd 9146, 4.

7. Union of South Africa, *Report on the natives of South West Africa and their treatment by Germany*, PP 1918, XVII, Cd 9146, 11. The opinions of a wide range of South West African chiefs and headmen (including, revealingly, the elders of the Bondelswarts of Warmbad, later the leaders of the rebellion) were also documented in *Correspondence relating to the Wishes of the Natives of the German Colonies as to their Future Government*, PP 1918, XVII, Cd. 9210, 10–21.

8. NAN, ADM 157, File W41, Gorges to De Jager, 21 Nov. 1917.

9. This material is found in NAN, ADM 157, W41. See esp. Gorges to Botha, 23 Nov. 1917; Report on the Conference of Magistrates and Police Officers, Windhoek, 28 Nov. 1917; Gorges to Minister of Defence, 20 April 1918; and reports by E. Manning, Magistrate, Keetmansoop, 12 March 1918, and T. L. O'Reilly, Military Magistrate, Omaruru, 6 March 1918.

10. NAN, ADM 157, W41, Gorges to Acting Prime Minister, 8 April 1919.

11. LNA, R11, 1/37014/1347, 'Statement by Mr. Hofmeyr to the Permanent Mandates Commission', 25 June 1924, 22, 25.

12. LNA, R41, Union of South Africa, South West Africa Territory, *Report of the Administrator for the Year 1920* (Cape Town, 1921), 15.

13. For the mandate administration's policies towards the German community and its response, Daniel Joseph Walther, *Creating Germans Abroad: Cultural Politics and National Identity in Namibia* (Athens, OH: Ohio University Press, 2002), 153–65.

14. Until recently, most standard accounts of South West Africa under the mandate were based very largely on official publications; these provide much useful material on government policy but relatively little information on African responses. See, e.g., Gail-Maryse Cockram, *South West African Mandate* (Cape Town: Juta and Co., 1976); I. Goldblatt, *History of South West Africa* (Cape Town: Juta & Co., 1971); and John H. Wellington, *South West Africa and its Human Issues* (Oxford: Clarendon Press, 1967). An exception is Ruth First's vivid and impassioned *South West Africa* (Harmondsworth: Penguin, 1963), which pays great attention to the histories and interests of various African groups. Much the best recent study is, however, Tony Emmett's 1987 dissertation, now published as *Popular Resistance and the Roots of Nationalism in Namibia, 1915–1966*, which thoroughly canvassed the Windhoek archives to provide a detailed portrait of labour

and social relations on the ground, and on which I have relied. Figures for the German population from Goldblatt, 200; for 1921, from 3 *PMCM*, 106.

15. The administration reported in 1923 that wages were 10–20 shillings per month, plus food, but that farmers were often unable to pay the wages; see Union of South Africa, South-West Protectorate, *Report of the Administrator for the Year 1922* (Cape Town: Cape Times Ltd., 1923), 21. The dog tax, in other words, amounted to between one and two months' wages for one dog, rising to the laughable amount of 10 pounds, or as much as one or two years' wages, for five dogs.

16. The Bondelswarts rising has received considerable scholarly attention. Arnold Toynbee discussed the event and the South African and League responses at some length in his account of mandatory administration in *Survey of International Affairs, 1920–1923* (London: Humphrey Milford, 1925), 404–17. In 1961 A. M. Davey surveyed contemporary and scholarly responses in *The Bondelzwarts Affair: A Study of the Repercussions, 1922–1959* (Pretoria: Communications of the University of South Africa, 1961). Most histories of Namibia also devote considerable attention to this rebellion. For an account that pays particular attention to the League response, see Cockram, *South West Africa Mandate*, 121–63; on the deterioration of the Bondelswarts' living conditions and the social causes of the revolt, see esp. Emmett, *Popular Resistance*, 111–24. The most gripping narrative account of the rising, one written with imaginative licence but considerable sympathy for Morris and his followers, is Richard Freislich, *The Last Tribal War: A History of the Bondelswart Uprising* (Cape Town: C. Struik, 1964).

17. 'Hottentot Rising. Rebels Bombed', *The Times*, 31 May 1922, 9.

18. NAN, ADM 158, W60, Smuts to Hofmeyr, 2 July 1922.

19. NAN, Acc. 312, File 19/73, Smuts to Hofmeyr, 5 July 1922.

20. RH, ASAPS Archives, G402, M. Hoskens to Harris, 26 July 1922 and 3 Aug. 1922; LNA, R41, 1/22331/15778, Buxton and Harris to Drummond, 3 Aug. 1922, and enclosing 'Crushing of the Bondelzwart Rebellion', *The African World*, 29 July 1922.

21. Charles Roberts, President of the Anti-Slavery Society, at its Annual Meeting, *ASRAF*, V, 13:2 (July 1923), 51.

22. 'Annual Meeting of the Society', *ASRAF*, V, 13:2 (July 1923), 51.

23. RH, ASAPS Archives, G402, Murray to Harris, 2 Nov. 1922 and 25 May 1923.

24. 'Good old British Flag!' *The International* (Johannesburg), 25 May 1923.

25. LNA, R10, 1/28258/1347, *Report of the Commission Appointed to Enquire into the Rebellion of the Bondelzwarts* (Cape Town, 1923).

26. LNA, R10, 1/29706/1347, CPM 49. 'Bondelzwarts Rising: Extracts from the Debate in the Union House of Assembly', 16.

27. 3 *PMCM*, 113–16.

28. Harris and Buxton's letter to Drummond of 23 July 1923 requesting that the PMC hear someone who could present the Bondelswarts' point of view is reprinted in 3 *PMCM*, Annex 8, 287–8.

29. LNA, R10, 1/29706/1347, CPM 49. 'Bondelzwarts Rising: Extracts from the Debate in the Union House of Assembly', 2.

30. 3 *PMCM*, 123. South Africa continued to use airplanes to intimidate allegedly insurrectionary natives, for which see Richard Dale, 'The Armed Forces as an Instrument of South African Policy in Namibia', *The Journal of Modern African Studies*, 18:1 (1980), 57–71.
31. 3 *PMCM*, 120.
32. 3 *PMCM*, 131–4.
33. 3 *PMCM*, 128–30.
34. LNA, S259, E. F. C. Lane, Cape Town, to Herbst, High Commission, London, 25 June 1923.
35. 3 *PMCM*, 134–7.
36. 3 *PMCM*, 183–7.
37. 3 *PMCM*, 201–4, and LNA, R11, 1/31364/1347, CPM 76, 'Opinion du membre portugais de la CPM sur l'Affaire du Bondelzwarts'.
38. The handwritten original of Theodoli's statement to his colleagues in LNA S284 1 (15), Theodoli to PMC members, 9 Aug. 1923.
39. 3 *PMCM*, 205–6; the draft of Theodoli's statement, mistitled 'Lugard', is in LNA S298(7).
40. RH, Lugard 136/6, Lugard, 'Bondelswarts'; a copy is also in LNA S298(7).
41. 3 *PMCM*, 203, and see LNA S284 1 (14), Lugard to Rappard, 15 Aug. 1923.
42. 3 *PMCM*, 207.
43. A.47.1923.VI, PMC, *Report on the Bondelzwarts Rebellion* (14 Aug. 1923).
44. C.550.1923.IV, PMC, *Comments of the Accredited Representative of the Union of South Africa on the Commission's Report on the Bondelzwarts Rebellion*, 23 Aug. 1923.
45. LNA, R10, 1/30798/1347, Lugard to Rappard, 7 Sept. 1923 (handwritten); typed copy in S298(7).
46. Fourth Assembly, Plenary Meeting, 26 Sept. 1923, *LNOJ*, Special Suppl. no. 13 (Oct. 1923), 92–3.
47. LNA, S263, File on 3rd meeting, 1923.
48. Minutes of the 27th session of the Council, 13 Dec. 1923, *LNOJ*, 5:2 (Feb. 1924), 339–41.
49. Sara Pienaar points out that South Africa's policy in South West Africa closely resembled its own policy in the Union, about which it was unapologetic, believing it to be right. See Sara Pienaar, *South Africa and International Relations between the Two World Wars: The League of Nations Dimension* (Johannesburg: Witwatersrand University Press, 1987), 126.
50. Fourth Assembly, Plenary Meeting, 26 Sept. 1923, *LNOJ*, Special Suppl. no. 13 (Oct. 1923), 92.
51. 4 *PMCM*, 114–15.
52. NAN, Acc. 312, 17/61, Hofmeyr to Smit, 6 Aug. 1924, and Smit to Hofmeyr, 5 July 1924.
53. The long struggle between the Rehobothers and the administration is documented fully in the League archives and absorbed a good deal of the PMC's

time. For their petition campaigns, see Tilman Dedering, 'Petitioning Geneva: Transnational Aspects of Protest and Resistance in South West Africa/Namibia after the First World War', *Journal of Southern African Studies*, 35:4 (Dec. 2009), 785–801, and for that history more generally, Rudolf G. Britz, Hartmut Lang, and Cornelia Limpricht, *A Concise History of the Rehoboth Basters until 1990* (Windhoek: Klaus Hess, 1999).

54. A. J. Christopher, 'Official Land Disposal Policies and European Settlement in Southern Africa, 1860–1960', *Journal of Historical Geography*, 9:4 (1983), 371.

55. Emmett, *Popular Resistance*, 105.

56. NAN, Acc. 312, 'The Visit of the Administrator to Warmbad', *Allgemeine Zeitung* (Windhoek), 9 Oct. 1926.

57. 14 *PMCM*, 90, 102, 104, 108, 109, 116.

58. 18 *PMCM*, 140–1.

59. 6 *PMCM*, 70.

60. The administration's resistance to spending on African needs was a constant theme in the PMC minutes; see, 22 *PMCM*, 368–9; 31 *PMCM*, 126–8; and 34 *PMCM*, 78, 323. Reinhard Kössler points out that the administration in the 1930s also began raiding the accounts into which the grazing fees collected from Africans were paid, which were to be used only for the reserves; see his 'From Reserve to Homeland: Local Identities and South African Policy in Southern Namibia', *Journal of Southern African Studies*, 26:3 (Sept. 2000), 447–62.

61. 14 *PMCM*, 101–4; see also Rappard's strenuous criticisms the previous year in 11 *PMCM*, 99.

62. 11 *PMCM*; and see also 26 *PMCM*, 61; 27 *PMCM*, 158–9.

63. The internal construction and policing of settler power and racial hierarchies in South West Africa between the wars has been explored most brilliantly in the essay collection, *Namibia under South African Rule: Mobility and Containment*, ed. Patricia Hayes, Jeremy Silvester, Marion Wallace, and Wolfram Hartmann (Oxford: James Currey, 1998); see esp. Robert J. Gordon, 'Vagrancy, Law & "Shadow Knowledge": Internal Pacification', 51–76.

64. Fourth Assembly, Plenary Meeting, 26 Sept. 1923, *LNOJ*, Special Suppl. no. 13 (Oct. 1923), 92–3.

65. 1 *PMCM*, 14, 31.

66. LNA, S298(7), Freire d'Andrade, 'Opinion du membre portugais de la CPM sur l'Affaire des Bondelswarts'; and 4 *PMCM*, 116; 6 *PMCM*, 69; 11 *PMCM*, 98.

67. The quotations are from Lugard. 5 *PMCM*, 27–8; 6 *PMCM*, 47–50.

68. The original handwritten drafts are in LNA, R74. All four memoranda were printed as annexes to 7 *PMCM*.

69. Sir Frederick Lugard, 'Economic Development of Mandated Territories in its Relation to the Well Being of the Natives', 7 *PMCM*, 194–7.

70. Freire d'Andrade, 'The Interpretation of that Part of Article 22 of the Covenant which Related to the Well-Being and Development of the Peoples of Mandated Territories', in 7 *PMCM*, 197–205.

71. 'Note by Sir F. Lugard on the Memorandum of M. Freire d'Andrade', and 'Reply by M. Freire d'Andrade on Sir F. Lugard's Note', in 7 *PMCM*, 206–9.

72. Frederick Lugard, *The Dual Mandate in British Tropical Africa* (1922; rpt. New York: Hamden, CT: Archon Books, 1965), 425–60, here at 431.

73. For that report see LNDM, Reel CPM-1, CPM 46, Bugge-Wicksell, 'A Comparative Study of Education in Mandated Territories', 23 March 1923; and two supplements CPM 46(a) dated 10 July 1923 and CPM 46(b) dated 19 July 1923. For the Commission's attitude to education, see also J. M. Barrington, 'The Permanent Mandates Commission and Educational Policy in Trust Territories', *International Review of Education*, 22:1 (1976), and Susan Pedersen, 'Metaphors of the Schoolroom: Women Working the Mandates System of the League of Nations', *History Workshop Journal*, 66 (2008), 188–207.

74. This was Bugge-Wicksell's conclusion after visiting Tuskegee, for which see LNDM, Reel CPM-7, CPM 623, Bugge-Wicksell, 'Memo regarding her visit to several coloured schools and universities in the Southern United States', 1927.

75. C. D. Rowley, 'The Occupation of German New Guinea 1914–1921', in W. J. Hudson, ed., *Australia and Papua New Guinea* (Sydney: Sydney University Press, 1971), 57–73.

76. For which see *Interim and Final Reports of the Royal Commission on Late German New Guinea, Parliamentary Papers (Australia)*, 1920–21, III.

77. For which see ANA, A457/1, Pethebridge to Defence, 3 Dec. 1915, and Johnston to Defence, 14 March 1919.

78. ANA, File A457/1, Trumble to Administrator, 9 April 1919, and PM's office to Administrator, Rabaul, 26 Sept. 1921.

79. See ANA Files A457/1 and A518/1 for particular cases; these, and the statistics on prosecutions of Europeans included in Australia's annual reports to the League of Nations, are much more revealing than the single government inquiry into abuse, undertaken in response to exposés published in the Sydney *Daily Telegraph* in 1923, which was largely a whitewash: see *Report of Inquiry into Allegations of Flogging and Forced Labour of Natives, by A. S. Canning*, in *Parliamentary Papers (Australia)*, 1923–24, vol. 4. Very little has been written until recently from archival sources about the New Guinea administration, but one exemplary piece (which also details the reasons Canning's inquiry was so unrevealing) is Roger C. Thompson, 'Making a Mandate: The Formation of Australia's New Guinea Policies, 1919–1925', *Journal of Pacific History*, 25:1 (1990), 68–94.

80. This was the view of Joseph Carrodus, Australia's representative in 1926, for which see Thompson, 'Making a Mandate', 81.

81. For Tanganyika's economic policy in the early 1920s, see esp. LNA, R40, 1/59624/15313, Report by His Britannic Majesty's Government to the Council of the League of Nations on the Administration of Tanganyika Territory for the Year 1926; 1/45468/15313, Donald Cameron, 'Agriculture and Labour' (5 Aug. 1926).

82. Charlotte Leubuscher, *Tanganyika Territory: A Study of Economic Policy under Mandate* (London: Oxford University Press, 1944), 22–5, 33.

83. Donald Cameron, 'Native administration' (1925), quoted in 9 *PMCM*, 137. Cameron expounded his philosophy of native administration at some length in Cameron, *My Tanganyika Service* (London: George Allen & Unwin, 1939), but for a thoughtful and critical summary of the system's character and effects, see John Iliffe, *A Modern History of Tanganyika* (Cambridge: Cambridge University Press, 1979), ch. 10.

84. LNA, R39, 1/29970/15313, 'African Territories under British Mandate' (7 Aug. 1923), 4. LNA, R40: 1/37084/15313, 'Draft Observations on the Administration of Mandated Territories. Tanganyika' (7 July 1924), 4; 1/44414/15313, 'Draft Observations. Tanganyika' (8 July 1925). 'Report to the Council on the Work of the 11th session', in 11 *PMCM*, 202–3, and 'Report', in 15 *PMCM*, 298.

85. 11 *PMCM*, 65, 203.

86. NA, FO 608/219/919, Note by Sir Charles Strachey, 18 Feb. 1919.

87. LNA, R1, 1/2371/161, 'Memorandum on the Colonial Mandates for the Late German Colonies from the Anti-Slavery and Aborigines Protection Society', 12 July 1919.

88. LNA, R60, 1/19802/19802, Anti-Slavery Society to Drummond, 28 March 1922, and Rappard to Harris, 31 March 1922.

89. 'The Land Question in Mandated Territories in Africa: Letter from the Anti-Slavery and Aborigines Protection Society', Annex 5 in 2 *PMCM*, 88–90.

90. The importance of Tanganyika's land legislation, and the process of its drafting, is treated in greater detail by Callahan, *Mandates and Empire*, 80–4.

91. British mandated Cameroons was divided in two and the northern portion again subdivided, so that by 1923 three separate reports were sent to the PMC. By 1925 there were two main divisions: Cameroons province in the South, and 'Northern Cameroons', which was subdivided into four portions, each being administered alongside the neighbouring Nigerian province. Togo was divided into two parts, a northern portion administered as part of the Northern Territories of Gold Coast, and the southern portion as part of Gold Coast Colony.

92. Callahan, *Mandates and Empire*, 104–21.

93. 2 *PMCM*, 90; see also J. H. Harris, 'Colonial Mandates and Native Rights', *The Manchester Guardian*, 18 March 1922.

94. 2 *PMCM*, 23–5, 30–2.

95. ASAPS, G404, Rappard to Harris, 15 Aug. 1922. Van Rees's memorandum, 'The System of State Lands in B and C Mandated Territories', was printed in 3 *PMCM*, Annex 2, 216–39.

96. 3 *PMCM*, 30, 144.

97. 'Legal Questions connection with the expressions "Domaine de l'Etat"…: Memorandum by the Legal Section of the Secretariat', Annex I in 4 *PMCM*, 163–8, and for the Commission's view, *Report on the Work of the Fourth Session*, 3.

98. See esp. Véronique Dimier's intelligent reading of mandates debates in '"L'internationalisation" du débat colonial: rivalités franco-britanniques autour de la Commission permanente des Mandats', *Outre Mers: Revue d'Histoire*, 89:336–7 (2002), 333–60.

99. 6 *PMCM*, 17–19, 25–7, 37.

## NOTES FOR CHAPTER 5

1. LC, Gilchrist Papers, Box 19, File: 'Quincy Wright'.

2. The authoritative account of politics in mandate Syria, one that pays considerable attention to the role of the rising in rechannelling the strategies of Syrian nationalists, is Philip S. Khoury, *Syria and the French Mandate: The Politics of Arab Nationalism, 1920–1945* (Princeton: Princeton University Press, 1987). Khoury, however, concentrates largely on urban notables, and as Michael Provence has pointed out, the revolt was predominantly rural; his *The Great Syrian Revolt and the Rise of Arab Nationalism* (Austin: University of Texas Press, 2005) provides a rich account of the social bonds and friendships among rural and non-elite populations that sustained the rising. Martin C. Thomas has mined the records of the Service des Renseignements—the intelligence network on which the mandatory administration relied—to provide much useful information on the perspectives of, and divisions within, that administration itself; see 'French Intelligence-Gathering in the Syrian Mandate, 1920–40', *Middle Eastern Studies*, 38:1 (Jan. 2002), 1–32. Stephen H. Longrigg's *Syria and Lebanon under French Mandate* (London: Oxford University Press, 1958), an account written with considerable sympathy for the Hashemite cause, is still useful. The account of the revolt given in the next few paragraphs draws on all four works.

3. Khoury, *Syria and the French Mandate*, 151, cites British sources to give an estimate of a rebel army of 8,000–10,000 men, but Provence, *The Great Syrian Revolt*, 62, points out that the British consul took those estimates from French sources, which wildly overestimated rebel strength in the early period. The total population of the Jabal Druze was only about 50,000 in the 1920s.

4. The complete text of al-Atrash's proclamation was included as an appendix to the 29 Sept. 1925 petition of the Syro-Palestinian Congress to the League (see, 8 *PMCM*, 191); Provence, *The Great Syrian Revolt*, 81–3, also reprints the proclamation in full.

5. The French claimed that they initially used only blank shells, a claim historians have largely repeated, but W. A. Smart, the British consul in Damascus, documented severe damage from live shells that first night. See, NA, FO 371/10852, E 7078, Smart to Chamberlain, 17 Nov. 1925.

6. NA, FO 371/10850, E 4692, Phipps (Paris) to FO, 9 Aug. 1925.

7. For French complaints of Sarrail's censorship and their reliance on the London press, see NA, FO 371/10851, Phipps to Chamberlain, 4 Aug. 1925.

8. 'The Druse Rebellion', *The Times*, 10 Aug. 1925.

9. 'Agitation against General Sarrail', *The Times*, 10 Aug. 1925.

10. See, e.g., 'L'affaire du Djebel Druse', *L'Asie Française*, 25:234 (Aug.–Sept. 1925), 249–56.

11. 'The Damascus Revolt', *The Times*, 22 Oct. 1925.

12. 'Damascus Riots. The Full Story. City Shelled for 48 hours. Famous Places Destroyed', *The Times*, 27 Oct. 1925. The *Times* article accords with the account of the rising and the bombardment given by the British Consul W. A. Smart in a long dispatch sent to the Foreign Office once the city was again calm (NA, FO 684/2, Smart to FO, Dispatch no. 220, 25 Oct. 1925), suggesting that he was its main source.

13. LNA, Box R21, 1/39401/4284, Lutfallah and Arslan, for the Syro-Palestinian Congress, to Giuseppe Motta, President of the 5th Assembly, 17 Sept. 1924.

14. Executive Committee of the Syro-Palestinian Congress, to Raoul Dandurand, President of the 6th Assembly, in 8 *PMCM*, Annex III, 174–97; and for Arslan, see William L. Cleveland, *Islam Against the West: Shakib Arslan and the Campaign for Islamic Nationalism* (Austin: University of Texas Press, 1985), 53, and Friedhelm Hoffmann, *Die Syro-Palästinensische Delegation am Völkerbund und Šakīb Arslān in Genf, 1921–1936/46* (Berlin: Lit, 2007), 121.

15. LNA, R23 and R24 have extensive files of such protests, some seventy of which were listed in Annex II, 8 *PMCM*, 171–3.

16. RH, Lugard Papers 129/4, Syrian American Society of the United States, *Memorandum on the Application of the Mandatory System of the League of Nations by France in Syria* (1926).

17. QW, Box 16, Folder 9, 'Investigation of the Operation of the Near Eastern Mandates' (report, 1926).

18. Quincy Wright, 'The Bombardment of Damascus', *The American Journal of International Law*, 20:2 (April 1926), 263–80.

19. J. O., *Débats (Chambre)*, 18 Dec. 1925, 4437–52; 20 Dec. 1925, 4501–56.

20. Smart's consular dispatches providing a vivid daily account of events in Damascus are in NA, FO 684/2 and in FO 371/10850–18052. See esp. his Dispatch no. 220 of 25 Oct. 1925, copies in FO 684/2 and in FO 371/10851, which is a full account of the bombardment, written about one week later when Smart had time to put together a full record, as well as Chamberlain's telegram approving his action, FO 684/2, Chamberlain to Smart, 26 Oct. 1925, and his letter commending his 'sound judgment, tact and courage', in FO 371/10852, E6891, Chamberlain to Smart, 9 Nov. 1925.

21. NA, FO 371/10851, E6673, Crewe (Paris) to FO, 31 Oct. 1925, and comment by W. Tyrrell on Dispatch 220, noting plan to read excerpts to M. de Fleuriau.

22. NA FO 371/10851, E6673, Crewe (Paris) to FO, 31 Oct. 1925.

23. 7 *PMCM*, 9–16.

24. For France's agreement, see 7 *PMCM*, 80–2.

25. 7 *PMCM*, 129–33.

26. For which see Cleveland, *Islam Against the West*, 53–4, and Hoffmann, *Die Syro-Palästinensische Delegation*, 123–5.
27. NA, FO 371/10851, E6771, Phipps to FO, n.d.
28. MAE, SDN 566, Avenol to Jouvenel, 17 Nov. 1925; and LC, Gilchrist Papers, Box 25, File: 'Mandates', Note by Gilchrist, 21 Nov. 1925.
29. Smart's dispatches (as well as those from Beirut) document the anti-British feeling in the French administration in Syria as well as repeated attacks on his own role; see NA, FO 371/10852, esp. E6967, Smart to FO, 12 Nov. 1925, and FO 371/10854.
30. See NA, FO 684/2, Dispatch no. 220, Smart to Chamberlain, 25 Oct. 1925, and Dispatch no. 136 (secret), Norman Mayers, Acting Consul General in Beirut, to Chamberlain, 27 Oct. 1925.
31. Smart was well aware that 'failure to secure compensation for such wanton damage inflicted on our Asiatic nationals would have unfortunate political repercussions for us in the East'. See NA, FO 684/2, Dispatch no. 217, Smart to FO, 24 Oct. 1925.
32. NA, FO 684/2, Dispatch no. 217, Smart to Chamberlain, 25 Oct. 1925. In later dispatches, Smart also asked the Foreign Office to try to prevent Transjordan from being used as a base by the rebels and to restrain the blistering criticisms of French behaviour appearing in the Arab press in Iraq, Egypt, and Palestine.
33. NA, FO 371/10852, E6890, Oliphant to Phipps, 9 Nov. 1925, and E7090, Phipps to Oliphant, 11 Nov. 1925; the account of Chamberlain and Amery's meeting with Jouvenel on 19 Nov. 1925 is in FO 371/10853, E7420.
34. NA, FO 371/10851, E6653, Memo by Lampson, 30 Oct. 1925, and comment by Chamberlain, 4 Nov. 1925.
35. MAE, SDN 566, Berthelot to Fleuriau, 18 Nov. 1925.
36. NA, CAB 24/175, C.P. 496 (25), Chamberlain to the Marquess of Crewe (Paris), 23 Nov. 1925.
37. RH, Lugard 119/4, Lady Lugard to Leo Amery, 22 Feb. 1926.
38. RH, Lugard 119/4, Lady Lugard to Leo Amery, 22 Feb. 1926.
39. MAE, SDN 566, Briand to Resnard, 1 Dec. 1925.
40. See the correspondence about Theodoli's untrustworthiness in MAE, SDN 566, de Caix to Berthelot, received 6 Jan. 1926; Resnard to Berthelot, 16 Jan. 1926; de Caix to Berthelot, 19 Jan. 1926.
41. NA, FO 371/11505, E459, Smart to Chamberlain, 11 Jan. 1926.
42. LNA, R24, 1/47643/4284, Notes about arrangements for Rome session.
43. Unfortunately, only the final (corrected) typescript made it back to Geneva; this can be found in LNA, R26. De Caix's comment on Roume's editing is in MAE, SDN 567, Robert de Caix, 'Note sur la session de la Commission des Mandats et sur son rapport à la Société des Nations' (13 March 1926).
44. RH, Lugard 119/4, Lugard to Lady Lugard, 16 and 17 Feb. 1926.
45. 8 *PMCM*, 12.
46. RH, Lugard 119/4, Lugard to Lady Lugard, 16, 17, and 18 Feb. 1926.

47. RH, Lugard 119/4, Lugard to Lady Lugard, 17 and 27 Feb. 1926.
48. RH, Lugard 119/4, Lugard to Lady Lugard, 2 March 1926.
49. RH, Lugard 119/4, Lugard to Lady Lugard, 21 Feb. 1926.
50. 8 *PMCM*, 45, 61.
51. 8 *PMCM*, 126.
52. 8 *PMCM*, 57, 87.
53. 8 *PMCM*, 61.
54. 8 *PMCM*, 156–60.
55. 8 *PMCM*, 140–1.
56. RH, Lugard 119/4, Lugard to Lady Lugard, 2 March 1926.
57. Smart reported 'much indiscriminate killing' by the French Army in October and widespread looting and burning of villages in November; see NA, FO 371/10852, Dispatch no. 221, Smart to FO, 26 Oct. 1925, and FO 684/2, Dispatch no. 228, 2 Nov. 1925.
58. RH, Lugard 119/4, Lugard to Lady Lugard, 21 Feb. and 2 March 1926.
59. MAE, SDN 566, de Caix to MAE, telegrams, 19 Feb. and 5 March 1926.
60. MAE, SDN 567, Berthelot to Jouvenel, telegram, 6 March 1926.
61. Given their origins and purpose, scholars coming across these reports in French and League archives should treat them most sceptically.
62. RH, Lugard 119/4, Lugard to Lady Lugard, 1 March 1926.
63. 'Report', in 8 *PMCM*, 198–208.
64. MAE, SDN, 567, Robert de Caix, 'Note sur la session de la Commission des Mandats et sur son rapport à la Société des Nations' (13 March 1926).
65. Council Meeting, 39th session, 5th meeting, 17 March 1926, in *LNOJ*, 7:4 (April 1926), 522–6.
66. BLPES, LNU Archives, Reel 431, vol. 5/44, Mandates Committee, 30 March 1926.
67. LC, Gilchrist Papers, Box 12, File: 'Fosdick, 1926–1928', Gilchrist to Fosdick, 17 March 1926.
68. LC, Gilchrist Papers, Box 19, File: 'Quincy Wright', Gilchrist to Wright, 22 March 1926.
69. LC, Gilchrist Papers, Box 19, File: 'Quincy Wright', Wright to Gilchrist, 5 April 1926.
70. LC, Gilchrist Papers, Box 19, File: 'Quincy Wright', Gilchrist to Wright, 3 May 1926.
71. LC, Gilchrist Papers, Box 19, File: 'Quincy Wright', Wright to Gilchrist, 17 May 1926.
72. Christine Manigand provides a rosy account of Jouvenel's administration in *Henry de Jouvenel* (Limoges: PULIM, 2000), 200–28.
73. NA, FO 371/11505, E459, Smart to Chamberlain, 11 Jan. 1926.
74. Dispatches from Smart in Damascus through this period (NA, FO 371/11506) provide a vivid picture of the French counter-insurgency; he and his successor noted the restraint of the rebels and the absence of sectarian killing.

75. LNA, S293 (3), Vaucher to Nansen, 27 Aug. 1926, enclosing 'Mémorandum sur la situation en Syrie et au Liban en Juillet/Aout 1926' (19 Aug. 1926).

76. 9 *PMCM*, 109–28; NA, CO 323/956/30, Minute by Clauson, 28 Aug. 1926.

77. De Caix, "L'Organisation donnée à la Syrie et au Liban, de 1920 à 1923 et la crise actuelle", in Gerard D. Khoury, *Une Tutelle coloniale: Le mandat français en Syrie et au Liban: Ecrits politiques de Robert de Caix* (Paris: Belin, 2006), 422.

78. MAE, SDN 568, Clauzel, 'Note pour M. Berthelot', 18 Nov. 1926.

79. The PMC had to wait a long time for these reports. Although de Caix stated that Jouvenel had decided to set up an inquiry immediately, in fact it was set in motion some seven months later in anticipation of the June 1926 PMC session. Jouvenel's report for 1925 was also, de Caix admitted, politically 'nulle'. For these wrangles over documentation, see MAE, SDN 567, de Caix to Clauzel, 27 May 1926, and de Caix, 'Note pour M. Philippe Berthelot', 26 May 1926; 9 *PMCM*, 110; MAE, SDN 568, de Caix to Briand, 2 Dec. 1926.

80. MAE, SDN 567, 'Note pour Monseiur Guerlet', 16 March 1926.

81. NA, CO 323/956/30, Minute by Clauson, 28 Aug. 1926; 'League Approves French Rule in Syria', *The New York Times,* 18 June 1926.

82. MAE, SDN 568, de Caix to Briand, 2 Dec. 1926.

83. 10 *PMCM*, 132.

84. 10 *PMCM*, 140, 146.

85. MAE, SDN 568, de Caix to Briand, 2 Dec. 1926.

86. LNA, R23, 1/47458/4284, B. F. Dawson, telegram, 8 May 1926, and Dawson to Secretary General, 2 June 1926.

87. LNA, R23, 1/47458/4284, Drummond to Catastini, 12 June 1926.

88. LNA, R23, 1/47458/4284, Dawson to Catastini, 18 June 1926.

89. LNA, R23, 1/47458/4284, Catastini to Dawson, 5 July 1926.

90. 8 *PMCM*, 148.

91. MAE, SDN 566, Berthelot to Sarrail, 30 Oct. 1925, and Sarrail to MAE, 30 Oct. 1925, and marginal comments.

92. LNA, R23, 1/47458/4284, Catastini to Dawson, 14 March 1927.

93. De Caix, 'L'Organisation donnée à la Syrie et au Liban, de 1920 à 1923 et la crise actuelle', in Khoury, *Une Tutelle coloniale*, 394–456.

94. NA, FO 371/10851, E6771, Phipps to FO, n.d.

## NOTES FOR CHAPTER 6

1. LNA, R 2324, 6A/25086/709, 'A Samoan National Protest voiced at Vaimoso on March the 5th, 1930, by High Chief Tuimaleali'ifano', in *The Samoan Massacre: December 28th, 1929* (Tasmania, 1930).

2. LNA, Box R32, 1/59448/9597, Bartlett to Catastini, 12 May 1927, enclosing Rowe to Bartlett, 29 April 1927.

3. LNA, R32, 1/59448/9597, Rowe to Theodoli, 1 June 1927, and enclosing Newton Rowe, 'The Samoa Mandate', *Foreign Affairs*, 8:12 (June 1927).

4. LNA, R32, File 1/59888/9597, Bartlett to Catastini, 3 June 1927, enclosing Westbrook to Bartlett, 2 May 1927.

5. LNA, R32, File 1/59888/9597, File 1/60890/9597, Buxton to Secretary of the Permanent Mandates Commission, 19 July 1927.

6. Theodoli mentioned the 1921 petition in 1927 (12 *PMCM*, 123), so its contents were known to the Commission by that time.

7. 12 *PMCM*, 105–8, 111, 127.

8. 12 *PMCM*, Annex 9, 'Reports on Petitions', 195–7, and 'Report', 203.

9. See 'The Maintenance of Authority in Native Affairs (no. 2) Ordinance', 1928, published in the *Supplement to the Western Samoa Gazette*, no. 74, 21 Feb. 1928, and *Legislative Council Debates*, 21 Feb. 1928, both in LNA, R2321, 6A/709/709, jacket 1. The second petition from the Anti-Slavery Society, dated 8 June 1928, is in LNA Box R2322, 6A/2713/709; those from Nelson, dated 29 March 1928, and the 8,000 Samoans, submitted 23 April 1928, are in R2322, 6A/2967/709.

10. Although protest movements in American Samoa were neither as widespread nor as harshly repressed as in the mandated territory, a 'Mau' was also active in American Samoa, where it won significant concessions from US authorities. See David A. Chappell, 'The Forgotten Mau: Anti-Navy Protest in American Samoa, 1920–1935', *Pacific Historical Review*, 69:2 (May 2000), 217–60.

11. USNA, Microfilm Class M336, Reel 161, 862m.00/48, Department of the Navy to the Department of State, enclosing Graham to the Department of the Navy, 29 June 1929.

12. Malama Meleisea, *The Making of Modern Samoa: Traditional Authority and Colonial Administration in the Modern History of Western Samoa* (Suva, Fiji: Institute of Pacific Studies, 1987), 1; see also his *Change and Adaptations in Western Samoa* (Christchurch, New Zealand: University of Canterbury, 1992).

13. A positive reading of the work of this Land Commission (which certainly disallowed more claims than it allowed) is given by J. W. Davidson, *Samoa mo Samoa: The Emergence of the Independent State of Western Samoa* (Melbourne: Oxford University Press, 1967), 64–5; for caveats, see Meleisea, *Making*, 44–5.

14. On German paternalism in Samoa, see Evelyn Wareham, *Race and Realpolitik: The Politics of Colonisation in German Samoa* (Frankfurt: P. Lang, 2002), 31–63, and George Steinmetz, 'The Uncontrollable Afterlives of Ethnography: Lessons from "Salvage Colonialism" in the German Overseas Empire', *Ethnography*, 5:3 (2004), 251–88.

15. On the 'half-castes' see esp. Toeolesulusulu D. Salesa, 'Half-Castes between the Wars: Colonial Categories in New Zealand and Samoa', *New Zealand Journal of History*, 34:1 (2000), 98–116; Meleisea, *Making*, ch. 7; and, for the German period, Wareham, *Race*, ch. 5.

16. For the military administration, see Mary Boyd, 'The Military Administration of Western Samoa, 1914–1919', *The New Zealand Journal of History*, 2:2 (Oct. 1968), 148–64; Meleisea, *Making*, 102–25; Davidson, *Samoa mo Samoa*, 93.

17. For the loss of the *Faipules*, see Meleisea, *Making*, 121; for Nelson, see Meleisea, *Making*, 174–5, and Davidson, *Samoa mo Samoa*, 94.

18. Boyd, 'Military Administration', 161–4.

19. USNA, Microfilm Class M336, Reel 162, 862m.01/12, Quincy Roberts to Secretary of State, 5 Aug. 1921.

20. ANZ, ACHK 16603, G48/33, S/8, 'A Humble Prayer to His Majesty George V. King of Great Britain & Ireland from the Government Councilors of British Samoa who Represent all the Districts and All the Natives of Western Samoa', 16 July 1921.

21. ANZ, ACHK 16603, G48/33, S/8, Prime Minister's Office to Governor General, 24 Aug. 1921; Governor General to Churchill, 26 Aug. 1921; Churchill to Governor General, 4 Nov. 1921. An account of Tate's efforts to return the petition is in USNA, Microfilm Class M336, Reel 162, 862m.01/12, Roberts to Secretary of State, 5 Aug. 1921.

22. A fair amount has been written on Richardson's administration and the emergence of the Mau. Davidson, *Samoa mo Samoa*, and Meleisea, *Making*, provide detailed accounts, although Davidson concentrates more on the political conflict with New Zealand and Meleisea more on its social impact. For a narrative account, with many interesting photographs, see Michael J. Field, *Mau: Samoa's Struggle Against New Zealand Oppression* (Wellington: A. H. and A. W. Reed 1984). This account draws on all three works.

23. *Imperial Conference, 1926, Appendices to the Summary of Proceedings*, PP 1926, Cmd. 2769, 188–9.

24. USNA, Microfilm class M336, Reel 161, 862m.00/20, Bryan to Secretary of the Navy, 3 Dec. 1926.

25. USNA, Microfilm class M336, Reel 163, 862.01/49, Roberts to Secretary of State, 25 Aug. 1927.

26. LNA, R32, 1/61825x/9597 (mislabelled 1/61281), CPM 686, 'Summary of the Report of the Royal Commission', 13 Dec. 1927.

27. Wellington's deepening concern about Richardson's judgement was aroused not only by his own confidential communications but still more by the frank telegrams sent by the Commodore of the ships sent to Apia. Although the government agreed to provide those forces, they stressed their anxiety about any use of force and insisted that Richardson's every move be cleared by Wellington. By the end of February, the Commodore was convinced that the conflict could not 'be settled under any circumstances by the present Administrator'; see ANZ, ACHK 16603, G48/37, Commodore to Naval Secretary, 29 Feb. 1928.

28. LNA, R2322, 6A/2090/709, Gilchrist, Memo for the Secretary General, 24 Feb. 1928, and note by Drummond, 27 Feb. 1928.

29. LNA, R2322, File 6A/875/709, jacket 1, John Roberts (solicitor) to Marquis Theodoli, 15 June 1928.

30. 13 *PMCM*, 110.

31. 13 *PMCM*, esp. 115–16 on Nelson, 122 and 125 on the limits of the administration's power, and 116–19 on the character of the Samoans.

32. 13 *PMCM*, 119.

33. 5 *PMCM*, 49.

34. 'New Zealand: The Trouble in Samoa', *Round Table*, 18 (Dec. 1927), 191–210; Nosworthy is quoted 203.

35. 13 *PMCM*, 115.

36. LNA, Box R2323, 6A/5037/709, CPM 755, 'Draft observations on Western Samoa. Text proposed by Lord Lugard', 25 June 1928.

37. 13 *PMCM*, 136.

38. 13 *PMCM*, 136.

39. 13 *PMCM*, 155.

40. 'Report', Annex 7, in 13 *PMCM*, 229–30.

41. LNA, Box R2322, 6A/2713/709, Buxton and Harris to Secretary General, 8 June 1928, reproduced as CPM 739.

42. ANZ, IT1, EX1/63, Pt. 1, Richardson to Parr, 2 July 1928, and Coates to Drummond, 27 Sept. 1928.

43. LNA, R2322, 6A/2713/709, CPM 762, 'Petitions dated July 19, 1927 and June 8, 1928, from the Anti-Slavery and Aborigines Protection Society: Report by Mr. Kastl'. With regard to the Society's first petition about the alleged deportation of native chiefs, the Commission simply reported that the chiefs had been banished but not deported from the territory, and that banishment was allowable by law.

44. J. V. Wilson to Drummond, 10 June 1927; Note by Drummond, 11 June 1927; Gilchrist to Catastini, 14 June 1927; Catastini to Drummond, 18 June 1927; Drummond to Catastini, 21 June 1927; all in LNA, R32, 1/29778/9597.

45. LNA, R32, 1/59448/9597, Coates to Secretary General, 13 Sept. 1927.

46. Arthur Garrels, the US Consul in Melbourne, told the State Department that, from what he had heard, Rowe's allegations were substantially true. See USNA, Microfilm M336, Reel 163, 862m.01/43, Garrels to State, 21 July 1927. The PMC criticized Parr for having misled them about the administration's competence; see 16 *PMCM*, 118, 122.

47. LNA, R2322, 6A/2712/709.

48. LNA, Box R2322, 6A/2967/709, 'The Petition of Olaf Frederick Nelson of Apia', 29 March 1928, quoted at paragraph 42.

49. 13 *PMCM*, 152–3.

50. LNA, Box R2323, 6A/5037/709, CPM 755, 'Draft observations on Western Samoa. Text proposed by Lord Lugard', 25 June 1928.

51. 'Report', 13 *PMCM*, Annex 7, 229–30; and see Palacios' objections, 155–7.

52. LNA, R2322, 6A/2967/709, petition submitted 23 April 1928.

53. LNA, R2323, 6A/4398/709, Coates to Secretary General, 24 April 1928, and 'Comment of General Sir George Richardson on the Petition of Certain Natives of the Territory', CPM 742 (14 June 1928).

54. 13 *PMCM*, 196.

55. 16 *PMCM*, 113–14.

56. LNA, Box R2322, 6A/875/709, O. F. Nelson, *Samoa at Geneva: Misleading the League of Nations* (Auckland: n.p., 1928), and *A Petition to Geneva: The Hon. O.F. Nelson again Appeals* (Auckland: National Printing Co., 1930).

57. Lugard, Report on petitions by Nelson, CPM 1161 (12 Nov. 1931) in LNA, Box R2322, 6A/875/709.

58. Taisi [O. F. Nelson], *What the Samoans Want* (1930), in LNA, Box R2322, 6A/875/709.

59. This is a point made by Meleisea, *Making*, 156, 175–6, 179. In 1934 legislation was passed allowing for the renunciation of 'European' status; see 35 *PMCM*, 24 Oct.–8 Nov. 1938, 160, 162.

60. 16 *PMCM*, 6–26 Nov. 1929, 118 (for Rappard), and 122 (for Dannevig); I discuss this language in more detail in Susan Pedersen, 'Metaphors of the Schoolroom: Women Working the Mandates System of the League of Nations', *History Workshop Journal*, 66 (2008), 188–207.

61. For Toynbee, see SFA, Rappard Papers, Box 1977/1354, Toynbee to Rappard, 16 April 1930.

62. RH, Perham Papers 36/3 and 36/5, *passim*; see also the posthumously published version of Perham's Pacific diary, *Pacific Prelude: A Journey to Samoa and Australasia, 1929* (London: Peter Owen, 1988).

63. RH, Perham Papers, 36/5/6 and 36/5/20.

64. RH, Perham Papers, 36/5/19.

65. 28 *PMCM*, 149, 153–4.

66. There are a number of accounts of this event, including Davidson, *Samoa mo Samoa*, 137–9. Government response to the killings can be followed through the Wellington archives.

67. ANZ, ACHK 16603, G48/37, S/17, Telegram, External Affairs to Administrator (Apia), 31 Dec. 1929.

68. LNA, BOX R2323, File 6A/16670/709, 'Telegram, dated January 2, 1930, from the New Zealand Government, relating to the riot which occurred at Apia on December 28th, 1929', C.5.M.2.1030.VI (6 Jan. 1930), and 'Telegrams dated January 28th and February 5, 1930, from the New Zealand Government relating to the riot which occurred at Apia on December 28th, 1929', C.125.M.43.1930.VI (6 Feb. 1930).

69. Allen's calumny is in ANZ, ACHK 16603, G48/37, S/17. Administrator to External Affairs, 3 April 1930. For the petition and the Mandates Commission's response, see LNA, Box R2324, File 6A/23388/709.

70. LNA, R2323, 6A/20424/709, Petition from Rev. A. John Greenwood; LNA, R2324, 6A/25086/709, correspondence with C. W. Owen; LNA R2324,

6A/23938/709, appeal by Hon E.A. Ransom; LNA R2324, 6A/23937/709, petition from Edwin William Gurr and William Cooper. For the Labour Party position, see Bruce Brown, *The Rise of New Zealand Labour* (Wellington: Milburn, 1962), 127.

71. LNA R2324, 6A/32498/709, 'Samoan Petition, 1931'.

72. A Mau appeal to Herbert Hoover of 11 May 1930, and the massive 1931 petition from the Mau Chiefs to the Tripartite Powers, together with various correspondence from the Mau supporter E.W. Gurr and the Women's International League for Peace and Freedom, can be found in USNA, Box 6835, 862m.01. US legal advisors insisted that, contrary to Mau assertions, Germany (and the US) held American Samoa in full sovereignty, so the Allies were within their rights turning it over to New Zealand under mandate.

73. Rappard Papers, Box 1977/1354, Sheepshanks to Rappard, 30 March 1930.

74. C. A. Berendsen explained the government's new policy to the PMC at the 30th session in 1936; see 30 *PMCM*, 108–12.

75. 28 *PMCM*, 145, 146, 149.

76. 30 *PMCM*, 108–26, 212; and see RH, Lugard Papers 139/1, Hailey to Lugard, 4 Nov. 1936.

### NOTES FOR PART III

1. AA, AE/II (2978) 948, Herbette to Hymans, 29 Sept. 1924.

2. AA, AE/II (2978) 948, Hymans to Herbette, 28 Oct. 1924. This exchange can also be found in MAE, SDN 545.

3. That note was appended to 'Letter from the German Government to the Secretary-General of the League', 12 Dec. 1924, in *LNOJ*, March 1925, 323–6.

4. PA, R29433, Memo (Secret), 14 April 1926.

5. Heinrich Schnee was an especially prolific and exigent propagandist, publishing a long series of books and articles defending Germany's colonial record and charging the new Allied administrations with neglect. Schnee, who was married to an Englishwoman, published several such works in English and French; see esp. *The German Colonies under the Mandates* (Berlin: Brönner in Nowawes, 1922), and *German Colonization, Past and Future: The Truth about the German Colonies* (London: G. Allen & Unwin, 1926). The *Koloniale Rundschau* in particular kept a watching brief over all the former German colonies and over the League's oversight regime. Historical accounts of the German colonial movement between the wars are proliferating. For an early account focused on the Nazi period in particular, see Wolfe W. Schmokel, *Dream of Empire: German Colonialism, 1919–1945* (New Haven and London: Yale University Press, 1964), and for economic plans, Dirk van Laak, *Imperiale Infrastruktur: Deutsche Planungen für eine Erschließung Afrikas 1880 bis 1960* (Paderborn: Ferdinand Schöningh, 2004).

6. PA, R95613, Von Bülow, 'Aufzeichnung', 6 Jan. 1926.

7. GStA PK,VI.HA, Schnee Papers, Box 31, Brückner to Schnee, 30 April 1925.

8. '...dass wir auch die uns noch nicht wieder zurückgegebenen früheren deutschen Schutzgebiete (abgesehen von dem japanischen Mandatsgebiet) wirtschaftlich in nicht zu langer Zeit so durchdringen, dass seine spätere Mandatsübertragung auf Deutschland nicht ausgeschlossen ist'. PA, R29433, Von Brückner, 'Richtlinien unserer Kolonialpolitik' (1924); see also van Laak, *Imperiale Infrastruktur*, 204–5.

9. 'zu einem in wesentlichen deutschen Lande würde', in PA, R29433.

10. PA, R29433, Seitz to von Schubert, 3 March 1925, enclosing 'Aufzeichnung über meine persönliche Auffassung der kolonialpolitishen Fragen'.

11. See PA R29433 Von Schubert to Seitz, 11 April 1925, and the related memos of 19 and 23 March 1925.

12. PA, R96524, 'Kontrolle des Völkerbundes über die Mandate', 12 Aug. 1926; see also R96528, 'Aufzeichnung. Zu Punkt 21 der Tagesordung der 43 Ratssitzung des Völkerbundes', III.a.1.8173/26 (27 Nov. 1926).

13. NA, CO 323/965/6, Note by T. K. Lloyd, 22 Sept. 1926. A joint meeting between Foreign and Colonial Office officials, held to outline policy for the 1926 Imperial Conference, also came down cautiously in favour. See NA, CO 323/956/33, 'Questions Connected with the Work of the Permanent Mandates Commission of the League of Nations: Memorandum Prepared for the Imperial Conference', Oct. 1926, 9–12.

14. NA, CO 323/956/33, Note by Austen Chamberlain, 19 Oct. 1926.

15. PA, R29434, Von Schubert to Consulate (Geneva), 1 Nov. 1926, and Aschmann (Geneva) to Von Schubert, 11 Nov. 1926.

16. NA, CO 323/956/34, Minute by Ormsby-Gore, 16 Nov. 1926.

17. LNA, S1608, no. 3, Drummond, 'Record of Interview', 17 Nov. 1926, very confidential.

18. PA, R29434, Note, 2 Dec. 1926.

19. PA, R29434, Stresemann to Embassies, 26 April 1927.

20. PA, R29434, Report, 7 June 1927.

21. AA, AE/II (2978) 948, Foreign Ministry to Colonial Ministry and Prime Minister, 19 May 1927.

22. PA, R96528, Stresemann Abschrift, 26 April 1927.

23. Minutes of the 45th session of the Council, *LNOJ*, July 1927, 791, and LNA, Box R8, 1/60184/248, Drummond to Theodoli, 18 June 1927.

24. *Reichstag Debates*, 326 sitting, 23 June 1927, 11005.

25. AA, AE/II (2978) 948, De Gaiffier to Foreign Ministry, 27 July 1927.

26. 11 *PMCM*, 133–40, 170–1, 178–83, 200; quoted 139–40, 180, 200.

27. LNA, S1608, no. 4, Memo by Gilchrist.

28. For information on Kastl, see LNA, S 1608, no. 4, jacket 1, note by Gilchrist, 9 Aug. 1927, and AA, AE/II (2978), 948, Everts to Vandervelde, 1 Sept. 1927.

29. For information on Ruppel, see LNA, R2327, 6A/19238/1143.

30. PA, R29434, Seitz to AA, 9 December 1927.

31. GStA PK, VI.HA, Schnee Papers, Box 31, Schnee to Stresemann, 9 Aug. 1927, and Stresemann to Schnee, 30 Aug. 1927.

32. NA, CO 691/100/27, Kastl to J. Scott, Chief Secretary to Government of Tanganyika Territory, 10 Aug. 1928, and Note by Lloyd.

33. See comments on Palacios in PA, R96515, German Embassy (Madrid) to Foreign Ministry, 12 March 1930, and on Rappard in PA, R96535, Dufour-Feronce to De Haas, 1 July and 2 July 1929.

34. NA, CO 323/986/1, G. Newlands to Ormsby-Gore, 1 Dec. 1927, recounting a conversation with Kastl in Berlin.

### NOTES FOR CHAPTER 7

1. George Louis Beer, *The English-Speaking Peoples: Their Future Relations and Joint International Obligations* (New York: Macmillan, 1917), ix.

2. The Hymans Report conferred 'a full exercise of sovereignty, in so far as such exercise is consistent with the carrying out of the obligations' of the Covenant on those holding B and C mandates, but explicitly declined to state where sovereignty resided. See 'Obligations falling upon the League of Nations under the terms of Article 22 of the Covenant (Mandates)', *LNOJ*, Sept. 1920, 334-41.

3. *H.L. Deb.*, vol. 50, 21 June 1922, col. 1046-7.

4. Minutes of the 18th session of the Council, 11th meeting, 17 May 1922, *LNOJ*, June 1922, 547.

5. Long treatises could be written (and, in the interwar years, were written) about the jurists' debate. For a cogent summary of the state of debate up to 1930, see Quincy Wright, *Mandates under the League of Nations* (1930; rpt. New York: Greenwood Press, 1968), 314-44.

6. RH, Lugard 119/4, Lugard to Lady Lugard, 20 Feb. 1926.

7. LNA, R6, 1/10005/248, see also S284 (1) 14, Lugard to Rappard, 15 Aug. 1923.

8. LNA, R6, 1/10779x/249, Dossier on Van Rees, Rappard, 'Note sur la Visite de Monsieur D. F. W. Van Rees, Membre Hollandais de la Commission Permanente des Mandats' (9 April 1921).

9. LNA, S1608, no. 3 (1921-29), File on Procedure, 'Nomination des Membres de la Commission permanente des Mandats comme rapporteurs pour des sujets spéciaux lors de l'examen des Rapports annuels des Puissance mandataire' (n.d. [1923]).

10. LNA, R8, 1/50162/248, Catastini to Merlin, 5 Dec. 1927.

11. For Van Rees's practice, and his demands on the Secretariat, see R2327, 6A/1365/1422.

12. D. F. W. Van Rees, *Les Mandats internationax: Le contrôle de l'administration mandataire* (Paris: Librairie Arthur Rousseau, 1927), and *Les Mandats internationaux: Les principes généraux du régime des mandats* (Paris: Librarie Arthur Rousseau, 1928); and for Lugard's comment, RH, Lugard 122/3, Lugard to Leggett, 22 Feb. 1937.

13. Van Rees, 'The System of State Lands in B and C Mandated Territories', in 3 *PMCM*, Annex II, 216–39.

14. 3 *PMCM*, Annex II, 219.

15. 3 *PMCM*, Annex II, 220–1.

16. 4 *PMCM*, 156–7.

17. LNA, R5, 1/47879/161, Gilchrist to Boheman, Ministry of Foreign Affairs, Stockholm, 20 Nov. 1925.

18. AA, AE II (3288) 1848, Hymans to Drummond, 17 Dec. 1920 and LNA, Box R9, 1/10301/1025, Rappard, 'Memorandum relative au projet de mandat belge', 14 Jan. 1921. Hymans claimed that the clauses were similar to those inserted in the Togo and Cameroon mandates. Rappard disagreed.

19. AA, AE/II (3243) 1424, File on German colonial claims, 1925–28, 'Note pour Monsieur le Ministre', 14 Dec. 1924.

20. AA, AE/II (3243) 1424, Marzorati to Colonial Minister, 16 Feb. 1925.

21. AA, AE/II (3243) 1424, Colonial Minister to Marzorati, 9 June 1925.

22. AA, AEII (3292) 1875, Halewyck de Heusch, 'Note pour Monsieur le Ministre', and Memo, 25 June 1924, and Minister of the Colonies to Governor General of the Congo, 28 June 1924, and to the Royal Commissioner of Ruanda-Urundi, 1 July 1924.

23. 'Projet de mandat belge', Marzorati to Minister of the Colonies, 2 Sept. 1924.

24. 'Projet de mandat belge', Halewyck de Heusch, 'Note pour M. le Secrétaire Général au sujet de la lettre de Monsieur Ryckmans à M. Camus' (confidential), 8 Jan. 1925.

25. AA, AE/II (3292) 1876, File on German Protests against 1925 Law, German Note of 28 March 1925.

26. AA, AE/II (3292) 1876, Note by Hymans, 27 April 1925.

27. AA, AE/II (3292) 1876, Note by J. Davignon, Chef du Cabinet de M. Hymans, 2 May 1925.

28. LNA, Box R9, 1/22769/1025, League Document C.593.1925.VI, 'Mandates. Administration of Ruanda-Urundi. Memorandum by the German Government' (29 Sept. 1925). This file also contains copies of Drummond's letter of 7 Oct. 1925 transmitting the note to the Belgian government. For the German text, see PA, R96512, Memorandum, 16 Sept. 1925.

29. LNA, Box R9, 1/22769/1025, J. Wouter, for the Minister of Foreign Affairs, to Eric Drummond, 16 Oct. 1925, and attached note, and Drummond to Hymans, 20 Oct. 1925.

30. 7 *PMCM*, 52–76 *passim*, and 'Report', in 7 *PMCM*, 215–16.

31. Minutes of the 37th session of the Council, *LNOJ*, Feb. 1926, 136–7.

32. PA, R96512, Aschmann, Consul (Geneva), to the Foreign Ministry, 23 Oct. 1925.

33. PA, R96528, 'Aufzeichnung. Zu Punkt 21 der Tagesordnung der 43 Ratssitzung des Völkerbundes' (27 Nov. 1926).

34. For Hanotaux's criticism, see Minutes of the 27th session of the Council, 27 Dec. 1923, in *LNOJ*, Jan. 1926, 334, and for Van Rees's response, LNA, R8,

1/36856/248, CPM 144 (1), 'Competence of the Mandates Commission. Memorandum by M.Van Rees' (24 June 1924). Lugard also wrote to Rappard saying that the issue of the PMC's competence should be addressed, but Drummond told Rappard it was best to let matters lie: the Commission's rights were clear, and he was certain the French would not raise the issue again. For this correspondence, see LNA S284 1 (14), Lugard to Rappard, 14 April 1924, and Rappard to Lugard, 29 April 1924, and LNA, S1608, no. 1, correspondence between Drummond and Rappard, 28 April 1924.

35. See, e.g., LNA, S1608, no. 1, Rappard to Secretary General, 'Record of an interview with Sir James Allen', 12 May 1924.

36. LNA, S284, File: Theodoli, Chamberlain to Theodoli, 13 Dec. 1925.

37. Alexander Cadogan, Permanent Secretary at the Foreign Office, had written to the League to ask for information about the petition process, implying that the process itself was encouraging ungrounded complaints. See LC, Gilchrist Papers, Box 25, File: 'Petitions: Rules of Procedure, 1925–1927', Gilchrist to Catastini and Secretary General, 9 Oct. 1925; Minute by Gilchrist, 15 Oct. 1925; and 'Procedure Adopted in Replying to Mandates Petitions', [1926]. For Chamberlain's criticisms, see minutes of the 39th session of the Council, meeting of 17 March 1926, in *LNOJ*, April 1926, 525–6.

38. PMC, 'Report', 9 *PMCM*, 216.

39. Minutes of the 41st session of the Council, 3rd meeting, 3 Sept. 1926, *LNOJ*, Oct. 1926, 1233–7; also Michael D. Callahan, *Mandates and Empire: The League of Nations and Africa, 1914–1931* (Brighton: Sussex Academic Press, 1999), 123–9.

40. NA, CO 323/956/33, Copy of Minute by Sir Austen Chamberlain, 19 Oct. 1926.

41. 'Questions connected with the work of the Permanent Mandates Commission of the League of Nations: Memorandum Prepared for the Imperial Conference' (Oct. 1926), in *Imperial Conference, 1926. Appendices to the Summary of Proceedings*, PP 1926, Cmd. 2769, 222–7. For drafts of the minutes, see NA, CO 323/956/33.

42. See the statements by Bruce, Coates, and Hertzog in *Imperial Conference, 1926. Appendices to the Summary of Proceedings*, PP 1926, Cmd. 2769, 135, 139, and *Imperial Conference, 1926. Summary of Proceedings*, PP, 1926, Cmd. 2768, 33.

43. MAE, SDN 567, De Caix, 'Note pour les services français de la Société des Nations', 14 Oct. 1926.

44. The communications from the mandatory powers, which were widely circulated, can be found in the League of Nations Microfilm Collection, Reel 6: CPM 524, 'Communication from the British Government dated November 8, 1926'; CPM 533, 'Letter from the South African Government'; CPM 534, 'Communication from the Government of New Zealand dated November 22nd 1926'; CPM 535, 'Communication from the French Government dated November 23rd 1926'; CPM 539, 'Communication from the Australian Government received December 2nd 1926'; CPM 540, Communication du Gouvernement japonais en date du 5 décembre 1926'; CPM 541,

'Communication from the Belgian Government dated December 3rd 1926'; CPM 545, 'Letter from the Australian Government'.

45. Minute of the 43rd session of the Council, meeting of 10 Dec. 1926, *LNOJ*, Feb. 1927, 153, and Minutes of the 44th session of the Council, meeting of 7 March 1927, *LNOJ*, April 1927, 348.

46. Minute of the 43rd session of the Council, meeting of 10 Dec. 1926, *LNOJ*, Feb. 1927, 152–3, and 11 *PMCM*, 200.

47. For the work on the questionnaire, see 3 *PMCM*, 14–7, and 6 *PMCM*, 45–6.

48. Orts supported hearing the Anti-Slavery Society on the Bondelswarts question (3 *PMCM*, 64–7); and Theodoli raised the question explicitly two years later (7 *PMCM*, 33–5).

49. 8 *PMCM*, 156–60.

50. LNA, Box R60, 1/51258/22099, CPM 405, 'Note by Sir Frederick Lugard on the procedure with regard to memorials or petitions' (15 May 1926).

51. 9 *PMCM*, 130; for the debate at this session, see 47–50, 52–6, 189–93.

52. NA, CO 323/959/5, Note by Lloyd, 18 Aug. 1926.

53. See the extensive clippings in LNA, Box R52, File 1/55141/16466, esp. 'The League and the Mandates', *Indian Social Reformer*, 18 September 1926; 'Quarreling about Mandates', *The Washington Post*, 8 September 1926; and the former German colonial Governor Heinrich Schnee, in the *Deutsche Allgemeine Zeitung*, 26 Sept. 1926.

54. Bodleian, Murray Papers, Box 199, fols. 44–6, Harris to Murray, 17 Sept. 1926.

55. RH ASAPS, G404, Harris to Olivier, 27 Sept. 1926.

56. BLPES Archives, LNU Archives, Microfilm Reel 431, Minutes of the Mandates Committee for 22 Oct. and for 3, 17 and 30 Nov. 1926. See also the articles in the LNU paper, *Headway*: 'Matters of Moment – Mandate Queries', Oct. 1926, 181; 'Mandate Troubles', Nov. 1926, 212–13, and Warren Postbridge, 'Mandates and Mandatories: Questions Great Britain does not like', Dec. 1926, 226; John Hills, 'Mandates and the League' (letter), *The Times*, 24 Nov. 1926; 'Power of Mandates Commission' (on the UDC protest), *The Manchester Guardian*, 20 Nov. 1926; 'League's Control of Mandates' (on the LNU protest), *The Manchester Guardian*, 6 Dec. 1926. For debate in Parliament, 65 *H.L. Deb.*, ser. 5, 17 Nov. 1926, cols. 644–72, and 200 *H.C. Deb.*, ser. 5, 14 Dec. 1926, cols. 2876–99.

57. The quotations are from BLPES Archives, LNU Archives, Microfilm Reel 431, 'Statement on the British Memorandum to the League Regarding Mandates Procedure', 1 Dec. 1926, and Sir Robert Hamilton in the Commons debate above, cols. 2888–92.

58. Quoting Cecil, 65 *H.L. Deb.*, 17 Nov. 1926, col. 661.

59. LC, Gilchrist Papers, Box 33, File: 'Trip to the US, 1927', Gilchrist, 'Note on the British Communication of November 8th, 1926'.

60. NA, CO 323/956/34, Minute by Ormsby-Gore, 16 Nov. 1926.

61. 'The Criticism of Mandatories', *The Manchester Guardian*, 5 Nov. 1926; and see 10 *PMCM*, 10–14.

62. 3 *PMCM*, 106–7, and 6 *PMCM*, 63–4.

63. 9 *PMCM*, 42.

64. 'Report', in 10 *PMCM*, 220.

65. Minutes of the 41st session of the Council, session of 3 September 1926, in *LNOJ*, Oct. 1926, 1235.

66. 'Mandates Debate: The Annexationist Interpretation', *The Manchester Guardian*, 22 Sept. 1926.

67. 'Report', in 10 *PMCM*, 182.

68. 'Report', in 10 *PMCM*, 182.

69. LC, Gilchrist Papers, Friis to Gilchrist, 23 March 1927; and Minutes of the 44th session of the Council, 7 March 1927, *LNOJ*, April 1927, 347.

70. Van Rees in 11 *PMCM*, 87–90.

71. For that interrogation, see Van Rees in 11 *PMCM*, 90–106, 175–6, and the 'Report', 204–5. For Van Rees's leadership on this issue, see LNA, Box R13, 1/60354/1347, CPM 612, 'South West African Railways. Note by M. Van Rees' (n.d. [1927]), and 1/60492/1347, CPM 611, 'Question of Sovereignty. Note by M. Van Rees' (n.d. [July 1927]).

72. LNDM, Directors' Meeting Minutes, Reel 3, Meeting no. 178, 29 June 1927.

73. Minutes of the 46th session of the Council, session of 8 Sept. 1927, *LNOJ*, Oct. 1927, 1119–20; QW, Addenda II, Box 8, Folder 5, Gilchrist to Wright, 24 Oct. 1927, and Wright to Gilchrist, 8 Dec. 1927.

74. Werth's opening speech was vetted by both the Prime Minister and by the High Commissioner. See NAN, Box 573, A59/16.

75. 14 *PMCM*, 66–7, 71–9, 99, 115–17, and 'Report', in 14 *PMCM*, 275.

76. Minutes of the 54th session of the Council, *LNOJ*, April 1929, 507.

77. 15 *PMCM*, 76–8.

78. 'Report', in 15 *PMCM*, 294.

79. Minutes of the 56th session of the Council, session of 6 Sept. 1929, *LNOJ*, Nov. 1929, 1467.

80. Minutes of the 57th session of the Council, session of 25 Sept. 1929, *LNOJ*, Nov. 1929, 1694.

81. The Secretariat member was Seymour Jacklin, the South African Treasurer of the League. For his role, and for an account of the controversy over sovereignty more generally, see Sara Pienaar, *South Africa and International Relations between the Two World Wars: The League of Nations Dimension* (Johannesburg: Witwatersrand University Press, 1987), 117–24.

82. PA, R96515, Dufour-Feronce to Köpke, 19 Dec. 1929.

83. Minutes of the 58th session of the Council, meeting of 13 Jan. 1930, *LNOJ*, Feb. 1930, 69–70; Annex 1184, 139.

84. Hertzog to Drummond, 13 March 1930, and Hertzog to Drummond, 16 April 1930, *LNOJ*, July 1930, 383–9.

85. LNA, R2327, 6A/7347/1143, 'Extract from the House of Assembly Debates of the Union of South Africa'.

86. *6 PMCM*, 60.

87. PA, R96513, 'Aufzeichnung: Souveränität über die Mandatsgebiete' (3 March 1927).

88. 14 *PMCM*, 80–3, 208–11; Van Rees and Kastl, 'South West Africa. Status of Non-Native Inhabitants', in 16 *PMCM*, 187–90; see also the statement by Von Schubert in the 13 Jan. 1930 meeting of the Council, *LNOJ*, Feb. 1930, 73.

89. NAN, Box 573, A59/16, Werth to Seitz, 19 Oct. 1928.

90. For Amery's role, see, Leo S. Amery, *My Political Life*, vol. 2, *War and Peace, 1914–1929* (London: Hutchinson, 1953), 360.

91. PA, R28600, Sthamer to Foreign Ministry, telegram, 11 April 1924.

92. *Indians in Kenya: Memorandum, PP* 1923, Cmd. 1922, 10.

93. Bodleian, MSS Milner 389, Amery to Philip Kerr, 14 March 1919.

94. 'A United East Africa: Mr. Amery on Recent Progress', *The Times*, 12 June 1926; also *The Leo Amery Diaries*, ed. John Barnes and David Nicholson, vol. 1 (London: Hutchinson, 1980), 457–8.

95. 'German Claim to Colonies', *The Times*, 28 June 1926.

96. *Future Policy in regard to East Africa, PP* 1927, Cmd. 2904, 5.

97. There are a number of accounts of the controversy over Closer Union. Amery, Cameron, and Grigg all told their side of the story in their memoirs: see Amery, *My Political Life*, vol. 2, 360–2, and *The Leo Amery Diaries*, vol. 1, *passim*; Donald Cameron, *My Tanganyika Service* (London: George Allen & Unwin, 1939), 223–35; and Lord Altrincham [Sir Edward Grigg], *Kenya's Opportunity* (London: Faber & Faber, 1955), 189–220. Margery Perham sketched out Lugard's very important role in *Lugard: The Years of Authority, 1898–1945* (London: Collins, 1960), 673–92. Robert Gregory tracks Labour policy on the question in *Sidney Webb and East Africa: Labour's Experiment with the Doctrine of Native Paramountcy* (Berkeley: University of California Press, 1962). Kenneth Ingham pays some attention to opinion within the various East African territories in *A History of East Africa* (London: Longman's, 1962), 310–23. The only study of the significant influence that Tanganyika's mandatory status exercised over the issue, to which I am indebted, is Michael D. Callahan, 'The Failure of "Closer Union" in British East Africa, 1929–31', *The Journal of Imperial and Commonwealth History*, 25:2 (1997), 267–93. Not enough attention has been paid, however, to the uniformly low opinion that the Colonial Office officials had of the plan (which certainly played a role in scuttling it); when asked to evaluate the Hilton Young proposals in January 1929, all thought the proposals undesirable, impractical, and possibly unconstitutional. On this issue, Colonial Under-Secretary Ormsby-Gore also stated frankly his utter opposition to Amery's hopes, writing that 'the one thing I care about is to prevent Uganda and Tanganyika Territory becoming Kenya or like Kenya', and that a uniform native policy in particular should be firmly opposed. See CAC, Amery Papers, AMEL 1/4/39, File 2, esp. the memos by Wilson (22 Jan. 1929) and Ormsby-Gore (16 Jan. 1929). Amery was unable to hear his office's warnings, as is clear from the minutes of the meetings in AMEL 1/4/39, File 1.

98. Tellingly, in his autobiography Cameron both insisted that 'the terms of the mandate did not trouble or preoccupy my mind in any way', since they were 'in complete accord with those with which I had become so accustomed in the administration of Nigeria', and recalled how he relied on those terms when opposing settlers' plans. See Cameron, *My Tanganyika Service*, 20, 85, 232.

99. RH, Lugard 9/1, Cameron to Lugard, 31 Jan. 1927.

100. 11 *PMCM*, 65–8.

101. RH, Lugard 9/1, Cameron to Lugard, 31 Jan. 1927.

102. Rappard in 21 *PMCM*, 32; see also Pierre Orts in 15 *PMCM*, 111–12.

103. *Report of the Commission on Closer Union of the Dependencies in Eastern and Central Africa*, PP 1928–9, Cmd. 3234, 224, 228.

104. For the elaboration of this argument, see PA, R29434, 'Die Hilton Young Commission' (30 Jan. 1929), De Haas, 'Aufzeichnung zum Bericht der Hilton-Young-Commission' (4 March 1929).

105. PA, R96530, 'Aufzeichnung über ein Besprechung mit Herrn Geheimrat Kastl' (2 April 1928). Kastl, it is worth noting, insisted on the value of building a common PMC front.

106. *Verhandlungen des Reichstages*, vol. 425, 94 Sitzung, 24 June 1929, 2877–8.

107. PA, R29434, 'Aufzeichnung für eine Unterhaltung mit dem englischen Botschafter über den Hilton-Young-Bericht' (2 Feb. 1929), and Note (4 Feb. 1929).

108. PA, R29434, Note (13 Feb. 1929). In an Aide-Memoire sent after the meeting, Britain denied that the Hilton-Young report was in violation of the mandate. See PA, R29434, Brückner, 'Aufzeichnung über die derzeitige Lage in Bezug auf die ostafrikanischen Unionspläne' (16 March 1929).

109. PA, R96530, 'Aufzeichnung über ein Besprechung mit Herrn Geheimrat Kastl' (2 April 1928).

110. PA, R96515, Dufour to Koepke, 19 July 1929.

111. 15 *PMCM*, 103–6, 167–70, 200–4, 292.

112. PA, R96515, 'Aufzeichnung für die 56 Tagung des Völkerbundsrates über die Britisch-Ostafrikanischen Unions-Bestrebungen' (28 Aug. 1929).

113. Minutes of the 56th session of the Council, *LNOJ*, Nov. 1929, 1470.

114. *Statement of the Conclusions of His Majesty's Government in the United Kingdom as regards Closer Union in East Africa*, PP 1929–30, Cmd. 3574, 16, and for the reiteration of 'native paramountcy', see *Memorandum on Native Policy in East Africa*, PP, 1929–30, Cmd. 3573.

115. Drummond thought that Lugard should not serve on the Joint Select Committee, since members of the Mandates Commission were not supposed to hold government office and also since he would be both on the body considering British policy and the body that would review that policy; but when Lugard retorted that he would resign from the PMC rather than from the Select Committee if membership in both were considered improper, Drummond swiftly backed down. For this see RH, Lugard 119/2, correspondence with Drummond from Oct.–Nov. 1930.

116. 'Report', in 18 *PMCM*, 201–2.
117. *Verhandlungen des Reichstages*, Bd. 428, 184 Sitzung, 26 June 1930, 5864, and 185 Sitzung, 27 June 1930, 5914–15; see British civil servants' notes about the depth of German concern in NA, FO 371/14948, W602.
118. Minutes of the 60th session of the Council, Meeting of 9 Sept. 1930, *LNOJ*, Nov. 1930, 1304, and for the German note, see NA, FO 371/14948, W9126, 'Aide Memoire' (4 Sept. 1930), and Callahan, 'Failure', 274.
119. PA, R28601, Schnee to Curtius, 19 Jan. 1931.
120. For the protests and petitions, see *Protest der deutschen Wirtschaft gegen die Einverleibung von Deutsch-Ostafrika in das Britische Reich* (1931); Hedwig von Bredow to PMC, 1 Oct. 1930; Schnee to Secretary General, 24 Jan. 1931; all in LNA, Box R2313, File 6A/21123/441.
121. RH, Lugard 141/1, Kastl to Lugard, 30 June 1930, and Lugard to Kastl, 4 July 1930.
122. RH, Lugard 122/3, Lugard to Leggett, 22 Feb. 1937.
123. NA, CO 822/28/4, Lugard to FO, 20 Oct. 1930, and Callahan, 'Failure', 277.
124. Callahan, 'Failure', 278.
125. Joint Committee on Closer Union in East Africa, *Report*, PP 1930–1, 7, 8, 15, 16.
126. See the petition from the Indian Association, 19 Sept. 1932, LNA, R4086, 6A/2774/722.
127. 22 *PMCM*, 135.
128. 23 *PMCM*, 46–52.
129. 23 *PMCM*, 35–43, 64–74, 77–80, 120–4, and 'Report', in 23 *PMCM*, 189–91.
130. AA, AE/II (2977) 939, Orts to Tschoffen, 8 July 1933.
131. 31 *PMCM*, 17.
132. 22 *PMCM*, Annex 8, 324.

## NOTES FOR CHAPTER 8

1. 7 *PMCM*, 65.
2. Detailed stipulations about economic equality were included in all 'B' mandate texts, although mandatory powers were allowed exemptions for core governmental services and political or security needs. The Anglo-Iraq Treaty of 1922 had a clause explicitly outlawing any economic discrimination between nationals of League states, but those clauses were heavily qualified in the Syrian mandate and stipulations about concessions were omitted from the Palestine mandate. Separate negotiations insisted upon by the United States extended identical rights to US nationals. For these provisions, see Benjamin Gerig, *The Open Door and the Mandates System* (London: George Allen & Unwin, 1930), 109–12.
3. For which see Richard A. Goodridge, '"In the Most Effective Manner"? Britain and the Disposal of the Cameroons Plantations, 1914–1924', *International Journal of African Historical Studies*, 29:2 (1996), 251–77.

4. Lugard insisted on the inquiry into the fate of German property: see Lugard, 'Ex-Enemy Estates in Mandated Territory', 3 *PMCM*, 286–7, and Lugard, 'Ex-Enemy Property in Mandated Territory', 7 *PMCM*, 159–60. When information came in, it became clear that while the British tried to sell the estates, the French largely exploited the right of preemption to take them over at fire-sale prices. See 'The Present Situation as regards "ex-enemy property" in Mandated Territories', 12 *PMCM*, 178–81.

5. The PMC collected information and discussed the issue across three sessions; see 3 *PMCM*, 76–7, 311; 5 *PMCM*, 154–62, 177–80; and 6 *PMCM*, 52–6, 117–19, 145, 151–8; for the Council decision, see Minutes, 35th session, 12th meeting, 15 Sept. 1925, in *LNOJ*, October 1925, 1363.

6. Lugard, 'Loans, Advances and Investment of Private Capital in Mandated Territories', in 5 *PMCM*, 177.

7. Bugge-Wicksell, 'Loans, Advances and Investments of Capital in Mandated Territories', 6 *PMCM*, 155.

8. For those reports, ANOM, SG Togo-Cameroun 24/217, esp. Neton to Foreign Ministry, 17 July 1920, and Governor-General AOF to Colonial Ministry, 9 July 1920.

9. PA, R29433, Memo by the Kolonial Abteilung on Seitz's memo of 3 March 1925 (19 March 1925).

10. For the French prohibition on German commerce in Togo and Cameroon, see ANOM, SG Togo-Cameroun 24/217, and for their efforts to retain that ban after Germany entered the League, see ANOM, SG Togo-Cameroun, 24/207; also Richard A. Joseph, 'The German Question in French Cameroun, 1919–1939', *Comparative Studies in Society and History*, 17:1 (Jan. 1975), 65–90.

11. Kastl's successor, Julius Ruppel, paid particularly close attention to French economic policies in Cameroon, a territory in which he had served, and insisted that the French practice of exempting (French) ships who held the contract to deliver mail from the port tax at Duala allowed those firms to monopolize shipment of other goods as well and hence violated the economic equality clause; see, e.g., 21 *PMCM*, 123–6, 131–3. Partly at his insistence, the PMC conducted an inquiry that revealed, not surprisingly, that mandatory powers granted concessions largely to their own nationals (although Tanganyika was something of an exception). See the PMC's inquiry into concessions, and the debates thereon, in 22 *PMCM*, 3 Nov.–6 Dec. 1932, 227–33, 253–4, 359–62, and the comments by Baron Aloisi (Italy) and Herr von Keller (Germany) to the 70th session of the Council on 24 Jan. 1933, in *LNOJ*, 14:2 (Feb. 1933), 190–1.

12. See, e.g., ANOM, SG Togo-Cameroun, 24/211, Bonnecarrère to Sarrault, 29 Jan. 1923, and Sarraut to Foreign Ministry, 20 March 1923.

13. For the slavery and forced labour conventions, see Suzanne Miers, *Slavery in the Twentieth Century: The Evolution of a Global Problem* (Walnut Creek, CA: Altamira Press, 2003), and for an analysis of the ILO's role in shaping a distinct set of codes to deal with 'native labour', Luis Rodríguez-Piñero, *Indigenous Peoples,*

*Postcolonialism, and International Law: The ILO Regime (1919–1989)* (Oxford: Oxford University Press, 2005).

14. Raymond Leslie Buell, *The Native Problem in Africa*, 2 vols. (New York: Macmillan, 1928).

15. The quotation about Buell is from RH, Lugard 9/1, Cameron to Lugard, 22 Oct. 1925, and the information about petitions from LC, Gilchrist Papers, Box 10, File: Buell (henceforth LC, GP10/B), Buell to Gilchrist, 27 April 1926.

16. Alfred Zimmern at the Geneva Institute for International Studies had received a draft copy and shared it with Henry Jouvenel, who passed it along to the Quai d'Orsay. The Quai then asked the preeminent French Africanist Henri Laboret for his views. Laboret's outraged summary, the vigorous protest against the book by Cameroon's Marchand, internal correspondence between the Quai and the Colonial Ministry, and efforts to have the book suppressed, can all be found in ANOM, AP 28. This episode is also discussed by Véronique Dimier, *Le Gouvernement des colonies, regards croisés franco-britanniques* (Brussels: Editions de l'Université de Bruxelles, 2004), 252–3.

17. LC, GP10/B, Buell to Gilchrist, 28 June 1927.

18. Buell, *Native Problem*, II, 345–6; and LC, GP10/B, 'Seventh Report to the Committee of International Research of Harvard University and Radcliffe', sent from Edea, French Cameroun, 16 March 1926, enclosed in Buell to Gilchrist, 30 March 1926.

19. The French government, furious to be again labelled the 'bad child' of the mandates regime, stiffly declined to submit observations on the petition (the British government, by contrast, replied in detail to every point); and at the fifteenth PMC session, the French representative Duchêne grew so heated on the matter that the Commission found it almost impossible to proceed. Only Rappard robustly defended Buell's impartiality, and the Commission weakly resolved that the allegations raised 'are either without foundation or have been the subject of investigation by the commission, and are not of a nature to justify any intervention by the Council'. Junod's petition, the responses from the man-datory powers, the discussion of those documents by the PMC, and the Commission's report and resolution, were all printed in full in 15 *PMCM*, 20–3, 143–5, 241–9, and 297. Buell thanked Rappard for his part in the debate: SFA, Rappard Papers, 1977/135 1, Buell to Rappard, 4 Sept. 1929.

20. LC, GP 10/B, Gilchrist to Buell, 6 Nov. 1925, and Buell to Gilchrist, 30 March 1926.

21. AA, AE/II (3288), 1849, Louis Franck, Memorandum, 15 June 1920. There are several good, detailed studies of Rwanda and Burundi under the Belgian man-date, and while most are based primarily on Belgian records, some also use oral histories and interviews to temper those often idealized sources. I have made use in particular of Jean Rumiya, *Le Rwanda sous le régime du mandat belge (1916–1931)* (Paris: Harmattan, 1992); Innocent Nsengimana, *Le Rwanda et le pouvoir européen (1894–1952): Quelles mutations?* (Bern: Peter Lang, 2003); Joseph Gahama,

*Le Burundi sous administration belge* (Paris: Karthala, 1983); Alison Des Forges, *Defeat is the Only Bad News: Rwanda under Musinga, 1896–1931* (Dissertation,Yale University, 1972; publ. Madison: University of Wisconsin Press, 2011); Catharine Newbury, *The Cohesion of Oppression: Clientship and Ethnicity in Rwanda, 1860–1960* (New York: Columbia University Press, 1988); David Newbury's luminous articles now collected in *The Land Beyond the Mists: Essays on Identity and Authority in Precolonial Congo and Rwanda* (Athens, OH: Ohio University Press, 2009), and the many works of Jean-Pierre Chrétien, esp. his *Burundi: L'histoire retrouvée. 25 ans de métier d'historien en Afrique* (Paris: Karthala, 1993), and *The Great Lakes of Africa: Two Thousand Years of History* (New York: Zone Books, 2003). For Franck's initial plans, see esp. Rumiya, *Rwanda*, 137–9, Nsengimana, *Rwanda*, 437–42, and Gahama, *Burundi*, 42–3.

22. 4 *PMCM*, 69.
23. Gahama, *Burundi*, 59.
24. For Classe and feudalism, see Rumiya, *Rwanda*, 133–5.
25. AA, AE/II (3288), 1849, Louis Franck, Memorandum, 15 June 1920.
26. *Rapport présenté par le gouvernement belge au Conseil de la Société des Nations au sujet de l'administration du Ruanda-Urundi pendant l'année 1925* (Brussels: n.p., 1926) 34. These reports will be cited henceforth as *Ruanda-Urundi Report [year]*.
27. Pierre Ryckmans, 'Le Problème politique au Ruanda-Urundi', *Bulletin de la Société belge d'Etudes et d'Expansion*, Feb. 1925, rpt. in Ryckmans, *Dominer pour Servir* (Brussels: Albert Dewit, 1931), 163, 165.
28. David Newbury stresses the sharp differences between ethnic identities, territorial identities, clientship forms, court power and military power in precolonial Rwanda and Burundi, insisting that these were in no way 'twin states' whose history can be conflated—although obviously those histories were forcibly entangled through the process of colonial rule. See his 'Precolonial Burundi and Rwanda: Local Loyalties, Regional Loyalties', in *The Land Beyond the Mist*, 281–339, here at 315.
29. *Ruanda-Urundi Report 1925* (Brussels, 1926), 64.
30. 5 *PMCM*, 65–7.
31. 5 *PMCM*, 67.
32. 'Report', in 5 *PMCM*, 216.
33. Van Rees laid out his views in the memorandum, 'What is the Forced or Compulsory Labour which is allowed in Territories under B and C Mandates and under what conditions is it allowed there?', in 7 *PMCM*, Annex 4b, 154–6.
34. For that Convention, see 'Slavery Convention (Geneva, September 25, 1926)', *LNOJ*, 7:12 (Dec. 1926), 1655–65, and, more generally, Miers, *Slavery*, 100–33.
35. The best account both of the Rwakayihura famine discussed below and the agricultural regime in Rwanda in the 1920s, to which I am indebted, is Anne Cornet, *Histoire d'une famine, Rwanda, 1927–30: Crise alimentaire entre tradition et modernité* (Louvain-La-Neuve: Université catholique de Louvain, 1996); see also

David Newbury, 'The "Rwakayihura" Famine of 1928–1929', in *Histoire sociale de l'Afrique de l'Est (XIXe–XXe siècle). Actes du colloque de Bujumbura (17–24 octobre 1989)* (Paris, 1991), 269–85.

36. *Ruanda-Urundi Report 1929* (Brussels, 1930), 79.

37. Very little has been written on these earlier famines, partly because Belgium kept them very quiet. Roger Botte, using the records of the 'White Fathers' missions, provides an account of their devastating impact. See Botte, 'Rwanda and Burundi, 1889–1930: Chronology of a Slow Assassination, Part 2', *The International Journal of African Historical Studies*, 18:2 (1985), 289–314.

38. 14 *PMCM*, 12.

39. SFA, Rappard Papers, Box 1977/135 3, J. E. T. Philipps to Rappard, 1 March 1929, enclosing J. E. T. Philipps to Sir William Gowers, 1 March 1929. Philipps, at the invitation of Stoffin, the energetic Belgian administrator in Gatsibu, had toured the famine districts and had a good sense of the extent of the calamity and the Belgian response.

40. J. E. Church, in *Ruanda Notes*, Jan. 1929; quoted in Cornet, *Histoire d'une famine*, 64.

41. 'A Stricken Land: Famine in the Ruanda', *The Times*, 16 April 1929, 17–18.

42. The Belgians never provided reliable estimates of mortality, although the PMC repeatedly asked for them. Anne Cornet uses mission and local records to arrive at this estimate, but she notes that Catholic missionaries estimated as many as 60,000 deaths (or about 20% of the population of the famine districts) and German propagandists 90,000 (or 30%). See Cornet, *Histoire d'une famine*, 40, 45.

43. Portage statistics from *Ruanda-Urundi Report 1931* (Brussels, 1932), and see Cornet, *Histoire d'une famine*, 53.

44. Ryckmans, 'Tribune libre: la famine', *Essor colonial et maritime*, 20 June 1929, rpt. in Ryckmans, *Dominer pour Servir*, 177.

45. See the Belgian reports, listed above, for 1927, 1928, and 1929, which contain maps drawn in July 1928, July 1929, and July 1930.

46. See, e.g., 'Famine Stricken Natives', *The Scotsman*, 1 April 1929; 'Lions on Famine Trail', *The New York Times*, 10 April 1929, 32; 'A Stricken Land', *The Times*, 16 April 1929, 17–18.

47. SFA, Rappard Papers, Box 1977/135 3, J. E. T. Philipps to Rappard, 1 March 1929, enclosing J. E. T. Philipps to Sir William Gowers, 1 March 1929.

48. Extensive reports to the Foreign and Colonial Offices from Belgian ambassadors in London, Paris, and Berlin tracking official and popular responses to German colonial claims can be found in AA, AE/II (3243) 1424.

49. At the autumn 1928 session, in answer to Kastl's criticisms, Orts stated that Belgium was happy to employ other nationals but had had no applications (see 16 *PMCM*, 134). Physicians from Kansas City to Latvia then wrote to the League offering their services, only to be told that they had to apply to Brussels; one stated he had done so, but had had no reply. For these see LNA Box R2342, File 6A/9006/5427. In fact, in 1929 the Belgian Colonial Ministry confirmed

internally its decision to employ only Belgian nationals, for which see Cornet, *Histoire d'une famine*, 75.

50. AA, AE/II (3300) 1936, Everts to Hymans, 27 April 1929, enclosing 'Die Zustände in Ruanda: "Das Land der lebenden und toten Skelette"', *Germania*, 24 April 1929. Note that the quotation in the title is from Church's article in *The Times*.

51. Heinrich Schnee, 'Die Hungersnot in Ruanda und die belgische Mandatverwaltung', *Koloniale Rundschau*, 1929, no. 12, 357–68.

52. 'The Ruanda Famine', *The Times*, 18 April 1929, 15; Cornet, *Histoire d'une famine*, 86–7.

53. Statistics from *Ruanda-Urundi Report 1928* (Brussels, 1929), 66–7; *Ruanda-Urundi Report 1929* (Brussels, 1930), 81.

54. A copy of that document was included as a preamble to the *Ruanda-Urundi Report 1930* (Brussels, 1931), 5–6.

55. *Ruanda-Urundi Report 1928* (Brussels, 1929), 67, and see Marzorati's comments on the native population's carelessness in 16 *PMCM*, 61.

56. 9 *PMCM*, 108.

57. Ryckmans, 'Tribune libre: la famine', *Essor colonial et maritime*, 20 June 1929, rpt. in Ryckmans, *Dominer pour Servir*, here at 180.

58. Jean-Pierre Chrétien, 'Féodalité ou féodalisation sous le mandat belge', in his *Burundi: L'histoire retrouvée*, 189–217.

59. Gahama, *Burundi*, 104.

60. See the discussions about consolidating fiefdoms and deposing chiefs, 19 *PMCM*, 126–7; 21 *PMCM*, 17–18; and 22 *PMCM*, 233–4.

61. Newbury, *Cohesion of Oppression*, 132, 153.

62. 'What is the Forced or Compulsory Labour which is allowed in Territories under B and C Mandates . . . Report by Mr. H.A. Grimshaw on the Memorandum by M. Van Rees', in 10 *PMCM*, 166.

63. Gahama, *Burundi*, 104, and Chrétien, *Great Lakes of Africa*, 270–2.

64. 24 *PMCM*, 73.

65. Resident Defawe to Governor-General, 2 May 1929, quoted in Gahama, *Burundi*, 81. For the Burundian monarchy more generally, see esp. René Lemarchand, 'Burundi', in René Lemarchand, ed., *African Kingships in Perspective: Political Change and Modernization in Monarchical Settings* (London: Frank Cass, 1977), 93–126.

66. AA, AE II (3292) 1875, Marzorati to the Minister of the Colonies, 2 Sept. 1924.

67. See the reports to the Governor-General from Marzorati (24 Jan. 1929) and Mgr. Classe (23 July 1929) about Musinga's alleged contacts with the British, in AA, RWA (1) 12; also the 'Note sur Musinga' (22 Dec. 1930) by Mortehan, Commissaire-General of Rwanda, RWA 1 (15). Just before Musinga's deposition, the Resident of Ruanda, O. Coubeau, wrote a detailed summary of the Belgian charges. See 'Rapport au sujet du Mwami Musinga' (6 Aug. 1931), AA, RWA 1 (10).

68. SFA, Rappard Papers, Box 1977/135 3, J. E. T. Philipps to Rappard, 1 March 1929, enclosing J. E. T. Philipps to Sir William Gowers, 1 March 1929.

69. David Newbury's work on those king-lists allows us to see them less as reliable records than as crucial instruments of legitimation; see his 'Trick Cyclists? Recontextualiziing Rwandan Dynastic Chronology', in *The Land Beyond the Mists*, 252–77.

70. One must infer Musinga's views from the accounts of his behaviour in the Belgian records above, but Alison Des Forges also used oral histories collected in the 1960s to paint a persuasive picture of the many ways Belgian rule had compromised Musinga's authority and his long efforts to combat those incursions; see Des Forges, chs. 7–9. For a focus on the key role of Christianity in delegitimizing the Rwandan monarchy, see René Lemarchand, 'Rwanda', in Lemarchand, ed., *African Kingships*, 67–92.

71. AA, AE II/(3296) 1885, File: 'Destitution du sultan Musinga, 1929–1932', Halewyck de Heusch, 'Propositions du Gouverneur du Ruanda-Urundi', 14 Aug. 1929.

72. Voisin's letter to Classe on 5 Jan. 1931, announcing his plan to depose Musinga and asking for his comments, is in RWA (1) 15. Classe's letter to Voisin of 15 Jan. 1931, agreeing that Musinga's deposition could only do good and recommending that he be made to leave Nyanza immediately, is in RWA (1) 16. The letter authorizing the removal of Musinga is in RWA (1) 15, Colonial Minister to Governor-General of Congo, 26 June 1931.

73. 21 *PMCM*, 18–19.

74. The deposition is discussed in Alison Des Forges, 'Defeat', 237–40. For the trouble caused by Musinga's automobile, see AA, RWA (1) 9, Voisin, Governor of Ruanda-Urundi (Usumbura), to Paradis, Delegate of the Resident (Nyanza), 18 Aug. 1930, and Paradis to Voisin, 17 Dec. 1930.

75. Reports sent by district officers are in AA, RWA (1) 15.

76. Ellen Gatti, *Exploring We Would Go* (New York: Charles Scribner's Sons, 1944), 76.

77. 24 *PMCM*, 74–5.

78. 22 *PMCM*, 253–6.

79. 30 *PMCM*, 130–52, *passim.*

80. Annual report for the Nyanza region, 1930, quoted in Rumiya, *Rwanda*, 228.

81. See esp. Hailey's critical statement to this effect, 35 *PMCM*, 51–2.

82. 26 *PMCM*, 149; 30 *PMCM*, 148.

83. Karuna Mantena, *Alibis of Empire: Henry Maine and the Ends of Liberal Imperialism* (Princeton: Princeton University Press, 2010).

84. 35 *PMCM*, 50–3, 63.

85. Mahmood Mamdani, *Citizen and Subject: Contemporary Africa and the Legacy of Late Colonialism* (Princeton: Princeton University Press, 1996). The claim for the colonial 'invention' of African traditions and structures began with (and sometimes involved a simplification of) Terence Ranger's classic essay, 'The

Invention of Tradition in Colonial Africa', in E. J. Hobsbawm and T. O. Ranger, eds., *The Invention of Tradition* (Cambridge: Cambridge University Press, 1983), 211–62; for an intelligent critique of this framework, see Thomas Spear, 'Neo-Traditionalism and the Limits of Invention in British Colonial Africa', *Journal of African History*, 44:1 (2003), 3–27.

86. For the convention see 'Convention concerning forced or compulsory labor', in International Labour Organization, *International Labour Conventions and Recommendations, 1919–1981* (Geneva: ILO, 1982), 29–36; and for the process of its negotiation, Miers, *Slavery*, 136–51. For the ILO's work on forced labour in general, see Daniel Roger Maul, 'The International Labour Organization and the Struggle against Forced Labour from 1919 to the Present', *Labour History*, 48:4 (2007), 477–500.

87. Hiroshi Shimizu, 'The Mandatory Power and Japan's Trade Expansion into Syria in the Inter-War Period', *Middle Eastern Studies*, 21:2 (April 1985), 152–71.


## NOTES FOR CHAPTER 9

1. LNA, S 284 1 (4), File: 'Kastl'.

2. 16 *PMCM*, 141.

3. For this correspondence, see *Policy in Iraq. Memorandum by the Secretary of State for the Colonies*, PP 1929–30, Cmd. 3440.

4. See Lord Cushenden's explanation to the 51st session of the Council, 1 Sept. 1928, in *LNOJ*, Oct. 1928, 1452.

5. I have reconstructed the political narrative from League and British archives but have also relied on three excellent studies: Peter Sluglett, *Britain in Iraq: Contriving King and Country, 1914–1932*, 2nd ed. (New York: Columbia University Press, 2007); Charles Tripp, *A History of Iraq*, 3rd ed. (Cambridge: Cambridge University Press, 2007); and Toby Dodge, *Inventing Iraq: The Failure of Nation Building and a History Denied* (New York: Columbia University Press, 2003). I am indebted to their work.

6. *Draft Mandates for Mesopotamia and Palestine as submitted for the Approval of the League of Nations*, PP 1921, Cmd. 1176.

7. LNA, R58, File 1/17516/17502, Fisher to the Council, 17 Nov. 1921.

8. LNA, S284 (1) (9), Ormsby-Gore file, Rappard to Ormsby-Gore, 29 May 1922.

9. *Iraq. Treaty with King Faysal*, PP 1922, Cmd. 1757, here at Article IV, and for the numerous subsidiary agreements, see *Protocol . . . and Subsidiary Agreements*, PP 1924, Cmd. 2120.

10. It is worth noting that many British officers in Iraq thought the promised four-year period simply 'a concession to extremist opinion', and fully expected the Treaty to be renewed. See C. J. Edmonds, *Kurds, Turks and Arabs: Politics, Travel and Research in North-Eastern Iraq, 1919–1925* (London: Oxford University Press, 1957), 414–15.

11. The discussion at the Council on 20 Sept. 1924, and the Council resolution accepting the Anglo-Iraq Treaty as giving effect to the mandate, were published by Britain as *Papers Relating to the Application to Iraq of the Principles of Article 22 of the Covenant of the League of Nations*, PP 1924–25, Cmd. 2317.

12. Wallace Lyon's memoir provides a vivid account of his work organizing support for the Iraqi case among the unenthusiastic Kurds; see D. K. Fieldhouse, ed., *Kurds, Arabs and Britons: The Memoir of Wallace Lyon in Iraq, 1918–1944* (London: I. B. Tauris, 2002), esp. 94–5. For Britain's role in the Mosul controversy, see Peter J. Beck, '"A Tedious and Perilous Controversy": Britain and the Settlement of the Mosul Dispute, 1918–1926', *Middle Eastern Studies*, 17:2 (April 1981), 256–76, and for a detailed account of the League mediation process, Aryo Makko, 'Arbitrator in a World of Wars: The League of Nations and the Mosul Dispute, 1924–1925', *Diplomacy & Statecraft*, 21:4 (2010), 631–49. For the resulting treaty, *Iraq. Treaty with King Faysal signed at Baghdad, 13th January, 1926*, PP 1926, Cmd. 2587.

13. Dobbs' views are mentioned in NA, CO 730/107/73, Memo by Hall, 29 Dec. 1926, and more fully in NA, CO 730/119/10, C.P. 173 (27), 8 June 1927, circulating Dobbs to Amery, 24 March 1927, and NA, CO 730/119/10, Dobbs to Amery, 31 March 1927.

14. Both quotations from NA, CO 730/107/73, Memo by Hall, 29 Dec. 1926. Horace Wilson also thought it would be nice to orchestrate a French refusal, see NA, CO 730/119/10, Minute by Wilson, 11 March 1927.

15. NA, CO 730/119/10, Minute by Hall, 29 June 1927, and NA, CO 730/120/1, Trenchard, 'Personal Note', 28 June 1927.

16. NA, CO 730/119/10, Minute by Amery, 15 March 1927, and C.P. 178 (27), 'Entry of Iraq into the League of Nations. Memorandum circulated by the Secretary of State for the Colonies', 9 June 1927.

17. NA, CO 730/120/1, Cabinet 38 (27), 4 July 1927, and Amery to Dobbs, 6 July 1927.

18. *Iraq. Treaty between the United Kingdom and Iraq signed at London, December 14, 1927*, PP 1927, Cmd. 2998.

19. 16 *PMCM*, 17–20.

20. NA, CO 730/150/3, Note by Clauson, received 28 Dec. 1929.

21. 16 *PMCM*, 33. For the discussion and report on the Bahai petition the previous year, see 14 *PMCM*, 189–90, 275–6. PMC consideration of the Bahai appeal turned into a hardy perennial, and the mandate ended with the issue still unresolved. Records of this international campaign are in LNA, R2314, 6A/7886/655.

22. 16 *PMCM*, 141.

23. 'Report', in 16 *PMCM*, 203.

24. Minutes of the 58th session of the Council, 13 Jan. 1930, *LNOJ*, Feb. 1930, 77, and of the 64th session, 4 Sept. 1931, *LNOJ*, Nov. 1931, 2058.

25. A preliminary report drafted by the Portuguese member, Count de Penha Garcia, 'General Conditions that must be fulfilled before the mandate regime

can be brought to an end in respect of a country placed under that regime', was published in 19 *PMCM*, Annex 8. The issue was discussed at the 20th session in June 1931, and a final report, also titled 'General Conditions that must be fulfilled...', was published in 20 *PMCM*, 228–30.

26. 20 *PMCM*, 152; LNA, R2346, 6A/16601/16601, CPM 1183, 'Contribution to the examination of the question of the general conditions required for the termination of the mandate regime... Note by M. Van Rees' (13 June 1931).

27. 20 *PMCM*, 228–9.

28. LNA, R2346, 6A/16601/16601, jacket 1, CPM 11997, 'General Question. Termination of a Mandate. Note by Lord Lugard' (20 June 1931).

29. De Penha Garcia, 'General Conditions' (1930).

30. 20 *PMCM*, 229.

31. NA, CO 730/152/7, Minute by Hall, 21 Nov. 1930; Minutes by Shuckburgh, 25 Nov. 1930, and Drummond Shiels, 2 Dec. 1930; and Bourdillon's 1929 pledge to wait for League consent, in 16 *PMCM*, 33.

32. NA, CO 730/152/7, Minute by Hall, 25 Oct. 1930; see also NA, CO 730/179/3, 'Memorandum: Attitude to be adopted by the British Accredited Representative at the forthcoming meeting of the Permanent Mandates Commission' (n.d. [Oct. 1931]).

33. *Special Report by His Majesty's Government... on the Progress of Iraq during the period 1920–1931* (London: HMSO, 1931). As the Colonial Office's J. E. Hall put it, material that was 'true' but might 'make a bad impression at Geneva' could be 'toned down', since the purpose of the report was to persuade the League that the Iraqi government was 'sufficiently enlightened' to be granted independence—advice that prefigures the notorious 'sexing up' of another Iraq dossier some seventy years later. See NA, CO 730/167/14, Note by Hall, 30 March 1931.

34. NA, CO 730/166/7, Note by Hall, 26 June 1931.

35. NA, CO 730/152/7, Minute by Flood, 27 Oct. 1930.

36. NA, CO 730/167/14, Cornwallis to Young, 22 March 1931.

37. Kedourie's coruscating analysis remains well worth reading: 'The Kingdom of Iraq: A Retrospect', in *The Chatham House Version and Other Middle-Eastern Studies* (New York: Praeger, 1970), 236–85.

38. NA, CO 730/152/7, Minute by Flood, 27 Oct. 1930.

39. PA, R96537, Grobba, 'Zu Punkt I der Tagesordnung des 58 Tagung des Völkerbundesrates' (23 Dec. 1929).

40. PA, R96543, Grobba, 'Zu Punkt 2 der Tagesordnung der 62. Tagung des Völkerbundsrates' (23 Dec. 1930).

41. PA, R96540, Grobba, 'XI Bundesversammlung. Punkt 2 Ziffer 8 II Mandats' (23 Aug. 1930).

42. PA, R96535, Kastl to Catastini, 8 Dec. 1928, enclosed in Grobba, 'Zu Punkt 2 der Tagesordnung der 54. Tagung des Völkerbundsrates. Mandate. Irak' (28 Feb. 1929); copy in LNA, S 284 1 (4), 'Kastl'.

43. *Treaty of Alliance between the United Kingdom and Iraq*, PP 1929–30, Cmd. 3627.
44. 19 *PMCM*, 87.
45. 21 *PMCM*, 77.
46. See Lugard's exchange with Humphrys in 20 *PMCM*, 130.
47. CO 730/170/4, Memo by Hall, 10 Nov. 1931.
48. The quotation from the German commission is from Timothy Mitchell, *Carbon Democracy: Political Power in the Age of Oil* (London:Verso, 2011), 48.
49. Hankey's comment is from BL, Cecil Papers, Add MS 51071, Hankey to Balfour, 12 Aug. 1918, secret. At San Remo the British had won French consent to their claim to the region only by agreeing to grant France a 25% share (in essence, the confiscated Deutsche Bank share) in any consortium established to exploit those holdings. For that oil agreement, see *Memorandum of Agreement between M. Philippe Berthelot . . . and Professor Sir John Cadman*, PP 1920, Cmd. 675.
50. The oil companies holding (from 1928) equal shares in any oil ventures inside the 'red line' (after granting 5% to Calouste Gulbenkian, the Armenian engineer who managed to retain an individual share of what became one of the world's most lucrative concerns) were: the D'Arcy Exploration Company (a British conglomerate of which the majority holder was Anglo-Persian Oil); Royal Dutch/Shell (combining British and Dutch oil interests); the Compagnie Française des Pétroles (of which the French government was the largest shareholder); and the Near East Development Corporation (a conglomerate of American firms, including Standard Oil). The complex and murky diplomacy around Middle East oil has been analysed from several perspectives, although the way the Mandates Commission emerged as one arena for negotiating those interests has largely escaped attention. I have benefited especially from Peter Sluglett's *Britain in Iraq*, Mitchell's *Carbon Democracy*, and Helmut Mejcher's works cited below.
51. Kastl's draft report is in LNA, R59, 1/62947/17502, CPM 674, 'Anglo-Persian Oil Concession. Report by M. Kastl' (7 Nov. 1927). For Kastl's revised report, 14 *PMCM*, 188, 213, and 247–9, and for the German Foreign Ministry's monitoring of this discussion, PA, R76851, 'Verlängerung der Konzession der Anglo-Persian Oil Company im Irak' (25 Oct. 1928).
52. 16 *PMCM*, 41–4.
53. Fritz Grobba claimed in his memoir that on a visit to Germany in 1930 Faysal himself solicited German support for the BOD. See Grobba, 'Deutsche Erdölinteressen in Arabien', in his *Männer und Mächte im Orient: 25 Jahre diplomatitischer Tätigkeit im Orient* (Göttingen: Musterschmidt, 1967), 85–94. Information about the Italian purchase is from 'Further communication to the Secretary-General dated September 19, 1929 from the British Oil Development Co., Ltd', in 18 *PMCM*, 179–80, and for the BOD more generally, Sluglett, *Britain in Iraq*, 112, 137–8, and 272, fn. 27, Helmut Mejcher, *Die Politik und das Öl im Nahen Osten*, vol. I (Stuttgart: Klett-Cotta, 1980), 37–42, and Mejcher, 'The International Petroleum Cartel (1928), Arab and Turkish Oil Aspirations

and German Oil Policy towards the Middle East on the Eve of the Second World War', in Klaus Jürgen Gantzel and Helmut Mejcher, eds., *Oil, the Middle East, North Africa and the Industrial States* (Paderborn: F. Schöningh, 1984), 29–59.

54. For this point, Sluglett, *Britain in Iraq*, 139.

55. For the petitions, reports, and debates, see 18 *PMCM*, 80–1, 177–84, and 19 *PMCM*, 90–2, 102–3, 122–4, 150–2, 177–84. For the British government's handling of the affair, see NA, CO 730/168/12.

56. For French diplomacy over the pipelines, see Peter A. Shambrook, *French Imperialism in Syria, 1927–1936* (Reading, UK: Ithaca Press, 1998), 55–8, and for the crucial American role mediating Anglo-French disagreement, Edward Peter Fitzgerald, 'Business Diplomacy: Walter Teagle, Jersey Standard, and the Anglo-French Pipeline Conflict in the Middle East, 1930–1931', *Business History Review*, 67:2 (Summer 1993), 207–45.

57. 20 *PMCM*, 144–9, 168–77, here at 147.

58. PA, R96543, Grobba, '64 Tagung des Völkerbundsrates. Punkt 2 der Tagesordnung', III O 2676 (22 Aug. 1931).

59. NA, CO 730/164/5, Bordonaro to Henderson, 6 July 1931.

60. NA, CO 730/164/5, Hall minute, 30 July 1931.

61. NA, CO 730/169/7, Hall minute, 9 Sept. 1931.

62. Foreign Office, Eastern Department, 'Iraq: Proposed Release from Mandatory Regime: Memorandum for British Representative on the Council of the League' (21 Jan. 1932), in *BDFA*, pt. II, ser. B, vol. 7, 376–7.

63. NA, CO 730/169/7, 'Record of interview between Lord Cecil and Signor Grandi', 2 Sept. 1931.

64. The Italian statement was agreed with the French and British beforehand in order to prevent public disagreements, but was still quite hard-hitting. See Minutes of the 64th session of the Council, 4 Sept. 1931, in *LNOJ*, Nov. 1931, 2049.

65. NA, CO 730/1704, Memo by Hall, 10 Nov. 1931.

66. Grobba's analysis of Germany's interest in opposing attempts to force Iraq to grant most-favoured-nation status to League states is in PA, R96543, Grobba, 'Zu Punkt 2 der Tagesordnung der 62. Tagung des Völkerbundrates' (23 Dec. 1930).

67. Minutes of the 64th session of the Council, 4 Sept. 1931, in *LNOJ*, Nov. 1931, 2052.

68. 21 *PMCM*, 77–8.

69. NA, CO 730/169/8, 'Notes of a meeting held in Mr. Rendel's room on Dec. 14th at 8:30 pm to consider the Permanent Mandates Commission's report to the Council on the release of Iraq from the Mandatory Regime', and, more generally, Foreign Office, 'Iraq: Proposed Release from Mandatory Regime', *BDFA*, pt. II, ser. B, vol. 7, 372–84.

70. For those rivalries, see Martin Thomas, *Empires of Intelligence: Security Services and Colonial Disorder after 1914* (Berkeley: University of California Press, 2008).

71. NA, CO 730/152/7, Note by Shuckburgh, 25 Nov. 1930, and Memo by Clauson, 19 Nov. 1930.

72. 20 *PMCM*, 33–8.

73. NA, CO 730/166/7, Note by Hall, 1 Sept. 1931.

74. The 'Wailing Wall' controversy is discussed in Chapter 12 below.

75. There are several excellent works on the League's Minorities Protection regime, but see esp. Carol Fink, *Defending the Rights of Others: The Great Powers, the Jews, and International Minority Protection, 1878–1938* (Cambridge: Cambridge University Press, 2006), and for Germany's role, Christoph Kimmich, *Germany and the League of Nations* (Chicago: University of Chicago Press, 1976), ch. 7. The process through which the 'minority' became an operative category in French-mandated Syria is illuminated in Benjamin Thomas White, *The Emergence of Minorities in the Middle East: The Politics of Community in French Mandate Syria* (Edinburgh: Edinburgh University Press, 2011).

76. Population figures are from Tripp, *A History of Iraq*, 31.

77. For that strategy of domination, see, esp., Pierre-Jean Luizard, 'Le Mandat britannique en Irak: Une rencontre entre plusieurs projets politiques', in Nadine Méouchy and Peter Sluglett, eds., *The British and French Mandates in Comparative Perspective* (Leiden: Brill, 2004), 361–84.

78. For a sensitive account of the emergence of fragile but pluralistic institutions in Hashemite Iraq, see Orit Bashkin, *The Other Iraq: Pluralism and Culture in Hashemite Iraq* (Stanford: Stanford University Press, 2009).

79. Acting High Commissioner H. W. Young told the PMC that he found a widespread belief among the Kurds that the League Council would provide for an independent Kurdish state upon Iraqi independence, although he had done his best to discourage such ideas. See 19 *PMCM*, 78–80.

80. LNA, R2316, 6A/22413/655, jacket 1, containing petitions of 27 July and 5 Aug. 1930.

81. LNA, R2316, 6A/22413/655, jacket 1, 'Observations, dated October 29th 1930, of the Mandatory Power'; see also Minutes of the 62nd session of the Council, 22 Jan. 1931, in *LNOJ*, Feb. 1931, 185.

82. LNA, R2316, 6A/22413/655, jacket 1, CPM 1081, Report by Rappard (13 Nov. 1930).

83. NA, CO 730/16/2, Humphrys to Passfield, 10 Feb. and 13 Feb. 1931, also K. Cornwallis, British Advisor, to the Minister of the Interior, 4 Feb. 1931.

84. For Turkish, Iraqi, and Persian collusion over the need to resist demands for Kurdish autonomy, see NA, CO 730/161/4, Humphrys to Passfield, 18 Feb. 1931, and NA, CO 730/161/1, Nuri to Humphrys, 25 Feb. 1931.

85. NA, CO 730/161/4, Passfield to Humphrys, 3 March 1931. Humphrys, however, had a good understanding of the symbiotic relationship between Kurdish unrest and Iraqi government repression. See NA, CO 730/161/1, Humphrys to Williams, editor of *The Near East*, 28 March 1931, private.

86. LNA, R2316, 6A/22413/655, CPM 1198, Rappard, 'Report on the various petitions emanating from Kurdish sources' (22 June 1931). David McDowall char-
acterizes Britain's retreat from promises of Kurdish autonomy and its delivery
of the Kurds into the hands of a unitary Iraqi state straightforwardly as a betrayal;
see McDowall, *A Modern History of the Kurds* (London: I. B. Tauris, 1996), ch. 8.

87. David Silverfarb gives the size of the Assyrian population as 28,000 in 1933
(*Britain's Informal Empire in the Middle East: A Case Study of Iraq, 1929–1941* [New
York: Oxford University Press, 1986], 45), a low estimate.

88. The very extensive petitions from Rassam, and later from the Mar Shimun, are
to be found in LNA, R2317 and R2318, 6A/22528/655.

89. LNA, R2317, 6A/22528/655, jacket 4, CPM 1208, 'Petitions dated September
23rd 1930 and December 9th 1930 from Captain Rassam…Report by M. Orts'
(26 June 1931).

90. LNA, R2318, 6A/22528/655, jacket 6, Mar Shimun to the League of Nations,
23 Oct. 1931 and 17 June 1932.

91. See esp. Hoare's initiation of two Commons debates over Iraq policy and protection of minorities in *H. C. Deb.*, vol. 242, 31 July 1930, cols. 800–817, and *H. C. Deb.*,
vol. 255, 23 July 1931, cols. 1784–1834; Dobbs letter to *The Times*, 10 July 1931;
A. T. Wilson, 'Peace in Iraq', *The Times*, 22 May 1931, and evidence of Wilson's
efforts in October 1931 to persuade the PMC (especially Lugard) to take a
strong stand against independence, in Rhodes House (Oxford), Lugard Papers
127/3.

92. For which see Gilbert Murray to Arthur Henderson, 14 Jan. 1931, and
'Confidential report of an interview by De Haller with Mr. Epstein of the
League of Nations Union', 6 Feb. 1931, both in LNA Box S284, file 2.

93. Ja'far al-'Askari to Major H. W. Young, 19 Aug. 1930, appended to the observations of the Mandatory Power on Kurdish petitions, 29 Oct. 1930; LNA Box
R2316, 6A/22413/655.

94. 20 *PMCM*, 122. British representatives consistently tried to discredit Rassam;
see, in addition to Humphrys' comments, Young's remarks in 19 *PMCM*, 79, and
NA, CO 730/166/7, Hall minute, 26 July 1931. Rassam, stung, protested to the
League, sending numerous letters about his character and good faith. See LNA,
R2317, 6a22528/655, jacket 4, Rassam to PMC Chairman, 17 Sept. 1931, and
jacket 5, Rassam to PMC Chairman, 23 Oct. 1931.

95. 20 *PMCM*, 135.

96. 20 *PMCM*, 135.

97. NA, CO 730/170/4, Memo by Hall, 10 Nov. 1931.

98. Much has been written on the Assyrian tragedy of 1933. A good account is
found in Silverfarb, *Britain's Informal Empire*, ch. 4. Fritz Grobba, then ambassador in Iraq and on confidential terms equally with the Mar Shimun and several
Iraqi ministers, provides an eyewitness account of perceptions and politics in
Baghdad during the crisis in 'Die Assyrische Tragödie', in his *Männer und Mächte
im Orient*, 75–85. Reports from Humphrys and other British officials in Iraq

about their efforts to mediate the crisis and quiet the levies in the first half of 1933 are in *BDFA*, pt. II, ser. B, vol. 8, 368–410 *passim*; reports of the August crisis, including Administrative Inspector R. S. Stafford's dispatch from Simmel giving a full account of the massacre, continue in *BDFA*, pt. II, ser. B, vol. 9, 204–357 *passim*, with Stafford's report at 223–4. Stafford later produced a comprehensive account, *The Tragedy of the Assyrians* (London: Allen & Unwin, 1935). The Iraqi government produced a Blue Book which sought to shift responsibility for the conflict from the Iraqi Army to the French and the Assyrians themselves; in LNA, R4064, see telegrams from Nuri al-Saʻid, 7 Aug. and 22 Aug. 1933, and Government of Iraq, *Correspondence Relating to Assyrian Settlement from 13 July 1932 to 5 August 1933* (Baghdad, 1933). The Mar Shimun's desperate appeals in July and August are in LNA, S1633.

99. NA, CO 730/169/8, Memo by Hall, 28 Nov. 1931.

100. 21 *PMCM*, Annex 22, 'Special Report of the Commission to the Council on the Proposal of the British Government with Regard to the Emancipation of Iraq', 222.

101. NA, CO 730/169/8, 'Memorandum' (n.d. [Dec. 1931]).

102. Minutes of the 66th session of the Council, 28 Jan. 1932, in *LNOJ*, March 1932, 471–9. The end of the Ottoman capitulations was made palatable through the introduction of a new judicial system with a statutory role for British judges. While the Council required Britain and Iraq to secure each state's consent to that regime, through this painstaking process the judicial immunities of foreigners in Iraq were finally abolished. For this work see LNA, R2315, 6A/10243/655.

103. LNA, R2319, 6A/35197/655, jackets 1 and 2, containing the minutes of the Committee appointed under the Council Resolution of 28 Jan. 1932. The declaration on employment of Kurdish officials made 'efficiency and knowledge of the language, rather than race' the qualification for appointment, and qualified the obligation to select officials from the population of the region with those fateful bureaucratic words, 'as far as possible'.

104. Carl Schmitt, 'Völkerrechtliche Formen des modernen Imperialismus', in *Positionen und Begriffe im Kampf mit Weimar—Genf—Versailles, 1923–1939* (1940; rpt. Berlin: Duncker & Humblot, 1994), 184–203. I have used the recent translation by Matthew Hannah, 'Forms of Modern Imperialism in International Law', in Stephen Legg, ed., *Spatiality, Sovereignty and Carl Schmitt: Geographies of the Nomos* (London: Routledge, 2011), 29–45, here at 30–1, 40, 44.

105. 'Großraum gegen Universalismus: Der völkerrechtliche Kampf um die Monroedoktrin', in *Positionen*, 335–43; trans. Matthew Hannah, 'Großraum versus Universalism: The International Legal Struggle over the Monroe Doctrine', in Legg, ed., *Spatiality*, 46–54.

106. Toynbee, 'The Settlement of Turkey and the Arabian Peninsula', 13 Nov. 1918, quoted in Gordon Martel, 'The Origins of the Chatham House Version', in Edward Ingram, ed., *National and International Politics in the Middle East: Essays in Honour of Elie Kedourie* (London: Frank Cass, 1986), 77–8.

107. Sluglett, *Britain in Iraq*, 140.
108. For Ponsot's efforts to craft a treaty that would fragment Syrian unity and preserve French hegemony, see Shambrook, *French Imperialism in Syria*, chs. 2–3. For German and Italian opposition, see the Council Minutes of 24 Jan. 1933', *LNOJ*, Feb. 1933, 190.
109. League records of its efforts to respond to the Assyrian crisis are in LNA, R2320, 6A/39025/655 and S1630 and 1633; see also the Council discussions of 5 and 15 Dec. 1932 in *LNOJ*, Dec. 1932, 1962–66 and 1984–85, and, for Lugard's guilt-ridden response, RH, Lugard 128/1.
110. Rappard to de Caix, 19 June 1936, quoted in Victor Monnier, *William E. Rappard: Défenseur des libertés, serviteur de son pays et de la communauté internationale* (Geneva: Slatkine, 1995), 449.

## NOTES FOR PART IV

1. LNA, S1628, File on Ruppel, Ruppel to Catastini, 14 Nov. 1933.
2. Much has been written on the Japanese in Manchuria, but for the ways in which it affected Japan's internationalism and its relations with Geneva, see Thomas Burkman, *Japan and the League of Nations: Empire and World Order, 1914–1938* (Honolulu: University of Hawaii Press, 2008), and Ian Nish, *Japanese Foreign Policy in the Interwar Period* (Westport, CT: Praeger, 2002), ch. 5.
3. For one statement of this view, see Luther H. Evans, 'Would Japanese Withdrawal from the League Affect the Status of the Japanese Mandate?', *The American Journal of International Law*, 27:1 (1933), 140–2.
4. For views of Japanese lawyers and the Japanese Foreign Office, see USNA, Box 6833, 862i.01/249, Grew to Secretary of State, 10 Feb. 1933. A translation of the Naval Affairs Information Bureau pamphlet, 'Japan's Withdrawal from the League of Nations and the Japanese Mandatory Administration over the South Sea Islands' (Feb. 1933), which forthrightly asserted that Japan held the islands in full sovereignty, is in 862i/01/272, Grew to Secretary of State, 3 May 1933.
5. USNA, Box 6833, 862i.01/276, [Prentiss Gilbert], 'General Discussion of the Political and Juridical Status of Areas under Mandate – with Special Reference to the Japanese Mandate' (8 Sept. 1933), 28.
6. NA, CO 232/1234/8, Note by Lee, 18 May 1933. In April 1933 the German Foreign Office intended to insist that since the League held ultimate authority over mandates, the Council and the PMC should be required to discuss the implications of Japan's withdrawal, but the Nazi takeover and German withdrawal put an abrupt end to those plans. See PA, R 96517, Memos by Renthe-Fink, 30 March 1933, and Memo of a departmental conference on the question, 25 April 1933.
7. USNA, Box 6834, 862i.01/301, Prentiss Gilbert, 'The Japanese Mandate', 15 Nov. 1934, 8–12.

8. Minutes of the 90th session of the Council, 22 Jan. 1936, in *LNOJ*, Feb. 1936, 79.

9. LNA, S1627, File on Sakenobe, De Haller to Avenol, 11 Nov. 1938.

10. The complaint is Orts': SFA, Rappard Papers, Box 1977/135 36, Orts to Rappard, 10 May 1937.

11. NA, CO 323/1332/9, Note by J. G. Lee, 2 July 1935.

12. RH, Lugard Papers, Box 122/2, Dannevig to Lugard, 10 May 1936.

13. RH, Lugard Papers, Box 122/2, Lugard to Dannevig, 15 May 1936.

14. PA, R102268, German Consulate, Geneva, to AA, 28 May 1936.

15. LNA, S1628, File on Theodoli, De Haller to Secretary General, 12 June 1936. De Haller went to considerable lengths to secure Theodoli's agreement to revise the minutes to disguise the extent of the disagreement; for which see LNA S1619, Note by De Haller, and, for the softened version, 29 *PMCM*, 168–71.

16. CZA, L22/960, Nahum Goldmann, 'Report about two conversations with Marchese Theodoli, Chairman of the Mandates Commission, in Rome on May 3rd and 4th, 1937'.

17. SFA, Rappard Papers, Box 1977/13 36, Orts to Rappard, 13 April and 10 May 1937; Rappard to Orts, 15 April and 7 May 1937.

18. RH, Lugard Papers, Box 122/2, Orts to Lugard, 18 May 1937, Lugard to Hailey, 19 May 1937, and Lugard to Orts, 21 May 1937. Theodoli finally resigned in December 1937.

19. MAE, SDN 556, Jules Laroche, French Ambassador in Brussels, to Yvon Delbos, Ministre des affaires étrangères, 22 April 1937.

20. CAC, AMEL 2/1/27 Pt. 2, Smuts to Amery, 9 Dec. 1937.

21. As Jean Monnet's successor as the French Deputy Secretary General, Avenol was the obvious successor to Drummond, but his entire unsuitability for the post led even the very correct Drummond to urge the Foreign Office to prevent his appointment, for which see BL, Cecil Papers, Add MS 51112, Drummond to Simon, 7 Jan. 1932; also, for Avenol more generally, James C. Barros, *Betrayal From Within: Joseph Avenol, Secretary-General of the League of Nations, 1933–1940* (New Haven: Yale University Press, 1969).

## NOTES FOR CHAPTER 10

1. There has been an explosion of work in recent years tracing connections between anti-colonial intellectuals and movements. That literature is now too vast to cite here, but for three works that capture some unexpected connections and effects, see Mrinalini Sinha, *Specters of Mother India: The Global Restructuring of an Empire* (Durham, NC: Duke University Press, 2006); Susan Pennybacker, *From Scottsboro to Munich: Race and Political Culture in 1930s Britain* (Princeton: Princeton University Press, 2009); Kris Manjapra, *Age of Entanglement: German and Indian Intellectuals across Empire* (Cambridge, MA: Harvard University Press, 2014).

2. Italy's cynical deployment of humanitarian and anti-slavery rhetoric is mentioned by George W. Baer in his standard history of the Italo-Ethiopian conflict, *Test Case: Italy, Ethiopia, and the League of Nations* (Stanford: Hoover Institution Press, 1976), but for two important new studies of how those ideologies suffused debates over Ethiopia, see Amalia Ribi, '"The Breath of a New Life"? British Anti-Slavery and the League of Nations', *Internationalism Reconfigured: Transnational Ideas and Movements Between the Wars*, ed. Daniel Laqua (London: I. B. Tauris, 2011), 93–113, and Jean Allain, 'Slavery and the League of Nations: Ethiopia as a Civilised Nation', *Journal of the History of International Law*, 8 (2006), 213–44.

3. For the 'mediatized' nature of the war, see Baer, *Test Case*, 43–5.

4. For a perceptive contemporary assessment of that non-white response, see Arnold Toynbee, *Survey of International Affairs, 1935*, vol. 2, *Abyssinia and Italy* (London: Oxford University Press, 1936), 106–12, and for mobilization in the United States, Britain, and even Japan, Clifford L. Muse, Jr., 'Howard University and U.S. Foreign Affairs during the Franklin D. Roosevelt Administration, 1933–1945', *The Journal of African-American History*, 87 (Autumn 2002), 403–15; S. K. B. Asante, 'The Impact of the Italo-Ethiopian Crisis of 1935–36 on the Pan-African Movement in Britain', *Transactions of the Historical Society of Ghana*, 13:2 (Dec. 1972), 217–27; Richard Pankhurst, 'Pro- and Anti-Ethiopian Pamphleteering in Britain during the Italian Fascist Invasion and Occupation (1935–1941)', *International Journal of Ethiopian Studies*, 1:1 (Summer-Fall 2003), 153–76; and J. Calvitt Clarke III, 'The Politics of Arms not Given: Japan, Ethiopia and Italy in the 1930s', in *Girding for Battle: The Arms Trade in a Global Perspective, 1815–1940*, ed. Donald J. Stoker, Jr., and Jonathan A. Grant (London: Praeger, 2003), 135–53. Ibrahim Sundiata provides an excellent account of African-Americans' earlier engagement with Liberia, that other precariously independent African state, in *Brothers and Strangers: Black Zion, Black Slavery, 1910–1940* (Durham, NC: Duke University Press, 2004).

5. CAC, NBKR 4/1, File 2, Noel Baker to Dalton, 12 Dec. 1935, and for Ormsby-Gore, see Toynbee, *Survey 1935*, 108.

6. Britain and France had sound reasons to wish to appease Italy, being desperate to prevent it from slipping into alliance with Germany, but their inability either to restrain Italian aggression or to condone it (given their League commitments) produced a prevaricating policy that estranged Italy without protecting either Ethiopia or the League. For a thorough discussion of the diplomacy of the conflict and its implications for the League, see Baer, *Test Case*; Zara Steiner, *The Triumph of the Dark: European International History, 1933–1939* (Oxford: Oxford University Press, 2011), ch. 3; and R. A. C. Parker, 'Great Britain, France and the Ethiopian Crisis, 1935–1936', *The English Historical Review*, 89:351 (April 1974), 293–332. Michael Callahan emphasizes rightly that British diplomats in particular wished to find a solution compatible with 'mandate' ideals, but it is worth noting that by doing so they again exposed how easily 'trusteeship' could

be used to cover nakedly imperial aims; after all, Italy too was eager to offer to abide by 'mandate principles' in Ethiopia. See Michael Callahan, *A Sacred Trust: The League of Nations and Africa, 1929–1946* (Brighton: Sussex Academic Press, 2004), 78–87.

7. The quotation is from 24 *PMCM*, 92; the 1938 population statistics (which were 65% native for the Caroline Islands and 95% native for the Marshall Islands) are from 35 *PMCM*, 184. Scholars agree that while Japan pursued development in its mandated territory much more aggressively than its peers, that development brought relatively few benefits to the islanders. For Japan's policy, see esp. David C. Purcell, Jr., 'The Economics of Exploitation: The Japanese in the Mariana, Caroline and Marshall Islands, 1915–1940', *The Journal of Pacific History*, 11:3 (1976), 189–211, and Mark R. Peattie, *Nan'yō: The Rise and Fall of the Japanese in Micronesia, 1885–1945* (Honolulu: University of Hawaii Press, 1988), esp. ch. 4.

8. Ralph J. Bunche, 'French Administration in Togoland and Dahomey,' Dissertation, Harvard University, 1934, 127.

9. For Murray's administration, see J. D. Legge, 'The Murray Period', in W. J. Hudson, ed., *Australia and Papua New Guinea* (Sydney: Sydney University Press, 1971), 32–56, and James Griffin, Hank Nelson, and Stewart Firth, *Papua New Guinea: A Political History* (Victoria: Heinemann Educational, 1979), 20–33.

10. This account is drawn from Heather Radi, 'New Guinea under Mandate 1921–1941', in Hudson, ed., *Australia and Papua New Guinea*, 74–137; Griffin et al., *Papua New Guinea*, 46–58; and Roger C. Thompson, 'Making a Mandate: The Formation of Australia's New Guinea Policies, 1919–1925', *Journal of Pacific History*, 25:1 (1990), 68–94. For mention of the high import of liquor (which was prohibited to natives), see 13 *PMCM*, 32.

11. The 1930 figures are from ANA, A518/1, AE 840/1/3, 'New Guinea and Papua – return of employment of natives', but are also provided each year in *New Guinea Report*. For bounties paid to recruiters in the goldfields, see Chinnery in 18 *PMCM*, 67, and Hortense Hallock, 'Life in New Guinea Goldfields', *Pacific Magazine*, Feb. 1932, and for a vivid portrait of the methods and morals of one recruiter, Margaret Matches, *Savage Paradise* (New York: The Century Co., 1931), 205–6.

12. 'Our Critics – the P.M.C.', *The Rabaul Times*, 3 Nov. 1933. W. J. Hudson notes that Australia harmed its own cause by allowing ill-informed braggarts like Sir Joseph Cook to meet with the suave diplomats of the Secretariat or the sagacious old foxes of the PMC. See Hudson, *Australia and the League of Nations* (Sydney: Sydney University Press, 1980), 139–44.

13. For Hubert's letters to Gilbert and Lady Mary Murray, see Francis West, ed., *Selected Letters of Hubert Murray* (Melbourne: Oxford University Press, 1970). For Lugard's and Rappard's use of such information, see RH, Lugard 138/1, Gilbert Murray to Lugard, 31 March 1928, and 13 *PMCM*, 21–2, 28. The Commission also questioned Australian representatives in 1927 and 1928 about

a punitive expedition that resulted in considerable loss of life; for which see Patricia O'Brien, 'Reactions to Australian Colonial Violence in New Guinea: The 1926 Nakanai Massacre in a Global Context', *Australian Historical Studies*, 43:2 (2012), 191–209.

14. *New Guinea Report 1921–22*, 52; see also Coleman in 18 *PMCM*, 46; Collins in 20 *PMCM*, 22.

15. See Cook in 6 *PMCM*, 85, and Carrodus in 9 *PMCM*, 22.

16. The fullest account of the relationship between anthropology and colonial administration in mandated New Guinea is I. C. Campbell, 'Anthropology and the Professionalization of Colonial Administration in Papua and New Guinea', *The Journal of Pacific History*, 33:1 (June 1998), 69–90, but for Chinnery in particular, see Geoffrey Gray, 'There are Many Difficult Problems: Ernest William Pearson Chinnery: Government Anthropologist', *The Journal of Pacific History*, 38:3 (Dec. 2003), 313–30, and for Radcliffe-Brown's time in Sydney, George W. Stocking, *After Tylor: British Social Anthropology, 1888–1951* (Madison: University of Wisconsin Press, 1995), 339–52.

17. I. C. Campbell stresses the innovative nature of Australian administration, but for an alternative view, see Radi, 'New Guinea under Mandate 1921–1941'.

18. See, e.g., Mead to Alfred Kroeber, 25 Feb. 1930, in *To Cherish the Life of the World: Selected Letters of Margaret Mead*, ed. Margaret M. Caffrey and Patricia A. Francis (New York: Basic Books, 2006), 245–6.

19. For which see Geoffrey Gray, '"Being Honest to My Science": Reo Fortune and J. H. P. Murray, 1927–1930', *Australian Journal of Anthropology*, 10:1 (1999), 56–76.

20. A. Le Breton Mount, 'How Should We Treat the New Guinea Natives?', *Pacific Islands Monthly*, 26 Jan. 1932, 30.

21. 18 *PMCM*, 63.

22. E. W. P. Chinnery, 'Applied Anthropology in New Guinea', in *New Guinea Report 1932–3*, 153–62, here at 159 and 161.

23. For the famous Rabaul strike and its aftermath, see Radi, 'New Guinea under Mandate 1921–1941', 117–18, and for the administration's report on the strike, *New Guinea Report 1928–9*, 105–9.

24. 18 *PMCM*, 62.

25. Margaret Mead, *Letters from the Field, 1925–1975* (New York: Harper & Row, 1977), 65.

26. 9 *PMCM*, 24; 11 *PMCM*, 56; 18 *PMCM*, 44–79 *passim*; 20 *PMCM*, 15; 25 *PMCM*, 41, 45; 29 *PMCM*, 17.

27. See, e.g., 3 *PMCM*, 165–6, 25 *PMCM*, 46.

28. 18 *PMCM*, 68.

29. 31 *PMCM*, 157.

30. For Leahy's life, see esp. Bob Connolly and Robin Anderson, *First Contact* (New York: Viking Penguin, 1987), *passim*; also James Griffin, 'Leahy, Michael James (Mick) (1901–1979)', *Australian Dictionary of Biography*, http://adb.anu.edu.au/

biography/leahy-michael-james-mick-7134/tet12311, accessed 10 July 2012, and Douglas E. Jones, 'Afterword', in Michael J. Leahy, *Explorations into Highland New Guinea, 1930–1935* (Tuscaloosa: University of Alabama Press, 1991), 245–50.

31. Kate Blackmer has drawn this map, but the approximation of Leahy's routes is taken from the maps found in Edward L. Schieffelin and Robert Crittenden, et al., *Like People You See in a Dream: First Contact in Six Papuan Societies* (Stanford: Stanford University Press, 1991), and of the area under government control from Griffin, Nelson, and Firth, *Papua New Guinea*, 51.

32. Michael Leahy and Maurice Crain, *The Land that Time Forgot: Adventures and Discoveries in New Guinea* (New York: Funk & Wagnalls, 1937), 150, 272.

33. Leahy always presented himself as his expeditions' leader, but Chinnery treated Taylor as the leader of that 1933 expedition; see, E. W. P. Chinnery, 'The Central Ranges of the Mandated Territory of New Guinea from Mount Chapman to Mount Hagen', *The Geographical Journal*, 84:5 (Nov. 1934), 398–412. Robin Radford's detailed account of the Upper Ramu area recovers a decade of work by German missionaries as well as earlier trips by prospectors before Leahy's expeditions; see Robin Radford, *Highlanders and Foreigners in the Upper Ramu: Tha Kainantu Area 1919–1942* (Melbourne: Melbourne University Press, 1987), esp. 76–7.

34. Jack Hides and Jim O'Malley's 1935 expedition into the Strickland and Purari valleys is the subject of Schieffelin and Crittenden's brilliant study, *Like People You See in a Dream*; for the later Hides-Leahy conflict, see 247; also Tim Bayliss-Smith, 'Papuan Exploration, Colonial Expansion and the Royal Geographical Society: Questions of Power/Knowledge Relations', *Journal of Historical Geography*, 18:3 (1992), 319–29.

35. Michael Leahy, 'The Central Highlands of New Guinea', *The Geographical Journal*, 87:3 (March 1936), 229–62; Leahy and Crain, *Land*, and Leahy, *Explorations*.

36. Connolly and Anderson, *First Contact*.

37. LNA, R4130, 6A/26211/4230, CPM 1878, Report from the Prime Minister's Office on the Anti-Slavery Society Petition, 17 May 1937, Annexure 'A'.

38. Connolly and Anderson, *First Contact*, 66.

39. Leahy, *Explorations*, 42–3, 150–3, Leahy and Crain, *Land*, 206–8. It is worth noting that the District Officer who investigated the killing of the miner Bernard McGrath concluded instead that McGrath was killed in revenge after he had enticed natives into his camp and shot them in cold blood for pilfering. For the much-discussed McGrath case, see ANA, A518/1, L841/1, pt. 2, E. Taylor, District Officer, to Director of District Services and Native Affairs, 17 March 1934, and the numerous letters from McGrath's sister holding the 'all-nigger administration, who will not allow natives to be shot' responsible for his death (Nerva Levy to Earle Page, 8 March 1935).

40. Leahy and Crain, *Land*, 126, 247.

41. Leahy and Crain, *Land*, 126–8.
42. Leahy, 'Central Highlands', 246, 260.
43. Leahy, *Explorations*, 77; Leahy and Crain, *Land*, 225.
44. Leahy, *Explorations*, 65, 77–8, 182–3; Leahy and Crain, *Land*, 225–6.
45. See, e.g., the cases of Lieut. B. C. Singleton and Captain Wittkopp, discussed in ANA, A457/1, 710/3, T. Griffiths to Department of Defence, 14 July 1920, and the case of Arthur Winstone, discussed in ANA, A518/1, N840/1/3.
46. Bob Connolly and Robin Anderson, *First Contact* (film, 1983).
47. For the lasting impact of the Leahys on the Highlands, Francesca Merlan and Alan Rumsey, *Ku Waru: Language and Segmentary Politics in the Western Nebilyer Valley, Papua New Guinea* (Cambridge: Cambridge University Press, 1991), 22–8. James Roy McBean points out that the Leahys' ongoing close connection with the Highlands is not discussed in the film *First Contact*, creating a sharper divide between 'then' and 'now' than actually exists; see McBean, 'Degrees of Otherness: A Close Reading of *First Contact*, *Joe Leahy's Neighbors*, and *Black Harvest*', *Visual Anthropology Review*, 10:2 (Autumn 1994), 54–70; and for the film more generally, Chris Ballard, 'Watching *First Contact*', *Journal of Pacific History*, 45:1 (June 2010), 21–36.
48. Goodenough in Leahy, 'Central Highlands', 261–2, and Bayliss-Smith, 'Papuan Exploration'.
49. LNA, R4130, 6a/26211/4230, Harris to S. M. Bruce, 22 June 1936, contained in Harris to Director, Mandates Section, 23 Oct. 1936; this correspondence was printed in *ASRAF*, 26:4 (Jan. 1937), 200–2.
50. 13 *PMCM*, 28.
51. Two-thirds of the territory was still outside effective control in the mid-1930s; see *New Guinea Report 1934–35*, 124.
52. Clashes were regularly discussed in the New Guinea reports, the PMC Minutes, the *Pacific Islands Monthly*, and the *Rabaul Times*. See also RH Lugard 138/5, Gilbert Murray to Lugard, 20 July 1935, and for a moving account of the life and death of one patrol officer, see Naomi M. McPherson, ' "Wanted: Young Man, Must Like Adventure", Ian McCallum Mack, Patrol Officer', in Naomi M. McPherson, ed., *In Colonial New Guinea: Anthropological Perspectives* (Pittsburgh: University of Pittsburgh Press, 2001), 83–110.
53. 27 *PMCM*, 17–19, 25.
54. For which see ANA, A518/1, AZ840/1/3, and 'Murder of Natives', *Pacific Islands Monthly*, 19 March 1936.
55. Leahy and Crain, *Land*, 273; Radford, *Highlanders*, 146.
56. ANA, A518/1, L841/1, pt. 2, Administrator, Rabaul, to Secretary, PM's Department, 28 Jan. 1937, and accompanying evidence. Leahy's statement and Taylor's report were also included in the Australian government's report on the Petition, copy in LNA, R2335, 6A/26211/4230.
57. 31 *PMCM*, esp. 157.

58. LNA, R2335, 6A/26211/4230, CPM 1904, 'Petition, dated November 19th, 1936, from Sir John Harris... Preliminary Report by Lord Hailey', 7 June 1937, and 31 *PMCM*, 80–2, 153–9.

59. 27 *PMCM*, 18, 28.

60. For example, in 1933 the Mandates Commission took up the question of 'the use of the cinematograph in view of the diversity of mentalities and civilisations', at the request of the Council and the Rome-based International Educational Cinematographic Institute, and urged that since 'such races are greatly attracted by cinema displays', it might be best to control their exposure to such media; see 23 *PMCM*, 14–16, 188, and LNA, R 2349.

61. 26 *PMCM*, 61.

62. 31 *PMCM*, 123.

63. Dannevig on Herero education, in 26 *PMCM*, 59.

64. LNDM, Reel CPM-17, CPM 2073 'General Statement Regarding Native Education and Social Services in African and South Seas Mandated Territories. Memorandum by Mademoiselle Dannevig', 21 June 1938.

65. NAN, SWAA Box 1980, A427/19, Botha to Secretary, SWA, 19 Feb. 1935.

66. NAN, Acc. 312, 19/72, Te Water to Hertzog, 15 June 1935.

67. For correspondence about the itinerary, NAN, SWAA Box 1980, File A427/19.

68. Allan D. Cooper, 'The Institutionalization of Contract Labour in Namibia', *Journal of Southern African Studies*, 25:1 (March 1999), 121–38.

69. On Hahn, see esp. Patricia Hayes, '"Cocky" Hahn and the "Black Venus": The Making of a Native Commissioner in South West Africa, 1915–46, *Gender & History*, 8:3 (Nov. 1996), 364–92.

70. Patricia Hayes, 'Northern Exposures: The photography of C. H. L. Hahn, Native Commissioner of Ovamboland, 1915–1946', in Wolfram Hartmann, Jeremy Silvester, and Patricia Hayes, eds., *The Colonising Camera: Photographs in the Making of Namibian History* (Cape Town: University of Cape Town Press, 1998), 171–87, quoted at 177. Copyright for Hahn's photographs remains with his family, and I have been unable to secure reproduction rights, but *The Colonising Camera* provides an impressive selection.

71. NAN, SWAA, Box 1980, A427/19, Hahn to Courtney-Clarke, 1 Aug. 1935.

72. 31 *PMCM*, 110–47 *passim*.

73. W. E. B. Du Bois, *The Souls of Black Folk* (1903; rpt. New York: New American Library, 1969).

74. For Bunche, see Brian Urquhart, *Ralph Bunche: An American Odyssey* (New York: Norton, 1993).

75. For which, see Alain Locke, 'The Mandates System: A New Code of Empire' (unpublished, 1928?), in Charles Molesworth, ed., *The Works of Alain Locke* (Oxford: Oxford University Press, 2012), 509–27; Rayford Logan, 'The Operation of the Mandate System in Africa', *The Journal of Negro History*, 13:4 (Oct. 1928), 423–77.

76. LC, Gilchrist Papers, Box 10, File 'Buell', Buell to Gilchrist, 28 June 1927.

77. Pearl T. Robinson analyses Bunche's debt to Buell in 'Ralph Bunche the Africanist: Revising Paradigms Lost', in Robert A. Hill and Edmond J. Keller, eds., *Trustee for the Human Community: Ralph J. Bunche, the United Nations, and the Decolonization of Africa* (Athens, OH: Ohio University Press, 2010), 69–90, to which I am indebted; see also Pearl T. Robinson, 'Ralph Bunche and African Studies: Reflections on the Politics of Knowledge', *African Studies Review*, 51:1 (April 2008), 1–16.

78. Robert Vitalis insightfully tracks the racial assumptions underlying the thinking of Buell and other early international relations scholars in 'Birth of a Discipline', in David Long and Brian C. Schmidt, eds., *Imperialism and Internationalism in the Discipline of International Relations* (Albany: State University of New York Press, 2005), 159–81.

79. Bunche, 'French Administration', 45, 73, 75; and for the epitome of that position, J. C. Smuts, *Africa and Some World Problems* (Oxford: Clarendon Press, 1930).

80. Bunche, 'French Administration', 347, 354.

81. Bunche, 'French Administration', 389.

### NOTES FOR CHAPTER II

1. 310 *H.C. Deb.*, 6 April 1936, cols. 2556–7.

2. 315 *H.C. Deb.*, 27 July 1936, col. 1177.

3. A great number of partisan and scholarly works were written about German colonial claims in the late 1930s, but for a useful summary of that debate from a British perspective, see Royal Institute for International Affairs, *Germany's Claim to Colonies*, Information Department Paper no. 23, 2nd ed. (London: RIIA, February 1939), and for an international view, Emanuel Moresco, *Colonial Questions and Peace* (Paris: League of Nations, International Institute for Intellectual Co-operation, 1939). For a bibliography of works related to colonies in the League of Nations Library as of 1939, see *Peaceful Change: Procedures, Population, Raw Materials, Colonies*, in *Proceedings of the Tenth International Studies Conference, Paris, June 28–July 3, 1937* (Paris: League of Nations, International Institute for Intellectual Co-operation, 1938), 644–66.

4. The most thorough account is Andrew J. Crozier, *Appeasement and Germany's Last Bid for Colonies* (London: Macmillan, 1988), but see also Martin Thomas, *Britain, France and Appeasement: Anglo-French Relations in the Popular Front Era* (New York: Berg, 1997), and, for France, Anthony Adamthwaite, *France and the Coming of the Second World War, 1936–1939* (London: Frank Cass, 1977).

5. Bodleian, Toynbee Papers, Uncat Box 117 for correspondence related to Berber's involvement in the International Studies Conference.

6. Arnold J. Toynbee, 'Peaceful Change or War? The Next Stage in the International Crisis', *International Affairs*, 15:1 (Jan.–Feb. 1936), 26–56.

7. The best study of the German colonial movement between the wars, which has informed the account given here, remains Wolfe W. Schmokel, *Dream of Empire: German Colonialism, 1919–1945* (New Haven and London: Yale University Press, 1964), although recently scholars have begun to pay more attention to the colonial movement both in the Wilhelmine and Weimar periods. For an overview, see Gisela Graichen and Horst Gründer, *Deutsche Kolonien: Traum und Trauma* (Berlin: Ullstein, 2007); for women's activism, Lora Wildenthal, *German Women for Empire, 1884–1945* (Durham, NC: Duke University Press, 2001); for Nazi colonial activism, Karsten Linne's copiously illustrated *Deutschland jenseits des Äquators? Die NS-Kolonialplanungen für Afrika* (Berlin: Ch. Links Verlag, 2008); and for an intelligent contemporary assessment, Mary Townsend, 'The Contemporary Colonial Movement in Germany', *Political Science Quarterly*, 43:1 (March 1928), 64–75. All mandatory powers also kept close tabs on German colonial revisionism through their ambassadors, consuls, and intelligence services.
8. NA, AIR 2/1732, quoted in J.V. Perowne, 'Memorandum Regarding German Colonial Aspirations' (20 June 1935), 14.
9. Schnee to Hitler, 20 March 1935, in *DGFP*, ser. C, vol. 3, 1033–7.
10. ANOM, AP 900, 'Revendications coloniales allemandes' (1936), 14. Schmokel, *Dream of Empire*, 10, estimates total membership at only 40,000 at the end of 1935.
11. Confidential reports sent to the French Colonial Ministry provide much information on the movement's activities. This paragraph relies heavily on Kachinsky, 'Rapport sur la question coloniale en Allemagne' (25 Aug. 1936), in ANOM, 1040, file on 'Revendications coloniales allemandes'.
12. For Schnee's objections to this plan, see GStA PK,VI.HA, Schnee Papers, Box 38, Schnee to Epp, 23 Nov. 1935.
13. ANOM, AP 1040, File: 'Revendications coloniales allemandes: Notes Rachinsky', Directives for colonial education issued by the Nazi Party's Office of Colonial Policy, 1936.
14. ANOM, AP 1040. These developments are covered in detail by Schmokel, *Dream of Empire*, but see also Mary E. Townsend, 'The German Colonies and the Third Reich', *Political Science Quarterly*, 53:2 (June 1938), 186–206.
15. Robert Boyce, rightly in my view, considers it impossible to explain the misguided policies of Britain and the USA during the 1920s and early 1930s without acknowledging the degree to which 'racial' assumptions about the superiority of Anglo-Saxons and Teutons to Latins and Slavs structured their thought. See Boyce, *The Great Interwar Crisis and the Collapse of Globalization* (London: Palgrave Macmillan, 2009), esp. 26–8, 57–9, 428–9.
16. For the very interesting case of Dawson, certainly the most indefatigable pro-German revisionist in England, see Stefan Berger, 'William Harbutt Dawson: The Career and Politics of an Historian of Germany', *The English Historical Review*, 116:465 (Feb. 2001), 76–113; for Rothermere's campaign in the

*Daily Mail*, see Crozier, *Appeasement*, 59–61 (although the date is mistakenly given as 1935 rather than 1934).

17. For which, see Adamthwaite, *France*, 111–72.

18. The first letter from Kelsall is in *Headway*, March 1935, 56. For replies, see (among others) 'Mandates are a Trust', April 1935, 62, and Lord Olivier, 'The Ex-German Colonies', June 1935, 112–13, and for pro-German statements, Elizabeth Yandell, 'Germany Must Expand—Or Disrupt the World!' June 1935, 115, Yandell 'Those German Colonies', Aug. 1935, 146, and Schnee, 'The German Colonial Problem', Oct. 1935, 196.

19. Mumford, 'The Mandates System and Germany', *Headway*, Aug. 1935, 146–7.

20. See, e.g., the letters from Henry T. Roberts, Oct. 1935, 198, and Wm J. Pearce, Feb. 1936, 37.

21. This was implied by Leonard Barnes, 'Germany's Colonial Claims', *Headway*, Sept. 1935, 165–6.

22. Lugard, 'Africa and the Powers', *The Times*, 19 and 20 Sept. 1935, and Lugard, 'The Claim to Colonies', *The Times*, 13 and 14 Jan. 1936. Lugard gave a talk making similar points to Chatham House on 3 Dec. 1935; this was printed as 'The Basis of the Claim for Colonies', *International Affairs*, 15:1 (Jan.–Feb. 1936), 3–25. The January *Times* articles were reprinted as 'The Claims to Colonies', *Journal of the Royal African Society*, 35:139 (April 1936), 115–22.

23. House of Commons debate of 5 Feb. 1936, quoted in *The Times*, 6 Feb. 1936, 7.

24. Amery noted in his diary that he had 'got on well' with Hitler, 'owing to the fundamental similarity of many of our ideas'. Entry for 13 Aug. 1935, in *The Empire at Bay: The Leo Amery Diaries, 1929–1945*, ed. John Barnes and David Nicholson (London: Hutchinson, 1988), 397.

25. 'An Inalienable Trust', *The Times*, 11 Feb. 1936, 8. Amery put much work into challenging the German case (see, e.g., 'General von Epp's Case Examined', *Journal of the Royal African Society*, 36:142 [Jan. 1937], 10–22) and cultivating joint Anglo-French resistance to revision (see CAC, AMEL, 1/5/51–2).

26. The count is from Schmokel, *Dream of Empire*, 90.

27. Toynbee played a key role in this campaign, not only because he had the intellectual agility necessary but also because of his close contacts with German academics and officials whom he thought sympathetic to 'internationalization', see esp. Bodleian, Toynbee Papers, Box 76, which contains correspondence with Fritz Berber and other German interlocutors, as well as with Noel-Buxton and other British allies. For one crucial intervention, see Noel-Buxton's motion in the Lords urging 'mandation' of colonies, 104 *H.L. Deb.*, 17 Feb. 1937, cols. 172–222; the 'National Memorial on Peace and Economic Cooperation' signed by some four hundred public figures, which included support both for a revision of the Ottawa accords and for an extension of the mandates system, in *The Times*, 11 Feb. 1937, 9; and the deputation to the Prime Minister in support of those aims, *The Times*, 23 March 1937.

28. ANOM, AP 1040, Kachinsky, 'Evolution de la question coloniale en Allemagne' (July 1937).

29. Crozier, *Appeasement*, 164.

30. 301 *H.C. Deb.*, ser. 5, 2 May 1935, col. 687; Crozier, *Appeasement*, 105–6; Callahan, *Sacred Trust*, 81.

31. NA, AIR 2/1732, J. V. Perowne, 'Memorandum Regarding German Colonial Aspirations' (20 June 1935).

32. Vansittart, Nov. 1935, quoted in Crozier, *Appeasement*, 126.

33. Crozier, *Appeasement*, 133.

34. The Plymouth Committee is discussed by Crozier, ch. 6, and by Callahan, *Sacred Trust*, 94–6, but see also the useful article by A. Edho Ekoko, 'The British Attitude towards Germany's Colonial Irredentism in Africa in the Inter-War Years', *Journal of Contemporary History*, 14:2 (April 1979), 287–307. The Committee's records can be found in NA, CO 323/1398.

35. NA, AIR 2/1732, E. N. Seyfret (Admiralty) to L. G. S. Payne (Air Staff), 21 March 1936. For Foreign Office views, see Crozier, *Appeasement*, 142–3.

36. NA, CO 323/1398, Note by Eastwood, 17 June 1936.

37. NA, CO 323/1398, CID, 'Transfer of a Colonial Mandate or Mandates to Germany: Report of a Sub-Committee' (Plymouth Committee Report) (9 June 1936).

38. 310 *H.C. Deb.*, 6 April 1936, cols. 3556–8; and see, e.g., Amery's plea for a categorical refusal to consider such claims in a deputation to the Prime Minister, CAC, AMEL 1/5/50, Statement, 'Deputation to the Prime Minister', 19 May 1936.

39. At the key foreign policy debate in July so many MPs wished to speak, including about the prospect of territorial transfer, that the government scheduled a supplementary session. For those debates, see 315 *H.C. Deb.*, 27 July 1936, cols. 1115–1224, and 31 July 1936, cols. 1904–74; the quotation from Eden is at col. 1132.

40. For the League Economic and Financial Organization, Patricia Clavin and Jens-Wilhelm Wessels, 'Transnationalism and the League of Nations: Understanding the Work of its Economic and Financial Organization', *Contemporary European History*, 14:4 (Nov. 2005), 465–92.

41. For the text of Hoare's speech, 'Britain and the League', *The Times*, 12 Sept. 1935, 7.

42. Schacht's strategies and achievements are clearly explained in Adam Tooze's marvellous history of Nazi economic policy, *The Wages of Destruction: The Making and Breaking of the Nazi Economy* (New York: Viking, 2006), chs. 2–3.

43. Hjalmar Schacht, 'Germany's Colonial Demands', *Foreign Affairs*, 15:2 (Jan. 1937), 223–34.

44. Plymouth Committee Report, 28–9; for British imperial economic integration in the 1930s, see also John Darwin, *The Empire Project: The Rise and Fall of the British World-System, 1830–1970* (Cambridge: Cambridge University Press, 2009), 431–9.

45. For Anglo-French consideration of Schacht's proposals, see Crozier, *Appeasement*, 197–206, Thomas, *Britain, France and Appeasement*, 68–9, 194–8.

46. For the League raw material inquiry, see Crozier, *Appeasement*, 211–15.

47. This was the position taken, for example, by the two economic experts who contributed to the LSE's 1937 lecture series on 'peaceful change', L. C. Robbins, 'The Economics of Territorial Sovereignty', and T. E. Gregory, 'The Economic Basis of Revisionism', in C. A. W. Manning, ed., *Peaceful Change: An International Problem* (London: Macmillan, 1937), 39–60 and 63–77; by Frederick Sherwood Dunn, who wrote a survey of the question for the American contingent of the International Studies Conference, *Peaceful Change: A Study of International Procedures* (New York: Council on Foreign Relations, 1937), and by J.B. Condliffe, the British economist who wrote one of the main publications to result from that conference, *Markets and the Problem of Peaceful Change* (Paris: International Institute of Intellectual Co-operation, 1938), among many others. See the excellent survey of this debate in Douglas Rimmer, 'Have-Not Nations: The Prototype', *Economic Development and Cultural Change*, 27:2 (Jan. 1979), 307–25, and for the sadly forgotten International Studies Conference, David Long, 'Who Killed the International Studies Conference?', *Review of International Studies*, 32 (2006), 603–22.

48. Condliffe, *Markets*, 55–6.

49. For that meeting, see Schmokel, *Dream of Empire*, 104–6; Tooze, *Wages of Destruction*, 239–43.

50. 'German Claim to Colonies: Führer's Renewed Demand', *The Times*, 4 Oct. 1937, 14; Vernon Bartlett, Gilbert Murray, Noel-Buxton, and A. J. Toynbee, 'The Question of Colonies', *The Times*, 7 Oct. 1937, 15.

51. 'The Claim to Colonies', *The Times*, 28 Oct. 1937, 17; 'A Sacred Trust', *The Manchester Guardian*, 10 Nov. 1937, 10; and for German reception of the latter article, MAE, SDN 547, François-Poncet to MAE, 11 Nov. 1937.

52. 107 *H.L. Deb.*, 17 Nov. 1937, cols. 115–72.

53. For that text, see BLPES, LNU Archives, Reel 431, Meetings of the Mandates Committee, 1 March 1938.

54. 'Memorandum: Conversation with Herr Hitler', included in Neurath to Henderson, 20 Nov. 1937, *DGFP*, ser. D. vol. 1, 55–67, here at 62.

55. 'Account by Lord Halifax of his Visit to Germany, November 17–21, 1939', *BDFA*, pt. II, ser. F, vol. 48, 360–70, here at 365. Andrew Roberts argues that Halifax let Hitler see how reluctant Britain was to try to restrain him in Eastern Europe; see *'The Holy Fox': A Life of Lord Halifax* (1991; rpt. London: Papermac, 1992), 67–75.

56. NA, Cab. 23/90A, Cabinet 43, 24 Nov. 1937.

57. The evolution of Chamberlain's plan is discussed by Crozier, *Appeasement*, ch. 8, and by Callahan, *Sacred Trust*, 141–6; for Schacht's proposal, see 'Account by Lord Halifax', 368.

58. Eden and Ormsby-Gore, quoted in Callahan, *Sacred Trust*, 144. There is some discussion of the Portuguese response in Crozier, *Appeasement*, 231–2, but diplomatic

correspondence reveals considerable anxiety and anger in Brussels as well. Only the Czechs, menaced by Germany and grasping at anything that might placate it, gave eager support to the prospect of colonial concessions—a stance that might have softened their French ally. See the various reports to the MAE in SDN 547, esp. Delacroix (Prague) to Delbos, 3 Dec. 1937.

59. Ribbentrop to Neurath and Hitler, 2 Dec. 1937, and to Neurath, 14 Dec. and 17 Dec. 1937, in *DGFP*, ser. D, vol. I, 91, 124–5, 131–4.

60. Memorandum by Neurath, 26 Jan. 1938, in *DGFP*, ser. D, vol. I, 190–1.

61. PA, R29990, Von Strempel to Weizsäcker, very secret, 11 Feb. 1938.

62. Memorandum by Ribbentrop, 1 March 1938, in *DGFP*, ser. D, vol. I, 228.

63. One record of this critically important conversation can be found in 'Notes of the Conversation between the Chancellor and the British Ambassador in the Presence of the Minister for Foreign Affairs, Herr von Ribbentrop, on March 3, 1938, in Berlin', in *BDFA*, pt. II, ser. F, vol. 49, 360–70, 47–52. I have, however, used the more direct and unambiguous English text sent to Henderson by the German Foreign Ministry, for which see 'Memorandum of the conversation between the Führer and the Royal British Ambassador in the Presence of Foreign Minister von Ribbentrop on March 3, 1938', enclosed in Ribbentrop to Henderson, in *DGFP*, ser. D, vol. I, 240–9.

64. BLPES, LNU Archives, Reel 431, Mandates Committee meeting, 9 Nov. 1938; see also the copy in Lugard 141/10, which also contains Lugard's note (read at the meeting) dissenting.

65. MAE, SDN 548, Corbin to MAE, 15 Dec. 1938.

66. CAC, AMEL 2/1/28, pt. 2, Amery to Halifax, 15 Nov. 1938; see also RH, Lugard 141/9, Lugard to MacDonald, 18 Nov. 1938, and his blunt chastisement of Harris for continuing to put forward proposals for colonial transfer, Lugard to Harris, 19 Dec. 1938.

67. Quoted in Adamthwaite, *France*, 297.

68. For a survey of that opinion, see John Perkins, ' "Sharing the White Man's Burden": Nazi Colonial Revisionism and Australia's New Guinea Mandate', *Journal of Pacific History*, 24:1 (April 1989), 54–69.

69. For PMC questions about this in 1932 and 1934, and the denials of the Japanese representatives (including the Japanese PMC members), see esp. 22 *PMCM*, 115–16, 299, 367, and 26 *PMCM*, 89–91, 96. It is worth noting that the unedited minutes of PMC discussions in 1932 and 1934 were handed confidentially to the US Consul in Geneva, Prentiss Gilbert, who passed them to the State Department, for which see USNA Box 6833, 852i.01/234–5, Gilbert to State, 15 Nov. and 3 Dec. 1932, and Box 6834, 862i.01/301, Gilbert to State, 15 Nov. 1934.

70. Allegations about fortification were reported to the League by one Richard Voigt, a German businessman working in Kobe, and by one Pablo Laslo (see LNA Box 4128, 6A/15250/3192, and Box 4129, 6A/36195/3192), and were raised in the *Pacific Islands Monthly*, 2 Feb. 1935. The US Office of Naval Intelligence tried to 'debrief' any visitors who made it to the mandated terri-

tories; their findings are summarized in Dirk Anthony Ballendorf, 'Secrets without Substance: U.S. Intelligence in the Japanese Mandates, 1915–1935', *Journal of Pacific History*, 19:2 (April 1984), 83–99. Professor Paul Clyde of the University of Kentucky, who spent some months travelling through the mandated islands in 1934, stated that he found no evidence of fortification, although he freely admitted that his research was facilitated by the Japanese Embassy and funded by a scholarship from the South Manchurian Railway (for which see USNA, Box 6833, 862i.01/296, Interview with Dr Paul Clyde, 18 Sept. 1934). In 1937 the American Consul in Yokohama interviewed a Norwegian ship captain whose vessel had sunk off the islands and who had been rescued by a Japanese vessel that had then called at several islands; he reported airport construction and considerable naval activity, with three Japanese destroyers in the harbour at Jaluit, but no fortifications in evidence; see USNA, Box 6834, 862i.01/329, Boyce to State, 25 June 1937.

71. For an intelligent survey of the controversy over fortification, see Richard Dean Burns, 'Inspection of the Mandates, 1919–1941', *Pacific Historical Review*, 37:4 (Nov. 1968), 445–62; also Mark Peattie, *Nan'yō: The Rise and Fall of the Japanese in Micronesia, 1885–1945* (Honolulu: University of Hawaii Press, 1988), 230–56. Burns points out, rightly, that the controversy persisted largely because while the Japanese may not have been openly fortifying the islands, the installations they were building could easily be turned to a military purpose; the question became one, then, of Japan's intended *future use* of those facilities. That said, other mandatory powers improved harbours, built radio towers, oil tanks, and airfields: what was unusual was Japan's determined secrecy about their activities.

72. Dirksen to Foreign Ministry, 15 Jan. 1938, *DGFP*, ser. D, vol. 1, 818–19.

73. Neurath to Dirksen, 18 Jan. 1938, in *DGFP*, ser. D, vol. 1, 822–3.

74. Perkins, 'Sharing the White Man's Burden', 68–9.

75. For PMC criticisms of the 'closer union' movement, see 23 *PMCM*, 82–3, and 26 *PMCM*, 48–52, 62–4. The handling of the 'incorporation' issue and of Nazi activities in the territory is discussed in Sara Pienaar, *South Africa and International Relations Between the Two World Wars: The League of Nations Dimension* (Johannesburg: Witwatersrand University Press, 1987), 136–52, quoted 141. For German irredentism in South Africa and Tanganyika, see Crozier, *Appeasement*, ch. 4; Callahan, *Sacred Trust*, esp. 65–70; Graichen and Gründer, *Deutsche Kolonien*, 399–417; Daniel Joseph Walther, *Creating Germans Abroad: Cultural Policies and National Identity in Namibia* (Athens, OH: Ohio University Press, 2002), 166–79.

76. William Kienzle, 'German-South African Trade Relations, in the Nazi Era', *African Affairs*, 78:310 (Jan. 1979), 81–90.

77. CAC, AMEL 2/1/27, pt. 2, Smuts to Amery, 18 May 1936; 'South Africa and German Colonies', *The Times*, 15 Sept. 1937; South African views on German claims are treated by Pienaar, 143–52.

78. For Pirow's entrepreneurial revisionism, see Crozier, *Appeasement*, 94–7, 156–7, and 269–70, quoted here 96.

79. There were 2,729 German and 2,100 British 'unofficials' in a total non-official population of 6,514; those numbers from John Iliffe, *A Modern History of Tanganyika* (Cambridge: Cambridge University Press 1979), 303. For the sisal industry, Nicholas Westcott, 'The East African Sisal Industry, 1929–49: The Marketing of a Colonial Commodity during Depression and War', *Journal of African History*, 25 (1984), 445–61, and Iliffe, *A Modern History*, 303–4, who notes that much of that sisal crop went to the continent.

80. USNA, Box 8637, 862s.00/3, Talbot Smith to State, 14 Oct. 1938.

81. RH, Lugard 141/9, Lugard to Joelson, 16 Nov. 1938, and Lugard to Himbury, 16 Nov. 1938.

82. ANOM AP 900, 'Revendications coloniales allemandes' (1936).

83. NA, FO 371/22514, File W3013, Williams (CO) to FO, 7 March 1938, enclosing Bourdillon to Ormsby-Gore, 10 Jan. 1938, and File W5302, Ormsby-Gore to Bourdillon, 19 April 1938.

84. For 1938 labour and population figures, see *Report by His Majesty's Government . . . on the Administration of the Cameroons under British Mandate for the year 1938* (London: HMSO, 1939), 69–72, 106–7; this paragraph also draws on David Gardinier's excellent article, 'The British in the Cameroons', in *Britain and Germany in Africa: Imperial Rivalry and Colonial Rule*, eds. Prosser Gifford and Wm. Roger Louis (New Haven: Yale University Press, 1967), 513–55, and Victor T. Le Vine, *Le Cameroun du mandat à l'indépendance* (Dakar: Présence Africaine, 1984), 156–61.

85. ANOM, SG Togo-Cameroun, 30/279, Bonnecarrère to Colonies, 27 Dec. 1933.

86. For PMC criticism, see 28 *PMCM*, 46–51. The union itself foundered partly on personal antagonism between Maurice-Léon Bourgine, the authoritarian Lieutenant-Governor of Dahomey who was to hold the position of Commissioner of Togo as well, and his independent-minded subordinate Léon Guismar, who strenuously and effectively opposed Bourgine's plans to move virtually the whole administration to Dahomey. For this conflict see ANOM, AP 605.

87. There are extensive files on surveillance of possible Germans and German sympathizers within Togo, Cameroun, and surrounding areas in ANOM, Togo-Cameroun, Boxes 27, 31, and 32; but see esp. 31/294, Marchand to Colonies, 21 May 1928 (for efforts to set up surveillance in Spanish territory), and Repiquet to Colonies, 2 Nov. 1934 (for the trial of a Germanophile Douala group). For the impact of that Franco-German antagonism on Cameroon, see Richard A. Joseph, 'The German Question in French Cameroun, 1919–1939', *Comparative Studies in Society and History*, 17:1 (Jan. 1975), 65–90.

88. ANOM, SG Togo-Cameroun, 27/238, Folder on Seitz.

89. For a survey of the diplomacy around the dispute, see Majid Khadduri, 'The Alexandretta Dispute', *The American Journal of International Law*, 39:3 (July 1945), 406–25, and for a vivid account of the way the entire process fostered ethnic

tensions, see Sarah D. Shields, *Fezzes in the River: Identity Politics and European Diplomacy in the Middle East on the Eve of World War II* (Oxford: Oxford University Press, 2011). Keith Watenpaugh illuminates the dispute's impact on Syrian nationalism in ' "Creating Phantoms": Zaki al-Arsuzi, the Alexandretta Crisis, and the Formation of Modern Arab Nationalism in Syria', *International Journal of Middle Eastern Studies*, 28:3 (Aug. 1996), 363–89. For Turkey's decision to join the League and diplomacy during the tense 1930s, see William Hale, *Turkish Foreign Policy, 1774–2000* (London: Frank Cass, 2000), ch. 2.

90. LNA S1628, File: Orts, Orts to De Haller, 13 Jan. 1937.

91. 36 *PMCM*, 222.

92. MAE, SDN 593, Note, 19 June 1939, 248–53. It is worth noting that De Caix had been in touch with De Haller (Director of the Mandates Section) before this session, essentially to work out the PMC's stance, which was simply to dissociate itself from the Alexandretta decision in the vain hope of limiting the damage to the mandates system itself. For this effort, see the spring 1939 correspondence between De Caix and De Haller in LNA S1609, File: France.

93. *Peaceful Change: Procedures, Population, Raw Materials, Colonies*, 417–18.

94. Those arguments were made by Fritz Berber of the Deutsches Institut für Aussenpolitische Forschung, the eminent French Africanist Henri Labouret, and the Belgian colonial *eminence grise* Octave Louwers, in *Peaceful Change: Procedures, Population, Raw Materials, Colonies*, 436–8, 445–6, 464–7.

95. *Peaceful Change: Procedures, Population, Raw Materials, Colonies*, 459–62.

96. *Peaceful Change: Procedures, Population, Raw Materials, Colonies*, 450–1.

97. This from LNA, R4137, 6A/27984/27984, Negro Welfare Association, London, to PMC, 7 April 1937, transmitting a protest from the Negro Welfare and Cultural Association, Port of Spain, but see also ANOM, AP 900/1, Comité National de Défense des Intérêts du Cameroun to Moutet, 12 Nov. 1937, and S. M. Kumaramangalam and K. Alleyne, 'What Mandates Mean', *Headway*, Jan. 1939, 21–3, and, more generally, Susan Pennybacker, *From Scottsboro to Munich: Race and Political Culture in 1930s Britain* (Princeton: Princeton University Press, 2009), esp. ch. 2.

## NOTES FOR CHAPTER 12

1. Arnold Toynbee, 'The Present Situation in Palestine', *International Affairs*, 10:1 (Jan. 1931), 58.

2. NA, CO 733/326/6, Ormsby-Gore to Wauchope, 24 Aug. 1937 (draft).

3. See Chapter 1 for the San Remo agreements and Chapter 3 for the approval of the mandate and the 1924 conflict.

4. Quoted in Walid Khalidi, introduction, *From Haven to Conquest* (Washington: Institute for Palestine Studies, 1987), lxxxiii.

5. Studies written during the League era tended to pay close attention to the work of the Mandates Commission; see, e.g., Nathan Feinberg, *Some Problems*

of the Palestine Mandate (Tel Aviv: Shoshani's Print Co., 1936), and Campbell L.
Upthegrove, Empire by Mandate (New York: Bookman Associate, 1954 [written
c. 1941]); there is also a large legal literature on the Palestine mandate. Accounts
written after the League's demise, by contrast, focus on London and Palestine
and pay only cursory attention to Geneva, exceptions being Roger Heacock,
'Le Système international aux prises avec le colonialisme: Les délibérations sur
la Palestine dans la Commission Permanente des Mandats de la Société des
Nations', in Nadine Méouchy and Peter Sluglett, eds., British and French
Mandates in Comparative Perspective (Leiden: Brill, 2004), 129–42, and Susan
Pedersen, 'The Impact of League Oversight on British Policy in Palestine', in
Rory Miller, ed., Palestine, Britain and Empire: The Mandate Years (London:
Ashgate, 2010), 39–65, from which parts of this chapter are drawn. For British
administration of Palestine during the first decade of the mandate, see Bernard
Wasserstein's authoritative The British in Palestine: The Mandatory Government
and the Arab-Jewish Conflict, 1917–1929 (1978; 2nd ed. Oxford: Blackwell, 1991),
and for the whole period, Tom Segev, One Palestine, Complete: Jews and Arabs
under the British Mandate (New York: Henry Holt, 1999), Gudrun Krämer, A
History of Palestine: From the Ottoman Conquest to the Founding of the State of Israel
(2002; English ed. Princeton: Princeton University Press, 2008), and Ilan Pappe,
A History of Modern Palestine: One Land, Two Peoples, 2nd ed. (Cambridge:
Cambridge University Press, 2006). For policymaking in London, see esp. N.A.
Rose, The Gentile Zionists: A Study in Anglo-Zionist Diplomacy, 1929–1939
(London: Routledge, 1973), and Michael J. Cohen, Palestine: Retreat from the
Mandate (New York: P. Elek, 1978).

6. Ze'ev Jabotinsky, 'The Iron Wall' (1923), excerpted in The Political and Social
Philosophy of Ze'ev Jabotinsky: Selected Writings, ed. Mordechai Sarig (London:
Vallentine Mitchell, 1999), 104–5.

7. J. C. Hurewitz, The Struggle for Palestine (1950; new ed. New York: Schoken
Books, 1976), p. 18.

8. CZA, S25, 2951, Jacobson to Stein, 14 Nov. 1928, and Rappard's draft report in
CZA, S25, 2951.

9. 7 PMCM, 102–5; 'Report', in 9 PMCM, 221–4; 11 PMCM, 117, 201.

10. Much has been written on the 1929 riots, the Passfield White Paper, and
MacDonald's letter to Weizmann effectively retracting it. For a good narrative
of the communal mobilizations prior to the riots and the riots themselves, see
Segev, One Palestine, chs. 13–15. Records in the Central Zionist Archives, L22/99
and S25/2951, make it clear that the Zionist Organization was trying quietly to
buy up the property facing the Western Wall in 1928 and to find a Christian
scholar to write a historical report establishing Jews' long-standing rights to the
Wall under Ottoman law, although that latter effort had to be abandoned when
the scholarly researches appeared 'to tell against rather than in favour of
the Jewish case' (CZA, S25/2951, 'Minutes of a Meeting . . . October 26, 1928',
and L. Stein, 'Wailing Wall—Further Petition to the Permanent Mandates

Commission: Memorandum for the Zionist Executive' [1929]). For a detailed and excellent account of the conflict focusing on Chancellor's failed land legislation in particular, see Kenneth W, Stein, *The Land Question in Palestine, 1917–1939* (Chapel Hill and London: University of North Carolina Press, 1984), chs. 3–4.

11. Minutes of the 56th League Council, 6 Sept. 1929, in *LNOJ*, 10:11 (Nov. 1929), 1465–72. For MacDonald's statement, see Weizmann to Ramsay MacDonald, 1 Sept. 1929, in *LPCW*, vol. 14, ed. Camillo Dresner (New Brunswick, NJ, 1978), 14, and Minutes of the 10th Assembly, 19 Sept. 1929, in *LNOJ*, Special Supplement no. 75 (Geneva, 1929), 127.

12. 16 *PMCM*, 108–10.

13. For which see 'Arab Grievances in Palestine', *The Times*, 11 April 1930, 9; 'Delegation's Statement', *The Times*, 14 May 1930, 15.

14. Weizmann to Felix Green, 5 Dec. 1929, 138–40, and Weizmann to Malcolm MacDonald, 21 May 1930, 307–8, enclosing the Weizmann-Faysal memorandum, both in *LPCW*, vol. 14.

15. Weizmann to Shuckburgh, 5 March 1930, *LPCW*, vol. 14, 239–43.

16. 17 *PMCM*, 121–4.

17. Weizmann to Rodolfo Foa, 14 May 1930, 283, Weizmann to Warburg, 15 May 1930, 286–96, both in *LPCW*, vol. 14.

18. 17 *PMCM*, 35–44.

19. 'Report', in 17 *PMCM*, 138, 140.

20. The questions of whether the riots were 'premeditated', of the Mufti's role, and of the swiftness and adequacy of the administration's response, remain contentious. Pinhas Ofer and Martin Kolinsky, working from Colonial Office records, argue that the Mufti was implicated in the violence but that the Shaw Commission downplayed his role because of the Palestine Administration's preference for conciliation; see Pinhas Ofer, 'The Commission on the Palestine Disturbances of August 1929: Appointment, Terms of Reference, Procedure and Report', *Middle Eastern Studies*, 21:3 (July 1985), 349–61; Martin Kolinsky, 'Premeditation in the Palestine Disturbances of August 1929?', *Middle Eastern Studies*, 26:1 (Jan. 1990), 18–34. Unfortunately, both mention the PMC's critical response to the Shaw report without noting the degree to which the PMC was itself influenced by (even ventriloquized) the Zionist position. Philip Mattar, also relying largely on British sources, insists on the Mufti's essentially moderate stance up until 1936; see Mattar, *The Mufti of Jerusalem: Al-Hajj Amin al-Husayni and the Palestinian National Movement* (New York: Columbia University Press, 1988), esp. 50–64.

21. 'Report', in 17 *PMCM*, 141–3.

22. Minutes of the 56th League Council, 6 Sept. 1929, in *LNOJ*, 10:11 (Nov. 1929), 1465–72.

23. 17 *PMCM*, 31, 56, 58, 62, 66, 70–1, 117.

24. 17 *PMCM*, 29.

25. 'Report', in 17 *PMCM*, 140–3.

26. 17 *PMCM*, 49–50, 82.

27. 'Report', in 17 *PMCM*, 145.

28. NA, CO 733/193/10A, Minutes by Clauson, 10 July 1930, and for MacDonald's statement, John Chancellor's transcript interview with the PM, 17 July 1930, quoted in Ofer, 'The Commission on the Palestine Disturbances', 354. Ofer suggests that the PMC report upset the British government because it 'demolished the umpire's image which Britain had been laboring so much to acquire' (357), but while this is certainly true, the PMC was hardly an impartial 'umpire' either.

29. 'Comments by the Mandatory Power', in 17 *PMCM*, 148–53. The British also managed to influence the Finnish member's report on the PMC's session; see the correspondence in NA, CO 733/193/10B.

30. Minutes of the 60th session of the Council, *LNOJ*, 11:11 (Nov. 1930), 1291–6.

31. For accounts stressing Weizmann's role, see, e.g., Segev, *One Palestine*, 335–41, and Rose, *Gentile Zionists*, ch. 1. Verbatim notes of Weizmann's meeting with the Cabinet on 18 Nov. 1930 are in Lugard 130/8.

32. 'Comments by the Mandatory Power', in 17 *PMCM*, 152, and Minutes of the 60th session of the Council, *LNOJ*, 11:11 (Nov. 1930), 1295–6; see also 'The Palestine Mandate', *The Times*, 9 Sept. 1930, 12.

33. For that Commons criticism, see esp. 245 *H.C. Deb.*, 17 Nov. 1930, cols. 45–210.

34. Weizmann girded himself for battle in Geneva immediately; see Weizmann to Herbert Speyer, 27 Oct. 1930, 12, and Weizmann to Lugard, 4 Nov. 1930, 32, in *LPCW*, vol. 15, ed. Camillo Dresner (New Brunswick, NJ, 1978).

35. Weizmann to Max Warburg, 16 Jan. 1930, in *LPCW*, vol. 14, 199.

36. For the transformation of Palestine in the early 1930s, see Krämer, *A History of Palestine*, ch. 11, and for immigration statistics, Roza El-Eini, *Mandated Landscape: British Imperial Rule in Palestine, 1929–1948* (New York: Routledge, 2006), 472.

37. For that deteriorating situation, see esp. Bernard Wasserstein, *On the Eve: The Jews of Europe Before the Second World War* (New York: Simon & Shuster, 2012), and for Poland in particular, Edward D. Wynot, Jr., ' "A Necessary Cruelty": The Emergence of Official Anti-Semitism in Poland, 1936–39', *AHR*, 76:4 (Oct. 1971), 1035–58.

38. On the New Zionist Organization, see esp. Laurence Weinbaum, *A Marriage of Convenience: The New Zionist Organization and the Polish Government, 1936–1939* (Boulder, CO: East European Monographs, 1993).

39. For which see Robert S. Wistrich, 'Zionism and its Jewish "Assimilationist" Critics (1897–1948)', *Jewish Social Studies*, new ser., 4:2 (Winter 1998), 59–111.

40. LNA S1609, File: France, De Caix to Rappard, 20 June 1935.

41. For the vexed issue of Nazi Germany's relationship with Arab nationalism, see esp. R. Melka, 'Nazi Germany and the Palestine Question', *Middle Eastern Studies*, 5:3 (Oct. 1969), 221–33; Lukasz Hirszowicz, 'Nazi Germany and the Palestine Partition Plan', *Middle Eastern Studies*, 1:1 (Oct. 1964), 40–65; David

Yisraeli, 'The Third Reich and Palestine', *Middle Eastern Studies*, 7:3 (Oct. 1971), 343–53; Francis Nicosia, 'Arab Nationalism and National Socialist Germany, 1933–1939: Ideological and Strategic Incompatibility', *International Journal of Middle Eastern Studies*, 12:3 (Nov. 1980), 351–72.

42. Much has been written on the land question in mandate Palestine, but for an illuminating account of the policies of the Jewish National Fund, purchaser of about 30% of total land in Jewish hands by 1937, see Kenneth W. Stein, 'The Jewish National Fund: Land Purchase Methods and Priorities, 1924–1939', *Middle Estern Studies*, 20:2 (April 1984), 190–205; figures at 191. And, for the impact on the Arab population, Yehoshua Porath, *The Palestinian Arab National Movement: From Riots to Rebellion*, vol. 2, *1929–1939* (London: Frank Cass, 1977), 82–7.

43. Quoted in Porath, *Palestinian Arab National Movement*, vol. 2, 34.

44. The most thorough account of those international ties in the 1930s is Weldon C. Matthews, *Confronting an Empire, Constructing a Nation: Arab Nationalists and Popular Politics in Mandate Palestine* (London: I. B. Tauris, 2006), although Porath's two-volume study also remains essential.

45. For those efforts, see esp. Yehoshua Porath, *In Search of Arab Unity, 1930–1945* (London: Frank Cass, 1986), ch. 2.

46. The complex diplomacy around the legislative council in the 1930s is best dealt with by Porath, *Palestinian Nationalist Movement*, vol. 2, 143–61.

47. Toynbee, 'Present Situation', 49, 54.

48. Weizmann to Herbert Samuel, 29 July 1920, in *LPCW*, vol. 10, ed. Bernard Wasserstein (New Brunswick, NJ, 1977), 2–5.

49. For an excellent account of the attitudes of official Zionists, revisionists, and the small group of bi-nationalist Zionists to the Legislative Council plans, see esp. Yehoyada Haim, 'Zionist Policies and Attitudes towards the Arabs on the Eve of the Arab Revolt, 1936', *Middle Eastern Studies*, 14:2 (May 1078), 211–31; also Israel Kolatt, 'The Zionist Movement and the Arabs', in *Essential Papers on Zionism*, ed. Jehuda Reinharz and Anita Shapira (New York: NYU Press, 1996), 617–47.

50. CZA, L22/856, Jacobson to Brodetsky, 5 Oct. 1932.

51. CZA, L22/856, Jacobson to Brodetsky, 8, 16, and 20 Nov. 1932.

52. 22 *PMCM*, 194–201.

53. CZA, L22/856, Jacobson to Brodetsky, 20 Nov. 1932.

54. 22 *PMCM*, 199, 363.

55. See, Nathan Feinberg, 'The Problem of the Legislative Council before the Permanent Mandates Commission', in *Some Problems of the Palestine Mandate*, 65–75.

56. The 1933–36 negotiations are covered in detail in Porath, *Palestinian Arab National Movement*, vol. 2, 147–59, who also notes at 149 that the Jewish agency informed Wauchope in 1935 that it would boycott even if granted parity with Arabs on the Council.

57. See, 99 *H.L. Deb.*, 26 Feb. 1936, col. 750–95, for Lord Snell's motion against the plan, and 310 *H.C. Deb.*, 24 March 1936, col. 1079–1150, for Wedgwood's motion.

58. Porath, *Palestinian National Arab Movement*, vol. 2, 158–9.

59. Orts insisted that the Commission's harsh criticism of the British unwillingness to provide full information on the rising appear in the published minutes, for which see 27 *PMCM*, 137–8.

60. In a talk at Chatman House, Emile Ghory made precisely that point: Ghory, 'An Arab View of the Situation in Palestine', *International Affairs*, 14:5 (Sept.–Oct. 1936), 688.

61. CZA, S25/4265, Goldmann to Ben-Gurion, 15 June 1936.

62. 29 *PMCM*, 145–6, and see RH, Lugard 131/5, Weizmann to Lugard, 29 Jan. 1936, and SFA, Rappard 1977/135 62, Weizmann to Rappard, 29 Jan. 1936.

63. For the role of the Arab states, see esp. M. J. Cohen, 'Origins of the Arab States' Involvement in Palestine', *Middle Eastern Studies*, 19:2 (April 1983), 244–52, and Norman Anthony Rose, 'The Arab Rulers and Palestine, 1936: The British Reaction', *Journal of Modern History*, 44:2 (June 1972), 213–31.

64. Poland urged Britain to grant more immigration permits to Palestine at the League Assembly in 1934; see 'The Palestine Mandate', *The Times*, 22 Sept. 1934, 11. See also Beck's statements at the 98th session of the Council, 14 Sept. 1937, in *LNOJ*, 18:12 (Dec. 1937), 889, 903.

65. See Statement by Comnene at the 102nd session of the Council, 17 Sept. 1938, in *LNOJ*, 19:11 (Nov. 1938), 850.

66. See Statement by Komarnicki at the 97th session of the Council, 27 May 1937, in *LNOJ*, May–June 1937, 300, and Weinbaum, *Marriage*, 110–16.

67. 312 *H.C. Deb.*, 18 May 1936, cols. 317–18, and 313 *H.C. Deb.*, 19 June 1936, cols. 1313–96.

68. Much has been written on the 1936–39 Arab revolt. For an account stressing the unsystematic response and the reluctance of the British authorities to crack down, see Charles Townshend, 'The Defence of Palestine: Insurrection and Public Security, 1936–1939', *The English Historical Review*, 103:409 (Oct. 1988), 917–49; for a more recent revisionist account stressing the brutality of Britain's response, Matthew Hughes, 'Lawlessness was the Law: British Armed Forces, the Legal System and the Repression of the Arab Revolt in Palestine, 1936–1939', in *Britain, Palestine and Empire: The Mandate Years*, ed. Rory Miller (London: Ashgate, 2010), 141–56, although Hughes has also maintained that, while brutal, the British were less harsh than comparable imperial regimes facing insurrections and rarely committed atrocities; see Matthew Hughes, 'The Banality of Brutality: British Armed Forces and the Repression of the Arab Revolt, 1936–39', *English Historical Reivew*, 124:507 (2009), 313–54. For Arab casualties, see Walid Khalidi, 'Note on Arab Casualties in the 1936–39 Rebellion', in Khalidi, ed., *From Haven to Conquest*, Appendix IV, 846–9.

69. Palestine Royal Commission, *Report*, PP 1936–37, Cmd. 5479, 363–4, 370–4.

70. Palestine Royal Commission, *Report, PP* 1936–37, Cmd. 5479, 375–6, 380–93.

71. For that background, see Penny Sinanoglou, 'British Plans for the Partition of Palestine, 1929–1938', *The Historical Journal*, 52:1 (2009), 131–52.

72. Palestine Royal Commission, *Report*, 395.

73. NA, CO 733/287/5, Note by O. G. R. Williams, 15 Dec. 1936; 'Report', in 29 *PMCM*, 207; and comments by Orts, Minutes of the 93rd session of the Council, 26 Sept. 1936, *LNOJ*, 17:11 (Nov. 1936), 1183.

74. NA, CO 733/287/5, Eden to Ormsby-Gore, 18 March 1937.

75. NA, CO 733/287/5, Rendel to League Secretary General, 6 July 1937.

76. 236 *H.C. Deb.*, 21 July 1937, cols. 2211–367.

77. NA, CO 733/326/6, Martin to Downie, 8 Aug. 1937.

78. CZA, Z4/32092, [Goldmann?] to Weizmann, 26 July 1937.

79. CZA, Z4/32092, Weizmann to Orts, 1 and 14 Aug. 1937.

80. National Library of Wales, Aberystwyth, Brogyntyn Papers, PEC 10/1/15, Ormsby-Gore to his mother, 16 Aug. 1937.

81. For that statement, 32 *PMCM*, 14–25; 'The League and Palestine', *The Observer*, 1 Aug. 1937; 'Mr Ormsby-Gore on Partition', *The Manchester Guardian*, 2 Aug. 1937.

82. Weizmann to Peel, 19 June 1937, in *LPCW*, vol. 18, ed. Aaron Kleiman (New Brunswick, NJ: Transaction Books, 1979), 3–22.

83. Weinbaum, *Marriage*, 106–10.

84. NA, CO 733/326/6, Ormsby-Gore to Wauchope, 24 Aug. 1937.

85. NA, CO 733/326/6, Hailey to Ormsby-Gore, 15 Aug. 1937.

86. NA, CO 733/326/6, Ormsby-Gore to Wauchope, 24 Aug. 1937.

87. 'Report', in 32 *PMCM*, 229–30.

88. 32 *PMCM*, 162–5.

89. See 'The Palestine Mandate', *The Times*, 6 Sept. 1937, 11, for one surprised reading.

90. RH, Lugard 131/5, Lugard to Lord Islington, 8 Sept. 1936.

91. 32 *PMCM*, 170.

92. 32 *PMCM*, 14, 186–7; Minutes of the 98th session of the Council, 14 Sept. 1937, *LNOJ*, 18:12 (Dec. 1937), 901.

93. For Zionist responses to the Peel Commission's proposals about population transfer, see Benny Morris, 'Revisiting the Palestinian Exodus of 1948', in Eugene L. Rogan and Avi Shlaim, (eds), *The War for Palestine,* 2nd ed. (Cambridge, 2007), 37–59. Weizmann also dilated on the importance of population transfer in a letter to Orts, 14 Aug. 1937, in *LPCW*, vol. 18, ed. Aaron Kleiman (New Brunswick, NJ, 1979), 185–7.

94. Weizmann's letters to Ormsby-Gore immediately after the Peel report set strict conditions for Jewish consent to the partition plan; by December, with that plan in danger, he was telling Léon Blum that the proposal was 'our greatest

triumph since the Balfour Declaration', see Weizmann to Ormsby-Gore, 15 June 1937, 118–19, 14 July 1937, 154–6, and 20 July 1937, 179–80; and Weizmann to Léon Blum, 31 Dec. 1937, 277–9, in *LPCW*, vol. 18. For the counter-productive results of Zionist diplomacy over partition, see Rose, *Gentile Zionists*, esp. 139–40; Cohen, *Palestine*, 34–8; and for Goldmann's illuminating account of this 'missed opportunity', Nahum Goldmann, *The Autobiography of Nahum Goldmann: Sixty Years of Jewish Life* (New York: Holt, Rinehart, and Winston, 1969), 179–81.

95. For the critical Commons debates over partition, see 332 *H.C. Deb.*, 8 March 1938, cols. 1737–94, 337 *H.C. Deb.*, 14 June 1938, cols. 79–189.

96. For Rappard's sharp questioning of Sir John Shuckburgh on the question of immigration, see 34 *PMCM*, esp. 49–50, 52, 56.

97. For Weizmann's claim that such restrictions were 'incompatible with the mandate', see Weizmann to Ormsby-Gore, 10 Dec. 1937, 253–6, and 21 Feb. 1938, 312–17, in *LPCW*, vol. 18.

98. Weizmann to Rappard, 29 Jan. 1938, *LPCW*, vol. 18, 297–8.

99. 'Report', in 34 *PMCM*, 228. For the intense negotiations around the discussion of the PMC's report at the 102nd session of the Council, see NA, FO 371/21888.

100. 'Comments of the Accredited Representative', in 34 *PMCM*, 240.

101. Rose, *Gentile Zionists*, 152.

102. Howard (Chanoch) Rosenblum, 'Promoting an International Conference to Solve the Jewish Problem: The New Zionist Organization's Alliance with Poland, 1938–1939', *The Slavonic and East European Review*, 69:3 (July 1991), 478–501, here at 487, 493.

103. CZA, L22/960, M. K. [Meir Kahany], 'Aus einem Gespräch mit dem polnischen Gesandten Komarnicki', 23 Nov. 1938.

104. *Palestine Statement of Policy*, PP, Cmd. 6019 (May 1939).

105. Weizmann to Rappard, 9 June 1939, in *LPCW*, vol. 19, ed. Norman Rose (New Brunswick, NJ, 1979), 112.

106. NA, CO 733/386/13, Interdepartmental Committee on Palestine, *passim*. The comment by Dufferin is from the 8th meeting, 11 Oct. 1938, the exchange between MacMichael and Bushe from the 4th meeting, 8 Oct. 1938.

107. 113 *H.L. Deb.*, 23 May 1939, col. 89.

108. For the Commons debates and votes, see 347 *H.C. Deb.*, 22 May 1939, cols. 1925–2056, and 23 May 1939, cols. 2129–97. Most of the Tory dissenters abstained, but some twenty prominent critics of the Chamberlain government, including Churchill, Amery, Harold Macmillan, and Vyvyan Adams, voted no. See 'Hundred Tories Abstain in Palestine Division', *The Manchester Guardian*, 24 May 1939, 11.

109. NA, CO 733/390/4, Butler Minute, 25 May 1939.

110. Weizmann to Solomon Goldman, 30 May 1939, *LPCW*, vol. 19, 91–5.

111. Weizmann to Rappard, 9 June 1939, *LPCW*, vol. 19, 111–12.

112. 36 *PMCM*, 98–9.

113. 36 *PMCM*, 121, 126–7.

114. 36 *PMCM*, 103, 113, 115.

115. 36 *PMCM*, 121.

116. For correspondence between Hankey and MacDonald about his appointment, see CAC, Hankey Papers, 9/1. Labour MPs Geoffrey Mander and Philip Noel-Baker objected to Hankey's appointment in the Commons, for which see NA, FO 371/24021.

117. Weizmann to Solomon Goldman, 30 May 1939, *LPCW*, vol. 19, 91–5.

118. CAC, Hankey Papers, 1/5, Diary, 18 April 1919.

119. CO 733/390/5, Hankey to MacDonald, 30 June 1939.

120. CO 733/390/5, Hankey to MacDonald, 30 June 1939.

121. 'Report', in 36 *PMCM*, 274–5.

122. NA, CO 733/390/5, Hankey to MacDonald, 30 June 1939; and see CAC, Hankey Papers 9/2, for the full text of Hankey's speech.

123. 'Comments of HMG', in 36 *PMCM*, 286–9.

124. 'Mandates Commission Rejects Palestine Policy', *The Manchester Guardian*, 18 Aug. 1939, 13; 'Zionist Congress Discusses Future Policy', *The Manchester Guardian*, 19 Aug. 1939, 6.

125. 111 *H.L. Deb.*, 8 Dec. 1938, cols. 412–67; Ormsby-Gore at col. 438.

126. LNA, S1608, no. 2, De Haller to Avenol, 3 April 1939.

## NOTES FOR THE CONCLUSION

1. LNA, S1626, no. 4, ' Réponse à la question posée au nom du secrétaire général ad intérim dans la note de Mr. Wilson du 29 Novembre 1939', 1 Dec. 1939.

2. NA, FO 371/24021, File W11508, Note by Randall, 27 July 1939, and FO 371/24022, File W14147, Note by Randall, 3 Oct. 1939.

3. For that discussion, 37 *PMCM*, 119–22, 129; and for the German protest, and British and French responses, Michael D. Callahan, *Sacred Trust: The League of Nations and Africa, 1929–1946* (Brighton: Sussex Academic Press, 2004), 178–80.

4. SFA, Rappard 1977/135 36, Orts to Rappard, 22 May 1940.

5. For Avenol's machinations in the spring of 1940, and Lester's important role, see esp. James C. Barros, *Betrayal From Within: Joseph Avenol, Secretary-General of the League of Nations, 1933–1940* (New Haven: Yale University Press, 1969), and Douglas Gageby, *The Last Secretary General: Sean Lester and the League of Nations* (Dublin: Town House, 1999).

6. For Lester's treatment at the conference, see Gageby, *The Last Secretary General*, 240–9. The standard account of wartime negotiations between the US and the UK over the future of empire remains Wm. Roger Louis, *Imperialism at Bay: The United States and the Decolonization of the British Empire, 1941–1945* (New York: Oxford University Press, 1978), but an extensive literature has developed on the impact of war on anti-colonial activism and colonial nationalism.

7. D. K. Fieldhouse's *Western Imperialism in the Middle East, 1914–1958* (Oxford: Oxford University Press, 2006), provides a good summary of the entire history, and the end of the Middle East mandate regimes, but for a more dramatic account see also Patrick Seale, *The Struggle for Arab Independence: Riad el-Solh and the Makers of the Modern Middle East* (Cambridge: Cambridge University Press, 2010).

8. See Stewart Firth's excellent summary of the war's effects on island populations, 'The War in the Pacific', in *The Cambridge History of the Pacific Islanders*, ed. Donald Denoon (Cambridge: Cambridge University Press, 1997), 291–323, and for New Guinea, Paul Ham, *Kokoda* (Sydney: Harper Collins, 2004).

9. The impact of the war on Africa is too large a topic to cover here, but for the crucial role of labour extractions in fuelling political demands, see esp. Frederick Cooper, *Decolonization and African Society: The Labour Question in French and British Africa* (Cambridge: Cambridge University Press, 1996), ch. 4.

10. Welles was forced out of State in 1943, but his important role in post-war planning is recovered in Christopher D. O'Sullivan, *Sumner Welles, Postwar Planning, and the Quest for a New World Order, 1937–1943* (New York: Columbia University Press, 2008).

11. On Gerig, Gerlof D. Homan, 'Orie Benjamin Gerig: Mennonite Rebel, Peace Activist, International Civil Servant, and American Diplomat, 1894–1976', *The Mennonite Quarterly*, Oct. 1999, at: http://www.goshen.edu/mqr/pastissues/oct99homan.html.

12. For the development of the trusteeship system, and of Bunche's work in particular, see esp. Brian Urquhart, *Ralph Bunche: An American Odyssey* (New York: Norton, 1993), 109–38, quoted 126; also Neta C. Crawford, 'Decolonization through Trusteeship: The Legacy of Ralph Bunche', in Robert A. Hill and Edmond J. Keller, eds., *Trustee for the Human Community: Ralph J. Bunche, the United Nations, and the Decolonization of Africa* (Athens, OH: Ohio University Press, 2010), 93–115. Stephen C. Schlesinger also emphasizes the roles of Edward Stettinius and Harold Stassen in *Act of Creation: The Founding of the United Nations* (Boulder, CO: Westview Press, 2003), ch. 14. Gilchrist provided his own account of the San Francisco agreements in his 'Colonial Questions at the San Francisco Conference', *American Political Science Review*, 39:5 (Oct. 1945), 982–92.

13. Anker's survey was reviewed by Rappard (see SFA, Rappard 1977/135 7, Rappard to Anker, 31 July 1944) and published in time for use at San Francisco; see *The Mandates System: Origin—Principles—Application* (Geneva: League of Nations, April 1945). For a list of materials supplied to Finkelstein, see LNA, R4178, File 6A/43974/43974.

14. Key documents on the trusteeship system—Chapters XI–XIII of the UN Charter, the Trusteeship Council's Rules of Procedure, and texts of the Trusteeship Agreements—are provided as annexes to H. Duncan Hall, *Mandates, Dependencies and Trusteeship* (Washington: Carnegie Endowment for International Peace, 1948), 335–85.

15. For the London discussions, see United Nation Preparatory Commission, Committee 4 (Trusteeship), *Summary Record of Meetings: 24 November–24 December 1945*, esp. meetings 5–6, pp. 12–15, on petitioning; meeting 7, pp. 16–17, on visits, and for the comment by Zeineddine (Syria), and meeting 14, p. 35, for the Ukrainian resolution.

16. Meredith Terretta, '"We Had Been Fooled into Thinking that the UN Watches over the Entire World": Human Rights, UN Trust Territories, and Africa's Decolonization', *Human Rights Quarterly*, 34:2 (May 2012), 329–60; Ullrich Lohrmann, *Voices from Tanganyika: Great Britain, the United Nations and the Decolonization of a Trust Territory, 1946–1961* (Berlin: Lit, 2007). For the work of newly independent states as advocates for decolonization and human rights at the United Nations, see also Roland Burke, *Decolonization and the Evolution of International Human Rights* (Philadelphia: University of Pennsylvania Press, 2010). Neta Crawford provides a nuanced account of how ethical arguments, advocacy groups, and political interests interacted to change the nature of colonial rule in *Argument and Change in World Politics: Ethics, Decolonization, and Humanitarian Intervention* (Cambridge: Cambridge University Press, 2002).

17. For a good summary of those early aims, see Benjamin Gerig, 'Mandates and Colonies', in *World Organization: A Balance Sheet of the First Great Experiment* (Washington: American Council on Public Affairs, [1942]), 211–30, and for African-American activism in particular, Penny M. Von Eschen, *Race Against Empire: Black Americans and Anti-Colonialism, 1937–1957* (Ithaca, NY, and London: Cornell University Press, 1997).

18. Charles K. Webster, quoted in Marika Sherwood, '"There is No New Deal for the Blackman in San Francisco": African Attempts to Influence the Founding Conference of the United Nations, April–July 1945', *The International Journal of African Historical Studies*, 29:1 (1996), 71–94, here at 90.

19. The classic account of those Anglo-American negotiations over the future of the British Empire remains Louis, *Imperialism at Bay*, but for an intelligent account of the steady paring down of the scope of trusteeship in particular, see John J. Sbrega, 'Determination versus Drift: The Anglo-American Debate over the Trusteeship Issue, 1941–1945', *The Pacific Historical Review*, 55:2 (May 1986), 256–80, and for the defeat of the newly independent states at San Francisco, Sherwood, 'There is No New Deal for the Blackman in San Francisco'.

20. For the complex legal history of South West Africa, see esp. Gail-Maryse Cockram, *South West African Mandate* (Cape Town: Juta and Co., 1976).

21. For these reservations, see Firth, 'The War in the Pacific', 319.

22. None other than Huntington Gilchrist laid the groundwork for the 'strategic trust' option in 'The Japanese Islands: Annexation or Trusteeship?', *Foreign Affairs*, 22 (1943–44), 634–42. The deplorable history of US, British, and French nuclear testing in the Pacific, and the impact on local populations (which the Trusteeship Council did little to mitigate), is ably summarized in Stewart Firth and Karin von Strokirch, 'A Nuclear Pacific', *The Cambridge History of the Pacific*

*Islanders*, ed. Donald Denoon (Cambridge: Cambridge University Press, 1997), 324–58.

23. The 'realist' cast of the trusteeship regime, in comparison to the 'idealist' cast of the mandates system, was noted by Rappard as early as 1946; see William Rappard, 'The Mandates and the International Trusteeship Systems', *Political Science Quarterly*, 61:3 (1946), 408–19, and for a useful recent comparison, Alexandru Gigorescu, 'Mapping the UN-League of Nations Analogy: Are there Still Lessons to Be Learned from the League?', *Global Governance*, 11 (2005), 25–42.

24. Rayford Logan, 'The System of International Trusteeship', *The Journal of Negro Education*, 15:3 (Summer 1946), 285–99; and SFA, Rappard 1977/135 148, Rappard to Sweetser, 8 Sept. 1945.

25. The Trusteeship system is only now beginning to get the kind of scholarly scrutiny it deserves. Early valuable studies include James N. Murray Jr., *The United Nations Trusteeship System* (Urbana: University of Illinois Press, 1957), and Ramendra Nath Chowdhuri, *International Mandates and Trusteeship Systems: A Comparative Study* ('s-Gravenhage: Martinus Nijhoff, 1955); for the point about the East-West conflict, see Murray, *The United Nations Trusteeship System*, 241–2. For an excellent recent overview of the geopolitical context of the regime, see Gordon W. Morrell's 'A Higher stage of Imperialism? The Big Three, the UN Trusteeship Council, and the Early Cold War', in R. M. Douglas, Michael D. Callahan, and Elizabeth Bishop, eds., *Imperialism on Trial: International Oversight of Colonial Rule in Historical Perspective* (Lanham, MD: Lexington Books, 2006), 111–38.

26. The literature on 'failed states' (especially in Africa) and on the relationship of colonization to state failure is too vast to survey here, but for three path-breaking works from very different perspectives see Basil Davidson, *Black Man's Burden: Africa and the Curse of the Nation State* (London: James Currey, 1992); Robert H. Jackson, *Quasi-States: Sovereignty, International Relations and the Third World* (Cambridge: Cambridge University Press, 1990); and Crawford Young, *The African Colonial State in Comparative Perspective* (New Haven: Yale University Press, 1994). The crisis of the post-colonial state has led to calls for heightened international intervention or a revival of the trusteeship regime, notably by politicians but also by international lawyers, e.g. Gerald B. Helman and Steven R. Ratner, 'Saving Failed States', *Foreign Policy*, 89 (Winter 1992), 3–20; Rosa Ehrenreich Brooks, 'Failed States, or the State as Failure?', *The University of Chicago Law Review*, 72:4 (Autumn 2005), 1159–96; Saira Mohamed, 'From Keeping Peace to Building Peace: A Proposal for a Revitalized United Nations Trusteeship Council', *Columbia Law Review*, 105:3 (April 2005), 809–40. For historically informed surveys of such efforts at international territorial administration or international state-building, see esp. Ralph Wilde, *International Territorial Administration: How Trusteeship and the Civilizing Mission Never Went Away* (Oxford: Oxford University Press, 2008), and Carsten Stahn, *The Law and*

*Practice of International Territorial Administration: Versailles to Iraq and Beyond* (Cambridge: Cambridge University Press, 2008).

27. LNA, R4178, 6A/43806/x, 'Extract from Report of the 1st Committee to the 21st session of the Assembly'.

28. Winifred Holtby, 'Better and Brighter Natives', in Paul Berry and Alan Bishop, eds., *Testament of a Generation: The Journalism of Vera Brittain and Winifred Holtby* (London: Virago, 1985), 181–5.

29. Hall, *Mandates, Dependencies and Trusteeship*, 3–26.

30. In this respect, my argument is similar to that advanced for the Cold War period by Odd Arne Westad, *The Global Cold War: Third World Interventions and the Making of Our Times* (Cambridge: Cambridge University Press, 2005).

31. SFA, Rappard 1977/135 31, Rappard to Lugard, 2 July 1942.

32. SFA, Rappard 1977/135 37, Rappard to Palacios, 30 Dec. 1946.

33. SFA, Rappard 1977/135 13, Catastini to Rappard, 1 Nov. 1945.

34. SFA, Rappard 1977/135 36, Rappard to Orts, 19 Nov. 1952.

35. SFA, Rappard 1977/135 36, Rappard to Orts, 11 May 1957.

36. Rappard, 'The Mandates and the International Trusteeship Systems', 416.

37. Archives Générales du Royaume, Brussels, Famille Orts Papers, File 389, 'Souvenirs de ma Carrière', 189–90.

38. SFA, Rappard 1977/135 62, Rappard to Vera Weizmann, 8 Nov. 1949.

39. SFA, Rappard 1977/135 36, Orts to Rappard, 13 Nov. 1952, and Rappard to Orts, 19 Nov. 1952.

# Works Cited

Multiple works by a single author are in order of publication date

### CONTEMPORARY PUBLISHED SOURCES, INCLUDING MEMOIRS, EDITIONS, AND LETTERS

Lord Altrincham [Sir Edward Grigg]. *Kenya's Opportunity*. London: Faber & Faber, 1955.

Amery, Leo S. 'General von Epp's Case Examined', *Journal of the Royal African Society*, 36:142 (January 1937), 10–22.

Amery, Leo S. *My Political Life*, vol. 2, *War and Peace, 1914–1929*. London: Hutchinson, 1953.

[Anker, Peter.] *The Mandates System: Origin—Principles—Application*. Geneva: League of Nations, 1945.

Antonius, George. 'The Machinery of Government in Palestine', *Annals of the American Academy of Political and Social Science*, 164 (November 1932), 55–61.

Antonius, George. *The Arab Awakening: The Story of the Arab National Movement*. London: Hamish Hamilton, 1938.

Azikwe, Ben. 'Ethics of Colonial Imperialism', *Journal of Negro History*, 16:3 (July 1931), 436–46.

Barnes, John, and David Nicholson, eds. *The Empire at Bay: The Leo Amery Diaries, 1929–1945*. London: Hutchinson, 1988.

Beer, George Louis. *The English-Speaking Peoples: Their Future Relations and Joint International Obligations*. New York: Macmillan, 1917.

Beer, George Louis. *African Questions at the Paris Peace Conference*. London: Dawsons of Pall Mall, 1968.

Berry, Paul, and Alan Bishop, eds. *Testament of a Generation: The Journalism of Vera Brittain and Winifred Holtby*. London: Virago, 1985.

Buell, Raymond Leslie. *The Native Problem in Africa*. 2 vols. New York: Macmillan, 1928.

Bunche, Ralph J. 'French Administration in Togoland and Dahomey', Dissertation, Harvard University, 1934.

Bunche, Ralph J. 'French Educational Policy in Togo and Dahomey', *Journal of Negro Education*, 3:1 (January 1934), 69–97.

Caffrey, Margaret M., and Patricia A. Francis, eds. *To Cherish the Life of the World: Selected Letters of Margaret Mead*. New York: Basic Books, 2006.

Cameron, Donald. *My Tanganyika Service*. London: George Allen & Unwin, 1939.

Carr, E. H. *The Twenty Year Crisis, 1919–1939: An Introduction to the Study of International Relations*. London: Macmillan, 1940.

Cecil, Robert. *The First Assembly: A Study of the Proceedings of the First Assembly of the League of Nations*. London: Macmillan, 1921.

Charteris, A. H. 'The Mandate over Nauru Island', *British Year Book of International Law*, 137 (1923–24), 137–52.

Chinnery, E. W. P. 'The Central Ranges of the Mandated Territory of New Guinea from Mount Chapman to Mount Hagen', *The Geographical Journal*, 84:5 (November 1934), 398–412.

Clyde, Paul H. *Japan's Pacific Mandate*. New York: Macmillan, 1935.

Condliffe, J. B. *Markets and the Problem of Peaceful Change*. Paris: International Institute of Intellectual Co-operation, 1938.

Davis, Harriet Eager. *Pioneers in World Order: An American Appraisal of the League of Nations*. New York: Columbia University Press, 1944.

de Madariaga, Salvador, *Morning without Noon*. Farnsworth, England: Saxon House, 1974.

Derso, Alois, and Emery Kelen. *Le Testament de Genève: 10 années de coopération internationale*. Paris: Georges Lang, 1931.

Du Bois, W. E. B. *The Souls of Black Folk*. 1903; rpt. New York: New American Library, 1969.

Dunn, Frederick Sherwood. *Peaceful Change: A Study of International Procedures*. New York: Council on Foreign Relations, 1937.

Edmonds, C. J. *Kurds, Turks and Arabs: Politics, Travel and Research in North-Eastern Iraq, 1919–1925*. London: Oxford University Press, 1957.

Emmet, E. 'The Mandate over South-West Africa', *Journal of Comparative Legislation and International Law*, 3rd series, 9:1 (1927), 111–22.

Evans, Luther H. 'The General Principles Governing the Termination of a Mandate', *The American Journal of International Law*, 26:4 (October 1932), 735–58.

Evans, Luther H. 'The Emancipation of Iraq from the Mandates System', *American Political Science Review*, 26:6 (December 1932), 1024–49.

Evans, Luther H. 'Would Japanese Withdrawal from the League Affect the Status of the Japanese Mandate?', *The American Journal of International Law*, 27:1 (1933), 140–2.

Evans, Luther H. 'International Affairs: The Japanese Mandate Naval Base Question', *American Political Science Review*, 29:3 (June 1935), 482–7.

Feinberg, Nathan. *Some Problems of the Palestine Mandate*. Tel Aviv: Shoshani's Print Co., 1936.

Fieldhouse, David, ed. *Kurds, Arabs and Britons: The Memoir of Wallace Lyon in Iraq, 1918–1944*. London: I. B. Tauris, 2002.

Gatti, Ellen. *Exploring We Would Go*. New York: Charles Scribner's Sons, 1944.

Gerig, Benjamin. *The Open Door and the Mandates System*. London: George Allen & Unwin, 1930.

Gerig, Benjamin. 'Mandates and Colonies', *World Organisation: A Balance Sheet of the First Great Experiment*. Washington: American Council on Public Affairs, [1942].

Gerig, Benjamin. 'Significance of the Trusteeship System', *Annals of the American Academy of Political and Social Science*, 255 (January 1948), 39–47.

Ghory, Emile. 'An Arab View of the Situation in Palestine', *International Affairs*, 14:5 (September–October 1936), 684–99.

Gilchrist, Huntington. 'The Japanese Islands: Annexation or Trusteeship?', *Foreign Affairs*, 22 (1943–44), 634–42.

Gilchrist, Huntington. 'Colonial Questions at the San Francisco Conference', *American Political Science Review*, 39:5 (October 1945), 982–92.

Gilchrist, Huntington. 'Trusteeship and the Colonial System', *Proceedings of the Academy of Political Science*, 22:2 (January 1947), 95–109.

Goldmann, Nahum. *The Autobiography of Nahum Goldmann: Sixty Years of Jewish Life*. New York: Holt, Rinehart and Winston, 1969.

Grobba, Fritz. *Männer und Mächte im Orient: 25 Jahre diplomatitischer Tätigkeit im Orient*. Göttingen: Musterschmidt, 1967.

Hales, James C. 'Some Legal Aspects of the Mandates System: Sovereignty; Nationality; Termination; Transfer', *Transactions of the Grotius Society*, 23 (1937), 85–126.

Hales, James C. 'The Creation and Application of the Mandates System', *Transations of the Grotius Society*, 25 (1939), 185–284.

Hales, James C. 'The Reform and Extension of the Mandates System: A Legal Solution of the Colonial Problem', *Transactions of the Grotius Society*, 26 (1940), 163–210.

Hall, H. Duncan. *Mandates, Dependencies and Trusteeship*. Washington: Carnegie Endowment for International Peace, 1948.

Howard-Ellis, C. [Konni Zilliacus]. *The Origin, Structure and Working of the League of Nations*. Boston: Houghton Mifflin, 1929.

Kelen, Emery. *Peace in their Time: Men Who Led Us In and Out of War, 1914–1945*. New York: Alfred A. Knopf, 1963.

Khoury, Gerard D. *Une Tutelle coloniale: Le mandat français en Syrie et au Liban: Ecrits politiques de Robert de Caix*. Paris: Belin, 2006.

[King, Henry, and Charles Crane], 'King-Crane Report on the Near East', *Editor & Publisher*, 55:27 (2 December 1922).

Koloniale Reichsarbeitsgemeinschaft. *Protest der deutschen Wirtschaft gegen die Einverleibung von Deutsch-Ostafrika in das Britische Reich*, n.p., 1931.

Labouret, Henri. *Le Cameroun*. Paris: Centre d'Etudes de Politique étrangère, 1937.

Leahy, Michael J. 'The Central Highlands of New Guinea', *The Geographical Journal*, 87:3 (March 1936), 229–62.

Leahy, Michael J. *Explorations into Highland New Guinea, 1930–1935*. Tuscaloosa: University of Alabama Press, 1991.

Leahy, Michael, and Maurice Crain. *The Land that Time Forgot: Adventures and Discoveries in New Guinea*. New York: Funk & Wagnalls, 1937.

*The Letters and Papers of Chaim Weizmann*, vols. 8–19. New Brunswick, NJ: Transaction Books, 1976–79.

Locke, Alain. 'The Mandates System: A New Code of Empire' (1928), in *The Works of Alain Locke*, ed. Charles Molesworth. Oxford: Oxford University Press, 2012, 509–27.

Logan, Rayford. 'The Operation of the Mandates System in Africa', *The Journal of Negro History*, 13:4 (October 1928), 423–77.

Logan, Rayford. 'The System of International Trusteeship', *The Journal of Negro Education*, 15:3 (Summer, 1946), 285–99.

Lugard, Frederick. 'The Problem of Colour in Relation to the Idea of Equality', *Journal of Philosophical Studies*, 1:2 (April 1926), 211–33.

Lugard, Frederick. 'The White Man's Task in Tropical Africa', *Foreign Affairs*, 5:1 (October 1926), 57–68.

Lugard, Frederick. 'Colonial Administration', *Economica*, 41 (August 1933), 248–63.

Lugard, Frederick. 'Africa and the Powers', *Journal of the Royal African Society*, 35:138 (January 1936), 4–17.

Lugard, Frederick. 'The Basis of the Claim for Colonies', *International Affairs*, 15:1 (January–February 1936), 3–25.

Lugard, Frederick. *The Dual Mandate in British Tropical Africa*, 1922; rpt. Hamden, CT: Archon Books, 1965.

Mair, L. P. 'Colonial Administration as a Science', *Journal of the Royal African Society*, 32:129 (October 1933), 366–71.

Manning, C. A. W., ed. *Peaceful Change: An International Problem*. London: Macmillan, 1937.

Matches, Margaret. *Savage Paradise*. New York: The Century Co., 1931.

Mead, Margaret. *Letters from the Field, 1925–1975*. New York: Harper & Row, 1977.

Moresco, Emanuel. *Colonial Questions and Peace*. Paris: League of Nations, International Institute for Intellectual Co-operation, 1939.

Nelson, O. F. *Samoa at Geneva: Misleading the League of Nations*. Auckland: n.p., 1928.

Nelson, O. F. *A Petition to Geneva: The Hon. O. F. Nelson again Appeals*. Auckland: National Printing Co., 1930.

Nelson, O. F. 'What the Samoans Want', reprinted from the *New Zealand Samoan Guardian*, 23 Oct. 1930.

'New Zealand: The Trouble in Samoa', *Round Table*, 18 (December 1927), 191–210.

Padmore, George. *Africa and World Peace*, 1937; rpt. London: Frank Cass, 1972.

Palacios, Leopoldo. *Los Mandatos internacionales de la Sociedad de Naciones*. Madrid: Librería General de Victoriano Suarez, 1928.

'Peaceful Change: Procedures, Population, Raw Materials, Colonies'. *Proceedings of the Tenth International Studies Conference, Paris, 28 June–3 July 1937*. Paris: League of Nations, International Institute for Intellectual Co-operation, 1938.

Perham, Margery. *Pacific Prelude: A Journey to Samoa and Australasia*, 1929. London: Peter Owen, 1988.

Perth, Lord [Sir Eric Drummond] et al. 'The Future of the Mandates: A Symposium', *African Affairs*, 43:173 (October 1944), 159–71.

Potter, Pitman B. 'League Publicity: Cause or Effect of League Failure', *Public Opinion Quarterly*, 2:3 (July 1938), 399–412.

Rappard, William. *International Relations as Viewed from Geneva*, 1925; rpt. New Haven: Yale University Press, 1975.

Rappard, William. 'The Practical Working of the Mandates System', *Journal of the British Institute of International Affairs*, 4:5 (September 1925), 205–26.

Rappard, William. *The Geneva Experiment*. London: Oxford University Press, 1931.

Rappard, William. 'The Mandates and the International Trusteeship Systems', *Political Science Quarterly*, 61:3 (1946), 408–19.

Rappard, William. 'Mandates and Trusteeships with Particular Reference to Palestine', *Journal of Politics*, 8 (1946), 520–30.

Ritsher, Walter H. 'What Constitutes Readiness for Independence', *American Political Science Review*, 26:1 (February 1932), 112–22.

Rowe, Newton. 'The Samoa Mandate', *Foreign Affairs*, 8:12 (June 1927).

Royal Institute for International Affairs. *Germany's Claim to Colonies*. Information Department Paper No. 23. 2nd ed., London: RIIA, February 1939.

Ryckmans, Pierre. *Dominer pour Servir*. Brussels: Albert Dewit, 1931.

*The Samoan Massacre: December 28th, 1929*. Tasmania: n.p., 1930.

Sarraut, Albert. *La Mise en Valeur des colonies françaises*. Paris: Payot, 1923.

Schacht, Hjalmar. 'Germany's Colonial Demands', *Foreign Affairs*, 15:2 (January 1937), 223–34.

Schmitt, Carl. 'Völkerrechtliche Formen des modernen Imperialismus', in *Positionen und Begriffe im Kampf mit Weimar—Genf—Versailles, 1923–1939*, 1940; rpt. Berlin: Duncker & Humblot, 1994.

Schnee, Heinrich. *The German Colonies under the Mandates*. Berlin: Brönner in Nowawes, 1922.

Schnee, Heinrich. *German Colonization, Past and Future: The Truth about the German Colonies*. London: G. Allen & Unwin, 1926.

Schnee, Heinrich. 'Die Hungersnot in Ruanda und die belgische Mandatverwaltung', *Koloniale Rundschau*, 1929, no. 12, 357–68.

Smuts, J. C. *The League of Nations: A Practical Suggestion*. New York: The Nation Press, 1919.

Smuts, J. C. *Africa and Some World Problems*. Oxford: Clarendon Press, 1930.

Stafford, R. S. *The Tragedy of the Assyrians*. London: Allen & Unwin, 1935.

Stoyanovsky, Jacob. *La Théorie générale des Mandats internationaux*. Paris: Presses universitaires de France, 1925.

Temperley, H. W. V. *The Second Year of the League: A Study of the Second Assembly of the League of Nations*. London: Hutchinson, 1922.

Theodoli, Alberto. *A Cavallo di Due Secoli*. Rome: La Navicella, 1950.

Townsend, Mary E. 'The Contemporary Colonial Movement in Germany', *Political Science Quarterly*, 43:1 (March 1928), 64–75.

Townsend, Mary E. 'The German Colonies and the Third Reich', *Political Science Quarterly*, 53:2 (June 1938), 186–206.

Toynbee, Arnold J. *Survey of International Affairs, 1920–1923*. London: Humphrey Milford, 1925.

Toynbee, Arnold J. 'The Present Situation in Palestine', *International Affairs*, 10:1 (January 1931), 38–68.

Toynbee, Arnold J. 'Peaceful Change or War? The Next Stage in the International Crisis', *International Affairs*, 15:1 (January–February 1936), 26–56.

Toynbee, Arnold J. *Survey of International Affairs, 1935*, vol. 2, *Abyssinia and Italy*. London: Oxford University Press, 1936.

Van Rees, D. F. W. *Les Mandats internationaux: Le contrôle de l'administration mandataire*. Paris: Librairie Arthur Rousseau, 1927.

Van Rees, D. F. W. *Les Mandats internationaux: Les principes généraux du régime des mandats*. Paris: Librairie Arthur Rousseau, 1928.

Weizmann, Chaim. *Trial and Error: The Autobiography of Chaim Weizmann*. New York: Harper & Brothers, 1949.

West, Francis, ed. *Selected Letters of Hubert Murray*. Melbourne: Oxford University Press, 1970.

Wright, Quincy. 'Sovereignty of the Mandates', *American Journal of International Law*, 17:4 (October 1923), 691–703.

Wright, Quincy. 'The United States and the Mandates', *Michigan Law Review*, 23:7 (May 1925), 717–47.

Wright, Quincy. 'The Bombardment of Damascus', *The American Journal of International Law*, 20:2 (April 1926), 263–80.

Wright, Quincy. 'National Sovereignty and Collective Security', *Annals of the American Academy of Arts and Sciences*, 186:1 (1936), 94–104.

Wright, Quincy. *Mandates under the League of Nations*. 1930; rpt. New York: Greenwood Press, 1968.

Yanaihara, Tadao. *Pacific Islands under Japanese Mandate*. New York: Oxford University Press, 1940.

SECONDARY SOURCES

### General

Adamthwaite, Anthony. *France and the Coming of the Second World War, 1936–1939*. London: Frank Cass, 1977.

Albrecht-Carrié, René. 'Italian Colonial Policy, 1914–1918', *The Journal of Modern History*, 18:2 (June 1946), 123–47.

Allain, Jean. 'Slavery and the League of Nations: Ethiopia as a Civilised Nation', *Journal of the History of International Law*, 8 (2006), 213–44.

Andrew, Christopher M., and A. S. Kanya-Forstner. 'France, Africa, and the First World War', *The Journal of African History*, 19:1 (1978), 11–23.

Andrew, Christopher M., and A. S. Kanya-Forstner, *France Overseas: The Great War and the Climax of French Imperial Expansion*. London: Thames and Hudson, 1981.

Anghie, Antony. 'Colonialism and the Birth of International Institutions: Sovereignty, Economy, and the Mandate System of the League of Nations', *NYU Journal of International Law and Politics*, 7 (2002), 513–634.

Anghie, Antony. *Imperialism, Sovereignty and the Making of International Law*. Cambridge: Cambridge University Press, 2004.

Arsan, Andrew. ' "This is the Age of Associations": Committees, Petitions, and the Roots of Interwar Middle Eastern Internationalism', *Journal of Global History*, 7 (2012), 166–88.

Arsan, Andrew, Su Lin Lewis, and Anne-Isabelle Richard. 'The Roots of Global Civil Society and the Interwar Moment', *Journal of Global History*, 7:2 (2012), 157–65.

Asante, S. K. B. 'The Impact of the Italo-Ethiopian Crisis of 1935–36 on the Pan-African Movement in Britain', *Transactions of the Historical Society of Ghana*, 13:2 (December 1972), 217–27.

Austen, Ralph A. 'Varieties of Trusteeship: African Territories under British and French Mandate, 1919–1939', in *France and Britain in Africa*, ed. Prosser Gifford and Wm. Roger Louis. New Haven: Yale University Press, 1971, 515–42.

Aydin, Cemil. *The Politics of Anti-Westernism in Asia: Visions of World Order in Pan-Islamic and Pan-Asian Thought*. New York: Columbia University Press, 2007.

Baer, George W. *Test Case: Italy, Ethiopia, and the League of Nations*. Stanford: Hoover Institution Press, 1976.

Bain, William. *Between Anarchy and Society: Trusteeship and the Obligations of Power*. Oxford: Oxford University Press, 2003.

Barrington, J. M. 'The Permanent Mandates Commission and Educational Policy in Trust Territories', *International Review of Education*, 22:1 (1976), 88–94.

Barros, James C. *Betrayal from Within: Joseph Avenol, Secretary-General of the League of Nations, 1933–1940*. New Haven: Yale University Press, 1969.

Barros, James C. *Office without Power: Secretary-General Sir Eric Drummond, 1919–1933*. Oxford: Clarendon Press, 1979.

Bellegarde-Smith, Patrick D. 'Dantès Bellegarde and Pan-Africanism', *Phylon (1960–)*, 42:3 (1981), 233–44.

Bendiner, Elmer. *A Time for Angels: The Tragicomic History of the League of Nations*. New York: Knopf, 1975.

Berger, Stefan. 'William Harbutt Dawson: The Career and Politics of an Historian of Germany', *The English Historical Review*, 116:465 (February 2001), 76–113.

Berman, Bruce, and John Lonsdale. *Unhappy Valley: Conflict in Kenya and Africa*. London: John Currey, 1992.

Benton, Lauren. 'From International Law to Imperial Constitutions: The Problem of Quasi-Sovereignty, 1870–1900', *Law and History Review*, 26:3 (2008), 595–619.

Borowy, Iris. *Coming to Terms with World Health: The League of Nations Health Organisation, 1921–1946*. Frankfurt: Peter Lang, 2006.

Boyce, Robert. *The Great Interwar Crisis and the Collapse of Globalization*. London: Palgrave Macmillan, 2009.

Brooks, Rosa Ehrenreich. 'Failed States, or the State as Failure?', *The University of Chicago Law Review*, 72:4 (Autumn 2005), 1159–96.

Burke, Roland. *Decolonization and the Evolution of International Human Rights.* Philadelphia: University of Pennsylvania Press, 2010.

Burton, Margaret E. *The Assembly of the League of Nations.* University of Chicago Press, 1941; rpt. NY: Howard Fertig, 1974.

Butler, Israel de Jesús. 'A Comparative Analysis of Individual Petition in Regional and Global Human Rights Protection Mechanisms', *University of Queensland Law Journal*, 23:1 (2004), 22–53.

Callahan, Michael D. *Mandates and Empire: The League of Nations and Africa, 1914–1931.* Brighton: Sussex Academic Press, 1999.

Callahan, Michael D. *A Sacred Trust: The League of Nations and Africa, 1929–1946.* Brighton: Sussex Academic Press, 2004.

Chowdhuri, Ramendra Nath. *International Mandates and Trusteeship Systems: A Comparative Study.* 's-Gravenhage: Martinus Nijhoff, 1955.

Clarke, J. Calvitt III. 'The Politics of Arms not Given: Japan, Ethiopia and Italy in the 1930s', *Girding for Battle: The Arms Trade in a Global Perspective, 1815–1940*, ed. Donald J. Stoker, Jr., and Jonathan A. Grant. London: Praeger, 2003, 135–53.

Clavin, Patricia. *Securing the World Economy: The Reinvention of the League of Nations, 1920–1946.* Oxford: Oxford University Press, 2013.

Clavin, Patricia, and Jens-Wilhelm Wessels. 'Transnationalism and the League of Nations: Understanding the Work of its Economic and Financial Organization', *Contemporary European History*, 14:4 (November 2005), 465–92.

Cohen, Albert. *Belle du Seigneur*, 1968; English ed. *Her Lover*, trans. David Coward. London: Penguin Classics, 2005.

Cohrs, Patrick. *The Unfinished Peace after World War I: America, Britain, and the Stabilisation of Europe, 1919–1932.* Cambridge: Cambridge University Press, 2006.

Conklin, Alice L. *A Mission to Civilize: The Republican Idea of Empire in France and West Africa, 1895–1930.* Stanford: Stanford University Press, 1997.

Cooper, Frederick. *Decolonization and African Society: The Labor Question in French and British Africa.* Cambridge: Cambridge University Press, 1996.

Cooper, John Milton. *Breaking the Heart of the World: Woodrow Wilson and the Fight for the League of Nations.* Cambridge: Cambridge University Press, 2001.

Cowan, Jane. 'Who's Afraid of Violent Language? Honour, Sovereignty and Claims-Making in the League of Nations', *Anthropological Theory*, 33:3 (2003), 271–91.

Craft, Stephen G.V. K. *Wellington Koo and the Emergence of Modern China.* Lexington: University Press of Kentucky, 2004.

Crawford, Neta. *Argument and Change in World Politics: Ethics, Decolonization and Humanitarian Intervention.* Cambridge: Cambridge University Press, 2002.

Crawford, Neta. 'Decolonization through Trusteeship: The Legacy of Ralph Bunche', in *Trustee for the Human Community: Ralph J. Bunche, the United Nations, and the Decolonization of Africa.* Athens: Ohio University Press, 2010, 93–115.

Crozier, Andrew J. 'The Establishment of the Mandates System, 1919–25: Some Problems Created by the Paris Peace Conference', *Journal of Contemporary History*, 14:3 (July 1979), 483–513.

Crozier, Andrew J. *Appeasement and Germany's Last Bid for Colonies*. London: Macmillan, 1988.

Darwin, John. *The Empire Project: The Rise and Fall of the British World-System, 1830–1970*. Cambridge: Cambridge University Press, 2009.

Davidson, Basil. *Black Man's Burden: Africa and the Curse of the Nation State*. London: James Currey, 1992.

Derrick, Jonathan. *Africa's 'Agitators': Militant Anti-Colonialism in Africa and the West, 1918–1939*. New York: Columbia University Press, 2008.

Dimier, Véronique. 'Direct or Indirect Rule: Propaganda around a Scientific Controversy', in *Promoting the Colonial Idea: Propaganda and Visions of Empire in France*, ed. Tony Chafer and Amanda Sackur. London: Palgrave, 2002, 168–83.

Dimier, Véronique. ' "L'Internationalisation" du débat colonial: Rivalités franco-britanniques autour de la Commission permanente des Mandats', *Outre Mers: Revue d'Histoire*, 89:336–7 (2002), 333–60.

Dimier, Véronique. *Le Gouvernement des colonies, regards croisés franco-britanniques*. Brussels: Editions de l'Université de Bruxelles, 2004.

Douglas, R. M., Michael D. Callahan, and Elizabeth Bishop. *Imperialism on Trial: International Oversight of Colonial Rule in Historical Perspective*. Lanham, MD: Lexington Books, 2006.

Dubin, Martin David. 'Towards the Bruce Report: The Economic and Social Programmes of the League of Nations in the Avenol Era', in *The League of Nations in Retrospect*. Berlin: W. de Gruyter, 1983, 42–72.

Dubin, Martin David. 'Transgovernmental Processes in the League of Nations', *International Organization*, 37:3 (1983), 469–93.

Dubow, Saul. 'Smuts, the United Nations and the Rhetoric of Race and Rights', *Journal of Contemporary History*, 43 (2008), 45–74.

Egerton, George W. *Great Britain and the Creation of the League of Nations*. Chapel Hill: University of North Carolina Press, 1978.

Ekoko, A. Edho. 'The British Attitude towards Germany's Colonial Irredentism in Africa in the Inter-War Years', *Journal of Contemporary History*, 14:2 (April 1979), 287–307.

Fields, Karen E. *Revival and Rebellion in Colonial Central Africa*. Princeton: Princeton University Press, 1985.

Fink, Carole. *The Genoa Conference: European Diplomacy, 1921–1922*. Chapel Hill: University of North Carolina Press, 1984.

Fink, Carole. *Defending the Rights of Others: The Great Powers, the Jews, and International Minority Protection, 1878–1938*. Cambridge: Cambridge University Press, 2006.

Firth, Stewart. 'The War in the Pacific', in *The Cambridge History of the Pacific Islanders*, ed. Donald Denoon. Cambridge: Cambridge University Press, 1997, 291–323.

Frecot, Janos, ed. *Erich Salomon 'Mit Frack und Linse durch Politik und Gesellschaft'*: *Photographien 1928–1938*. Halle, Leipzig, and Passau: Schirmer/Mosel, 2004.

Gageby, Douglas. *The Last Secretary General: Sean Lester and the League of Nations*. Dublin: Town House, 1999.

Gorman, Daniel. *The Emergence of International Society in the 1920s*. Cambridge: Cambridge University Press, 2012.

Graichen, Gisela, and Horst Gründer. *Deutsche Kolonien: Traum und Trauma*. Berlin: Ullstein, 2007.

Grant, Kevin. 'Trust and Self-Determination: Anglo-American Ethics of Empire and International Government', in *Critiques of Capital in Modern Britain and America: Transatlantic Exchanges*, ed. Mark Bevir and Frank Trentmann. London: Palgrave, 2002, 151–73.

Grant, Kevin. *A Civilized Savagery: Britain and the New Slaveries in Africa, 1884–1926*. New York: Routledge, 2005.

Grant, Kevin. 'Human Rights and Sovereign Abolitions of Slavery, c. 1885–1950', in *Beyond Sovereignty: Britain, Empire and Transnationalism, c. 1880–1950*, ed. Kevin Grant, Philippa Levine, and Frank Trentmann. London: Palgrave Macmillan, 2007, 80–102.

Grant, Kevin. 'The British Empire, International Government, and Human Rights', *History Compass*, 11:8 (2013), 573–83.

Grayson, Richard S. *Austen Chamberlain and the Commitment to Europe: British Foreign Policy, 1924–29*. London: Frank Cass, 1997.

Grigorescu, Alexandru. 'Mapping the UN-League of Nations Analogy: Are There Still Lessons to be Learned from the League?', *Global Governance*, 11 (2005), 25–42.

Haas, Ernst B. 'The Reconciliation of Conflicting Colonial Policy Aims: Acceptance of the League of Nations Mandate System', *International Organization*, 6:4 (November 1952), 521–36.

Hale, William. *Turkish Foreign Policy, 1774–2000*. London: Frank Cass, 2000.

Helman, Gerald B., and Steven R. Ratner, 'Saving Failed States', *Foreign Policy*, 89 (Winter, 1992–1992), 3–20.

Hodge, Joseph Morgan. *Triumph of the Expert: Agrarian Doctrines of Development and the Legacies of British Colonialism*. Athens, OH: Ohio University Press, 2007.

Homan, Gerlof D. 'Orie Benjamin Gerig: Mennonite Rebel, Peace Activist, International Civil Servant, and American Diplomat, 1894–1976', *The Mennonite Quarterly*, vol. 73, no. 4, October 1999.

International Labour Organisation, *International Labour Conventions and Recommendations, 1919–1981*. Geneva: ILO, 1982.

Jackson, Peter. 'Tradition and Adaptation: The Social Universe of the French Foreign Ministry in the Era of the First World War', *French History*, 24:2 (2010), 164–96.

Jackson, Robert H. *Quasi-States: Sovereignty, International Relations and the Third World*. Cambridge: Cambridge University Press, 1990.

Janken, Kenneth Rogert. *Rayford W. Logan and the Dilemma of the African-American Intellectual.* Amherst: University of Massachusetts Press, 1993.

Kimmich, Christoph. *Germany and the League of Nations.* Chicago: University of Chicago Press, 1976.

Kinnear, Mary. *Woman of the World: Mary McGeachy and International Cooperation.* Toronto: University of Toronto Press, 2004.

Knock, Thomas J. *To End All Wars: Woodrow Wilson and the Quest for a New World Order.* Princeton: Princeton University Press, 1992.

Kuehl, Warren F., and Lynne K. Dunn. *Keeping the Covenant: American Internationalists and the League of Nations, 1920–1939.* Kent, OH: Kent State University Press, 1997.

Lake, Marilyn, and Henry Reynolds. *Drawing the Global Colour Line: White Men's Countries and the International Challenge of Racial Equality.* Cambridge: Cambridge University Press, 2008.

Lang, Michael. 'Globalization and Global History in Toynbee', *Journal of World History,* 22:4 (December 2011), 747–83.

Laqua, Daniel, ed. *Internationalism Reconfigured: Transnational Ideas and Movements Between the World Wars.* London: I. B. Tauris, 2011.

Lauren, Paul Gordon. *The Evolution of International Human Rights: Visions Seen.* Philadelphia: University of Pennsylvania Press, 1998.

*The League of Nations in Retrospect: Proceedings of the Symposium.* Berlin: W. de Gruyter, 1983.

L'Estoile, Benoît de. 'Internationalization and "Scientific Nationalism": The International Institute of African Languages and Cultures between the Wars', in Helen Tilley with Robert J. Gordon, ed., *Ordering Africa: Anthropology, European Imperialism and the Politics of Knowledge.* Manchester: Manchester University Press, 2007, 95–116.

Legg, Stephen, ed. *Spatiality, Sovereignty and Carl Schmitt: Geographies of the Nomos.* London: Routledge, 2011.

Lewis, David Levering. *W. E. B. Du Bois: Biography of a Race, 1868–1919.* New York: Henry Holt, 1993.

Lewis, David Levering. *W. E. B. Du Bois: The Fight for Equality and the American Century, 1919–1963.* New York: Henry Holt, 2000.

Linne, Karsten. *Deutschland jenseits des Äquators? Die NS-Kolonialplanungen für Afrika.* Berlin: Ch. Links Verlag, 2008.

Lloyd, Lorna. *Peace through Law: Britain and the International Court in the 1920s.* London: Royal Historical Society, 1997.

Löhr, Isabella, and Roland Wenzlhuemer. *The Nation State and Beyond: Governing Globalization Processes in the Nineteenth and Early Twentieth Centuries.* Heidelberg: Springer, 2013.

Long, David. 'Who Killed the International Studies Conference?', *Review of International Studies,* 32 (2006), 603–22.

Long, David, and Brian C. Schmidt. *Imperialism and Internationalism in the Discipline of International Relations.* Albany: State University of New York Press, 2005.

Louis, Wm. Roger. 'The United States and the African Peace Settlement of 1919: The Pilgrimage of George Louis Beer', *The Journal of African History*, 4:3 (1963), 413–33.

Louis, Wm. Roger. *Great Britain and Germany's Lost Colonies, 1914–1919*. Oxford: Clarendon Press, 1967.

Louis, Wm. Roger. 'The United Kingdom and the Beginning of the Mandates System, 1919–1922', *International Organization*, 23:1 (1969), 73–96.

Louis, Wm. Roger. *Imperialism at Bay: The United States and the Decolonization of the British Empire, 1941–1945*. New York: Oxford University Press, 1978.

Louis, Wm. Roger. *Ends of British Imperialism: The Scramble for Empire, Suez and Decolonization*. London: I. B. Tauris, 2006.

Mamdani, Mahmood. *Citizen and Subject: Contemporary Africa and the Legacy of Late Colonialism*. Princeton: Princeton University Press, 1996.

Manela, Erez. *The Wilsonian Moment: Self-Determination and the International Origins of Anticolonial Nationalism*. Oxford: Oxford University Press, 2007.

Manigand, Christine. *Les Français au service de la Société des Nations*. Bern: Peter Lang, 2003.

Manjapra, Kris. *Age of Entanglement: German and Indian Intellectuals across Empire*. Cambridge, MA: Harvard University Press, 2014.

Mantena, Karuna. *Alibis of Empire: Henry Maine and the Ends of Liberal Imperialism*. Princeton: Princeton University Press, 2010.

Maul, Daniel Roger. 'The International Labour Organization and the Struggle against Forced Labour from 1919 to the Present', *Labour History*, 48:4 (2007), 477–500.

Mazower, Mark. *No Enchanted Palace: The End of Empire and the Ideological Origins of the United Nations*. Princeton: Princeton University Press, 2009.

Mazower, Mark. *Governing the World: The History of an Idea*. New York: Penguin, 2012.

McCarthy, Helen. *The British People and the League of Nations: Democracy, Citizenship and Internationalism, c. 1918–45*. Manchester: Manchester University Press, 2011.

Méouchy, Nadine, and Peter Sluglett, eds. *British and French Mandates in Comparative Perspective*. Leiden: Brill, 2004.

Metzger, Barbara H. M. 'The League of Nations and Human Rights: From Practice to Theory', Dissertation, University of Cambridge, 2001.

Metzger, Barbara H. M. 'Towards an International Human Rights Regime during the Inter-War Years: The League of Nations' Combat of Traffic in Women and Children', in *Beyond Sovereignty: Britain, Empire and Transnationalism, c. 1880–1950*, ed. Kevin Grant, Philippa Levine, and Frank Trentmann. London: Palgrave Macmillan, 2007, 54–79.

Miers, Suzanne. *Slavery in the Twentieth Century: The Evolution of a Global Problem*. Walnut Creek, CA: Altamira Press, 2003.

Miller, Carol. 'The Social Section and Advisory Committee on Social Questions of the League of Nations', in *International Health Organizations and Movements*, ed. Paul Weindling. Cambridge: Cambridge University Press, 1995, 154–76.

Mitrany, David. *A Working Peace System: An Argument for the Functional Development of International Organization*. New York: Oxford University Press, 1944.

Mohamed, Saira. 'From Keeping Peace to Building Peace: A Proposal for a Revitalized United Nations Trusteeship Council', *Columbia Law Review*, 105:3 (April 2005), 809–40.

Momirov, Aleksandar. 'The Individual Right to Petition in Internationalized Territories: From Progressive Thought to an Abandoned Practice', *Journal of the History of International Law*, 9 (2007), 203–31.

Monnier, Victor. *William E. Rappard: Défenseur des libertés, serviteur de son pays et de la communauté internationale*. Geneva: Slatkine, 1995.

Moorhouse, Frank. *Grand Days*. Sydney: Pan Macmillan, 1993.

Moorhouse, Frank. *Dark Palace*. New York: Knopf, 2000.

Morrell, Gordon W. 'A Higher State of Imperialism? The Big Three, the UN Trusteeship Council, and the Early Cold War', in *Imperialism on Trial: International Oversight of Colonial Rule in Historical Perspective*, ed. R. M. Douglas, Michael D. Callahan, and Elizabeth Bishop. Lanham, MD: Lexington Books, 2006, 111–38.

Murray, James N., Jr. *The United Nations Trusteeship System*. Urbana: University of Illinois Press, 1957.

Muse, Clifford L. Jr. 'Howard University and U.S. Foreign Affairs during the Franklin D. Roosevelt Administration, 1933–1945', *The Journal of African-American History*, 87 (Autumn 2002), 403–15.

Nish, Ian. *Japan's Struggle with Internationalism: Japan, China and the League of Nations, 1931–33*. New York: Kegan Paul International, 1993.

Nish, Ian. *Japanese Foreign Policy in the Interwar Period*. Westport, CT: Praeger, 2002.

Nordqvist, Liv Wicksell. *Anna Bugge Wicksell: En Kvinna fore sin tid*. Malmö: Liber Förlag, 1985.

Northedge, F. S. *The League of Nations: Its Life and Times*. Leicester: Leicester University Press, 1986.

O'Sullivan, Christopher D. *Sumner Welles, Postwar Planning, and the Quest for a New World Order, 1937–1943*. New York: Columbia University Press, 2008.

Omissi, David. *Air Power and Colonial Control: The Royal Air Force, 1919–1939*. Manchester: Manchester University Press, 1990.

Parker, R. A. C. 'Great Britain, France and the Ethiopian Crisis, 1935–1936', *The English Historical Review*, 89:351 (April 1974), 293–332.

Pearce, Robert. *Sir Bernard Bourdillon: The Biography of a Twentieth-Century Colonialist*. Oxford: Kensal Press, 1987.

Pedersen, Susan. 'Settler Colonialism at the Bar of the League of Nations', in Caroline Elkins and Susan Pedersen, eds, *Settler Colonialism in the Twentieth Century* (New York: Routledge, 2005), 113–34.

Pedersen, Susan. 'The Meaning of the Mandates System: An Argument', *Geschichte und Gesellschaft*, 32:4 (October–December 2006), 560–82.

Pedersen, Susan. 'Back to the League of Nations', *American Historical Review*, 112:4 (October 2007), 1091–117.

Pedersen, Susan. 'Metaphors of the Schoolroom: Women Working the Mandates System of the League of Nations', *History Workshop Journal*, 66 (2008), 188–207.

Pedersen, Susan. 'Getting out of Iraq—in 1932: The League of Nations and the Road to Normative Statehood', *American Historical Review*, 115:4 (October 2010), 975–1000.

Pedersen, Susan. 'Samoa at Geneva: Petitions and Peoples before the Mandates Commission of the League of Nations.' *Journal of Imperial and Commonwealth History*, 40:2 (June 2012), 231–61.

Pennybacker, Susan. *From Scottsboro to Munich: Race and Political Culture in 1930s Britain*. Princeton: Princeton University Press, 2009.

Perham, Margery. *Lugard: The Years of Authority, 1898–1945*. London: Collins, 1960.

Peter, Ania. *William E. Rappard und der Völkerbund: Ein Schweizer Pionier der internationalen Verständigung*. Bern: Lang, 1973.

Rajagopal, Balakrishnan. *International Law from Below: Development, Social Movements, and Third World Resistance*. Cambridge: Cambridge University Press, 2003.

Ranger, T. O. 'The Invention of Tradition in Colonial Africa', in *The Invention of Tradition*, ed. E. J. Hobsbawm and T. O. Ranger. Cambridge: Cambridge University Press, 1983, 211–62.

Ranshofen-Wertheimer, Egon F. *The International Secretariat: A Great Experiment in International Administration*. Washington: Carnegie Endowment for International Peace, 1945.

Renoliet, Jean-Jacques. *L'Unesco oubliée: La Société des Nations et la coopération intellectuelle, 1919–1946* (Paris: Publications de la Sorbonne, 1999).

Ribi, Amalia. ' "The Breath of a New Life"? British Anti-Slavery and the League of Nations', *Internationalism Reconfigured: Transnational Ideas and Movements Between the World Wars*, ed. Daniel Laqua. London: I. B. Tauris, 2011, 93–113.

Richard, Anne-Isabelle. 'Competition and Complementarity: Civil Society Networks and the Question of Decentralizing the League of Nations', *Journal of Global History*, 7:2 (2012), 233–56.

Rietzler, Katharina. 'Experts for Peace: Structures and Motivations of Philanthropic Internationalism in the Interwar Years', in *Internationalism Reconfigured: Transnational Ideas and Movements between the Wars*, ed. Daniel Laqua. London: I. B. Tauris, 2011, 45–65.

Rimmer, Douglas. 'Have-Not Nations: The Prototype', *Economic Development and Cultural Change*, 27:2 (January 1979), 307–25.

Roberts, Andrew. *'The Holy Fox': A Life of Lord Halifax*, 1991; rpt. London: Papermac, 1992.

Robinson, Pearl T. 'Ralph Bunche and African Studies: Reflections on the Politics of Knowledge', *African Studies Review*, 51:1 (April 2008), 1–16.

Robinson, Pearl T. 'Ralph Bunche the Africanist: Revising Paradigms Lost', in *Trustee for the Human Community: Ralph J. Bunche, the United Nations, and the Decolonization of Africa*, ed. Robert A. Hill and Edmond J. Keller. Athens, OH: Ohio University Press, 2010, 69–90.

Rodríguez-Piñero, Luis. *Indigenous Peoples, Postcolonialism, and International Law: The ILO Regime (1919–1989)*. Oxford: Oxford University Press, 2005.

Rovine, Arthur W. *The First Fifty Years: The Secretary-General in World Politics, 1920–1970*. Leyden: A. W. Sijthoff, 1970.

Rucker, ' "A Negro Nation within the Nation": W. E. B. Du Bois and the Creation of a Revolutionary Pan-Africanist Tradition', *The Black Scholar*, 32:3/4 (Autumn 2002), 37–46.

Sbrega, John J. 'Determination versus Drift: The Anglo-American Debate over the Trusteeship Issue, 1941–1945', *Pacific Historical Review*, 55:2 (May 1986), 256–80.

Schlesinger, Stephen C. *Act of Creation: The Founding of the United Nations*. Boulder, CO: Westview Press, 2003.

Schmokel, Wolfe W. *Dream of Empire: German Colonialism, 1919–1945*. New Haven and London: Yale University Press, 1964.

Schneer, Jonathan. *The Balfour Declaration: The Origins of the Arab-Israeli Conflict*. New York: Random House, 2010.

Schneider, Michael A. 'The Intellectual Origins of Colonial Trusteeship in East Asia: Nitobe Inazô, Paul Reinsch and the End of Empire', *American Asian Review*, 17:1 (Spring 1999), 1–48.

Scott, George. *The Rise and Fall of the League of Nations*. New York: Macmillan, 2003.

Sherwood, Marika. ' "There is No New Deal for the Blackman in San Francisco": African Attempts to Influence the Founding Conference of the United Nations, April–July 1945', *The International Journal of African Historical Studies*, 29:1 (1996), 71–94.

Shilliam, Robbie. 'What about Marcus Garvey? Race and the Transformation of Sovereignty Debate', *Review of International Studies*, 32 (2006), 379–400.

Sinha, Mrinalini. *Specters of Mother India: The Global Restructuring of an Empire*. Durham, NC: Duke University Press, 2006.

Skran, Claudena M. *Refugees in Inter-War Europe: The Emergence of a Regime*. Oxford: Clarendon Press, 1995.

Sluga, Glenda. *Internationalism in the Age of Nationalism*. Philadelphia: University of Pennsylvania Press, 2013.

Spear, Thomas. 'Neo-Traditionalism and the Limits of Invention in British Colonial Africa', *Journal of African History*, 44:1 (2003), 3–27.

Stahn, Carsten. *The Law and Practice of International Territorial Administration: Versailles to Iraq and Beyond*. Cambridge: Cambridge University Press, 2008.

Stedman, Andrew David. ' "A Most Dishonest Argument": Chamberlain's Government, Anti-Appeasers, and the Persistence of League of Nations Language before the Second World War', *Contemporary British History*, 25:1 (2011), 83–99.

Steiner, Zara. *The Lights That Failed: European International History, 1919–1933*. Oxford: Oxford University Press, 2007.

Steiner, Zara. *The Triumph of the Dark: European International History, 1933–1939*. Oxford: Oxford University Press, 2011.

Stocking, George W., Jr. *After Tylor: British Social Anthropology, 1888–1951*. Madison: University of Wisconsin Press, 1995.

Strachan, Hew. *The First World War in Africa*. Oxford: Oxford University Press, 2004.

Sundiata, Ibrahim. *Brothers and Strangers: Black Zion, Black Slavery, 1914–1940*. Durham, NC: Duke University Press, 2003.

Terretta, Meredith. ' "We had been fooled into thinking that the UN watches over the whole world": Human Rights, UN Trust Territories, and Africa's Decolonization', *Human Rights Quarterly*, 34:2 (May 2012), 329–60.

Thomas, Martin. *Britain, France and Appeasement: Anglo-French Relations in the Popular Front Era*. New York: Berg, 1997.

Thomas, Martin. 'Albert Sarraut, French Colonial Development and the Communist Threat', *Journal of Modern History*, 77:4 (December 2005), 917–55.

Tilly, Helen, with Robert J. Gordon, ed. *Ordering Africa: Anthropology, European Imperialism, and the Politics of Knowledge*. Manchester: Manchester University Press, 2007.

Tooze, Adam. *The Wages of Destruction: The Making and Breaking of the Nazi Economy*. New York: Viking, 2006.

Unger, Gérard. *Aristide Briand: Le ferme conciliateur*. Paris: Fayard, 2005.

Upthegrove, Campbell L. *Empire by Mandate*. New York: n.p., 1954.

Urquhart, Brian. *Ralph Bunche: An American Odyssey*. New York: Norton, 1993.

Van Ginneken, Anique H. M. 'Volkenbondsvoogdij: Het Toezicht van de Volkenbond op het Bestuur in Mandaatgebieden, 1919–1940', Dissertation, University of Utrecht, 1992.

Van Ginneken, Anique H. M. *Historical Dictionary of the League of Nations*. Lanham, MD: Scarecrow Press, 2006.

Van Laak, Dirk. *Imperiale Infrastruktur: Deutsche Planungen für eine Erschließung Afrikas 1880 bis 1960*. Paderborn: Ferdinand Schöningh, 2004.

Vitalis, Robert. 'The Graceful and Generous Liberal Gesture: Making Racism Invisible in American International Relations', *Millennium: Journal of International Studies*, 29:2 (2000), 331–56.

Vitalis, Robert. 'Birth of a Discipline', in David Long and Brian C. Schmidt, eds, *Imperialism and Internationalism in the Discipline of International Relations*. Albany: State University of New York Press, 2005, 159–81.

Von Eschen, Penny M. *Race Against Empire: Black Americans and Anticolonialism, 1937–1957*. Ithaca, NY, and London: Cornell University Press, 1997.

Walters, Francis P. *A History of the League of Nations*. Oxford: Oxford University Press, 1952.

Wasserstein, Bernard. *On the Eve: The Jews of Europe Before the Second World War*. New York: Simon & Shuster, 2012.

Webster, Andrew. 'The Transnational Dream: Politicians, Diplomats and Soldiers in the League of Nations' Pursuit of International Disarmament, 1920–1938', *Central European History*, 14:4 (November 2005), 493–518.

Weltsch, Robert. 'A Tragedy of Leadership (Chaim Weizmann and the Zionist Movement', *Jewish Social Studies*, 13:3 (July 1951), 211–26.

Wertheim, Stephen. 'The League of Nations: A Retreat from International Law?', *Journal of Global History*, 7:2 (2012), 210–32.

Westad, Odd Arne. *The Global Cold War: Third World Interventions and the Making of Our Times*. Cambridge: Cambridge University Press, 2005.

Wilde, Ralph. *International Territorial Administration: How Trusteeship and the Civilizing Mission Never Went Away*. Oxford: Oxford University Press, 2008.

Wildenthal, Lora. *German Women for Empire, 1884–1945*. Durham, NC: Duke University Press, 2001.

Wintzer, Joachim. *Deutschland und der Völkerbund, 1918–1926*. Paderborn: Ferdinand Schöningh Verlag, 2006.

Wolf, Hans-Georg. 'British and French Language and Educational Policies in the Mandate and Trusteeship Territories', *Language Sciences*, 30 (2008), 553–74.

Wright, Jonathan. *Gustav Stresemann: Weimar's Greatest Statesman*. Oxford: Oxford University Press, 2002.

Yearwood, Peter. *Guarantee of Peace: The League of Nations in British Policy, 1914–1925*. Oxford: Oxford University Press, 2009.

Young, Crawford. *The African Colonial State in Comparative Perspective*. New Haven: Yale University Press, 1994.

Zilliacus, Stella. *Six People and Love*. New York: John Day, 1957.

## 'A' Mandates

### Middle East General

Alkhazragi, Hussein D. 'Un Petit Prince à la SDN: La lutte du roi Hussein du Hedjaz pour l'indépendance des provinces arabes de l'empire ottoman', *Relations Internationales*, 146 (2011–12), 7–23.

Fieldhouse, D. K. *Western Imperialism in the Middle East, 1914–1958*. Oxford: Oxford University Press, 2006.

Fisher, John. 'Syria and Mesopotamia in British Middle Eastern Policy in 1919', *Middle Eastern Studies*, 34:2 (April 1998), 129–70.

Fisher, John. *Curzon and British Imperialism in the Middle East, 1916–1919*. London: Frank Cass, 1999.

Fisher, John. 'Lord Robert Cecil and the Formation of a Middle East Department of the Foreign Office', *Middle Eastern Studies*, 42:3 (2006), 365–80.

Fromkin, David. *Peace to End All Peace: The Fall of the Ottoman Empire and the Creation of the Modern Middle East*. New York: Henry Holt, 2001.

Hoffmann, Friedhelm. *Die Syro-Palästinensische Delegation am Völkerbund und Šakīb Arslān in Genf, 1921–1936/46*. Berlin: Lit, 2007.

Mouton, Marie-Renée. 'Le Congrès syro-palestinien de Genève', *Relations Internationales*, 19 (Autumn 1979), 313–28.

Reynolds, Michael A. *Shattering Empires: The Clash and Collapse of the Ottoman and Russian Empires, 1908–1918*. Cambridge: Cambridge University Press, 2011.

Seale, Patrick. *The Struggle for Arab Independence: Riad el-Solh and the Makers of the Modern Middle East*. Cambridge: Cambridge University Press, 2010.

Thomas, Martin. *Empires of Intelligence: Security Services and Colonial Disorder after 1914*. Berkeley and Los Angeles: University of California Press, 2008.

*Palestine and Transjordan*

Alon, Yoav. 'Tribal Shaykhs and the Limits of British Imperial Rule in Transjordan, 1920–46', *Journal of Imperial and Commonwealth History*, 32:1 (January 2004), 69–92.

Alon, Yoav. *The Making of Jordan: Tribes, Colonialism and the Modern State*. London: I. B. Tauris, 2007.

Ayyad, Abdelaziz A. *Arab Nationalism and the Palestinians, 1850–1939*. Jerusalem: PASSIA, 1999.

Cohen, Michael J. *Palestine: Retreat from the Mandate: The Making of British Policy, 1936–45*. New York: P. Elek, 1978.

Cohen, Michael J. 'Origins of the Arab States' Involvement in Palestine', *Middle Eastern Studies*, 19:2 (April 1983), 244–52.

Cohen, Michael J. *The Origins and Evolution of the Arab-Zionist Conflict*. Berkeley: University of California Press, 1987.

El-Eini, Roza I. M. *Mandated Landscape: British Imperial Rule in Palestine, 1929–1948*. New York: Routledge, 2006.

Gilmour, David. 'The Unregarded Prophet: Lord Curzon and the Palestine Question', *Journal of Palestine Studies*, 25:3 (Spring 1996), 60–8.

Haim, Yehoyada. 'Zionist Policies and Attitudes towards the Arabs on the Eve of the Arab Revolt, 1936', *Middle Eastern Studies*, 14:2 (May 1078), 211–31.

Hirszowicz, Lukasz. 'Nazi Germany and the Palestine Partition Plan', *Middle Eastern Studies*, 1:1 (October 1964), 40–65.

Hughes, Matthew. 'The Banality of Brutality: British Armed Forces and the Repression of the Arab Revolt, 1936–39', *English Historical Reivew*, 124:507 (2009), 313–54.

Hughes, Matthew. 'Lawlessness was the Law: British Armed Forces, the Legal System and the Repression of the Arab Revolt in Palestine, 1936–1939', in *Britain, Palestine and Empire: The Mandate Years*, ed. Rory Miller. London: Ashgate, 2010, 141–56.

Huneidi, Sahar. 'Was Balfour Policy Reversible? The Colonial Office and Palestine, 1921–23', *Journal of Palestine Studies*, 27:2 (Winter 1998), 23–41.

Huneidi, Sahar. *A Broken Trust: Herbert Samuel, Zionism, and the Palestinians*. London: I. B. Tauris, 2001.

Hurewitz, J. C. *The Struggle for Palestine*, 1950; new ed. New York: Schocken Books, 1976.

Khalidi, Rashid. *Palestinian Identity: The Construction of Modern National Consciousness*. New York: Columbia University Press, 1997.

Khalidi, Walid, ed. *From Haven to Conquest*. Washington: Institute for Palestine Studies, 1987.

Kolatt, Israel. 'The Zionist Movement and the Arabs', in *Essential Papers on Zionism*, ed. Jehuda Reinharz and Anita Shapira. New York: NYU Press, 1996, 617–47.

Kolinsky, Martin. 'Premeditation in the Palestine Disturbances of August 1929?', *Middle Eastern Studies*, 26:1 (January 1990), 18–34.

Krämer, Gudrun. *A History of Palestine: From the Ottoman Conquest to the Founding of the State of Israel*, 2002; English ed. Princeton: Princeton University Press, 2008.

Mattar, Philip. *The Mufti of Jerusalem: Al-Hajj Amin al-Husayni and the Palestinian National Movement*. New York: Columbia University Press, 1988.

Matthews, Weldon C. *Confronting an Empire, Constructing a Nation: Arab Nationalists and Popular Politics in Mandate Palestine*. London: I. B. Tauris, 2006.

Melka, R. 'Nazi Germany and the Palestine Question', *Middle Eastern Studies*, 5:3 (October 1969), 221–33.

Miller, Rory, ed. *Palestine, Britain and Empire: The Mandate Years*. London: Ashgate, 2010.

Nicosia, Francis. 'Arab Nationalism and National Socialist Germany, 1933–1939: Ideological and Strategic Incompatibility', *International Journal of Middle Eastern Studies*, 12:3 (November 1980), 351–72.

Pappe, Ilan. *A History of Modern Palestine: One Land, Two Peoples*, 2nd ed. Cambridge: Cambridge University Press, 2006.

Pedersen, Susan. 'The Impact of League Oversight on British Policy in Palestine', in *Palestine, Britain and Empire: the Mandate Years*, ed. Rory Miller. London: Ashgate, 2010, 39–65.

Porath, Yehoshua. *The Palestinian Arab National Movement: From Riots to Rebellion*, vol. 2, *1929–1939*. London: Frank Cass, 1977.

Porath, Yehoshua. *In Search of Arab Unity, 1930–1945*. London: Frank Cass, 1986.

Rogan, Eugene L., and Avi Shlaim, eds. *The War for Palestine*, 2nd ed. Cambridge: Cambridge University Press, 2007.

Rose, Norman A. 'The Arab Rulers and Palestine, 1936: The British Reaction', *Journal of Modern History*, 44:2 (June 1972), 213–31.

Rose, Norman A. *The Gentile Zionists: A Study in Anglo-Zionist Diplomacy, 1929–1939*. London: Routledge, 1973.

Rosenblum, Howard (Chanoch). 'Promoting an International Conference to Solve the Jewish Problem: The New Zionist Organization's Alliance with Poland, 1938–1939', *The Slavonic and East European Review*, 69:3 (July 1991), 478–501.

Segev, Tom. *One Palestine, Complete: Jews and Arabs under the British Mandate*. New York: Metropolitan Books, 2000.

Sherman, A. J. *Mandate Days: British Lives in Palestine, 1918–1948*. Baltimore: Johns Hopkins University Press, 2001.

Sinanoglou, Penny. 'British Plans for the Partition of Palestine, 1929–1938', *The Historical Journal*, 52:1 (2009), 131–52.

Smith, Barbara J. *The Roots of Separatism in Palestine: British Economic Policy, 1920–1929*. Syracuse, NY: Syracuse University Press, 1993.

Smith, Charles. 'Communal Conflict and Insurrection in Palestine', in *Policing and Decolonization: Politics, Nationalism and the Police, 1917–1965*, ed. David M. Anderson and David Killingray. Manchester: Manchester University Press, 1992, 62–83.

Stein, Kenneth W. 'The Jewish National Fund: Land Purchase Methods and Priorities, 1924–1939', *Middle Estern Studies*, 20:2 (April 1984), 190–205.

Stein, Kenneth W. *The Land Question in Palestine, 1917–1939*. Chapel Hill and London: University of North Carolina Press, 1984.

Townshend, Charles. 'The Defence of Palestine: Insurrection and Public Security, 1936–1939', *The English Historical Review*, 103:409 (October 1988), 917–49.

Wasserstein, Bernard. '"Clipping the Claws of the Colonizers": Arab Officials in the Government of Palestine, 1917-48', *Middle Eastern Studies*, 13:2 (May 1977), 171–94.

Wasserstein, Bernard. *The British in Palestine: The Mandatory Government and the Arab-Jewish Conflict, 1917–1929*, 1978; 2nd ed. Oxford: Basil Blackwell, 1991.

Wasserstein, Bernard. *Herbert Samuel: A Political Life*. Oxford: Oxford University Press, 1992.

Weinbaum, Laurence. *A Marriage of Convenience: The New Zionist Organization and the Polish Government, 1936–1939*. Boulder: East European Monographs, 1993.

Wheatley, Natasha. 'Mandatory Interpretation: Legal Hermeneutics and the New International Order in Arab and Jewish Petitions to the League of Nations', *Past and Present*, no. 227 (May 2015).

Wilson, Mary C. *King Abdullah, Britain and the Making of Jordan*. Cambridge: Cambridge University Press, 1987.

Wistrich, Robert S. 'Zionism and its Jewish "Assimilationist" Critics (1897–1948)', *Jewish Social Studies*, new series, 4:2 (Winter 1998), 59–111.

Wynot, Edward D. Jr. '"A Necessary Cruelty": The Emergence of Official Anti-Semitism in Poland, 1936–39', *American Historical Review*, 76:4 (October 1971), 1035–58.

Yisraeli, David. 'The Third Reich and Palestine', *Middle Eastern Studies*, 7:3 (October 1971), 343–53.

*Syria and Lebanon*

Cleveland, William L. *Islam Against the West: Shakib Arslan and the Campaign for Islamic Nationalism*. Austin: University of Texas Press, 1985.

Eldar, Dan. 'France in Syria: The Abolition of the Sharifian Government, April–July 1920', *Middle Eastern Studies*, 29:3 (July 1993), 487–503.

Firro, Kais M. *Inventing Lebanon: Nationalism and the State under the Mandate*. London: I. B. Tauris, 2003.

Gelvin, James L. *Divided Loyalties: Nationalism and Mass Politics in Syria at the Close of Empire*. Berkeley: University of California Press, 1998.

Jackson, Simon. 'Diaspora Politics and Developmental Empire: The Syro-Lebanese at the League of Nations', *Arab Studies Journal*, 21:1 (Spring 2013), 166–90.

Khadduri, Majid. 'The Alexandretta Dispute', *The American Journal of International Law*, 39:3 (July 1945), 406–25.

Khoury, Philip S. *Syria and the French Mandate: The Politics of Arab Nationalism, 1920–1945*. Princeton: Princeton University Press, 1987.

Longrigg, Stephen H. *Syria and Lebanon under French Mandate*. London: Oxford University Press, 1958.

Moubayed, Sami. *Syria and the USA: Washington's Relations with Damascus from Wilson to Eisenhower*. London: I. B. Tauris, 2012.

Provence, Michael. *The Great Syrian Revolt and the Rise of Arab Nationalism*. Austin: University of Texas Press, 2005.

Rafez, Abdul-Karim. 'Arabism, Society, and Economy in Syria, 1918–1920', in *State and Society in Syria and Lebanon*, ed. Youssef M. Choueiri. Exeter: University of Exeter Press, 1993, 1–26.

Shambrook, Peter A. *French Imperialism in Syria, 1927–1936*. Reading, UK: Ithaca Press, 1998.

Shields, Sarah D. *Fezzes in the River: Identity Politics and European Diplomacy in the Middle East on the Eve of World War II*. Oxford: Oxford University Press, 2011.

Shimizu, Hiroshi. 'The Mandatory Power and Japan's Trade Expansion into Syria in the Inter-War Period', *Middle Eastern Studies*, 21:2 (April 1985), 152–71.

Thomas, Martin C. 'French Intelligence-Gathering in the Syrian Mandate, 1920–40', *Middle Eastern Studies*, 38:1 (January 2002), 1–32.

Watenpaugh, Keith. ' "Creating Phantoms": Zaki al-Arsuzi, the Alexandretta Crisis, and the Formation of Modern Arab Nationalism in Syria', *International Journal of Middle Eastern Stuides*, 28:3 (August 1996), 363–89.

White, Benjamin Thomas. *The Emergence of Minorities in the Middle East: The Politics of Community in French Mandate Syria*. Edinburgh: Edinburgh University Press, 2011.

Zamir, Meir. *The Formation of Modern Lebanon*. Ithaca and New York: Cornell University Press, 1985.

Zamir, Meir. 'Faisal and the Lebanese Question, 1918–20', *Middle Eastern Studies*, 27:3 (July 1991), 404–26.

Zamir, Meir. *Lebanon's Quest: The Road to Statehood, 1926–1939*. London: I. B. Tauris, 2000.

*Iraq*

Bashkin, Orit. *The Other Iraq: Pluralism and Culture in Hashemite Iraq*. Stanford: Stanford University Press, 2009.

Beck, Peter J. ' "A Tedious and Perilous Controversy": Britain and the Settlement of the Mosul Dispute, 1918–1926', *Middle Eastern Studies*, 17:2 (April 1981), 256–76.

Dodge, Toby. *Inventing Iraq: The Failure of Nation Building and a History Denied*. New York: Columbia University Press, 2003.

Fitzgerald, Edward Peter. 'Business Diplomacy: Walter Teagle, Jersey Standard, and the Anglo-French Pipeline Conflict in the Middle East, 1930–1931', *Business History Review*, 67:2 (Summer 1993), 207–45.

Kedourie, Elie. 'The Kingdom of Iraq: A Retrospect', in *The Chatham House Version and Other Middle-Eastern Studies*. New York: Praeger, 1970, 236–85.

Luizard, Pierre-Jean. 'Le Mandat britannique en Irak: Une Rencontre entre plusieurs projets politiques', in *The British and French Mandates in Comparative Perspectives/*

*Les Mandats français et anglais dans une perspective comparative*, ed. Nadine Méouchy and Peter Sluglett. Leiden: Brill, 2004, 361–84.

Makko, Aryo. 'Arbitrator in a World of Wars: The League of Nations and the Mosul Dispute, 1924–1925', *Diplomacy & Statecraft*, 21:4 (2010), 631–49.

McDowall, David. *A Modern History of the Kurds*. London: I. B. Tauris, 1996.

Mejcher, Helmut. *Die Politik und das Öl im Nahen Osten*. Stuttgart: Klett-Cotta, 1980.

Mejcher, Helmut. 'The International Petroleum Cartel (1928), Arab and Turkish Oil Aspirations and German Oil Policy towards the Middle East on the Eve of the Second World War', in *Oil, the Middle East, North Africa and the Industrial States*, ed. Klaus Jürgen Gantzel and Helmut Mejcher. Paderborn: F. Schöningh, 1984, 29–59.

Mitchell, Timothy. *Carbon Democracy: Political Power in the Age of Oil*. London: Verso, 2011.

Silverfarb, David. *Britain's Informal Empire in the Middle East: A Case Study of Iraq, 1929–1941*. New York: Oxford University Press, 1986.

Sluglett, Peter. *Britain in Iraq: Contriving King and Country, 1914–1932*, 2nd ed. New York: Columbia University Press, 2007.

Townshend, Charles. *Desert Hell: The British Invasion of Mesopotamia*. Cambridge, MA: Harvard University Press, 2011.

Tripp, Charles. *A History of Iraq*, 3rd ed. Cambridge: Cambridge University Press, 2007.

Vinogradov, Amal. 'The 1920 Revolt in Iraq Reconsidered: The Role of Tribes in National Politics', *International Journal of Middle Eastern Studies*, 3:2 (April 1972), 123–39.

## 'B' Mandates

### Cameroon

Austen, Ralph A., and Jonathan Derrick, *Middlemen of the Cameroons Rivers: The Duala and their Hinterland, c. 1600–c. 1960*. Cambridge: Cambridge University Press, 1999.

Eckert, Andreas. *Die Duala und die Kolonialmächte: Eine Untersuchung zu Widerstand, Protest und Protonationalismus in Kamerun vor dem Zweiten Weltkreig*. Münster and Hamburg: Lit, 1991.

Gardinier, David. 'The British in the Cameroons', in *Britain and Germany in Africa: Imperial Rivalry and Colonial Rule*, ed. Prosser Gifford and Wm. Roger Louis. New Haven: Yale University Press, 1967, 513–55.

Goodridge, Richard A. ' "In the Most Effective Manner"? Britain and the Disposal of the Cameroons Plantations, 1914–1924', *International Journal of African Historical Studies*, 29:2 (1996), 251–77.

Joseph, Richard A. 'The Royal Pretender: Prince Douala Manga Bell in Paris, 1919–1922', *Cahiers d'Etudes Africaines*, 14:54 (1974), 339–58.

Joseph, Richard A. 'The German Question in French Cameroun, 1919–1939', *Comparative Studies in Society and History*, 17:1 (January 1975), 65–90.

Le Vine, Victor T. *Le Cameroun du mandat à l'indépendance.* Dakar: Présence Africaine, 1984.

Yearwood, Peter J. ' "In a Casual Way with a Blue Pencil": British Policy and the Partition of Kamerun, 1914–1919', *Canadian Journal of African Studies,* 27:2 (1993), 218–44.

*Togo*

Amenumey, D. E. K. *The Ewe Unification Movement: A Political History.* Accra: Ghana Universities Press, 1989.

Lawrance, Benjamin N. 'Language between Power, Power between Languages: Further Discussion of Education and Policy in Togoland under the French Mandate, 1919–1945', *Cahiers d'etudes africaines* (2001), 517–40.

Lawrance, Benjamin N. 'Bankoe v. Dome: Traditions and Petitions in the Ho-Asogli Amalgamation, British Mandated Togoland, 1919–1939', *Journal of African History,* 46 (2005), 243–67.

Lawrance, Benjamin N. *Locality, Mobility, and 'Nation': Periurban Colonialism in Togo's Eweland, 1900–1960.* Rochester, NY: University of Rochester Press, 2007.

Lawrance, Benjamin N. 'Petitioners, "Bush-Lawyers" and Letter-Writers: Court Access in British Occupied Lome', in Benjamin N. Lawrance, Emily L. Osborn, and Richard L. Roberts, eds. *Intermediaries, Interpreters and Clerks: African Employees and the Making of Colonial Africa.* Madison: University of Wisconsin Press, 2006.

*Rwanda and Burundi*

Botte, Roger. 'Rwanda and Burundi, 1889–1930: Chronology of a Slow Assassination, Part 2', *The International Journal of African Historical Studies,* 18:2 (1985), 289–314.

Chrétien, Jean-Pierre. *Burundi: L'histoire retrouvée. 25 ans de métier d'historien en Afrique.* Paris: Karthala, 1993.

Chrétien, Jean-Pierre. *The Great Lakes of Africa: Two Thousand Years of History.* New York: Zone Books, 2003.

Cornet, Anne. *Histoire d'une famine.* Louvain-La-Neuve: Université catholique de Louvain, Centre d'histoire de l'Afrique, 1996.

Des Forges, Alison. 'Defeat is the Only Bad News: Rwanda under Musinga, 1896–1931', Dissertation, Yale University, 1972; publ. Madison: University of Wisconsin Press, 2011.

Gahama, Joseph. *Le Burundi sous administration belge.* Paris: Karthala, 1983.

Kabagema, Innocent. *Ruanda unter deutscher Kolonialherrschaft, 1899–1916.* Frankfurt: Peter Lang, 1993.

Lemarchand, René, ed. *African Kingships in Perspective: Political Change and Modernization in Monarchical Settings.* London: Frank Cass, 1977.

Louis, Wm. Roger. *Ruanda-Urundi, 1884–1919.* Oxford: Clarendon Press, 1963.

Newbury, Catharine. *The Cohesion of Oppression: Clientship and Ethnicity in Rwanda, 1860–1960.* New York: Columbia University Press, 1988.

Newbury, David. 'The "Rwakayihura" Famine of 1928–1929', in *Histoire sociale de l'Afrique de l'Est (XIXe–XXe siècle). Actes du colloque de Bujumbura (17–24 octobre 1989),* Paris, 1991, 269–85.

Newbury, David. *The Land Beyond the Mists: Essays on Identity and Authority in Precolonial Congo and Rwanda.* Athens, OH: Ohio University Press, 2009.

Nsengimana, Innocent. *Le Rwanda et le pouvoir européen (1894–1952): Quelles mutations?* Bern: Peter Lang, 2003.

Rumiya, Jean. *Le Rwanda sous le régime du mandat belge (1916–1931).* Paris: L'Harmattan, 1992.

### Tanganyika

Callahan, Michael D. 'The Failure of "Closer Union" in British East Africa, 1929–31', *The Journal of Imperial and Commonwealth History,* 25:2 (1997), 267–93.

Gregory, Robert. *Sidney Webb and East Africa: Labour's Experiment with the Doctrine of Native Paramountcy.* Berkeley: University of California Press, 1962.

Iliffe, John. *A Modern History of Tanganyika.* Cambridge: Cambridge University Press, 1979.

Ingham, Kenneth. *A History of East Africa.* London: Longman's, 1962.

Leubuscher, Charlotte. *Tanganyika Territory: A Study of Economic Policy under Mandate.* London: Oxford University Press, 1944.

Lohrmann, Ulrich. *Voices from Tanganyika: Great Britain, the United Nations and the Decolonization of a Trust Territory, 1946–1961.* Berlin: Lit, 2007.

Westcott, Nicholas. 'The East African Sisal Industry, 1929–49: The Marketing of a Colonial Commodity during Depression and War', *Journal of African History,* 25 (1984), 445–61.

## 'C' Mandates

### South West Africa/Namibia

Bley, Helmut. *Namibia under German Rule,* new ed. Hamburg: Lit, 1996.

Britz, Rudolf G., Hartmut Lang, and Cornelia Limpricht, *A Concise History of the Rehoboth Basters until 1990.* Windhoek: Klaus Hess, 1999.

Christopher, A. J. 'Official Land Disposal Policies and European Settlement in Southern Africa, 1860–1960', *Journal of Historical Geography,* 9:4 (1983), 369–83.

Cockram, Gail-Maryse. *South West African Mandate.* Cape Town: Juta and Co., 1976.

Cooper, Allan D. 'The Institutionalization of Contract Labour in Namibia', *Journal of Southern African Studies,* 25:1 (March 1999), 121–38.

Dale, Richard. 'The Armed Forces as an Instrument of South African Policy in Namibia', *The Journal of Modern African Studies,* 18:1 (1980), 57–71.

Davey, A. M. *The Bondelzwarts Affair: A Study of the Repercussions, 1922–1959.* Pretoria: Communications of the University of South Africa, 1961.

Dedering, Tilman. 'Petitioning Geneva: Transnational Aspects of Protest and Resistance in South West Africa/Namibia after the First World War', *Journal of Southern African Studies,* 35:4 (December 2009), 785–801.

Emmett, Tony. *Popular Resistance and the Roots of Nationalism in Namibia, 1915–1966.* Basel: P. Schlettwein, 1999.

First, Ruth. *South West Africa.* Harmondsworth: Penguin, 1963.

Fisch, Maria. *Die südafrikanische Militärverwaltung (1915–1920) und die frühe Mandatszeit (1920–1936) in der Kavango-Region/Namibia*. Cologne: Rüdiger Köppe Verlag, 2004.

Freislich, Richard. *The Last Tribal War: A History of the Bondelswart Uprising*. Cape Town: C. Struik, 1964.

Goldblatt, I. *History of South West Africa*. Cape Town: Juta & Co., 1971.

Hayes, Patricia. ' "Cocky" Hahn and the "Black Venus": The Making of a Native Commissioner in South West Africa, 1915–46', *Gender & History*, 8:3 (November 1996), 364–92.

Hayes, Patricia. 'Northern Exposures: The photography of C. H. L. Hahn, Native Commissioner of Ovamboland, 1915–1946', in *The Colonising Camera: Photographs in the Making of Namibian History*, ed. Wolfram Hartmann, Jeremy Silvester, and Patricia Hayes. Cape Town: University of Cape Town Press, 1998, 171–87.

Hayes, Patricia, Jeremy Silvester, Marion Wallace, and Wolfram Hartmann, eds, *Namibia under South African Rule: Mobility and Containment*. Oxford: James Currey, 1998.

Kienzle, William. 'German-South African Trade Relations, in the Nazi Era', *African Affairs*, 78: 310 (January 1979), 81–90.

Kössler, Reinhard. 'From Reserve to Homeland: Local Identities and South African Policy in Southern Namibia', *Journal of Southern African Studies*, 26:3 (September 2000), 447–62.

Pienaar, Sara. *South Africa and International Relations between the Two World Wars: The League of Nations Dimension*. Johannesburg: Witwatersrand University Press, 1987.

Walther, Daniel Joseph. *Creating Germans Abroad: Cultural Policies and National Identity in Namibia*. Athens, OH: Ohio University Press, 2002.

Wellington, John H. *South West Africa and its Human Issues*. Oxford: Clarendon Press, 1967.

*Western Samoa*

Boyd, Mary. 'The Military Administration of Western Samoa, 1914–1919', *The New Zealand Journal of History*, 2:2 (October 1968), 148–64.

Brown, Bruce. *The Rise of New Zealand Labour*. Wellington: Milburn, 1962.

Chappell, David A. 'The Forgotten Mau: Anti-Navy Protest in American Samoa, 1920–1935', *Pacific Historical Review*, 69:2 (May 2000), 217–60.

Chaudron, Gerard. 'New Zealand's International Initiation: Sir James Allen at the League of Nations, 1920–1926', *Political Science*, 64:1 (2012), 62–80.

Davidson, J. W. *Samoa mo Samoa: The Emergence of the Independent State of Western Samoa*. Melbourne: Oxford University Press, 1967.

Field, Michael J. *Mau: Samoa's Struggle Against New Zealand Oppression*. Wellington: A. H. and A. W. Reed, 1984.

Lawson, Stephanie. *Tradition versus Democracy in the South Pacific: Fiji, Tonga and Western Samoa*. Cambridge: Cambridge University Press, 1996.

Meleisea, Malama. *The Making of Modern Samoa: Traditional Authority and Colonial Administration in the Modern History of Western Samoa*. Suva, Fiji: Institute of Pacific Studies, 1987.

Meleisea, Malama. *Change and Adaptations in Western Samoa*. Christchurch, New Zealand: University of Canterbury, 1992.

Salesa, Toeolesulusulu D. 'Half-Castes between the Wars: Colonial Categories in New Zealand and Samoa', *New Zealand Journal of History*, 34:1 (2000), 98–116.

Steinmetz, George. 'The Uncontrollable Afterlives of Ethnography: Lessons from "Salvage Colonialism" in the German Overseas Empire', *Ethnography*, 5:3 (2004), 251–88.

Wareham, Evelyn. *Race and Realpolitik: The Politics of Colonisation in German Samoa*. Frankfurt: P. Lang, 2002.

*Nauru*

Anghie, Antony. ' "The Heart of my Home": Colonialism, Environmental Damage, and the Nauru Case', *Harvard International Law Journal*, 34:2 (Spring 1993), 445–506.

Cushman, Gregory T. *Guano and the Opening of the Pacific World: A Global Ecological History*. Cambridge: Cambridge University Press, 2013.

Thompson, Roger C. 'Edge of Empire: Australian Colonization in Nauru, 1919–1939', in *Pacific History: Papers from the 8th Pacific History Association Conference*, ed. Donald H. Rubinstein. Mangilao: University of Guam Press, 1992, 273–80.

Weeramantry, Christopher. *Nauru: Environmental Damage under International Trusteeship*. Melbourne: Oxford University Press, 1992.

*New Guinea*

Ballard, Chris. 'Watching *First Contact*', *Journal of Pacific History*, 45:1 (June 2010), 21–36.

Bayliss-Smith, Tim. 'Papuan Exploration, Colonial Expansion and the Royal Geographical Society: Questions of Power/Knowledge Relations', *Journal of Historical Geography*, 18:3 (1992), 319–29.

Campbell, I. C. 'Anthropology and the Professionalization of Colonial Administration in Papua and New Guinea', *The Journal of Pacific History*, 33:1 (June 1998), 69–90.

Connolly, Bob, and Robin Anderson, *First Contact*. Film: 1983; Book: New York: Viking Penguin, 1987.

Gray, Geoffrey. ' "Being Honest to My Science": Reo Fortune and J. H. P. Murray, 1927–1930', *Australian Journal of Anthropology*, 10:1 (1999), 56–76.

Gray, Geoffrey. 'There are Many Difficult Problems: Ernest William Pearson Chinnery: Government Anthropologist', *The Journal of Pacific History*, 38:3 (December 2003), 313–30.

Griffin, James. 'Leahy, Michael James (Mick) (1901–1979)', *Australian Dictionary of Biography*, http://adb.anu.edu.au/biography/leahy-michael-james-mick-7134/tet12311, accessed 10 July 2012.

Griffin, James, Hank Nelson, and Stewart Firth. *Papua New Guinea: A Political History*. Victoria: Heinemann Educational, 1979.

Ham, Paul. *Kokoda*. Sydney: Harper Collins, 2004.

Hudson, W. J., ed. *Australia and Papua New Guinea*. Sydney: Sydney University Press, 1971.

Hudson, W. J., ed. *Australia and the League of Nations*. Sydney: Sydney University Press, 1980.

Jones, Douglas E. 'Afterword', in Michael J. Leahy, *Explorations into Highland New Guinea, 1930–1935*. Tuscaloosa: University of Alabama Press, 1991, 245–50.

McBean, James Roy. 'Degrees of Otherness: A Close Reading of *First Contact, Joe Leahy's Neighbors*, and *Black Harvest*', *Visual Anthropology Review*, 10:2 (Autumn 1994), 54–70.

McPherson, Naomi M., ed. *In Colonial New Guinea: Anthropological Perspectives*. Pittsburgh: University of Pittsburgh Press, 2001.

Meaney, Neville. *Fears and Phobias: E. L. Piesse and the Problem of Japan*. Canberra: National Library of Australia, 1996.

Merlan, Francesca, and Alan Rumsey. *Ku Waru: Language and Segmentary Politics in the Western Nebilyer Valley, Papua New Guinea*. Cambridge: Cambridge University Press, 1991.

O'Brien, Patricia. 'Reactions to Australian Colonial Violence in New Guinea: The 1926 Nakanai Massacre in a Global Context', *Australian Historical Studies*, 43:2 (2012), 191–209.

Perkins, John. 'Sharing the White Man's Burden: Nazi Colonial Revisionism and Australia's New Guinea Mandate', *Journal of Pacific History*, 24:1 (April 1989), 54–69.

Radford, Robin. *Highlanders and Foreigners in the Upper Ramu: Tha Kainantu Area 1919–1942*. Melbourne: Melbourne University Press, 1987.

Rowley, C. D. 'The Occupation of German New Guinea, 1914–1921', in *Australia and Papua New Guinea*, ed. W. J. Hudson. Sydney: Sydney University Press, 1971, 57–73.

Schieffelin, Edward L., Robert Crittenden, et al. *Like People You See in a Dream: First Contact in Six Papuan Societies*. Stanford: Stanford University Press, 1991.

Thompson, Roger C. 'Making a Mandate: The Formation of Australia's New Guinea Policies, 1919–1925', *Journal of Pacific History*, 25:1 (1990), 68–94.

Willis, Ian. 'Rabaul's 1929 Strike!', *New Guinea*, 5:3 (September/October 1970), 6–24.

*Japanese mandated islands*

Ballendorf, Dirk Anthony. 'Secrets without Substance: U.S. Intelligence in the Japanese Mandates, 1915–1935', *Journal of Pacific History*, 19:2 (April 1984), 83–99.

Beasley, W. G. *Japanese Imperialism, 1894–1945*. Oxford: Oxford University Press, 1987.

Burkman, Thomas W. *Japan and the League of Nations: Empire and World Order, 1914–1938*. Honolulu: University of Hawaii Press, 2008.

Burns, Richard Dean. 'Inspection of the Mandates, 1919–1941', *Pacific Historical Review*, 37:4 (November 1968), 445–62.

Denoon, Donald, ed. *The Cambridge History of the Pacific Islanders*. Cambridge: Cambridge University Press, 1997.

Higuchi, Wakako. 'Japan and War Reparations in Micronesia', *The Journal of Pacific History*, 30:1 (1995), 87–98.

Myers, Ramon H., and Mark R. Peattie. *The Japanese Colonial Empire, 1895–1945*. Princeton: Princeton University Press, 1984.

Peattie, Mark R. *Nan'yō: The Rise and Fall of the Japanese in Micronesia, 1885–1945*. Honolulu: University of Hawaii Press, 1988.

Purcell, David C., Jr. 'The Economics of Exploitation: The Japanese in the Mariana, Caroline and Marshall Islands, 1915–1940', *The Journal of Pacific History*, 11:3 (1976), 189–211.

Rattan, Sumitra. 'The Yap Controversy and its Significance', *The Journal of Pacific History*, 7 (1972), 124–36.

Schencking, J. Charles. 'Bureaucratic Politics, Military Budgets and Japan's Southern Advance: The Imperial Navy's Seizure of German Micronesia in the First World War', *War in History*, 5:3 (1998), 308–26.

# Illustration Credits

Albert Harlingue/Roger-Viollet/The Image Works: 5.1
Alexander Turnbull Library, New Zealand: 6.1; 6.2, 6.3, 6.5 (Photographer: Alfred James Tattersall); 6.4 (Photographer: Francis Gleeson)
Archives de la Ministère des Affaires Etrangères, Gouraud Papers: 1.5, 1.6, 1.7, 5.3
Bodleian Library of Commonwealth and African Studies, Lugard Papers: Frontispiece (122/1); 4.5 (160/12/f.1)
Bundesarchiv, Germany: 1.3 (Photographer: Walther Dobbertin); 8.1, 11.6
Geheimes Staatsarchiv Preußischer Kulturbesitz, Schnee Papers: 11.2
Imperial War Museum: 1.4
Library of Congress, George Grantham Bain Collection: 1.1; G. Eric and Edith Matson Collection: 1.8, 1.9, 3.2, 5.2, 5.5, 9.1, 9.2, 12.1, 12.2, 12.3, 12.4, 12.5, 12.6, 12.8
Mary Evans/Süddeutsche Zeitung Photo: 7.1, 11.1, 11.4, 11.5
Moorland-Spingarn Research Center, Howard University Archives: 10.5
Namibian National Archives: 4.2, 4.3, 4.4
National Library of Australia: 10.1 (Photographer: Sarah Chinnery); 10.2, 10.3, 10.4 (Photographer: Michael Leahy)
Rapport présenté par le Gouvernement belge au Conseil de la Société des Nations au sujet de l'Administration du Ruanda-Urundi: 8.2 (1928); 8.3 and 8.4 (1929)
Stadtarchiv Stadt Freiburg: 11.3
University of Chicago Library, Quincy Wright Papers: 5.4
UNOG Library, League of Nations Archives, Geneva: 2.1, 2.2, 3.1, 4.1, III.1, III.2, 12.7
Wikipedia.com (public domain): 1.2

# Index